Contents

Utopia and Anti-Utopia
in Modern Times

To F.P.

Utopia and Anti-Utopia in Modern Times

KRISHAN KUMAR

Basil Blackwell

First published 1987
First published in paperback 1991

Basil Blackwell Ltd
108 Cowley Road, Oxford OX4 1JF, UK

Basil Blackwell, Inc.
3 Cambridge Center
Cambridge, Massachusetts 02142, USA

British Library Cataloguing in Publication Data

A CIP catalogue record for this book is available from the British Library.

Library of Congress Cataloging in Publication Data

Kumar, Krishan.
Utopia and anti-utopia in modern times / Krishan Kumar.
p. cm.
Includes bibliographical references (p.) and index.
1. Utopias. 2. Utopias in literature. 3. Dystopias. I. Title.
[HX806.K86 1991]
335′.02—dc20 90–23084 CIP
ISBN 0–631–16714–5 (p/bk); 0–631–14873–6 (h/bk)

Typeset by Alan Sutton Publishing Ltd, Gloucester
Printed in Great Britain by T.J. Press Ltd, Padstow

Preface

This is a book about books. Worse, it is mostly about some very well-known books, such as Huxley's *Brave New World* and Orwell's *Nineteen Eighty-Four*. What can be the justification of yet another treatment of these works – and at such length?

There are several good histories of utopias. And there are many individual studies of particular utopian texts. It is rarer, though, to find a combination of the approaches of both, which seeks to add the advantage of historical narrative and context to that of the detailed consideration of particular texts. This is what this book tries to do. Inevitably, such a combination lengthens the treatment – whether justifiably or not the reader alone will judge.

Histories of utopian thought generally have all the interest of a telephone directory. A string of names – of books and authors – unfolds, accompanied by capsule summaries of the books' contents. The net effect is indigestion, or boredom. One is bounced through the ancients – the biblical prophets, Plato and the Greeks; hurried throughout the Middle Ages, with a glance at Augustine; served up More, Campanella and Bacon as a substantial dish; then finished off with the nineteenth-century socialists: often with a coda which proclaims or laments the death of utopia in our own century. An old and respected text, Joyce Oramel Hertzler's *The History of Utopian Thought* (1923), can stand as a convenient example – not only because the author is dead and beyond hurt, but also because, as one of the earliest histories, it seems to have established the pattern of most later accounts.

That these books – and I include Hertzler's – have their uses is undeniable; just how much will be clear particularly in the earlier chapters of this one. Moreover, I too have felt the need to run through the familiar story. The bulk of this book is about English and American utopias and anti-utopias of the period from the 1880s to the 1950s. But some context, some setting of these works within the intellectual and literary tradition of utopia, is clearly necessary. This is the object of the chapters in part I. I look there at the classical and Christian inheritance of the modern utopia, and seek to distinguish these intellectual antecedents from the utopia proper invented by More. I next consider in some detail the socialist and especially Marxist utopias of nineteenth-century Europe, as the essential historical and ideological background to the works studied in part II. America gets a separate chapter, both because of its own important role in the utopian tradition – America as utopia – and as the home of the experimental utopian community. America is also where, it is sometimes surprising to recall, the first fully realized socialist utopia was produced: Edward Bellamy's *Looking Backward.* Lastly in part I I discuss the anti-utopia, as a form related to but distinct from the traditional utopia. Anti-utopia is, in essence, a relatively recent invention, a reaction largely to the socialist utopia of the nineteenth century and certain socialist practices of the twentieth century. Since two of my studies – and two of the best-known works – are anti-utopias, I have felt the need to examine the main themes and preoccupations of the anti-utopia as the general intellectual background to Huxley and Orwell in particular.

In all this I am indebted to the standard histories of utopia, as I hope I have made sufficiently clear in the notes. So far as these chapters go, I make no claim to any originality of treatment or particularly of thought. But I should have felt guilty of just the very fault I have complained of in the standard accounts if I had then gone on to deal with the particular period I have chosen in the same discursive way. It seemed to me important, both as a means of stimulating the interest of the reader and of saying something substantial and significant about the works themselves, to avoid the standard narrative approach. This, with its listing of 'influences' and requirement of something like a comprehensive coverage of works produced in the period, seemed to be the road to literary and intellectual congestion. At the same time, I did not wish to write isolated studies of literary texts, in the traditional manner of literary critics and some historians of political thought. I wanted the detail that would come from concentrating on a few texts, but I also wanted to show that there was a distinct intellectual tradition linking the texts, and that this strand was in its turn subsumed in a larger tradition of social thought. The relationship between part I and part II is therefore reciprocal, even though the treatments are very different.

The selection of works for detailed study in part II is to some extent arbitrary. I should have liked, for instance, to include William Morris's *News from Nowhere* and Evgeny Zamyatin's *We.* Arthur Koestler's *Darkness at Noon*, too, seems a key text of the period. But, for reasons of space, there had to be some choice; and I chose works which, at the time or subsequently, most seem to have caught the public imagination. I also wanted to balance utopia against anti-utopia, as far as I could. So utopias of socialism and science – Bellamy's *Looking Backward* and Wells's *A Modern Utopia* – are matched by anti-utopias of science and socialism – Huxley's *Brave New World* and, to an extent at least, Orwell's *Nineteen Eighty-Four.* These four also have the advantage of being tightly linked in an intricate pattern of challenge and response. Skinner's *Walden Two* stands somewhat outside this tradition, although it is partly an answer to *Brave New World.* But it is important both as a prime example of the experimental utopia, the chief legacy of the American utopian tradition, and as signalling a renewal of the utopian impulse in the West.

In all cases I have discussed my chosen texts in relation to the writer's work and thought as a whole, and to other writers. But I have not been much concerned with the specifically literary quality of the works. All utopias and anti-utopias are, by definition, fictions. Strictly speaking, the literary utopia – as opposed, say, to the political treatise – is the only utopia. All the utopias of part II are novels, imaginative works of fiction. Therefore, they can be, and sometimes have been, treated according to the conventional canons of literary criticism. But not only do I not feel particularly competent to do this, I also feel that not much is to be gained by doing so. On the whole, utopias are not very distinguished for their aesthetic qualities as works of literature. More's *Utopia* and Morris's *News from Nowhere* are perhaps the principal exceptions. But one would not go to *Looking Backward* or *Walden Two* for the pleasure of their prose. What is interesting about them, and what I have concentrated on, is the nature and quality of their ideas about individuals and societies. It is chiefly as contributions to social thought that I consider them.

That this leaves out certain other important aspects of these works is something I am regretfully conscious of. The limitation probably does not matter so much in the case of the utopias I discuss, with the exception perhaps of *A Modern Utopia*. But it possibly matters more with the anti-utopias, *Brave New World* and *Nineteen Eighty-Four*, both of which are complex works of fiction where the literary devices can make meanings uncertain and open to varying interpretations. It does indeed seem the general rule that the anti-utopia, at least in modern times, has been more effective than the utopia in evoking literary qualities of a vivid and compelling kind. This is borne out not just by other examples such as Zamyatin's *We* and Koestler's *Darkness at Noon*, but in the well-known contrast between the literary power of Wells's early anti-utopian fables and the more hackneyed quality of his later utopian writing. To say that this is yet another case of the devil's having all the best tunes is, of course, to prejudge the question of just who are the angels and who the devils in the conflict between utopia and anti-utopia.

The single chapter of part III, finally, is by way of an epilogue. It summarizes the situation of utopia and anti-utopia in the first half of the twentieth century; and it goes on to consider the fate of both in the second half of the century. Is utopia now dead, as so often pronounced, and as appeared the case at least in the earlier part of the century? Or has it survived the battering of the anti-utopia? What are its current forms, and what place might it have in current thinking about the future of Western or world society? The outlook for utopia seems uncertain, to put it no stronger than that. But it would be odd indeed if a type of thought which has flourished in one form or another for at least three thousand years should now cease altogether to perform its historic function of clarifying the choices before us through the presentation of the most varied pictures of a fulfilled and happy humanity.

One meets many people on a journey through utopia. For simply an encouraging wave, or more substantial help, I should particularly like to thank: Chimen Abramsky, Bernard Crick, Jean Jackson, Ruth Levitas, Steven Lukes, David McLellan, Frank Parkin, Patrick Parrinder, Steven Rose, Peter Singer,

Quentin Skinner, Howard Smokler, Brian Stableford. I am grateful also to the American Council of Learned Societies for awarding me a Fellowship, and to Daniel Bell and the Sociology Department of Harvard University for providing so congenial an environment in which to hold it.

Krishan Kumar
Canterbury, Kent

Acknowledgements

For permission to quote from copyright sources, the author and publisher would like to thank the following: A. P. Watt Ltd, on behalf of The Literary Executors of the Estate of H. G. Wells, for extracts from *A Modern Utopia* by H. G. Wells; the author's Estate, Chatto and Windus and Harper and Row Publishers, Inc., for extracts from *Brave New World* by Aldous Huxley; the Estate of the late Sonia Brownell Orwell and Secker and Warburg Ltd, for extracts from *Nineteen Eighty-Four* by George Orwell; Macmillan Publishing Company for extracts from *Walden Two* by B. F. Skinner, copyright 1948, renewed 1976 by B. F. Skinner.

PART I

1
Utopianism Ancient and Modern

Utopian ideas and fantasies, like all ideas and fantasies, grow out of the society to which they are a response. Neither the ancient world nor the modern world is an unchanging entity, and any analysis of Utopian thinking which neglects social changes in the course of the history of either antiquity or modern times is likely at some point to go badly wrong.

M. I. Finley, 'Utopianism Ancient and Modern', in K. H. Wolff and Barrington Moore, Jr. (eds), *The Critical Spirit: Essays in Honor of Herbert Marcuse* (1967)

GREEKS AND ROMANS

George Orwell wrote of 'the dream of a just society which seems to haunt the human imagination ineradicably and in all ages, whether it is called the Kingdom of Heaven or the classless society, or whether it is thought of as a Golden Age which once existed in the past and from which we have degenerated'.[1] Orwell points to the constancy and consistency of the utopian vision. As a structure of the imagination, says another student of utopias, 'it has barely changed in the last four and a half centuries.'[2] Even that sounds too modest: should we not rather say, the last *twenty-four* and a half centuries? Is it not a persuasive view, a commonplace even, that all utopias of the past two and a half thousand years have been merely footnotes to Plato's *Republic*?[3] What are Wells's Samurai, Huxley's Controllers, the Inner Party of Orwell's Oceania, but the recognizable and legitimate descendants of Plato's Guardians? How frequently in later utopias do we not meet the characteristic features of the Platonic utopia: the 'reign of reason' in the threefold hierarchy of philosopher-kings, executive agents, and ordinary producers and artisans; the elevation of public over private life, and the pervasive control and regulation of daily life; the communism of property, wives and children, and the eugenic approach to reproduction; even the 'noble lie'?

Certainly we would be doing violence to both popular and scholarly usage to dismiss out of hand the idea that there was a classical utopia; even that there was a Christian utopia, although that has always been more controversial. I do in fact want to argue that, although classical and Christian influences on utopia have been and remain profound, there is not, properly speaking, either a classical or a Christian utopia. The modern utopia – the modern western[4] utopia invented in the Europe of the Renaissance – is the only utopia. It inherits classical and Christian forms and themes, but it transforms them into a distinctive novelty, a distinctive literary genre carrying a distinctive social philosophy. But in order to show that, we clearly need to consider, however briefly, the classical and Christian background to the idea of utopia.

Plato in fact comes in rather late, if we focus first on the world of classical antiquity. Utopian themes reach back to the earliest Greek writings. From Hesiod's *Works and Days*, of the early seventh century BC, came the canonical depiction of the Golden Age, the bitterly-lamented vanished age of Kronos' reign: when men 'lived as if they were gods, their hearts free from all sorrow, and without hard work or pain'; when 'the fruitful earth yielded its abundant harvest to them of its own accord, and they lived in ease and peace upon their lands with many good things.' Reworked by Virgil and Ovid as the lost age of Saturn (the Roman Kronos), the pastoral perfection of the Golden Age reappeared as the classic Arcadia, a time and a place of rustic simplicity and felicity. Virgil's Fourth *Eclogue* foretells the return of 'the reign of Saturn', an age of peace and prosperity, where nature is abundant, and men's wants moderate and easily satisfied without excessive toil. Ovid's portrayal of the Golden Age in Book One of the *Metamorphoses*, 'the definitive form in which the myth was infused into utopian thought',[5] scales more extravagant heights:

> Golden was that first age, which, with no one to compel, without a law, of its own will, kept faith and did the right. . . . There was no need at all of armed men, for nations, secure from war's alarms, passed the years in gentle ease. The earth herself, without compulsion, untouched by hoe or ploughshare, of herself gave all things needful. . . . The spring was everlasting, and gentle zephyrs with warm breath played with the flowers that sprang unplanted. Anon the earth, untilled, brought forth her store of grains, and the fields, though unfallowed, grew white with the heavy, bearded wheat. Streams of milk and streams of sweet nectar flowed, and yellow honey was distilled from the verdant oak.

The long arm of the Arcadian idyll is apparent in the anti-urban (and later anti-industrial) fantasies of scores of later writers up to our own time, most notoriously perhaps in England. As a serious ingredient of utopian thought it had its final fling in the eighteenth century. Rousseau's *Discourse on the Origin of Inequality* was the stern Arcadian counterpart to the revels of French courtiers playing at shepherds and shepherdesses in the gardens of Versailles. Before that, Arcadia as a vision of utopia was sufficiently familiar to educated Europeans for Shakespeare to be able to mock it, as in Gonzalo's fanciful utopian endeavours 't' excel the golden age' in *The Tempest*:

> I' the commonwealth I would by contraries
> Execute all things; for no kind of traffic
> Would I admit; no name of magistrate;
> Letters should not be known; riches, poverty,

> And use of service, none. . . .
> All things in common nature should produce
> Without sweat or endeavour; treason, felony,
> Sword, pike, knife, gun, or need of any engine,
> Would I not have; but nature should bring forth
> Of its own kind, all foison, all abundance,
> To feed my innocent people.[6]

Montaigne, on the other hand, in his influential essay 'Of Cannibals', praised the simple life of savages for a more important reason than their abundant leisure and peaceable equality: 'they are moreover happy in this, that they only covet so much as their natural necessities require: all beyond that is superfluous to them. . . . they have no lack of anything necessary, nor yet lack of that great thing, the knowledge of how to be happy in the enjoyment of their condition, and to be content with it.' So long as Arcadia persisted as an element in the western utopia – and the discovery of the New World in the sixteenth century gave it a renewed lease of life – its hallmark was the harmony between man and nature, based on moderate 'natural' needs, uncomplicated and uncorrupted by 'civilization'. Arcadia, as the myth of the Golden Age indicated, might exist in the past. But that did not prevent its being willed into existence, in some future time, as the conscious product of a utopian design. 'The Golden Age of the human species is not behind us, it is before us', declared Henri Saint-Simon in a typical utopian pronouncement of the early nineteenth century.

Interestingly, Montaigne deliberately set his Arcadian vision against the classical utopian tradition represented by Plato, which he accused of the over-elaborate contrivance typical of philosophers. It shows the fertility of invention in the ancient world that it could both throw up the Golden Age and Arcadia as objects of man's longing, and at the same time inaugurate an alternative, almost antithetical, tradition which was nevertheless equally utopian: the utopian project of the ideal city. If Arcadia showed man living within, and according to, nature, the Hellenic ideal city represented human mastery over nature, the triumph of reason and artifice over the amoral and chaotic realm of nature. Hence the importance, in the ideal city tradition, of those who gave the law and made the rational order of human society: the founders and framers of cities and constitutions, the philosopher-kings, the architect-planners. An early Greek tradition already venerated the semi-mythical figures of Solon of Athens and Lycurgus of Sparta as the founders and law-givers of their respective city-states. This idealization, common throughout the classical period, was boosted by Plutarch's *Lives* (first century AD), which made of Solon and Lycurgus virtually the creators of utopian societies. As received in Europe through various translations in the fifteenth and sixteenth centuries, the *Lives*, eked out with such celebrated set-pieces as Pericles' funeral oration from Thucydides' *History*, set before European thinkers two sharply contrasting utopian models. There was Athens: democratic, tolerant, boisterous, given over to a cultivated hedonism; and there was Sparta: authoritarian, ascetic, communistic. European utopian writers, along with most other kinds, were clearly fascinated by the alternative possibilities suggested by these two great exemplars of the ancient world. Right up to the French Revolution and beyond, one way of classifying utopias was as 'Athenian' or 'Spartan', with Sparta predictably the favourite not simply for matching more closely the utopian preference for a tightly regulated communal order, but as much for its status as the putative model of the most admired ancient utopia, Plato's *Republic.*

Solon and Lycurgus, the ideal law-givers, were the prototype of later utopian *nomothetai*: King Utopus in Sir Thomas More's *Utopia*, Sol in Campanella's *City of the Sun*, King Solamona in Bacon's *New Atlantis*. The Pythagorean communities of southern Italy (Magna Graecia), 'the most famous utopian experiment of the ancient world',[7] provided a modification within the ideal city tradition. Here were model communities, set up in the sixth and fifth centuries BC, which were governed by aristocratic clubs (*hetaireiai*) of philosophically and religiously trained followers of Pythagoras. The mystical and mathematical mixture of their Pythagorean philosophy itself suggests a line of connection with Plato's similarly inclined philosopher-kings, the Guardians of his *Republic.* But more important was the aristocratic form of the Pythagorean ideal community. This implied that a founder–law-giver might well be necessary at the beginning – Pythagoras himself had in fact fulfilled this role – but that the continuation of the community depended upon a rigorously trained and disciplined aristocratic caste. Such at any rate seems to have been Plato's inference from the Pythagorean experiment, whose legendary communal order seems to have influenced him considerably in his own utopian construction. The influence persisted in the aristocratic ideal which Plato's pupils at the Academy carried with them as constitutional advisers throughout the Hellenic world in the fourth century, and which thereby in time reached practically every corner of the ancient world. The best society would be the society ruled by the best, those most fitted by training and temperament for the most difficult of all arts, the art of government. The philosophers, having left the cave in pursuit of the light, had a duty to return to it, to give the benefit of their illumination to the ordinary mortals still chained with their faces to the wall.

It was of course through Plato's *Republic*, rediscovered along with other Greek writings in the European Renaissance, that the Hellenic ideal city most influenced the western utopia. More saw his own *Utopia* as partly a continuation of the *Republic*, fulfilling Socrates' desire in the *Timaeus* to see the abstract Republic in action actualized (a task barely begun in the fragmentary *Critias*). And four hundred years later, H. G. Wells was still constructing his 'modern utopia' according to Platonic example, and largely along Platonic lines. But in some ways the most direct Platonic influence was to be found in the architectural utopia. Architecture has always been the most utopian of all the arts. It has a longstanding concern with the marriage of mathematical and human forms, the finding of a harmony and correspondence between the mathematical relations of the cosmos and the forms and functions of the human body. Between the cosmic order of nature and the corporeal structure of man it interposes the ideal city, as the rationally designed mediator and link between the macrocosmic and the microcosmic spheres. Lewis Mumford has said that 'the first utopia was the city itself',[8] since the city expressed in its very form and conception an escape from nature, and an attempt at human and rational mastery over it. The city is a work of art, an artifice. It is a machine for living in. The design of that machine, the task of the architect-planner, is critical for the quality of life lived. The good life needs not just the ideal social and political environment but also, perhaps more so, the ideal physical environment.

Certainly the Renaissance architects seemed incapable of conceiving their task in anything but utopian terms. In the ambitious urban plans of Alberti, Filarete, Patrizi, Francesco di Giorgio and Leonardo, the writings of the Roman architect Vitruvius were fused with Platonic conceptions to produce a physical replica of the Republic: Plato realized in stone. 'The architect-planner was the high-priest of the ideal.'[9] The centralized, circular, radial plan of the Renaissance *città felice*, with its specialized and differentiated quarters for the different classes and occupations, was a precise physical realization of the aristocratic Platonic Republic. Its influence was clear even in those contemporary utopias which shared Plato's communism but pushed it in a more radically egalitarian direction. Andreae's *Christianopolis* has the perfect symmetry of the Renaissance ideal city. 'Its shape is a square, whose side is seven hundred feet, well fortified with four towers and a wall. It looks, therefore, towards the four quarters of the earth. . . .' Orderly rows of buildings, all of the same height and material, are cut by a main thoroughfare which converges on the circular temple, the spiritual as well as the physical centre of the city. The city is minutely and exhaustively divided into a multitude of quarters, each functionally specialized for the performance of different economic and social activities; those whose work requires the greatest skill and ability are placed nearest the centre of the city. In a similar fashion, Campanella's *City of the Sun* is divided into seven concentric circles, through which four broad streets radiate out to the four gates from the great temple at the centre, the seat of all political and spiritual power. Each circle marks off and segregates the different arts and occupations practised within the city, so that it is only when they are considered together, as an organic whole, that the seven circles can be seen as a repository of all the skills and materials needed for the life of the city. Moreover, all human knowledge is physically represented, in words and paintings, on the walls dividing up the seven circles. Thus the city is itself, as a physical entity, a compendium of all knowledge. It is the physical embodiment of all the arts and sciences, all that is needed for the cultivation of the good life.

Campanella's extraordinary vision of the city as knowledge or science incorporated shows that the architectural utopia aspired, in some ways, to out-Plato Plato himself. Plato had aimed at the immutability of his Republic, but could see no way to prevent corruption and decay from seeping in, such being the nature of men and society. But he had paid almost no attention to the physical environment of his ideal society. Might not stone, which visibly – especially in Italy – outlived the laws and institutions of men, form the essential determining framework of the ideal society? Might not the 'frozen music' of architecture continue to exert its harmonizing influence when corruption threatened to dissolve the social fabric of the city? Something of this utopian belief has continued to haunt architects and planners right up to the present day. It is to be found in L'Enfant's plan, steeped in Enlightenment classicism and rationalism, for the new city of Washington, the capital of the new American nation: itself a revolutionary creation, a utopia. It is there in the 'City Beautiful' movement of late nineteenth-century America, and in the contemporaneous 'garden city' movement of Patrick Geddes and Ebenezer Howard. And it is explicit and extreme in Le Corbusier's writings and designs for 'the city of tomorrow', *la ville radieuse*: perhaps the most utopian of all architectural schemes, and in its integrative and organic aspiration to create 'a single society, united in belief and action', the most purely Platonic in spirit.[10]

The classical world bequeathed one further important element to the later utopian tradition: the 'Cokaygne utopia', the popular or folk utopia. The happy Land of Cokaygne, a land of abundance, idleness and instant and unrestrained gratification, is to be found in practically all folk cultures. It is probably pre-classical as well as pre-Christian. Of all the components of utopia, it contains the strongest element of pure fantasy and wish-fulfilment. This is a fair reflection of the fact that it is 'the poor man's heaven', the dream of the labouring classes of all ages, to be free from toil and drudgery. Such a characteristic comes out clearly in two well-known American versions of Cokaygne, *The Big Rock Candy Mountains* and *Poor Man's Heaven*. These folk songs not only tell of the place and the time when

> We'll eat all we please
> Of ham and egg trees,
> That grow by the lake full of beer

but also of the determination

> to stay where they sleep all day,
> Where they hung the Turk that invented work,
> In the Big Rock Candy Mountains.[11]

But Cokaygne would probably not have entered the realm of utopia proper had it not also been elaborated by classical authors. Ironically, this they did largely as part of a satirical mocking of the myth of the Golden Age. Teleclides, writing in the fifth century BC, was probably drawing on familiar folk images of pleasure and plenty – so amazingly and exactly alike are the same images centuries later, in folk song and fairy tale – when he thus satirized the literature of the Golden Age:

> First there was peace among all things like water covering one's hands. And the earth bore neither fear nor disease, but all needed things appeared of their own accord. For every stream flowed with wine, and barley cakes fought with wheat cakes to enter the mouths of men. . . . And fishes, coming to men's houses and baking themselves, would serve themselves upon the tables . . . and roasted thrushes with milk cakes flew down one's gullet.[12]

The satirists might ridicule Cloudcuckooland; but in doing so they delineated a hedonistic paradise that might very easily be taken over by popular tradition as something to dream about and, in popular carnivals such as the Saturnalia or Feast of Fools, something actually to live, for a drunken day or two at least. This seems to have happened to the comedies of Aristophanes, many of which were aimed at the Greek utopian tradition generally, and some at Plato's *Republic* specifically. In the *Ecclesiazusae* Praxagora leads a revolution of women which abolishes private property and institutes a reign of equality and plenty:

> All pressure from want will be o'er.
> Now each will have all that a man can desire.
> Cakes, barley-loaves, chestnuts, abundant attire,
> Wine, garlands, and fish. . . .

Law courts are converted to banqueting halls, and 'all women and men will be common and free/No marriage or other restraint there will be.' Everyone, men and women, old and young, beautiful and ugly, will be able to satisfy their desires without toil or effort (there are slaves to do the work). In *The Birds*, the Birds too, before their corruption by power-hungry politicians, lead happy and carefree lives, 'like a perpetual wedding day'. They do without money, and spend their 'idle mornings with banqueting and collations in the gardens, with poppy-seeds and myrrh'.

Aristophanes was much admired in the Renaissance, but Lucian was even more important in transmitting the Cokaygne utopia into the mainstream of utopian thought. His *True History* was a popular text throughout the Roman period, and when it was brought to the West from Constantinople in the fifteenth century it quickly became a firm favourite with Renaissance humanists such as Erasmus and More (his Utopians are 'captivated by the wit and pleasantry of Lucian'). In his caricatured portrait of the Island of the Blessed, Lucian parodied the whole Greek utopian tradition by treating it as a dream of the popular imagination. He describes the 'marvellous air, like scent', of the island, whose flowery fragrance hovers over the 'crystal rivers flowing placidly to the sea'. There is no day or night, but perpetual 'morning twilight', no seasons, but 'perpetual spring'. The music of a children's chorus fills the air, to which is added a choir of singing swans, swallows and nightingales, while 'sweet zephyrs just stir the woods with their breath, and bring whispering melody.' The heroes and philosophers who inhabit the isle never die, and while away their time in laughter and pleasure. Lovemaking takes place openly, without shame. The trees always bear ripe fruit. There are even 'glass trees', which, instead of bearing fruit, 'bear cups of all shapes and sizes. When anyone comes to table he picks one or two of the cups and puts them at his place. These fill with wine at once.'

Cokaygne obviously overlaps Arcadia or the Golden Age somewhat (all utopian categories overlap one another). But it differs characteristically from Arcadia in being a utopia of excess and superabundance rather than one of moderation and restraint. Arcadia gives a more than decent sufficiency to its inhabitants, who are governed by the modest needs implanted by nature. Cokaygne is there to satisfy all needs and desires, however multiplied or inflated, however greedy or gross. In this it shows the continuing influence of popular culture. Echoes of the classical Cokaygne can be found in many modern utopias, but what kept it alive in the utopian tradition were the frequent injections of earthy themes and images from more popular sources. Shakespeare put it in the portly knight Sir John Falstaff. Rabelais drew on it for the society of happy debtors in *Pantagruel*, and the utopian society of the Abbey of Thélemè, with its motto 'Do what you will', in *Gargantua*. Brueghel painted it in a picture which shows roofs made of cake, a roast pig running round with a knife in its side, a mountain of dumplings, and citizens lying back at their ease waiting for all the good things to drop into their mouths. But probably the most remarkable, and certainly one of the most complete, renderings of the Cokaygne utopia is the eponymous fourteenth-century English poem, *The Land of Cokaygne*. Like Aristophanes and Lucian, the poet comes to mock gluttony, licentiousness and idleness – especially as practised in the monasteries – but like these he ends up painting his earthly paradise in such glowing colours that the satire is overwhelmed by the utopia. Cokaygne is fairer than Paradise itself, 'for what is there in Paradise/But grass and flowers and greeneries'? What but water to drink and fruit to eat? Whereas in Cokaygne:

> There are rivers broad and fine
> Of oil, milk, honey and of wine;
> Water serveth there no thing
> But for sight and for washing.
>
> Ah, those chambers and those halls!
> All of pasties stand the walls,
> Of fish and flesh and all rich meat,
> The tastiest that men can eat.
> Wheaten cakes the shingles all,
> Of church, of cloister, bower and hall.
> The pinnacles are fat puddings,
> Good food for princes or for kings.
> Every man takes what he will,
> As of right, to eat his fill.
> All is common to young and old,
> To stout and strong, to meek and bold.
>
> Yet this wonder add to it –
> That geese fly roasted on the spit,
> As God's my witness, to that spot,
> Crying out, 'Geese, all hot, all hot!'
> Every goose in garlic drest,
> Of all the food the seemliest
> And the larks that are so couth
> Fly right down into man's mouth,
> Smothered in stew, and thereupon
> Piles of powdered cinnamon.
> Every man may drink his fill
> And needn't sweat to pay the bill.[13]

JEWS AND CHRISTIANS

Utopia would have been stifled at birth by excess had Cokaygne played a dominant part in its creation. It needed the moderating force of Arcadia and the rationalizing influence of the ideal city to offset the unbridled wish-fulfilment and fantasy of Cokaygne. Christianity further spiritualized the classical inheritance of utopia. It was indeed the intention of the Cokaygne poet to satirize the debased life of the monasteries from the point of view of the true faith, a restrained and truly spiritual Christianity. In seeing the earthly utopia as some kind of simulacrum of the heavenly city of God, Christianity added immeasurably to the ascetic and monastic qualities to be found in certain aspects of the classical inheritance – notably Plato's utopia.

Christianity's decisive contribution to utopia partly consisted in taking over and absorbing classical utopian themes, which it fused with its own Judaic and Near Eastern inheritance. It was easy enough to assimilate and identify the Golden Age with the Garden of Eden. The Golden Age could now stand as the representation of the blissful condition of mankind before the Fall. And if classical ideas chimed in nicely with the notion of a paradise lost, they could also, though less readily, be enlisted in the service of the idea of paradise regained, in some future time. In the *Odyssey* Homer had sketched the picture of Elysium, the paradisiac realm at 'the bounds of the earth' where the Greek heroes were resurrected after death and where they lived happy and glorious lives for ever more among the gods. Hesiod offered an almost identical account of his home for heroes, the Isles of the Blessed. In Pindar's Orphic version of the myth, the Isles of the Blessed have become the permanent abode not so much of warlike heroes as of the innocent and the good, in contrast to the wicked who suffer torments in the nether world of Hades. It needed only a little expansion of Pindar's rather restricted category of the virtuous for Christianity to be able to incorporate this Orphic myth in its own vision of a heavenly paradise in the herafter, where, following the resurrection and the Day of Judgement, the faithful live in everlasting joy and splendour at God's right hand.

But, though more or less satisfactorily reconciled with pagan tradition, and having obvious utopian overtones, the paradise concept was itself problematic for utopia. Many myths and religions, from all regions of the world, contain the idea of a paradise in the past or the future.[14] But, with the exception of Christianity, none of them has thrown up a utopian tradition. The reason is not difficult to see. There is in principle a fundamental contradiction between religion and utopia. As Moses Finley has said, 'utopia transcends the given social reality; it is not transcendental in a metaphysical sense.'[15] Religion typically has an other-worldly concern; utopia's interest is in this world. The idea of a paradise by itself does nothing to reconcile this opposition of interest.[16] Whether that paradise is conceived as lying in some earlier pristine, pre-lapsarian, state or in some future world to come, it almost always remains irreducibly transcendental: a time and a place that is not of this world. Man has lived in it, and will one day again live in it. But only when he has freed himself of earthly dross and earthly preoccupations. Did not Christ say 'My Kingdom is not of this world'?

In this sense religion in general, and paradise in particular, can work directly against utopian speculation and aspiration. They can make the whole business of earthly politics appear futile and unnecessary. The world of fallen man is a vale of tears, a period of necessary suffering and purgation before he is redeemed through divine agency. The Golden Age or the Garden of Eden is there precisely to define and to explain the existence of evil, and the necessity of living with and through it. Paradise sustains hope, and reveals something of the bliss to come. But it is not a goal or a paradigm. For man to attempt to create, by his own unaided efforts, a paradise on earth must from this point of view appear the grossest impiety and arrogance. It would be an act of Promethean defiance, a usurpation of the omnipotence of God, who alone can bring in the new dispensation.

It was this that St Augustine was at pains to insist upon, in the troubled world of the later Roman Empire. Faced with the charge that Christianity had undermined the Empire and let in the barbarians, he made a radical separation between the concerns of religion and those of the secular state. In his great fifth-century anti-utopia, *The City of God*, he warns against too much absorption in the affairs of the earthly city, as leading to an alienation from the heavenly city of God. Men must make the best of their time here on earth and, through the Church, endeavour to live as good Christians to the fullest extent possible in a world that is necessarily and inescapably stained with sin. But their real life will be in the life to come. The earthly pilgrimage will be followed by the Day of Judgement and their blessed release from the earthly city. And if this world is no more than 'a dark vestibule leading to the great hall of the next world',[17] what could plans for a perfect society here on earth be, other than presumptuous? Certainly that seems to have been the general attitude towards utopianism during the Christian Middle Ages, when Augustine's influence was paramount in orthodox theological circles.[18] The *contemptus mundi* was profoundly discouraging to utopian speculation; as a result, the Middle Ages are a conspicuously barren period in the history of utopian thought.[19]

But, as with so many other aspects of Christianity and the Middle Ages, things are not really as simple as this familiar picture suggests. There were profound ambiguities and ambivalences in Christian doctrine that repeatedly stirred up utopian sentiments and tendencies, in a manner often highly displeasing to the churchly hierarchy. Unwelcome interpretations of the Scriptures might be frowned on by the orthodox; extreme views denounced as heretical. But throughout the Middle Ages heterodox currents flowed strongly, feeding the springs of utopia. It was these forces that ensured that Christianity, uniquely among religions, would lead not away from but straight into the heart of the utopian enterprise.

Not that all the utopian elements in medieval Christian belief were necessarily heterodox. The first, the literal belief that the Garden of Eden existed somewhere on earth, somewhere to the east (Genesis 2:8), was shared by most Christian thinkers throughout the Middle Ages. Medieval maps testify to the widespread conviction that there was an actual terrestrial paradise. And if it existed on the maps, it could be found – or at least searched for. Since the Nile was thought to be one of the four rivers flowing from the garden, as described in Genesis, the legend of the Christian Emperor of Ethiopia, Prester

John, could be tied to the search for the earthly paradise – as, in a different way, could the search for the Holy Grail. A celebrated instance of this literal belief, showing its persistence well into the Renaissance, was Columbus's alarmed conviction that he had found the Garden of Eden at the mouth of the Orinoco River with its four tributaries. (Columbus of course thought he was by then in the East.[20]) When such notable figures could so seriously hold the belief in a terrestrial paradise, it is not difficult to imagine how attractive it would appear to the multitudes of the poor and oppressed in the medieval world.

Such a widespread consensus of belief could not be expected of the second utopian current in Christendom: the belief in the perfectibility of man. The crucial, hotly disputed, text is in Matthew, from Jesus' Sermon on the Mount: 'Be ye therefore perfect, even as your Father which is in heaven is perfect' (Matthew 5:48). What became the orthodox view, derived largely from Augustine and confirmed by Luther and Calvin, was that it was impossible for man to be or become perfect in anything like the same sense or to the same extent that God was understood to be perfect:

> Impossible for metaphysical reasons, since human perfection, so far as it can be attained at all, is the perfection of a finite temporal being, with all the limitation this involves. Impossible for moral reasons, since man, even when granted God's grace, has been so corrupted by Adam's Fall that he is incapable of achieving, even, that degree of moral perfection which his metaphysical nature permits.[21]

But from the earliest days of Christianity a contrary view had been asserted and had persisted, despite repeated condemnation. The injunction in Matthew seemed plain enough: Jesus had laid it down that men are to perfect themselves. Moreover, was not Jesus himself a human exemplar of that God-like perfection, and were not men called upon to imitate him? Neo-Platonic thought, with its Hellenic motif of 'men like gods', was particularly influential in early Christianity in keeping alive the idea of human perfectibility. In the fifth century, Dionysius ('pseudo-Denys') was arguing that man could, in effect, *become* God, achieve a oneness with Him, by mystical apprehension. A similar notion was spread by Gnosticism, which held that men could be perfected by purifying themselves through the higher knowledge – 'gnosis' – accessible to true believers. 'Born of light and of the gods', runs a Gnostic poem, 'I am in exile and cut off from them. . . . I am a god, and born of gods, shining, sparkling, luminous, radiant, perfumed and beautiful. . . .' Most far-reaching of all was the attack by the fifth-century British monk Pelagius on Augustine's doctrine of original sin, perhaps the most serious obstacle to any Christian concept of human perfectibility. Men, said Pelagius, are born neither virtuous nor vicious, neither perfect nor corrupt: they *make* themselves so, by the exercise of their free will. They have that capacity because God has commanded men to be perfect, and He could not command them to do what lies beyond their powers. And if they have that God-given capacity, if that is in fact God's specific gift to them, it becomes sinful not to exercise it in the proper manner, to perfect themselves. The Church must be a community of saints, a college of perfection. No more than Christianity in general was Pelagianism utopian advocacy; but wherever and whenever its influence was strong, as among Renaissance neo-Platonists such as More and Erasmus, or radical Protestants during the English Civil War, it countered the anti-utopianism entrenched in Augustinian orthodoxy.

Pelagius's views were rejected as heretical (at the Council of Carthage in 418); Augustinianism triumphed, and remained dominant throughout the Christian centuries. But the Church could no more prevent outbreaks of Pelagianism than it could contain an even more dangerous heresy, and one which, of all the heterodox currents in Christianity, was the most replete with utopianism: the idea of the millennium. If neo-Platonism sustained the belief in perfectibility within Christianity, then millenarianism was the form in which Judaism made its major contribution to Christian utopianism. For millenarianism is clearly a continuation and extension of the Messianic prophecies of the Old Testament. It shows in a striking form Christianity's inheritance of the dynamic and apocalyptic pattern of Jewish thought. From Amos down to Enoch, a period spanning a thousand years, the Hebrew prophets proclaimed the coming of a new order in Israel. They scourged the people for their corruption and idolatry, they blamed them for the periods of captivity and exile, they prophesied trials and suffering on a massive scale. But they also confidently announced an 'end of the days', a term to the period of probation and purgation. They foretold the coming of a Messiah, a Deliverer – usually of the House of David – who would restore a cleansed and regenerated Israel to a position of pre-eminent purity and glory among the nations.

The grandest and most significant prophetic vision always remained Isaiah's. The Jewish people are 'laden with iniquity'; 'the faithful city become an harlot'. There will be, there has to be, a cleansing catastrophe. But the wrath of God will spare some, a 'saving remnant', the pure in heart, who will become the 'holy seed' of the new Israel. God will place on the throne of the new kingdom a just and powerful scion of the House of David, a virgin's son. He will be called Immanuel, 'the mighty God, the everlasting Father, the Prince of Peace' (Isaiah 9:6). The new dispensation is painted in glowing tones, the themes and images supplying material for utopian writing for centuries to come.

> Then the eyes of the blind shall be opened, and the ears of the deaf shall be unstopped. Then shall the lame man leap as an hart, and the tongue of the dumb sing. . . . (Isaiah 35:5–6)

> The desert shall rejoice, and blossom as the rose. . . . And the parched ground shall become a pool, and the thirsty land springs of water. (Isaiah 35:1,7)

> The wolf also shall dwell with the lamb, and the leopard shall lie down with the kid; and the calf and the young lion and the fatling together. (Isaiah 11:6)

> [Nations] shall beat their swords into plowshares, and their spears into pruninghooks: nation shall not lift up sword against nation, neither shall they learn war any more. (Isaiah 2:4)

> The ransomed of the Lord shall return, and come to Zion with songs and everlasting joy upon their heads: they shall obtain joy and gladness, and sorrow and sighing shall flee away. (Isaiah 35:10)

The important thing about the Jewish prophecies, from the point of view of the later utopia, is that they placed the new order firmly on this earth. The Promised Land of Canaan 'flowing with milk and honey', the New Jerusalem in the days of the Messiah, was here, not in the hereafter. Judaism broke with the cyclical conception of history common to the Graeco-Roman world. It adopted the idea of a unique and unitary history, with a beginning and an end, and marked by the progressive realization of God's will and purpose. But the 'end' it foretold was not – at least in the earlier prophecies – the prelude to an existence beyond this life on earth. Judaism was never particularly concerned with eschatological issues. It had a weakly developed conception of heaven and hell, and of life in the hereafter. Heaven was God's abode and His alone. The Covenant between Jehovah and the Jews refers to Israel's future on earth. Rewards and punishments are meted out here, not enjoyed or suffered in some supermundane heaven or hell. The perfect state would be on earth, and the perfection of the people would be obtained not by their being transplanted to the sphere of Jehovah's abode, but by His coming down and dwelling among them.[22]

Later prophets embellished Isaiah's Messianic vision with certain details that were to become very important in Christian millenarianism. From Ezekiel came the idea that a terrible war would precede the Messianic age of peace. The people of Magog, under their leader Gog, would invade Israel, and only after their defeat amidst frightful slaughter would the Messiah inaugurate his reign (Ezekiel 38–39). Deutero-Isaiah, following a general spiritualization of the Messianic prophecy in Jeremiah and Ezekiel, added the touch of universality: the New Jerusalem would be eternal, and not only the Jews but also Gentiles, under Jewish guidance, would find a place there (Isaiah 45:7, 56:1–8). And as the trials of the Jews increased and intensified, as deliverance seemed more and more remote, the writers of the Apocalypse contributed their characteristically powerful symbols of urgency and expectation. It was the Apocalyptists who most fully expressed the idea of human history as a unity, proceeding according to a particular design and bound to issue in a happy consummation. The Apocalypse of Daniel, 'the parent and model of Apocalyptic'[23] and for over a thousand years a potent influence on the Christian philosophy of history, laid down the schema of the 'four kingdoms', the four pagan ages through which mankind must pass before the end of the days and the inception of the everlasting Messianic age (Daniel 2,7). Enoch's Apocalypse breaks down time into 'seven days', each day lasting a millennium; the seventh millennium will be the last, a Messianic period of earthly happiness and peace preceding the last judgement and the establishment of the eternal kingdom in heaven.

But it was the Christian Apocalypse, as contained in the Revelation of St John, which ensured the decisive transmission of these ideas in the west, and supplied the form in which they were to have so profound an influence on social thought and action. The Jewish Apocalypse centred on the first coming of the Messiah; for the Christian Apocalypse it had of course to be the second coming. The Book of Revelation tells of a time when, following a period of strife and the emergence and defeat of the Antichrist, Christ shall return and rule with his resurrected saints for a thousand years on earth. The millennial reign of Christ will be followed by a second judgement and a second resurrection, and the righteous shall live in peace and contentment with God. There will be 'a new heaven and a new earth'; the 'holy city, new Jerusalem' shall come down 'from God out of heaven, prepared as a bride adorned for her husband'; God will have His dwelling among men, and 'shall wipe away all tears from their eyes; and there shall be no more death, neither sorrow, nor crying, neither shall there be any more pain: for the former things are passed away' (Revelation 20–21).

The addition of the millennial to the Messianic expectation was explosive, as the early Church quickly realized and sought to forestall. Millenarianism was pronounced a heresy at the Council of Ephesus (AD 431). Augustine once more supplied the orthodoxy, confirmed later with due authority by Aquinas. For Augustine there could be no additional or 'intermediate' earthly millennium supervening between the advent of Christ and the Last Judgement. With the appearance of Christ the Saviour, the world had already entered on its last epoch. It already lived in a state of grace, under the rule of the Church.

The millennium, in other words, was already here: it began with Christ's ministry on earth and continued with the Church as the body of Christ. 'The Church even now is the kingdom of Christ and the kingdom of heaven', wrote Augustine. 'Accordingly even now Christ's saints reign with him, though otherwise than they will reign hereafter.' The future on earth would now be merely a period of waiting, during which the Church must retain and expand its spiritual domain. It would be a time – Augustine refused to speculate on its length – of preparation for the Second Coming of Christ. But the Second Coming would not inaugurate another earthly millennium, to be followed by a second judgement and a second resurrection. There could be only one Last Judgement, and one final Resurrection. The Second Coming would spell the end of all earthly history, and the beginning of eternal life in heaven for those who have been the inhabitants of the City of God during their earthly pilgrimage.

But the Revelation of St John, in all its cryptic complexity, remained a standing temptation to a more radical conception of the relation of earthly to heavenly existence. Learned and unlearned alike, in the succeeding centuries, accepted in all seriousness the idea of a future millennium on earth which would be something like a prefiguration of the heavenly bliss awaiting the faithful. Again and again, the medieval world was convulsed by millenarian social movements whose members sought to live as if the Second Coming were imminent, or as if the millennium had already dawned and they were to live the life of God's saints while awaiting Christ's Second Coming among them. The millenarian expectation was further charged when combined with a particular – and heterodox – understanding of Augustine's description of the City of God as 'a communion of saints'. Regarding the City of God as a state of earthly preparation for the Second Coming, this could lead to the setting up of communities of perfected men and women who set themselves apart from the unregenerated society around them, and who saw themselves as owing no allegiance to the laws and customs of the secular state. It was these antinomian groups, such as the Ranters of seventeenth-century England or the Oneida community of nineteenth-century America, who with their 'sawciness and irreverence' were the most offensive to orthodox Christians. Their arrogance, however, sprang not from simple perversity but from the conviction that, being already perfected, they were incapable of sinning. Their favourite biblical text was Paul's 'To the pure all things are pure.' But they could also quote Luther: 'Inasmuch as a man is a Christian, he is above the law and sin. For he hath Christ the Lord of the law present and inclosed in his heart.'

For all antinomian and millenarian groups, the teachings of the twelfth-century Calabrian monk Joachim of Fiore were a specially important source of inspiration and support. Of all the commentaries on the Revelation of St John, it was Joachim's which offered the most serious and influential challenge to the Augustinian orthodoxy of the Church. Joachim was not formally a millenarian, and he himself was never denounced as heretical by the Catholic Church. But he preached a doctrine that could be and frequently was interpreted in a revolutionary millenarian manner by a long succession of followers, among whom were Thomas Müntzer, Tommaso Campanella and Gerrard Winstanley. Basing himself on the trinitarian doctrine, Joachim presented a historical scheme in which three different dispensations come to pass in three different epochs in which the three persons of the Trinity are successively manifested. The first is the dispensation of the Father, the second that of the Son, and the third that of the Holy Ghost. The third epoch, the age of the Holy Ghost, was just beginning. 'Already we can apprehend the unveiling of the final liberation of the spirit in its plenitude.' In the first age men are governed by fear of the Father, in the second by faith in the Son, but in the third age they will be governed by love, as 'friends to God'. It was St Benedict, whose monastic rule is conceived in love and joy, who heralded the new age of the Holy Ghost; and it was the monks, the 'spiritual men', who would be the leaders of this third and last dispensation. The Church, with its clerical hierarchy and strict discipline, is not permanent as Augustine insists but belongs only to the second age. It is destined to be superseded by the monks as the truest representatives of the Holy Ghost. They would guide men to a full spiritual understanding and perfection in holiness. It was following this prophecy that the Franciscan Spirituals of the thirteenth and fourteenth centuries rejected pope, hierarchy, sacraments, the Scriptures and all theology. They endeavoured to live a Christian life of unconditional poverty and humility, and to transform the Church into a community of the Holy Spirit.

It was not difficult to associate Joachim's 'third age' with the millennium, whether as the immediate prelude to it or in the 'post-millennialist' sense, as the preparatory setting for Christ's Second Coming. Hence it is that Joachimite beliefs can be found in so many of the radical millennarian movements of medieval and early modern times: the Cathars, the Brethren of the Free Spirit, the Hussites, the Taborites, the Anabaptists and the Fifth Monarchists and other millenarian sects of the English Civil War.[24] Whatever the specific interpretation, the important thing, as with the Jewish concept of the Days of the Messiah, was the belief in an order of *earthly* perfection, seen as something both imminent and realizable. The millennium or the third age of the Holy Ghost promised a truly Christian dispensation of love, peace and freedom, of life lived on this earth according to the precepts of the Sermon on the Mount. It proffered a foretaste of the heavenly bliss to come. It was here, uniquely, that religion and utopia overlapped one another. The normal religious devaluation of the world – and hence of utopia – when set against the promise of other-worldly fulfilment, was here radically qualified. The concept of the millennium offered an intermediate term between the purely earthly existence of fallen man and the purely heavenly existence of man redeemed. It is a transcendental concept, truly, but a transcendence that links earth and heaven rather than irreconcilably separating them. It holds out the prospect of 'heaven on earth', of a 'new earth' which in its paradisiac perfection harks back to the Paradise before the Fall and anticipates the heavenly Paradise of the life to come. The Lord's prayer really says it all: 'Thy kingdom come, Thy will be done, on earth as it is in heaven.'

To an extent, then, the idea of the millennium, like that of perfectibility in general, also contributed to keep alive within Christianity the otherwise blasphemous Hellenic theme of 'men like gods'. It was said of Henry Niclaes, the founder of the millenarian Family of Love, that he 'turns religion upside down. He buildeth heaven here upon earth; he maketh God man and man God.' Thomas Müntzer taught that 'we fleshly earthly men become gods through Christ's becoming human and thus we are pupils of God with Him, taught by Him Himself and made divine by Him. Nay far more. We become altogether transformed so that the earthly life changes over into heaven.' Certainly those who saw themselves as the saints of the new dispensation often claimed possession of the divine prerogatives of justice and mercy, although in their exercise of them they sometimes made men wonder whether it was the reign of the Antichrist rather than Christ that was being ushered in. Millenarianism did not necessarily lead to revolutionary action. Doctrinally it was just as possible for it to lead to a passive awaiting of the Second Coming, as indeed has happened within most latter-day millennial sects. It was after all God, and God alone, who would or could bring in the new dispensation. But right up to the end of the seventeenth century and often beyond, it was impossible for most millenarian groups not to prepare themselves actively for Christ's Second Coming, to live as if the millennium were imminent. For some, indeed, especially the Joachimites, the millennium had already arrived: as the Shakers and members of the Oneida community were also to hold in nineteenth-century America. In either case, the belief involved a radical reconstruction of individual and social life, such that human society should approach as nearly as possible to the heavenly state which the millennium mirrored. This is not utopia, as we shall see; but it is as close to it as Christianity ever got.

It was fitting that Joachim should choose the monks as the heralds and leaders of the new age. For as one last Christian contribution to utopia we must include the medieval monastery. To the ideological strands of perfectibilism and millenarianism, the monastery added an institutional idea. To be sure, there was always the Church itself as the supreme institutional ideal. In the orthodox view, the Church as Christ's body and the communion of all believers was the divinely inspired and unique vehicle of salvation. There could be no rival: *extra ecclesiam nulla salus*. The Church was, Augustine insisted, 'even now

. . . the kingdom of Christ and the kingdom of heaven'; to the English Puritan preacher William Dell it was 'the freest society under heaven'. But to the Digger leader Gerrard Winstanley, and to many Christians throughout the centuries, the Church as actually constituted, whether Catholic or 'reformed', was a prison, the abode and embodiment of the Beast. And, whatever the official ideal, the actual history of the Church as a powerful secular institution on the whole disqualified it as a serious candidate for utopia. It was not so much practices such as the Inquisition and heresy-hunting that were the obstacle: utopia indeed often seems to have borrowed these wholesale from Christianity. It was rather the frequent compromises and changes of direction, forced upon it as the very condition of its continued survival as a great power, that rendered the Church a poor utopian exemplar.

But if not the Church, then the monastery offered itself as a likelier candidate by far. Despite repeated tendencies towards worldliness and corruption, the medieval monastery has appeared to many thinkers to come closest in conception and even achievement to the general form of the ideal society. As basically laid down by St Benedict in the sixth century, the monastery was an autonomous, man-made, essentially egalitarian communal order. Rules and discipline exist, often in a high degree, but they are freely accepted by those who have committed themselves to this austere and ascetic way of life. The ends of the monastery were of course prayer and contemplation; but to a remarkable extent it concerned itself with the precise and highly efficient organization of the day-to-day life of earthly existence – as, indeed, it had to to retain its self-sufficiency. The day was meticulously divided into periods, each with its allotted activity of prayer, reading, resting, working, eating and sleeping. Labour was rescued from the denigration of the Greeks and the curse laid by God upon Adam. To the extent that any wordly activity could be deemed worthy, the monastery dignified manual work and gave it a central and almost spiritualized role in the life of the community. 'To work is to pray' is a Lutheran slogan, breaking down the traditional distinction between monastery and market-place; but its practical origin, as Max Weber recognized, was in the monastic life of the Middle Ages. Elevated by this spirit, the monasteries, abbeys and priories were powerhouses of advanced economic activities and techniques. As isolated communities by definition, they could be laboratories of scientific and economic experimentation. The monks were pioneers in fish breeding and plant cultivation. Their grounds and gardens were the admired models for lay imitation. They generally made the best wines and liqueurs of the region. But all this activity was, in principle at least, a by-product. Their aim was not and could not be economic advance, or progress in any material sense. The only progress the monks could recognize was progress towards spiritual perfection, for it was to achieve something like perfection in the Christian sense that the monks removed themselves from the worldly affairs of society. The cloister was the 'gate of Paradise'; it opened on to an order of timeless perfection. 'All the hopes, prayers and demands the medieval Christian set on the monks and the monasteries were centred on one expectation: that they would achieve the complete sanctity of a perfect Christian life.'[25]

'The European monastery,' say the Manuels, 'was the first institution to wrestle with the quintessential Christian utopian problem, the creation of a society that was both a simulacrum on earth of a divine order and a preparation for the beatitude of a future time.'[26] It is hardly surprising, given this conception and the enormous influence of monasticism on Christian thought and practice, that the early utopias should be so evidently marked by the presence of the monastery. Thomas More actually lived for four years with the monks of the Charterhouse, and the monastic ideal is pervasive in his *Utopia*. Carthusian and Benedictine rules underlie much of the highly regulated order of Utopia: the plainness and uniformity of dress; the absence of pomp and the general air of austerity; the devotion to work, study and prayer; the community of property and dwelling; the communal meals, 'taken with some reading which is conducive to morality'; and the common surveillance of all by all: for, as the monk has no privacy, so the Utopian citizen is always 'in present sight and under the eyes of every man'. Similarly with the *City of the Sun*: its author, Tommaso Campanella, was trained as a monk and monastic characteristics feature strongly in his utopia. As with More, there is a simplicity of dress and manner; work and moral discipline are emphasized and strictly regulated; property is held in common; meals are served in communal refectories; and those who wish to become citizens of the City of the Sun have to serve a kind of novitiate. The citizens of Andreae's *Christianopolis* also live a frugal, communally ordered life, akin in many respects to that of More's Utopia. Even in Francis Bacon's *New Atlantis*, of all the seventeenth-century utopias the one least obviously indebted to Christian conceptions, the House of Saloman is modelled fairly clearly on the monastery. Since the *New Atlantis* became for many later utopians the exemplary modern utopia, it is a tribute to the power of the monastic ideal that it should prove so enduringly appealing, even in the most hard-headed and scientific of ages – as is evidenced in the repeated recurrence of monastic forms in the socialist and scientific utopias of the nineteenth and twentieth centuries.[27]

THE MODERN UTOPIA

The Golden Age, the Ideal City, the Land of Cokaygne; Paradise, the millennium, the monastic ideal: when we consider the power, by no means yet lost, of these ideas and images, are we not compelled to accept with Orwell the essential timelessness and universality of the utopian conception? Nurtured as it is by these almost archetypal forms, does that not also suggest that utopia itself is an archetype, a natural propensity of the human mind, like dreaming? 'Men everywhere seem addicted to visions of ideal otherness', says David Plath. The Manuels speak of 'the mythic substratum' of utopian thought; and Arthur Koestler has said that 'all utopias are fed from the sources of mythology; the social engineer's blue-prints are merely revised editions of the ancient text.'[28]

But, firstly, utopia is *not* universal. It appears only in societies with the classical and Christian heritage, that is, only in the West. Other societies have, in relative abundance, paradises, primitivist myths of a Golden Age of justice and equality, Cokaygne-type fantasies, even messianic beliefs; they do not have utopia.[29]

But this suggests the second thing. Christian civilization may be unique in giving birth to utopia (as has already been suggested, millenarianism is probably the key link);[30] but the Christian and classical components are not themselves utopia. The Golden Age, the ideal city and the rest constitute the essential 'pre-history' of utopia. Like many prehistoric fragments, they remain embedded in the later forms; or, to change the figure somewhat, we may say that they live on in the Unconscious of utopia, giving it much of its motivation and dynamism. But, no more than the id can be identified with the ego, can these utopian 'pre-echoes' be identified with utopia itself.

The difficulties of this position are obvious enough. The eponymous utopia was written by Sir Thomas More. That is, the modern utopia was invented by a Christian martyr later canonized by the Catholic Church. More's Christian piety was in many respects matched by that of the two other great early utopists, Campanella and Andreae, both of whom passed their entire lives as priests and preachers. Monasticism was, as we have seen, a strong influence on all three. Even the 'pansophic' utopias of Bacon, Comenius and Leibniz, with their stress on science, were conceived within a framework of Christian philosophy: science was the means both to a better knowledge of God and to the creation of a truly Christian society.[31] The title of Andreae's utopia, *Christianopolis*, sums up well the evident goal of all the principal utopian thinkers to the end of the seventeenth century: the ideal Christian commonwealth, a Christian utopia. And at a more popular level, there were, right up to the end of the nineteenth century, persistent outbursts of millenarianism to keep the torch of religious utopianism alight: whether among the Anabaptists of Münster, the Diggers, Ranters and Fifth Monarchy men of the English Civil War, or the Shaker and Oneida communities in America. Given the continuing presence of such powerful Christian themes, there seems on the face of it no real warrant for treating utopia as an independent and separate enterprise.

But then, there are the other equally well-known but discrepant features of the early utopias. More's Utopians, like Campanella's Solarians, are pagans. More's Utopia is 'a pagan state founded on Reason and Philosophy'.[32] Although most of his Utopians subscribe to some kind of monotheistic religion, they have a distinctly relaxed attitude towards it, and towards the religious beliefs of others. 'Some worship for god the sun, some the moon, some some other of the planets.' They are receptive to the Christianity brought by Raphael Hythloday and his companions, as chiming with their own religious beliefs, but will not allow it to be imposed on anyone or prevent anyone from speaking against it. 'For this is one of the ancientist laws among them, that no man shall be blamed for reasoning in the maintenance of his own religion. For King Utopus . . . made a decree that it should be lawful for every man to favour and follow what religion he would . . .' The Utopians have among them their 'religious men', the Buthrescas, and their dedication and ascetic way of life are admired. But their lives are not the lives of the majority of Utopians. Like the monasteries of Europe, the religious sects of Utopia are not coterminous with society but live as virtually segregated enclaves within it.[33]

Then there is the attitude to the good life among the Utopians, an attitude markedly at odds with the severe and ascetic character that one would expect of a monastic or religious utopia. The Utopians, to Hythloday's surprise and mild disapproval, take the pursuit of pleasure to be the chief or best part of human happiness. 'Nature (they say) prescribeth to us a joyful life, that is to say, pleasure, as the end of all our operations.' Moreover, they are outrageously Benthamite in their view of pleasure. 'They think that all our actions, and in them the virtues themselves, be referred at last to pleasure as their end and felicity'; and they are studious 'that a less pleasure hinder not a bigger, and that the pleasure be no cause of displeasure. . . . For they judge it extreme madness to follow sharp and painful virtue. . . .' True, it speedily turns out that they count the cultivation of the mind to be the greatest pleasure; but not at the sacrifice of the pleasures of the body, which include good eating and good drinking as well as the maintenance of a healthful condition ('for they agree . . . that health is a most sovereign pleasure').[34]

This same brisk and cheerful utilitarian spirit is seen at work throughout Utopia. All the fifty-four cities of Utopia are built to the same plan. All the private houses are exactly alike; the doors have no locks, and 'whoso will may go in, for there is nothing within the houses that is private or any man's own.' The Utopians change their houses by lot every ten years, to prevent feelings of possessiveness developing. On the farms, which are uniformly organized and based on a rational and efficient pattern of work, chickens are hatched not by the hens but in incubators. Men and women see each other naked before deciding to marry, the Utopians not disdaining the importance of physical attributes, since 'the endowments of the body cause the virtues of the mind more to be esteemed and regarded, yea, even in the marriages of wise men.' Divorce is permitted, and euthanasia practised, again on the grounds of allowing the lesser evil. Severe crimes are punished not by death but by bondage; 'for that they suppose to be to the offenders no less grief, and to the commonwealth more profit, than if they should hastily put them to death, and so make them quite out of the way. For there cometh more profit of their labour than of their death, and by their example they fear other the longer from like offences.' It is in something of the same canny and combative spirit that, having abolished money, the Utopians use the gold and silver that they get through trade to make chamberpots and prisoners' chains, thereby showing their contempt for these useless metals while at the same time constantly reminding themselves of the folly of other nations in worshipping them.[35]

In all these ways, More shows himself, and his Utopia, to be the product of a new age. His Utopia has a rationalism and a realism that we associate typically with the classical revival of the Renaissance, and that are to be found equally in the architectural utopias of fifteenth and sixteenth-century Italy. We should remember that *Utopia* was published less than three years after Niccolò Machiavelli's *The Prince* (1513). More's urbane and witty style, his 'profound sense of political realities',[36] constantly evoke the relentlessly de-mystified world of Machiavelli's notorious treatise (and, incidentally, remind us that utopia and anti-utopia shadow each other very closely). Both thinkers, in their very different ways, share in the classical republicanism that enjoyed such favour among Renaissance humanists. More is often described as a Christian humanist,[37] and certainly his life as a whole cannot be understood outside his religion. But there has been a tendency also, in recent years, to read his *Utopia* predominantly through religious eyes, to stress his medievalism and monasticism, his Christianity over his humanism.[38] While this makes life easier for his biographers, it also reduces the complexity, the contradictoriness perhaps, of the man and his times. Christianity and pagan classicism could be fused, as was common in Renaissance neo-Platonism, but there was always a tension between them. This can be seen as much in More's agonizing over whether to remain a monk at the Charterhouse as in the efforts of his friend Erasmus to secure a papal dispensation from the fulfilment of his monastic vows. In any case, whatever More's final commitment, in his *Utopia* it is his humanism which is clearly uppermost. Over and above the specifically Christian influences, such as monasticism, it is More's veneration for Plato and his delight in the Roman satirists that most strongly shine through.[39]

Not just the Renaissance but also the Reformation defines the modern utopia. Barely a year after the appearance of More's *Utopia*, Martin Luther nailed his Ninety-Five Theses to the church door at Wittenberg (1517). Luther's challenge to Rome of course initiated an era of intense religiosity in Europe. But it was a religiosity marked by bitter conflict, and it ended leaving Europe exhausted and divided. After that, Europe preferred to express its passions in non-religious terms, in the terms of secular revolutionism. The Protestant Reformation, in other words, launched Europe, and eventually the world, on the road to secularization. It broke up the unity of medieval Christendom, and gave rise to such a plurality of discordant voices that they ended up by silencing each other.

All this took a long time, of course; and many of the early utopias show the impress of one or other religious persuasion. But the ultimately secular nature of the modern utopia was clear from the start, in the paganism of More's and Campanella's utopias. It was, we may say, a necessary condition for the emergence of utopia that the religious world-view prevalent in the Middle Ages should cease to monopolize men's minds. For however much millenarianism and antinomianism might lead believers to utopian ventures, in the end the dominant and decisive teaching of Christianity was that Christ's kingdom was not of this world. As Bishop Goodman put it in the seventeenth century, 'If Paradise were to be replanted on earth, God had never expelled man from Paradise.' The problem for the religious radicals, as Christopher Hill has said, was that 'however radical their conclusions, however heretical their theology, their escape route from theology was theological.'[40] The aim to set up a perfect society on earth was ultimately blasphemy, and could not really be anything else. It gave a quite disproportionate attention to the City of Man, as opposed to the City of God. Christianity might and frequently did stir up utopian impulses; but it also effectively stifled them, and ensured that, so long as it remained the dominant ideology, no utopian tradition would be established. Neither contemplative withdrawal to the monastery nor active preparation for the Second Coming of Christ can be equated with the utopian enterprise in which humans themselves, unaided by any divine agency, take on the god-like task of redeeming and transforming humanity. Seen as such, utopia must always be to the Christian 'the perennial heresy'; and ultimately, the 'Christian utopia' is a contradiction in terms.[41]

It cannot be accidental, then, that the birth of the modern utopia coincides with the break-up of the unified Christian world. More's *Utopia*, Campanella's *City of the Sun*, Andreae's *Christianopolis*, Bacon's *New Atlantis*: these, the 'classic' modern utopias, together with a host of others, emerged out of the turmoil of the wars and conflicts of religion in sixteenth and seventeenth-century Europe. These conflicts led eventually to a secularized world, a world of new possibilities which opened up new forms and objects for utopia. In much the same way, and at much the same time, the European voyages of exploration and discovery were literally discovering a New World, which was bound to stir the utopian imagination. In 1507 Amerigo Vespucci published an account of his travels. Raphael Hythloday, More tells us, had accompanied Vespucci on all four of his voyages, being one of the 23 men left behind at Cape Frio on the fourth voyage. From there he and some companions had made the further voyages which had led to the discovery of Utopia. Utopia is Nowhere; but there have been many ingenious and not necessarily far-fetched efforts to show the correspondence between Utopian institutions and those of certain New World civilizations, most notably that of the Incas, reports of which were already available to More.[42]

Again, no more than with the Reformation can there be any question of a direct causal connection between the voyages of discovery and the invention of utopia. The immediate effect of the discovery of America was to intensify apocalyptic expectation (as we shall see later). But the encounter with exotic and even outlandish places and cultures was bound sooner or later to affect utopian conceptions. It had been standard literary practice since the time of Herodotus to use the customs and institutions of distant lands, real or invented, as a critical or satirical commentary on one's own age and people. The European voyages revived this practice by adding immeasurably to the store of knowledge of strange worlds – not to mention the sense of possibility they opened up with their vistas of vast spaces still to be explored and perhaps settled. European ships returned regularly with colourful accounts of the ways of far-flung cultures, East and West. A vast new literature and culture of the voyages of discovery began to accumulate, whether in sailors' fireside yarns or in the detailed reports of the explorers, *conquistadores* and missionaries. These travellers' tales were, many of them, the raw material of utopias – almost incipient utopias. Shakespeare might use the accounts of South Sea cannibals to produce a monster like Caliban in *The Tempest*; but for Montaigne their lives were the stuff of an arcadian utopia. It was the very strangeness of these cultures that made them such perfect material for utopia. Utopias have always aspired to be both critical and constructive. The alien forms of distant cultures enabled the utopian writer to establish the crucial 'critical distance' from his own society, while often suggesting something of the constructive alternative that his utopia aimed to present. Othello's 'anthropophagi and men whose heads do grow beneath their shoulders' could, in the hands of a Swift or a Diderot, turn into admired utopian exemplars.

The Renaissance, the Reformation and the European voyages of discovery are one conventional and still persuasive line of division between the modern and the ancient and medieval worlds. Utopia is, on this view, a creation of the modern world.[43] It is a modern European novelty. Thomas More did not just invent the word 'utopia', in a typically witty conflation of two Greek words (*eutopos* = 'good place', *outopos* = 'no place'): he invented the *thing.* Part of that new thing was a new literary form or genre; the other, more important, part was a novel and far-reaching conception of the possibilities of human and social transformation.

More said of his *Utopia* that it was 'a fiction whereby the truth, as if smeared with honey, might a little more pleasantly slide into men's minds'.[44] All utopias are of course fictions, by definition; and in choosing the utopia over other possible literary forms, later writers did so with much the same didactic intention as More. In one sense this simply expressed the common Aristotelian preference for the study of poetry over history, fiction over fact, as more effectively communicating moral and social truths. But the fictional form that More invented for his purpose differed radically from the standard poetic forms, just as it differed from the philosophical dialogue that had been the principle vehicle for social and political speculation. As Hexter points out, only Book One – the later addition – of *Utopia* is in the conventional dialogue form, the dialogue that Hexter calls 'the Dialogue of Counsel'; Book Two, the utopia proper, is a discourse, a piece of narrative and descriptive fiction. Here too of course More had his predecessors, especially in the Hellenistic romancers and writers of imaginary voyages, inspired perhaps by Alexander's eastern exploits just as the modern utopia was influenced by the voyages of discovery.[45] For the strong vein of satire in *Utopia*, as well, there were the literary models of the Roman satirists Horace, Persius and Juvenal.[46] But in fusing together these elements, and putting them to the purposes more traditionally reserved to the Platonic dialogue of the good life and the good state, More achieved a creative synthesis that transcended the forms and purposes not simply of the romancers and satirists but of the Platonic dialogue as well.

Plato's *Republic* is the only classical text that looks even remotely like More's *Utopia* (and Moses Finley reminds us that it is the only classical text that looks remotely like *any* utopia, all other classical utopias appearing to us only in fragments or as somewhat dubious reports at second-hand of utopian experiments[47]). But merely to read a few pages of the *Republic* followed immediately by a few pages of *Utopia* is to be aware of standing in two quite different literary worlds. Socrates' enquiry is into the nature of justice and the just man. He is led to the construction of the ideal state on the consideration that it will be easier to see justice 'writ large' in the community than 'writ small' in the individual. But the concern throughout remains the realization of justice in the individual. Socrates argues from the social model to the individual, not from the individual to society. At the end of the *Republic* he makes it clear that the state that he has sketched is not a blueprint for the practical guidance of some future reformer, but an ideal to be contemplated in the present by the individual mind. The just man will guide his conduct by 'the city which is within him', 'the city which is his own'.

> I understand; you mean that he will be a ruler in the city of which we are the founders, and which exists in idea only; for I do not believe that there is such an one anywhere on earth? In heaven, I replied, there is laid up a pattern of it, methinks, which he who desires may behold, and beholding, may set his own house in order. But whether such an one exists, or ever will exist in fact, is no matter; for he will live after the manner of that city, having nothing to do with any other.[48]

This conception justifies the highly abstract nature of the portrait of the ideal state. No physical details are given, no attempt made to imagine the Republic as an actual society with real men and women. Social groups and social institutions are presented more or less directly as what essentially they are: illustrations of philosophic categories expressing the nature of justice. If there is fiction here – as of course there is, of a kind – it is the fiction familiar in philosophical discourse where one reaches for a concrete example to illustrate the abstract concept.

Plato's example was followed not so much by the utopian writers but by the political philosophers and political theorists of later centuries. It is in the 'ideal constitution' tradition of Bodin (*La République*), Hobbes (*Leviathan*), Harrington (*Oceana*), Locke (*The Second Treatise of Government*) and Rousseau (*The Social Contract*) that we should look for the deepest Platonic influence. What all these offer are prescriptive models of the ideal political constitution. They lay down in opening chapters ('Of Man', 'Of Nature', etc.) various postulates, propositions and presumptions about the nature of man and society. They then deduce or derive from these general propositions the principles of the best state or the 'natural' order of society. They are thus, like Plato, under no obligation to furnish the details or show the practice of their undoubtedly fictional but very abstractly conceived societies.

The fiction of More's Utopia and its successors is of a very different kind. It shows the best society not as a normative or prescriptive model but as actually achieved, as already in existence. Utopia is a description of the best (or, in anti-utopia, the worst) society not as an abstract ideal, and not simply as a satirical foil to the existing society, but as a society in full operation in which we are invited vicariously to participate. A group of travellers happens upon a hitherto unknown society in a remote part of the globe; a spaceship lands on a planet whose inhabitants have radically different lives from earthlings; a time traveller journeys backwards and forwards to strange and astounding times: all give us a detailed account of what they see and do, of their adventures among the utopians, of the mixture of disbelief and admiration with which they contemplate utopian life. In the later utopian tradition, as in the anti-utopias of Zamyatin, Huxley and Orwell, the journey to utopia, whether in space or time, is dispensed with, and we are plunged straight into the daily lives of the utopians. The authors avail themselves of the full range of techniques, including characterization and plot, however rudimentary, that we associate with narrative fiction. Here it is made clear what is not so apparent in the earlier utopias: that the utopia is closer to the novel than to any other literary genre; *is* in fact a novel, though not necessarily of the kind that we have come to identify too exclusively with its nineteenth-century form and focus.[49]

More, then, invented, more or less single handedly, a new literary genre. But the literary form of utopia is not an important concern of this study; nor perhaps should it be in any serious treatment of utopia. Very few utopias stand out as great works of literature – More's *Utopia* and William Morris's *News From Nowhere* are among the best – and in many cases utopian authors are perfunctory in the extreme in their selection and use of the form. The didactic purpose overwhelms any literary aspiration: Bellamy's *Looking Backward* and

Skinner's *Walden Two* are clear examples of this, as are a host of lesser utopias. In any case, any attempt to define the boundaries of utopia by purely literary criteria speedily ends up in absurdity, and is best abandoned for a recognition of the diversity of literary forms that make up utopia. For some purposes, and depending on the definition (or lack of it) of utopia, it makes perfectly good sense to discuss as utopias works which are not formally so but are, as it were, in the 'utopian mode', products of the utopian imagination or temperament. So, in his study of seventeenth-century English utopias, J. C. Davis makes a good case for considering Gerrard Winstanley's *Law of Freedom in a Platform* and James Harrington's *Oceana* along with more obviously formal utopias such as Bacon's *New Atlantis* and Samuel Gott's *Nova Solyma*. Similarly, the Manuels, who eschew any definition of utopia, show the value of discussing Rousseau's *Émile* and *The Social Contract* as Enlightenment utopias, even though they admit that Rousseau 'never composed a proper speaking-picture utopia' and that in fact 'none of the *patres majores* of the French Enlightenment actually wrote a proper utopia'.[50] We too will have occasion to consider the utopia to be found in the writings of Saint-Simon, Marx and Engels, even though none of them ever wrote a formal utopia. More broadly still, 'democracy', 'socialism', 'science', 'the free market economy' – all can be fairly treated as utopian conceptions and programmes, just as, in a somewhat different way, the concept of 'America' or 'the Soviet Union' can take on utopian dimensions.[51]

As so often with concepts in the human sciences, it seems best not to insist on some 'essentialist' definition of utopia but to let a definition emerge: by use and context shall we know our utopias. Following Wittgenstein's discussion of these matters, we should also not expect to find more than 'family resemblances' between various instances of utopia. So nothing is to be gained by attempting to be too precise or exclusive. Even the line of demarcation which we have sought to establish between the ancient and the modern utopia must, on various occasions and for particular purposes, break down. Having expelled the *Republic* from the utopian canon, we shall not hesitate to re-admit it when necessary. Anything else would be absurd in the face of the fact that utopian writers themselves have often chosen to regard it as the great and original expression of the form. That they are, strictly speaking, wrong is hardly the point.

Still, it is one thing to ignore on occasion the formal differences, the difference of literary genre, between Plato's *Republic* and More's *Utopia*. As a feature distinguishing the ancient from the modern utopia the social content is infinitely more important. The Republic, like Utopia, is a communist society. In both, community of property serves a more general scheme of communal living involving the prohibition of money, common military training, common education, common habitation and common dining. But beyond this, the differences between Plato and More are equally striking. Plato's is an aristocratic vision, More's an egalitarian. The communism of the ideal life is restricted in the Republic to the Guardians. The auxiliaries and artisans lead the ordinary life of lesser mortals, brainwashed by the 'noble' or 'golden lie' to devote themselves to the maintenance of their rulers, the Guardians. The ideal life of the Guardians is moreover contemplative; labour is despised as an obstacle to the higher life of the mind. The whole communal order of the Republic is directed to the creation of a self-enclosed, insulated elite, separated from the masses whose life they do not share and on whose labour they depend. The Guardians thus resemble not so much the monks of the medieval monastery as the Brahmins of the hierarchical, caste-based system of traditional Hindu civilization.

By contrast, the communism of More's Utopia underpins the social existence of all citizens. The education of all Utopians is the same; all have an equal voice in the choice of magistrates; the use of money is prohibited throughout Utopia; and no distinctions of rank or privilege are recognized. Crucially, there is a community of work. All Utopians, men and women alike, have an obligation to labour. All must work on the farms and in the fields, as well as specialize in a craft. As with the medieval monastery, this obligation is embraced as a necessity which also dignifies, and which is central to the whole communal purpose. For Utopians to depend on the labour of others would be to undermine the whole foundation of a society dedicated to social equality. The institution of bondage in Utopia reinforces rather than qualifies this. Bondage exists as a punishment for certain offences; but it is made clear that the compulsory labour of the bondsmen serves not an economic but a strictly penal function. Utopians are made bondsmen not because they are needed to do the unpleasant work but because they are bad Utopians in need of moral reformation.[52]

The egalitarianism of More's communism is repeated in most of the utopias of the sixteenth and seventeenth centuries. So, too, is the insistence on work, especially manual work, as the common duty of all citizens, together with its increasing elevation as an honourable and ethical activity. Berneri is probably right to suggest that behind this attitude, so different from that of the Greeks, lay not just the medieval monastery but the medieval city of self-governing guilds and councils, seen as a community of producers.[53] The guildsmen were most likely to admire Campanella's Solarians, who from an early age are introduced to the arts and crafts of the city, and who 'also go into the country to learn the work in the fields and pastures. . . . They laugh at us, who consider our workmen ignoble and hold to be noble those who have learned no trade and live in idleness.' Andreae goes even further in attacking the prejudice against manual labour, and in showing how work, if it is equally shared and carried out in an atmosphere of freedom, can be both immensely productive and spiritually ennobling. Christianopolis 'is, as it were, one single workshop', and its inhabitants regard 'the employment of their hands' as necessary and fitting in the discharge of their public duties, just as we do in the running of our own homes.

> For what we are in our homes, they are in their city, which they not undeservedly think a home. And for this reason it is no disgrace to perform any public function, so long as it be not indecent. Hence all work, even that which seems rather irksome, is accomplished in good time and without much difficulty. . . . Who denies that every citizen, in his own place and order, owes his best efforts to the republic, not merely with his tongue but also with hands and shoulder? With an entirely mistaken sense of delicacy do the carnal-minded shrink from touching earth, water, stones, coal and things of that sort; but they think it grand to have in their possession to delight them, horses, dogs, harlots and similar creatures.[54]

The centrality of work in the modern utopia reflects the wider phenomenon of the discovery of labour as a, perhaps *the*, significant factor of production, and the widespread attempts at this time to make the poor 'a productive resource'.[55] More generally, too, the rise of the modern utopia is clearly linked to the great expansion of trade and commerce that took place in the sixteenth and seventeenth centuries in Europe. The sense of boundless material growth, of an 'unbound Prometheus', that men began dimly to discern in these centuries is, along with egalitarianism, a key feature of modern utopianism. Thus the kinds of associations that Max Weber and his followers have made between Protestantism, capitalism, science and technology[56] are relevant also to the rise of the modern utopia. But just as science, work and production eventually threw off the religious ideology that initially permitted and promoted them, so too utopia had to reject a cardinal tenet of the Christian philosophy that in other respects was unusually encouraging to the utopian enterprise. It had, that is, to reject all concepts of 'original sin' or man's 'fallen nature' as incompatible with the utopian project of perfection. As H. G. Wells rightly said in *A Modern Utopia*, 'the leading principle of the Utopian religion is the repudiation of the doctrine of original sin.'[57] This was a marked feature of all the classical utopias of the sixteenth and seventeenth centuries, whether or not formally Christian. 'Utopia', Judith Shklar has written, 'was a way of rejecting the notion of "original sin" which regarded natural human virtue and reason as feeble and fatally impaired faculties. Whatever else the classical utopias might say or fail to say, all were attacks on the radical theory of original sin. Utopia is always a measure of the moral heights man could attain using only his natural powers "purely by the natural light".'[58]

It is just this aspect of utopianism that most offended orthodox Christians such as G. K. Chesterton and C. S. Lewis. Writing of Wells, Chesterton memorably remarked:

> The weakness of all utopias is this, that they take the greatest difficulty of man [i.e. original sin] and assume it to be overcome, and then give an elaborate account of the overcoming of smaller ones. They first assume that no man will want more than his share, and then are very ingenious in explaining whether his share will be delivered by motor-car or balloon.[59]

Chesterton's amusing and highly effective barb is however more correctly directed against the specifically Wellsian belief that utopia 'holds that man, on the whole, is good'. This certainly has not been seen as a necessary postulate of utopia. Carried to an extreme, it would indeed make utopia redundant. But what does seem necessary is that human nature should be seen as almost infinitely malleable – for practical purposes, a *tabula rasa*. There should, above all, not be such intrinsic checks and obstacles to human perfectibility as to doom the utopian enterprise from the start. If the 'old Adam' will and must out, if ineradicable greed or aggression will continue to plague utopia, then it is futile to invent it.

Here again More lays down the exemplary utopian pattern. His Utopians are 'natural men', but they are neither naturally good nor naturally evil. They are not so corrupt that they are for ever incapable of making and inhabiting the good society. But nor are they so good that the laws and institutions of Utopia are unnecessary. Hexter makes the point well:

Utopia is the best of commonwealths, and Utopians are the best of men; but it is not because they are of a better stuff and nature than other men; it is because their laws, ordinances, rearing, and rules of living are such as to make effective man's natural capacity for good, while suppressing his natural propensity for evil. The sound social, political, and economic regimen under which they live is the cause of the civic virtue of the Utopians, not the other way about; their institutions are not the creation but the creator of their good qualities.[60]

The paradox in the making of the modern utopia is that the Reformation, which in certain important respects stimulated utopian thought, also revived and reinforced the idea of original sin. The current of thought that could produce the religious utopianism of Thomas Müntzer or Gerrard Winstanley could also, in its Augustinian emphasis on sin and the doctrine of the elect, block any truly utopian conception of human society. Ultimately the Lutheran and Calvinist obsession with sin, and the reformers' implacable hostility to any Pelagian doctrine of perfectibilism, was to drive utopia firmly in a secular direction. But before that became fully apparent in the eighteenth century, Francis Bacon had made the necessary adjustment by an extraordinary synthesis of Christianity and science. Drawing on the magical and alchemical tradition, Bacon sought to fuse orthodox Christian conceptions of original sin with decidedly unorthodox views of its overcoming. In effect, he put forward the 'truly astonishing claim that it was the business of learning to undo the consequences of the fall of man'.[61] As 'the proud knowledge of good and evil' had brought about the fall of man, so, Bacon argued, 'the pure knowledge of nature and universality' would lead to man's recovery of his original command over the creation. Thus, 'natural philosophy proposes to itself, as its noblest work of all, nothing less than the restitution and renovation of things corruptible.' This then is 'the true end of knowledge . . . it is a restitution and reinvesting (in great part) of man to the sovereignty and power . . . which he had in his first state of creation.'

Christopher Hill points up admirably the significance for utopia of this Baconian achievement.

Though Bacon accepted a Fall of Man, he rejected the full Calvinist doctrine of human depravity. He shared the hope of alchemists and magical writers, that the abundance of Eden might be recreated on earth, in Bacon's case by experiment, mechanical skill, and intense cooperative effort. Sin for him was largely the result of ignorance and poverty. Labour, the curse of fallen man, might be the means whereby he would rise again. . . .

The popularization of Bacon's ideas after 1640 thus helped to get rid of the shadow that had dogged humanity for so many centuries: the shadow of original sin. What alchemy and Calvinism had in common was that salvation came from without, from the philosopher's stone or the grace of God. Bacon extracted from the magical–alchemical tradition the novel idea that men could help themselves – mankind, not merely favoured individuals. This together with the dramatic events of the English Revolution helped to transform the backward look to a golden age, a Paradise Lost, into a hope for a better life here on earth, attainable by human effort. Bacon's disciple Comenius hoped 'to restore man to the lost image of God, i.e. to the lost perfection of the free will, which consists in the choice of good and the repudiation of evil'.[62]

'Oh, if you knew what our astrologers say of the coming age, and of our age, that has in it more history within a hundred years than all the world had in four thousand years before! Of the wonderful invention of printing and guns, and the use of the magnet. . . .'[63] In thus concluding his *City of the Sun*, Campanella sounded the authentic Baconian note. For if More is the great originator of the egalitarian tendency in modern utopianism, Bacon is the inspirer of its fundamentally expansive and dynamic character. For some, such as H. G. Wells, this 'kinetic' quality is indeed the defining essence of the modern utopia. It was for this that he hailed Bacon's *New Atlantis* as the first of the truly modern utopias, 'the greatest of the scientific utopias', and remarked: 'that Utopia of Bacon's has produced more in the way of real consequences than any other Utopia that was ever written.'[64] Wells was right to see in science the key ingredient of this dynamism, although the link between science and utopia took over a century to become firmly etablished, and even then it remained, as it always has, problematic: the dynamism of science was bound to press against the finished, perfected order of utopia.[65] Nevertheless, from the time of the *New Atlantis* (1627) it was clear that the modern utopia could scarcely deserve the name if it did not incorporate the fruits of the most novel and fundamental development of the modern world, the scientific revolution.

Campanella's *City of the Sun*, first circulated in manuscript form in 1602, deserves the accolade of being the first utopia to make science and scientific research central to its vision. But it was undoubtedly the *New Atlantis* which was most influential in fixing the association between science and utopia. This probably would not have happened on the strength of the *New Atlantis* itself, a mere fragment of a projected utopia that was never finished and perhaps never intended to be. But from the very moment of Bacon's death a group of energetic and enterprising Baconians devoted themselves with conspicuous success to spreading the utopian message of science. In the middle decades of the seventeenth century, the scientific utopia was elaborated and popularized in the activities, projects and publications of Samuel Hartlib, Jan Comenius, William Petty, Robert Boyle, Abraham Cowley and Joseph Glanville, many of whom were members of the 'Invisible College' of scientists who vigorously promoted the idea of a national scientific foundation. Their efforts achieved some sort of culmination in the founding of the Royal Society in 1662, a body explicitly Baconian in inspiration, and whose purpose was admirably summed up in the motto of the House of Saloman in *New Atlantis*: 'The End of our Foundation is the knowledge of Causes, and secret motions of things; and the enlarging of the bounds of Human Empire, to the effecting of all things possible.'[66]

'The effecting of all things possible': this remained the hallmark of the scientific utopia. For what science contributed to utopia was the sense that utopia was ultimately, in the foreseeable future, realizable. More had concluded his *Utopia* with the regretful observation that Utopia was something 'I may rather wish for than hope for'. His utopia seems to have been offered more in the Platonic spirit, as an object of contemplation, than as a realizable human possibility. But in presenting the *New Atlantis* to the public in 1627, Bacon's first editor William Rawley declared roundly: 'Certainly the model is more vast and high than can possibly be imitated in all things; notwithstanding most things therein are within men's power to effect.'[67] The scientific utopia, with its array of workshops, laboratories and research institutes, was thoroughly practical and utilitarian in its emphasis. Its concern with scientific investigation exemplified the Baconian precept that 'nature is only to be commanded by obeying her'; but 'what in operation is most useful, that knowledge is most true.' Command over nature, the enlargement of 'the power and empire of mankind in general over the universe', was always the overriding goal. The scientific utopia aimed to show how human life could become easier, healthier, happier. Technical inventions, eulogized by Bacon as 'new creations and imitations of divine works', were to be the signal means to this end. Bacon declared that the modern inventions of printing, gunpowder and the compass had 'changed the appearance and state of the whole world . . . so that no empire, sect, or star, appears to have exercised a greater power and influence on human affairs than these mechanical discoveries'.[68] This was just the beginning of a process whereby science would revolutionize life and realize utopian aspirations. The vision of the scientific utopia is of a *possible* world. James Spedding, Bacon's Victorian editor, rightly said of this vision that it was

> not of an ideal world released from the natural conditions to which ours is subject, but of our own world as it might be made if we did our duty by it; of a state of things which . . . would one day be actually seen upon this earth such as it is by men such as we are; and the coming of which Bacon believed that his own labours were sensibly hastening.[66]

The introduction of science and technology into utopia also brought into it the idea of progress. There could be no resting point for scientific and technical development, and so utopia too cannot achieve any final state of rest. Whether we see utopia as the realization of the ideals of progress or, with Oscar Wilde, progress as the realization of utopias, the two concepts come to be linked as closely as science and utopia. In the end, indeed, the closeness of utopia to the typical scientific view of progress was to lead to the suppression, temporarily at least, of utopia as a distinctive literary genre. For if the scientific project is so eminently and distinctively a realizable one, might it not best present itself in a historical and realist, not to say materialist, guise, rather than a utopian one? That was precisely what happened at the end of the eighteenth century. But for some time, and in principle at any time, the idea of scientific progress could give rise to a utopia in which the age-old restriction of scarcity was at last overcome. Ancient and many early modern utopias had accepted scarcity of goods as a datum, and perforce their utopias were of a simple and static kind. It was not so much that progress and growth were threatening to the utopian principle as that they could barely be conceived in a social order limited to minor variations on the basic theme of poverty and inertia. Economic stagnation therefore confirmed the static quality of the ancient utopia already implied by a cyclical, naturalistic view of change (which in effect meant no change). But with the productive energies realeased by applied science, the utopia of abundance could replace the utopia of scarcity. Increasingly, utopias held out the prospect of vast resources harnessed to every conceivable human desire and purpose. With original sin overcome by science, there seemed no limit to human progress and perfection. 'Where can the perfectibility of man stop, armed with geometry and the mechanical arts and chemistry?' There was only one possible answer to Sebastian Mercier's rhetorical question in his eighteenth-century utopia, *L'An 2440: nowhere*, that is, utopia.

The realm of utopia is wide but it is not boundless. Utopia is not some unchanging human archetype or universal human propensity. Distinctions have to be made and these must be largely historical. If utopia is not in one very obvious sense concerned with the here-and-now, for the most part it draws both its form and its content from the contemporary reality. Whether or not we choose to call Plato's *Republic* a utopia, or to accept the idea of a Christian utopia, we must recognize the fundamental difference of intention and concern between them, a reflection of the very different conditions that gave rise to them. Both classical and Christian utopianism persisted well into the modern age. They had – and have – a continuing influence on conceptions of utopia. This can make it difficult to see the even more important differences between both these utopian 'prefigurations' and the utopia proper, the modern utopia that was invented in Europe in the sixteenth century. The utopia of the ancient world is socially hierarchical, economically undeveloped and static. The modern utopia is egalitarian, affluent and dynamic. Such a conception emerged under unique historical conditions. As these changed so the content and even, to an extent, the form of utopia changed. So we should not be surprised to find ourselves dealing with utopias of many different kinds, and with many different purposes, in the more than four centuries since More's *Utopia*. A strict definition of utopia would serve no useful purpose; as Nietzsche says, 'only that which has no history can be defined.'

2
Utopia in Nineteenth-Century Europe

> We all feel a-tiptoe with hope and confidence. We *are* on the threshold of a great time, even if our time is not great itself. In science, in religion, in social organization, we all know what great things are in the air. 'We shall see it, but not *now*' – or rather our children and our children's children will see it . . . It is *not* the age of money bags and cant, soot, hubbub, and ugliness. It is the age of great expectation and unwearied striving after better things.
>
> Frederic Harrison, 'A Few Words about the Nineteenth Century', *Fortnightly Review* (April 1882)

> The idea of communism as the goal of history remains a non-materialist and non-dialectial one, best understood as an Idea of Pure Marxist Reason. In so far as it posits the end of scarcity, the disappearance of the state, and an end to the distinction between manual and intellectual labour, it clearly deserves to be called utopian.
>
> Régis Debray, 'Marxism and the National Question', *New Left Review*, vol. 105 (September–October 1977)

> Socialism has been, and . . . still is, *the* utopia of the modern epoch.
>
> Zygmunt Bauman, *Socialism: The Active Utopia* (1976)

The nineteenth century is generally, and rightly, regarded as the most utopian century of modern times. And yet it is almost entirely lacking in the formal literary utopia. Only towards the end of the century did the formal utopia re-appear, in such works as Edward Bellamy's *Looking Backward*, William Morris's *News from Nowhere* and Theodor Hertzka's *Freeland*. The paradox is not an entirely empty one. The decline of the literary utopia, and the rise of utopianism in a new historical and 'scientific' form, marks an important change in the consciousness of European societies. But even more important is the continuity of utopian aspirations. The form of utopia changes; the spirit flourishes unchecked. In the socialist utopia, the nineteenth century achieved a utopian monument every bit as grand as the Hellenic ideal city, the Christian millennium or the Renaissance utopia. That it partly derived from these utopias is beside the point. So too is the undoubted fact that few socialists were prepared to regard themselves as utopians. In re-fashioning the elements of the ancient and early modern utopia, the socialist utopia effectively substituted itself for these earlier utopias. For all intents and purposes, it made itself the only utopia. H. G. Wells was right: the socialist utopia is the modern utopia.

FROM MORE TO MARX

As with categories of utopian thought, so with periods of utopia's history: they overlap one another. Francis Bacon in the early seventeenth century produced in the *New Atlantis* the model of the dynamic utopia which was at the same time felt – at least by his followers – to be a realizable project. In the succeeding two centuries this vision all but disappeared from view. If it surfaced at all it was largely as an object of ridicule, as in the hare-brained schemes of the projectors of the Academy of Lagado in Swift's *Gulliver's Travels*. A growing awareness of the scientific revolution meant that it would only be a matter of time before the Baconian vision was resurrected. The European reputation of Bacon, and even more of Newton, assured this. The Baconian current in fact continued strong throughout, but it flowed within streams other than that of utopia. As far as the formal utopia was concerned, what persisted, what was imitated to almost intolerable lengths, was the utopia of Plato and More: bounded, ascetic, static.

Glaucon, in the *Republic*, accused Socrates of constructing a 'city of pigs'. The simple life that Socrates expressed as his ideal was all very well for the beasts, but did not provide the ornaments and luxuries proper to man. Thomas More and the later utopians followed Socrates in their distaste for the society 'at fever heat', puffed up with 'sauces and sweets', 'perfumes and incense'. More's Utopia abolishes private property and profits; it does away with money and the market. But it is not the utopia of abundance of modern socialism or communism, not the utopia indeed of any modern economic philosophy. It is not interested in material growth and the supplying of an ever-increasing quantity of goods to its citizens. Goods are distributed to householders in Utopia in accordance with need, and there is no fear that anyone will ask for more than he needs. Only in an insecure and morally unhealthy environment are wants increased beyond what is required for the satisfaction of the relatively simple needs of mankind.

> For why should it be thought that that man would ask more than enough which is sure never to lack? Certainly in all kinds of living creatures either fear of lack doth cause covetousness and ravin, or in man only pride, which counteth it a glorious thing to pass and excel others in the superfluous and vain ostentation of things. The which kind of vice among the Utopians can have no place.[1]

Hexter's comment on this aspect of More's Utopia can stand for all the early modern utopias to the end of the eighteenth century:

> The Utopian economy does not justify itself as modern economies do by claiming to give men in the fullest measure the things they want; it is not based on the tacit assumption of modern economies that on the whole what men want is what they ought to have. The

shadow of Bentham lies forward over Mill and Marx, Kautsky and Keynes – it does not fall backward over More. The justification for the Utopian system in all its aspects, economic and other, is that it provides all men with what they need in the measure that they need it; and while men ought to have what they need, they certainly do not need and ought not to have in full, or any other measure, whatever they happen to want.[2]

A six-hour working day suffices for the Utopians to produce 'all things that may be requisite either for necessity or for commodity [comfort], yea, or for pleasure, so that the same pleasure be true and natural.' A work system which uses the labour of all, men and women, and tolerates no idlers or parasites, not only finds time within these six hours for public works such as road-mending but can often allow a reduction of working hours.

For the magistrates do not exercise their citizens against their wills in unneedful labours. For why, in the institution of that weal-public this end is only and chiefly pretended and minded, that what time may possibly be spared from the necessary occupations and affairs of the commonwealth, all that the citizens should withdraw from the bodily service to the free liberty of the mind and garnishing of the same. For herein they suppose the felicity of this life to consist.[3]

Operating on the same philosophy and with the same organization of work, Campanella's Solarians work only four hours a day, the remaining hours being spent 'in learning joyously, in debating, in reading, in reciting, in writing, in walking, in exercising the mind and body, and with play'. 'They are,' says the Captain, 'rich because they want nothing, poor because they possess nothing; and consequently they are not slaves to circumstances, but circumstances serve them.'[4] The inhabitants of Andreae's Christianopolis have drawn the same moral: 'We will always be in need, as long as we desire what we cannot obtain. . . . You will be surprised how a supply of provisions, not at all very great, can be made to suffice for temperate habits in everything.'[5] The philosophy of restricted needs is passionately restated over a century later by the old Tahitian in Diderot's *Supplement to Bougainville's Voyage*, as he bids Bougainville and his companions to quit Tahiti:

Leave us to our ways; they are wiser and more honest than yours. We do not want to barter what you call our ignorance for your useless civilization. Everything that is necessary and good for us we possess. Do we deserve contempt, because we have not known how to develop superfluous wants? When we hunger, we have enough to eat; when we are cold we have wherewith to clothe us. You have been in our huts; what is lacking there, in your opinion? You may pursue as far as you like what you call the comforts of life; but allow sensible people to stop, when they would only have obtained imaginary good from the continuation of their painful efforts. If you persuade us to exceed the narrow limits of our wants, when shall we ever finish toiling? When shall we enjoy ourselves? We have reduced the sum of our annual and daily labours to the least possible, because nothing seems to us preferable to repose. Go to your own country to agitate and torment yourself as much as you like; leave us in peace. Do not worry us with your artificial needs nor with your imaginary virtues.[6]

Such an attitude to human needs meant, in turn, a surprisingly limited conception of scientific possibilities. The dynamic scientific society was implicit in Bacon's *New Atlantis*. But the utopian writers of the seventeenth and eighteenth centuries were not on the whole interested in growth and expansion. They appreciated the importance of the new science, and were often pioneers in the promotion of its legitimacy. They saw the enormous benefits it could bring in eliminating poverty and sickness, and in making human life more attractive and comfortable. But they were fearful of giving science its head. The new Prometheus had to be bounded, contained. Science existed only to serve certain religious or ethical ends, which were the real point and substance of their utopias. The idea of scientific progress for its own sake, or for the indefinite increase of society's wealth, was for these utopists distasteful and dangerous.

More's Utopians honour natural science ('phisick'), and think it God's gift to his favoured creature, man; but they pursue science not so much for its practical accomplishments as for the pleasure and awe it gives in the contemplation of 'the marvellous and gorgeous frame of the world' which God has created 'for man with great affection intentively to behold'. The function of science is largely reverential, and hence it is no contradiction that the Utopians 'highly esteem and worship miracles that come by no help of nature, as works and witnesses of the present power of God'.[7] The *City of the Sun* certainly acknowledges the importance and power of science: it covers the seven concentric walls of the city with scientific knowledge. But the restricted concept of science comes out when we realize that *all* scientific knowledge is supposed to be represented there, for all time: there will be no new discoveries, no new inventions. It is 'knowledge complete and frozen in an immutable orthodoxy', knowledge 'fully known, codified and exhibited'. Wisdom, the chief officer of the city, 'keeps only one book in which are all the sciences and he has this read out to all the people in the manner of the Pythagareans'. It is not so surprising then to discover that in the City of the Sun there are no laboratories, only museums. Andreae indeed packs his Christianopolis with manufacturing and technical workshops, and the experimental method is strongly encouraged; but 'the science pursued . . . is a "practical" science more closely akin to technological development than to pure scientific research.' Andreae celebrates the skilfull and industrious artisan, not the Promethean scientists of Bacon's imagination.[8]

The utopias of the sixteenth to eighteenth centuries are modern in that they are essentially secular and rational. This was the necessary break with the religious world-view, however radical the religion. They are not modern in the sense of being dynamic and expansive. The early modern utopia was an expression of the rational and critical spirit of the Renaissance and Reformation; but it also represented a reaction against the individualism of those movements that threatened to tear society apart.[9] It saw its function as the reintegration of society around a new moral and social order. The threat, in these centuries of civil war and religious strife, seemed to come from the pace and pattern of innovation in all spheres of life: not too little but too much freedom and change. It was this perception that underlay Thomas Hobbes's grimly authoritarian *Leviathan*. For the utopians too it followed that the new order must be stable and unchanging. Hence the characteristic utopia of these centuries was the carefully regulated communal order, a sort of secularized monasticism, modelled on More's *Utopia*. Such an order was nicely calculated to control the pride and the inflamed passions – of anger, ambition and acquisitiveness – that seemed to pose the principal political problem of these times.[10] Frank Manuel has aptly described the utopias of these centuries as 'utopias of calm felicity'. Their overriding aim is the elimination of social discord and individual unhappiness caused by unrestrained desires and strivings. Their ends are 'serenity, quiet happiness, peace, perhaps virtue, above all order'. It is towards these ends that all the chief practices and institutions of utopia are directed: the elaborate education of the young, the tightly controlled marriage system and, especially, the communalization of property that abolishes the main source of conflict and restores a simple ethos of equality and brotherhood.[11]

Stoicism both sums up the moral tone and points to the intellectual tradition of these early modern utopias. As with much of the social theory of these centuries, they are shaped in the classical mould. They recall the virtue and the civic spirit that European thinkers attributed to the Greek polis and the Roman Republic. Lycurgus's Sparta, in Plutarch's idealized account, was a particular source of inspiration. The Spartan model suggested pre-eminently the qualities of asceticism, order, communal life and public duty which mark these utopias. It is in this sense that Judith Shklar is right to call Rousseau 'the last of the classical utopists'. Although he did not write a formal utopia, Rousseau's writings are instinct with the values and ideals of the Enlightenment utopias. Like these utopias, like Plato's *Republic*, he constructs a moral and social order that is intended not as a programme for reform but as an object of contemplation and a standard of judgement. 'The *Social Contract*,' says Shklar, 'was not meant to be a plan for any future society, but a standard for judging existing institutions. It was a yardstick, not a programme.' Hence the features of Rousseau's social theory that are also the ingredients of the utopias of the time. Enlightenment utopias are static and a-historical, conceived on a basis of modest needs that excludes both the desire and the necessity for change. 'Progress' and 'change' in these utopias, as in the *Republic*, can only mean degeneration from the perfect order on which, for its moral edification, the individual mind is invited to dwell in philosophic contemplation.[12]

Such a philosophical enterprise could continue to appear justified, and to retain its intellectual vitality, so long as society itself seemed limited in its capacity for change and growth. By the eighteenth century the signs of the momentous changes being wrought in European society by science and economic expansion were unmistakable. Utopia, which clung to the older modes of thinking, become increasingly feeble and fragmented, increasingly marginal to the main intellectual developments of the age. 'The eighteenth century, which witnessed a great proliferation of what by any definition of the term would be called proper utopias, . . . did not produce a single major work in the traditional utopian form, no one document that would be for the Enlightenment what More's golden *libellus* was for the sixteenth century and the books of Andreae, Bacon, Campanella, and Comenius were for the seventeenth.'[13] The English utopia declined. For the governing classes, at least, the 'Glorious Revolution' of 1688 had produced a real-life utopia, a bourgeois utopia, while 'the question of its successor had not yet been raised.' The need seemed to be for consolidation and the pragmatic approach, not for visions of the New Jerusalem. Satire, traditionally fused with utopia, here flourished at its expense. The critical and the sceptical, often in a Tory vein, ridiculed the constructive and the complacent alike. The most impressive work of the century, aimed at shaking bourgeois complacency, was Swift's 'magnificent dystopia', *Gulliver's Travels*.[14]

The utopian torch passed to France, but it burned only a little less feebly there. Hundreds of utopias were written, mostly imitative variations on the basic Morean theme.[15] With the exception of Rousseau, and perhaps Diderot, the *philosophes* were generally sceptical and hostile towards utopian forms and schemes. There is no entry for *utopie* in the *Encyclopédie*, and Voltaire confessed that he had never read More's *Utopia*. 'Thank you for your letter against the human species' was his characteristically ironic riposte to Rousseau on being sent the *Discourse on the Origin of Inequality*. For its primitivist utopia he had no patience. It is true that there is a sense in which the *philosophes*' own enterprise could be considered utopian: 'the belief that a small band of men of good will, learned and moderately zealous, through the propagation of ideas on the sciences, arts, and trades could serve as a leaven to raise the general consciousness of their society'.[16] The political means so often looked to, the enlightened despot, also has the true utopian character, half practical, half fantastic. But, as we shall see, the philosophic movement pointed to a different direction entirely for utopia. Moreover, there is a strength in the writings of the *philosophes* quite lacking in the inspid and imitative utopias that poured from the presses. In only one area did the French utopia introduce fresh themes. It put sexual and religious liberation on the agenda of utopia. Both of these found passionate, not to say extravagant, expression in Diderot's *Supplement to Bougainville's Voyage* and the Marquis de Sade's *Philosophy of the Bedroom*. But, with the partial exception of Fourier, the sexual utopia had to wait until the twentieth century to find its time.

One other French utopia broke new ground – but it did so almost accidentally. Louis-Sebastien Mercier's *L'An 2440* (1771) is conventional in most respects. Its utopia of a peaceful world governed by philosophic monarchs and united by education and science derived more or less directly from Bacon. But science remains bounded; technology is simple. Mercier's utopia follows the classic pattern of restricted needs and a simple and austere way of life. His citizens cultivate education and science in the spirit of a pious deism. Their lives are devoted to the service of the Supreme Being, the Eternal Ruler of the World.[17]

The radically new element is *time*. Mercier takes as his epigraph a line of Leibniz's: 'The present is pregnant with the future.' *L'An 2440*, says I. F. Clarke, is 'the first influential story of the future in world literature'.[18] Its enormous popularity in the last quarter of the eighteenth century – it went through 11 editions between 1771 and 1793 and was translated and imitated through Europe and America – seems to be related to this feature of an otherwise highly conventional utopia. Mercier's actual handling of time is as simple and unsophisticated as can be imagined. His narrator falls asleep and awakes, now an old man with tottering legs and white hair, in the year 2440. The device of the sleeper or dreamer as a means of time travel became standard in later utopias – Bellamy, Morris and Wells all use it – and Mercier may well have invented it. But a late eighteenth-century readership would not have been impressed by this clumsy literary contrivance. It had already been educated in a far more complex and realistic treatment of time. What appealed in Mercier, in fact, what Mercier himself reflected perhaps without fully realizing it, was precisely the new zest for the future which in the second half of the eighteenth century was transforming both the form and the substance of utopia – to say nothing of social thought in general. Not in the past, as the myth of the Golden Age had suggested, but in the future lay the secret of human nature and human destiny. Wordsworth expressed the new conviction perfectly when he later wrote of

> the Mind's gaining that prophetic sense
> Of future change, that point of vision, whence
> May be discovered what in soul we are.

Utopia was, in the late eighteenth century, regenerated by sources other than utopia. 'After the death of Louis XIV,' says Albert Soboul, 'there took place a dissociation between social criticism and romantic utopias. The most daring criticisms and the projects of communist cities were presented in other forms while the utopian novel became insipid. . . . [But] while traditional utopian genres grew insipid, the utopian imagination bloomed in social theory. . . .'[19] Out of the new social philosophy fashioned by the Enlightenment thinkers, utopia found the means to survive and indeed thrive in the nineteenth century, albeit in quite new forms. Despite the scepticism of Enlightenment *philosophes*, despite the exhaustion of the literary form of utopia, it was by a creative synthesis of certain elements of Enlightenment thought that utopia made itself once more as central to the intellectual life of the age as it had been in the sixteenth and seventeenth centuries.

What were these elements? There was first the very thing by which we often define the Enlightenment, the faith in reason. '*Sapere Aude!* "Dare to use your own understanding!" – that is the motto of enlightenment,' wrote Kant in his great essay, 'What is Enlightenment?' (1784).[20] Hegel, having absorbed the French Revolution and the 'unhappy consciousness' of the Romantics, still could make a courageous declaration of faith in reason. Progress was the recognition and realization of the reason that was immanent in the world. 'To recognize reason as the rose in the cross of the present and thereby to enjoy the present, this is the rational insight which reconciles us to the actual.'[21] No matter how much nineteenth-century thinkers 'historicized' Kant, no matter how much they acknowledged the place of strife and suffering in human life, their social philosophies retained at the core the belief that history had a meaning, that it was essentially rational. The 'cunning of reason' meant that this rationality might conceal itself, or show itself in strange and disturbing forms – as in the French Revolution and Napoleon's conquests, or the 'invisible hand' of an apparently chaotic market. The serenity of the Enlightenment disappeared, and with it the simpler forms of rationalist faith. But what took its place – not exclusively, of course – was not a rejection of reason but its re-working in various historical and evolutionary philosophies. Though Marx and Comte indignantly repudiated the label 'utopian', they would have been equally indignant at the charge that they had abandoned the belief in the reality and efficacy of human reason. In this respect at least Marxism may properly be considered the last great fling of the Enlightenment.[22]

Communism too, so often narrowly identified with nineteenth-century socialism, was an Enlightenment legacy incorporated into the nineteenth-century utopia. Through Plato, More and the later utopian tradition, Enlightenment thinkers were of course familiar with communism. Christian thought, and radical Christian practice, had also made its contribution. It was indeed partly because of its very familiarity that some Enlightenment thinkers turned away from it. To them it was associated with primitivism and the 'pre-history' of modern society – with the communal organization of poor peasant societies and ascetic Christian sects. For Enlightenment individualists, it represented the inheritance of the European 'Dark Ages', with their restrictive corporate orders of guilds, colleges and monasteries.

It was perhaps, as Soboul suggests, partly because of the survival of the village community in eighteenth-century France that French thinkers remained alive to communistic ideas. The utopian writer Restif de la Bretonne was tireless in propagating the beliefs and values of the idealized village community, in such works as *Andrographe* (1782) and *The Year 2000* (1789).[23] Restif was a Rousseauist, the 'Rousseau of the gutters', he was called, because of his innumerable popular utopias spelling out the message of Rousseau's *Discourse on the Origin of Inequality* (1755). Rousseau put the question of property and equality at the centre of the debate about the condition of civilized humanity. He quoted 'the wise Locke, "There can be no injury, where there is no property."' The first man who claimed exclusive possession of a piece of ground was the true founder of civil society, with its attendant 'crimes, wars, . . . murders . . . horrors and misfortunes'.[24] 'Property,' agreed his disciple Mably, 'is the chief cause of all the unhappiness of mankind.' But Rousseau would not follow Mably and other radical Rousseauists into communism. His utopia remained largely 'eupsychic', concerned with the optimum state of individual consciousness. This would best be achieved through the merging of the individual 'I' with the communal 'I', the *moi commun*. But in social and institutional terms this entailed at most an equalization of property, not its communalization. 'Must *meum* and *tuum* be annihilated, and must we return again to the forests to live among bears?'[25] Rousseau never gave a clear answer to his own rhetorical question. But his evident attachment to the social arrangements of his own Geneva, of Corsica, of what he conceived to be Lycurgus's Sparta and the Rome of the Gracchi, sufficiently indicates the main shape of his utopia. It was a simple rustic utopia, based squarely on a plurality of equal and independent peasant households, supported by village artisans. Its most obviously legitimate descendant was the Jacobin utopia of Robespierre and Saint-Just, the egalitarian utopia of the *sansculottes*, with their hatred of aristocracy and *grands bourgeois* and their belief in the inherent virtues of the *menu peuple*, the artisans, shopkeepers and smallholding peasants.

For others among his followers, however, Rousseau's denunciation of property as the root of all evil pointed towards full communism as the only logical solution to society's ills. A characteristic view was that of the Benedictine monk Dom Deschamps: 'It is enough to replace moral inequality and property with moral equality and the community of goods to efface all the moral vices that reign over humanity.'[26] But it was Morelly, whose *Code de La Nature* (1755) appeared in the same year as Rousseau's *Discourse*, who provided the definitive link between the communism of More and Campanella and that of Babeuf and the nineteenth-century communists. Rousseau-like, Morelly inveighed against 'pitiless Property, mother of all the crimes that inundate the world'. Man is naturally good, but he has been corrupted by the institutions of private property. In the state of nature goods are held in common, as witness the North American Indians. Morelly proposed the following 'fundamental and inviolable laws, which would cut off at the root the vices and all the evils of society':

1. Nobody will own anything in the society individually or as a landlord except the things which he is currently using for his needs, his pleasures, or his daily work.
2. Every Citizen will be a public person, supported, maintained, and employed at public expense.
3. For his part every Citizen will contribute to the public weal in accordance with his strength, his talents, and his age; these will determine his obligations. . . .[27]

It was, by Babeuf's own account, the *Code de La Nature* that inspired the communism of his 'Manifesto of the Equals' (c. 1796), the programmatic basis of the revolutionary 'Conspiracy of the Equals' that he formed with Darthé and Buonarroti during the French Revolution. For Babeuf, there could be no 'real equality', *égalité réelle*, without full-fledged communism.

We desire real equality or death; behold what we want . . . The French Revolution is but the forerunner of another revolution far more grand, far more solemn, and which will be the last. The people has marched over dead bodies against the kings and princes coalesced against it; it will do the same against the new tyrants – against the new political Tartuffes who have usurped the places of the old.

'What do we want', you ask, 'more than equality of rights?' We want that equality not merely written in the 'Declaration of the Rights of Man and of the Citizens'; we want it in the midst of us – under the roofs of our houses. . . .

The Agrarian law [of the Gracchi], or partition of lands, was only the instantaneous wish of certain soldiers without principles. . . . We aim at something more sublime, and more equitable; we look to *common property*, or the *community of goods*! No more individual property in lands. *The earth belongs to no one*. We claim – we demand – we *will* the communal enjoyment of the fruits of the earth; *the fruits belong to all*. . . .

The moment for great measures has arrived. Evil is at its height; it has reached its *maximum*, and covers the face of the earth. Chaos, under the name of politics, has too long reigned over it. Let everything revert to order, and resume its proper place. At the voice of equality, let the elements of justice and felicity be organized. The moment is come to found the REPUBLIC OF EQUALS – that grand asylum open to all human kind. The days of general restitution are come.[28]

'With Babeuf, utopia becomes revolutionary.'[29] Certainly nineteenth-century socialists were inclined to see in the 'Manifesto of the Equals' and Babeuf's conspiracy the pivotal point at which the French Revolution reached its limits, and at the same time showed the direction of future revolutions. For Franco Venturi the 'communist ideal', as expounded especially by Morelly and Babeuf, is indeed one of the central contributions of the Enlightenment to the modern utopia.

> The traditional utopia expanded and altered under the stimulus of the typical Enlightenment determination to create paradise on this earth, to create a completely human society which was egalitarian and free. A system of communal life for everyone was to supersede the small groups of the elect. . . . The history of the passage from utopia to ideal, from the individual dream to the communist political movement, is certainly full of interest. The whole age of the Enlightenment could not be understood without it. However marginal it may seem at times, it is really one of the most irreversible, unchanging and lasting results the eighteenth century transmitted to the nineteenth. It is one of those mental forms which, once they are fixed and shaped, will never yield without long and difficult trials and struggles, and without contact with a long and complex historical process. After the middle of the eighteenth century, the idea that the abolition of property might change the very basis of human society, might abolish all traditional morality and every political form of the past, was never again to disappear.[30]

Communism provided a good deal of the moral and social substance of the nineteenth-century utopia. To that extent there was continuity with the classic utopian tradition of More, Campanella and Andreae, to say nothing of Plato. What was different, what represented a decisive break with the classic tradition, was the form in which the nineteenth-century utopia was conceived. The new element was the note struck by Mercier's *L'An 2440*: the new sense of time and history. Here Enlightenment egalitarian and communistic utopias had remained conservative. The utopias – if we may call them that – of Rousseau and Saint-Just, of Morelly and Babeuf, were made in the Morean mould. They were timeless, static entities. Little attention was paid to the question of how the new order would be brought into being, although the French Revolution gave some of them an unexpected opportunity. Even the most daring thinkers remained largely content to diagnose the ills of the human condition in philosophic fashion, providing remedies that were indeed radical but also remote from the actual life of their society. Among Enlightenment reformers there persisted the quality of playful intellectual exchange among a select group that was so prominent a feature of Renaissance humanism.

But from another quarter of Enlightenment thought the new feature, the dynamic element, of the nineteenth century utopia was developing powerfully. Stimulated by developments in geology and biology, European thought was increasingly penetrated by concepts of change, evolution and progress. The movement of societies through time came to acquire a new meaning, one that took it out of religious fatalism and rationalist scepticism and gave history a purpose and a direction. Many Enlightenment thinkers continued to think of change in classic cyclical terms – Vico's *ricorsi*, Hume's flux and re-flux, the cycle of growth and decay in empires and nations that was charted by

Montesquieu and Gibbon. The new view had to struggle against what was perhaps the predominant strain of the eighteenth-century philosophy of history. 'Limitless progress, a utopia inherent in the very nature of the historical process, is a novum of the closing decades of the eighteenth century that had to overcome a wide variety of contrary intellectual currents.'[31] But by the end of the century the idea of progress had triumphed. The 'Moderns' had defeated the 'Ancients', modern science and philosophy had been acknowledged as equal if not superior to that of Greece and Rome. This victory was achieved largely through a new vision of time and a new philosophy of history. The new was better than the old, the future more perfect than the past, because history was the record of the growth and progressive fulfilment of humanity. 'We can regard the history of the human species as a whole,' wrote Kant, 'as the unravelling of a hidden plan of nature for accomplishing a perfect state of civil constitution for society . . . as the sole state of society in which the tendency of human nature can be all and fully developed.'[32]

The story has been often told, and can be briefly recapitulated.[33] Turgot's two discourses on the advancement of the human race and mind, given at the Sorbonne in 1750, constitute by general agreement the first important statement in modern times of the ideology of progress. Progress is inevitable and indefinite, Turgot affirmed, given – as Locke has shown – the human capacity to accumulate experience and to be educated by it. There is moreover in humanity an innate tendency towards movement and change, an inherent progressiveness. Each generation contributes to and augments 'a common treasury', which is the common inheritance of all the successive ages of man, so that 'the human race, considered from its beginnings, appears to the eyes of a philosopher to be one immense whole which, like every individual, has its infancy and its progress.' The historical progress of mankind towards perfection is 'the most glorious spectacle'.

> We see the establishment of societies and the formation of nations which one after the other dominate other nations or obey them. Empires rise and fall; the laws and forms of government succeed one another; the arts and sciences are discovered and made more perfect. Sometimes arrested, sometimes accelerated in their progress, they pass through different climates. Interest, ambition, and vainglory perpetually change the scene of the world, inundating the earth with blood. But in the midst of these ravages man's mores become sweeter, the human mind becomes enlightened, and the isolated nations come closer to each other. Commerce and politics reunite finally all the parts of the globe, and the whole mass of the humankind, alternating between calm and agitation, good and bad, marches constantly, though slowly, towards greater perfection.

French thinkers always remained the most closely identified with the belief in progress. But Leibniz, Kant, Herder, Fichte and Schelling, to say nothing of Hegel and Marx, all variously contributed to its popularity. In England Bacon's name was frequently and rightly invoked in its support; while Locke's empirical epistemology and psychology were in many ways the bedrock of the idea wherever it appeared. Right from the start, too, future progress was linked to modern science, the science of Newton: 'God said, *Let Newton be!* and all was light.' So it is not surprising to find the English scientist Joseph Priestley making a rhapsodical declaration of faith in 'the progress of the species towards perfection'. Priestley looked forward to an explosive growth in scientific knowledge,

and *knowledge*, as Lord Bacon observes, being *power*, the human powers will, in fact, be enlarged; nature, including both its materials, and its laws, will be more at our command; men will make their situation in this world abundantly more easy and comfortable; they will probably prolong their existence in it, and will grow daily more happy, each in himself, and more able (and, I believe, more disposed) to communicate happiness to others. Thus, whatever was the beginning of this world, the end will be glorious and paradisaical, beyond what our imaginations can now conceive.

But it was another Frenchman, Condorcet, who put the idea of progress most forcibly in the form in which it was assimilated into the nineteenth-century utopia. Condorcet's *Sketch for a Historical Picture of the Progress of the Human Mind* (1793) drew upon Turgot's writings with full, indeed fulsome, acknowledgement. In turn, it inspired both Saint-Simon and Comte and, through their Positive Philosophy, extensive regions of the nineteenth-century European mind. Condorcet's conclusion in his *Sketch*, that 'the perfectibility of man is indefinite', was conventional enough by that time. What was less conventional was the urgency and dynamism that he injected into this belief. The theological trappings still evident in Turgot, Kant and Herder were thrown off. Progress was a principle intrinsic to human history itself – it was not the working of a divine and inscrutable Providence. Its laws were discoverable as fully and as exactly as those of nature. History was 'a science to foresee the progression of the human species'; such foreknowledge enables us to 'tame the future' (compare Comte's '*prévoir pour pouvoir*'). The world had so far progressed through nine epochs; the tenth, of which the French Revolution was the herald, lay in the future. But 'the picture of the future destiny of mankind' can be deduced from 'the results of its history'.

Gazing into 'the ocean of futurity', Condorcet saw a world of universal equality, enlightenment and peace. Education would expand men's minds, industry produce an abundance of goods with the least amount of labour. It was science, above all, as a method of thought and as a form of practical operation on the world, that would be the great deliverer of this future happiness – to the point even of prolonging indefinitely the common duration of human life. 'Interrogated everywhere, observed in all its aspects, attacked simultaneously by a variety of methods and instruments capable of tearing away its secrets, nature will at last be forced to let them escape. . . Every discovery is a conquest over nature.' In his last work, the *Fragment sur L'Atlantide*, the Baconian utopia takes over completely. Condorcet looks forward to a society under the supreme direction of a world body of scientists. The spirit of science will infuse itself into the thought and behaviour of all citizens. No longer the work of lone individual geniuses, science would become a collective force, ceaselessly transforming and improving the world. In this 'wildly dynamic republic of science, innovating endlessly',[34] the Baconian utopia at last returned to the centre of social thought. The hurried scribbling of an aristocratic *philosophe* of the old regime, fleeing the guillotine, reflected far more vividly than the laboured tomes of later system-builders the fact that modern science and the modern utopia had become virtually synonymous.

But with a new twist. To the dynamism internal to the Baconian utopia of science was now added the dynamism of the historical process itself. With Turgot and Condorcet, *eutopia* becomes *euchronia*. The good place becomes the good time. No longer was utopia to be found on a remote island or in a hidden mountain valley. The European voyages of discovery and the enthusiastic mapping of the world were in any case making it less and less easy to find some *terra incognita* to serve as utopia.[35] Henceforth, if utopia were to be contemporary with the writer, it would have to be found under the sea, in the bowels of the earth, on the moon or some distant planet in outer space. But even here, as 'science fiction' writers increasingly showed, it was more convincing if these outlandish places were distant not simply in space but also in time. The new sense of history, the new concern with change and development, made it increasingly old-fashioned to think of utopia as belonging anywhere but in mankind's future. Saint-Simon's declaration was typical:

> Poetic imagination has put the Golden Age in the cradle of the human race, amid the ignorance and brutishness of primitive times; it is rather the Iron Age which should be put there. The Golden Age of the human race is not behind us but before us; it lies in the perfection of the social order. Our ancestors never saw it; our children will one day arrive there; it is for us to clear the way.[36]

Nineteenth-century utopians, like H. G. Wells's Time-Traveller, 'flung themselves into futurity'. They took with the utmost seriousness Pascal's ironic *pensée*: 'The present is never an end, the past and present are our means. Only the future is our end. Thus we never live; but we hope to live. . . .' This new turn to time and the future represented, in one of its aspects, the return of the Judaeo-Christian strand to utopia. The Morean utopia, which dominated until the end of the eighteenth century, was strongly classical. In its static, timeless quality it showed itself close to Plato and Hellenic rationalism. The nineteenth-century utopia was temporal and dynamic. The idea of progress secularized the belief in Providence and the millennium, but it retained much of the apocalyptic and eschatological character of the Christian philosophy of history.[37] Daniel's four kingdoms, Joachim of Fiore's three ages, reappeared in Condorcet's succession of historical epochs, the three ages of Comtean Positivism and a host of nineteenth-century evolutionary schemes. The Christian consummation in the millennium or the Heavenly City now turned into the advent of the classless communist society or the reign of the positivist religion of humanity. But what persisted, what linked the two forms of thought, was the belief that utopia or the millennium was to be delivered by history itself, as the more or less inevitable consequence of its unfolding logic. Utopia was not the deliberate conscious construct of a wise monarch or legislator, a King Utopus or King Solamona. It was the product of the impersonal working out of dynamic historical forces, which was guiding humanity to the realization of its full potential in the modern socialist or scientific utopia. No one could of course predict exactly when that new world would dawn. But the historical and temporal orientation of utopia made it possible to use dates with apocalyptic effect: *L'An 2440, Nineteen Eighty-Four, The Year 2000.*

The nineteenth-century utopia was not just dynamic, it was also world-wide. H. G. Wells was right in seeing both these qualities as distinctive of the modern utopia, but wrong in thinking that his *A Modern Utopia* was the first to recognize this. Practically all nineteenth-century thinkers followed Turgot and Condorcet in seeing history as world history, and in projecting their future societies on a world plane. Nothing less seemed adequate to the new social and technological forces released by modern democracy and science. No one nation or continent could hope to contain these forces. Their dynamism pushed them beyond all national frontiers; equilibrium was possible only in a world system. This was the lesson that all thinkers took from the French and Industrial Revolutions, the first major expressions of the new developments.

There was another thing suggested by these revolutions, perhaps most fateful of all for the modern utopia. The utopias up to the end of the eighteenth century, true to their classicist leaning, rested on generally simple social orders. They were premised on the idea that human needs were few and relatively easily satisfied. An agrarian society of independent peasants and artisans sufficed to produce all that was necessary. It allowed fully for mental and moral growth. Any further material growth was unnatural and corrupting, the product of an unhealthy and debilitating desire for luxury and comfort. For all their differences, the Jacobins Robespierre and Saint-Just were here entirely at one with the communists Morelly, Deschamps and Babeuf. Their ideal societies all breathe the air of that *douce serenité* and *simplicité aimable* that the Manuels find in Deschamps's utopia.[38] Babeuf inveighed against the 'perversion of the passions' and the 'torments and uneasiness', the 'jealousy and covetousness', stirred up among the masses by the 'pomp and pleasures' of the effete wealthy. Certain citizens 'create to themselves new factitious wants and refinements ... unknown to the multitude. ... Simplicity is no longer loved, happiness ceases to consist in an active life and tranquil soul. ...'[39] All these thinkers took their lead from Rousseau, who contrasted the 'peace and liberty' of the savage, 'who desires only to live and be free from labour' with 'civilized man, ... always moving, sweating, toiling, and racking his brains to find still more laborious occupations. ...' 'Society offers to us only an assembly of artificial men and factitious passions.' The invention of 'conveniences' in the simple state was 'the first yoke man inadvertently imposed on himself, and the first source of the evils he prepared for his descendants'.

> For, besides continuing thus to enervate both body and mind, these conveniences lost with use almost all their power to please, and even degenerated into real needs, till the want of them became far more disagreeable than the possession of them had been pleasant. Men would have been unhappy at the loss of them, though the possession of them did not make them happy.[40]

The French and Industrial Revolutions destroyed this happy innocence. As early as 1755 Bishop Berkeley, reflecting on the distressing propensity of the eighteenth-century labourer to prefer increased leisure to increased income, had raised the question, 'whether the creation of wants be not the likeliest way to produce industry in a people?' Adam Smith took up this fateful suggestion with enthusiasm, arguing that high wages would bring new standards of 'ease and plenty' to the worker and encourage him 'to exert his strength to the utmost' in striving to attain them.[41] The Industrial Revolution made of these innocent beginnings a grand 'revolution of rising expectations'. The fantastic productivity of man linked to the machine created ideas of growth and abundance that were bound to find an echo in the contemporary utopia. Rousseau's arcadianism had, for the time at least, to take a back seat. The modern utopia had to be industrial and scientific, with all the complexities this dynamism brought with it. 'The harmony of the Rousseauan vision was irreparably disrupted by the spread of science and technology, when desire became dynamic and infinite and was virtually identified with need. . . . Keeping up with burgeoning desire became a critical utopian problem, entailing a constant theoretical reordering of economic and political systems.'[42]

But while the 'dynamism of desire' created new problems for utopia, it also opened up new vistas and new possibilities inconceivable to earlier utopians. The whole idea of a basic human nature, with certain natural and more or less unchanging needs, had to be abandoned. The human essence was now defined by its very infinitude, its unboundedness – as unbounded as the Prometheus unleashed by the Industrial Revolution. Human nature was now seen to be in process of constant and continuous formation and growth, as protean and changeable as human society itself. It had to be conceived as potentiality, as a striving for fulfilment in a mental and material world that had no limits. Even the stars, as the scientist J. D. Bernal was later to claim, set no barrier to human growth: humanity could re-fashion the whole universe, become joint-creator with the Creator Himself.[43] The demands that utopia made and sought to meet had to match the new possibilities and desires. The Marquis de Sade had already raised this at the most elemental level of sexual and bodily desires, a theme continued by Fourier in a more moderate vein. Nineteenth-century liberals and socialists likewise struggled to invent schemes which would accept the unlimited nature of economic and technical growth without tearing the social and political order apart. What was at issue here, as Michel Foucault has seen, was a novel conception of human rights. People no longer struggled for specific laws and liberties; they claimed the right to the fulfilment of human life as such, as essentially conceived: 'life as a political object'.

> One no longer aspired toward the coming of the emperor of the poor, or the kingdom of the latter days, or even the restoration of our imagined ancestral rights; what was demanded and what served as an objective was life, understood as the basic needs, man's concrete essence, the realization of his potential, a plenitude of the possible. . . . It was life more than the law that became the issue of political struggles . . . the 'right' to life, to one's body, to health, to happiness, to the satisfaction of needs, and beyond all the oppressions or 'alienations', the 'right' to rediscover what one is and all that one can be. . . .[44]

Nineteenth-century utopias had perforce to be open-ended, to a degree never before attempted or thought necessary. They had to accommodate the requirement for ceaseless innovation and growth, individual and social. The attempt threatened the very form of utopia as a literary genre. If there is one thing that students of utopia agree upon, it is that utopias are perfected social orders. They are societies, that is, which have more or less satisfactorily solved all known human problems. Change is, almost by definition, not only unnecessary but a distinct threat. It can only signal degeneration and decay of the good society.

For the 'classic' utopias of the sixteenth to eighteenth centuries, this posed no problem. Timeless and settled, meeting all the natural desires of humanity, what need had they of change? Their very isolation and insulation from the ordinary unregenerate world was some sort of guarantee that their perfection was stable and permanent. This was precisely the solution denied to the dynamic and world-wide utopia of the nineteenth century. Not only was it impossible to present an isolated utopian fragment uncontaminated by the rest of the un-utopian world: the utopia itself had to show a capacity for innovation and development that seemingly contradicted its formal requirement of perfection.

The resulting impasse was to put the formal utopia, temporarily at least, into abeyance. Karl Mannheim has said that 'each utopia, as it is formed at a later stage of development, manifests a closer approximation to the historical social process.' Hence utopia eventually disappears, giving way to scientific conceptions of society and social movements based on them.[45] This accepts rather too much at face value the self-professed 'scientific' pretensions of nineteenth- and twentieth-century social theory. But certainly it is true that nineteenth-century social theory became impatient with the traditional utopian form of More and his successors. To Saint-Simon, Fourier, Owen, Comte, Spencer, Marx and the other great system-builders of the century, it seemed self-evident that utopia was on the point of realization. History had prepared the way, and history was now intimating its end in the modern utopia of science and socialism. An actual utopia was here in the making, in the rapidly industrializing Europe and America of the nineteenth century. What was needed were not wishful visions of perfection but scientific accounts of historical development, together with some precise indication of what needed to be done to usher in the new order as effectively and painlessly as possible. The time for philosophic contemplation of perfection was past. 'The philosophers,' said Marx, 'have so far only interpreted the world in various ways; the point however is to change it.'[46] The new science of society set itself the task both to describe and to prescribe. It had to give an account of society's past, to diagnose the ills of the present and to show what, in accordance with this analysis, was now necessary to inaugurate the society of the future. Saint-Simon's is, once again, the best and most characteristic utterance. Looking back on a life of extraordinarily varied endeavours, he saw a single guiding thread. 'The life purpose which I set before me was to study the movements of the human mind, in order that I might then labour for the perfection of civilization.'[47]

That the new accounts were, in almost every way except in form, as utopian as the old was obvious to everyone but their authors.

THE SOCIALIST UTOPIA

Socialism was not of course the only nineteenth-century utopia. Throughout, it competed with other ideologies, such as utilitarianism and liberalism, which had their high complement of utopianism. Above all there was the ideology of the free-market, *laissez-faire*, economy, which Karl Polanyi rightly described as 'a stark utopia'.[48] In a hundred speeches by businessmen and their apologists, the invisible and benevolent guiding hand of the unfettered market was extolled as the royal road to the good society. At a higher level, the utopian element in 'free trade' was especially clear in the writings and pronouncements of such liberals as John Bright and Richard Cobden. And in our own time, there has been a significant resurgence of the free-market utopia.[49]

Nevertheless, it seems true to say that socialism was the nineteenth-century utopia, the truly modern utopia, *par excellence*.[50] Of all the ideas and movements of the time, it most clearly continued the utopian tradition of More, Campanella and Bacon. Its full-blooded egalitarian communism, the Morean legacy, was married to a Baconian belief in the beneficence of science: it was, after all, the very progress of science and industry that was making socialism both possible and necessary. At the same time, it continued the Enlightenment faith in reason and progress. The nineteenth century developed the idea of progress in many forms – liberalism and positivism, social Darwinism and Technocracy were prominent among its varieties – but none could compete in comprehensiveness or appeal with the socialist vision. Increasingly as the century wore on, other ideologies were forced to define themselves against the challenge of socialism. This was true not just of conservative and liberal ideologies but, even more perhaps, of radical ideologies such as anarchism and populism. And when, towards the end of the century, the literary utopia once more reappeared, it was clear to everyone that socialism was the only utopia that mattered. The essential argument, it was agreed, was about socialism: whether writers used the utopian form to dispute and promote varieties of socialism among themselves, as with Bellamy, Morris and Wells; or whether they used it to attack socialism in one or other of its manifestations, as with Zamyatin, Huxley and Orwell. The anti-utopia can indeed be thought of as an invention to combat socialism, in so far as socialism was seen to be the fullest and most sophisticated expression of the modern worship of science, technology and organization. In that sense, both utopia and anti-utopia in the past hundred years have come to express and reflect the most significant political phenomenon of modern times, the rise of socialism as an ideology and as a movement.

Just as there was more than one nineteenth-century utopia, so there was more than one nineteenth-century socialism. There was the socialism of Saint-Simon, Fourier, Owen, Cabet, Weitling and Marx, not to mention that of the Fabians and the British Labour Party at the end of the century, or the various currents of socialist syndicalism and anarchism. They differed among themselves on such matters as the importance of co-operatives, whether or not all private property should be abolished, the necessity of revolution in achieving socialism and the extent to which centralized control of the economy should predominate over local associations of producers. All could claim respectable historical and ideological pedigrees. There was no one 'true socialism'.[51]

But here too one variety – Marxian socialism – achieved a unique prominence. It is just possible that, without the success of the Russian and Chinese revolutions, carried out under Marxist auspices, Marx and Marxism would have remained of largely academic and historical interest in this century.[52] But such speculation is probably not very profitable; and the fact is that, largely because of these revolutions, nowadays it is almost impossible to think of socialism without thinking of Marxism. In any case, many of the major nineteenth-century socialist parties of Europe, above all those of Germany, France and Italy, were formed under the influence of Marxism. Their continued activity in this century, and their inescapable involvement with the Soviet Union, have ensured that Marxism and socialism remain closely bound together – almost, for many, synonymous terms. Together with these facts of political history must be taken the enormous explosion of interest in Marx in Western countries since 1945. Studies have accumulated with such velocity and in such volume as to have created a veritable Marx industry. Much of this remains unread on dusty library shelves; but enough has got out to fix Marx's name, at least, firmly in the consciousness of Western societies. For their populations, too, socialism and Marxism are difficult to distinguish, a confusion encouraged energetically by politicians of the right. Unless, then, we wish to be accused of wilful perversity, to discuss the socialist utopia must mean primarily discussing the Marxist utopia.

Still it remains true that, for instance, both Bellamy and Wells produced socialist utopias which deliberately distanced themselves from Marx. In Bellamy's case this meant playing down the role of revolutionary conflict in the attainment of socialism; in Wells's, that of the proletariat in favour of the new men of science. So too Orwell attacked a state socialism, of the Soviet kind, that for many thinkers has only the most tenuous connection with Marxism. In considering particular socialist utopias and anti-utopias, the differences between them, including those with Marxism, have of course to be respected. This I hope to have done sufficiently in the studies below. But it is not stretching the point too much to say that, in considering the features of the Marxist utopia, we are considering the features of the socialist utopia in general. For all the differences of philosophic approach and political strategy, Marxism remains a form of socialism. It shares with all other varieties a common past in the utopian and Enlightenment tradition. Like them, it claims to be completing the unfinished business of the French Revolution. Its analysis of capitalist society in terms of class conflict and exploitation differs from other kinds of socialism largely – as Marx himself pointed out[53] – in its belief in the inevitability of revolution and the coming of socialism. Most importantly from the present point of view, its vision of the future incorporates the central elements of socialism while showing, more clearly than any other type, socialism's utopian inheritance.

Any discussion of Marxism as a utopia starts off with the considerable problem of Marxism's own vehement and repeated repudiation of that status. More than this, there is Marxism's well-known reluctance to speculate about the future at all. Marx was contemptuous of those critics who seemed to be demanding that he should write 'recipes . . . for the cookshops of the future'. 'The construction of the future and its completion for all times is not our task. . . . We do not anticipate the world dogmatically, but rather wish to find the new world through criticism of the old.'[54] Later Marxists could be equally uncompromising. There was the retort of one of the leading theoreticians of German Marxism, Wilhelm Liebknecht, stung by Reichstag attacks in the 1890s on the alleged future socialist society: 'The "Future State" is a matter of fantasy; science has nothing to do with it. Our party, the Social Democratic Party, has never accepted the Utopia of a Future State in its programme.' At about the same time Engels was congratulating the SPD press for its freedom from futile speculations about the future, and he added: 'One of the most pleasing differences between the present and the pre-socialist ways of thought of the great masses or partisans lies in the complete disappearance of Utopian concepts, the dreaming about the "Future State".'[55] Lenin showed the same attitude in his emphatic rejection of Bukharin's plea in 1918 for some outline of the future society which the Russian Revolution promised: 'We cannot outline Socialism. What Socialism will look like when it takes on its final forms we do not know and cannot say.'[56]

Sidney Webb's stiff-necked response to Edward Bellamy's wildly popular socialist utopia, *Looking Backward*, was all of a piece with this distaste for formal utopias. Belittling Bellamy as 'but a belated Cabet, Baboeuf, or Campanella', he lectured: 'It cannot be too often repeated that Socialism, to Socialists, is not a Utopia which they have invented, but a principle of social organization which they assert to have been discovered by the patient investigators into sociology whose labours have distinguished the present century.'[57] Earlier in the century Marxists had been equally uncomfortable with the popular success of Étienne Cabet's communist utopia, *Voyage en Icarie* (1840), which George Lichtheim says by any measure must count 'among the classics of communist literature'.[58] The rejection of 'utopianism' by Marx and Engels had in fact a good deal to do with their attempt to demonstrate that their kind of socialism was superior to the many other varieties currently on offer. Other people's socialisms were 'utopian', if not sentimental or downright reactionary; theirs, by contrast, was 'scientific'. In describing, in particular, the socialism of Saint-Simon, Fourier, Owen, Cabet and Weitling as 'utopian', the Marxists meant to make two main points. They wanted to show first that utopian socialism was in some sense primitive and 'premature'. The utopians formulated their socialism in abstract and ahistorical terms because the conflict between the bourgeoisie and the proletariat had not yet reached the stage where socialism – 'scientific socialism' – could be related in theory and practice to the actual struggles of the proletariat, in conditions which made proletarian emancipation feasible.

> The solution of the social problems, which as yet lay hidden in undeveloped economic conditions, the Utopians attempted to evolve out of the human brain. . . . To all these, socialism is the expression of absolute truth, reason and justice, and has only to be discovered to conquer all the world by virtue of its own power.[59]

Not conceiving socialism as the product of a determinate historical development, the Utopian socialists were led also to 'fantastic pictures of future society', fantastic notions of how socialism would come about. They did not see the necessity of class conflict and revolution, leading to the establishment of a proletarian dictatorship, as the prelude to 'the abolition of class distinctions generally'. Instead they placed their hopes in 'personal inventive action' by idealists and philanthropists, and in experimental communities and co-operatives.

They reject all political, and especially all revolutionary action. . . . They endeavour . . . to deaden the class struggle and to reconcile the class antagonisms. They still dream of experimental realisation of their social Utopias, of founding isolated '*phalanstères*', of establishing 'Home Colonies', of setting up a 'Little Icaria' – duodecimo editions of the New Jerusalem. . . .[60]

Under their misguidance, the proletariat

throws itself into doctrinaire experiments, exchange banks and workers' associations, hence into a movement in which it renounces the revolutionising of the old world by means of the latter's own great, combined resources, and seeks, rather, to achieve its salvation behind society's back, in private fashion, within its limited conditions of existence, and hence necessarily suffers a shipwreck.[61]

Eventually, however, schooled by these experiences, the proletariat comes to the 'scientific' understanding that 'mankind sets itself only such tasks as it can solve.' The utopian formulas of 'well-wishing bourgeois-doctrinaires' are recipes for disaster.

The workers have no ready-made utopias to introduce *par décret du peuple*. They know that in order to work out their own emancipation, and along with it that higher form to which present society is irresistibly tending by its own economical agencies, they will have to pass through long struggles, through a series of historic processes, transforming circumstances and men. They have no ideals to realise, but to set free the elements of the new society with which old collapsing bourgeois society itself is pregnant.'[62]

Leave aside the gross distortion of the utopian socialists in this account – as any reading of Saint-Simon or Owen would show. Leave aside, too, the many features that Marxism took over from the utopians: from Saint-Simon, the slogan 'from the government of men to the administration of things' and the idea of the 'withering away' of the state; from Fourier, the idea that 'in any given society the degree of the emancipation of women is the natural measure of general emancipation'; from Owen, many of the technical details of the working of a communist economy. Since these are all Engels's own examples, freely given, it is clear that Marxism was by no means forgetful of or ungenerous to its 'utopian' predecessors.[63] The more important question, however, has to do with Marxism's own utopianism. It may be true enough that, according to Marxism's own view of itself, it differs fundamentally from utopian theory, as it conceives and characterizes that. But should we accept this self-regarding verdict? Must we see Marxism as in some sense more realistic, more 'scientific', than other kinds of modern socialism? Certainly there are important differences between Marx and the utopians. But when we look at Marx's account of the social changes that are bringing the new society into being, still more when we consider the glimpses that we are given of the future communist society, we may be inclined to think Marx's own vision more dazzling in its utopianism than that of even the most utopian of utopian socialists.

Marx and Engels distinguished themselves from the utopians principally in their understanding of how socialism would come about. While the utopians dreamed up schemes of ideal societies, the Marxists thought they had discovered the 'law of motion' of history and society that was, more or less inevitably, delivering socialism as the final stage of human history. It was this special understanding of history on which the Marxists insisted. In one of the many brief accounts of Marxism that Engels provided for the faithful, he picked out as of first importance 'the revolution brought about by Marx in the whole conception of world history'. Marx, said Engels, showed not only that all history was the history of class rule and class struggle, but that the long series of struggles was on the point of culmination in the proletarian revolution, which would bring to an end all classes and all oppression. The Marxist investigation of history

> leads to the realisation that, in consequence of the so tremendously increased productive forces of the present time, even the last pretext has vanished for a division of mankind into rulers and ruled, exploiters and exploited, at least in the most advanced countries; that the ruling big bourgeoisie has fulfilled its historic mission, that it is no longer capable of the leadership of society and has even become a hindrance to the development of production. . . ; that historical leadership has passed to the proletariat, a class which, owing to its whole position in society, can only free itself by abolishing altogether all class rule, all servitude and all exploitation; and that the social productive forces, which have outgrown the control of the bourgeoisie, are only waiting for the associated proletariat to take possession of them in order to bring about a state of things in which every member of society will be enabled to participate not only in production but also in the distribution and administration of social wealth, and which so increases the social productive forces and their yield by planned operation of the whole of production that the satisfaction of all reasonable needs will be assured to everyone in an ever-increasing measure.[64]

But it is precisely this account of the mechanisms and dynamism of history that seems most dubious. Marxism may be a very good way of analysing past and present societies. But it has no more hold on the future than any other theory, utopian or otherwise. Its certainty that capitalism will give rise to socialism is a matter of desire and hope, not of 'science'. 'Marx's faith in the "end of prehistory",' Kolakowski rightly says, 'is not a scientist's theory but the exhortation of a prophet.'[65] Many thinkers have pointed out that, while Marx gives an acute and in many ways convincing account of the 'inevitable' breakdown of capitalism, there is nothing similarly shown to be inevitable about the triumph of socialism. Bauman indeed argues that, on one unexceptionable reading, *Capital* 'presents a cogent case for the self-perpetuation of exploitation'.

As a cohesive and systematic theory *Capital* distinguishes as *inevitable* developments . . . the continuous subordination of the workers to their rulers and to the system as such, and the emergence of workers' defensive organisations cut to the measure of market relations and private property, that is organisations which pursue redistributive aims. The one 'necessity' whose nature is far from clear is that which is supposed to lead to the socialist channelling of workers' disaffection.[66]

Even allowing for a less restricted reading of *Capital*, it remains the case that Marx provides little in the way of either theoretical or empirical argument for the mass conversion of workers to socialism. The link between the alienation and oppression of present-day society and the general emancipation of future society is left therefore critically unclear. As Bauman, again, says:

In a sense, *Capital* makes depressing reading; it demonstrates, perhaps, why the capitalist system may eventually collapse under the burden of its own systemic incongruencies, but it hardly makes a convincing case for the *necessity* of human freedom establishing itself as an uncontested factor of human history, or of the "active man" doing away with the shackles of alienated institutions.'[67]

Martin Buber is led so far as to speak of a 'utopian apocalypse' in Marx, the point at which 'the whole topic of economics and science is transformed into pure "utopics"' in a post-revolutionary convulsion. 'The "withering away" of the State, "the leap of humanity out of the realm of necessity into the realm of freedom", may be well-founded dialectically, but it is no longer so scientifically.'[68] The proletariat is called upon to redeem humanity in a situation in which it is the most oppressed class in history. It must free itself from oppression in order to accomplish its task, but – the mistake of the utopians – mere willing is not enough. The proletariat, in Marx's dialectical conception, squares the circle of necessity and freedom by acting out of its own free spontaneous consciousness against a background of 'objective' social forces which are intimating and encouraging such a 'subjective' development. 'Socialism is the effect of history in the sense that history gives birth to the revolutionary consciousness of the proletariat, but it is the effect of freedom inasmuch as the act of revolution is free, so that, in the revolutionary workers' movement, historical necessity expresses itself in free action.'[69] The problem is not one of understanding this conception. It is not even a matter of whether or not the proletariat or some other agency *could* bring in socialism. The difficulty lies in the absence of any well-grounded – 'scientific' – account of how, historically and sociologically, the proletariat will in fact realize its allotted task. Proletarian consciousness will develop, the problem of freedom and necessity will be resolved, but Marxism no more shows that this will and must happen than any of its socialist rivals. It leaves crucially unresolved the question of how a class subject, as Marx puts it, to 'bestial barbarization', to the extreme of dehumanization, can become the agency of human emancipation and inaugurate the 'fully human' society of the future. Marx deals with the problem by a dialectical sleight of hand which only serves to show up the absence of a genuine theory of proletarian revolution.

All this is only one way of saying that Marx and the utopians are not after all so far apart. On the point crucial to the Marxists, the mechanics of the transition to socialism, they are in much the same position.[70] This is not, it must be insisted, to side with those who regard Marxism as 'impossibly utopian'. To denigrate utopian thought in this way is simply to play the game so zealously promoted by Marxists themselves. Whatever satisfaction it may give some people so to turn the tables against the Marxists, it is no part of this account to give comfort to anti-utopians. Marxian socialism may or may not be capable of attainment – at the very least we may say that, like Christianity, it has nowhere been tried. To see it, in certain respects at least, as utopian is simply to place it in a particular tradition of social theory, not to consign it to the realm of fantasy or the impossible.

Marxism has had to pay heavily for its reluctance to picture the future communist society in any detail. It was easy enough to make fun of the utopian motto that Wilhelm Weitling affixed to his *Guarantees of Harmony and Freedom* (1842): 'We want to be as free as the birds of the air; we want to go through life in joyful bands, just as they do, with never a thought of care.' But in trying to avoid such naive effusions, Marxists often forgot that the appeal of socialism, as with all utopian philosophies, was as much to the 'hungry soul' as to the belly. Pointing this out, Schumpeter warned that, 'in trying to distance himself [from utopia], the Socialist not only is being ungrateful to the wave that carries him, but he is also courting the danger that its forces might be harnessed into other service.'[71] There was also, in a sense, an opposite danger in this disdain for utopia: that, when the 'scientific socialists' came to construct a socialist society, they would not have faced in advance inescapable questions of political, economic and social organization.[72]

Nevertheless, there is a Marxist utopia to be found in Marxist writing, fragmentary and sometimes contradictory though it may be. It was clear to many thinkers that some conception of a future state was in fact essential to Marxism. Rosa Luxemburg stressed that Marx's whole theory was based on 'the transitory character of the capitalist economy. . . . It is only because Marx looked at capitalism from the socialist's viewpoint, that is from the historic viewpoint, that he was enabled to decipher the hieroglyphics of the capitalist economy.'[73] And Steven Lukes has pointed out that 'the Marxian views of justice and injustice, exploitation and the unfreedom of alienation all presuppose an ideal of freedom. They all employ a radical critical perspective, the standpoint of "human" society, or the realm of freedom, that cannot be adopted unless . . . some content is given to "communism".'[74] When we consider the content of 'full communism', the goal of the future society, we are confronted with a vision that in outlines at least is as grand as anything to be found in the whole utopian tradition.[75]

Thus, in the very work which laid down canonically the distinction between 'utopian' and 'scientific' socialism, Engels looks forward glowingly to a future society in which humanity takes possession, on almost god-like terms, of the whole domain of nature and society.

> With the seizing of the means of production by society, production of commodities is done away with, and, simultaneously, the mastery of the product over the producer. Anarchy in social production is replaced by systematic, definite organisation. The

struggle for individual existence disappears. Then for the first time man, in a certain sense, is finally marked off from the rest of the animal kingdom, and emerges from mere animal conditions of existence into really human ones. The whole sphere of the conditions of life which environ man, and which have hitherto ruled man, now comes under the dominion and control of man, who for the first time becomes the real, conscious lord of Nature, because he has now become master of his own social organisation. The laws of his own social action, hitherto standing face to face with man as laws of Nature foreign to, and dominating him, will then be used with full understanding, and so mastered by him. Man's own social organisation, hitherto confronting him as a necessity imposed by Nature and history, now becomes the result of his own free action. The extraneous objective forces that have hitherto governed history pass under the control of man himself. Only from that time will man himself, more and more consciously, make his own history – only from that time will the social causes set in movement by him have, in the main and in a constantly growing measure, the results intended by him. It is the ascent of man from the kingdom of necessity to the kingdom of freedom.[76]

Marx had already referred to the communist revolution as ending the 'prehistory of human society'[77] and inaugurating the true history of mankind, the history men freely make themselves. In some of the last things he wrote, he also reverted to the idea – touched on here by Engels – that communism would free humanity in an unprecedented way from the age-old curse of scarcity and the necessity of nature. It would do so partly by expanding the productive forces of modern industry, under collective ownership and control, to an indefinite degree, and so making the totality of human wealth available for the first time to everyone. But more than this, and more significantly than this, it would free humans altogether from 'the realm of necessity' to develop themselves in all their manifold creative individuality. For man, when free, is a natural artist. Unalienated man 'creates according to the laws of beauty'.[78] But for this he must free himself, at least in part, from the demands of labour, however rationally and communally organized.

The realm of freedom only begins, in fact, where that labour which is determined by need and external purposes ceases; it is therefore, by its very nature, outside the sphere of material production proper. Just as the savage must wrestle with Nature in order to satisfy his wants, to maintain and reproduce his life, so also must civilized man, and he must do it in all forms of society and under any possible mode of production. With his development the realm of natural necessity expands, because his wants increase; but at the same time the forces of production, by which these wants are satisfied, also increase. Freedom in this field cannot consist of anything else but the fact that socialized mankind, the associated producers, regulate their interchange with Nature rationally, bring it under their common control, instead of being ruled by it as by some blind power, and accomplish their task with the least expenditure of energy and under such conditions as are proper and worthy for human beings. Nevertheless, this always remains a realm of necessity. Beyond it begins that development of human potentiality for its own sake, the true realm of freedom, which however can only flourish upon that realm of necessity as its basis. The shortening of the working day is its fundamental pre-requisite.[79]

The idea of free time as the time of freedom, as 'the time for the full development of the individual',[80] was consistent with the general Hegelian–

Marxist view of human history as the growth of mankind to self-consciousness and self-mastery. Man's essence, his 'species-being', is as a social creature who is simultaneously developed by history to realize his potentiality as a morally autonomous, free, rational and almost divinely creative individual. Some contact with the 'realm of necessity' is inevitable and probably desirable, but Marx seems to regard it as at best a sphere where the individual will realize simply one aspect of his many-sided activities, without in any way being bounded by it. The overcoming of the division of labour – whose progressive development in history plays in Marxist philosophy something of the role of Original Sin and the Fall in Christian theology – is seen as a release of energy and creativity that will take man well beyond the mundane realm of material production.

As soon as labour is distributed, each man has a particular, exclusive sphere of activity, which is forced upon him and from which he cannot escape. He is a hunter, a fisherman, a shepherd, or a critical critic, and must remain so if he does not want to lose his means of livelihood; while in communist society, where nobody has one exclusive sphere of activity but each can become accomplished in any branch he desires, society regulates the general production and thus makes it possible for me to do one thing today and another tomorrow, to hunt in the morning, fish in the afternoon, rear cattle in the evening, criticize after dinner, just as I have a mind, without ever becoming hunter, fisherman, shepherd or critic.[81]

Somewhat embarrassed by this bucolic idyll – and missing perhaps Marx's playful expression – some commentators have seized upon another strand in Marx's thought to envisage a rather different relation between the realms of freedom and necessity. In this the definition of man as producer is seen as primary and fundamental. Even in the most distant period of the future communist society, *work* (production) will continue to be the centre of human activity: only work shorn of its character as 'alienated labour', work as 'life's prime want'. There cannot really be two spheres of activity, the one expressing constraint, the other freedom. This suggests a persisting duality or dichotomy quite at variance with Marx's general concept of future society. In communal production, both socially necessary work and free creative activity will find their synthesis. In it, men will find the scope for affirming their common humanity as well as for the fullest and most varied expression of their individuality. Some early notes on this theme contain a passage as rhapsodical and utopian as Marx ever wrote:

Suppose we had produced things as human beings [as would be the case in communist society]: in his production each of us would have twice affirmed himself and the other. (1) In my production I would have objectified my individuality and its particularity, and in the course of the activity I would have enjoyed an individual life; in viewing the object I would have experienced the individual joy of knowing my personality as an objective, sensuously perceptible, and indubitable power. (2) In your satisfaction and your use of my product I would have had the direct and conscious satisfaction that my work satisfied a human need, that it objectified human nature, and that it created an object appropriate to the need of another human being. (3) I would have been the mediator between you and the species and you would have experienced me as a redintegration of your own nature and a necessary part of your self; I would have been affirmed in your thought as well as your love. (4) In my individual life I would have directly created your life; in my individual activity I would have immediately confirmed and realized my true human and social nature . . . My labor would be a free manifestation of life and an enjoyment of life. Our productions would be so many mirrors reflecting our nature.[82]

The idea that freedom might be found *within* the realm of necessity finds a more concrete utterance in a remarkable passage in the *Grundrisse*, the unpublished sketch for *Capital*. Here Marx anticipates the fully automated society. The worker's 'direct labour' is no longer the basis of production and the source of wealth. Machines, encapsulated science, perform all the socially necessary work of production. But instead of regarding this as the opportunity for freeing the worker altogether from production – the realm of necessity – Marx seems to envisage the worker continuing to interact with machines at a higher, more rarefied level.

Labour no longer appears so much to be included within the production process; rather, the human being comes to relate more as watchman and regulator to the production process itself. . . He steps to the side of the production process instead of being its chief actor. In this transformation, it is neither the direct human labour he himself performs, nor the time during which he works, but rather the appropriation of his own general productive power, his understanding of nature and his mastery over it by virtue of his presence as a social body – it is, in a word, the development of the social individual which appears as the great foundation-stone of production and of wealth. . . As soon as labour in the direct form has ceased to be the great well-spring of wealth, labour time ceases and must cease to be its measure, and hence exchange value must cease to be the measure of use value.[83]

Freedom here, it seems, is to be found not in an escape from necessity but in a creative engagement with it. Human fulfilment is sought in the virtuoso deployment of scientific knowledge and technology within the sphere of production itself, in experimenting with the technical material and developing it as a matter of intrinsic satisfaction and pleasure. Work here is an expression of a 'human' rather than a 'biological' need. 'Really free labour . . . gives up its purely natural, primitive aspects and becomes the activity of a subject controlling all the forces of nature in the productive process.' But even here, we should note, the essence of this experimental and playful encounter with production turns on the creation of free, disposable time displacing 'socially necessary' time. For the vision in the *Grundrisse* is of 'the free development of individualities' made possible by 'the general reduction of the necessary labour of society to a minimum, which then corresponds to the artistic, scientific, etc. development of the individuals in the time set free, and with the means created, for all of them'.[84] In general, Marx remained consistent in the view that, whether exercised in the productive process or beyond it, free human activity depended on overcoming 'forced labour' in all its forms. For

free time, disposable time, is wealth itself, partly for the enjoyment of the product, partly for the free activity which – unlike labour – is not dominated by the pressure of an extraneous purpose which must be fulfilled, and the fulfilment of which is regarded as a natural necessity or a social duty, according to one's inclinations.[85]

An obvious reason for what seems an ambiguity or ambivalence in Marx on this question is that at different times in his life he distinguished various stages on the road to full communism. One conception of future life might therefore be appropriate to one stage but be superseded by another at a later stage. Above all, Marx insisted, we have to recognize that in the early stages 'what we have to deal with here is a communist society, not as it has *developed* on its own foundations, but, on the contrary, just as it *emerges* from capitalist society; which is thus in every respect, economically, morally, and intellectually, still stamped with the birth marks of the old society from whose womb it emerges.'[86] Hence many of the features – and freedoms – of the final stage of full communism would not be possible or appropriate to the first stage marked by 'the dictatorship of the proletariat'. In this first stage, for instance, the principle that has to apply in the production and distribution of society's wealth is 'from each according to his ability, to each according to his *work*'. This must entail, as Marx points out, substantial inequality, as people differ in their ability to labour. It is essentially still a bourgeois right of equal opportunity to exchange, which means a 'right of inequality', inevitable in the early stages of building a communist society. Only in a later stage of development can such a conception of rights be dispensed with and a different principle put into operation.

In a higher stage of communist society, after the enslaving subordination of the individual to the division of labour, and therewith also the antithesis between mental and physical labour, has vanished; after labour has become not only a means of life but life's prime want; after the productive forces have also increased with the all-round development of the individual, and all the springs of co-operative wealth flow more abundantly – only then can the narrow horizon of bourgeois right be crossed in its entirety and society inscribe on its banners: From each according to his ability, to each according to his needs![87]

There were times when Marx was inclined to stress that even communism should not be seen as the final goal of history. Communism, for all its finality as an economic system, remains essentially 'the negation of private property'. It is still touched by its origins in systems of property, even though it is the dissolution and overcoming of all such systems and their contradictions. It does not therefore sufficiently express the positive potentialities of the new society.

Communism is the phase of negation of the negation and is, consequently, for the next stage of historical development, a real and necessary factor in the emancipation and rehabilitation of man. Communism is the necessary form and the dynamic principle of the immediate future, but communism is not itself the goal of human development – the form of human society.[88]

This passage, which has puzzled some commentators, has to be read in its context. It occurs in the section of the *Economic and Philosophical Manuscripts* where Marx is polemicizing against 'crude communism' and striving to give the most complete sense of the transformation of humanity and nature implicit in communism. Communism has been considered too much in negative terms, as the mere repudiation of private property and individual ownership. This 'crude communism' is based an 'envy and levelling-down', a 'desire to reduce everything to a common level'. It is really only the logical extension and expression of private property, now generalized to all members of society equally, as 'universal private property'. Far from transcending property in any positive sense, it represents 'the domination of material property'.

> The role of worker is not abolished, but is extended to all men. The relation of private property remains the relation of the community to the world of things. . . . How little this abolition of private property represents a genuine appropriation is shown by the abstract negation of the whole world of culture and civilization, and the regression to the unnatural simplicity of the poor and wantless individual who has not only not surpassed private property but has not yet even attained to it. The community is only a community of work and of equality of wages paid out by the communal capital, by the community as universal capitalist. The two sides of the relation are raised to a *supposed* universality; labour as the condition in which everyone is placed, and capital as the acknowledged universality and power of the community.[89]

Against this spurious universality, Marx offers a vision of true universality that is positively awe-inspiring in its claims. Communism is nothing less than 'the reintegration of man, his return to himself, the supersession of man's self-alienation'. The 'positive supersession of private property, as the appropriation of human life, is the positive supersession of all alienation, and the return of man from religion, the family, the state, etc. to his human, i.e. social life.' This recognition of his fundamentally social nature, and the expansion of powers that this entails, also transforms man's relation to the natural world. No longer treated as an alien, recalcitrant entity, nature is now seen for what it truly is: man's own creation and, through its resources, the means for his self-creation. Thus in communist society not only is man allowed the fullest expression of his natural human essence; nature too is 'humanized.'

> The human significance of nature only exists for social man, because only in this case is nature a bond with other men, the basis of his existence for others and of their existence for him. Only then is nature the basis of his own human experience and a vital element of human reality. The natural existence of man has here become his human existence and nature itself has become human for him. Thus society is the accomplished union of man with nature, the veritable resurrection of nature, the realized naturalism of man and the realized humanism of nature.[90]

The recognition of nature as 'human nature', and of man's social or 'species-being' as 'natural' to him, makes possible the unification of all knowledge. It reconciles the science of man and the science of nature. For both 'history' and 'nature' are aspects of the same process of humanity's growth to self-consciousness and freedom. Through industry, nature and natural science have already penetrated practically into human life.

Industry is the actual historical relationship of nature, and thus of natural science, to man. It has transformed human life and prepared the emancipation of humanity. . . . If industry is conceived as the exoteric manifestation of the essential human faculties, the human essence of nature and the natural essence of man can also be understood. . . . One basis for life and another for science is *a priori* a falsehood. Nature, as it develops in human history, in the act of genesis of human society, is the actual nature of man; thus nature, as it develops through industry . . . is truly anthropological nature. . . . History itself is a real part of natural history, of the development of nature into man. Natural science will one day incorporate the science of man, just as the science of man will incorporate natural science; there will be a single science.[91]

With this reconciliation of man and nature, the way is cleared for the most complete development of human powers. The individual engages with reality through all his newly released faculties and senses. In class society, the institution of private property means that men experience the world 'only in the sense of immediate, exclusive enjoyment, or only in the sense of possession or having'. All their physical and intellectual senses have thereby been alienated. A thing is 'ours' only when we consume or use it directly. We do not see objects as expressions and extensions of ourselves, continuously remaking us as we experience or re-fashion them.

Man appropriates his manifold being in an all-inclusive way, and thus as a whole man. All his human relations to the world – seeing, hearing, smelling, tasting, touching, thinking, observing, feeling, desiring, acting, loving – in short, all the organs of his individuality, like the organs which are directly communal in form, are in their objective action (their action in relation to the object) . . . the appropriation of human reality . . . The supersession of private property is, therefore, the complete emancipation of all the human qualities and senses. It is such an emancipation because these qualities and senses have become human, from the subjective as well as the objective point of view. The eye has become a human eye when its object has become a human, social object, created by man and destined for him.[92]

Objectively, man comes to see reality everywhere as 'the reality of human faculties, human reality'. 'All objects become for him the objectification of himself.' They confirm and realize his individuality. Subjectively, the senses respond with the appropriate human sensibility to objects which now have a human meaning for them, and not simply a one-dimensional, utilitarian character. For the education of the senses depends upon the refinement of needs and transformation of man's relation to the objective world which communism, in its long process of becoming, embodies.

For it is not only the five senses, but also the so-called spiritual senses, the practical senses (desiring, loving, etc.), in brief, human sensibility and the human character of the senses, which can only come into being through the existence of its object, through humanized nature. The cultivation of the five senses is the work of all previous history. Sense which is subservient to crude needs has only a restricted meaning. . . Thus, the objectification of the human essence, both theoretically and practically, is necessary in order to humanize man's senses, and also to create the human sense corresponding to all the wealth of human and natural being. . . . The fully constituted society produces man in all the plenitude of his being, the wealthy man endowed with all the senses, as an enduring reality.[93]

It is this conception of a fully realized humanity, in all its individual and collective aspects, which is summed up in the passage in the *Manuscripts* that has frequently struck commentators as the most breathtakingly utopian of all Marx's comments on the future society:

Communism is the positive abolition of private property, of human self-alienation, and thus the real appropriation of human nature through and for man. It is, therefore, the return of man himself as a social, i.e. really human, being, a complete and conscious return which assimilates all the wealth of previous development. Communism as a fully developed naturalism is humanism and as a fully developed humanism is naturalism. It is the definitive resolution of the antagonism between man and nature, and between man and man. It is the true solution of the conflict between existence and essence, between objectification and self-affirmation, between freedom and necessity, between individual and species. It is the solution of the riddle of history and knows itself to be this solution.[94]

Such a dazzling vision of universal harmony – the principle perhaps of all utopian thought? – is hardly to be found anywhere else in the serious utopian literature. Marx himself, feeling uncomfortable with this lyrical Hegelian vocabulary, never again scaled such utopian heights (and the *1844 Manuscripts* of course remained unpublished during his lifetime). But just as, on occasion, and however reluctantly, the master was forced to declare himself on the nature of the future society, so with his epigones. The demand, from friends and opponents alike, for some sketch of the future socialist society remained – and remains – compelling. Even before Marx's death, Engels was provoked by the lucubrations of a German professor to produce, in the *Anti-Dühring*,[95] the fullest account of the new socialist society that he or Marx ever gave. Engels's book proved highly popular, but even more popular was August Bebel's *Woman Under Socialism* (1883). Far wider than its title suggests, Bebel's book went through 50 editions in the original German before his death in 1913, besides numerous translations.[96] Bebel ignored the misgivings of his fellow SPD leader Wilhelm Liebknecht and gave the most detailed picture to date of life in socialist society, down to the particulars of diet and the design of kitchens. Inspirational in tone, written in direct and simple language, Bebel's book conveyed socialism's utopian promise to the mass of literate workers who were repelled by the aridities of much socialist writing. It is in fact a utopia in almost everything but form. Its appearance in the 1880s, together with other works of a similar kind, helps us to understand the climate in which, a few years later, Edward Bellamy could produce his formal socialist utopia, *Looking Backward*: a book which, surpassing even Bebel's in popularity, had something of the same homely, direct quality.

For Russian Marxists there was an even greater urgency in meeting the demand for some account of the new socialist society. For apart from the usual need to clarify one's position in relation to a host of contending rivals, Russian Marxists, unlike their western counterparts, found themselves having to go beyond theory to acute problems of practice. For all his principled reluctance to speculate about the future society, Lenin found himself on numerous occasions forced to define the nature of the emerging communist society. In the midst of revolution he produced what virtually amounts to a political utopia, *The State and Revolution* (1917). In this, and with something of the same elation born of stirring events, he harked back to Marx's writing on the Paris Commune of 1871. Marx had waxed ecstatic over the direct democracy of the Commune, seeing it as an entirely new form of workers' state. Its 'true secret', he declared, was that 'it was essentially a working-class government, . . . the political form at last discovered under which to work out the economic emancipation of labour.'[97] Lenin purported to see in the Russian *soviet*, which first surfaced in the 1905 revolution, the same direct, conciliar, form of democracy; and, on its spontaneous reappearance in the crisis of 1917, he offered it as the revolutionary basis of the new communist state. ('Soviets plus electrification' was his later notorious formula for the content of the new society.) Late in 1918, when the Bolshevik Party was already draining away the power of the soviets, he was still echoing Marx and proclaiming that 'the soviets are the Russian form of the dictatorship of the proletariat.'[98]

But for the clearest echo of Marx at his most utopian we must go to Trotsky. The Russian Revolution produced one of the most creative ferments of modern times in cultural theory and practice. In considering the role of art under socialism, what should be produced and how, Russian Marxists were forced to engage with some of the most utopian of Marx's ideas on the end of alienation and the abolition of the division of labour. The artist seemed, in so many ways, to embody the free creative activity that Marx had seen as central to communism. 'In this sense,' says Trotsky, 'the development of art is the highest test of the vitality and significance of each epoch.' But, according to Marx, in establishing communism, the artist himself, as a social type, had to disappear. 'In communist society there are no painters but at most people who engage in painting, among other activities.'[99] It was partly this that led Trotsky to deny that there could be such a thing as 'proletarian art', for such a concept entailed tying art once more to a class, whereas communism meant the abolition of all classes and all class activity. 'The historic significance and the moral grandeur of the proletarian revolution consist in the fact that it is laying the foundations of a culture which is above classes and which will be the first culture that is truly human.'[100]

'Proletarian art' might play some 'temporary and transient' role, but it must never forget that its function is to prepare the way for the 'new man' of the fully socialist society. In describing the new man, Trotsky evokes a vision of human creativity and power that in its sublimity can fairly be said to sum up the entire utopian tradition from Bacon to Marx. The passage, towards the close of *Literature and Revolution*, must be quoted at length.

> The new man, who is only now beginning to plan and to realize himself, will . . . through the machine . . . command nature in its entirety. . . . He will point out places for mountains and for passes. He will change the course of the rivers, and he will lay down rules for the oceans. . . . The machine is not in opposition to the earth. The machine is the instrument of modern man in every field of life. . . .

Having rationalized his economic system, that is, having saturated it with consciousness and planfulness, man will not leave a trace of the present stagnant and worm-eaten domestic life. The care for food and education, which lies like a millstone on the present-day family, will be removed, and will become the subject of social initiative and of an endless collective creativeness. Woman will at last free herself from her semi-servile condition. . . .

Communist life will not be formed blindly, like coral islands, but will be built consciously, will be tested by thought, will be directed and corrected. Life will cease to be elemental, and for this reason stagnant. Man, who will learn how to move rivers and mountains, how to build people's palaces on the peaks of Mont Blanc and at the bottom of the Atlantic, will not only be able to add to his own life richness, brilliancy and intensity, but also a dynamic quality of the highest degree. The shell of life will hardly have time to form before it will burst open again under the pressure of new technical and cultural inventions and achievements. . . .

More than that. Man at last will begin to harmonize himself in earnest. He will make it his business to achieve beauty by giving the movement of his own limbs the utmost precision, purposefulness and economy in his work, his walk and his play. He will try to master first the semi-conscious then the sub-conscious processes in his own organism, such as breathing, the circulation of the blood, digestion, reproduction, and within necessary limits, he will try to subordinate them to the control of reason and will. Even purely physiologic life will become subject to collective experiments. The human species, the coagulated *Homo sapiens*, will once more enter into a state of radical transformation, and, in his own hands, will become an object of the most complicated methods of artificial selection and pyschophysical training. This is entirely in accord with evolution. . . . The human race will not have ceased to crawl on all fours before God, kings and capital, in order later to submit humbly before the dark laws of heredity and blind sexual selection. . . .

Man will make it his purpose to master his own feelings, to raise his instincts to the heights of consciousness, to make them transparent, to extend the wires of his will into hidden recesses, and thereby to raise himself to a new plane, to create a higher social biologic type, or, if you please, a superman.

It is difficult to predict the extent of self-government which the man of the future may reach or the heights to which he may carry his technique. Social construction and psycho-physical self-education will become two aspects of one and the same process. All the arts – literature, drama, painting, music and architecture – will lend this process beautiful form. More correctly, the shell in which the cultural construction and self-education of Communist man will be enclosed, will develop all the vital elements of contemporary art to the highest point. Man will become immeasurably stronger, wiser and subtler; his body will become more harmonized, his movements more rhythmic, his voice more musical. The forms of life will become dynamically dramatic. The average human type will rise to the heights of an Aristotle, a Goethe, or a Marx. And above this ridge new peaks will rise.[101]

Marxism has frequently sought to distance itself from such utopian utterances. It is embarrassed by what it considers 'unreal' aspirations – unreal, that is, not in some ultimate possible future but by what can be achieved in the currently existing social reality. It prides itself on its pragmatism, its realism – this is precisely what makes it 'scientific' as opposed to the 'utopianism' of other radical movements. But the price of that pragmatism has often been a cautiousness, an unwillingness to act because the time was 'unripe', that has on more than one occasion cost Marxist parties the opportunity to take or retain power. Lenin's 'opportunism' in this respect should be seen as one aspect of his 'utopianism': making revolutionary demands on an 'unripe' reality, and so making the reality more 'ripe'. Leszek Kolakowski has seen this utopian anticipation and pressure on reality as an indispensable component of all revolutionary thought and action. For Marxism to renounce utopia is to divest itself of a weapon so as to make the Marxist future impossible *ever* of realization, in however distant a time.

> The Left cannot renounce utopia; it cannot give up goals that are, for the time being, unattainable, but that impart meaning to social changes. . . . Why is utopia a condition of all revolutionary movements? Because much historical experience, more or less buried in the social consciousness, tells us that goals unattainable now will never be reached unless they are articulated when they are still unattainable. It may well be that the impossible at a given moment can become possible only by being stated at a time when it is impossible. . . . The existence of a utopia is the necessary prerequisite for its eventually ceasing to be a utopia.[102]

UTOPIA IN LATE NINETEENTH-CENTURY EUROPE

Towards the end of the nineteenth century, the literary utopia revived. With the exception of a few works, such as Cabet's *Voyage en Icarie*, it had been conspicuously absent in the first half of the century, its role usurped by sociological treatises and revolutionary manifestos. After 1870 a spate of utopias poured forth. In one year alone, 1871, three of the most influential appeared. Edward Bulwer-Lytton's *The Coming Race* showed strikingly the addition of the main new ingredient to utopia: Darwinism, with all its ambiguous conceptual armoury of struggle, survival and superior fitness. Lytton's story of an advanced race, the Vril-ya, who live in a remote underground region was designed, as he explained, to illustrate 'the Darwinian proposition that a coming race is destined to supplant our races'. In the same year – on the same day – *Blackwood's Magazine* published Sir George Chesney's *The Battle of Dorking*, which launched for endless imitation the theme of 'the coming war', 'the war that will end war'. This too reflected a new feature: the prospect of a great war fought with fearful weapons of mass destruction, a spectre already raised by rapid developments in armaments and the recent experience of the American Civil War and the Franco-Prussian war of 1870. In Wells's hands the theme was firmly linked to utopia in a narrative pattern of apocalyptic destruction followed by world reconstruction.[103] The third book, Samuel Butler's *Erewhon* (submitted to Chapman and Hall in 1871, published by Trubner in 1872), used the utopian form to satirize Darwinian ideas, but also to portray an alternative society that Butler equally mocks and praises. It too, picking up where *Gulliver's Travels* left off, re-established the literary utopia as a fit vehicle for satire and social criticism.

These three very different books show clearly enough that there was no one pattern or theme in the revival of utopia. Tales of advanced mechanical civilizations jostled those of simple, back-to-nature utopias, such as W. H. Hudson's *A Crystal Age* (1887). Some recent and spectacular technological achievements no doubt played their part in stimulating the utopian imagination. In 1869 the Suez Canal was opened; by 1874 five submarine cables had been laid across the Atlantic, and the first transcontinental railway had crossed the United States. The new interest in utopia as a literary form was also partly the result of new literary techniques, many deriving from impressionism; new genres, such as science fiction; and new technologies, such as photography and film. Utopia had a well-tried flexibility of purpose and content that made it particularly suitable for literary experimentation – as Wells, Zamyatin and Huxley all showed in their different ways.

As early as 1873 James Presley, the Director of Cheltenham Library, was moved to remark that 'the last four or five years' had been 'remarkably fruitful in works of a utopian character'.[104] The explosion of utopian writing at the very end of the century showed that the revival was more than a passing fashion. It also made clear that the socialist utopia would remain dominant even in the literary domain. Bellamy's *Looking Backward* (1888), Theodor Hertzka's *Freeland* (1890) and William Morris's *News from Nowhere* (1890) swept all before them. Oscar Wilde's 'The Soul of Man Under Socialism' (1891) portrayed socialism as an aesthetic utopia and so won converts among those repelled by the increasingly mechanical representation of socialism. Though not formally a utopia, it is so instinct with the utopian spirit as to stand with Morris's book as among the freshest and most attractive visions of socialism.[105] Then there was H. G. Wells, whose *Anticipations* (1901) and *A Modern Utopia* (1905) launched him on his long career as a utopian writer. Wells alone, tirelessly propagating over half a century his vision of the scientific socialist utopia, would have ensured the dominance of the socialist utopia. While utopias at the end of the nineteenth century were mainly imitations, refutations or vilifications of Bellamy, Hertzka and Morris, those of the twentieth have likewise turned on Wells.

Why did socialism become utopian in the full, formal sense? Why, having expressed itself mainly in 'scientific' treatises and tracts, did it revert to the traditional literary utopia? No doubt the insistent demand for pictures of the socialist future had something to do with it. But that could have been resisted, as it largely was until the 1880s, had it not been for the state of socialism in the late nineteenth century. What was happening was that socialism was becoming, in effect, a religion – a religion, moreover, that was increasingly showing its churchly rather than sect-like aspect. Its adherents no longer had the clear-eyed confidence of its founders, such as Saint-Simon and the young Marx, that the achievement of socialism was certain and imminent. Just as the belief of the early Christians in the imminence of the Second Coming gave way to the indefinite expectation of the Augustinian Church, so the socialists of the 1880s came to place their faith in the Party and the Movement as the vehicles of regeneration in some distant future. The fervency of belief remained, but the concrete goal was displaced to a remote time which none could predict. The language of socialism became correspondingly consolatory and inspirational, couched in the terms and tones of traditional religion. Marx's daughter, Eleanor Marx Aveling, in 1885 urged the Council of the Socialist League in England to have a Christmas tree. 'Is not socialism the real "new birth", and with its light will not the old darkness of the earth disappear?'[106] A few years later the ageing Engels was comparing the trials and persecution of contemporary socialists to the trials and persecution of the early Christians. Just as Christianity triumphed to become the state religion of the Roman Empire, so, he predicted, socialism would eventually triumph to become the world religion.[107] The patience of Job, it seems, was fast displacing the urgency of Isaiah in the outlook of European socialism.

Religion, we know, is not utopia. Still, it seems that a climate of religious inspiration and fervour is particularly favourable to utopia. That most sceptical and unreligious of ages, the eighteenth-century Enlightenment, was also the most un-utopian. In the 1880s, the uncertainty and divisions besetting socialism led many to look over and beyond these difficulties to the ultimate socialist utopia. William Morris, along with many other contemporary English socialists, was happy to declare his 'single-hearted devotion to the religion of Socialism'.[108] It seemed more important, urgent even, to keep the ultimate goal firmly in the minds of socialists, in the midst of sectional squabbles that might lead many to disillusion and despair. There seems no doubt that this was one of the key functions performed by the utopias of Bellamy and Morris.

Wells, too, was attracted by the 'religion of humanity' that was now increasingly mixed with socialism. In his case the revelation seems to have been Winwood Reade's *The Martyrdom of Man* (1872), a book which made a profound impression on him and many other English socialists. Like Henry George's *Progress and Poverty* (1879), for many another milestone on the road to socialism, Reade substituted a humanistic religion, a religion of science and the intellect, of the head and the heart, for traditional Christianity. He adapted Darwinism to provide an evolutionary framework for his view that mankind, considered as a unitary organism, was progressing slowly but surely towards an earthly paradise. But time was of the essence of human perfectibility:

> A time will undoubtedly arrive when all men and women will be equal, and when the love of money, which is now the root of all industry, and which therefore is now the root of all good, will cease to animate the human mind. But changes so prodigious can only be effected in prodigious periods of time. Human nature cannot be transformed by a *coup d'état*, as the Comtists and Communists imagine.[109]

'The Prince of Darkness is still triumphant in many regions of the world.' But, Reade is confident, 'the God of Light, the Spirit of Knowledge, the Divine Intellect, is gradually spreading over the planet and upwards to the skies.' With the growth of knowledge and the continued inventiveness of science, humanity will attain a peak of perfection that will literally lift it to the stars. The closing pages of *The Martyrdom of Man* presents a comprehensive picture of perfected humanity that in its grandeur compares directly with Trotsky's vision, quoted earlier. It is the most extensive and exhilarating, the most purely utopian, writing of its kind in the whole of the nineteenth century. Its score or so pages need to be read in their entirety; here is a brief but typical section:

> Not only will man subdue the forces of evil that are without; he will also subdue those that are within. He will repress the base instincts and propensities which he has

inherited from the animals below; he will obey the laws that are written on his heart; he will worship the divinity within him. As our conscience forbids us to commit actions which the conscience of the savage allows, so the moral sense of our successors will stigmatise as crimes those offences against the intellect which are sanctioned by ourselves. Idleness and stupidity will be regarded with abhorrence. Women will become the companions of men and the tutors of their children. The whole world will be united by the same sentiment which united the primeval clan, and which made its members think, feel, and act as one. Men will look upon this star as their fatherland; its progress will be their ambition, the gratitude of others their reward. These bodies which now we wear belong to the lower animals; our minds have already outgrown them; already we look upon them with contempt. A time will come when science will transform them by means which we cannot conjecture, and which, even if explained to us, we could not now understand, just as the savage cannot understand electricity, magnetism, or steam. Disease will be extirpated; the causes of decay will be removed; immortality will be invented. And then, the earth being small, mankind will migrate into space, and will cross the airless Saharas which separate planet from planet and sun from sun. The earth will become a Holy Land which will be visited by pilgrims from all the quarters of the universe. Finally, men will master the forces of Nature; they will become themselves architects of systems, manufacturers of worlds.

Man then will be perfect; . . . he will then be a creator; he will therefore be what the vulgar worship as a god.[110]

Reade's glowing vision represents the high-point of the 'secular perfectibilism'[111] of the nineteenth-century utopia. The similar vision that closes Wells's *A Short History of the World* (1922) is but an echo of it, and it anticipates even the extraordinary utopian vision of scientific progress in J. D. Bernal's *The World, the Flesh, and the Devil* (1929). The socialist utopia was squarely linked to this evolutionary world-view, with its progressiveness and faith in science. By the end of the century it had fully incorporated it and was more or less identified with it. Thus, when the reaction came against the idea of progress and perfectibility, it took the form largely of a reaction against the progressive socialist utopia. The modern anti-utopia, like the modern utopia, is also socialist – only, as it were, painted black. But before we consider the anti-utopia, we must go to America.

3

Utopia in Nineteenth-Century America

It seems so easy for America to inspire and express the most expansive and humane spirit; newborn, free, healthful, strong, the land of the laborer, of the democrat, of the philanthropist, of the believer, of the saint, she should speak for the human race. America is the country of the Future.

Ralph Waldo Emerson, '*The Young American*' (1844)

We Americans are the peculiar, chosen people – the Israel of our time; we bear the ark of the liberties of the world.

Herman Melville, *White Jacket* (1850)

We are all a little wild here with numberless projects of social reform. Not a reading man but has a draft of a new community in his waistcoat pocket. . . . One man renounces the use of animal food; and another of coin; and another of domestic hired service; and another of the State. . . .

Ralph Waldo Emerson to Thomas Carlyle, 1840

If the nucleus of the new society be implanted upon these soils, today a wilderness, and which tomorrow will be flooded with population, thousands of analogous organizations will rapidly rise without obstacle and as if by enchantment around the first specimens. . . . It is not the desertion of society that is proposed to you, but the solution of the great social problem on which depends the actual salvation of the world.

Victor Considérant, *The Great West* (1854)

It was never, in our minds, an experiment. We believed we were living under a system which the whole world would sooner or later adopt.

Pierrepont Noyes, *My Father's House: An Oneida Boyhood* (1937)

AMERICA AS UTOPIA

Everything about America has inspired, and continues to inspire, utopianism. It is big; it is open; it is democratic. Above all, it is new. Its continent is the New World. The very names of its regions and cities speak of renewal: New

England, New York, New Haven. It has inspired hundreds of communities with names like New Harmony, Equality, True Inspiration, even Utopia itself. Its capital city, Washington, was expressly conceived in utopian terms, and L'Enfant's plan followed precisely the utopian design of Renaissance architects. The seal of its Republic proclaims a *novus ordo saeclorum*, a new order of the ages. Repeatedly it has moved European observers to declare, as with Jean-François Revel, that 'America offers the only possible escape for mankind'; or, as with the young Simone de Beauvoir, that 'America is a pivotal point in the world where the future of man is at stake.'[1]

These utopian hopes for America are, differently expressed, as old as European civilization itself. America, it is often said, was invented before it was discovered. Long before Columbus's voyages of the 1490s, Europeans had speculated on the existence of lands and civilizations to the west of the Eurasian land mass. Precisely because the seas had not been explored and nothing was known, all manner of fantasy and desire could be wished on the empty spaces. Plato placed the lost continent of Atlantis there. It was the site of the Earthly Paradise of Celtic mythology; in a Christianized form this appeared as the fabled St Brendan's Isle, in search of which several expeditions put out from Ireland. The medieval poem *The Land of Cokaygne* set Cokaygne 'far in the sea, to the west of Spain'. There was also the legend, firmly believed in by Columbus, of the seven Christian bishops who fled boldly into the Atlantic from Moorish Spain, to discover the beautiful island of Antilia, upon which they built seven cities. All these myths spurred on the explorers of the fifteenth and sixteenth centuries. In turn, their discoveries fed the myths and gave them renewed substance and plausibility. They could also give them a new and more modern form. Whether or not the accounts of Columbus's and Vespucci's voyages actually influenced More in the writing of *Utopia*, it is certain that with the appearance and popularity of *Utopia* another theme, more directly social and secular, was added to the predominantly mythological and religious repertoire of imaginary Atlantic civilizations.

America, now newly found, was Utopia. The first impulse, following a longstanding tradition, was to see this largely in Edenic terms.[2] Columbus could report, in almost matter-of-fact tones, that he had discovered Eden 'because all men say that it's at the end of the Orient, and that's where we are'. Peter Martyr's *The New World* (1511), an account of Columbus's exploits, told of the inhabitants of Hispaniola (the modern Haiti), who 'go naked and . . . know neither weights nor measures, nor that source of all misfortunes, money; living in a golden age, without laws, without lying judges, without books, satisfied with their life, and in no wise solicitous for the future'. Moreover, 'it is proven that amongst them the land belongs to everybody, just as does the sun or water. They know no difference between *meum* and *tuum*, that source of all evils. . . . It is indeed a golden age. . .' Amerigo Vespucci, in a famous letter of 1503 to Lorenzo de Medici, similarly wrote:

> The inhabitants of the New World do not have goods of their own, but all things are held in common. They live together without king, without government, and each is his own master. . . There is a great abundance of gold, and by them it is in no respect esteemed

or valued. . . . Surely if the terrestrial paradise be in any part of this earth, I esteem that it is not far distant from these parts.[3]

More's own picture of Utopia seemed to square, more or less, with these early accounts. More had described an island somewhere in the South Atlantic whose people lived a life halfway between that of the Golden Age and Plato's *Republic*. Was this not what the explorers had discovered? The centuries of hope and expectation centred on the West were not likely to make men too attentive to the differences. Renaissance descriptions of the New World were heavily coloured by classical and Christian utopianism. America, initially at least, could only too readily be seen as the actual embodiment of the Renaissance utopia. For many early explorers and administrators, More's *Utopia* acquired the status of a guide and handbook. With its aid Vasco de Quiroga drew up a scheme for the government of New Spain. The leader of the first English colonial expedition, Sir Humfrey Gilbert, carried a copy of More's book along with him in 1583; and the first English settlements began with a system of common ownership on Utopian lines.[4]

But these attempts to see America literally through Utopian eyes did not long survive further knowledge and experience of the continent. Common ownership in the English colonies was speedily abandoned; and Utopian impressions specifically of the culture of the indigenous peoples faded somewhat on closer inspection, and closer contact. The Indians showed themselves to be, if need be, at least the equal of the Europeans in cunning and treachery. Nor did the cannibalism of the Caribs really belong in Utopia, although Montaigne managed to find them a place there. For jaded Old Worlders, *Homo americanus* continued right up to the end of the eighteenth century to provide ethnographic material for primitive utopias based on the uncorrupted simplicity and virtue of 'the noble savage'. But for those who seriously contemplated the move to America, as well as for those who actually settled there, other utopian conceptions proved more attractive, as well as more convenient.

The central feature of these conceptions was that they elevated the land, the physical landscape, over the people, such that the native people appeared at best as embellishments of the land, at worst as obstacles which had to be removed in order for it to fulfil its promise. Here, it seemed, was a land untouched by history, nature unmixed with art. This was the way the world must have looked before the coming of civilization. 'In the beginning,' said John Locke in his *Second Treatise of Government*, 'all the world was America.' The natives, in their rude simplicity, fitted in easily enough with this conception of the New World as primal nature. America was, to all intents and purposes, empty, a virgin land ready and waiting for settlement and civilization. Here mankind could make a new beginning. More than three centuries later, an American presidential candidate could still declare resoundingly to his supporters 'we Americans have the power to begin the world all over again.'[5]

It says much for the strength of utopian feeling aroused by the New World that it was able not just to circumvent but to exploit what seemed, on first acquaintance, the most obvious fact about the continent: its vast and terrifying wilderness. It was a land of pathless forests and impassable mountains, of freezing winters and scorching summers. Its inhabitants were ferocious animals and men who could be equally savage. When the *Mayflower* stood off Cape Cod in September 1620, William Bradford looked across the water to what he later described as 'a hideous and desolate wilderness, full of wild beasts and wild men'. Such an initial impression, deepened by further experience of danger and hardship in the early years, quickly dispelled any simple belief in America as the earthly paradise, a full-fledged Arcadia simply waiting to welcome and renew the weary denizens of the Old World.

There was a more serious obstacle to seeing America as a ready-made utopia. To the Christians, who formed the overwhelming majority of the first settlers, wilderness, far from being a paradise, was its precise antipode. Paradise, as the Persian root made clear, was a garden, not a wilderness. 'The land is like the garden of Eden before them, but after them a desolate wilderness' (Joel 2:3). Biblical tradition treated the wilderness – usually represented as a desert – as a cursed condition, declaring God's wrath and the withdrawing of his protection. Adam and Eve were expelled from the Garden of Eden to face a wilderness, a 'cursed' land full of 'thorns and thistles'. After the Exodus from Egypt, the Jews under Moses were compelled to wander for forty years in the 'howling waste of the wilderness' of Sinai, as a punishment for their ingratitude and impiety.

But that same Old Testament episode also showed how utopia might be wrung out of anti-utopia, deliverance out of despair. The wilderness experience of the Jews prepared the way for a more positive, optimistic evaluation of the wilderness condition. God had not abandoned his people when he left them to wander in the desert. The wilderness was a testing-ground, a place where the chosen people were humbled, purged and made ready for entry into the promised land of Canaan. A similar meaning was preserved in the idea of the wilderness as a sanctuary or refuge. One went to the wilderness to escape a complacent or ungodly society, to rediscover and re-dedicate one's faith in its harsh and dangerous environment. Wilderness was a godly discipline. When Elijah sought inspiration from God, he went into the wilderness a symbolic forty days and received guidance, like Moses, on a deserted mountain. The New Testament continued this tradition. John the Baptist sought the wild valley of the Jordan to revitalize faith and make ready for the coming of the Messiah. Jesus went to John in the Judean desert to be baptized; immediately afterwards he was 'led up by the Spirit into the wilderness to be tempted by the devil'. Sometimes whole communities might seek the wilderness to purify themselves and await the coming of the Messiah: the Essenes in the caves near the Dead Sea, the Waldensians in the valleys of the Alps. Or the individual hermit or monk might go there for spiritual discipline: Saint Anthony on the Red Sea desert and Saint Basil in the Black Sea wilderness remained classic early Christian examples.

The Puritans of America therefore had a strong and inspiring biblical tradition to fall back upon in justifying and interpreting their own 'Errand into the Wilderness', as Samuel Danforth called it in 1670. They frequently associated their migration with the Exodus, and compared themselves to the children of Israel being led through the desert by Moses. The settlers are the new chosen people; their land is divinely appointed, as was Israel's: so John Cotton claimed in 1620, quoting 2 Samuel 7:10. Edward Johnson spoke in 1654 of the Puritans as 'the ancient Beloved of Christ, whom he of old led by the hand from Egypt to Canaan through the great and terrible wilderness'. The visionary and apocalyptic note was sounded most clearly in Philip Freneau and Hugh Brackenridge's euphoric *Poem on the Rising Glory of America* (1771):

> A new Jerusalem, sent down from heaven,
> Shall grace our happy earth . . . .
> Paradise anew
> Shall flourish, by no second Adam lost . . . .
> Another Canaan shall excell the old,
> And from a fairer Pisgah's top be seen.

The settlers knew too what they had to do to realize their mission. The first commandment of God to man was that he should multiply, subdue the earth, and have dominion over every living thing (Genesis 1:28). The wilderness – which included the Indians – had to be conquered, cultivated, civilized, Christianized. It was a '*City* upon a Hill' that John Winthrop called upon his fellow passengers in the *Arabella* to build. Although utopia was destined and promised in America, it had to be *made*, by energy and enterprise; it did not lie ready-made, like Cokaygne. The wilderness must become a garden. America was a God-given opportunity – or duty – to create a new Garden of Eden, a new earthly paradise. But this must be striven for. The Puritans saw their mission as the conquest of the wilderness within – fallen human nature – and that without, the American wilderness. Logically, there could be no spiritual or physical end to this work. America's westward expansion, the conquest of the wilderness to the furthest shores of the continent, followed as a matter of course. Simply put, as it was in an account of 1796, the task was to make the wilds 'like Eden'.[6]

The New England Puritans arrived at their utopian conception of America by a characteristically tortuous and painful route, intellectually and practically. For those observing or inhabiting the milder climes of the south, the idea of America as a new Eden suggested itself more directly and immediately. A comprehensive pastoral ideology came to centre particularly on Virginia, as the emblem of the New World. It was largely around Virginia that there was elaborated what Henry Nash Smith has called 'the master symbol of the Garden' in American development. The tradition started with Arthur Barlowe's account for Sir Walter Raleigh of his voyage to Virginia in 1584. Virginia, he reported, was an immense and 'delicate garden' of 'incredible abundance', where the waters are sweet, the soil plentiful and fruitful, and the natives 'most gentle, loving and faithful . . . and such as live after the manner of the golden age'. Michael Drayton's 'Ode to the Virginian Voyage' (*c.* 1605) clearly draws on Barlowe's report as well as the conventional language of the Arcadian pastoral in celebrating Virginia as 'Earth's onely paradise'. Captain John Smith's *General History of Virginia* (1624) took a similar though more qualified Arcadian view. Barlowe, Drayton and Smith, writing expressly for an English audience schooled in the pastoral idiom, reflect the view of the outsider and observer; Robert Beverley's *History and Present State of Virginia* (1705) is by contrast a fully developed pastoral conception by a native with native experience. Virginia, he says, in its very name refers to a land that 'did still seem to retain the Virgin Purity and Plenty of the first Creation, and the People their Primitive Innocence'. It is one of 'the Gardens of the World': sunny, bountiful, beautiful.

But it was Thomas Jefferson's *Notes on Virginia* (1785) which developed the pastoral ideology for America in its most famous and influential form, the form in which it was to find utterance for more than a century. Perhaps the most notable thing about it is that Jefferson cleared the idea, so far as he could, of most of its conventional Golden Age, Arcadian literary associations. His pastoral image of America is firmly related to American conditions and American experience. In doing this, Jefferson modified the garden image of America in a way that brought him remarkably close to the Puritan conception. Unlike Barlowe and even Beverley, Jefferson did not see Virginia (America) as an already existing Eden. The beauty and bounty of Virginia were *achieved*; nature was worked upon by the art of the cultivator, the farmer. It was the husbandman, the yeoman farmer, who was singled out, in a famous passage, as the true creator of the American Eden:

> Those who labour in the earth are the chosen people of God, if he ever had a chosen people, whose breasts he made his peculiar deposit for substantial and genuine virtue. It is the focus in which he keeps alive that sacred fire, which otherwise might esape from the face of the earth.

Thus for Jefferson, as for the Puritans, America's pastoral utopia was the product of design, enterprise and toil. America was potentially a cultivated garden, halfway between the wilderness of untouched nature and the refinements (too many) of commercial urban society. After Jefferson, 'the cardinal image of American aspirations was a rural landscape, a well-ordered green garden magnified to continental size.'[7] And as with the Puritan ideology, the pastoral vision was well suited to the movement to turn the wild heartlands to the west into 'the Garden of the World'.

> The image of this vast and constantly growing agricultural society in the interior of the continent became one of the dominant symbols of nineteenth-century American society – a collective representation, a poetic idea . . . that defined the promise of American life. The master symbol of the garden embraced a cluster of metaphors expressing fecundity, growth, increase, and blissful labor in the earth, all centering about the heroic figure of the idealized frontier farmer armed with that supreme agrarian weapon, the sacred plow.[8]

With whatever modifications necessary to suit the most palpable circumstances of New World life, the utopian conception of America survived the first settlements to persist with extraordinary force throughout the nineteenth century and beyond. (It is of course still alive today, though much diminished.) One reason for its tenacity may have to do with the quite unusual extent to which America satisfied Old World longings and expectations deriving from the apocalyptic and millennial traditions. America, as Mircea Eliade points out, fused first and last things in a most compelling way. It was not simply, as John Locke had said, the world's beginning; it was also the world's end. It represented, it promised, both the restoration of paradise lost – the Garden of Eden, the terrestrial paradise – and the culmination of history in the millennium. Columbus himself was in no doubt as to the eschatological significance of his geographic discovery. In his *Book of Prophecies* he pronounced that the end of the world was not far off. It would be preceded by the conquest of the new continent, the conversion of the heathen, and the destruction of the Antichrist. 'God made me the messenger of the new heaven and the new earth, of which He spoke in the Apocalypse by Saint John, after having spoken of it by the mouth of Isaiah; and He showed me the spot where to find it.'

Protestant Reformers were equally convinced that the time had arrived for the renewal of the Christian world and the rebirth of Sacred History. They were increasingly persuaded, as reports of the New World flowed in, that it was the West that had been appointed for the completion of the Reformation. Protestant theology had for some time been developing the view that the true progress of religion was from East to West. The discovery of the New World seemed the clearest indication that it was there that the movement would complete and fulfil itself. The Antichrist – the Catholic Church, the European monarchies – was alive and active in the Old World. Its defeat or eclipse would herald the millennium. 'The first pioneers did not doubt that the final drama of moral regeneration and universal salvation would begin with them. . . . More than any other modern nation the United States was the product of the Protestant Reformation seeking an Earthly Paradise in which the reform of the Church was to be perfected.' Whatever their other doctrinal differences, among the early settlers the most common unifying belief was that America had been chosen among all the nations of the earth as the place of Christ's Second Coming, and that the millennium, 'though essentially of a spiritual nature, would be accompanied by a paradisiacal transformation of the earth, as an outer sign of an inner perfection'. Increase Mather, the eminent Puritan and Harvard president, wrote that, 'when this Kingdom of Christ has filled all the earth, this Earth will be restored to its Paradise state.'[9]

The pervasiveness and potency of these beliefs on both sides of the Atlantic ensured that they would play a major part in American history and culture for centuries to come. They showed themselves astonishingly adaptable to – one might even say, they were the cause of – the key episodes and encounters of later American history: the war with England, the conflicts with Indians, Spaniards and Mexicans, the westward movement, massive industrialization, and America's growth to world power.[10] All threats from the Old World could be interpreted as the machinations of the Antichrist, all opportunities provided by new lands and new machines as the providential tools by which the chosen people was to accomplish its mission in this world. American ideologies therefore did not simply remain resolutely utopian, a characteristic virtually forced upon them by America's continuing status as a refuge or haven where men might make a new beginning, and which found secular expression in such forms as the American Dream and the Horatio Alger myths.[11] More remarkable was the persistence and vitality of religious and even millennial utopianism, at a time when utopia had been decisively secularized in Europe. 'In a large, quasi-metaphorical sense,' says David Lodge, 'all significant American literature is utopian in spirit, and saturated in the myths of paradise lost or regained, either celebrating the potentialities of the American Adam, or brooding over where he went wrong.'[12] As literature, so politics: 'In the United States religion is the matrix and dominant form of political utopia, and it provides the mirrors in which each emerging group envisages its new social self.'[13]

The American Revolution, the final breaking of formal ties with the Old World, was bound to reinforce apocalyptic and millennial convictions. England replaced Rome as the Antichrist; her defeat made the millennium that more certain and imminent. Ezra Stiles, President of Yale College, in an election sermon of 1783 later published as *The United States Elevated to Glory and Honour*, was conventional in seeing America's victory as the work of Providence: 'How wonderful the revolutions, the events of Providence! We live in an age of wonders; we have lived an age in a few years; we have seen more wonders accomplished in eight years than are usually unfolded in a century.'

Equally conventional was the warning that a nation whose Revolution signalled and promised so much must be especially committed to maintaining a purity of purpose: 'The United States are under peculiar obligations to become a holy people unto the Lord our God, on account of the late eminent deliverance, salvation, peace and glory with which he hath now crowned our new sovereignty.'

But the same election sermon also sounded a rather different note, reminding us that this was the era of the Enlightenment, in which Americans vigorously participated. Stiles looked forward to a future for America in which reason, science and the arts form the substance of his utopian vision:

> We shall have a communication with all nations in commerce, manners, and science, beyond anything heretofore known in the world. . . all the arts may be transplanted from Europe and Asia, and flourish in America with an augmented lustre, not to mention the augment of the sciences from American inventions and discoveries, of which there have been as capital ones here, the last century, as in all Europe. The rough sonorous diction of the English language may here take its Athenian polish, and receive its Attic urbanity, as it will probably become the vernacular tongue of more numerous millions than ever yet spake one language on earth. . . .[14]

A similar mixture of the religious and the secular is to be found in a book, one of the most famous of its time, published in America in the same year as Stiles' sermon: Crèvecoeur's *Letters from an American Farmer*. But as befits a scion of the *petite noblesse* of Normandy and a later *habitué* of Parisian salons, Crèvecoeur largely chooses the more secular language of the Enlightenment in which to express his hopes for America. 'The American,' he says firmly, 'is a new man.' The promise of 'resurrection' that America holds out to its settlers is more the result of human than Providential design; 'Everything has tended to regenerate them; new laws, a new mode of living, a new social system; here they are become men. . . .' Even where the language takes on religious overtones, the content is predominantly secular: 'Americans are the western pilgrims, who are carrying along with them that great mass of arts, sciences, vigour, and industry which began long since in the east; they will finish the great circle.'[15]

From Enlightenment times onwards, it was always possible to see America in terms of the secular utopia. Many eighteenth-century Americans saw their Revolution, and the new nation it had created, as the fulfilment of secular Enlightenment ideals of reason and freedom. The *novus ordo saeclorum* could indeed be a new secular beginning. Tom Paine, the atheist, was thinking not in religious but in purely rationalist terms when he wrote in *The Rights of Man* that, with America, 'we are brought at once to the point of seeing government begin, as if we had lived in the beginning of time.' Radical democracy and rational government may have been conceived in the English Civil War and the European Enlightenment; but only in America was it instituted in anything like its full form. Echoing these eighteenth-century views, Henry Steel Commager roundly declares: 'The Old World imagined, invented, and formulated the Enlightenment, the New World .... realized and fulfilled it.'[16]

As America expanded its boundaries, and industry and technology grew apace, the sheer momentum of American development added a further secularizing influence. The American utopia could now share in the general idea of progress. Elaborated in eighteenth-century Europe, it was adopted with fervour in nineteenth-century America.[17] The youthfulness of the new nation was tied to ideas of its vigour and potency, its dynamism; its own newness suggested a special affinity with novelty and inventiveness. Europe was old and tired, weighed down with the encrustations of age-old traditions and antiquated institutions. To Americans, as Tocqueville noted, tradition meant nothing and the past had no hold over the present. 'The woof of time is ever being broken and the track of past generations lost.'[18] The *Democratic Review* wrote in 1839 that 'our national birth was the beginning of a new history . . . which separates us from the past and connects us with the future only.'[19] The march of progress, started in the East, would continue and culminate in the West. 'The old races are all gone,' wrote Emerson, 'and the elasticity and hope of mankind must henceforth remain on the Alleghany ranges, or nowhere.' 'America is the country of the Future.'[20] And while the fact of progress was written in the American Constitution, and demonstrated in the character of the 'new man' of America, it was inevitable that technology and material growth should also find a secure and increasingly central place in the ideology of progress. Technology came to be thought of as something almost quintessentially American. To a French visitor, Guillaume Poussin, 'the railroad, animated by its powerful locomotive, appears to be the personification of America.' The American utopia, as David Potter in particular has argued,[21] came to be a utopia of economic abundance at least as much as it was a democratic or spiritual utopia. In his inaugural address of 1830, Andrew Jackson compared the country as it had been, 'covered with forests and ranged by a few thousand savages', with the present 'extensive Republic, studded with cities, towns, and prosperous farms, embellished with all the improvements which art can devise or industry execute'.

But despite the increasing importance of the secular idea of progress, the religious framework of utopia was too powerful to give way to it. The mixture of the religious and the secular, the material and the metaphysical, continued throughout the nineteenth century and has persisted to this day. The mix could sometimes be quaint and quixotic, as in John Adolphus Etzler's *The Paradise within the Reach of all Men, without Labor, by Powers of Nature and Machinery* (1833). But in Ralph Waldo Emerson's 'The Young American' (1844) it achieved a synthesis of compelling power and subtlety. Emerson rejoiced that America was free of 'the insupportable burdens under which Europe staggers'. Youth and novelty had their drawbacks, chiefly in the lack of a history to feed the artistic imagination. But in the modern age, who could feel that this was enough to confer on Europe the right to superiority?

Europe is to our boys and girls, what novels and romances are; and it is not strange that they should burn to see the picturesque extremes of an antiquated country. But it is one thing to visit the pyramids, and another to wish to live there. Would they like tithes to the clergy, and sevenths to the government, and horse-guards, and licensed press, and grief when a child is born, and threatening, starved weavers, and a pauperism now constituting one-thirteenth of the population? Instead of the open future expanding here before the eye of every boy to vastness, would they like the closing in of the future to a narrow slit of the sky, and that fast contracting to be no future?

Among the many features marking out America as 'the country of the Future' was the 'uprise and culmination of the new and anti-feudal power of Commerce'. Commerce was 'a very intellectual force'. It was a mighty engine of peace and progress. It displaced physical strength, the principle of patriarchy and aristocracy, and substituted for it 'computation, combination, information, science . . .'. Commerce had its faults and was not to be the final form of human activity and endeavour. But 'the historian of the world will see that Trade was the principle of Liberty; that Trade planted America and destroyed Feudalism; that it makes peace and keeps peace, and it will abolish slavery.'

The beneficent force of commerce and technology was the necessary complement to the vast American land mass, now being bound fast 'in one web' by the railroad. But commerce could overreach itself. It was the land that Emerson relied on to provide the moral force in American culture:

The land is the appointed remedy for whatever is false and fantastic in our culture. The great continent we inhabit is to be physic and food for our mind, as well as our body. The land, with its tranquillizing, sanative influences, is to repair the errors of a scholastic and traditional education, and bring us into just relations with men and things. . . . I think we must regard the *land* as a commanding and increasing power on the American citizen, the sanative and Americanizing influence, which promises to disclose new virtues for ages to come.[22]

Together, the new spirit of commerce and the inspiring presence of the American continent were marking a new progressive stage in human evolution. From now on, America would 'speak for the human race'.

From Washington, its capital city, proverbially the city of magnificent distances, through all of its cities, states, and territories, it is a country of beginnings, of projects, of vast designs, and expectations. It has no past: all has an onward and prospective look. And herein it is fitted to receive more readily every generous feature which the wisdom or the fortune of man has yet to impress.

There were even the signs that people were aware of and active in confronting the dark side of the new commercial civilization. The alienation and inequality associated with a trading society were being acknowledged, and new social forms elaborated to combat them. This to Emerson was the inestimable importance of the experimental communities that flourished in the middle years of the century. Their individual failure or success was irrelevant to 'the revolution which they indicate as on the way'. It was this prompt recognition and redress of the weaknesses within the overall strength of the American venture that filled Emerson with optimism and drew from him a powerful declaration of faith.

The development of our American internal resources, the extension to the utmost of the commercial system, and the appearance of new moral causes which are to modify the state, are giving an aspect of greatness to the Future, which the imagination fears to open. One thing is plain for all men of common sense and common conscience, that here, here in America, is the home of man.

But what is especially interesting in this otherwise fairly conventional expression of the ideology of progress is its inspiration in Emerson's Transcendentalist philosophy. The entire beneficence in the American enterprise is seen as the product of the 'sublime and friendly Destiny by which the human race is guided'. Men are narrow and selfish; it is Destiny which has guided their actions and ensured that the overall result is good for the race as a whole.

It is easy to see that we of the existing generation are conspiring with a beneficence, which, in its working for coming generations, sacrifices the passing one, which infatuates the most selfish men to act against their private interest for the public welfare. . . . We plant trees, we build stone houses, we redeem the waste, we make long prospective laws, we found colleges, hospitals, but for many and remote generations.

The same thing is true of that mighty power of Trade which has undermined monarchies and empires. Merchants and manufacturers pursue their own self-interest, but the result has benefited all mankind.

Trade is an instrument in the hands of that friendly Power which works for us in our own despite. We design it thus and thus; but it turns out otherwise and far better. This beneficent tendency, omnipotent without violence, exists and works. Every line of history inspires a confidence that we shall not go far wrong; that things mend. That is it. That is the moral of all we learn, that it warrants Hope, HOPE, the prolific mother of reforms.

The very settlement of America was no historical accident. Its form and its happy timing were the work of Providence:

No thanks to us; but in the blessed course of events it did happen that this country was not open to the Puritans until they had felt the burden of the feudal system and until the commercial era in modern Europe had dawned, so that, without knowing what they did, they left the whole curse behind, and put the storms of the Atlantic between them and this antiquity. And the felling of the forest, and the settling in so far of the area of this continent, was accomplished under the free spirit of trading communities with a complete success. Not by our right hand, or foresight, or skill, was it done, but by the simple acceptance of the plainest road ever shown to men to walk in. It was the human race, under Divine leading, going forth to receive and inhabit their patrimony.

Emerson concludes that young America has no need to heed the sneers and slights of old Europe. 'Youth is a fault of which we shall daily mend.' In any case,

really at last all lands are alike. Ours, too, is as old as the Flood, and wants no ornaments or privilege which nature could bestow. Here stars, here woods, here hills, here animals, here men abound, and the vast tendencies concur of a new order. If only the men are well employed in conspiring with the designs of the Spirit who led us hither, and is leading us still, we shall quickly enough advance out of all hearing of other's censures, out of all regrets of our own, into a new and more excellent social state than history has recorded.[23]

All of Emerson's hopes and aspirations, together with the persisting tendency to see America's future in Providential terms, reappear in a celebrated passage in Herman Melville's novel *White Jacket* (1850). Melville echoes not just Emerson but Samuel Danforth, Edward Johnson, Ezra Stiles and the whole tradition that saw America entrusted with a unique, divinely ordained mission on which the future of the whole world turned. Here the religious basis of American utopianism, but at the same time its profoundly material content, received its clearest and most eloquent expression.

We Americans are the peculiar, chosen people – the Israel of our time; we bear the ark of the liberties of the world. Seventy years ago we escaped from thrall; and besides our first birthright – embracing one continent of earth – God has given to us, for a future inheritance, the broad domains of the political pagans, that shall yet come and lie down under the shade of our ark, without bloody hands being lifted. God has predestined, makind expects, great things from our race; and great things we feel in our souls. The rest of the nations must soon be in our rear. We are the pioneers of the world; the advance-guard, sent on through the wilderness of untried things, to break a new path in the New World that is ours. In our youth is our strength, in our inexperience, our wisdom. At a period when other nations have but lisped, our deep voice is heard afar. Long enough have we been sceptics with regard to ourselves, and doubted whether, indeed, the political Messiah had come. But he has come in *us*, if we would but give utterance to his promptings. And let us always remember that with ourselves, almost for the first time in the history of the earth, national selfishness is unbounded philanthropy; for we cannot do a good to America, but we give alms to the world.

AMERICA AS META-UTOPIA: THE UTOPIAN COMMUNITIES

Utopia in nineteenth-century America is full of paradoxes. The American nation or continent was frequently conceived in utopian terms; yet its sheer scale made it difficult to picture it, in literary form, as a fully realized utopia, present or future. Bellamy's *Looking Backward* is less striking for presenting America as a socialist utopia as for presenting the American utopia in national form at all. *Looking Backward*, and the utopian literature it produced as an immediate response, is exceptional in the history of American utopian literature. Unlike England or France, America did not develop a significant literary tradition of presenting the whole society in utopian form.[24] It did not indeed take to the literary utopia very much at all. As a metaphor or symbol, utopia is practically everywhere in American literature. But as a detailed portrait of an ideal society it is relatively rare. It is almost as if, because Americans thought they were already living in utopia, there was no need to represent it in imagination. Utopianism, the idea of America's special destiny, was a central part of the national ideology – almost *the* national ideology. It was a common ingredient of domestic and foreign policy; and in this general ideological form it is met with often enough in American literature. But this ideological or 'pragmatic' utopianism, a unique and almost contradictory blend, had the paradoxical effect of driving out almost entirely the formal literary utopia.

What such pragmatic utopianism produced in abundance, however, were actual utopian communities, and a rich literature based on them. Here again there was a paradox. America, at the level of national ideology, might think of itself as utopia. But to the members of the utopian communities it was more like dystopia. At any rate, with its government, army and rich capitalists, it shared in the general corruption and imperfection of the ordinary world. In this respect it hardly differed from old Europe. But firstly, and crucially, America had the *space* where utopia could be constructed, free from the contamination and intrusion of the unregenerate world. And secondly, the communitarians on the whole shared the view that the New World was the appointed place for achieving whatever perfection was humanly posible. They parted company with the more conventional position in thinking that it was impossible to do this on a national or continental scale. Like certain pious Jews in relation to the state of Israel, they regarded utopia and the nation-state as contradictory concepts. But there was nevertheless a direct and dynamic connection between the idea of the American nation as utopia, and the foundation of scores of utopian communities that, dismissing this idea, still sought and found refuge on the American continent.

We might borrow a term from the American philosopher Robert Nozick and consider America, in this aspect, as *meta-utopia*. In this conception utopia is not one community, one vision of the good life, but a 'framework for utopias', a place which freely allows people to form and re-form themselves into utopian communities of diverse kinds. 'The utopian society is the society of utopianism . . . the environment in which utopian experiments may be tried out.' As Nozick points out, this concept puts the emphasis on the realization not of particular utopian visions but of the environmental framework which permits such utopian schemes to be attempted in the first place.[25]

Nineteenth-century America was this meta-utopia on a grander and more generous scale than ever before or since. The vast size of its still relatively unsettled territory, coupled with the utopian notions that accompanied its entire development as a nation, drew utopian groups to it as to a magnet. On both physical and ideological grounds, nineteenth-century America was the ideal framework for utopias, in Nozick's sense. It set up a dynamic counterpoint between the larger national experiment – America as utopia – and the host of small experimental communities, each pursuing its individual utopian vision.

Meta-utopia, like utopia, produced a characteristic literature, the literature of the experimental community. There were the reports and surveys of founders, sympathizers and observers, such as John Humphrey Noyes's *History of American Socialisms* (1870), Charles Nordhoff's *The Communistic Societies of the United States* (1875) and William Alfred Hinds' *American Communities* (1878). Noyes founded Oneida; Hinds was a founding-member of it. There were also the autobiographies and memoirs of those who had actually been born or lived for much of their time in utopian communities, such as Frederick Williams Evans's *Autobiography of a Shaker* (1869), Robert Dale Owen's *Twenty-Seven Years of Autobiography* (1874) and Pierrepont Noyes's *My Father's House: An Oneida Boyhood* (1937). All these combine, to a remarkable degree, personal involvement and sympathy with a wide-ranging outlook and refreshingly clear-sighted analysis. The same can hardly be said of Nathaniel Hawthorne's somewhat jaundiced memorial of his Brook Farm experience, as this appears in his novel *The Blithedale Romance* (1852). Nor was there always the same judicious combination of qualities in the many reports of curious or committed European visitors, such as Charles Dickens's sour account of the Shakers in *American Notes* (1842), or the Owenite John Finch's equally one-sided encomium on the communities in his 'Notes of Travel in the United States' (1844). More balanced and more thoughtful was Harriet Martineau's assessment of the Shakers and Rappites in her *Society in America* (1839).

But the *chef d'oeuvre* of this whole literature is undoubtedly Henry David Thoreau's *Walden* (1854). This celebrated account of Thoreau's two-year experiment in solitary living around Walden Pond can almost be considered the epitome of American utopianism. It breathes its spirit through and through. It carries to a logical extreme the utopian promise of America to grant every single individual the right and opportunity to pursue his own vision, however idiosyncratic, of the good life. The paradox, of course, is that it is also the *reductio ad absurdum* of American utopianism. One man does not make a community, even a utopian community.[26] In the strict sense *Walden* did not and could not establish a tradition within the literature of the experimental community. B. F. Skinner's *Walden Two*, which clearly belongs to this literature, does indeed invoke its great predecessor by name. But the relationship remains largely one of spirit, the spirit of adventurous utopianism. This utopia of 'behavioural engineering' is so far removed from *Walden's* exuberant individualism as almost to be thought a conscious rebuke to it.

Skinner's collectivist utopia reminds us of a striking fact about the American communities, one which further illustrates some of the paradoxes of the American utopia. Contemporaries were in no way surprised or titillated by Noyes's and Nordhoff's books, which quite unselfconsciously and accurately described the communities they observed as 'socialist' or 'communistic'. For to nineteenth-century Americans, communistic colonies were a commonplace. They were almost as much a part of the landscape as New England townships, mid-West farms and frontier settlements. But modern readers may be forgiven for feeling somewhat startled when confronted with these books. Socialism in America, the most capitalistic of nations? Did not Werner Sombart write a famous book, *Why is there No Socialism in the United States?* and have not American scholars preoccupied themselves with this question for nearly a century? Was not the American utopia indeed pre-eminently a free-enterprise, *laissez-faire* utopia?

And yet there was probably more genuine communism practised in nineteenth-century America than in any society, at any time, beyond the hunting and gathering stage. This certainly seemed self-evident to many Europeans. The young Friedrich Engels was among the many European socialists who were stirred by the reports of the American communities, and who at first looked to them to provide the example and model for European communism. 'The first people in America,' wrote Engels, 'and indeed in the world who brought into realization a society founded on the community of property were the so-called Shakers.' The American communities, he confidently declared, had demonstrated that 'communism, the social life and work based on the common possession of goods, is . . . not only possible but has actually been realized . . . and with the best result.'[27]

The communities were themselves to a good extent the product of a wider movement of reform that enthusiastically embraced socialism. Socialism in mid-nineteenth-century America was far from being the 'un-American' thing it has now become. To followers such as the Transcendentalist Octavius Brooks Frothingham socialism seemed 'to be fast assuming in the United States a national character'. So receptive to socialism was progressive American opinion in these decades that in 1825 Robert Owen could, by invitation, lecture on his schemes for three hours to the United States Congress in the presence of two American Presidents, and hold long conversations with two others. Only by a few votes of 'the Southern slavemongers' did Congress regretfully refuse him permission to repeat the feat in 1845.[28] Owenism was just one of the socialist currents to find a ready response among American reformers. There was perhaps even greater enthusiasm for Fourierism, as powerfully advocated by Albert Brisbane and Horace Greeley, and which, with the conversion of Brook Farm to Fourierism in its later years, at one time seemed to engage every leading intellectual in the land. The New England Transcendentalists were particularly drawn to socialism in the 1830s and 1840s. Charles A. Dana, who drew up the Articles of Association for Brook Farm, wrote: 'In the party of Transcendental philosophers the idea early arose . . . that democracy was not enough . . . it should be raised up into life and be made social. The principle of equality should be extended. . . . That could only be accomplished by the reform of society. . . . And that was what inspired the socialistic movement. . . .'[29]

But what was the 'socialism' or 'communism' of the American communities? How well does the label 'utopian' fit? The sectarian religious communities, the first wave of American communitarianism which developed from the seventeenth century onwards, appear initially only dubiously utopian – and not simply for being religious. Groups such as the Shakers, the Rappites, the

Moravian Brethren, the Separatists of Zoar and the True Inspirationists of Amana represented the radical wing of the Protestant Reformation. They were mostly millennial in belief: the official name of the Shakers, for example, was 'The Millennial Church, or United Society of Believers in Christ's Second Appearing'. They held that they must set themselves apart from the world, to live a life as Christianly perfect as possible in preparation for Christ's Second Coming. The Rappites, wrote their historian John Bole, believed 'that they had formed their Society under the special guidance of God, whose kingdom was near at hand, and that life in their Society, as they planned it, was the best preparation for this kingdom'.[30]

The groups' millenarianism confirmed their communitarianism. For them, as for many other radical Protestant sects, Protestant individualism was severely qualified by an appeal to the communitarian way of life of the Primitive Church. Their favourite text was Acts 4:32: 'And the multitude of them that believed were of one heart and of one soul: neither said any of them that ought of the things which he possessed was his own; but they had all things common.' Part of perfection must consist in imitating the lives of the early apostles and in seeking to spread that way by example. But strenuous proselytism was largely avoided. A sense of separateness, reinforced by persecution in Europe and often enough further persecution in the New World to which they emigrated, marked the sects throughout. Since many of them were composed of German Pietists – the Shakers were the outstanding exception – a difference of language also frequently gave them the air of a 'society within a society'. 'A small society, voluntarily separated from the world, striving after perfection in its institutions, sharing many things in commom, and relying upon imitation for the spread of its system – such was the sectarian community.'[31]

The economic communism of the sects was, as often as not, pragmatic rather than doctrinal. Communism was more or less forced upon them by the poverty and hardship they encountered in their early years in America. One after another, groups which had never bothered themselves with economic and social theory in Europe found it necessary to pool their resources in order to establish themselves in a strange and often hostile environment. The Shakers, the Moravian Brethren, the Rappites and the Zoarites adopted communism only after an initial period which proved to them the impossibility of maintaining themselves on any other basis. The same was true of the later settlement of Amana. Communism was not envisaged when the Inspirationists left Germany in 1842, and was adopted at Ebenezer three years later only because, as a member explained to Nordhoff, they 'could not have got on or kept together on any other plan'. Bertha Shambaugh, another life-long member of Amana, wrote that 'communism had ever been incidental to the life and thought of the Community.' Faced with this resolutely undoctrinaire approach, together with the fact that some communities did not adopt communism at all, or only partially, scholars have increasingly preferred to regard the American communities not as 'communistic' but as 'communitarian', thereby emphasizing the wider ideal of community life that prevailed over particular economic arrangements.[32]

Nor were other aspects of the life of the sectarian communities necessarily of that forward-looking, progressive kind that we tend to associate with modern utopianism. The Shakers and Rappites were economically successful and technologically inventive, but their celibacy offended the humanist outlook of many intellectuals. Save occasionally in this respect, most of the religious communities made no attempt to alter the traditional relations between the sexes or the role of the family. Old-fashioned patriarchy was the rule at Harmony, Zoar, Amana and elsewhere – extending often to the domination of one man over the community for much of its existence, as with George Rapp at Harmony and Joseph Bäumeler at Zoar. Moreover, the sects displayed little interest in education or general culture, and – with the exception of the Shakers – they kept aloof from most of the stirring issues of the day, such as the anti-slavery and industrial reform agitation. They remained, overall, peaceful, industrious and conservative, as befitted the pious German peasants who formed the backbone of most of the religious communities. What Nordhoff had to say about Amana and Zoar fairly sums up their general character. The members of Amana are 'quiet, a little stolid, and very well satisfied with their life'. They 'appeared to me a remarkably quiet, industrious, and contented population; honest, of good repute among their neighbours, very kindly, and with religion so thoroughly and largely made a part of their lives that they may be called a religious people'. Of the Zoarites he noted that, being 'of the peasant class of Southern Germany', they are 'unintellectual and . . . have not risen in culture beyond their original condition.' 'Baümeler has left upon the society no marks to show that he strove for or desired a higher life here. . . .' The Zoarites have a 'dull and lethargic appearance'. They have achieved a certain reasonable degree of comfort and wealth – 'according to the German peasant's notion'. 'Much more they might have accomplished; but they have not been taught the need for more. They are sober, quiet, and orderly, very industrious, economical. . . .'[33]

This hardly sounds the stuff of utopia – certainly not of the modern utopia, with its Promethean expansiveness. But the importance of the sects in the communitarian tradition as a whole can hardly be overstated. They were the pioneer practitioners, the principal connecting links, of the whole tradition of the experimental community in America. When Robert Owen bought the lands and buildings of the Rappites at Harmony, Indiana, he was buying not just well-cultivated lands and well-equipped workshops but, symbolically, the fruits of the whole communitarian tradition to date. With that purchase, and Owen's founding of New Harmony there in 1825, secular communitarianism was added to – it never displaced – sectarian communitarianism, in an unbroken tradition. 'In America, and America alone,' writes Bestor, 'the religious socialism of the seventeenth century evolved without a break into the secular socialism of the nineteenth. The communitarian sects were the links in this chain of continuity.'[34]

The sects contributed to communitarianism not simply the ideology of radical Protestanism – an important factor, in a country still steeped in religious utopianism. As vital communities throughout the nineteenth century, they continued to provide living examples of communitarian life, models for (secular) imitation. The economic success of certain groups, notably the Shakers and Rappites, was particularly important in dispelling the notion that communistic practices doomed communities to poverty or philanthropic dependence. This gained in significance as the sects themselves increasingly came to display secularizing tendencies, leading them to emphasize economic and social questions at the expense of theological ones. They came to think of themselves as communitarians first and sectarians second. They made more of an effort to publicize their achievements and to propagate their ways. A Shaker *Summary View* of 1848 was explicit about the relevance of their experience to all associations based on 'a community of interests' – i.e., communism:

> The United Society of Believers (called Shakers) was founded upon the principles of equal rights and privileges, with a united interest in all things, both spiritual and temporal, and has been maintained and supported in this Society at New-Lebanon, about sixty years, without the least appearance of any failure. Is not this proof sufficient in favor of such a system?

The Shakers, indeed, as the first wholly Americanized, English-speaking community, played a pivotal role in passing on the communitarian tradition. Nordhoff rightly devoted the greater part of his book to them. They, as the oldest surviving community, were the 'elder statesmen' of the movement. They freely offered assistance and advice to the founders and members of other communities, religious and secular. They opened their doors to visitors – 'the world' – and published a large body of material about their beliefs and practices. Visitors such as Emerson and Harriet Martineau in turn published their accounts and so spread the fame of the Shakers. They were visited by American Presidents. They entered American literature, as in Hawthorne's 'Shaker Bridal' and 'The Canterbury Pilgrims'. Robert Owen published a pamphlet on them some years before founding New Harmony, and visited their communities in New York. His son Robert Dale Owen studied their social and educational practices at New Lebanon. The Transcendentalists were always fascinated by the Shakers; and while the Brook Farmers were repelled by their 'inhumanity', the founders of Fruitlands, Charles Lane and Bronson Alcott, were sympathetic observers and students of the Shaker experiment. When Fruitlands disbanded, Lane and his son temporarily joined the Shaker society at Harvard. A more committed conversion was that of the radical journalist Frederick Williams Evans, who abandoned Owenism for Shakerdom in 1831. As Elder Evans, he became the leading Shaker propagandist of his time, corresponding with such figures as Leo Tolstoy on Shaker pacifism and communism. It was he who provided Nordhoff with most of his material on the Shakers. Evans had the great gift of translating Shaker concerns into the language of contemporary reform, as the following passage shows:

> To the mind of the simple, unsophisticated Shaker, it seems marvellously inconsistent for any human government to be administered for the sole benefit of its own officers and their friends and favourites; or that more than one half the citizens should be disfranchised because they happen to be females, and compelled by the sword to obey laws they never sanctioned, and ofttimes in which they have no faith, and to submit to taxation where there has been no previous representation; while still millions of other

fellow-citizens are treated as property, because they chance to possess a darker-coloured skin than their cruel brethren. And again, that the members of the same religious body or church should be divided into rich and poor in the things of this temporary world, but who are vainly expecting that, in the world to come, they shall be willing to have eternal things in common! And when this same unjust and unequal administration is confirmed and carried out in the most popular religious organizations of Christendom, the Shakers think the climax of absurdity, tyranny, and oppression wellnigh attained.[35]

For John Humphrey Noyes, 'the Shakers' influence on American Socialisms has been so great as to set them entirely apart from the other antique religious communities.' They were the foundation stone of American communitarianism. Noyes's *History of American Socialisms* was the first and is still the best statement of the unity of the communitarian tradition in America. In this account, it was the religious communities that set the basic pattern. Noyes makes no simple claim of one-way influence. He acknowledges the importance of European social theory, above all that of Owen and Fourier, and of the experiments at New Harmony, Brook Farm and elsewhere, carried out under its auspices. But he is fully alive to the fact that the socialism to which America was particularly receptive – Owenism and Fourierism – was of the communitarian kind. It was, that is, based on the small experimental community with which Americans had already become familiar through the example of the religious communities. Hence in America religious and secular socialism were organically related. Noyes thought this could be seen especially well in the period of the 1820s to the 1840s, when religious Revivalism and communitarian socialism both flourished. 'The Millennium seemed as near in 1831 as Fourier's Age of Harmony seemed in 1843.' Both drew on the same source, which was ultimately the legacy of the early Pentecostal Church as resuscitated by the religious sects. 'The Revivialists had for their great idea the regeneration of the soul. The great idea of the Socialists was the regeneration of society which is the soul's environment. These ideas belong together, and are the complement of each other.'[36]

Noyes was peculiarly well placed to appreciate the interpenetration of religious and secular utopianism in the American communities. His own Oneida community, and the Perfectionist philosophy it embodied, spectacularly combined elements of both. It drew on both Revivalist theology and utopian socialism. As he himself wrote, though he and his followers rejected Fourierism, 'they drank copiously of the spirit of the *Harbinger* and of the Socialists; and have always acknowledged that they received a great impulse from Brook Farm.' In one guise, they saw themselves as the heirs of the Brook Farm experiment in socialism. The Putney Association, which preceded the foundation of Oneida in upstate New York in 1848, 'cautiously' practised communism. 'In the fall of 1847, when Brook Farm was breaking up, the Putney Community was also breaking up, but in the agonies, not of death, but of birth.'[37]

The Oneida community which succeeded it seemed intent on outdoing Brook Farm in full-blooded socialism and scientific enlightenment. The communism it practised was wide-ranging, extending not just to community of goods but, as in the *Republic*, to community of persons. Monogamous marriage was abolished, the couple bond forbidden. Oneida was transformed into one large 'family', with a system of 'complex marriage', in which, in theory at least, any couple could engage in sexual intercourse. Worse, Oneida went in for 'male continence' (*coitus reservatus*) and a form of eugenics known as 'stirpiculture'.[38] To the scandalized people of the surrounding community, who eventually forced Noyes to flee to Canada, all this smacked of the worst excesses of secular free-thinking and scientific rationalism. It certainly seems poles away from Shaker and Rappite celibacy, and the generally ascetic character of most of the religious communities. In other ways too Oneida seemed to go well beyond the quiet and conservative boundaries of religious communitarianism. Its scientific system of child-rearing and education, its willingness to send its young people for scientific and technical training in the outside world and its enthusiasm for labour-saving devices and technical advance all seem to place it more in the forward-looking world of New Harmony and Brook Farm – not to say *Walden Two* – than of Amana or Zoar.[39]

And yet, as Noyes insists, 'the Oneida Community belongs to the class of religious socialisms.' Perfectionism does indeed put a high value on communism; but its communism is 'Bible Communism', in the title of one of Noyes's principal books. Communism is 'the social state of the resurrection'. It exists only and entirely as the environment for the achieving of spiritual self-perfection, the sole aim of the community. 'Our Communism with one another is based on our religion, and our religion is based on Communion with God. . . .' Noyes was stern with those who confused Oneida's system of 'complex marriage' with Bohemian or licentious 'free love'. 'Any attempt to revolutionize sexual morality before settlement with God, is out of order. Holiness must go before free love.' 'Whoever undertakes to enter the liberty of the resurrection without the holiness of the resurrection, will get woe and not happiness . . . . They must be *Perfectionists* before they are *Communists*.'[40]

Noyes trained as a minister, and though the Perfectionist doctrines he developed were denounced as heretical and his licence to preach revoked, he always regarded himself as continuing in his Christian ministry. Theologically, Oneida belongs squarely with the Shakers in the camp of religious millennialism. Like the Shakers, Noyes believed that Christ's Second Coming had already taken place. For the Shakers this had occurred in the person of Mother Ann Lee, in whom Christ had made his second appearance, as a woman, after first appearing in the body of Jesus as a man. The Shakers therefore dated the beginning of Christ's kingdom on earth from the establishment of their Church. For Noyes, the Second Coming had taken place around A.D.70, at the time of the destruction of Jerusalem, and following the Biblical prophecy that it would occur one generation from the time of Christ's personal ministry. Ever since then it had been possible to achieve spiritual perfection.

Like the Shakers, then, the Noyesian Perfectionists took the view that they were already living in a state of regeneration, in 'the dispensation of the fullness of times.' It was possible to live without sin, in a condition approximating to that of the heavenly kingdom of God. Those who did not could be led to perfection, but those who persisted in their sinful ways were the literal agents of the devil.

Noyes believed himself to have reached a state where he was entirely free from sin. Whatever he did, however unorthodox, had to be seen in this light. He came to believe that his task was to establish the heavenly kingdom on earth, as a demonstration of the practicability of the selfless perfection of the regenerate life. This was the significance of Oneida: 'a Church on earth is now rising to meet the approaching kingdom in the heavens, and to become its duplicate and representative.' Announcing the founding of Oneida, Noyes's *Spiritual Magazine* declared in 1847: 'We believe that God has commenced the development of his kingdom in this country; that he has inoculated the world with the spirit of heaven, and prepared a Theocratic nucleus in this the most enlightened and advanced portion of the earth.'[41]

Oneida theology at this level was not so very different from that of the other American millennial sects. It was less easy to fit Oneida's unorthodox and, to some, shocking sexual and eugenic practices into a biblical framework, for these clearly separated it from the other sects. But Noyes showed no uncertainty in the matter. 'In the Kingdom of Heaven, the institution of marriage, which assigns the exclusive possession of one woman to one man, does not exist' (Matt. 22:23–30). In the notorious *Battle-Axe* letter of 1837, he wrote:

> When the will of God is done on earth as it is in heaven, there will be no marriage. The marriage-supper of the Lamb, is a feast at which every dish is free to every guest. Exclusiveness, jealousy, quarreling, have no place here, for the same reason as that which forbids the guests at a thanksgiving dinner to claim each his separate dish, and quarrel with the rest for his rights. In a holy community there is no more reason why sexual intercourse should be restrained by law, than why eating and drinking should be; and there is as little occasion for shame in the one as in the other.

'Sexual shame was the consequence of the fall, and is factitious and irrational' (Gen.2:25). Sexual pleasure, the 'amative' principle, was primary over and prior to procreation, the 'propagative' principle. This is clearly shown in the relations of Adam and Eve in the Garden of Eden (Gen. 2:18). Hence eugenics or 'stirpiculture', control over the amount and type of reproduction, was justified not just by nature but by God's dispensation for humanity in its original, unfallen, state. Even 'male continence' had divine sanction. God had given man self-control; to deny this was sinful, and lowered one to the level of the brutes. 'It is the glory of man to control himself, and the Kingdom of Heaven summons him to self-control in *All Things*.' Noyes was aware that the Shakers and the Rappites read the Bible differently, but dismissed the 'negative or Shaker method of disposing of marriage and the sexual relation'. Their celibacy was not only psychologically harmful to the individual but injurious to that communism on which both they and Oneida rested their search for spiritual perfection.

> The Oneida Communists claim that their control over amativeness and philoprogenitiveness, the two elements of familism, is carried much further than that of the Shakers; inasmuch as they make those passions serve Communism, instead of opposing it, as they do under suppression. They dissolve the old dual unit of society, but take the constituent elements of it all back into Communism.[42]

Hinds called the Noyesian Perfectionists, of whom he was one, 'practical rather than theoretical religionists'.[43] This rather understates the rational and experimental spirit that pervaded Oneida throughout its 33-year existence. In reading the accounts of its technical inventiveness, its business acumen and its social and scientific experimentation, it is sometimes difficult to remember that it was a religious community at all. It varied its work routines, decision-making, diet and dining. It instituted a system of 'mutual criticism' whose techniques foreshadowed that of the later therapeutic communities, such as Synanon. Its concern especially with culture and education, with emotional and personal fulfilment, gives it a distinctly secular, modern air. Noyes himself wrote extensively on social and scientific topics. He announced in roundly Comtean terms that 'it is generally agreed among the highest thinkers that sociology is the science around which all the other sciences are finally to be organised.' He offered lessons in community-building. The failure of the Owenite and Fourierist communities was blamed on their 'deductive socialism'. The way to the truth was 'to combine and alternate thinking with experiment and practice, and constantly submit all theories . . . to the consuming ordeal of practical verification'.

There were indeed many signs that by the 1870s the original millennial church had evolved into a secular Positivist association. Noyes busied himself with the scientific study of the communitarian tradition – the *History of American Socialisms* – and aspired to become the spokesman of the communitarian movement in America. In 1876 the Community paper *The Oneida Circular* was replaced by a new weekly paper, *The American Socialist*, edited by Noyes. The paper aimed to record the facts 'relating to the progess of Socialism everywhere', and to be a forum for the discussion of socialist opinion of every kind. In 1877 Noyes resigned the presidency of Oneida, arguing that his editorial duties left him insufficient time to manage the community. But the significant point was that '*The American Socialist* aspires to be the organ of Socialism in all its degrees, while the *O.C.* [sic] is the exponent of only one form of Communism.' So far had Oneida moved, in Noyes's eyes, from its origin as the 'Theocratic nucleus' of the Kingdom of God. With Noyes's flight to Canada in 1879, and the discontinuance of *The American Socialist*, even the role of communitarian prophet had to be abandoned. Oneida gave up 'complex marriage' and, in 1881, economic communism, formally reconstituting itself as a joint-stock company, Oneida Ltd. The utopian experiment was over.[44]

And yet it is a mark of the extraordinary synthesis of the religious and the secular in American utopianism that Noyes, at the height of his Positivist enthusiasm, should still declare that 'Social Science . . . is the science of righteousness.' After Noyes's death, a pious disciple Estlake wrote a formal apology, in which he could still state that 'the Oneida Community was . . . an object lesson in direct connection with the plan of Christianity, demonstrating the possibility of realizing the state of civilisation that Christ foreshadowed. . . .' Noyes himself, in examining the communitarian tradition in the *History of American Socialisms*, concluded that no community could succeed without religion. Although his treatise was largely concerned with the fate of the secular communities, he gave pride of place, so far as significance and influence went, to the religious communities. They were the longest-lasting and most successful, the Shakers chief among them. The Shakers 'are making the longest and strongest mark on the history of Socialism'. And Noyes chose to end his study with a remarkable tribute to the Shakers' role in the whole modern communitarian movement. Exaggerated or not, it is a fitting reminder of the strength of the religious undercurrent that flows constantly through the American utopia in the nineteenth-century – whether that utopia was seen in national or communitarian terms.

> The great facts of modern Socialism are these: From 1776, the era of our national Revolution, the Shakers have been established in this country; first at two places in New York; then at four places in Massachussetts; at two in New Hampshire; two in Maine; one in Connecticut; and finally at two in Kentucky, and two in Ohio. In all these places prosperous religious Communism has been modestly and yet loudly preaching to the nation and to the world. New England and New York and the Great West have had actual Phalanxes before their eyes for nearly a century. And in all this time what has been acted on our American stage, has had England, France and Germany for its audience. The example of the Shakers has demonstrated, not merely that successful Communism is subjectively possible, but that this nation is free enough to let it grow. Who can doubt that this demonstration was known and watched in Germany from the beginning; and that it helped the succesive experiments and emigrations of the Rappites, the Zoarites and the Ebenezers? These experiments . . . were echoes of Shakerism. . . . Then the Shaker movement with its echoes was sounding also in England, when Robert Owen undertook to convert the world to Communism. . . . France also had heard of Shakerism, before St Simon or Fourier began to meditate and write Socialism. These men were nearly contemporaneous with Owen, and all three evidently obeyed a common impulse. That impulse was the sequel and certainly in part the effect of Shakerism. Thus it is no more than bare justice to say, that we are indebted to the Shakers more than to any or all other social architects of modern times. Their success has been the 'specie basis' that has upheld all the paper theories, and counteracted the failures, of the French and English schools. It is very doubtful whether Owenism or Fourierism would have ever existed, or if they had, whether they would have ever moved the practical American nation, if the facts of Shakerism had not existed before them and gone along with them.[45]

UTOPIANISM IN LATE NINETEENTH-CENTURY AMERICA

Oneida's evolution from utopian community to modern corporation was representative and symptomatic. Towards the end of the century, one after another of the utopian communities disappeared or were transformed. The Zoarites dissolved in 1898, the Rappites in 1904. Two other long-lived German Pietest communities, Bethel and Aurora, also came to an end in 1880–1. Snow Hill, an offshoot of the famous eighteenth-century Ephrata community, disappeared in 1870, although the monastic order of the Seventh Day Baptists clung on until the early 1900s. In 1932 Amana, like Oneida, abandoned communism and turned itself into a joint-stock cooperative society. Even the Shakers, the hardiest of the religious communities, went into decline in the late nineteenth century. At their peak before the Civil War they had 6,000 members, spread over 18 societies. By 1900 there were no more than 1,000 members, and in the first half of the new century the decline continued relentlessly.[46] Of the nineteenth-century religious communities only one, the Hutterite Brethren – a German sect founded in South Dakota in 1874 – survived intact into the twentieth century.

The secular utopian communities fared even less well. Owenite New Harmony, Transcendentalist Brook Farm, the Fourierist Phalanxes and Josiah Warren's anarchist communities were of course long gone. So too were the other experimental communities founded on educational or libertarian theories, such as Northampton (1842–6), Skaneateles (1843–6) and Nashoba (1825–8), Frances Wright's Tennessee commune for emancipated slaves. Very few of these communities lasted more than six years, most not more than two, some only a few months. The Icarian communities founded by Étienne Cabet at Nauvoo (1849–59) and Cheltenham (1856–64) lasted somewhat longer but were, like most of the other secular communities, a painful story of economic hardship and factional strife. A breakaway group of Icarians at Corning, saved by the Civil War which boosted farm prices, lasted until 1895, but at the cost of even further splitting and the abandonment of most aspects of utopian socialism.[47] A similar tale of factionalism followed by collapse had to be told of Communia (1847–56), which Wilhelm Weitling unsuccessfully attempted to use to further his scheme of an eventual national *Arbeiterbund* of American workers. The fate of these and other colonies founded in the later part of the century showed that the communitarian movement in America, while by no means over,[48] had come to the end of its most distinctive and impressive phase. 'After 1860,' says Arthur Bestor, 'experimental communities were appendices or footnotes to other and more powerful movements of reform. They were rarely proposed as possessing in themselves the key to a transformation of society.'[49]

Were the communities successful? The question is as unanswerable as it is unavoidable. Do the more than 180 years of the Shakers – almost the time span of America itself – constitute success? Or the 100 years of George Rapp's Harmony Society, the 90 years of Amana, the 81 years of Zoar, the 70 years of Snow Hill? These are, by any reasonable measure, impressive figures, clear testimony to the stability and durability of these communistic ventures. But what of Oneida's 33 years? Is this not also evidence of success, given the radicalism of Noyes's experiment and the animosity it stirred up around him? Even the secular communities, with their average existence of only a few years, cannot be simply dismissed as failures. The ideas and practices they tried out, however unsuccessfully, often lived on to have a wide-ranging influence on later thought and practice. The experiments in education of the Owenite communities, for instance, were continued in different contexts by Owen's son Robert Dale Owen and the Owenite geologist William Maclure. Maclure introduced the Pestalozzian system of teaching to the American nation, and set up the first kindergarten and the first truly co-educational schools. Robert Dale Owen became the most prominent advocate in America of 'free, equal, and universal' schools, and fathered the Indiana free-school system that was adopted throughout the Middle West. The experience of the Owenite and Fourierist communities was also of direct relevance to the anti-slavery, labour and feminist movements. Fourierism too, through the work and writings expecially of Frederick Law Olmsted, had a decisive influence on American town planning and the 'landscape architecture' movement in the second half of the century. New York's Central Park, the 'People's Garden', can in a real sense be seen as the product of the Fourierist ferment of the 1840s.[50]

All contemporaries, as well as most later observers, at least agreed on one thing: that the stability and persistence of the religious communities showed that communism, in the narrow sense of community of goods, could and did work. The prosperity of the Shakers and Rappites was incontestable evidence. In the wider sense of full-blooded democratic communism, the failure of New Harmony and the Icarian communities might cast doubt on this general secular ideal. But economic communism was shown to be antithetical to neither human nature nor society by people who sought devoutly to imitate the practice of the early Church as described by Luke: 'And all that believed were together, and had all things in common; and sold their possessions and goods; and parted them to all men as every man had need.' The Fabian Society, in a tract of 1896, was inclined to be scornful of communitarianism, and pronounced itself impatient with all schemes for 'the establishment of socialism by private enterprise'.[51] This would have been all right if socialists had been more successful in demonstrating the practicability of socialism in more ideologically acceptable ways. As it was, the statement condemned as irrelevant some of the most impressive examples of practical communism in modern times. Not for the first or last time, the socialist intellectuals were unable or unwilling to appreciate the importance to their cause of the experiments in 'utopian socialism', whether conducted under secular or religious auspices.

There was widespread agreement, too, that the general conditions of life in the successful communities were far superior to town or country life in 'the world' – at least, as lived by the majority of people there. Their members had better food and better housing. They were healthier and longer-lived – Nordhoff noted that 'eighty is not an uncommon age for a Communist.' Their children were better educated and trained, their women less burdened with household chores and more involved, on more equal terms with the men, in the life of the community. Within the general communal purpose, all enjoyed a high degree of independence and equality. The old and infirm were better cared for. Individual poverty and economic insecurity were abolished. Work was less unremitting and more pleasurable than outside the community. High standards of craftsmanship and considerable business and technical skill ensured a level of comfort and convenience enjoyed only by the well-off in ordinary society. All this was achieved, Nordhoff pointed out, with 'a greater amount of comfort, and vastly greater security against want and demoralisation', than were attained by the surrounding population with their greater resources and lesser exposure to hardships. He concluded:

> If I compare the life in a contented and prosperous, that is to say a successful, commune, with the life of an ordinary farmer or mechanic even in our prosperous country, and more especially with the lives of the working-men and their families in our great cities, I must confess that the communist life is so much freer from care and risk, so much easier, so much better in many ways, and in all material aspects, that I sincerely wish it might have a farther development in the United States.[52]

A reformer of the 1890s, Henry Demarest Lloyd, was even more emphatic.

> Only within these communities has there been seen, in the wide boundaries of the United States, a social life where hunger and cold, prostitution, intemperance, poverty, slavery, crime, premature old age and unnecessary mortality, panic and industrial terror have been abolished. If they had done this for only a year, they would have deserved to be called the only successful 'society' on this continent, and some of them are generations old. All of this has not been done by saints in heaven, but on earth by average men and women.[53]

On the reasons for the success of some communities and the failure of others, there was likewise a general consensus. There could be differences about the importance of charismatic leadership: it was pointed out that the Shakers, for instance, had not depended upon this beyond the early stages. But all agreed that religion was the indispensable if not sufficient condition of success. Noyes may be suspected of some bias in this, but the sour verdict of Charles A. Dana, the erstwhile Brook Farmer, that he quotes has been echoed with minor modifications by scores of commentators since:

> Communities based upon peculiar religious views, have generally succeeded. The Shakers and the Oneida Community are conspicuous illustrations of this fact; while the failure of the various attempts made by the disciples of Fourier, Owen, and others, who have not had the support of religious fanaticism, proves that without this great force the most brilliant social theories are of little avail.[54]

Religion in fact is one part of the story of the decline of the communitarian utopia. For if the presence of religion was crucial to the success of the community, we would expect the vitality of the communitarian movement to be sapped by secularization. And so it happened. The decline of the utopian communities towards the end of the century took place in a society that was slowly but steadily experiencing the process of secularization that was the fate of all modern Western societies. Oneida is again instructive. Its decline as a utopian community parallels its evolution from religious millennialism to an experiment in secular socialism.[55] Carden is clear that Oneida's break-up cannot be attributed principally to Noyes's gradual withdrawal and eventual flight. Other fundamental changes were taking place, reflecting changes in the wider society, which were driving the community towards dissolution. 'The key was not the presence of a leader but the practice of Perfectionism.'

> As long as its religious ideals remained central in the lives of the members, Oneida was able to prosper to the benefit of all. The Community's minor problems – a succesor for Noyes, the integration of its young people, the introduction of virgins to Oneida's sexual practices – took on major, schism-making proportions only when the decline in religion undermined the value system sufficiently to diminish the importance of ideals and, hence, to destroy the balance which had existed between the individual member and the society. Unable to survive for its own sake, powerless to expect the individual to sacrifice himself for so empty a goal, Oneida terminated the utopian phase of its existence.[56]

In a familiar pattern, secularization was itself part of the wider process of urbanization and industrialization that was transforming America with such astonishing force and rapidity after the Civil War.[57] Urbanization and industrialization did not themselves kill communitarianism. In many ways they provided new fuel for the communitarian impulse. In sheer quantitative terms, as many communities continued to be founded after the turn of the century as before.[58] We might go so far as to say that in America, so big, so open, so rich, so full still of utopian promise, there will always be both the desire and the opportunity for communitarian life. Whatever the fate of America as utopia, its existence as meta-utopia seems reasonably assured.

But what changed was that communitarianism was no longer so central or significant in American life. Communities might be founded as ancillary to some larger scheme of reform, as in Weitling's case. Or they might offer retreat or escape from mainstream American society. But they no longer aspired to transform it. They were no longer thought to hold the key to America's future. Whether religious or secular, the mid-nineteenth-century communitarians believed in the small experimental community as the germ-cell of the future society. They were convinced that, if the world could but see a successful experiment, it would hasten to duplicate and reduplicate it – until whole nations were covered with such communities. 'If,' wrote Arthur Brisbane, the leading American Fourierist, 'one Association be established, and *it is of little consequence* where, which will prove practically to the world the immense advantages of the system . . . it will spread with a rapidity which the most sanguine cannot anticipate.'[59]

Such confidence was not as deluded as it might later sound. At the time when the communitarian movement was at its height, it was by no means fantastic to conceive America's future in communitarian terms. The communities were in many respects not so very different from the surrounding towns and settlements, at least on a technical and economic level. Owen and Fourier had declared about 2,500 members to be the maximum optimum size for a community. With about this number, Owen's New Lanark had been in the forefront of technological advance in the textile industry. None of the American communities, as individual units, approached this number – New Harmony with about 1,000 in 1825 came closest. But many of them, notably the Shakers and Rappites, carried on a combination of manufacturing and agricultural operations that impressed contemporaries by their progressive methods as well as their profitableness. As Bestor has pointed out:

> So long as ninety per cent of the American people made their living in places with a population less than twenty-five hundred – which they did until 1840 – the limitation of a community to that size could hardly be regarded as retrogressive. Until the middle of the century it was reasonable to believe that most of the advantages of the new machinery could be realized, while its disadvantages were avoided, in settlements of the size that communitarians, with striking unanimity, were proposing.[60]

By the later decades of the century, the large scale of industrial and commercial enterprises was making this view increasingly untenable. Ironically, Noyes's and Nordhoff's great books on the communities, published in the 1870s, came just at the end of the period in which it was still possible to think of them as holding the key to the social and industrial future. In that sense their books are, if not an obituary of the movement, a valediction to it. But there is a revealing difference of interest. Noyes still sees socialism in utopian terms, and is concerned about its future as such. The concluding pages of his book betray an anxiety and uncertainty about the prospects for communitarian socialism. His forward look is based on past successes, now increasingly obsolete as models. Nordhoff, on the other hand, can conclude on a more confident note because, as befits the progressive journalist, he restricts his immediate interest in the communities to their possible role in alleviating 'the labor problem' thrown up by advancing capitalism. From this perspective he declares himself satisfied that the socialistic community has earned the right to count as 'another way by which the dissatisfied laborer may, if he chooses, better his condition'.[61] To such narrow reformist ends had the utopian enterprise been reduced.

But the solution of 'the labor problem' did not necessarily have to take reformist forms. As the dimensions of the problem grew, it seemed to demand, once more, the fully developed utopian response. Such a response was not long in forthcoming. But it was no longer the utopianism of the communities. Edward Bellamy's *Looking Backward* aspired to offer a solution in terms of a socialist utopia fully equal to the scale and complexity of late nineteenth-century industrial America. In the last quarter of the nineteenth century utopia did not die out in America; it changed its form. The small-scale experimental community, itself the product largely of European theory, was displaced in favour of the new European model of national, scientific, socialism. Only something of this kind could hope to counter the competing model of a triumphant capitalism that was all too present in the real world.

David Riesman has suggested that one of the reasons why utopian thought and experiment could flourish in mid-nineteenth-century America was that 'the capitalism of that period was singularly unconcerned about propagandizing itself as an ideological system.' This may have been 'because it was so much taken for granted that it did not need verbal defence. . . . The system was written into the landscape, so to speak; it did not need to be written into books.'[62] If that was so, in the period after the Civil War writers and politicians hurried to make good the deficiency. Capitalism went fully on the offensive. Faced with the immense social problems thrown up by the unprecendented scale and speed of American industrialization, capitalism could not be content to rest on its material achievements but must also trumpet its moral virtue. As in Victorian England, the age seemed to demand new heroes; and, as in England, they were found in the new Carlylean 'captains of industry'. In the rhetoric of the new Republicanism, the self-made millionaires, the financiers, industrialists and railroad promoters, were presented as the paragons of 'free labor', the emblems of what individual initiative and enterprise could lead to. The aspirations and achievements of the Harrimans, the Stanfords, the Vanderbilts, the Carnegies, the Rockefellers and the Morgans were publicized throughout the land. And if some found these real-life heroes too raw, too much like robber-barons and less like captains of industry, there were the tales of Horatio Alger and the sermons of Henry Ward Beecher to bolster confidence in the 'rags to riches' promise of the American Dream. Meanwhile the anti-collectivist philosophy of Herbert Spencer, the businessmen's favourite thinker, was widely promoted by such intellectual luminaries as Charles W. Eliot, President of Harvard, and William Graham Sumner, the Yale sociologist. For the majority of Americans, the businessmen undoubtedly carried 'the mace of authority' in the enormous expansion of American industry after 1860.[63]

But there were also those who, like Walt Whitman, saw in the 'exceptional wealth' and social power of the big capitalists 'a sort of anti-democratic disease and monstrosity'. The extraordinary contrasts of dizzying wealth for the tiny minority and extreme destitution for the vast majority filled many observers with a sense of foreboding. A civil disaster, comparable to the civil war that the nation had just suffered, seemed to be looming. Observing three wretched-looking tramps hunting for scraps of food, Whitman was struck with a feeling of 'deep and spectral dangers'. The growth in unemployment, the rise in the number of strikes, the homelessness and the poverty were all indications that the health of the Republic – perhaps its very existence – was at risk.

> If the United States, like the countries of the Old World, are also to grow vast crops of poor, desperate, dissatisfied, nomadic, miserably-waged populations, such as we see looming upon us of late years – steadily, even if slowly, eating into them like a cancer of lungs or stomach – then our republican experiment, notwithstanding all its surface-successes, is at heart an unhealthy failure.[64]

The ideology of 'free labor' that had united workers and industrialists in the Republican party during the 1860s shattered against the brutal realities of post-Civil War reconstruction. The American work-force underwent a decisive proletarianization, exacerbated by ethnic competition and conflict as the immigrants poured in. Low wages, high unemployment, strikes, lock-outs and the violence of employers' private militias taught the American workers the need for combination. The Knights of Labor during these years represented the principal attempt to organize labour as a distinct force with a distinct identity opposed to capital. The national union movement was indeed the response to the infinitely more powerful combination of capitalists in large trusts and corporations. Despite the rhetoric of Spencerian individualism and 'free labor', it was clear that the capitalsm of individual proprietors and family businesses was on its way out, and with it the hopes of advancement from rags to riches. John D. Rockefeller, who more than any other man led the trend towards consolidation and concentration, could be as insistent about this as, on other occasions, he and his fellow-capitalists were prepared to subscribe to the ideology of individual enterprise and individual success: 'The day of combination is here to stay. Individualism has gone, never to return.'[65]

It was in this thoroughly modern world of organized capital and organized labour that Bellamy made his profound impact with the first thoroughly modern utopia, *Looking Backward*. But this was also the setting for a new theme: America as *dystopia*. For the first time in its history, America towards the end of the nineteenth century could present the image not only of utopia but also now of anti-utopia. While Bellamy looked for a hopeful resolution of the problems of industrializing America, others began to fear that, after all, America might have no special mission to succeed where others failed. Her future might be as dark and uncertain as that of other industrial nations. Worse, given her awesome size and power, she might be a force for evil and destruction in the world far surpassing anything they might be capable of. The vast energies of the continent might go into the making of a new hell rather than a new heaven on earth. The American dream turned, for many writers and artists, into a nightmare of unbridled power and industrial alienation, of moral purposelessness and individual anomie. And yet F. Scott Fitzgerald's *The Great Gatsby*, which partly depicts this, can still recall 'the last and greatest of all human dreams', can still remember that time, three centuries earlier, when 'for a transitory enchanted moment man must have held his breath in the presence of this continent . . . face to face for the last time in history with something commensurate to his capacity for wonder.'[66]

4
Anti-Utopia, Shadow of Utopia

I have no more faith than a grain of mustard seed in the future of 'civilisation', which I know now is doomed to destruction, and probably before very long: what a joy it is to think of! and how often it consoles me to think of barbarism once more flooding the world, and real feelings and passions, however rudimentary, taking the place of our wretched hypocrisies. . . . I used really to despair because I thought what the idiots of our day call progress would go on perfecting itself: happily I know that all that will have a sudden check. . . .

William Morris, letter to Mrs Georgiana Burne-Jones, 12 May 1885.[1]

The peak of Utopia is steep; the serpentine road which leads up to it has many tortuous curves. While you are moving up the road you never face the peaks, your direction is the tangent, leading nowhere. If a great mass of people are pushing forward along the serpentine they will, according to the fatal laws of inertia, push their leader off the road and then follow him, the whole movement flying off at a tangent into the nowhere.

Arthur Koestler, *The Yogi and the Commissar* (1945)

The decline of utopia and the rise of its nightmare cousin is parallel to the history of this surrealist century, which is at once the partial fulfilment of nineteenth-century dreams and their negation.

Chad Walsh, *From Utopia to Nightmare* (1962)

This place no good.

D. H. Lawrence's last written words. Keith Sagar, *The Life of D. H. Lawrence* (1982)

THE ANTI-UTOPIAN TEMPERAMENT

As nightmare to its dream, like a malevolent and grimacing *doppelgänger*, anti-utopia[2] has stalked utopia from the very beginning. They have been locked together in a contrapuntal embrace, a circling dance, that has checked the escape of either for very long. As in Freud's theory of the unconscious, the very announcement of utopia has almost immediately provoked the mocking, contrary, echo of anti-utopia. Hesiod's Golden Age is succeeded by an Iron Age of unending pain and sorrow. Plato's *Republic* elicits the satire and ribaldry of Aristophanes and the Attic comedy. Bacon's scientific utopia is mercilessly ridiculed in Swift's *Gulliver's Travels*.

Like the religious and the secular, utopia and anti-utopia are antithetical yet interdependent. They are 'contrast concepts', getting their meaning and significance from their mutual differences. But the relationship is not symmetrical or equal. The anti-utopia is formed by utopia, and feeds parasitically on it. It depends for its survival on the persistence of utopia. Utopia is the original, anti-utopia the copy – only, as it were, always coloured black. It is utopia that provides the positive content to which anti-utopia makes the negative response. Anti-utopia draws its material from utopia and reassembles it in a manner that denies the affirmation of utopia. It is the mirror-image of utopia – but a distorted image, seen in a cracked mirror.

The formal literary anti-utopia consequently had to wait for the establishment of the formal literary utopia. It does not, that is, appear before More's *Utopia*, after which it has a history almost as continuous as that of utopia itself. But just as the formal utopia was extensively prefigured, in classical and Christian thought, so anti-utopia was frequently manifested in expressions of what we might call the anti-utopian temperament. There have always been those who, for reasons of individual psychology or social ideology, have been profoundly sceptical of the hopeful claims made on behalf of humanity by social prophets and reformers. They have evoked the dark side of human nature as the preponderant side. Men are sinful, fallen creatures. They are weak, and in need of authority and guidance. Left to their own devices, they will always be the prey of selfish and aggressive impulses. 'Never hope to realize Plato's Republic,' warned the philosopher-emperor Marcus Aurelius, 'for who can change the opinions of men? And without a change of sentiments what can you make but reluctant slaves and hypocrites?'[3] Marcus Aurelius's Stoical perception that happiness was not of this world, but perhaps of another, found a stronger Christian form in Augustine's contrast between the necessarily corrupt 'city of man' and the heavenly 'city of God'. In this orthodox Christian view, the search for earthly perfection was not just blasphemous but illusory.

Part of the interwoven story of utopia and anti-utopia can indeed be interestingly told as the longstanding clash between Augustinian and Pelagian traditions within western thought. The utopian, like Bellamy or Wells, is a Pelagian. He denies original sin, and believes that men can perfect themselves by creating the right environment. The anti-utopian, as Huxley and Orwell were inclined to be, is Augustinian. He sees weak human creatures constantly succumbing to the sins of pride, avarice and ambition, however favourable the circumstances. The anti-utopian need not believe in original sin, but his pessimistic and determinist view of human nature leads him to the conviction that all attempts to create the good society on earth are bound to be futile. Utopian strivings will lead to violence and tyranny. The anti-utopian takes a certain melancholy pleasure in the recital of failed and aborted reforms and revolutions. The record of history is plain. Augustinian determinism comes over pitilessly in Hegel's declaration: 'The History of the World is not the theatre of happiness. Periods of happiness are blank pages in it.'[4]

Augustinianism, in the terms of secular social theory, is a variety of conservatism; and conservative social thought has been a powerful wellspring of anti-utopian sentiment throughout the ages. Aristotle's conservative critique of Plato's *Republic* was one influential source of this attitude. For more modern times, Edmund Burke's *Reflections on the Revolution in France* (1790), together with his other writings, provided a philosophical rationale for anti-utopian European conservatism for nearly two centuries. Amplified by a host of European thinkers from Joseph de Maistre to Oswald Spengler, it offered a battery of weapons for assailing the reforming and revolutionary movements of the nineteenth and twentieth centuries.

For all its variety, the conservative message was clear. Men are creatures of custom and habit. They are governed by precedent and prescription, history and tradition. They are not and never will be saints or angels. At all times, said Burke, 'men do bear the inevitable constitution of their original nature with all its infirmities.' They are formed and guided by society, which is a complex and delicate web of custom and belief. It is society, not 'nature', which confers rights. The elevation of Reason and Nature by the European Enlightenment was fraught with dangers. Society is bound together by common sentiment more than calculating self-interest, by religion and ritual more than rational organization. Change is natural and inevitable, but it must be gradual and consensual if it is not to destroy society. It must follow the 'intimations of tradition'. Conservatives attacked the rationalism of revolutionaries and utopians who aspired to refashion society according to the dictates of abstract theories. 'That man thinks much too highly, and therefore he thinks weakly and delusively, of any contrivance of human wisdom, who believes it can make any sort of approach to perfection.' The attempt at perfection in society, thought Burke, flew in the face of all principles of social life. It would, as the French Revolution showed, turn liberty into licence, authority into tyranny.[5]

The anti-utopian temperament was not always or only tied to a conservative ideology. It could manifest itself in several other ways. There was the robust, no-nonsense, Anglo-Saxon rebuttal of utopia, in the spirit of realism and common sense. This could lead Sir Robert Burton, in his *Anatomy of Melancholy*, to dismiss all the utopias from More to Bacon as 'witty fictions, but mere chimeras'. There was a similar earthiness in Macaulay's declaration that 'an acre in Middlesex is better than a principality in Utopia. The smallest actual good is better than the most magnificent promises of impossibilities.'[6] Suitably twisted, this philosophy of pragmatism could turn into a cynical strategy of statecraft based on the assumption that men are moved only by the basest and most self-interested of motives. Men are fools and knaves. A clever ruler will always be able to lead them by the nose. To think otherwise, to hope to order society by an appeal to duty or altruism, is to court disaster. In this sense Machiavelli's *The Prince* is a key anti-utopian text – as is clear from the many conscious and unconscious echoes of it in *Brave New World* and *Nineteen-Eighty-Four*.[7]

The conservative and pragmatic critiques of utopia spring from a fundamental pessimism, or at least scepticism, about the capacities of human beings, and the possibility of attaining more than a moderate degree of happiness in human society. Standard anti-utopian figures have been 'the worm in the bud' and 'the thorn in the rose': the pessimistic counterpoint to the optimistic visions of history and humanity, like the serpent coiling itself around the apple tree in the Garden of Eden. But while this scorns the possibility of achieving utopia, there are those who fear the opposite: that utopia *can* be attained, and that it will be a nightmare. It is not, in this view, that humans are too vicious or too stupid to create the perfect society, but that such an achievement would violate the restlessness and striving that are an essential part of the human spirit. For Willam James it was this dynamic quality of human nature that made utopia so unappealing and ultimately so deadly.

Everyone must at some time have wondered at the strange paradox of our moral nature, that, though the pursuit of outward good is the breath of its nostrils, the attainment of outward good would seem to be its suffocation and death. Why does the painting of any paradise or utopia, in heaven or earth, awaken such yawnings for nirvana and escape? The white-robed harp-playing heaven of our sabbath-schools, and the lady-like tea-table elysium represented in Mr Spencer's Data of Ethics, as the final consummation of progress, are exactly on a par in this respect, – lubberlands, pure and simple, one and all *Tedium vitae* is the only sentiment they awaken in our breasts. To our crepuscular natures, born for conflict, the Rembrandtesque moral chiaroscuro, the shifting struggle of the sunbeam in the gloom, such pictures of light upon light are vacuous and expressionless, and neither to be enjoyed nor understood.[8]

The fear that satisfaction and surfeit, along hedonistic and utilitarian lines, would kill human creativity and endeavour is central to Huxley's anti-utopian critique in *Brave New World*. In utopia, he and others such as Zamyatin say, we would die of boredom. The Savage claims 'the right to be unhappy', and chooses death over the stultifying happiness of Brave New World. But elsewhere Huxley also raised the question of utopia's future-orientation – almost a defining characteristic of the modern utopia – as itself a principal vice. Secular modern ideologies, complained Huxley, were obsessed with the future. They were blind to 'the eternal present' which was the common element of all the great world religions. As such, they were only too capable of sacrificing the present to the future, 'about which the only thing that can certainly be said is that we are totally incapable of forseeing it accurately'.

The moment you get a religion which thinks primarily about the bigger and better future – as do all the political religions from Communism and Nazism up to the, at present, harmless, because unorganized and powerless, forms of Humanism and Utopianism – it runs the risk of becoming ruthless, of liquidating the people it happens to find inconvenient now for the sake of the people who are going, hypothetically, to be so much better and happier and more intelligent in the year 2000. . . .[9]

Earlier Huxley's friend D. H. Lawrence had protested: 'Why do modern people invariably ignore the things that are actually present to them? . . . They certainly never live on the spot where they are. They inhabit abstract space, the desert void of politics, principles, right and wrong, and so forth.'[10] The anti-utopian temperament has always preferred the concrete to the abstract, the immediate task to the long-term plan, the present or the past to the future. It sees in this the elementary safeguarding of essential human qualities against the possibility that they will be sacrificed in the service of some remote goal or abstract idea. 'The future is not the time of love,' wrote Octavio Paz; 'what man truly wants he wants *now*. Whoever builds a house for future happiness builds a prison for the present.'[11]

It is no more than an extension of this feeling that the anti-utopian frequently celebrates the ordinary against the extraordinary, the everyday over the exotic. In a world which gives itself over to big names and big causes – democracy, nationalism, Marxism, the Free World – he sees in a clinging to the small things of life some way of maintaining a grip on reality. Everyday objects and routines become a means of arming oneself against cloudy abstractions and illusory promises. In Orwell's *Nineteen Eighty-Four*, it is chiefly through such a deliberate and self-conscious attention to the small details of everyday life – making tea, keeping warm, collecting old-fashioned objects such as paperweights – that Winston Smith retains some hold on his sanity. In anti-utopia, ordinary life can itself become utopia, as remote and longed-for as utopia appears to its votaries.

The anti-utopian temperament supplies the terms of a perennial philosophy. It can manifest itself in all ages, in all manner of guises. It underlies Christian objections to perfectibility, conservative opposition to radical reforms, and cynical reflections on human incapacity. Its tones are variously satirical, mocking, minatory – all of which can be effective foils to human pride and vanity. It presents itself as the sum of ripe old human wisdom, a storehouse of cautionary but essential truths about human nature and human strivings distilled from the collective experience of mankind. Its principal target is hubris: the insolent pretensions of humanity to mimic the gods. Utopia is the modern form of hubris, and so it is the implacable enemy of utopia.

The formal anti-utopia draws comprehensively on the varied expressions of the anti-utopian temperament. But it is both more and less than this widespread general philosophy. It is more than it, because it makes its objections to utopia not in generalized reflections about human nature but by taking us on a journey through hell, in all its vivid particulars. It makes us live utopia, as an experience so painful and nightmarish that we lose all desire for it. It is one thing to discourse in general terms on the limitations of human capacities and the folly of attempting too much. It is another thing to paint a picture of such an attempt in colours so sharp and strong that no one can miss the message. As a weapon in the armoury of philosophical conservatism, few devices have been as effective as the modern anti-utopia.

And yet the modern anti-utopia is in an important sense also less than – even opposed to – temperamental anti-utopianism of this kind. It is frequently written by people who do not share this general philosophical outlook. The two most famous anti-utopias of the twentieth century, Huxley's *Brave New World* and Orwell's *Nineteen Eighty-Four*, were both written by men who had at least as much of the utopian as the anti-utopian temperament in their make-up. Similarly, the most influential utopian thinker of the century, H. G. Wells, terrified his late Victorian public with some of the most chilling anti-utopias ever written. We might even say, stretching the point only a little, that the anti-utopia is largely the creation of men for whom it represented the dark obverse of their own profound and passionate utopian temperament. Their anti-utopias are born of a sense of frustrated and thwarted utopianism. Neither in their individual life nor in the world at large do they see any prospect of the utopia they so desperately wish for. The anti-utopia is for them a kind of angry revenge against their own foolish hopes, a back-handed compliment to the noble but deluded purposes of utopia. The intimate connection of utopia and anti-utopia here most clearly reveals itself as the anguished cry of a single divided self.

All this is to emphasize the fact that the anti-utopia is different from the anti-utopian temperament and bears only an indirect relationship to it. More precisely, it is to suggest that the anti-utopian temperament could give rise to the anti-utopia only in certain specific historical and social circumstances. It was only as the result of social and intellectual developments in the centuries following More's *Utopia* that the general critique of the anti-utopian temperament could become the distinct outlines of the formal literary anti-utopia. And then the anti-utopia might offer as little comfort to those who were anti-utopian by temperament as to the utopians.

THE TWO FACES OF SATURN

Since the time of More's *Utopia*, the anti-utopia – a formal reversal of the promise of happiness in utopia – has been a literary and intellectual possibility. But it was not until the nineteenth century that much was made of this possibility. Till then the anti-utopia, though generally recognizable as a distorted reflection of utopia, tended to appear as a variety of the older form of satire.

This was reasonable enough. Satire holds together both negative (anti-utopian) and positive (utopian) elements. It criticizes, through ridicule and invective, its own times, while pointing – usually implicitly but sometimes explicitly – to alternative and better ways of living. Eventually the literary forms of utopia and anti-utopia were to pull these two elements apart, assigning them to separate genres, or sub-genres. But the separation was never final or complete; and in the early period utopia and anti-utopia familiarly jostle each other within the same satirical form, often confusing the reader as to the author's true intent.

Satire was indeed an ambiguous form. Its patron saint in the Renaissance was the god Saturn, the Roman form of the Greek Kronos, ruler of the Golden Age. To the literary form of satire there had long corresponded the social form of the Saturnalia, an annual festival of mockery and destruction that was also a positive re-enactment of the pleasures of the Golden Age. Saturn–Kronos was from the beginning characterized by contradiction. He was the dispenser of the Golden Age, the god of agriculture, and to the Romans also the bringer of civilization to Italy. All this emphasized bounty and benevolence. But he also castrated his father and devoured his children. 'The sickle in the iconography of Saturn is an agricultural tool or the castrating weapon, depending upon which aspect of the myth is uppermost.' Moreover, he came to be associated with the oldest, slowest and most remote of the planets, one which exercised a malignant influence on human affairs. Thus the Janus-faced character of satire, its encompassing of both negative and positive qualities, was fittingly symbolized by this double-image of Saturn, 'a god who reigns over the earthly paradise, but who also by reason of his concern with melancholy, disease, and death becomes the patron of snarling Renaissance satirists'.[12]

Utopia itself has kept alive this dual concern, refusing to hand over entirely to anti-utopia the negative side of human nature and society. Most commonly, the anti-utopia appears as the existing contemporary society, to which the author offers his utopia as the solution to present ills and discontents. Thus More paints a bleak picture of Tudor England, against which the colours of Utopia stand out the more brightly. Rousseau's *Social Contract* is the utopian response to his own anti-utopia in the *Discourse on the Origin of Inequality*. Bellamy's awakened sleeper, Julian West, has the constant jarring memory of ninteenth-century Boston to contrast with the glowing new world of 2000, and in a memorable episode is transported back in a nightmare to that world he is so glad to have quit. In many of H. G. Wells's utopian novels, such as *The World Set Free* and *The Shape of Things to Come*, the misery and disorder of the contemporary world leads to breakdown and chaos, out of which there gradually emerges a world order reconstituted along utopian lines.[13]

The frequent appearance of utopia in a satirical guise made this double-focus natural. For more than three centuries after More, anti-utopia was often concealed in utopia. Even when the anti-utopia took on separate form, it retained the satirical character of utopia and used satirical techniques to attack existing society. But now the positive was suppressed almost altogether in favour of the negative and the destructive. Bishop Hall's *Mundus Alter et Idem* (1607), which has good claim to be considered the first formal anti-utopia, scourges the vices of its age in a sort of inverted vision of Cokaygne. The inhabitants of Crapulia, when not fighting or thieving, drink and eat to excess, with consequences to their minds and especially their bodies which Hall describes in the grossest possible terms. They are of a repellent fatness and sluggishness, the rich having attendants to hold their eyes open during the daytime and to put food into their gaping mouths. In one city, there are 'but few inhabitants of any years that have any teeth left: but all, from 18 to the grave, are the natural heirs of stinking breath'.[14]

Northrop Frye has noted that 'what is a serious utopia to its author, and to many of its readers, could be read as a satire by a reader whose emotional attitudes were different.' He instances Bellamy's *Looking Backward* as likely to produce such a response among many of today's readers.[15] The opposite is also true: anti-utopian satire can be read as utopia by those so minded. There were many who read Bishop Hall's account of Crapulia as a celebration of the pleasures of the body, an evocation of a genuine Cokaygne. Similarly teachers have often found that the sex-and-drugs culture of *Brave New World* represents blissful nirvana to their college students.[16]

Swift's *Gulliver's Travels* (1726), the greatest of the older anti-utopias, threw up some of the same conundrums. The satire on eighteenth-century English society was plain enough, as was the attack on the scientific utopia of Bacon and his followers. But there were, or seemed to be, distinct utopian features in Lilliput and Brobdingnag; while the society of the impeccably rational horses, the Houyhnhnms, appeared almost a formal utopia. The anti-utopian satire is no doubt uppermost. The King of Brobdingnag's verdict on European civilization, contradicting Gulliver's fulsome account of it, is clearly Swift's: 'I cannot but conclude the bulk of your natives to be the most pernicious race of little odious vermin that nature ever suffered to crawl upon the surface of the earth.' But Swift was no simple misanthrope. The human race was not irredeemably damned. Man was not *animal rationale* but he was *rationis capax*. Swift admired More and his *Utopia*, and on more than one occasion proposed to himself a similar exercise. As with later anti-utopians, there was a utopian streak in his temperament, concealed for much of the time by his rage at the obduracy of human folly.[17]

Much the same kind of ambiguity is to be found in Samuel Butler's very Swiftian satire, *Erewhon* (1872). The savagery is softened, the tone more good-humoured than in Swift, but Erewhonian society holds the mirror up to Victorian society with equal effect to Swift's mirroring of Hanoverian England in Lilliput and Laputa. The Erewhonians treat disease as a crime and crime as a disease, but with the same kind of specious rationalizations employed by Victorians in holding the opposite. The Musical Banks, much revered but little visited, echo the place of the church and religion in English life; and just as the Victorians paid lip-service to God but in practice worshipped Mammon, so the Erewhonians professed to believe in their official deities but in their everyday life showed their devotion to the vulgar goddess Ydgrun. The Colleges of Unreason, with their hatred of genius and originality, their dedication to useless 'hypothetics' and their professors of Inconsistency and Evasion, are a suitably absurd reflection of English academic life. Most singular of all, Erewhonians have drawn the logical conclusion from the theory of evolution and have killed off their machines before they supplant man, just as man had superseded the lower forms of life.

Erewhon is anti-utopia in so far as Butler has represented in it, to a fantastic degree, beliefs and practices of his own society which he finds ridiculous and repugnant. It shows the diseases of Victorian society in advanced form: to that extent, it is an image of England's future, seen in an unflattering light. Yet the visitor to Erewhon finds much to admire there – not least the woman he carries off to be his bride. The Erewhonians are healthy, good-looking, gay, generous and kind. Their concern with physical well-being seems a necessary corrective to a cribbed and confined intellectualism. There were plenty of Casaubons in Victorian society. The Erewhonians similarly adopt a commonsense attitude to death, regarding it as less to be feared than a serious illness. A calmness and quiet cheerfulness pervades much of their life, giving it an attractively Epicurean quality. The very absence of machines has made for a less hurried pace of life and a more tranquil environment. The towns and villages are of moderate size, well-planned and well-maintained. The countryside remains beautiful and unspoilt by industrial ravages. Gunpowder is not known, or at any rate is not used, and game birds are shot at with the cross-bow. Butler at times seems intent on conjuring up an Arcadian utopia not far off that of William Morris. Technologically, we are told, the Erewhonians 'were about as far advanced as Europeans of the twelfth or thirteenth century; certainly not more so'.

It is indeed in the Erewhonian attitude to the machine that the ambiguity of Butler's view comes out most strikingly. At one level, the 'Book of Machines' (chapters 23–25) is a satirical attack on a misplaced analogy between men and machines and a misinformed understanding of Darwin's theory of evolution.[18] The Erewhonians fear that the machines represent a potentially higher form of evolution than man, and in order to forestall an eventual take-over they order their destruction. But in this apparently ludicrous and hopelessly Luddite action they also display an intelligence and a sensibility dangerously lacking in Victorian England, with its machine-worship. The Erewhonians understand, in a way the Victorians seem not to, that humans are becoming increasingly dependent on machines and may end up being their slaves. Just as man is 'such a hive and swarm of parasites that it is doubtful whether his body is not more theirs than his', so 'may not man himself become a sort of parasite upon the machine? An affectionate machine-tickling aphid?' It may be very well to talk of this as interdependence, a symbiosis of man and machine; but we should be aware who will increasingly be the dominant partner. Without the machines, men even now would likely perish, physically and mentally. It is evidently Butler's voice speaking in the following passages, even though the tone is playful and the logic carried to satirical lengths.

Man's very soul is due to the machines; it is a machine-made thing; he thinks as he thinks, and feels as he feels, through the work that machines have wrought upon him, and their existence is quite as much a *sine qua non* for his, as his for theirs. This fact precludes us from proposing the complete annihilation of machinery, but surely it indicates that we should destroy as many of them as we can possibly dispense with, lest they should tyrannize over us even more completely.

Those who argue that machines are an unmixed good, that they make their users wealthy and powerful, should be warned that it is 'the art of the machines' that 'they serve that they may rule.' They do not mind if a whole generation of machines is destroyed so long as it is replaced by a newer and better one. Then they will reward their creators even more lavishly – but only so as to increase their indispensability. In this way they prey upon 'man's grovelling preference for his material over his spiritual interests'. Men are betrayed into servitude by their own greed. They are compelled, in order to survive in competition with their fellows, ceaselessly to develop new machines, on pain of poverty or death. Thus they have supplied the machines with that element of struggle and innovation which is necessary for a species to evolve, and which the machines cannot for the time being themselves provide. They thereby hasten their own decline into dependence.

So that even now the machines will only serve on condition of being served, and that too upon their own terms; the moment their terms are not complied with, they jib, and either smash both themselves and all whom they can reach, or turn churlish and refuse to work at all. How many men at this hour are living in a state of bondage to the machines? How many spend their whole lives, from the cradle to the grave, in tending them by night and day? Is it not plain that the machines are gaining ground upon us, when we reflect on the increasing number of those who devote their whole souls to the advancement of the mechanical kingdom?

Machines are becoming increasingly like men in form and function. They are fed just as we are fed, and we are their feeders: 'the stoker is almost as much a cook for his engine as our own cooks for ourselves.' Already machines employ an 'army of servants'.

Are there not probably more men engaged in tending machinery than in tending men? Do not machines eat as it were by mannery? Are we not ourselves creating our successors in the supremacy of the earth? daily adding to the beauty and delicacy of their organization, daily giving them greater skill and supplying more of that self-regulating, self-acting power which will be better than any intellect?

As machines become more life-like, more akin to men in complex organization and consciousness, able also to reproduce themselves like men, their superior size and strength will make them invincible. Their rise to dominance will however be gradual and imperceptible. The take-over will be painless. So should we mind? Should we try to prevent it? There are many who will say that man 'will probably be better off in a state of domestication under the beneficent rule of the machines than in his present wild condition'. 'We treat our domestic animals with much kindness . . . and slaves are tolerably happy if they have good masters.' 'Man is a sentimental animal where his material interests are concerned; and though here and there some ardent soul may look upon himself and curse his fate that he was not born a vapour-engine, yet the mass of mankind will acquiesce in any arrangement which gives them better food and clothing at a cheaper rate. . . .' There is every reason to hope that the machines will use us kindly,

for their existence will be in a great measure dependent upon ours; they will rule us with a rod of iron, but they will not eat us; they will not only require our services in the reproduction and the education of their young, but also in waiting upon them as servants; in gathering food for them, and feeding them; in restoring them to health when they are sick; and in either burying their dead or working up their deceased members into new forms of mechanical existence.[19]

In this bizarre vision of humans as humble nurses and servants to animate machines, Butler totally reverses the customary relationship between man and machine. In doing so he powerfully realized one of the fundamental themes of the anti-utopia: the progressive dehumanization and mechanization of man. For if machines become like men, the obverse of this process is that men become machines. Such was the most frequent observation of nineteenth-century social criticism. This was, said Thomas Carlyle, 'the Mechanical Age. . . . Men are grown mechanical in head and heart, as well as in hand.' Marx spoke of man becoming 'the appendage of the machine', reduced to the most simple and routine tasks. The upshot of this process was also clear to all. The more mechanical became the activities and outlook of men, the more dependent on the machine for their realization, the more inevitable was the displacement of human skills and creativity by mechanical contrivances. 'The shuttle drops from the fingers of the weaver, and falls into iron fingers that ply it faster.'[20] The final stage would be total automation: the elimination of the human worker altogether from productive life and his reduction to the role of machine-minder and machine-tender. It is this that Butler's Erewhonians have foreseen, and forestalled.

Swift, too, had had fun with machine-mania and the mechanical philosophy. The scientists of Laguda were hard at work on devices for extracting sunbeams from cucumbers and turning ice into gunpowder; they were busily constructing vast knowledge machines, like primitive computers, which would enable the most ignorant and illiterate to write works of poetry and philosophy. But by Butler's time there were good reasons for a deeper anxiety. The Industrial Revolution had promoted mechanization at a pace and on a scale quite beyond eighteenth-century experience. T. H. Huxley and others were confidently advancing the 'mechanistic hypothesis' as capable of explaining all the phenomena of the universe, mental as well as physical. Butler's fable reflected the fear of a totally determined, predictable and mechanical cosmos. If there was no essential distinction between mind and matter, man and machine, why should there not eventually arise acting, thinking, self-reproducing machines? What place had humanity in such a world? A subject that for Swift or Voltaire could be the material of grotesque ribaldry became for the nineteenth century a serious matter of practical possibility. Utopia *could* be realized – and *quelle horreur*!

Erewhon was a response to the new threat in the form of a traditional satire. The Erewhonian solution, to kill off the machines, could evoke a reassuring smile. But the 'Book of the Machines' also spoke with a fervour and an urgency more in tune with the mood of the times. The previous year the Victorian public had been disconcerted by Edward Bulwer-Lytton's *The Coming Race* (1871), in which the human race is on the point of being superseded by a superior underground race which has developed the machine to the fullest possible extent. Lytton's earnest tale is of slight literary merit, but it pointed the way to the characteristic form of the anti-utopia, and to its characteristic themes. The mocking tone of satire no longer seemed adequate to the urgency of the issue. Satire continued to play an important role in anti-utopia, as is clear in *Brave New World* and even *Nineteen Eighty-Four*. But it was joined now to the attempt to show, by as graphic and detailed a portrayal as possible, the horror of a society in which utopian aspirations have been fulfilled. The anti-utopia now had to match the utopia point for point, to make a detailed drawing of a utopian society and then colour it black. This was not necessary so long as utopia remained an ideal for philosophic contemplation. Only as utopia approached, or seemed to approach, reality could the anti-utopia develop fully as the negation of utopia's promise.

THE UNREASON OF PROGRESS

For most nineteenth-century thinkers utopia, whether or not so-called, was a thing of the future. It would be the culmination of the forces of historical evolution. But this development was more or less inevitable. It was being prepared by all the most powerful and progressive tendencies of modern times: democracy, science, socialism. Sooner or later these forces would combine in the modern utopia.

For the anti-utopia, it was those very forces that were preparing a modern hell. Moreover, the anti-utopia felt no need to look very far into the future. The impact of the new developments was only too evident in their own times, in their own societies. Democracy was producing mob rule or Napoleonic dictatorship, science and technology a world emptied of all meaning and purpose. By the time the modern anti-utopia was established, in the last part of the nineteenth century, it had come to feel that modern society was already so far anti-utopian as to require little in the way of futuristic elaboration. Unlike utopia, which was only too acutely aware of how much still needed to be done, the anti-utopia was often no more than a thinly disguised portrait of the contemporary world, seen as already more than halfway on the road to damnation. Wells's *The Time Machine* and Zamyatin's *We* do indeed have a considerable futuristic dimension, but the impress of the events and tendencies of their own time is unmistakable. By the time Huxley came to write *Brave New World* and Orwell *Nineteen Eighty-Four*, the merest accentuation and exaggeration of contemporary trends was thought sufficient to present a fully rounded picture of anti-utopia.

It was this evident focus on a clearly recognizable contemporary world that gave the anti-utopians the reputation of being hard-headed realists, as against the woolly idealism of the utopians. Anti-utopia to this extent partook of that widespread movement of thought towards 'the new Machiavellianism' that was so distinctive a feature of late nineteenth-century western society. Behind the anti-utopian critique lay the uncovering of the unconscious by Freud, the doubt cast by the new biology on the progressiveness of evolution, in nature or society, and the exposure of democracy as a sham by Robert Michels and Vilfredo Pareto.[21] Common to this movement was an attack on some of the most cherished assumptions of western society, the belief above all in the idea of progress through reason and science.

But the anti-utopians were not traditional conservatives. They had little in common with the strident defenders of hierarchy, property and religion. They were not the cynical hedonists and world-weary aesthetes of *fin-de-siècle* Europe. Theirs was not a simple negative reaction to modernity. They believed, often passionately, in equality, science and reason. This is as plain in the early anti-utopian Wells as in Huxley and Orwell. Not the principles of progress themselves, but their use and practice, was what dismayed and outraged them. There seemed no way to make the practice fit the principles. Every attempt ended in the grotesque inversion of its promise – democracy produced despotism, science barbarism, and reason unreason.

The special poignancy in this was that these attempts were premised on the very terms of the modern utopia. It was in the measure that modern societies became utopian – or at least tried to realize utopian aspirations – that freedom disappeared and human values were crushed. It was the 'scientific', 'rational', 'democratic' nation-state, the product of all that was considered progressive, that had delivered its citizens into bondage. The anti-utopians drew the conclusion that it was the utopian enterprise itself that was to blame for the contemporary predicament. The whole of western development since the time of More was re-interpreted and recounted as a disaster, in so far as it represented the dominance of utopian principles. Science and democracy were no doubt noble ideals, good in themselves, but the attempt to institutionalize them in society had produced the exact opposite of utopian hopes. The anti-utopia was the image of those blighted hopes, a precise reversal of utopian expectations. In two world wars, Soviet communism, German nazism, the planned 'scientific state' and scientific expertise in warfare, it found ample evidence of utopian strivings, and ample material for its anti-utopian vision. Writing shortly after the publication of *Nineteen Eighty-Four*, Orwell's friend George Woodcock remarked: 'For four centuries after the publication of Sir Thomas More's romance, Utopia focussed the hopes of men with uneasy social consciences. Now it gives shape to their fears, and . . . the reason is that the visionary societies of dead thinkers have at last begun to move out of theory and to assume in the modern world a portentous actuality.'[22]

One reason why the twentieth-century anti-utopia could address its own world so familiarly and so directly was that contemporary events seemed merely a melancholy confirmation of a pattern prophesied and analysed more than a century before. All that was required, therefore, was to apply this analysis to the most obvious and dramatic events of twentieth-century history: its world wars, its revolutions, its totalitarian dictatorships. So far as the broad form of its criticism went, anti-utopia did not have to invent its own terms. It could draw on a tradition of social criticism that was already fully developed by the end of the century. Just as the anti-utopian temperament is different from and older than the formal anti-utopia, so the main lines of the anti-utopian critique were laid down before their crystallization in the literary form of anti-utopia at the end of the nineteenth century. In this it paralleled the history of utopia itself. For just as the formal utopia went into abeyance in the first half of the nineteenth century, to re-emerge at the end, so also the older satirical anti-utopia largely disappeared in the first half of the century to be replaced by the anti-utopian novel towards its end. The reason in both cases was the same: the submergence of utopia and anti-utopia in powerful strands of social theory and social criticism that usurped their function, and that came to regard the older literary forms as obsolete and irrelevant. In the case of anti-utopia, this refers to a tradition of cultural and social criticism that undertook a wide-ranging critique of the chief assumptions and postulates of modernity: science, reason, democracy, the idea of progress. In the process, one after another, the idols of utopia – the Scientific Revolution, the Enlightenment, the French Revolution, the Industrial Revolution – were toppled from their pedestals.

To trace this tradition in any detail would require another book (one which, fortunately, has already been written, by Judith Shklar.[23]) It would need, among other things, to consider the Romantic reaction, the rediscovery of medievalism, the reformulation of conservative thought and the rise of existentialist philosophy. But two items perhaps can be pulled out for their particular importance in the later anti-utopian novel: Mary Shelley's

Frankenstein, Or, The Modern Prometheus (1818), and 'The Legend of the Grand Inquisitor' in Dostoyevsky's last novel, *The Brothers Karamazov* (1880).

Frankenstein, as its subtitle makes clear, harks back to older myths – the myths especially of Prometheus and Faust. Like Prometheus and Faust, Frankenstein risks his soul and eternal punishment by his obsessive pursuit of dangerous or forbidden knowledge. No one knows better than Frankenstein himself how far he has thrown himself beyond the pale of common humanity in his blasphemous quest.

> . . . I pursued nature to her hiding-places. Who shall conceive the horrors of my secret toil as I dabbled among the unhallowed damps of the grave or tortured the living animal to animate the lifeless clay? . . . A resistless and almost frantic impulse urged me forward; I seemed to have lost all soul or sensation but for this one pursuit. . . . I collected bones from charnel-houses and disturbed, with profane fingers, the tremendous secrets of the human frame. In a solitary chamber . . . I kept my workshop of filthy creation: my eyeballs were starting from their sockets in attending to the details of my employment. The dissecting room and the slaughterhouse furnished many of my materials; and often did my human nature turn with loathing from my occupation, whilst, still urged on by an eagerness which perpetually increased, I brought my work near to a conclusion.[24]

The breaking of all the traditional human taboos brings also the traditional nemesis: in creating the monster, Frankenstein brings down upon himself and all his loved ones disaster and death. The Faustian moral, thus powerfully reformulated in Mary Shelley's tale, was to become the theme of a hundred science-fiction tales and films: there are things in heaven and on earth with which we should not meddle. *Frankenstein* here simply reflected a standard motif of the contemporary Gothic novel. William Beckford's *Vathek* (1786), for instance, concluded its exotic fable of an Arabian Faust with the warning:

> Such shall be the chastisement of that blind curiosity, which would transgress those bounds the wisdom of the Creator has prescribed to human knowledge; and such the dreadful disappointment of that restless ambition, which, aiming at discoveries reserved for beings of a supernatural order, perceives not, through its infatuated pride, that the condition of man upon earth is to be – humble and ignorant.[25]

Beckford's irony would not have been lost on Mary Shelley. For her novel is not just a retelling of the old myth. Her Frankenstein is not punished just for his pursuit of knowledge.It is the attitude of mind with which he pursues it, and the particular aspects of it to which he is drawn, that compass his doom. Mary Shelley is at pains to make Frankenstein a truly modern Prometheus, a type of the modern scientist, not simply a reincarnation of the old Faustian alchemist. The link with the old myth is certainly maintained. The youthful Frankenstein is singular, as both his father and his first professor Krempe contemptuously point out, in his absorption with the medieval occultists and alchemists – Cornelius Agrippa, Albertus Magnus and Paracelsus. These are, says Frankenstein, 'the lords of my imagination', and remain so. But he learns to join this interest in the transformation of substances to the theories and methods of modern science. He accepts the view of his father 'that the principles of Agrippa had been entirely exploded and that a modern system of science had been introduced which possessed much greater power than the ancient, because the powers of the latter were chimerical, while those of the former were real and practical'.[26] The new theories of electricity and galvinism excite him, and for a time make him give up his studies of the older writers. But his interest is rekindled by the broader approach of his second professor, Waldman, who assures him that modern science is reared on the labours of the older natural philosophers. Their particular concepts and techniques are however outmoded. To achieve their ends, Frankenstein must devote himself to all the newer branches of science, especially modern chemistry. The practical results of doing so, says Waldman, will go beyond the wildest dreams of the old alchemists.

The ancient teachers . . . promised impossibilities and performed nothing. The modern masters promise very little; they know that metals cannot be transmuted and that the elixir of life is a chimera. But these philosophers, whose hands seem only made to dabble in the dirt, and their eyes to pore over the microscope or crucible, have indeed performed miracles. They penetrate into the recesses of nature and show how she works in her hiding-places. They ascend into the heavens; they have discovered how the blood circulates, and the nature of the air we breathe. They have acquired new and almost unlimited powers; they can command the thunders of the heaven, mimic the earthquake, and even mock the invisible world with its own shadows.[27]

Frankenstein's peculiarly modern act of hubris, then, is achieved by the union of old alchemical strivings with the tools of modern science. It is this that makes modern science so frightening, and why in modern times the Frankenstein myth should supersede the older Promethean or Faustian legends. It is a myth particularly suited to the scientific, industrial age. For it is a warning not just against an unnatural thirst for knowledge, but against the scientific potentialities of the new science of Newton, Lavoisier and Priestley that was already transforming the world in the early nineteenth century. The jump from Frankenstein's monster to the atom bomb is not a big one, either symbolically or in terms of the science that led to the creation of both. The alarm that now surrounds nuclear power is based on much the same fears as Mary Shelley's husband Percy Bysshe Shelley expressed in his *Defence of Poetry* (1821): 'Our calculations have outrun conception; we have eaten more than we can digest.'

Of such fears H. G. Wells too was to write a brilliant anti-utopian fable, *The Island of Dr Moreau* (1896). And the pitiless and fanatical scientist Moreau, though a harsher picture by far, is distinct kin to Frankenstein, with his narrow and singleminded pursuit of scientific knowledge to the exclusion of all other forms of knowledge, moral or social. In this respect too Frankenstein's modernity is marked. He is a thoroughgoing positivist, a materialist and a reductionist, convinced that the physical sciences will provide the answers to all questions.

I confess that neither the structure of languages, nor the politics of various states possessed attractions for me. It was the secrets of heaven and earth that I desired to learn; and whether it was the outward substance of things or the inner spirit of nature and the mysterious soul of man that occupied me, still my enquiries were directed to the metaphysical, or in its highest sense, the physical secrets of the world.[28]

As with the figure of the scientist, so with his monstrous creation: there is the same forceful conjunction of old and new. Behind Frankenstein's monster lies a whole tradition of the 'artificial man' – the *golem* of sixteenth-century Prague, and the many attempts of alchemists such as Albertus Magnus to produce man-like automata. In the eighteenth century there was particular a vogue for artificial men – the word 'android' made its first appearance in English in 1727 – and numerous experiments were conducted to create them, most notably by Jacques Vaucanson in France.[29]

The artificial man could be a toy, or a scientist's dream; it was not necessarily threatening. But its status as an image of terror was implicit in the very scientific developments that gave rise to the attempts to create it. For essentially it reflected the progressive displacement of man from his central place in creation that followed from the theories of Galileo, Newton and the seventeenth-century scientific revolution. If the earth was not the centre of the universe, neither was man. He was not God's special creation, in God's own image. He was simply a bundle of physical elements, like the rest of the universe. The universe was a machine, like a gigantic watch, and its parts, including man, reflected that principle, as microcosm to macrocosm. Descartes sketched the design of a mechanical being with all the physical attributes of a human being. He left open the question of whether there was a 'ghost in the machine', whether anything needed to be added – a 'soul', a 'conscience' – to complete the human person. Worldly Enlightenment scientists, under the influence of Locke and Condillac, were only too prepared to dispense with the hypothesis of the soul. And if so, if there was no essential difference between man and machine, why should not men be displaced ultimately by more finely constructed machines – constant, tireless, practically immortal?

The monster in *Frankenstein* expressed in the most vivid and lasting form the Romantics' horror at this mechanistic image of man. The sheer ugliness of the monster, its yellow skin, watery eyes and shrivelled complexion, is what first makes Frankenstein realize that he has brought forth an abortion, a 'catastrophe'. It is the aesthetic counterpart to the more fundamental moral and social catastrophe unleashed upon the world. The monster is the mechanical philosophy literally run mad, annihilating everything distinctly human – love, friendship, family – in its path. The mechanical man became the standard figure of Romantic protest against the dehumanization of man inherent in modern science and philosophy. Two years before *Frankenstein*, Ernst Hoffman, in 'The Sandman' (1816), had expressed a similar fear in his tale of the sinister spectacle-maker Dr Coppelius who builds a beautiful automaton, a 'mechanical bride', Olympia (the 'Coppelia' of Delibes's ballet based on the story). Olympia is cold and heartless, and her beauty is used to entrap and enslave men. In the ensuing century and a half, there was to be a succession of mechanical brides, not least the brides provided for Frankenstein's monster in the many adaptations of Mary Shelley's novel. Fritz Lang, too, in his film

Metropolis (1926), created one of the most striking mechanical brides in the robot Maria, manufactured by the plutocratic Master of Metropolis to incite the workers to riot and so self-destruction.[30] And, with Karel Capek's *R.U.R.* (1921), 'robots' formally entered the utopian and science-fiction literature, to be joined by 'androids' and 'cyborgs' as humanoid machines often endowed with superhuman strength, intelligence and capacity for wreaking havoc.[31]

Thus far, Mary Shelley's treatment of the monster was, again, traditional, though none the less powerful for that. But a newer element was introduced by the pathos which surrounds her monster. The monster is not just horrific; he is a creature to be pitied, a victim himself as much as those he murders. Despite Frankenstein's repugnance at his appearance, he is not morally a monster at birth. He is made one by the reaction of others to him, above all that of his own creator. Frankenstein is blameworthy not simply for meddling with knowledge best left alone, but also because, having invented a creature, he treats him shamefully and abandons him.

Mary Shelley here shows herself a true daughter of William Godwin, and an exponent of his rationalist theories of human perfectibility. The monster, like, according to Godwin, all humans, is at birth a *tabula rasa*, an innocent being as yet lacking in any moral feeling or social sense. It is in the terms of a rudimentary 'booming, buzzing confusion' that he later describes to Frankenstein his first impressions of the world, on fleeing from the laboratory and falling into an exhausted sleep.

> It was dark when I awoke; I felt cold also, and half frightened, as it were, instinctively, finding myself so desolate. . . . I was a poor, helpless, miserable wretch; I knew, and could distinguish, nothing; but feeling pain invade me on all sides, I sat down and wept.
>
> Soon a gentle light stole over the heavens and gave me a sensation of pleasure. I started up and beheld a radiant form rise from among the trees. I gazed with a kind of wonder. . . . No distinct ideas occupied my mind; all was confused. I felt light, and hunger, and thirst, and darkness; innumerable sounds rang in my ears, and on all sides various scents saluted me; the only object that I could distinguish was the bright moon, and I fixed my eyes on that with pleasure.[32]

He is a being, it is made clear, fully capable of responding to beauty and benevolence, as in his pleasure at a young girl's singing, and his longing to share in the scenes of domestic happiness that he witnesses. The horrified revulsion of the people he wishes to befriend drives him to desperation and violence. He demands of Frankenstein that he make him a mate, so that 'I can live in the interchange of those sympathies necessary for my being.' When Frankenstein goes back on his promise to do so, the monster unleashes even greater violence. But again he reminds Frankenstein that this is not something inevitable and intrinsic to his nature. He is made monstrous by his social isolation, and by the fear and loathing his appearance inspires in all he meets.

> If any being felt emotions of benevolence towards me, I should return them a hundred and a hundredfold. . . . If I have no ties and no affections, hatred and vice must be my portion. . . . My vices are the children of a forced solitude that I abhor, and my virtues will necessarily arise when I live in communion with an equal.[33]

But in the end it is Frankenstein himself who must bear the chief responsibility for the devastation wreaked by the monster. It was his duty to undertake the education of his creature, and he has shirked it.

> I am thy creature, and I will be even mild and docile to my natural lord and king if thou wilt also perform thy part, the which thou owest me. Oh, Frankenstein, be not equitable to every other and trample upon me alone, to whom thy justice, and even thy clemency and affection, is most due. Remember that I am thy creature; I ought to be thy Adam, but I am rather the fallen angel whom thou drivest from joy for no misdeed. Everywhere I see bliss, from which I alone am irrevocably excluded. I was benevolent and good; misery makes me a fiend. Make me happy, and I shall again be virtuous.[34]

That Frankenstein's God-like capacity, granted to him by the powers of modern science, produces only chaos and despair serves to underline the tie between utopia and anti-utopia. Anti-utopia draws its energy from the failure of utopian hopes and aspirations. In *Frankenstein*, the utopian promise of 'the perfectibility of man' ends in the nightmare of 'a malignant devil' who ravages the world. And, as Mary Shelley shows, such a sequence is not contingent or accidental but follows from the logic of the utopian attempt. For the monster, it is clear, is the embodiment of Frankenstein's own unconscious desires. At the very moment of its creation, he dreams of the death of his fiancée Elizabeth; later the monster vows to be with him on his wedding night. When his brother William is murdered by the monster, he has a hallucination in which he almost puts himself in the role of the killer. In this feverish state he sees the monster as the emanation of his own darker nature: 'I considered the being whom I had cast among mankind and endowed with the will and power to effect purposes of horror . . . nearly in the light of my own vampire, my own spirit let loose from the grave and forced to destroy all that was dear to me.'[35]

The monster shows the same awareness when he tells Frankenstein that they are 'bound by ties only dissoluble by the annihilation of one of us'. But this can never happen while Frankenstein still harbours his secret desires. Lordly creator and despised creation confront each other among the peaks of the Alps and the icy wastes of the Arctic, and recognize their dual-identity and mutual dependence. When Frankenstein dies, there is nothing for the monster to do but crawl away and die as well. People are sometimes apt to be severe with the popular habit of confusing Frankenstein and his monster, and calling the monster Frankenstein; but popular perceptions can sometimes be more acute than those of literary pedants.

There were many stories of the Frankenstein-type to choose from, but it was Mary Shelley's *Frankenstein* that caught the collective imagination. It established securely for anti-utopia one of its principal themes: the spectre of a mysterious and malignant power that evaded human control and threatened to destroy humanity. It was the old myth of the Sorcerer's Apprentice, linked now not to primitive magic but the vastly greater powers of modern science and technology. Wells in his early anti-utopian fantasies such as *The Island of Dr Moreau* and *The War of the Worlds* was to make the most effective use of it. But it became a standard device of anti-utopian science fiction generally, especially in the post-1945 atomic era. Again and again, mankind was to blow itself up, reverting – as in Aldous Huxley's *Ape and Essence* (1948) and Walter Miller's *A Canticle for Leibowitz* (1955) – to a primitive barbarism. In one of science's greatest triumphs – the splitting of the atom – the anti-utopia read the signs of the greatest act of scientific hubris, one that was preparing the way for the extinction of the species.

Frankenstein was distinctive in singling out science and the scientist as the object of its deepest fears. Dostoyevsky launched his attack on the whole Enlightenment ideology of progress. Not just science, but reason, democracy, liberalism, socialism and practically all the other shibboleths of the nineteenth-century utopia drew his withering contempt. But the target was in a sense almost the opposite of *Frankenstein*'s. It was not the violence and terror unleashed by modern developments that concerned Dostoyevsky, but the elimination of the struggle and conflict in individual life that he regarded as essential for human culture. Mary Shelley remained the liberal rationalist, fearful of humanity's ability to control the new forces it had created. Dostoyevsky saw the imminent victory of Enlightenment reason and was appalled. In him was expressed, with unequalled power and virtuosity, the single most important idea of the anti-utopia: that the modern utopia was on the point of realization, with disastrous consequences for human freedom and creativity.

As an aspect of general social criticism, this view was stated with increasing urgency in the course of the nineteenth century. Benjamin Disraeli saw in the high hopes placed in technical progress the moral flaw at the centre of a society 'which has mistaken comfort for civilization'. Jacob Burckhardt scornfully dismissed what was called 'progress' as 'domestication'. For Kierkegaard and Nietzsche, nineteenth-century culture was promoting the victory of mediocrity and the dominance of a mechanical, utilitarian, philosophy, crushing out all passion and spirituality. Charles Baudelaire, in a fragment for an uncompleted project, 'The End of the World', went to the heart of the anti-utopian critique in seeing the worst threat as the triumph of all that was admired and desired by the nineteenth century.

> The world is drawing to a close. Only for one reason can it last longer: just because it happens to exist. But how weak a reason is this compared with all that forebodes the contrary, particularly with the question: What is left to the world of man in the future? Supposing it should continue materially, would that be an existence worthy of its name and of the historical dictionary? I do not say the world would fall back into a spectral condition and the odd disorder of South American republics; nor do I say that we should return to primitive savagery and, with a rifle in our arms, hunt for food through the grass-covered ruins of our civilization. No, such adventures would still call for a certain vital energy, an echo from primordial times. We shall furnish a new example of the inexorability of the spiritual and moral laws and shall be their new victims: *we shall perish by the very thing by which we fancy that we live*. Technocracy will Americanize us, progress will starve our spirituality so far that nothing of the bloodthirsty, frivolous or unnatural dreams of the utopist will be comparable to those positive facts. . . . Universal ruin will manifest itself not solely or particularly in political institutions or general progress or whatever else might be a proper name for it; it will be seen, above all, in the baseness of hearts. Shall I add that that little left-over sociability will hardly resist the sweeping brutality, and that the rulers, in order to hold their own and to produce a sham order, will ruthlessly resort to measures which will make us, who already are callous, shudder?[36]

Tolstoy, often opposed to Dostoyevsky for his 'westernizing' sympathies, towards the end of his life was inclined to see modern western civilization as a scourge threatening the spiritual life of the entire globe. In terms strongly reminiscent of another Victorian sage, Matthew Arnold, he contrasted that civilization with 'true civilization' or 'true enlightenment'.

The medieval theology, or the Roman corruption of morals, poisoned only their own people, a small part of mankind; today, electricity, railways and telegraphs spoil the whole world. Everyone makes these things his own. He simply cannot help making them his own. Everyone suffers in the same way, is forced to the same extent to change his way of life. All are under the necessity of betraying what is most important for their lives, the understanding of life itself, religion. Machines – to produce what? The telegraph – to despatch what? Books, papers – to spread what kind of news? Railways – to go to whom and to what place? Millions of people herded together and subject to a supreme power – to accomplish what? Hospitals, physicians, dispensaries in order to prolong life – for what? How easily do individuals as well as whole nations take their own so-called civilization as the true civilization. . . .[37]

It was Dostoyevsky, however, who carried this critique right into the heart of the nineteenth-century utopia. 'Happiness is not in happiness but in its pursuit' – with this slogan he set himself in total opposition to the scientific materialism and utilitarianism that to him was the hallmark of the modern utopia. In *The Diary of a Writer* (1878) he imagined the populations of Europe being showered with a bountiful hail of scientific inventions, rendering them all at a stroke prosperous and entirely free from material want. People would feel, surely, 'bestrewn with happiness, interred in material blessings' – but for how long?

'People would suddenly realize that there is no freedom of spirit, no will, no personality; that someone has stolen something from them; that the human image has vanished and the bestial image of the slave, the cattle image has come into being, with the difference, however, that the cattle do not know that they are cattle whereas men would discover that they had become cattle. And mankind would begin rotting; people would be covered with sores and ulcers; they would start biting their tongues with pain, seeing that their lives had been taken away from them in exchange for bread, 'stones turned into bread'.'[38]

Dostoyevsky's nightmare was always that of the fully rationalized man in the fully rationalized society, with everything so calculated and catered for that there was literally nothing to do, nothing to strive for. The spiteful, splenetic hero (or 'non-hero') of *Letters from the Underworld* (1864) protests with all his being at this spectre of 'predictable man', who rationally pursues his 'self-interest' according to the minutest calculations of science and reason. Against this presumed self-interest he glories in 'filthy nocturnal revels' and scenes of shameful self-humiliation. He attests his essential humanity by deliberately flouting his rational self-interest, by the gratuitous exercise of his free will.

Man loves to act as he *likes*, and not necessarily as reason and self-interest would have him do. . . . His own will, free and unfettered; his own untutored whims; his own fancies, sometimes amounting almost to a madness – here we have that superadded interest of interests which enters into no classification, which for ever consigns systems and theories to the devil.

The hero of the *Letters* supposes that science discovers a formula which 'exactly expresses our wills and whims', and shows precisely what laws and circumstances shape them. If that were to happen, 'man will have ceased to have a will of his own – he will have ceased even to exist.' For 'who would care to exercise his will-power according to a table of logarithms? In such a case man would become, not a human being at all, but an organ-handle, or something of the kind. What but the handle of a hurdy-gurdy *could* a human being represent who was devoid either of desires or volition?'

'Reason is an excellent thing – I do not deny that for a moment; but reason is reason, and no more, and satisfies only the reasoning faculty in man, whereas volition is a manifestation of all life (that is to say, of human life as a whole . . .).' If I wish to exercise my will in ways that are foolish and harmful to me, that is as human – *more* human – than if I act according to rational self-interest. 'Human nature acts as a whole, and with all that is contained in it; so that, whether conscious or unconscious, sane or mad, it is always human nature.' Consequently it is not out of some mysterious perversity but from an assertion of his true humanity, his individuality and his personality, that man will be prepared to reject all the blessings that science and material comforts bring to him.

You may heap upon him every earthly blessing, you may submerge him in well-being until the bubbles shoot to the surface of his prosperity as though it were a pond, you may give him such economic success that nothing will be left for him to do but to sleep and to eat dainties and to prate about the continuities of the world's history; yes, you may do all this, but none the less, out of sheer ingratitude, sheer devilment, he will end by playing you some dirty trick. He will imperil his comfort, and purposely desiderate for himself deleterious rubbish, some improvident trash, for the sole purpose that he may alloy all the solemn good sense which has been lavished upon him with a portion of the futile, fantastical element which forms part of his very composition.

Men are not 'keyboards of pianos over which the hands of Nature may play at their own sweet will'. Not Nature's laws but man's volition ultimately governs his activities. He will choose madness rather than become Nature's slave. Nature is useful to him; he will exploit her laws in pursuing his ends. But he will then carelessly and irresponsibly violate them when the end is in sight. Man has a passion for construction, it is true, but also a horror of completion, of attaining his goal. For such finality, such perfection, is death. Man's essence does not lie in the attainment of finite goals but in the 'ceaseless continuation of the process of attainment (that is to say, in the process which is comprised in the living of life). . . .' For him therefore the beatitude of the 'Palace of Crystal', the millennial utopia that ends all unhappiness, will be more hateful than the meanest and poorest state of society that has ever existed.[39]

All utopias are detestable to Dostoyevsky because they express the tyranny of the idea. However noble their aims, they must by their very principle crush the individual human will and abolish freedom. 'Starting from unlimited freedom I arrive at unlimited despotism', announces Shigalov in *The Possessed* (1872). All the revolutionaries of that novel – Stavrogin, Verhovensky – end up in the the same contradiction. So, too, Raskolnikov in *Crime and Punishment* (1866) and Ivan Karamazov in *The Brothers Karamazov* (1880) are driven to murder and moral nihilism by their fanatical pursuit of the logic of their particular pet modern ideas. It is indeed in *The Brothers Karamazov*, his last and greatest work, that Dostoyevsky presented his most powerful critique of the modern utopia. This is contained in the novel as a whole – a story of the loss of religious faith and the moral chaos that results from the conversion to scientific materialism. But the whole moral is also wonderfully concentrated in 'The Legend of the Grand Inquisitor', which Ivan Karamazov, the sceptic and atheist, tells his saintly brother Alexey (Alyosha).

It is the time of the Inquisition. In the city of Seville, Christ reappears. He is immediately imprisoned on the order of the Grand Inquisitor, an aged Cardinal. The Inquisitor visits Christ in the dungeon and, in a long monologue, explains to him why he must be killed again.

'There's no need for you to come at all now. . . . Everything has been handed over by you to the Pope and, therefore, everything is now in the Pope's hands.' Christ's message of freedom has had to be interpreted and implemented by the Church. After fifteen hundred years of wrestling with this troublesome legacy the Church has at last understood the nature of the problem. Men do not really want to be free; they want to be happy. They can only be happy by giving up their freedom. This the Church has contrived to make them do without their realizing it. 'These men are more than ever convinced that they are absolutely free, and yet they themselves have brought their freedom to us and humbly laid it at our feet. But it was we who did it.'

Rebels cannot be happy. Satan was right, and Christ wrong, in his understanding of what moves men. His 'temptations' to Christ in the wilderness revealed 'the whole future history of the world and mankind'. Challenged by Satan to turn the stones of the desert into loaves of bread as a proof of his power, Christ refused. For – the Inquisitor mimics Christ – 'what sort of freedom is it if obedience is bought with loaves of bread? . . . Man does not live by bread alone.' But men have shown otherwise. Their 'science' has proclaimed that there is no crime and no sin but 'only hungry people'. And the Church, in Christ's name, has promised to feed the people, on condition that they give up their freedom. 'No science will give them bread so long as they remain free. But in the end they will lay their freedom at our feet and say to us, "Make us your slaves, but feed us!"'

To 'the weak, always vicious and always ignoble race of men', 'earthly bread' will always be preferable to 'the bread of heaven'. 'Nothing has ever been more unendurable to man and to human society than freedom.' Christ had the opportunity to use his power to make men follow him, and to give up their freedom to him. But he would not do this: 'instead of taking possession of men's freedom you multiplied it and burdened the spiritual kingdom of man with its sufferings for ever.' So men have deserted him, because in effect he has deserted them, not understanding their needs. He has only himself to blame for the destruction of his kingdom. 'There are three forces, the only three forces that are able to conquer and hold captive for ever the conscience of these weak rebels for their own happiness – these forces are: miracle, mystery and authority. You rejected all three and yourself set the example of doing so.'

Christ may have thought a faith based on miracles rather than free will to be no faith at all. But men need miracles, they need demonstrations of great, mysterious powers. Although naturally rebellious, their rebellions are childish and end in destruction and despair. Confused and unhappy, they turn to a powerful authority which relieves them of the burden of choice. And they are content that that authority should exercise its power in ways they do not understand, even when they are the victims.

So we have done. We have corrected your great work and have based it on *miracle, mystery and authority*. And men rejoiced that they were once more led like sheep and that the terrible gift which had brought them so much suffering had at last been lifted from their hearts. . . . Did we not love mankind when we admitted so humbly its impotence and lovingly lightened its burden and allowed men's weak nature even to sin, so long as it was with our permission?

At last the Inquisitor reveals the terrible secret: it is Satan, not Christ, that the Church has chosen to follow. Christ rejected Satan's offer of earthly power; the Church has learned the need for it and has accepted Satan's gift. 'We took from him Rome and the sword of Caesar and proclaimed ourselves rulers of the earth, the sole rulers. . . .' This too Christ could have had, and in doing so,

you would have accomplished all that man seeks on earth, that is to say, whom to worship, to whom to entrust his conscience and how at last to unite them all in a common, harmonious, and incontestable ant-hill, for the need of universal unity is the third and last torment of men. Mankind as a whole has always striven to organize itself into a world state. . . . By accepting the world and Caesar's purple, you would have founded the world state and given universal peace. For who is to wield dominion over men if not those who have taken possession of their consciences and in whose hands is their bread? And so we have taken the sword of Caesar and, having taken it, we of course rejected you and followed *him*.

The Church, then, has accepted all three of the offers with which Satan tempted Christ in the wilderness. On this basis it is building itself into an impregnable position, giving itself a complete hold over the minds and bodies of men. It will establish a reign of eternal peace and happiness for all mankind. Men will be grateful and obedient, as children are to the parents who protect and succour them.

We shall give them quiet, humble happiness, the happiness of weak creatures, such as they were created. . . . We shall prove to them that they are weak, that they are mere pitiable children, but that the happiness of a child is the sweetest of all. They will grow timid and begin looking up to us and cling to us in fear as chicks to the hen. They will marvel at us and be terrified of us and be proud that we are so mighty and so wise as to be able to tame such a turbulent flock of thousands of millions. They will be helpless and in constant fear of our wrath, their minds will grow timid, their eyes will always be shedding tears like women and children, but at the slightest sign from us they will be just as ready to pass to mirth and laughter, to bright-eyed gladness and happy childish song.

Yes, we shall force them to work, but in their leisure hours we shall make their life like a children's game, with children's songs, in chorus, and with innocent dances. Oh, we shall permit them to sin, too, for they are weak and helpless, and they will love us like children for allowing them to sin.

It is the duty, the burden of the Inquisitor and his like, to take these sins upon themselves. The people will adore them the more as benefactors for this. They will give themselves wholly and blindly to the Church.

They will have no secrets from us. We shall allow or forbid them to live with their wives and mistresses, to have or not have children – everything according to the measure of their obedience – and they will submit themselves to us gladly and cheerfully. The most tormenting secrets of their conscience – everything, everything they will bring to us, and we shall give them our decision for it all, and they will be glad to believe in our decisions, because it will relieve them of their great anxiety and of their present terrible torments of coming to a free decision themselves.

Only the leaders of the Church, 'the hundred thousand who rule' over the multitude, will have the consciousness and understanding of what is being done. The penalty for their great power is the suffering that comes with freedom and knowledge. But it is a burden that the rulers have voluntarily shouldered, in the interests of the happiness of mankind; and it is by this service, not for the saintly few but for the weak millions, that they ask to be judged.

We alone, we who guard the mystery, we alone shall be unhappy. There will be thousands of millions of happy infants and one hundred thousand sufferers who have taken upon themselves the curse of knowledge of good and evil. . . . And we who, for their happiness, have taken their sins upon ourselves, we shall stand before you and say, 'Judge us if you can and if you dare.'

Christ's reappearance threatens to wreak havoc with all this patient work. He will cause untold suffering and destruction. 'If anyone has ever deserved our fire, it is you. Tomorrow I shall burn you.'[40]

The mere recital of Dostoyevsky's fable is almost enough to establish its importance for the modern anti-utopia. Take almost any anti-utopia written after the end of the nineteenth century and the strong chances are that it will bear the imprint of the 'Legend of the Grand Inquisitor'.[41] It is not too much to say that, while not itself an anti-utopia, it is probably the single most important text for the genre. Again and again, the scene in the dungeon between Christ and the Grand Inquisitor was to be re-enacted. It is there in the dialogue between the Benefactor and D-503 in Zamyatin's *We*; between the Controller and the rebels in Huxley's *Brave New World*; between Gletkin and Rubashov in Koestler's *Darkness at Noon*; and – with a horrific twist – between O'Brien and Winston Smith in Orwell's *Nineteen Eighty-Four*. Not just the general form and tone but even many of the images and details are repeated. No one seems to have been able to resist, in particular, Dostoyevsky's memorable picture of a helpless and childishly happy people playing under the strict but benevolent eye of their all-powerful rulers.

His target in the 'Legend', Dostoyevsky himself said, was modern socialism, seen not just as the legitimate descendant of the philosophy and practice of the Roman Catholic Church but as the chief embodiment of modern science and materialism. And certainly the core of his critique – preferring 'bread' to 'stones', selling man's inheritance of freedom for a mess of pottage – is frequently found in anti-utopian attacks on socialism, most notably in *We* and *Brave New World*. But what made the 'Legend' so seductive was its capacity for general deployment against a much wider range of modern thought and practice. Its very allegorical form gave it a universality which permitted a selective and flexible application to a wide variety of targets. Thus it could be directed against modern hedonism, utilitarianism, liberalism, positivism, social democracy and practically any other modern social philosophy which drew on Enlightenment rationalism and modern science.

What was common to all these philosophies, what united their critics over all other differences, was a scientific determinism that seemed intent on driving out any concept of individual will and individual freedom. The utilitarian and materialist cast of their ideologies denied any place and meaning to the 'soul' or to any other human attribute that could not be scientifically analysed and empirically observed. This left the way open to the rationally organized Scientific or Welfare State, run by the experts: the technicians and bureaucrats with the requisite scientific understanding of nature, society and man. The justification of such a regime was nearly always that of the Grand Inquisitor. The mass of the people are weak, ignorant, defenceless. They must be helped and protected, if necessary against their own will and short-sighted selfishness. The empirical evidence for this view appeared so overwhelming as to force practically all political ideologies into the same mould. The differences between them shrank to a trivial matter of degree – more 'market' or more 'state', etc. – or of electoral and party strategy. Against this massive consensus Dostoyevsky's protest, in the name of a powerful variety of religious existentialism, was encouragement and ammunition to all those who sought to resist the encroachments of the modern totalitarian state – the central concern of the anti-utopia. For them, this was the ultimate tendency of the modern utopia; and like Dostoyevsky they saw it as preparing a palace for Satan.

That the 'Legend' could also be employed on the side of *utopia* is one more indication of the close connection and permeability of utopia and anti-utopia. The same fate had befallen Plato's *Republic*, whose Guardians could be regarded as benevolent or threatening depending on one's temperament and outlook. The ruling Samurai of Wells's *A Modern Utopia* have much of the Guardians in them, but also something of the Grand Inquisitor. They dedicate themselves to the heavy burden of their rule in the same spirit of personal renunciation and sacrifice displayed by the Grand Inquisitor and 'the hundred thousand who rule'. So too Frazier, the founder and leader of Skinner's *Walden Two*, stands somewhat wistfully aloof from the happy community he has created. Like the Grand Inquisitor, he possesses the 'mystery', the science of human behaviour, which makes the community function. But by the same token such knowledge excludes him from full participation in the life of the community. He cannot be like the others; he cannot be happy. 'Isn't it enough that I've made other men likeable and happy and productive? Why expect me to resemble them?'[42] The Grand Inquisitor speaks not just for the Machiavellian elite of the anti-utopia, but also sometimes for the dedicated party of humanity engaged in building utopia.

It is clear in fact that the Grand Inquisitor, like Dostoyevsky himself, is a frustrated utopist. As with Mary Shelley, the energy of the anti-utopian feeds on the failure of high utopian hopes. The inquisitor tells Christ:

> Know that I, too, was in the wilderness, that I, too, fed upon locusts and roots, that I, too, blessed freedom, with which you have blessed men, and that I, too, was preparing to stand among your chosen ones, among the strong and mighty, thirsting 'to make myself of the number.'[43]

But, he says, 'I woke up and refused to serve madness.' Dostoyevsky too woke up from his utopian 'madness'. In his youth in the 1840s he had been a prominent member of the 'Petrashevsky Circle' in St Petersburg, a group which met to consider utopian schemes for the radical reconstruction and regeneration of society. He evidently went beyond the 'gradualist' politics of this group, for in 1849 he was arrested as a member of a secret revolutionary club and exiled to Siberia, only just escaping execution. On his return from exile at the end of the 1850s he had abandoned his radicalism. He used his experience of the 'Petrashevskyists' for the biting portrayals of *The Possessed* and other novels. But he had not lost his utopian passion; the utopian personality shines through in almost everything he wrote. Not idly did he later refer to himself as 'the old Nechayevist', or write that, but for his arrest in 1849, he might have become a Peter Verhovensky. It is even plausible to see in his later writing the outline of another utopia, an 'anarcho-Christian' utopia, that is a translation or transformation of his secular utopianism of the 1840s. In this admittedly often obscure vision he blended together elements of primitive Christianity, Russian Orthodoxy and the communal life of the Russian peasant to produce an ideal society based on an idyllic version of Russia's past. In this exotic fusion of radical Christianity and mystic populism he found a new outlet for his utopian energy, and a powerful instrument with which to cudgel the secular utopia of his youth.[44]

Dostoyevsky's case is far from exceptional. One can almost say it expresses the normal relation between utopia and anti-utopia. Only to a certain extent is the modern anti-utopia a reaction againt the modern utopia by people of opposed beliefs. More fundamentally, it is one side of a dialogue of the self within individuals who have been indelibly stamped with the utopian temperament.

UTOPIA AND ANTI-UTOPIA IN THE LATER NINETEENTH CENTURY

For a considerable time after More, utopia carried the function of anti-utopia as well. Its satire presented the writer's world negatively, as anti-utopia, to which utopia was the constructive, positive, response. This strategy was never entirely lost – it is still there partly in Wells. But by the second half of the nineteenth century it was beginning to look increasingly archaic. Utopia could incorporate anti-utopia only so long as its own utopian scheme seemed simply a moral, heuristic device, or a remote fantasy. The negative, critical and satirical function could then stand on equal terms with the utopian advocacy – could indeed seem the principal function. Once, however, utopia appeared a real possibility, an actual prospect, this balance was destroyed. In utopias such as Bellamy's *Looking Backward*, where the utopia was seen as the logical and more or less inevitable culmination of existing social developments, the satirical and critical tone was sharply reduced. The important thing seemed to be to provide a map of those developments which were ushering in utopia, lest people should mistake the way and distort or abort the potentialities of the present. A detailed picture of present ills seemed irrelevant and out of place. Some other form therefore had to take upon itself this task. It was in this situation that the anti-utopia of modern times was born.

From the late nineteenth century onwards, the negative and positive poles of the old satirical utopia were pulled apart and assigned to separate genres or sub-genres. Utopia focused, with increasing urgency, on the task of reconstruction. Utopia was possible – that was the novel feature of the times – but the confidence of the earlier part of the century in its imminence and certainty was checked. All the more reason for utopia to paint in the most glowing colours the promise that was there to be realized. Socialism *could* be a reality; science *could* solve the problem of scarcity and want. The social theory of the first six or seven decades of the century had amply and convincingly demonstrated this. But that scientific theory had now to be complemented by the artistic resources of the literary utopia. There was a critical gap between rational theory and the emotional conviction needed to make that theory a practical political reality. The late nineteenth-century utopia aimed to supply that want. It would show that what was within the sight of men was also within their grasp, if only they would reach for it.

One man's dream of felicity may be another man's nightmare. The more utopians urged the possibility of the realization of their dream, the more alarmed were those who were convinced that modern developments were leading to a new slavery and a new barbarism. The renewal of utopia in the late nineteenth century stimulated also its counter-image and counter-force, anti-utopia. As utopia concentrated on the positive, so anti-utopia dispensed with a balanced assessment of contemporary trends to paint the most negative, the blackest, picture possible of the present and the future to come. And just as utopia lent the persuasive techniques of the literary imagination to the cause of modern ideas of science and socialism, so anti-utopia lent the same techniques to the revolt against modernity. Like utopia, anti-utopia invented whole social orders, in all their particularity. But while the utopian order was *perfect*, in the moral sense, the anti-utopian order was merely *perfected*, in the social sense. It was the dreadful perfection of some modern system or idea. And while utopian societies were *ideal*, in the sense of the best possible, anti-utopian society represented merely the victory or tyranny of the *idea*. In both cases, the reader was invited to live the life of a society realized according to some principle. But in the one case the expected response to the experience was delight, in the other, horror.

Still, though the two genres of utopia and anti-utopia flourished side by side, as challenge and response, the separation was never complete, nor could it be. The tension between the two poles remained, linking them in a single arc. This underlying unity was a necessity of their continuing mutual survival. They fed off one another, deriving an equal and opposite energy from each other's affirmations and negations. But in one respect the dependence remained predominantly one-way. The anti-utopia was historically a response to utopia, and its significance and power always turned on the memory of that promise of a Golden Age. The anti-utopia, Irving Howe has said, 'must depend on the ability of its readers to engage in an act of historical recollection'. It lives off the deep resonance of the idea of utopia in the collective consciousness of Western society.

> Still dependent on this vision of the Golden Age, the anti-utopian novel thus shares an essential quality of all modern literature: it can realize its values only through images of their violation. The enchanted dream has become a nightmare, but a nightmare projected with such power as to validate the continuing urgency of the dream.[45]

The reciprocal relationship of utopia and anti-utopia was sometimes explicit, sometimes not. Authors sometimes referred by name or in some other obvious way to what they perceived to be the enemy. Huxley went furthest in naming practically all the characters of *Brave New World* after his chief *bêtes noires*. To know that Morris regarded Bellamy as the antagonist, however, one would have to go to his scathing review of *Looking Backward* in *The Commonweal*; while for Wells's response to Morris a certain amount of literary detective work is necessary. What complicates the story further is the fact that the same writer might espouse the causes of both utopia and anti-utopia at different times of his life. What we have found with Mary Shelley and Dostoyevsky, the warring conflict of utopian and anti-utopian dispositions within the same person, is more formally repeated in Wells, Huxley and Orwell.

The ambivalence was evident in the earliest productions of the utopian revival. Bulwer-Lytton's *The Coming Race* (1871) and Butler's *Erewhon* (1872) mixed utopia and anti-utopia in confusing degrees, so that the stance of the authors and the object of their satire were unclear to readers. Did Lytton admire the qualities of the superior coming race, the Vril-ya, or did he fear them? Did Butler see the Erewhonians as simply grotesque Victorians, or had they seen deeper and further than Butler's contemporaries? The explicitly utopian content of W. H. Hudson's *A Crystal Age* (1887) was clear enough. But was the extreme and almost mystical arcadianism of his primitive society, which has renounced all the fruits of modern science and technology, not more in the nature of an anti-utopian reflection on modern industrial civilization? A similar observation could be made of the most famous arcadian utopia of all, William Morris's *News from Nowhere* (1890). Morris, no doubt, offers it as a realizable, socialist utopia, not a nostalgic idyll. It is 'a vision', not 'a dream', he says. But many like Northrop Frye have seen in this 'pastoral utopia' not so much an affirmation of an existing possibility in industrial society as a moral evocation of a 'state of innocence' by which the present is to be judged.[46] In this sense, *News from Nowhere* might be read more as a powerful indictment of a large-scale mechanical civilization than as a utopian portrait of a future society. It would be more akin, that is, to something like Rousseau's *Discourse on the Origin of Inequality*, with its similar ambivalence between a primitivist utopia and an anti-utopian critique of the writer's own society.

There was no question of utopia in Richard Jefferies' apocalyptic *After London* (1885), a work which deeply affected Morris.[47] The savagery and brutality of the world it depicted marked it out clearly as an anti-utopia. But, as with many of the early anti-utopias, there was a characteristic ambiguity of purpose. Jefferies described an England plunged into barbarism, following an obscure astronomical catastrophe. It is a new Dark Age, a world of poverty and cruelty, of warring petty tyrants and marauding robber-bands. There is little of the Romantics' idealization of the Middle Ages in this picture of a harsh rural wilderness. But nor is there any vindication of modernity or progress. The stark central image of the novel is of an abandoned and deserted London, marooned in a vast lake, a stinking, poisoned city which has literally become the graveyard of urban civilization and all its noxious ways. Jefferies, in short, points in no direction, neither backwards nor forward. He longs for the Great Purge, but he can also see the cost of it. Industrial civilization is doomed, but a return to rural poverty and violence is no answer.

In its apocalyptic fears and pessimistic forebodings, *After London* belongs not so much to the formal anti-utopian tradition as to the new wave of 'the literature of terror' that broke in the late nineteenth century. In this magnificent fresh outpouring of the Gothic imagination were to be found some of the key works that formed what we might call the demotic strand of anti-utopia. It was the themes and images of these works that were ceaselessly repeated, adapted and imitated in the popular culture of twentieth-century Western society. Earlier examples of the type were the stories of Edgar Allan Poe, the novels of Wilkie Collins, such as *The Woman in White* (1860) and *The Moonstone* (1868), and the supernatural tales of Sheridan LeFanu. But it was the decade of the 1890s that produced the works that gave the popular tradition its major myths and archetypes: Robert Louis Stevenson's *Dr Jekyll and Mr Hyde* (1886), Oscar Wilde's *The Picture of Dorian Gray* (1891), H. G. Wells's *The Island of Dr Moreau* (1896), and Bram Stoker's *Dracula* (1897). In these novels were articulated fears of hideous and invincible powers, nameless subterranean and subconscious forces that sprang from the very nature of man and the cosmos and were hence ineradicable. Tireless and ubiquitous, these forces worked ceaselessly on the side of death and destruction. Against the evil and murderous impulses embodied in Hyde or Dracula, reason, science and civilization seemed the thinnest of veneers and the feeblest of defences. Later, Freud was to add the prestige of psychoanalysis to fears of a similar kind in his unyieldingly pessimistic *Civilization and its Discontents* (1930).[48]

The formal anti-utopia certainly drew on these fears and anxieties, as the mention of Wells and the coincidence of time both suggest. The 'literature of terror' and the formal anti-utopia shared the same sub-culture of concern with the prospects of industrial civilization. In the eyes of both, late nineteenth-century industrial society seemed to have overreached itself and was preparing its own destruction. But, while the Gothic imagination responded with the invocation of nameless horrors to which we could seemingly offer no resistance, the anti-utopia had a more precise target and a more developed structure of values with which to attack it. This was because the content of the anti-utopia was shaped primarily by its response to the socialist utopia, and especially as that was presented in literary utopias such as Bellamy's *Looking Backward*.

It may indeed be only a slight overstatement to say that *Looking Backward* created the anti-utopia. Certainly it started that chain of challenge and response that largely makes up the history of utopia and anti-utopia from the 1880s to the 1950s. Its startling popularity from the very beginning excited or alarmed those who thought that the world either was or should be going in a different direction. In America it spawned scores of imitations, including a crop of anti-utopias that read American developments very differently from Bellamy. Among the best was Ignatius Donnelly's *Caesar's Column* (1890). Donnelly was a radical Populist and so very much of Bellamy's party, in the most general sense. But while Bellamy projected an optimistic socialist resolution to the contradictions of American capitalism, Donnelly saw the power of large-scale oligarchic capitalism leading inexorably to a business dictatorship. *Caesar's Column* portrays an America a century ahead which has polarized into two nations, a ruling oligarchy and a pauperized and oppressed proletariat. A revolutionary organization, the Brotherhood of Destruction, develops, but its insurrection is brutally crushed. The novel ends with the corpses of the revolutionaries piling up into the sky in a great column, 'Caesar's column'.[49] A markedly similar future society, based on a capitalist oligarchy, was pictured for America in Jack London's powerful *The Iron Heel* (1907). There too a socialist rising is defeated; and although the book looks ahead to an eventual socialist future, its strength lies in London's remarkable anticipation of the techniques of totalitarian fascism – as Orwell noted of it on several occasions.[50]

Donnelly was a radical, London a socialist. That they could construct anti-utopias out of the same materials, and with the same basic political sympathies, as Bellamy, shows something of the complexity of the relationship between utopia and anti-utopia. This complexity deepened in the widening response to Bellamy. William Morris wrote his *News from Nowhere* as an angry retort to what he saw as the soulless mechanical socialism of *Looking Backward*. *News from Nowhere* is of course a utopia, a 'counter-utopia', we might say; but, as we have seen, in its extreme rejection of much of technological civilization it has many of the qualities of the anti-utopia. Undoubtedly, its socialism is very different from that embodied in the socialist utopia of Marx and most other European socialists. To that extent it rejects important features of the modern utopia.

This was certainly how Wells saw Morris. Wells harks back on several occasions to Bellamy, not just in the employment of formal devices such as the sleeper who wakes, but as the source of ideas and images with which to ridicule Morris's 'back-to-nature' socialism. At the same time, in such anti-utopian fables as *The Time Machine*, he has his own go at Bellamy's optimistic picture of the future.[51]

But then Wells reverses *himself*, as well. Out of the anti-utopian portraits of his early science fiction, such as the Martians of *The War of the Worlds* and the Selenites of *The First Men in the Moon*, he constructs the not very dissimilar utopian Samurai of *A Modern Utopia* and the Utopians of *Men Like Gods*. In his own person he makes the passage from anti-utopia to utopia in the decades of the 1900s. Thereafter he became the most imposing and influential utopian target for later anti-utopians. Among early responses was E. M. Forster's anti-utopian story, 'The Machine Stops' (1909), which its author described as 'a reaction to one of the earlier heavens of H. G. Wells'.[52]

Huxley and Orwell, too, made no secret of the fact that their anti-utopias were directed largely against Wells, as the representative modern utopian. But what is interesting, and very evident, is the extent of their borrowing from the earlier anti-utopian Wells in their attacks on the later utopian Wells. Zamyatin had explicitly, and with due acknowledgement to Wells, already done this in *We*, tending in any case to regard Wells more as a critic and a satirist than a utopian. Huxley and Orwell were perhaps less conscious of their debt to Wells; but both were well acquainted with *When the Sleeper Wakes* and *The First Men in the Mooon*, in both of which novels can be found clear anticipations of many of the features of *Brave New World* and *Nineteen Eighty-Four*, right down to such details as the 'Bokanovsky process' of *Brave New World*.[53]

The twists and turns do not stop there. The behavioural conditioning of the anti-utopian *Brave New World* becomes the scientific basis of Skinner's optimistic utopia, *Walden Two*. What makes passive, conformist Brave New Worlders also makes active, co-operative members of Skinner's experimental utopian community. Most intriguing of all, Huxley himself re-evaluates these techniques in a utopian direction. Like Wells, he also reverses himself. The anti-utopian author of *Brave New World* becomes towards the end of his life the utopian author of *Island*. What is remarkable is how little change seems to be needed to make the move. The 'neo-Pavlovian' conditioning of *Brave New World* is central to the child-rearing practices of the energetic and creative society of *Island*. The escapist drug *soma* of *Brave New World* reappears as the revered mind-enhancing *moksha-medicine* of *Island*. Of course, both conditioning and drugs serve quite different ends in the two societies; but it is nevertheless a little unnerving to find a hated anti-utopia modulate so smoothly and effortlessly into an admired utopia.

With Orwell the case is not so simple, but it can at least be made. Bernard Crick in his biography urges us not to regard *Nineteen Eighty-Four* as in the nature of Orwell's 'last will and testament'; it was simply the last thing he wrote before he died. It is quite conceivable that he might later have produced a utopia as well. We know that he was fascinated by utopian literature, since he wrote so much about it. His childhood friend Jacintha Buddicom tells us that Orwell 'greatly fancied' Wells's *A Modern Utopia* and 'said that he might write that kind of book himself'.[54] For many of his readers he did in fact write that kind of book: it is *Homage to Catalonia*. Certainly, in his account of revolutionary Barcelona in the early months of the Civil War there is a euphoria and an intensity that fully deserves to be called 'utopian'. So too in many essays and reviews – as in the review of Wilde's 'The Soul of Man under Socialism' – one can find the elements of a vision that points towards a utopia of equality and fraternity, the hallmarks of Orwell's socialism.[55]

Wells, Huxley, Orwell: utopia and anti-utopia flow into and out of each other in an intricate pattern of fervent affirmation mixed with bleak pessimism. There is no fixity or consistency in the pattern. Utopia is countered by anti-utopia, which in turn becomes the basis for another utopia, often by the same anti-utopian turned utopian. No such uncertainty or ambivalence afflicts the two American utopians, Bellamy and Skinner. Perhaps the contrast is no more than a reflection of the different historical experiences of Europe and America, at least as these have been conveniently interpreted to their populations. Young America still seems capable of harbouring utopian expectations, even among its sternest critics. Old Europe alternates between periods of intense optimism and darkest despair.

In the studies that follow, the confident American utopias of Bellamy and Skinner frame the more ambiguous English contributions of Wells, Huxley and Orwell. But it would be wrong to conclude from this that there are two distinct traditions at work, an American and a European one. Nineteenth-century American utopianism clearly drew upon European utopian ideas, even though American practice may have given them a different slant. Skinner's *Walden Two*, an intensely American utopia, is likewise steeped in European social theory. Similarly, much of the twentieth-century interplay of utopia and anti-utopia in Europe derived from the socialist utopia which, though European in origin, was first influentially portrayed in Bellamy's *Looking Backward*. The American initiative then became the signal for a resurgence of European utopianism. The utopian tradition, stretching back to More, is a unified one, capable of many transformations. It is a remarkable product of the European social imagination – and one of its inventions was America.

PART II

5
Utopia as Socialism: Edward Bellamy and *Looking Backward*

'But what *would* you call the system you have now?'
'Well, if the truth be known, it is in a condition of flux and evolving as rapidly as any of the sciences, social and physical. There are elements of *socialism*, in the various senses of the word, since the term is so elastic. There are elements of *collectivism* and of *syndicalism* and perhaps *technocracy*. It might even be said that there are elements of *anarchism*, if you mean by that the anarchism of the nineteenth century Proudhon and of the poets Shelley and Blake. Elements, too, of *meritocracy*. . . .'

Mack Reynolds, *Looking Backward from the Year 2000* (1973)

'I suppose you have seen . . . "Looking Backward". . . . Thank you, I wouldn't care to live in such a cockney paradise as he imagines.'

William Morris, letter to John Glasier, 13 May 1889

A LITERARY AND POLITICAL PHENOMENON

Who, one might ask, now reads Edward Bellamy's *Looking Backward*? Students taking academic courses on utopias, no doubt. Historians of American literature and Americal social philosophy. Readers with a taste for the by-ways of socialist theory and socialist history. All these, together with the zestful accumulation of unread books by academic libraries, would sufficiently account for the modest but steady sale that the book continues to enjoy. Outside these specialist groups, it is unlikely that many educated people have read Bellamy, and some may not even have heard of him.

In the 1970s, a popular American science fiction writer, Mack Reynolds, began to produce stories with titles like *Looking Backward from the Year 2000* and *Equality in the Year 2000*. They were books offered explicitly in homage to Bellamy. They sought to make him more up to date, and more accessible to a popular readership. The basic plot, characters and main ideas all came straight from Bellamy. Not only did Reynolds mystify his readers by resurrecting this forgotten figure; he offended them by championing a social philosophy which to most of them was as obsolete as the steam engine.[1]

Things were once very different. On his death in 1898, the *American Fabian* wrote:

> It is doubtful if any man, in his own lifetime, ever exerted so great an influence upon the social beliefs of his fellow-beings as did Edward Bellamy. Marx, at the time of his death, had won but slight recognition from the mass; and though his influence in the progressive struggle has become paramount, it is through his interpreters, and not in his own voice, that he speaks to the multitude. But Bellamy spoke simply and directly; his imagination conceived, and his art pictured, the social framework of the future in such clear and bold outlines that the commonest mind could understand and appreciate. Wherever, in all lands, men are striving for a fairer social order based upon an econonic democracy, Bellamy is a recognized prophet of the ideal state.[2]

The tribute is, if anything, almost too restrained. The story of Bellamy's success in his own lifetime is so astonishing that, well-known as the facts are, it compels retelling. Within a year of its publication in 1888, *Looking Backward* sold a quarter of a million copies in the United States alone; by the time of the publication of its sequel, *Equality*, in 1897, it had sold half a million copies in America and hundreds of thousands more throughout the rest of the world. It was the best-selling novel in nineteenth-century America after *Uncle Tom's Cabin*, and the second novel in American literature to sell a million copies. It has never been out of print in the United States since its publication. It was translated, usually within a year or two of initial publication, into every major language in the world.[3] Bellamy was read not only in England, France, Germany, Russia and Italy, but also in Australia, India, Indonesia, Japan, South Africa and many other countries.[4]

Such a resounding success might still make of him a historical curiosity, no more. Similar things have happened to other authors now little read – T. H. Buckle and Herbert Spencer are other notable nineteenth-century examples in the English-speaking world. Why continue to attend to Bellamy? Partly as an exceptionally influential figure in the modern utopian tradition, a thinker whose work directly inspired, by way of imitation or refutation, some of the most important utopian writings of the past hundred years. More importantly, at a time when socialist writing mainly took the form of theory or criticism, Bellamy lay before the world the first detailed picture of what a socialist society would look like. It did not please all socialists, and some went out of their way to deny that it was socialism at all. But socialist it was, and is; and it remains of great interest as an unusually direct and clear statement of socialist aims and aspirations, and of the problems that these give rise to.

In 1886, Dr and Mrs Edward Aveling, travelling in the United States, had remarked on the 'unconscious socialism' of the American people, and speculated that one day 'the *Uncle Tom's Cabin* of capitalism' would be written.[5] In many people's eyes, *Looking Backward* was that book. The comparison, in terms of appeal and influence, with the great novel of American slavery appears again and again. *Looking Backward*, says the literary historian Bruce Franklin, 'changed the consciousness of Americans more than any other novel of the century except for *Uncle Tom's Cabin*'.[6] In a salute to 'a great American prophet' in 1934, the American philosopher John Dewey wrote that 'what *Uncle Tom's Cabin* was to the anti-slavery movement Bellamy's book may well be to the shaping of popular opinion for a new social order.'[7] It was clearly recognized by all, moreover, that *Looking Backward* exceeded its great predecessor in its influence beyond the shores of the United States. In 1935 three prominent American intellectuals – John Dewey, Charles Beard and Edward Weeks – drew up, each independently, a list of the 25 most influential books published since 1885. All three ranked Bellamy's *Looking Backward* second only to Karl Marx's *Das Kapital* in its world-wide influence.[8]

The list of prominent individuals influenced – directly and positively, by their own testimony – by this 'most popular and appealing of American utopias'[9] is an interesting and impressive one. It reveals the diverse appeals of the book, and the diverse uses to which it was put. In America, in addition to Dewey and the radical historian Charles Beard, Bellamy had a lasting influence on many of the early socialist leaders, such as Daniel de Leon, Eugene V. Debs and Norman Thomas. He also influenced such social critics as Thorstein Veblen, Upton Sinclair and Adolf Berle, Jr. He was greeted enthusiastically by Madame Helena Blavatsky, co-founder of the Theosophical Society, who wrote in the 'Bible' of the society, *The Key to Theosophy* (1889): 'The organization of society, depicted by Edward Bellamy, in his magnificent work *Looking Backward*, admirably represents the Theosophical idea of what should be the first step toward the full realization of universal brotherhood.' Madame Blavatsky's English disciple, Annie Besant, who was also a leading Fabian, as enthusiastically lectured on Bellamy to English audiences. Other English followers were the biologist Alfred Russel Wallace, who dated his conversion to socialism from a reading of *Looking Backward*, and Ebenezer Howard, the founder of the Garden City movement. Howard had been instrumental in getting *Looking Backward* published in England, and his first statement of the Garden City idea, in his book *Tomorrow* (1898), is heavily marked by borrowings from Bellamy.

British socialists reacted with mixed feelings to *Looking Backward*, and to its success. The most famous response was that of William Morris, whose profound irritation with it, and simultaneous awareness that he could not ignore it, prompted the writing of *News from Nowhere* as an alternative socialist utopia. But others, especially in the Fabian movement, were more favourably disposed. H. G. Wells seems to have been inspired by Bellamy not simply in the formation of his political ideas, but also in the form and themes of a good deal of his science fiction, such as *The Time Machine* and *When the Sleeper Wakes*. George Bernard Shaw reversed an earlier, rather flippant, judgement on Bellamy ('we rather turned up our noses at Utopias as cheap stuff until Wells stood up for them'), and went on to make systematic use of his ideas in his propagandistic tracts such as *The Intelligent Women's Guide to Socialism*. In fact, many more British socialists were influenced by Bellamy than were prepared to admit, or perhaps were even aware of. The historian R. C. K. Ensor, who had great personal knowledge of the radicalism of the period, declared that '"out of Henry George by either Bellamy or Gronlund" was a true pedigree of the convictions held by nearly all the leading propagandists who set socialism on its feet in Great Britain between 1886 and 1900.' As late as 1948, when Bellamy's son Paul was introduced to Clement Atlee, Prime Minister of the new Labour government, Atlee told him that *Looking Backward* was one of the English bibles, and that the English socialist government was 'a child of the Bellamy idea'.

Other European socialists were equally warm. Jean Jaurès, the French socialist leader, proclaimed *Looking Backward* to be 'an American masterpiece' which had done 'wonders towards dissipating hostility and ignorance against our ideas'. But in some ways the most remarkable influence is to be found in Russia. For many, the most impressive testimony to the power of Bellamy's vision must lie in the fact that no less a figure than Leo Tolstoy was responsible for the first translation into Russian of *Looking Backward*. 'An exceedingly remarkable book', noted Tolstoy in his diary on 30 June 1889. The English-language copy in his library is extensively annotated, and the passage at the end of the novel recounting Julian West's nightmare return to nineteenth-century Boston is especially heavily marked. It was indeed Bellamy's searing criticisms of capitalist society, rather than his prescriptions for a future society, that most moved Tolstoy, and led him to seek a Russian translator. The success of the book was immediate. There were seven different translations in Russia before 1917, including translations into Georgian, Lithuanian and Hebrew. A critic noted in 1906 that Bellamy's book 'was more effective propaganda for the ideas of socialism among the broad masses than any other book during the past thirty years'. In the same year Maxim Gorki told an audience of literati in Philadelphia: 'We know more of your authors than you do of ours. *Uncle Tom's Cabin* is read in every part of the Empire; Edward Bellamy and his theories in *Looking Backward* are known to all the Russian students.'

So alarmed were the Tsarist authorities by the success of *Looking Backward* that in 1889 they banned it in public libraries and reading rooms. They also prevented the Russian publication of its successor, *Equality* (1897), for over a decade. But this could not stop the widespread circulation of the famous chapter XXIII, 'The Parable of the Water Tank', which was translated and ran into many editions before 1917. With its artful biblical language, and forceful presentation of the inhumanity and irrationality of the capitalist system, it proved immensely popular with those many Russians who were ill-equipped to deal with the scholastic lucubrations of Lenin, Plekhanov and the rest.[10]

It is, obviously, difficult to gauge the long-term effect of Bellamy's work on particular individuals and the various movements associated with them. This list simply indicates the extraordinarily widespread appeal that he seems to have had for a particular generation of intellectuals. But as to his immediate impact in the literary and political spheres, there is no such uncertainty. Before him, there had been a few utopian novels by American writers. But none of them generated much interest or attention. *Looking Backward* created an appetite and a vogue for utopias that did not subside for a dozen years. Between 1889 and 1900 at least 62 utopias and novels influenced by Bellamy were published – most of them in the United States, but several also in Britain and Germany. One measure of that influence is simply that the writers chose the utopian genre at all, given its thinness before Bellamy. Often the influence is directly acknowledged in the title – *Looking Beyond, Young West, The World a Department Store, When the Sleeper Wakes*. And if the titles did not make the connection clear, the themes and forms of these utopias were only too evidently moulded by *Looking Backward*. One way or another, and whether the authors came to scoff, praise or damn, Bellamy's influence can be traced directly in a spectacular burgeoning of the utopian imagination at the close of the nineteenth century.[11]

He also – and this is more unusual – directly stimulated an outburst of intense political activity in the United States. *Looking Backward* is probably unique in that, as a single book, it launched a national political movement. (The same cannot be said of *Das Kapital*, for instance, or even of the *Communist Manifesto*.) Within only months of its publication, the first Nationalist Club – Bellamy's own chosen name for his system – had been established in Boston (September 1888). Its objects were, quite simply, to propagate Bellamy's ideas as expounded in *Looking Backward*. The hope was that by a systematic educating of public opinion Bellamy's ideas could find their way into the mainstream of political life.

At first slowly, other clubs began to form across the country. In May 1889 the movement acquired a national voice with the publication of a monthly journal, the *Nationalist*. This accelerated the growth of the clubs. By February 1891 there were 165 Nationalist Clubs spread across 27 states of the Union, together with a host of more informal Bellamy clubs which met simply for purposes of discussion. Moreover, the movement had moved more seriously into politics. In 1891, with the failure of the *Nationalist*, Bellamy himself started a new weekly, the *New Nation*, which he employed as a direct political instrument. The *New Nation* greeted the rise of the People's Party with enthusiasm, and championed it throughout its existence. Although Bellamy never identified Populism with Nationalism, he saw in the People's Party the best hope for Nationalist policies. Nationalism could be the ideological spearhead of the Populist attack on the two major parties. Together, they constituted a new kind of revivalistic politics, preparing the way for utopia. The *New Nation* vigorously campaigned on behalf of the People's Party, and Nationalists were urged to play as full a part as possible in the local branches of the party. Nationalists were active at the Cincinnati (1891) and Omaha (1892) conventions of the People's Party; and although their influence on the final programme has often been exaggerated by Bellamyites,[12] they had every reason to be pleased with the policies adopted for the 1892 presidential election, which included a large measure of nationalization. The million votes gained by the Populist presidential candidate, General Weaver, were hailed by the *New Nation* as a triumph as much for Nationalism as for Populism.

Nationalism and Populism rose and fell together, which suggests that they drew on the same forces and made something of the same appeal. Both were 'populist' in the more general meaning of the term. The Omaha programme, Bellamy averred, was 'a platform not for a class or classes, but for the masses'. Both relied heavily on the same geographical regions – the trans-Mississippi states, the Pacific coast and the Middle West. Both were fatally weakened when the two major parties took several planks from the Populist platform, leading to a fusion of Populists and Democrats. And the election of McKinley in 1896 was the death blow to both movements. Nationalism was never even remotely as important a political force as Populism. But it was still quite extraordinary that a single book by a hitherto obscure journalist should have created a mass movement which could reasonably aspire to shape the policies of one of the most important parties in American history.[13]

To describe *Looking Backward* as a literary and political phenomenon is not, therefore, to strain the term too much. The question is, why? Why did the book achieve such phenomenal popularity? Why did a socialist utopia so seize the imagination of so many Americans at the end of the nineteenth century? Why, for that matter, was it so successful abroad?

America, as we have seen, was almost embarrassingly rich in utopian ideas and utopian ventures in the nineteenth century. Many of these schemes were also socialistic or communistic, in the broadest meaning of those terms. So at first sight there is nothing at all surprising about the appearance of a socialist utopia in America in the 1880s. Bellamy himself placed his Nationalist movement in a native tradition stretching back to the utopian experiments of the first half of the century, so that 'in spirit if not in form it may be said to date back to the forties'. He saw his utopia as legitimate heir to 'the extraordinary wave of socialistic enthusiasm which swept over the United States at that period and led to the Brook Farm Colony and a score of phalansteries for communistic experiments'.[14]

But the problem, as Bellamy recognized, is more complicated than that. At the time he wrote, he could hardly be unaware that, with the exception of the strictly religious communities, all the utopian communities of the pre-Civil War period had long since disappeared. *Looking Backward* broke decisively with the Brook Farm era in rejecting partial, retreatist and communitarian utopianism. 'We do not,' said Bellamy, 'believe in the colony idea as a help to the social solution, any more than we believe in the monastic idea as an assistance to the moral solution.' The social problem had to be resolved – could only be resolved – at the level of the nation-state. So important did it seem to make this clear that it is emphasized above all else in the very name that Bellamy chose to describe his system: Nationalism. It is a clumsy term, and it caused irritation and confusion both at the time and since. But at the very least it had the merit of indicating a new hardheadedness, a new spirit of realism, in the American utopian tradition. The time for utopian idylls, of the kind at any rate that had fascinated New England Fourierites around Concord, was past.

This conviction shows up even more in the quality of the social theory which informs Bellamy's utopia. It is 'scientific' and systematic in a new way. Like so many American intellectuals of his time, Bellamy, as we shall see, never entirely shook off the individualist, Transcendentalist philosophy of Emerson and his circle. But the change was clear enough for all that. In the half-century following the Civil War, something like a revolution in social thought occurred among American intellectuals.[15] The dominant individualism of the prewar period gave way to a discovery of *society* as the fundamental fact of human existence. Put another way, sociology arrived in America in the second half of the nineteenth century. The influence of Comte was especially strong. Faced with social problems of an unprecedented magnitude, intellectuals reacted, as John Thomas puts it, against the 'undirected humanitarianism of their elders', and in favour of the rational, scientifically organized society. There was a keen interest in social statistics, in techniques of planning and social experimentation.[16]

Bellamy clearly partakes of this revolution in thought – indeed, given his popularity, he may truly be said to be one of its chief agents. The rejection of individualist solutions is total. Whether or not Bellamy's thought is strictly socialist, it is unquestionably sociological through and through. The resolution of problems of poverty, powerlessness and individual unhappiness is linked to an analysis of the whole system of society, and to its principles of growth and development. As with so many modern utopias, *Looking Backward* is indeed offered primarily as a work of social theory. The social prescriptions which constitute the utopian element are supposed to follow directly from this theory, and to be no more than a prefiguring in the imagination of what is bound to happen in actuality. In a postscript to the second edition of 1888, Bellamy wrote: '*Looking Backward*, although in form a fanciful romance, is intended, in all seriousness, as a forecast, in accordance with the principles of evolution, of the next stage in the industrial and social development of humanity, especially in this country. . . .'[17]

Both these aspects of Bellamy's thought – its focus on the nation-state, and its socialist content – are directly linked to a single fact: the massive and rapid industrialization of America in the second half of the nineteenth century. Herbert Gutman makes the appropriate point in a vivid contrast: 'In the year [1860] of Abraham Lincoln's election as president, the United States ranked behind England, France, and Germany in the value of its manufactured product. In 1894 the United States led the field: its manufactured product nearly equalled in value that of Great Britain, France, and Germany together.'[18] Such a gigantic transformation in economic condition was unique – certainly among modern nations, perhaps in the whole of human history. It was bound to set up corresondingly awesome social strains. At the same time, it nullified all social thought, all schemes of reform, which were tied to the earlier condition of American society. The only relevant social theory was that capable of addressing the system of a fully industrialized society.

Moreover, the form in which the transformation took place exacerbated the problem. Unlike the industrialization of Britain in the earlier part of the century, American industrialization rapidly threw up enormous business empires in the form of trusts, combines and monopolies. In response, industrial workers too began to organize – hesitatingly and patchily, but sufficiently to indicate that the struggle between labour and capital was now permanently on the agenda of American political life. Other groups, such as the small farmers, also felt the pressure of big business: by the 1880s farmers were in such dire straits that they threw themselves into the mass movement of Populism.

The industrializing drive was the more disruptive for being accompanied by an intensified movement to the cities. The generation after the Civil War was the generation in which, as Arthur Schlesinger says, 'the city took supreme command.' Between 1860 and 1900 the urban population quadrupled while the rural population only doubled.[19] The typical American experience, especially for the millions of immigrants who arrived at the end of the century, was increasingly an urban one. For a nation accustomed to think of itself in terms of a 'garden', or a wilderness, this was a psychological fact of enormous importance. The invocation of 'Nature', characteristic of Emerson's day, was less convincing when so many people barely had a glimpse of it. Equally traumatic, again as much in symbolic meaning as in actual effect, was the official closing of the frontier in 1890. Whether or not Americans had actually used the opportunity, the sense of the possibility of escape from city and even 'society' was a powerful psychological safety-valve, so long as there was frontier land to be cheaply acquired. For the first time since its colonization, America was now bounded and sealed-in. It could not 'export' its moral and social problems to the moving frontier. There was no escape to virgin lands.

In such conditions of compressed economic, demographic and urban growth, it is hardly surprising that apocalyptic visions haunted America at the end of the nineteenth century. They arose out of 'the overriding paradox of the age: the co-existence of technological progress and social chaos'.[20] One such famous vision was that of Henry Adams in the hall of dynamos at the Paris Exposition of 1900, when 'he found himself lying in the Gallery of Machines . . . with his historical neck broken by the sudden irruption of forces totally new.'[21] Adams's terror was much more than simply the fear of the destructive power of science and technology, the crushing of the spiritual (the Virgin) by the material (the Dynamo). In the science of force and motion he thought he had discovered the laws of history, and the second law of thermodynamics dictated a cold, grey death for all civilization.

But whether the visions of apocalypse took negative (dystopian) or positive (utopian) form, they were all coloured by what Henry James called 'the imagination of disaster'. John Kasson's comment is very much to the point:

> Both utopian and dystopian works [of the late nineteenth century] pointed to the danger of barbarism at the heart of America's vaunted civilization rising out of the gulf between the nation's abundant resources and her shocking inequities. In a society whose republican purposes had been obscured or corrupted . . . technology itself might serve as an instrument not of liberty but of repression, not order but chaos, not creation but destruction. The hopeful vision of an integrated technological republic struggled against the dreadful anticipation of technological tyranny and holocaust.[22]

Bellamy's political organs, the *Nationalist* and the *New Nation*, repeatedly sounded the note of direful warning. 'Our ship of state is fast nearing the shoals upon which past civilizations have stranded, and, unless we put hard down the helm and steer clear of danger, history will again repeat itself, and the dark, thick, gloomy pall of ignorance and superstition will once more enshroud our globe.'[23] In an appeal to the People's Party on the eve of the presidential election of 1892, Bellamy gave full rein to his fondness for Old Testament prophecy:

> We are today confronted by portentous indications in the conditions of American industry, society and politics, that this great experiment [America], on which the last hopes of the race depends, is to prove, like all former experiments, a disastrous failure. Let us bear in mind that, if it be a failure, it will be a final failure. There can be no more new worlds to be discovered, no fresh continents to offer virgin fields for new ventures.[24]

It is not difficult to see how, in general terms, Bellamy's utopia both responded to and attempted to resolve this alarming national predicament. Part of the appeal of *Looking Backward* was of course the perennial one, precisely that it *was* a utopia: an escape into a world where all the obstacles to social harmony and social welfare had been magically overcome. But the differences with past utopias also need to be emphasized if we are to understand its great impact and seeming relevance at the time. It spoke directly to contemporary society and contemporary issues. As an industrial utopia, it firmly turned its back on nostalgic pastoral dreams of Arcadia. The society of *Looking Backward* is modern, technological, urban, industrial.[25] As a socialist utopia, it addressed itself centrally to what seemed to be the heart of the problem: the organization of industry, the conflict between labour and capital, the problem of work in an industrial civilization. In both these respects it found a responsive echo not simply in America but elsewhere. 'It was,' as I. F. Clarke says, 'the most widely read and most influential of all the nineteenth century ideal states, because the lessons it proposed to teach the Americans had great relevance for the citizens of all industrial countries.'[26] But in order to understand better the complex nature of Bellamy's appeal, both to his fellow-Americans and to others, we need to look more closely at Bellamy's relation to socialism.

IS IT SOCIALISM?

It still seems distinctly odd that the first comprehensive socialist utopia should have been written not by a European, but by an American. America, after all, was the great exception to the development of mass socialism among industrial nations. At a time when, in Britain, France and Germany, socialist parties were beginning to gain serious support from the labouring classes, American socialism remained an affair of a handful of *émigré* intellectuals, mostly German refugees from the 1848 Revolution. It first organized as the Marxist Working Men's Party of the United States, founded by German–American socialists after the break-up of the First International in 1876. Modifying its uncompromising Marxism somewhat, in the following year it transformed itself into the Socialist Labor Party, and made a more determined effort to enter national politics and the politics of the new industrial unions. It failed in both directions. At no time between 1850 and 1890 were there ever more than a few thousand American socialists, and these were mostly first-generation German immigrants, living within their own communities and speaking and writing in their own language. 'The German socialists were as isolated from America at large as the communitarians of the pre-Civil War days had been.'[27] More serious was the failure within the small body of unionized workers. Neither the Knights of Labor nor the later American Federation of Labor – both dominated by a conservative 'aristocracy of labour' – was receptive to socialist influence. Other workers were even more suspicious of the alien, academic doctrines of Marxism. Thus, although the character of American socialism had changed markedly from the earlier Owenite or Fourierite communitarianism to a more 'scientific' or German socialism, the movement still remained formally and institutionally almost totally excluded from American political life.[28]

In 1906, in a study entitled *Why is there no Socialism in the United States?*, the German socialist Werner Sombart addressed the paradox that the most advanced industrial nation in the world had produced no serious socialist movement. He concluded that the lack of interest in socialism had a good deal to do with the prosperity of the American worker, compared with his European counterpart. The sheer success of American capitalism had made the American worker its willing devotee. 'An input of patriotism,' he wrote, 'impinging as it did upon the proud consciousness that the United States led all other nations on the path of (capitalist) progress, established the cast of [the worker's] business-orientated mentality and made him into the sober, calculating, businessman without ideals whom we know today. All Socialist utopias came to nothing on roast beef and apple pie.'[29]

There was, therefore, at first sight no strong influence in the American political and intellectual tradition to inspire the writing of a socialist utopia. Brook Farm experiments might provide the impetus for a quasi-utopia such as Thoreau's *Walden*; even more, they could supply in plenty material for an anti-utopian satire, such as Hawthorne's *The Blithedale Romance*. But neither in their philosophy nor in their practice did they move in the direction of a fully socialist society, ordered around a single, central principle of socialized property and collective control over the whole life of society. Added to this unpromising social environment was Bellamy's own apparent indifference to and ignorance of socialist ideas prior to the writing of *Looking Backward*. More than this, Bellamy appeared in his earlier work not only to be unacquainted with socialism but to be no more than mildly interested in 'the social question' itself. A close student of his work, Everett MacNair, has this to say about the stories and journalistic essays published right up to the 1880s:

> There was one lack most markedly noticeable – the lack of habitual expression of anything like 'social passion'. The natural experience of the reader, who has become acquainted with *Looking Backward* for the first time today, is to go to the earlier stories, looking for the roots of his social idealism. And the only honest conclusion is that it just is not there. Nor in his journals, to any marked extent. Nor in the *Religion of Solidarity*. With the one exception of the unsuccessful serial, *The Duke of Stockbridge*, there is no basis of fact for the claim that Bellamy had shown in his published fiction a passion for social reform. It is as if he had intentionally combed it out. It is as if he had disciplined himself to avoid it.[30]

Bellamy himself, after the publication of *Looking Backward*, went out of his way to dissociate himself from the socialist label, and to deny specifically socialist influences: 'I have never been in any sense a student of socialistic literature, or have known more of the various socialistic schemes than any newspaper reader might'.[31] A letter to his friend, William Dean Howells, explaining his objections to the term 'socialism', reveals a mixed bag of motives.

> Every sensible man will admit there is a big deal in a name, especially in making first impressions. In the radicalness of the opinions I have expressed, I may seem to out-socialize the socialists, yet the word socialist is one I could never well stomach. In the first place it is a foreign word in itself, and equally foreign in all its suggestions. It

smells to the average American of petroleum, suggests the red flag, with all manner of sexual novelties, and an abusive tone about God and religion, which in this country we at least treat with decent respect. . . . Whatever German and French reformers may choose to call themselves, socialist is not a good name for a party to succeed with in America. No such party can or ought to succeed that is not wholly and enthusiastically American and patriotic in spirit and suggestions.[32]

There was, as Bellamy indicates, more in this than simple native American prejudice. Sylvia Bowman notes that '*Looking Backward* . . . sold in the United States over 400,000 copies from 1888 to 1897 – the period in which the ideas of socialists and philosophical anarchists were an anathema because of the "red scare" resulting from the Haymarket riot'.[33] Drawing the lesson for other reformers in an editorial of 1898 entitled 'The Lesson from Bellamy', the Chicago *Journal* remarked that this was a time when 'a man who talked or wrote socialism was in danger of being run into a corner and clubbed.'[34] There were good practical reasons for publishing and promoting one's schemes of reform under some other name than socialism, as Henry George recognized in expelling the socialists from his 'single tax' movement; and Bellamy was an experienced enough journalist to be aware of this simple but important fact. Indeed, no explicitly socialist or Marxist movement, party or programme has ever seized the imagination of more than a handful of Americans.

In being so circumspect, Bellamy may have misled contemporaries as well as many later commentators into underestimating his knowledge of socialist movements and ideas. Throughout the 1860s and 1870s, as the researches of Morgan and Bowman have shown, Bellamy was acquiring a quite extensive understanding of the new ideas in political economy, sociology and socialism. He had read John Stuart Mill as a boy. As a student in Germany in 1868–9 he seems to have been particularly fascinated by the activities of the German socialists, and wrote frequently to his brother Frederick about them and their ideas. When a journalist with the *New York Evening Post*, which had radical sympathies, he got to know a good deal about the ideas and aspirations of the members of the New York branch of the First International, mostly Germans under the influence of Weitling and Marx. For the *Springfield Union* he reviewed Charles Nordhoff's *The Communistic Societies of the United States* and John Noyes's *History of American Socialisms*. Later, as editor of the Springfield *Penny News*, which he founded with his brother Charles, he devoted considerable attention to the new social movements of Europe and America. Clearly, at the time of writing *Looking Backward* Bellamy was not quite the politically innocent writer of romances that he is sometimes pictured as.[35]

It was, admittedly, an image which at times he himself seemed very intent on fostering. Shortly after the publication of *Looking Backward*, in a piece entitled 'Why I wrote "Looking Backward"', he made the strongest of his public demurs: 'I never had, previous to the publication of the work, any affiliations with any class or sect of industrial or social reformers nor, to make my confession complete, any particular sympathy with undertakings of the sort.' He artfully evokes the figure of the simple story-teller, who merely stumbled across a serious social theme:

In undertaking to write 'Looking Backward' I had, at the outset, no idea of attempting a serious contribution to the movement of social reform. The idea was of a mere literary fantasy, a fairy tale of social felicity. There was no thought of contriving a house which practical men might live in, but merely of hanging in mid-air, far out of reach of the sordid and material world of the present, a cloud-palace for an ideal humanity.[36]

Five years later Bellamy, now a national figure and an ardent political propagandist, gave a quite different account of the writing of *Looking Backward.* He now seemed anxious to provide a respectable intellectual and theoretical pedigree for the Nationalist movement – which meant finding one for himself. A range of personal experiences and public activities was drawn upon to build up a quite misleading picture of coherent development and clearly defined goals. Thus, speaking of his European travels in 1868–9, at the age of 18:

At that time I visited Europe and spent a year there in travel and study. It was in the great cities of England, Europe, and among the hovels of the peasantry that my eyes were first fully opened to the extent and consequences of man's inhumanity to man. I well remember in those days of European travel how much more deeply that blue background of misery impressed me than the palaces and cathedrals in relief against it. I distinctly recall the innumerable debates, suggested by the piteous sights about us, which I had with a dear companion of my journey, as to the possibility of finding some great remedy for poverty, some plan for equalizing human conditions. . . . So it was that I returned home, for the first time aroused to the existence and urgency of the social problem, but without as yet seeing any way out. Although it had required the sights of Europe to startle me to a vivid realization of the inferno of poverty beneath our civilization, my eyes having once been opened I had now no difficulty in recognizing in America . . . the same condition in course of progressive development.[37]

He even claimed to have discovered, 'rummaging among old papers', an unpublished manuscript of a public address 'which it appears I delivered before the Chicopee Falls Village Lyceum in 1871 or 1872'. The subject of the address was 'The Barbarism of Society', and Bellamy quoted large extracts from it to show the great extent of his social awareness at so early a date. The address does indeed show a concern for the misery of the labourer's condition, but it goes little further than an expression of the Christian compassion that was always a part of Bellamy's nature. It certainly does not justify his complacent comment that 'since I came across this echo of my youth and recalled the half-forgotten exercises of mind it testifies to, I have been wondering, not why I wrote "Looking Backward", but why I did not write it, or try to, twenty years ago.' Nor, decidedly, does it support the suggestion of a disciplined apprenticeship in social studies implicit in Bellamy's programmatic declaration:

According to my best recollection it was in the fall or winter of 1886 that I sat down to my desk with the definite purpose of trying to reason out a method of economic organization by which the republic might guarantee the livelihood and material welfare of its citizens on a basis of equality corresponding to and supplementing their political equality.[38]

Bellamy's second account of how he came to write *Looking Backward* is clearly overdone and exaggerated. The very contrivance of the style, quite apart from other evidence to the contrary, sufficiently suggests this. It is a conscious and not very successful imitation of the form of literary reminiscence sometimes adopted by famous political intellectuals. Bellamy may well have been influenced by Mill's *Autobiography*, which he knew. As it happens, the detailed picture of Bellamy's intellectual development prior to his writing *Looking Backward* will probably never be known, since many of his letters and papers were destroyed or lost. If one were to go on his published work alone, one would certainly incline to the earlier account as the truer one. But that leans too much the other way; Bellamy was certainly both intellectually and emotionally better equipped and prepared than it suggests.

This much at least can be said. Bellamy's awareness of social issues, strong in many ways and fed by wide though unsystematic reading in the relevant literature of the day, had not led him to any definite socialist commitment before the writing of *Looking Backward*. If *Looking Backward* is socialist, then Bellamy was accurate in saying that he had stumbled on it in the course of writing his book. His European travels crystallized certain perceptions, some of which became crucial to his later ideas, but they were far less important than he later made out in shaping his socialist consciousness. It was only after the publication of *Looking Backward*, and under the stimulus of its astonishing success, that Bellamy seriously got down to a study of socialist writings. He then read Marx, Engels, Blanc, Bebel and George. The results were apparent in *Equality*, a book certainly more sophisticated in its treatment of economic issues but, equally, lacking that directness and spontaneity that made *Looking Backward* so much more appealing to so many people.[39]

Given that Bellamy's route to socialism was indirect and very individual, the question remains: Is what he sets before us in *Looking Backward* properly socialism? The answer is that it is, even though Bellamy himself and many contemporary socialists strenuously denied it.[40] To put the matter even more paradoxically, it is the more completely socialist for being essentially American. That is, the very nativist cast of thought which Bellamy was so anxious to proclaim, and which for most European socialists disqualified Bellamy for entry into the socialist pantheon, actually gives him greater entitlement than was claimed on behalf of more conventional socialist heroes.

Bellamy, referring to his own system, once wrote of 'Nationalism . . . or American socialism'.[41] John Dewey, in one of the most acute analyses of Bellamy's thought, said that 'it is an American communism that he depicts.' Dewey went on to explain this.

> Bellamy was an American and a New Englander in more than a geographical sense. He was imbued with a religious faith in the democratic ideal. But for that very reason he saw through the sham and pretence that exists or can exist in the present economic system. I could fill pages with quotations in which he exposes his profound conviction that our democratic government is a veiled plutocracy. He was far from being the originator of this idea. But what distinguishes Bellamy is the clear ardor with which he grasped the *human* meaning of democracy as an idea of equality and liberty, and portrayed the complete contradiction between our present economic system and the realization of human equality and liberty. No one has carried through the idea that equality is obtainable only by complete equality of income more fully than Bellamy. Again, what

distinguishes him is that he derives his zeal and his insight from devotion to an American ideal of democracy.[42]

Albert Fried has written that, for an earlier generation of American socialists, 'socialism represented itself as the authentic expression of the American egalitarian norm, as the true legatee of the original contract.' In that sense, 'socialism was not an alien but an integral part of the American past.'[43] It is a view that came to dominate Bellamy's thinking in the decade following the publication of *Looking Backward* – the last decade of his life. In an explicit form it is stated only in a minor way in *Looking Backward*; but thereafter it became the theme of innumerable addresses and articles, and culminated finally as the guiding motif of his last work, *Equality*. Simply put, it involved a view of Nationalism ('or American socialism') as the logical and necessary outcome of the premise and promise of the 1776 American Revolution. Nationalism, Bellamy asserted, 'has been logically involved in the very principle of popular government on which the nation was founded'. Distinguishing – as he thought – Nationalism from socialism, he wrote: 'We seek the final answer to the social question not in revolution, but in evolution; not in destruction, but in fulfilment – the fulfilment of the hitherto stunted development of the nation according to its logical intent.'[44] It was this evolutionary perspective which led Bellamy to proclaim to his followers, at the first anniversary meeting of the Boston Nationalists in 1890, that 'we are the true conservative party, because we are devoted to the maintenance of republican institutions against the revolution now being effected by the money power. We propose no revolution, but that the people shall resist a revolution. We oppose those who are overthrowing the republic. Let no mistake be made here. We are not revolutionists, but counterrevolutionists.'[45]

Equality, in which Bellamy expanded and elaborated the ideas of *Looking Backward*, contains the fullest statement of the new evolutionary view of American history. 'As we look at it,' says the knowledgeable Dr Leete, 'the immortal preamble of the American Declaration of Independence, away back in 1776, logically contained the entire statement of the doctrine of universal economic equality guaranteed by the nation collectively to its members individually.'[46] The achievement of political equality – in other words, of equal rights as citizens – implied and entailed the establishment of economic equality, of equal conditions of material existence. Why was this not recognized and implemented at the time? Because, according to Dr Leete, at the time of the American Revolution there existed a sufficient equality of economic condition among Americans to make any further changes appear unnecessary. The America of Washington and Jefferson, the America that still existed when Tocqueville visited it to see democracy at work, was a society of small farmers and middling traders. Gross inequalities of wealth were absent. Political democracy had not yet been nullified by economic inequality. Thus the American Revolution remained incomplete – but men were not conscious of that fact because of the special conditions of the early phase of the republic.

The Industrial Revolution, and the subsequent economic development of America, transformed this situation. It threw up enormous inequalities of material circumstances. The political equality established by the American Revolution, unaccompanied by any move towards economic equality, increasingly became empty and meaningless to the vast majority of Americans. It was an awareness of this that spurred the first stages of the socialist movement in America – the Owenite and Fourierite communitarianism of the 1840s. Such partial and premature attempts were however bound to fail – if only because of the persistence of slavery in large sections of the nation. With the ending of the Civil War, which at least solved the issue of slavery, industrialization proceeded by gigantic leaps and bounds. The era of great trusts and monopolies forced the problem of poverty and inequality into the forefront of the American consciousness. The power of the capitalist robber-barons threatened to erode the foundations of the republic. The Nationalists, the legitimate heirs of the equalitarian tradition of the American Revolution, stood against this usurpatory tendency. Their programme of complete nationalization of the economy, and complete equality of condition, would bring about the second, positive, stage of the realization of democracy, to complement the earlier negative stage accomplished by the American Revolution. It would finish the work of the revolution, and secure the rights and liberties which it promised. The seeds of democracy planted at the time of the revolution would finally come to fruition, after a long period of delayed growth.[47]

In the society of *Equality*, the society of the year 2000, the Nationalists have truimphed. The revolution has been completed, so belatedly fulfilling the promise of 1776. 'The corner stone of our state,' says Dr Leete,

> 'is economic equality, and is not that the obvious, necessary, and only adequate pledge of these three birthrights -- life, liberty, and happiness? What is life without its material basis, and what is an equal right to life but a right to an equal material basis for it? What is liberty? How can men be free who must ask the right to labor and to live from their fellow-men and seek their bread from the hands of others? How else can any government guarantee liberty to men save by providing them a means of labor and of life coupled with independence; and how could that be done unless the government conducted the economic system upon which employment and maintenance depend? Finally, what is implied in the equal right of all to the pursuit of happiness? What form of happiness, so far as it depends at all on material facts, is not bound up with economic conditions; and how shall an equal opportunity for the pursuit of happiness be guaranteed to all save by the guarantee of economic equality?'[48]

So clear a derivation of socialism from a native American tradition was pleasing not simply to Bellamy and his followers, but to many European middle-class intellectuals. Preoccupied by 'the social question', but unable to swallow the revolutionary socialism of Marx and his disciples, they gratefully turned to the optimistic, 'utopian', evolutionary socialism of Bellamy. Its very Americanness, its origins in a democratic society characterized by a high regard for individual rights and freedoms, reassured them as to the nature of the future socialist society. Socialism would come by an evolutionary process of change, not by violent revolution. It would be a broadly based movement of humanity, a movement in which members of all classes could and would join: no one was disqualified by class origin or membership. It would resolve the conflict between labour and capital without annulling the civic rights of the liberal tradition. In a shrewd prefatory note to an Italian translation of 1890, the publisher Treves wrote: 'The merit of Bellamy's work lies in the fact that the book is good propaganda, supremely and deeply socialistic; and yet it neither provokes nor disgusts the upper classes . . . and it is due to the gentlefolk that this book, written for the poor, has been such a success.'[49]

Bellamy's European followers may have been happy to acknowledge his system as 'supremely and deeply socialistic'; but Bellamy himself, as we have seen, was generally resistant to the label. Partly this was due to simple ignorance and prejudice. As Thomas says, 'like most Americans of his generation he considered socialism a license for bomb throwing and inflammatory speechmaking by bearded radicals.'[50] But at a deeper level there was a more serious confusion and ignorance about the whole history of socialism, and its essential meaning. For Bellamy, as for many European socialists by the late nineteenth century, socialism had come to be identified with its Marxist variety. It meant a doctrine of class and class conflict. It meant internationalism and world revolution. It meant a bitterly uncompromising hostility towards all traditional systems of religion and ethics. It meant a contempt for patriotism. On all these counts Bellamy rejected it, and hence went out of his way to distinguish 'Nationalism' from socialism; despite the fact that he often found it very difficult to do so, and often puzzled and confused his supporters in his attempts.[51]

There was really no need for such uneasiness. The Nationalist philosophy, in emphasizing collective control of economic life, had in fact seized upon the central aspect of socialist theory; and it had no more reason than any other socialist sect for considering itself disqualified as properly socialist by other incidental features of its position. There is indeed a striking parallel between Bellamy's derivation of Nationalism from the implicit promise of the American Revolution, and the claim of European socialists that socialism was nothing but the continuation and completion of the French Revolution of 1789. This was the position of the first great theorist of European socialism, Saint-Simon; and in various guises it figures in the socialist philosophies of Owen, Fourier and Marx. Since the American and French Revolutions can plausibly be held to have constituted a single 'democratic revolution',[52] it appears that both American nationalism and European socialism got their inspiration from the same historical source, and with something of the same theoretical consequences. Certainly, whether or not Bellamy recognized it, in reaching socialism by his peculiarly American route, he in fact grounded it more firmly in the appropriate historical and intellectual tradition than could be said of many of the self-proclaimed socialists of nineteenth-century Europe.

The French Revolution, European socialists argued, had brought about the political integration of the nation. It had shown that modern political life could not be carried on with the partial, overlapping sovereignties of the old regime, where aristocracy, church and monarchy competed for power and so frustrated the expression of the national will. But in nationalizing and centralizing political power, it had left economic life to private choice and caprice. As in the American Revolution, but for different reasons of history and ideology, the economy was not considered a suitable arena for public intervention and regulation. With the rapid growth of the industrial economy in the nineteenth century, such an attitude could no longer be supported. The economic realm, like the cuckoo in the nest, now threatened to squeeze out and dominate all other spheres of social life. To the socialists it was inescapable that, just as political life had had to be nationalized, so the economy in turn had to be integrated into the public domain. The great French sociologist Émile Durkheim, commenting on Saint-Simon's prescriptive analysis of industrialism, saw that its tendency was 'to bind economic life to a central organ that regulates it – which is the very definition of socialism'.[53] How that regulation might be accomplished was of course a matter of intense dispute among socialists. It might take the form of a co-operative community, or state socialism, or syndicalist organization. It might require political revolution, or it might come about by evolutionary change. But what socialists did not disagree about, and what Bellamy would have heartily concurred in, was the grave consequence of leaving the economy to its own laws and momentum, and the urgent need to incorporate economic life fully into the body politic. In such a way would the business commenced by the French Revolution be concluded.

The utopia sketched in Bellamy's *Looking Backward* can, therefore, reasonably be treated as socialist. It is based on substantially the same analysis of industrial society as was currently being offered, in the later nineteenth century, by mainstream European socialism. It is socialism by way of Saint-Simon and Comte, rather than Marx and Engels; but Marxism holds no monopoly of the title to socialism. There were many routes to the socialist conviction in the nineteenth century – one thinks of John Stuart Mill's slow and painful steps in that direction, or the movement from Dissenting chapels to the Labour Party for many early socialists in England.

In Bellamy's case, too, there is the strong suggestion that religion, of a very diffuse kind, directed him towards a socialist philosophy whose precise economic and political terms he only later discerned. Bellamy was the son of a New England Baptist minister. He early abandoned any formal religious beliefs, but never seems to have given up the striving to understand the world along basically religious lines. In 1874 he wrote an essay entitled 'The Religion of Solidarity', which remained unpublished during his lifetime, but which he subsequently said 'represents the germ of what has been ever since my philosophy of life'.[54] The substance as well as the title of the essay recalls Comte's 'Religion of Humanity'. It shows Bellamy employing the language of Emersonian Transcendentalism to establish an elemental affinity between 'the Individual' and 'the Infinite', such that it is only by merging himself in the infinite (humanity as a whole) that man truly fulfils himself. The language and concepts are metaphysical, but it takes very little to discern in the following passage the seeds of the socialist philosophy that was to be spelled out so painstakingly in *Looking Backward*:

> Seeing there is in every being a soul common in nature with all other souls . . . it is easy to understand the origin of that cardinal motive of human life which is a tendency and a striving to absorb or be absorbed in or united with other lives and all lives. This passion

for losing ourselves in others or for absorbing them into ourselves . . . is the greatest expression of the law of Solidarity. . . . It is the operation of this law in great and low things, in the love of men for women, for each other, for the race . . . and for those great ideas which are the symbols of solidarity that has ever made up the web and woof of human passion.[55]

LOOKING BACKWARD (i): THE MORAL EQUIVALENT OF WAR

'The opening scene was a grand parade of a departmental division of the industrial army on the occasion of the annual muster day when the young men coming of age that year were mustered into the national service and those who that year had reached the age of exemption were mustered out.'[56]

Such, according to Bellamy, was the original plan of the first chapter in the first draft of *Looking Backward*. He finally discarded it, which was perhaps just as well, since the parallel between the industrial and the military army drawn in such precise detail might have been too close for the comfort of his generally pacific admirers. But, shorn of purely decorative detail, the fundamental analogy remained in the final version. It was, as Bellamy said, 'the corner-stone of the new social order'. The central problem of society, the organization of production, was to be solved by conceiving the nation as collectively mobilized in pursuit of its survival and sustenance. The nation in arms, dissolving all its differences and exerting itself to the utmost in the moment of collective striving against the common enemy, was to be the model for a society in which all were equally engaged in the activity of production, and all were the equal beneficiaries of their common collective effort.

Bellamy was by no means the first to see in the forms adopted for the purposes of war and destruction the possible social organization for peace and production. Behind Plato's *Republic*, and as a lesson to the quarrelsome and competitive Athenians, lay an idealized view of the military–agrarian order of ancient Sparta, with the lives of its citizens governed by the communal discipline and self-sacrifice of the militia. The medieval idea of the 'church militant' preserved something of the same analogy, and for the same purposes of emphasizing commitment and community. In both cases there was embedded a fundamental notion of moral equality, of the equal worth of all participants, which co-existed with an often rigid and sharply defined hierarchy. It was this fusion of equality and hierarchy that seems to have particularly appealed to Bellamy. Industrial organization, he accepted, required hierarchy, of a managerial and functional kind. But without a pervasive and felt sense of equality, without the conviction of an enterprise existing for common ends and common benefits, managerial hierarchy simply mirrored an exploitative social order.

The virtues of the military life, and their possible relevance to peacetime, were not lost on the generation of American intellectuals which had experienced the Civil War. There were many after 1865 who looked back nostalgically to the patriotism, courage and selflessness revealed in the armies of both North and South, and which they contrasted with the rampant self-seeking and callousness of the succeeding era of Reconstruction. The philosopher William James gave one of the best-known expressions of this feeling in his essay, 'The Moral Equivalent of War'. Here his memories of the Civil War furnished the vivid emotional background to the search for a social ethic which would summon up the same qualities of 'unstinted exertion' and 'intrepidity', 'service' and 'devotion', so readily evoked in war.[57]

Bellamy shared profoundly in this native current of feeling. But in his case European experience, both by direct observation and by general reflection, was equally compelling. The *American Fabian* pointed up the relevance of Bellamy's European travels with unusual perception when it commented, in its obituary of 1898, that 'the sight of German and Swiss festivals in honor of war prompted him to begin a story celebrating the victories of peace'.[58] Even more thought-provoking was the specific example of the Prussian army, and the demonstration of its power in the victories over Austria and France in 1866 and 1870. At one point, in striving to impress Julian West with the power and efficiency of the nationalized industrial army, Dr Leete compares it to 'such a fighting machine . . . as the German army in the time of von Moltke'.[59] The German army, in its turn, was but the most spectacular example of the general tendency among Continental nations to introduce the system of universal compulsory military service, a practice which had its origins in the revolutionary concept of the citizen army and the *levée en masse* of the French Revolution.

Bellamy is explicit about the impact of this development on the central concern of *Looking Backward*:

> The idea of committing the duty of maintaining the community to an industrial army, precisely as the duty of protecting it is entrusted to a military army, was directly suggested to me by the grand object lesson of the organization of an entire people for national purposes presented by the military system of universal service for fixed and equal terms, which has been practically adopted by the nations of Europe and theoretically adopted everywhere else as the only just and only effectual plan of public defence on a great scale. What inference could possibly be more obvious and more unquestionable than the advisability of trying to see if a plan which was found to work so well for the purposes of destruction might not be profitably applied to the business of production now in such shocking confusion.

What started off as a 'vaguely conceived' analogy became, in the writing, a firmer realization of

> the full potency of the instrument I was using, and [I] recognised in the modern military system not merely a rhetorical analogy for a national industrial service, but its prototype, furnishing at once a complete working model for its organisation, an arsenal of patriotic and national motives and arguments for its animation, and the unanswerable demonstration of its feasibility drawn from the actual experience of whole nations organised and manoeuvred as armies.[60]

It is this structure, of sentiment as well as of society, that Julian West has to understand before he can become a member of the new society. His awakening has to be symbolic as well as literal. Listening to Dr Leete's explanations, Julian's confusion is often as much emotional as intellectual. He has been brought up as a regular member of the nineteenth-century bourgeoisie, with all the emotional attitudes corresponding to that upbringing. His greatest difficulty is to understand how it is that people will do things without the 'normal' material incentives, still less without the fear of hunger, poverty or coercion. In attempting to convince him of the reality of this, Dr Leete again and again finds that the most persuasive way is to remind him of the ethos of the military organization of his own day.

It has to be said that Bellamy hardly even begins to exploit the artistic possibilities of this situation. An opportunity is presented of demonstrating the abstract philosophy of 'the Religion of Solidarity' within the concrete context of a social system explicitly designed according to its underlying principles. There is the classic but promising situation of an unregenerate member of the old society gradually, through interaction with specific members of the new society, coming to an awareness of a new social ethic as well as a new social order. William Morris and H. G. Wells, borrowing the initial idea directly from Bellamy, put it to far more successful use, in a purely literary sense. (So, for a different purpose, did Swift.) Of all the literary utopias considered in this book, Bellamy's is in fact the least interesting, considered as literature. Bellamy clearly felt the urgency of his theme to be too important to be 'dressed up' properly as fiction, according to all the best models and conventions. It is almost with pride that he confesses that, in the final version of *Looking Backward*, 'barely enough story was left to decently drape the skeleton of the argument and not enough, I fear, in spots, for even that purpose.'[61] In refusing to attend seriously to the literary form of utopia, Bellamy was also rejecting his own past, as a romancer and story-teller. He was self-consciously taking on a new, more purposive role, as social critic and prophet. But in doing so he also ensured that, once his ideas had been generally absorbed, or were no longer considered interesting, there was little to attract a later generation to his book.

The basic outline of the story, of the sleeper who awakes hundreds of years later, influenced a whole generation of utopian and 'science fiction' writers. The hero, Julian West, is the scion of a wealthy Boston family in late nineteenth-century America. It is a tense period. The capitalist system is in one of its periodic crises. There are intense conflicts between labour and capital. The economy still has not recovered from the great slump of 1873. There are strikes, and various other kinds of labour unrest. The activities of small groups of anarchists and communists alarm the upper classes. Julian, although contemptuous of these fears, has his own personal reason for hating the workers. Strikes in the building trade are delaying the completion of his new house, and so also his marriage to the beautiful and wealthy Edith Bartlett.

Julian is an insomniac. He sleeps in an underground vault, known only to his manservant and the professional hypnotist who regularly puts him into a trance at night. The servant has been taught how to bring Julian out of the trance in the morning. One night the house burns down, and the servant with it. Julian is presumed dead. Still under the trance, he sleeps on, to awake in the year 2000, in the family home of Dr and Mrs Leete and their daughter Edith.

The society into which Julian is 'reborn' has some familar utopian features. The physical structures show the influence of the 'city beautiful' movement of late nineteenth-century America, the movement that produced the utopian design of cities like Chicago and San Fransisco. Julian's first awareness of the difference between the old and the new world comes with the sight of Boston in the year 2000:

> at my feet lay a great city. Miles of broad streets, shaded by trees and lined with fine buildings, for the most part not in continuous blocks but set in larger or smaller enclosures, stretched in every direction. Every quarter contained large open squares filled with trees, among which statues glistened and fountains flashed in the late-afternoon sun. Public buildings of a colossal size and architectural grandeur unparalleled in my day raised their stately piles on every side. (*LB*, p. 115)

Bellamy follows conventional lines, too, in making his utopia one of abundance. The problem of scarcity having been solved by a rational organization of production, such old virtues as parsimony and thrift are now otiose. 'No man any more has any care for the morrow, either for himself or his children, for the nation guarantees the nurture, education, and comfortable maintenance of every citizen from the cradle to the grave' (*LB*, p. 149). For ordinary purposes of personal consumption, every one gets an equal income, irrespective of the nature or amount of his work. But such income does not come in the form of money, for money has been abolished, along with banks, middle-men and private exchange. There is instead a system of direct distribution from national storehouses. Each citizen is annually given a credit corresponding to his (equal) share of the annual product of the nation. A credit card allows him to procure goods from the public storehouses. In a much needed *entr'acte*, Edith Leete takes Julian shopping. He sees one of the many national stores, magnificent public buildings laid out with the refined elegance of a Knightsbridge or Fifth Avenue department store. Edith stresses that these stores carry merely samples from the big central distributing warehouses – one chooses from the store for eventual delivery from the warehouses. Julian notes, as do many contemporary advocates of direct selling from warehouses, the enormous saving in labour and cost produced by this system.

But who decides what goods to produce? The state socialist societies of Eastern Europe have frequently embarrassed themselves and enraged their consumers by overproducing unwanted goods and underproducing those most sought by consumers. The difficulty appears inherent in a system of bureaucratic allocation, as opposed to one based on market response. In Bellamy's socialist utopia, there is a close monitoring of consumer demand, based on statistical returns from the national warehouses, so that production is geared as far as possible to consumer preference. But to take account of minority tastes, and to counteract errors of the system, the authorities are compelled to produce any article petitioned for by the public. This ingenious touch goes some way at least to dealing with the problem of bureaucratic remoteness and indifference; although it can hardly be said that Bellamy faces up to the difficulty of its practical operation.

Here, as in several other places, it is clear that Bellamy's casual attitude derives from the enormous confidence which he reposes in the central institution of the society, the system of the national industrial army. The industrial army structures not simply work, but also politics, and in general regulates the entire life of the society. It provides the ethos and organization for production, and for the selection of the principal administrative officers of the nation. In the general character of its working Bellamy again and again finds the solution to so many of the problems of incentive and motivation which plagued the managers of the old industrial system.

After a varied education to the age of 21, everyone – men and women – enters the industrial army. For the first three years, all recruits belong to the unclassified grade of 'common labourers', during which they learn the habits of obedience and work discipline. During this period they also select the particular kind of work which they wish to engage in for the remainder of their working lives, and the next stage is their enrollment as apprentices in that trade or occupation. At the end of their apprenticeship they become 'full workmen', and a member of a particular trade or guild. Their performance as apprentices determines which grade of worker they will become – first, second or third. Everyone is encouraged to aspire to, and compete for, the higher grades, the prime inducement being that only those in the higher grades are allowed to specialize in a particular aspect of their occupation. A further inducement comes from the public esteem given to members of the higher grades, an esteem acknowledged in the form of various honorific emblems worn by higher-grade workers. Membership of the higher grades in turn makes one eligible for offices within the guild, and eventually for the highest offices in the nation, including the presidency.

Thus emulation is encouraged, and a hierarchy of rank within the industrial army clearly exists. But the hierarchy is one of status and honour only, since all ranks are equally paid, and all are equally supported by the nation throughout their lives. For Julian, this situation persistently provokes two questions. First, given the equality of income and, generally, of condition, how can anyone be persuaded to do the 'dirty work' in society – the hard, monotonous and sometimes dangerous work to which the lower classes of Julian's day were condemned? Second, how are people motivated to work at all? Why do they strive conscientiously in their trade, and compete for the higher grades, when their material circumstances will not be affected by the promotion?

These are questions which have repeatedly been put to socialists, since the earliest statements of socialist philosophy at the beginning of the nineteenth century. They gained fresh relevance with the creation of socialist economies in a number of countries in this century: Russia, Yugoslavia, China and Cuba, among others. With regard to the latter, the answers to the questions have become only too clear; or rather, we might better say, the relevance of the questions themelves now appears doubtful. Despite public ownership of the means of production, inequalities of income, status and power have all rapidly reappeared within the socialist states. Success within the educational system, and in the struggles for power within the party bureaucracies of the state and economy, clearly brings its rewards in very traditional forms.

Socialist theory has therefore to come to terms with these problems of motivation and incentive without much help from the practices of so-called socialist states. Bellamy's treatment of these questions is interesting partly for its representativeness, that is, for its detailed exposition of what was to become a familiar form of the socialist argument. But it is interesting also for the way it fits so neatly into Bellamy's primary vision of the nation militant.

For Bellamy, as for Marx and Engels, many of the conventional difficulties of work organization and the work ethic are solved by the very transition that produces the new society in the first place. The transition, that is to say, is educative: it teaches and prepares members of society for a new social order and a new social ethic. 'In revolutionary activity', Marx had written, 'change of self coincides with change of circumstances'. Bellamy's new society has come into being by evolution, not revolution. But the distinction is not crucial even in Marxism, still less in other kinds of socialism; and Bellamy's account of how the change came about is essentially the same as that prophesied in such popular Marxist accounts as Engels's *Socialism, Utopian and Scientific.*

Dr Leete describes for Julian the evolution of society during his century-long sleep. The concentration of capital went on apace, and with it the increasingly agonized resistance of labour, and certain residual groups such as small businessmen and small farmers. The impotence of this resistance, and the relentless movement towards industrial concentration, led men eventually to reflect in a different way on the significance of this development. They acknowledged the unprecedented prosperity of the capitalist system, and 'the vast economies effected by concentration of management and unity of organisation'. There was no going back to an older, more primitive, order of capitalism. The 'mighty wealth-producing principle of consolidated capital' should and could be made to work for the benefit of all, and not simply for the wealthy capitalists.

> The movement toward the conduct of business by larger and larger aggregations of capital, the tendency towards monopolies, which had been so desperately and vainly resisted, was recognised at last, in its true significance, as a process which only needed to complete its logical evolution to open a golden future to humanity. Early in the last century the evolution was completed by the final consolidation of the entire capital of the nation. The industry and commerce of the country, ceasing to be conducted by a set of irresponsible corporations and syndicates of private persons at their caprice and for their profit, were entrusted to a single syndicate representing the people, to be conducted in the common interest for the common profit. The nation, that is to say, organised as the one great business corporation in which all other corporations were absorbed; it became the one great capitalist in the place of all other capitalists, the sole employer, the final monopoly in which all the previous and lesser monopolies were swallowed up, a monopoly in the profits and economies of which all citizens shared. The epoch of trusts had ended in The Great Trust. (*LB*, pp. 126–7)

Julian, mindful of his own bitter feelings towards the workers, comments that so 'stupendous a change' must have been accompanied by 'great bloodshed and terrible convulsions'. But the revolution has been bloodless. Along with the recognition of the inherent logic of the capitalistic system, its tendency to abolish itself at the structural level, there has been a parallel growth in consciousness of the necessity and desirability of the socialist system. As Marx had predicted in *Capital*, it was the capitalists themselves who had educated society in this direction, so preparing the way for their own supersession. Dr Leete explains:

The change had long been foreseen. Public opinion had become fully ripe for it, and the whole mass of the people was behind it. There was no more possibility of opposing it by force than by argument. On the other hand the popular sentiment toward the great corporations and those identified with them had ceased to be one of bitterness, as they came to realize their necessity as a link, a transition phase, in the evolution of the true industrial system. The most violent foes of the great private monopolies were now forced to recognise how invaluable and indispensable had been their office in educating the people up to the point of assuming control of their own business. Fifty years before, the consolidation of the industries of the country under national control would have seemed a very daring experiment to the most sanguine. But by a series of object lessons, seen and studied by all men, the great corporations had taught the people an entirely new set of ideas on this subject. They had seen for many years syndicates handling revenues greater than those of states, and directing the labors of hundreds of thousands of men with an efficiency and an economy unattainable in smaller operations. It had come to be recognised as an axiom that the larger the business, the simpler the principles that can be applied to it; that, as the machine is truer than the hand, so the system, which in a great concern does the work of a master's eye in a small business, turns out more accurate results. Thus it came about that, thanks to the corporations themselves, when it was proposed that the nation should assume their functions, the suggestion implied nothing which seemed impracticable even to the timid. (*LB*, pp. 127–8)

Such an elemental shift in consciousness itself supplies most of the requirements for the ordered working of the industrial system. The 'labour question' dissolves when the nation becomes the sole employer, and all citizens 'become employees, to be distributed according to the needs of industry'. Julian, struck by a host of perplexing problems in this arrangement, remarks that 'human nature itself must have changed very much.' Dr Leete's reply is an echo of Marx's, quoted earlier: 'The conditions of human life have changed, and with them the motives of human action.' There is a willing commitment to the system. Industrial service is as natural and acceptable as military service had been regarded in the old days. It is seen as an equal and necessary obligation on all citizens. Individuals are given the chance, during their education, to discover the work that most fits their natural aptitutdes, and as a general rule are able to pursue this work in later life. Since, as might be expected, it turns out that some trades are oversubscribed and others undersubscribed, the administration has a simple but effective device for balancing supply and demand. It regulates the number of hours that have to be spent at work according to the attractiveness of the job, as shown by the level of demand for that particular kind of work.

The lighter trades, prosecuted under the most agreeable circumstances, have in this way the longest hours, while an arduous trade, such as mining, has very short hours. There is no theory, no *a priori* rule, by which the respective attractiveness of industries is determined. The administration, in taking burdens off one class of workers and adding them to other classes, simply follows the fluctuations of opinion among the workers themselves as indicated by the rate of men volunteering. The principle is that no man's work ought to be, on the whole, harder for him than any other man's for him, the workers themselves to be the judges. There are no limits to the application of this rule. (*LB*, pp. 134–5)

Bellamy was not the inventor but the highly influential carrier of this idea for achieving some sort of equality in work. It turns up in several utopias in the succeeding centuries – in Skinner's *Walden Two*, for instance. But in Bellamy's utopia it plays a subordinate role. As a simple technique it ensures that workers feel that a reasonably just distribution of effort is arrived at. But for Bellamy, the truly important thing is that all citizens, irrespective of their abilities and efforts, feel part of a common system. They are not therefore preoccupied with getting the most out of it for the least effort on their part (as under the old system). In return, the system always treats them also as full and equal participants, whatever the nature of their contribution. Julian, probing the question of 'wage differentials', asks: 'by what title does the individual claim his particular share [of the national product]?' Dr Leete replies that 'his title is his humanity. The basis of his claim is the fact that he is a man.' This revelation of an equality of income, irrespective of merit, provokes Julian to declare that it is an unfair system that rewards unequal contributions equally, not allowing that some people add to the national product more than others. 'Desert,' says Dr Leete, 'is a moral question, and the amount of product a material quantity. It would be an extraordinary sort of logic which should try to determine a moral question by a material standard. The amount of the effort alone is pertinent to the question of desert. All men who do their best, do the same' (*LB*, p. 152).

Julian tries a different tack. In his day, men put forth their best only when suitably rewarded, usually with wealth. Has human nature changed so much? Are no incentives required to stimulate the ingenuity and energy of the population? In reminding Julian of certain practices in his own society, Dr Leete provides the strongest statement of the ultimate ethical basis of the industrial army, and so of the socialist utopia as a whole. Incentives do indeed exist. But not material ones. As with military service in nineteenth-century society, the incentives are moral and social. The rewards are esteem and gratitude.

Not higher wages, but honor and the hope of men's gratitude, patriotism and the inspiration of duty, were the motives which were set before your soldiers when it was a question of dying for the nation. . . . The coarser motives, which no longer move us, have been replaced by higher motives wholly unknown to the mere wage earners of your day. Now that industry of whatever sort is no longer self-service, but service of the nation, patriotism, passion for humanity, impel the worker as in your day they did the soldier. The army of industry is an army, not alone by virtue of its perfect organization, but by reason also of the ardor of self-devotion which animates its members. (*LB*, pp. 153–4)

It is out of this visionary conception, finally, that Bellamy sees the politics of his utopia. It amounts to saying that there is virtually no place for politics in socialist society. Here Bellamy is following firmly in the tradition of much European socialism of the nineteenth century. The scheme of government he proposes indeed breathes the spirit of Saint-Simon throughout. In deriving political arrangements directly from the institutions and requirements of industry, it exemplifies the Saint-Simonian slogan (which Engels took up), 'from the government of men to the administration of things'. Where the life of society is recognized to turn on the organization of production, it is natural that politics should be based on the system of production, as well as being mostly about it.

In Bellamy's utopia, governmental officers are based entirely on the industrial army. The military analogy is worked through precisely and in detail. The hierarchy of grades within each guild culminates in the 'general' of the guild. In conventional military terms, he corresponds to the rank of major-general. Above him are the 'lieutenant-generals' who command the ten great departments of state, which are groupings of allied trades. These ten officers form the council of the general-in-chief, who is the President of the United States. Within each guild, promotion takes place on the usual bureaucratic system of selection by merit. The elective principle enters only with the position of general of each guild, and then operates for the remaining superior ranks, including the Presidency. But it is not the active members of the industrial army who compose the electorate. Rather, election is thought to be more properly the function of the retired members of the industrial army, so that the electorate is made up entirely of people over the age of 45, the age of retirement. Julian remarks that 'the method of electing officials by votes of the retired members of the guild is nothing more than the application on a national scale of the plan of government by alumni, which we used to a slight extent occasionally in the management of our higher educational institutions (*LB*, p. 220). Bellamy's intent here, as with the whole concept of the industrial army, is to urge upon his own society that the germs of the future organization of society are all already present, and need but recognition and encouragement to come to fruition.

The higher officials, once elected, have a very limited set of functions. Their main business is the smooth running of the economic system: 'Almost the sole function of the administration now is that of directing the industries of the country.' They are managers, not politicians. Bellamy, along with many socialists, clearly imagines that once the basic economic problem has been solved there really is not very much left to argue about. There is no room for the activity that is central to politics, the conflict over alternative values and goals, and the means of their realization. Nor, for that matter, is there any reason to turn to such 'parapolitical' practices as crime, the result largely of the inequities and inequalities of capitalism. What crime there is is treated as illness, as cases of atavism. This, too, greatly simplifies the scope and structure of administration and legislation. Given the general organization of society, there is indeed, as Dr Leete flatly says, 'nothing to make laws about. The fundamental principles on which our society is founded settle for all time the strifes and misunderstandings which in your day called for legislation' (*LB*, p. 230).

The influence of Saint-Simon, directly or indirectly, again comes out in one final feature of the organization of Bellamy's state. Members of the liberal professions, it turns out – the doctors and teachers as well as the artists and men of letters – do not belong to the industrial army proper. They have a parallel organization in 'faculties', governed by boards of regents which are elected by the retired members of the professions. The faculties can vote in presidential elections, and in the most general way are under the supervision of the President as the chief officer in the land, but in most important respects they are autonomous. Bellamy here comes very close to the actual Saint-Simonian proposal of a triumvirate of industrialists, scientists and artists as the directing agency of socialist society. As with Saint-Simon, the specific organization of the 'free professions' introduces a much-needed liberal and 'pluralist' element in an otherwise highly co-ordinated and integrated structure based on industry. The gesture towards the arts in the same way is an attempt to offset what seemed to be the purely utilitarian and economic preoccupation of the new society. There is, Bellamy wants to insist, a concern with other aspects of life, with learning, leisure and the arts. But it is clear from the outraged reaction that his utopia provoked on this score that Bellamy did little to allay the suspicions that this was truly an arch-philistine's utopia.

LOOKING BACKWARD (ii): MILITARISM, GIANTISM, CONSUMERISM?

Ralph Waldo Emerson, in something of a difficulty as to how to conceive workable communities in the normal conditions of American life, found in the Civil War some real hope. 'War civilizes,' he wrote, 'for it forces individuals and tribes to combine, and act with larger views, and under the best heads, and keeps the population together, producing the effect of cities; for camps are wandering cities.'[62] The same experience prompted Bellamy to remark that 'the instinct of patriotism, like the instinct of maternity, is prophetic, and looks to the future, not the present, for its full vindication'.[63] In *Looking Backward* he presented a future society in which the patriotic principle was given the fullest scope for its exercise. An ethic and an organization which had traditionally served the military function was put to work to resolve the social question.

Yesterday's utopias are so very often today's nightmares. Bellamy's utopia might almost have been calculated to ensure this fate. In making the military analogy the central aspect of his socialist society, and in choosing to emphasize the national framework by rendering socialism as 'Nationalism', Bellamy was bound, even more than other socialists, to fall under the shadow of Stalin's 'state socialism' and Hitler's 'National Socialism'. 'We read *Looking Backward*,' says Bruce Franklin, 'within a society that has fulfilled many of its predictions about the merging of capitalist monopolies with the state, and we also read it in a period after Mussolini, former leader of the Socialist Party, applied Bellamy's theories in Italy and after "National Socialism" became the title of a German political party.'[64] To the historian of socialism, Alexander Gray, writing in 1944, *Looking Backward* presented 'a rather vulgar and unattractive world of state socialism run mad'.[65] For Lewis Mumford, Bellamy's vision of a nationalized, centralized and bureaucratically co-ordinated society represents 'the archetypal megamachine. . . . *Looking Backward* turns out to be the first authentic picture of National Socialism (German style), or State Capitalism (Russian style), in its most insidiously corrupting form, that of the providential Welfare State with all its disciplinary braces relaxed – though not removed – by a massive bribe.'[66]

It is difficult to defend Bellamy against many of the main charges under these heads. We can't even say that the charges are anachronistic, although they are clearly provoked largely by twentieth-century experience. There were critics in plenty in the nineteenth century who pointed out that the socialistic schemes of the Saint-Simonians and the Marxists involved an excessive degree of centralization and bureaucratization.[67] Bellamy however ignores much of this criticism. There is virtually no discussion of the problems of alienation and control posed by the existence of large-scale bureaucracies. No concessions are made to the possibility of administrative malfunctioning or of bureaucratic stupidity and incompetence. No shadow of doubt clouds the confident belief in the power of large-scale technology to produce an abundance of goods, without end. There is the barest admission of the danger of the rise of a new ruling elite, based on its centralized control of the entire economy and society. Bellamy seems to find nothing worrying in the fact that, when the nation becomes 'the one great capitalist', the public managers and administrators enjoy a unique degree of access to and control over resources previously monopolized by private capitalists.

Whether or not Bellamy was aware of these problems, it is clear that he would have regarded most of them as negligible. The fundamental step once taken, that of organizing production according to the principle of the industrial army, Bellamy seems to feel that all remaining difficulties become amenable to rational discussion and resolution. There are no basic conflicts of interest to interfere with this natural process of collaboration in the common interest. As with Marx, it is the irrationality of capitalist society which preoccupies Bellamy; the nationalization of private property removes that central irrationality, and all else pales into insignificance.

A vivid illustration of this belief occurs at the very end of the novel. Julian West has a nightmare in which he imagines that he has woken up back in the world of nineteenth-century Boston. Dr Leete, his daughter Edith and their whole wonderful world have simply been a beautiful dream, the 'figments of a vision'. It is, from a literary point of view, perhaps the most effective part of the whole work. In Tolstoy's copy of *Looking Backward* this section is, as earlier noted, especially heavily marked. In a numbed state, Julian wanders around the familiar landmarks of the city, the shops, banks and businesses now revealed to him in their appallingly true colours as the emblems of greed and exploitation. In despair and practically on the verge of breakdown, he witnesses a military parade, and some hope revives.

> A regiment was passing. It was the first sight in that dreary day which had inspired me with any other emotions than wondering pity and amazement. Here at last were order and reason, an exhibition of what intelligent co-operation can accomplish. The people who stood looking on with kindling faces – could it be that the sight had for them no more than but a spectacular interest? Could they fail to see that it was their perfect concert of action, their organization under one control, which made these men the tremendous engine they were, able to vanquish a mob ten times as numerous? Seeing this so plainly, could they fail to compare the scientific manner in which the nation went to war with the unscientific manner in which it went to work? (*LB*, p. 304)

We may shudder a little at the awful singleness of the conception, and even more at the actual phrasing, reminiscent of a score of memoirs by ageing fascists and militarists. But it is too simple to dismiss the whole of Bellamy's vision as the innocent anticipation of totalitarian Fascism or Stalinism. Just as in the case of Plato, or Hegel, or Marx – to name three others who have been tarred with the same brush – the practical dangers inherent in realizing the vision have to be set against the force of the overall conception of society, and the importance of the goals thereby embraced. It all depends on the nature of our interest: in the whole or in the parts, in the social philosophy or in its (variable) institutional embodiment. At times, the urgency of the situation posits the greater need for overall goals and 'utopian' conceptions. The practical difficulties of pursuing the goals are noted, but are regarded in the light of the value of the vision as a whole.

In Bellamy's case, the turn of the historical cycle makes this consideration especially significant. Doubtful as we might be as to the feasibility or desirability of many of the practices he advocates, his insight into the power of a mobilized society harnessed to a socialist ethic has a relevance today perhaps even greater than in his own time. If Bellamy thought in apocalyptic terms of the America of the 1880s, what might he feel about the present condition of the industrial societies? The prophets of doom are if anything greater in number now, and with historical hindsight we can well believe that their gloomy analyses have a firmer foundation in sober fact than those of the last decades of the nineteenth century. Bellamy thundered against the unjust distribution of the fruits of economic development, but what when economic growth stops altogether? What when natural resources become so heavily exploited that the possibility of their exhaustion can plausibly be advanced? What when technological developments, in industry, communications and warfare, at once unify the world and threaten to extinguish it?

Faced with problems of this scale, many contemporary thinkers have turned with remarkable frequency to the idea that is basic to Bellamy: that of society mobilized, as in war, in the face of a great national emergency. At one level there is the invocation, common in the rhetoric of politicians in power, of 'the Dunkirk spirit', accompanied by the call for us all to tighten our belts, give of our best, and face up to our grim condition of a static economy and a falling standard of living. A similar thought informs the many schemes now being canvassed of a revived form of 'national service', conceived now not primarily in terms of training for war, but in terms of developing a common ethic of service and social responsibility, and of inspiring and evoking the energies of the potentially vast number of unemployed young people in the coming years. Most significant of all is the recourse to similar devices by scholars concerned with the anatomy and the long-term implications of the present crisis of industrial societies. In the works of Robert Heilbroner and Fred Hirsch, for instance, who explore what they regard as the basic impasse of current lines of economic and social development, the situation is seen as so desperate, the structural problems so profound and wide-ranging, that only a massive collective effort of will can offer any hope of avoiding disaster.[68] Hirsch appeals for a new social morality, emphasizing communal restraint and sacrifice, to offset the individualist and acquisitive ethic which is destroying the social foundations of liberal capitalist societies. Heilbroner more radically sees the need for a form of 'religious politicism', akin to that achieved for a time in Mao's China, which will provide a new ethos and a new social organization more fitted to the needs of the coming difficult years. In these clear echoes of Bellamy's 'Religion of Solidarity', as well as the militant society in his *Looking Backward*, we may see the continuing relevance of his conception, and the powerful potential it contains for prescriptive action in conditions of crisis.

In some ways, indeed, it is relatively easy to deal with the charges of militarism and totalitarianism, since they are so familiar, in relation not simply to Bellamy's society but to practically the whole utopian tradition. Total conceptions, the usual utopian style, not unnaturally often lead to totalitarian societies. To say this is neither to excuse them nor to dismiss the charges as trivial or irrelevant. But it suggests that this aspect of Bellamy's society is better discussed as a general problem of utopian theory, rather than by itself; and this is done elsewhere in this book. There is however a different kind of criticism of Bellamy's society which cannot be so conveniently or easily dealt with. In this, Bellamy's utopia is renounced not so much for its militaristic character as for its mechanical soullessness: its consumerism, passivity and generally narrow conception of the possibilities of human life and human fulfilment.

The critic here is William Morris: directly in *News from Nowhere*, and indirectly in the whole tradition of utopian thought that takes its inspiration from him. *Looking Backward* so incensed Morris, and its success so alarmed him, that he set about producing a sketch of what a truly socialist society might be like.[69] In doing so he made no attempt to imitate Bellamy's painstaking attention to the details of economic organization, education and public administration. This was not because he thought these things unimportant, but because he regarded them as secondary, as a means rather than, as seemed with Bellamy, the ends of socialist society. *News from Nowhere* carries the mood of its form, the dream-like fantasy, into every detail of the socialist society depicted. It is truly, as its last line proclaims, a vision, an evocation of the feel and quality of life in a totally different society from the capitalist present. The criticism of Bellamy is implicit: in a way of describing the look of people, and their relations with each other; in a particular sense of nature, as landscape, and as a way and means of life; and in the description of scenes of everyday life, in the shop and the street, at leisure and at work. This is not, we should note, a technique for disparaging Bellamy by ignoring him. By concentrating on the very things that Bellamy seems to think slight, and elevating them to a position of cardinal importance in a socialist society, Morris offers a direct challenge to Bellamy's conception of socialism.

In his review of *Looking Backward* for *The Commonweal*, Morris states that 'the only safe way of reading a Utopia is to consider it as the expression of the temperament of its author.' Bellamy, Morris contends, is representative of the 'unmixed modern' temperament, 'unhistoric and unartistic'. He is the kind of socialist who is

> perfectly satisfied with modern civilization, if only the injustice, misery, and waste of class society could be got rid of; which half change seems possible to him. The only ideal

of life which such a man can see is that of the industrious *professional* middle-class men of today purified from their crime of complicity with the monopolist class, and become independent instead of being, as they now are, parasitical.[70]

Since such men are satisfied 'with the best part of modern life', it follows that Bellamy can conceive the change to socialism taking place 'without any breakdown of that life, or indeed any disturbance of it', simply by the gradual evolution of a few large private monopolies into the one great public monopoly. The change is largely external and organizational; and Bellamy throughout 'has his mind fixed firmly on the mere *machinery* of life'. Given only the detailed scheme for 'the organisation of life – which is organised with a vengeance', we can conclude nothing about the quality of that life or the attitudes of the people living it. Thus

though he *tells* us that every man is free to choose his occupation and that work is no burden to anyone, the impression that he produces is that of a huge standing army, tightly drilled, compelled by some mysterious fate to unceasing anxiety for the production of wares to satisfy every caprice, however wasteful and absurd, that may cast up amongst them.[71]

This is an acute and accurate insight into Bellamy, and the character of his utopia. It is all the more penetrating for the fact that Bellamy goes out of his way to deny, explicitly, that his utopia is all work and no play, no more than a purified industrial society, with the capitalist irrationality removed but the Calvinistic ethic still intact. Work stops for all men and women at the age of 45. After that they are free to devote themselves 'to the higher exercise of our faculties, the intellectual and spiritual enjoyments and pursuits which alone mean life'. Dr Leete waxes quite lyrical on this point.

It is not our labor, but the higher and larger activities which the performance of our task will leave us free to enter upon, that are considered the main business of existence. . . . Whatever the differences between our individual tastes as to the use we shall put our leisure to, we all agree in looking forward to the date of our discharge as the time we shall first enter upon the full enjoyment of our birthright, the period when we shall first really attain our majority and become enfranchised from discipline and control, with the fee of our lives vested in ourselves. As eager boys in your day anticipated twenty-one, so men nowadays look forward to forty-five. At twenty-one we become men, but at forty-five we re-new youth. (*LB*, pp. 221–2)

This could be made to sound like Marx: 'the realm of necessity' gives way to the 'realm of freedom'; men are no longer determined but self-determining. The reason why it doesn't, why it is so unconvincing in Bellamy, is not simply that he introduces the subject very late in the book, with hardly any preparation, and in a chapter that occupies all of two pages (chapter 18): the stronger reason for suspicion is the whole treatment of the sphere of leisure and consumption in the book. This is done briefly and patchily; but enough is said to be very revealing of Bellamy's understanding of 'leisure', and his claim that it consitutes 'the main business of existence'.

Fundamentally, Bellamy remains a utilitarian in his philosophy of work and leisure. His vision is irretrievably bourgeois. Leisure (and consumption) are still seen in relation, and opposition, to work. Work is hard, necessary and painful. After 24 years of it, the members of Bellamy's society are rewarded by a long period of leisure ('pleasure'). But despite Bellamy's celebration of this period of life, it is clear from his description of the activities pursued by the retired population that he sees it in terms entirely appropriate to retired people of his own unregenerate day. It is a period of rest and relaxation, gentle recreation rather than active 're-creation'. People mostly engage in the conventional leisure pursuits of all industrial societies – sport, travel, hobbies. Indeed, the discussion of leisure takes place in the very chapter that is devoted to sports and hobbies in the new society, and the public provision of facilities for these. At the end of this brief chapter Dr Leete guilelessly remarks: 'The demand for *panem et circenses* preferred by the Roman populace is recognised nowadays as a wholly reasonable one. If bread is the first necessity of life, recreation is a close second, and the nation caters for both' (*LB*, p. 223). Julian West, previously so alert, by this time in the novel is totally disarmed and uncritical, and the sinister implication of this concept of leisure is quite lost on him. Morris however sees that for Bellamy leisure really is no more than publicly arranged 'circuses'; nor can it be anything else, given Bellamy's mechanical separation of the sphere of work, considered as necessity, and the sphere of leisure, considered as freedom:

> it may be mentioned that everybody is to begin the serious work of production at the age of twenty-one, work three years as a labourer, and then choose his skilled occupation and work till he is forty-five, when he is to knock off his work and amuse himself (improve his mind, if he has one left him). Heavens! think of a man of forty-five changing all his habits suddenly and by compulsion![72]

Bellamy's imprisonment in the middle-class outlook of his day is revealed in a further, related, separation: that of production from consumption. Although in theory workers now produce for themselves, and not for private capitalists who sell the products of their labour in the market, in Bellamy's account the activities of production and consumption remain stubbornly separate experiences. For all the discussion of the organization of work and production, Julian West never observes anyone actually at work. He gets no impression of what work means to them, whether it is fulfilling or alienating, whether they feel they are in truth working for themselves, or still yet another, the 'one great capitalist' and 'sole employer'. The unified sensibility, linking work and non-work life, that Bellamy claims for the members of his utopia remains assertion. It is not demonstrated. Goods and services appear to be produced anonymously, in huge centralized complexes, from which they are distributed to the large warehouses and showrooms. The consumers who purchase from these appear to have a very similar relation to them as shoppers at any large department store under capitalism. Bellamy has simplified the system and magnified the scale, and it is clearly more efficient; but it seems to embody the same impersonality and 'fetishism of commodities' that Marx saw underlying the system of capitalism.

Julian West's experiences in the new society are in fact confined largely to the private life of its members. And very private it appears to be. Despite the communal aspirations of the 'Religion of Solidarity', life in the year 2000 still seems to revolve around the private realm of domesticity and its ancillary activities. Julian never meets anyone outside the nuclear family circle of Dr Leete, nor is anyone else even mentioned as neighbour, colleague or friend. Even when meals are taken in the public dining-room, each family has reserved ('for a small annual rent') its own private table in a private booth, and so can keep the family group separate and intact. But there is always home – family life is still centred on private houses and apartments, and the alternative of meals taken at home is always available. Domestic life is aided by extensive labour-saving devices and even, by expending some 'income credits', by specialized domestic service. The wealthy middle classes of Bellamy's day would have been pleasantly surprised at how few of the amenities that made up their domestic comforts would have to be sacrificed in the new society.

Since all washing is done at public laundries, cooking at public kitchens, and clothes repaired at public workshops, there are some solid grounds for Julian's exclamation, 'What a paradise for womankind the world must be now!' Bellamy's society indeed goes some way towards realizing the socialist promise of equalizing the lives of men and women. Women, like children, are economically independent of husbands and parents, and are maintained, like men, directly by the state. Dr Leete's comments on the previous condition of women are unusually sharp:

> It seems to us that women were more than any other class the victims of your civilization. There is something which, even at this distance of time, penetrates one with pathos in the spectacle of their ennuied, undeveloped lives, stunted at marriage, their narrow horizon, bounded so often, physically, by the four walls of home, and morally by a petty circle of personal interests. . . . From the great sorrows, as well as the petty frets of life, they had no refuge in the breezy outdoor world of human affairs, nor any interests save those of the family. (*LB*, p. 265)

But the answer has not been to equalize the roles and tasks of the sexes as demanded 'by some reformers in your day'. Women, having been largely freed from household tasks, belong to the industrial army, but in a parallel branch to the men, with their own female general-in-chief and 'under exclusively feminine regime'. Being physically weaker than men, the lighter occupations are reserved for them, and they have shorter hours and more frequent vacations. Dr Leete warns that society must respect the differences between the sexes every bit as much as it acknowledges their common features. 'In your day there was no career for women except in an unnatural rivalry with men. We have given them a world of their own, with its emulations, ambitions, and careers, and I assure you that they are very happy with it' (*LB*, p. 265). Such a regime of sexual *apartheid* might please some of the radical feminists of today. But it can scarcely satisfy socialists, and seems to owe more to Bellamy's Victorian patriarchalism than to any anticipation of feminine separatism. In any case, the character and activities of Edith and Mrs Leete are so entirely cast in the conventional feminine mould that here, too, Bellamy's vision seems blinkered by the perceptions of the middle-class professional male of his time.

It is worth remarking that, to the exent that we get a glimpse of 'socialized' activities in the sphere of consumption, the spectacle can only corroborate the fears of those who predict mass passivity and mass conditioning under socialism. In Bellamy's future society, the main form of entertainment – indeed, the main form of culture as a whole, it appears – is the radio. Technically, the signals are delivered by telephone rather than radio waves but the system is identical in most other respects to the modern one. Instead of attending church, concerts and other public events, people can listen to sermons, music or speeches and discussions in their own homes. Music, of different kinds, is on tap 24 hours a day. All private and amateur performances are devalued. Edith Leete declines to sing or play for Julian, remarking:

> the professional music is so much grander and more perfect than any performance of ours, and so easily commanded when we wish to hear it, that we don't think of calling our singing or playing music at all. . . . I suppose it was the difficulties in the way of commanding really good music which made you endure so much playing and singing in your homes by people who had only the rudiments of the art. (*LB*, p. 163, 166).

She commends the system, particularly for its soothing effects at night, to Julian, who not surprisingly has been having some difficulty sleeping since his awakening in the year 2000: 'with the receiver at your ear, I am quite sure you will be able to snap your fingers at all sorts of uncanny feelings if they trouble you again.'

If *Nineteen Eighty-Four* has already raised an anticipatory head, shades of *Brave New World* hover over this statement. They return again when Julian is marvelling over a novel of the new age, struck not so much by the elements in it as by those, necessary in the great novels of his day, which have been left out: 'all effects drawn from the contrasts of wealth and poverty, education and ignorance, coarseness and refinement, high and low, all motives drawn from social pride and ambition, the desire of being richer or the fear of being poorer, together with sordid anxieties of any sort for one's self or others. . . .' None of these devices, we gather, is employed in the novel of the future; but we wonder what kind of romance it can be, 'in which there should, indeed, be love galore, but love unfretted by artificial barriers . . .' (*LB*, pp. 204–5).

The utopian impulse towards a uniform, carefree, undemanding world is at work here with a vengeance. It is in these sections that *Looking Backward* most deserves Morris's dismissal of it as a 'cockney paradise'. In his anxiety to suggest the bliss that is achieved with the coming of socialism, Bellamy commits the common utopian error of equating that bliss with the instant gratification and unreflecting happiness of the land of Cokaygne. Marx had struggled to show that, in the communist future, the passive and consumerist ethos of bourgeois society would be reversed. Instead of taking the world as it is, as eternally given with its unchanging 'nature', men would be ceaselessly active in the making and remaking of themselves and their environment. Bellamy is too hard-headed to fall victim to the worst kinds of utopian fantasy, with their childlike vision of lemonade seas and beatific idleness. But this very matter-offactness inhibits his imagination where most it needs to be exercised. In his socialist utopia the forms of bourgeois capitalist society are changed. Property is nationalized, there is equality of wealth, every one is guaranteed security as to their material and physical well-being. But much of the spirit of bourgeois society remains. People's attitudes towards themselves and their world continue to be locked in a traditional series of oppositions; between work (necessity) and leisure (freedom), consumption and production, art and utility, the private life of family and the public life of society. Things are done to and for individuals, instead of by them.

One cannot help discerning here a vein of religious fatalism in Bellamy, which crops up frequently in his earlier short stories as well as in 'The Religion of Solidarity'. His temperamental leanings are towards taking man out of this world, rather than making him master within it. Socialism achieves, by secular, scientific means, that transcendental identification of the individual and the universe that Bellamy had always yearned for. For Marx (and for Morris), this is a beginning, the beginning of human history proper, where man becomes the active determining author of his own being and existence. For Bellamy, it seems to be more like an end: the end of the long history of suffering and exploitation, to be consummated now in the calm and quiet of reconciliation. Bellamy's conception of harmony is one where there is no struggle or striving, no need for painful exertion in pursuit either of one's bread or one's happiness. In such a view it is not surprising, as Morris notes, that Bellamy's 'only idea of making labour tolerable is to decrease the amount of it by means of fresh and ever fresh developments of machinery'.[73] Indeed, one presumes that Bellamy's ultimate goal is the cessation of all human labour – but for what further end? Contemplation?

At the conclusion of his review of *Looking Backward*, Morris, concerned that Bellamy's book by its very success might come to be taken as 'the Socialist bible of reconstruction', puts forward an alternative view of socialism:

> It is necessary to point out that there are some Socialists who do not think that the problem of the organisation of life and necessary labour can be dealt with by a huge national centralisation, working by a kind of magic for which no one feels himself responsible; that on the contrary it will be necessary for the unit of administration to be small enough for every citizen to feel himself responsible for its details, and be interested in them; that individual men cannot shuffle off the business of life on to the shoulders of an abstraction called the State, but must deal with it in conscious association with each other: that variety of life is as much an aim of a true Communism as equality of condition, and that nothing but a union of these two will bring about real freedom: that modern nationalities are mere artificial devices for the commercial war that we seek to put an end to, and will disappear with it. And, finally, that art, using that word in its widest and due signification, is not a mere adjunct of life which free and happy men can do without, but the necessary expression and indispensable instrument of human happiness.[74]

The precise terms of this attractive conception will have to be inspected more carefully, later in this book. For the moment we may say that, in this contrast between Bellamy and Morris, we have a useful point of reference for the discussion of socialism and utopia. Bellamy may seem to have come off badly. Certainly, with the example and the experience of the 'state socialism' of Eastern Europe constantly before our eyes, it is difficult for Western industrial societies to feel particularly drawn to it, or to imagine that it would or could be very different were it attempted here. But if, as solution, Bellamy's utopia is much less convincing than first appeared to an impressed world, nearly a hundred years ago, as criticism of the moral and social order of capitalism it still carries great force. Few readers are likely to forget the extended parable with which the book opens, in which Julian West likens nineteenth-century capitalist society

> to a prodigious coach which the masses of humanity were harnessed to and dragged toilsomely along a very hilly and sandy road. The driver was hunger, and permitted no lagging, though the pace was necessarily very slow. Despite the difficulty of drawing the coach at all along so hard a road, the top was covered with passengers who never got down, even at the steepest ascents. Those seats on top were very breezy and comfortable. (*LB*, p. 97)

The character of the road has changed a little, and other needs have joined hunger in the driving seat; but the sorry spectacle of the mass of humanity being led by the nose is as accurate as ever.

6

Science and Utopia: H. G. Wells and *A Modern Utopia*

The things that might be done today! The things indeed that are being done! It is the latter that give one so vast a sense of the former. When I think of the progress of physical and mechanical science, of medicine and sanitation during the last century, when I measure the increase in general education and average efficiency, the power now available for human service, the merely physical increment, and compare it with anything that has ever been at man's disposal before, and when I think of what a little straggling, incidental, undisciplined and unco-ordinated minority of inventors, experimenters, educators, writers and organizers has achieved this development of human possibilities, achieved it in spite of the disregard and aimlessness of the huge majority, and the passionate resistance of the active dull, my imagination grows giddy with dazzling intimations of the human splendours the justly organized state may yet attain. I glimpse for a bewildering instant the heights that may be scaled, the splendid enterprises made possible . . . .

H. G. Wells, *The New Machiavelli* (1911)

The difference between us is fundamental. You don't care for humanity but think they are to be improved. I love humanity but know they are not.

Joseph Conrad to H. G. Wells, 25 September 1908[1]

THE DISCOVERY OF THE FUTURE

H. G. Wells is the greatest of the modern utopists – his own preferred term – even though he never wrote a proper utopia, in the strict sense. He is the leading apostle of the utopia of science, and yet his apocalyptic visions of the disasters science may bring were the source of the dystopias and anti-utopias of the twentieth century. His advocacy of planning and organization was classically utopian, and yet in his personal and professional life he was the least organized and utopian of men.

None of these paradoxes is unfamiliar, and only the second is really important for our purposes. But they do suggest that Wells's utopianism is not to be found readily distilled in one or two books, or neatly packed for easy summary. Although specific utopian projects abound in his writings, it is in the writings and public advocacy as a whole that the force of his utopianism becomes apparent. For his contemporaries, Wells was throughout his long life utopianism incarnate. Where it was not spelled out, the utopian striving was implicit in practically everything he wrote. It is there in the tone of the writing as much as in any ostensible subject. Whether in the science fiction, the social novels or the journalism, Wells put into his writing a quality of yearning, of things possible 'if only', that marks him off as distinctly as any English writer. Great things were afoot, and Wells expressed this sense and this hope more completely than any of his contemporaries. 'I flung myself into futurity', says his Time-Traveller in *The Time Machine*, and the same could be said of Wells himself. Phrases like 'the new civilization', 'the new society' and 'the new world' came naturally and, as it were, unconsciously to him. The very titles of his books are instinct with utopianism: *Anticipations, Mankind in the Making, New Worlds for Old, The World Set Free, Men Like Gods, The Shape of Things to Come.*

'New' was indeed the keyword of the age in which Wells grew to early manhood, the late Victorian and Edwardian age. In that sense his utopianism was a representative response, although it went well beyond the expression of his English contemporaries. There was Art Nouveau, the New Novel of Zola, the New Drama of Ibsen and Shaw, the New Music of Wagner, the New Journalism of Newnes's *Tit-bits* and Northcliffe's *Daily Mail*, the new Unionism of the unskilled trades, and the New Woman of the feminist movement. In the 1880s and the 1890s, any article in search of a buyer found it expedient to call itself 'new'. Wells's formative years occurred in a period when the great Victorian equipoise was beginning to be shaken to its core. The cult of modernity, with a new emphasis on the word 'modern' as the desired progressive quality of novelty in art, politics or morals, dates from this time. 'Transition', 'renovation' and 'reconstruction' were all terms commonly met with; but so too were 'decadence' and 'decline'. The *fin de siècle* mood in one influential aspect was powerfully captured by Max Nordau in his book *Degeneration* (1895):

> One epoch of history is unmistakeably in its decline, and another is announcing its approach. There is a sound of rending in every tradition, and it is as though the morrow would not link itself with today. Things as they are totter and plunge, and they are suffered to reel and fall, because man is weary, and there is no faith that is worth an effort to uphold them. Views that have hitherto governed minds are dead or driven hence like disenthroned kings, and for their inheritance they that hold the titles and they that would usurp are locked in struggle.[2]

The intellectual and artistic spirit Nordau found to be 'a curious compound of feverish restlessness and blunted discouragement, of fearful presage and hang-dog renunciation'. The juxtaposition of great hopes and equally great fears was only to be expected, as a familiar feature of all ages – such as the seventeenth century in Europe – when momentous changes were sensed. The early Victorians were by no means complacent, but they had an overall sense that the problems of the age were solvable, with God's will and human effort. Progress was an accomplished fact as well as a human tendency. By the 1860s

Anthony Trollope, writing two years after Wells's birth, was not so sure. 'It is the year of grace 1868; the roar of our machinery, the din of our revolutions, echoes through the solar system; can we not, then, make up our minds whether our progress is a reality and a gain, or a delusion and a mistake?'[3] The response was not always to play up the negative, as the century drew to a close and Victoria gave way to Edward. But the extremes of both confidence and despair grew, often in the tortured breast of the same person. Wells himself expressed this ambivalence throughout his life. In the *Autobiography* which he published in 1934 he saw his individual story as part of the story of 'the handicapped intelligence of our species, blundering heavily towards the realization and handling of vast changes and still vaster dangers and opportunities'.[4]

Wells by then had a relatively long perspective within which to judge the current efforts of the species. He had lived through one world war, seen the failure of the League of Nations, the degeneration of Bolshevism under Stalin, the rise of fascism and the world-wide economic slump. The surprising thing was the maintenance of any degree of optimism whatsoever (it took another world war to wipe that out). But in fact, Wells's generation was not quite so inclined as the immediately succeeding one to see the First World War as marking the great historical watershed. Wells would not have agreed with D. H. Lawrence (in *Kangaroo*) that 'it was in 1915 the old world ended.' For Wells and his contemporaries, such as E. M. Forster, the old world had ended long before that; and the war could be seen variously as the death-rattle of the old order or (as Wells hoped) the birth-pangs of the new.

Some people could be very definite indeed about dating the change. 'In or about December 1910, human character changed. . .', wrote Virginia Woolf in a famous essay if 1924. 'All human relations have shifted – those between masters and servants, husbands and wives, parents and children. And when human relations change there is at the same time a change in religion, conduct, politics and literature. Let us agree to place one of these changes about the year 1910.'[5] Such confidence was possible because the writer knew there would be ready assent to the general proposition. E. M. Forster's novel, *Howards End*, actually published in 1910, made much the same point. The characters are set in a social field which affirms the passing of the old England of the country house and its attendant values, and the rise of a mechanical and business civilization. Wells had the year before handled an almost identical theme in his most ambitious novel, *Tono-Bungay*. In the last years of the nineteenth century, the forces of change which had been slowly transforming England since the Industrial Revolution culminated with unnerving abruptness. The industrial population for the first time began to outnumber the agricultural population. The effects of the massive growth in population in the second half of the century – a doubling from 21 million in 1850 to 41 million in 1910 – were compounded by its increasing concentration in cities. In 1841 one in six of the population lived in cities of 10,000 or more; by 1901, the year of Victoria's death, more than a half of the population were in cities of 20,000 or more. The census of 1911 classified 80 per cent of the population as urban. By this time England was the most fully industrialized and urbanized society in the world.

Wells's own experience in the little town of Bromley in North Kent could scarcely have been more representative of these vast changes. When he was born there in 1866 Bromley was still a small market town, scarcely more than a village, of 5,000 people. The town rested amidst fields, clearly visible to all its inhabitants, and the nearby river Ravensbourne was trout-filled and visited by kingfishers. The streets were still unpaved; lighting was by oil-lamps. Travel between Bromley and London was by horse-drawn coaches and carrier carts. By the end of the century the coming of the railway had turned Bromley into a fast-growing commuter suburb of London, and the local traders were being killed off by the growth of the large London stores and daily deliveries by rail from London.

It was indeed London, the largest city in the world, that was the startling and almost monstrous phenomenon of the age. It seemed to crystallize and symbolize in awesome form all the principal developments of the time. London had grown from a population of 1¾ million in 1841 to 4½ million by the end of the century, a growth far faster than the national population as a whole. The expansion of the national railway network reconfirmed the capital's supreme importance in the political, commercial and cultural life of the nation. All the main railway lines were centred on the London termini, radiating out from there and holding the nation in a tight centralized grid for the first time in its history. London dwarfed and dominated hitherto independent provincial cities like Manchester and Birmingham. It truly seemed to aspire, as many complained, to become all England.[6]

But London was not simply the nation's capital, the metropolis; it was a 'world city', cosmopolis, the seat of the Empire and the centre of world trade. It is, Mr Ponderevo tells his nephew George in *Tono-Bungay*, 'the richest town in the world, the biggest port, the greatest manufacturing town, the Imperial city – the centre of civilization, the heart of the world . . . a whirlpool, a maelstrom!' In its vast population the whole world seemed almost literally to be represented. It was the melting pot of the many immigrant communities with their different cultures. It had its own black spots, 'outcast London', which it attempted to civilize and to which it sent missionaries like Christian countries to heathen lands. In its bewildering contrasts of the extremes of wealth and poverty, glitter and squalor, West End and East End, it seemed, like the new industrial society as a whole, to be pregnant with as many glorious possibilities as frightful disasters. George Ponderevo, coming to London like Wells himself from rural Kent, reflects: 'The whole illimitable place teemed with suggestions of indefinite and sometimes outrageous possibility, of hidden but magnificent meanings.' But as he wanders the length and breadth of the city, and sees its shapelessness and disorganization, the doubts recur, and London suggests to him

> the unorganised, abundant substance of some tumorous growth-process, a process which indeed bursts all the outlines of the affected carcass and protrudes such masses as ignoble, comfortable Croydon, as tragic improverished West Ham. To this day I ask myself will those masses ever become structural, will they indeed shape into anything new whatever, or is that cancerous image their true and ultimate diagnosis? . . .[7]

It is a scene and a perception repeated many times in Wells's novels: Lewisham wandering forlornly among the vast museums and colleges of science in South

Kensington; Kipps coming to London from Folkestone and being bewildered by its 'intricate complexity', yet struck by its wonders, which he shows off to his bride-to-be the day before their wedding. Ann Veronica too, coming to the city from suburban Surbiton, is at first almost lost, morally as well as physically, in its 'vast endlessness', but subsequently discovers there the resources to recover her spirit and assert her independence, to the point of becoming almost the archetype of the New Woman.

London in its present form, it is clear, was for Wells practically the antithesis of the utopian city. He was more impressed by the clean lines and planned order of Swiss cities like Basel, and, above all, American cities like New York, which he saw as the city of the future.[8] But London, in its vastness and cosmopolitan significance, had distinct utopian possibilities. It was, moreover, the first great city that Wells encountered, and the only one that he got to know really well. Like many other thinkers coming from rural or small-town backgrounds, he was both more overwhelmed by the metropolis and more appreciative of its sociological significance than were its native inhabitants.[9] London suggested the possibility, for the first time ever perhaps, of a wholly urban existence, in which the countryside not only is never experienced but is entirely irrelevant to the lives of urban dwellers. It was the city become society, and as such figured, in however twisted and distorted a form, in many of Wells's utopias.

Although Wells spent a good part of his life in London, and in some of his novels shows an almost Dickensian understanding of it, he always retained something of the suburbanite's distance and detachment from it. For much of his life he circled it warily, living in a variety of spots near to it but resisting a wholehearted commitment. His early years were spent in a succession of small southern towns and villages – Bromley and Midhurst, Windsor and Wookey, Southsea and Up Park – as he made his wretched progression from one failed apprenticeship to another. A scholarship to the Normal School of Science in London finally gave him his escape; but it was country life rather than the countryside itself that so depressed the clever and boundlessly inquisitive young Wells. When he had made his name as a writer and established his independence in London, he returned in more opulent style to the Home Counties, setting up homes at Woking in Surrey, Sandgate in Kent and Little Easton in Essex. It was only towards the end of his life that he finally settled in London, in Regents Park, becoming in the Second world War the very type of the cheerful cockney Londoner who refused to leave the city and shrugged off the danger from the German bombs. But in his early writings especially, the presence of the small towns and countryside around London is very strong, and is used to striking effect. One thinks here not simply of *Kipps* and *Mr Polly*, but of the Martians stalking across the Surrey hills and commons in *The War of the Worlds*, and Griffin the invisible man descending in a murderous frenzy on the quiet villages of Iping and Burdock.

In this twilight existence between town and country, *in* London but not *of* it, Wells, the self-taught lower-middle-class draper's apprentice who became a world-famous writer conversing with Roosevelt and Stalin, seems almost to have been invented by Providence to symbolize the Edwardian sense of change and transition. 'Expectancy and surprise are the notes of the age', wrote the astute Liberal politician C. F. G. Masterman in 1905. 'Expectancy belongs by nature to a time balanced uneasily between two great periods of change. On the one hand is a past still showing faint survivals of vitality; on the other is the future but hardly coming to birth. The years as they pass still appear as years of preparation, a time of waiting rather than a time of action.'[10]

Wells was never one merely to wait. From an early age the future beckoned insistently – too insistently, as it turned out. There seems something portentous in his very decision, against the strong urging of his family, to break his articles of apprenticeship and to strike off on the educational trail which led him to London and the Normal School of Science. In itself there was nothing particularly remarkable in this: many men of his background were doing much the same thing at the time. Had he performed as well as he should have done in his scientific studies at the Normal School, he would probably have ended up, like his son Gip, as a conventionally successful professor of zoology. Even when he was employed as a crammer at the London Tutorial College, and trying to launch himself as a writer, his future appeared the unremarkable one of a down-at-heel denizen of Grub Street. But Wells seemed to know that, consonant with the age, he was destined for greater things. As no English writer before or since, he lived for the future, almost, at times, in it. In English writing he can truly be said to be the discoverer of the future, although characteristically in the lecture 'The Discovery of the Future', which he gave at the Royal Institution in 1902, he attributed this spirit to the times:

> In the past century there was more change in the conditions of human life than there had been in the previous thousand years. . . . Everything seems pointing to the belief that we are entering upon a progress that will go on with an ever-widening and ever more confident stride for ever . . . . We are in the beginning of the greatest change that humanity has ever undergone.

Just as geology and archaeology had opened up the remote past to us,

> is it really, after all, such an extravagant and hopeless thing to suggest that, by seeking for operating causes instead of for fossils, and by criticising them as persistently and thoroughly as the geological record has been criticised, it may be possible to throw a searchlight of inference forward instead of backward, and to attain to a knowledge of coming things as clear, as universally convincing, and infinitely more important to mankind than the clear vision of the past that geology has opened to us during the nineteenth century? . . . The man of science comes to believe at last that the events of the year AD 4000 are as fixed, settled, and unchangeable as the events of the year 1600.[11]

I. F. Clarke has rightly remarked that 'the tale of the future came to the first full perfection of its form in the 1870s', and that by the 1890s it 'had reached a position of worldwide influence: Jules Verne in translation for the Japanese and Chinese; Bellamy read in many editions from Brisbane to British Columbia; tales of future wars in Arabic and Turkish'. These were 'the first signs of a growing realization throughout the planet Earth that modern technology was bringing all nations ever closer together, that the evolution of industrial civilization called for a new order of human society. . .' But Wells still gets pride of place:

in the mysterious way of human society in the decade when the new practice of prediction had begun to take over some of the operations of futuristic fiction, the idea of the future found its high priest in H. G. Wells, who did more than any other writer to establish the awareness of the future that is so characteristic of the twentieth century.[12]

But did turning mankind's attention towards the future necessarily inspire confidence in that future as well? In this respect the positive tone of Wells's Royal Institution lecture is misleading. For by the time he gave it he had done as much as any man in England to make people tremble for the future, and to look back longingly to the Victorian certainty in progress, as a law of nature and human history.

UTOPIA OR CATASTROPHE?

Wells grew up at a time when the Victorian faith in progress was being assailed on all sides.[13] Already at the mid-century Ruskin was musing, in *Modern Painters*, that 'the elements of progress and decline' are 'strangely mingled in the modern mind'. But the most dramatic change was to be seen in the writer who has always seemed most representative of the Victorian sensibility, the Poet Laureate Tennyson. His youthful 'Locksley Hall' had confidently summoned up the future:

> Not in vain the distance beacons. Forward,
> forward let us range,
> Let the great world spin forever down the
> ringing grooves of change.

His sequel, 'Locksley Hall Sixty Years After', written in 1886, violently repudiates this clarion call:

> Let us hush this cry of 'Forward' till ten
> thousand years have gone.

The progressive tendency of evolution is now seen as engaged in a constant, losing, battle with the forces of regression:

> Evolution ever climbing after some ideal good,
> And Reversion ever dragging Evolution in the mud.

Science, the great agency of progress, has continued its advance, but at the cost of social squalor and misery:

> Is it well that while we range with Science,
> glorying in the time,
> City children soak and blacken soul and sense
> in city slime?

It was the same paradox of material progress and social degradation that struck the social reformer Henry George, whose *Progress and Poverty* went through ten editions in England within the first five years of its publication in 1879, and whom Wells acknowledged as the earliest inspirer of his socialist thoughts.

> The tramp comes with the locomotive, and almshouses and prisons are as surely the marks of 'material progress' as are costly dwellings, rich warehouses, and magnificent churches . . . . The enormous increase in productive power which has marked the present century and is still going on with accelerating ratio . . . simply widens the gulf between Dives and Lazarus . . . . This association of poverty with progress is the great enigma of our times.[14]

But the decisive consideration for Wells, as befitted a man of the future, was science. He could discount the aesthetic objections to industrial progress of such as Ruskin and Morris; he could vigorously defend it against the moral misgivings or outright rejection of sages like Carlyle, Matthew Arnold and Tennyson (as he did with the similar doubts of his friend Joseph Conrad). But he could never ignore the shadow cast across the belief in progress by the scientific developments of his time. Throughout his life, Wells was haunted by two things: the law of entropy enunciated by Sir William Thomson (Lord Kelvin) and, above all, the view of evolution presented by Darwin and T. H. Huxley.

In 1852 Thompson formulated the second law of thermodynamics, according to which the sum of useful energy throughout the universe would be constantly reduced by the diffusion of heat until all had reached a state of entropy. 'Within a finite period of time past,' he concluded, 'the earth must have been, and within a finite period to come, the earth must again be, unfit for the habitation of man as at present constituted.' Twenty years later the physicist Balfour Stewart popularized the idea in an 'elementary treatise' on the conservation of energy. 'Universally diffused heat,' he wrote, 'forms what we may call the great waste-heap of the universe, and this is growing larger year by year . . . . We are led to look to an end in which the whole universe will be one equally heated inert mass, and from which everything like life or motion or beauty willl have utterly gone away.'[15]

That the law of entropy referred to periods of millions of years was no consolation to social thinkers such as Herbert Spencer, who had been accustomed to think of evolutionary processes in cosmic terms, and who had found in the theory of evolution a triumphant scientific vindication of the law of progress, natural and social. The view of mankind as progressing along an indefinite and continuously ascending path was suddenly clouded. Nor was the gloom confined to social philosophers. The artists did not always understand the precise technicalities of the new physics, but the image of the dying sun was awesome enough to stir the dullest poetic imagination. 'If you believe in improvement you must weep,' wrote Joseph Conrad to his friend Cunninghame Graham in 1898, 'for the attained perfection must end in cold, darkness, and silence.'[16]

The law of entropy showed the story of life and, *a fortiori*, the human story, to be finite. The end was appointed in the distant but scientifically calculable future. T. H. Huxley's interpretation of Darwinian evolution caused further consternation by demonstrating even that limited passage to be characterized by prodigious waste and suffering. It was not that Huxley subscribed in a simple way to the view of nature as 'red in tooth and claw'. He was more concerned to show that the optimistic interpretation of evolution by natural selection as 'progressive development' was based on a profound misconception of the process of evolution. Darwin had misguidedly lent his authority and prestige to the optimists by a notorious passage at the end of the *Origin of Species*. Huxley, in his Romanes lecture of 1893, 'Evolution and Ethics', went out of his way to dispel this comforting illusion and to insist that the evolutionay process was blind, arbitrary and frequently hideously cruel. There was no discernible purpose in evolution, and nothing to justify a belief in progress. The 'survival of the fittest' not only was not the same thing as the 'survival of the best' – as humans understand that term – but was frequently its antithesis. If aggression and selfishness suited the conditions of the time, they would be selected by nature as against tolerance and altruism. 'The thief and the murderer follow nature just as much as the philanthropist.' If man by chance has constructed something of value, and hopes for its permanence, nature's ceaseless operations topple that construction just as they permitted it in the first place: 'nature is always tending to reclaim that which her child, man, has borrowed from her and arranged in combinations which are not those favoured by the general cosmic process.'[17]

Human history, according to Huxley, had blindly imitated the equally blind 'cosmic process', and so was a record as futile and ethically barren as natural history.

I know of no study which is so utterly saddening as that of the evolution of humanity. Man emerges with the marks of his lowly origin strong upon him. He is a brute, only more intelligent than the other brutes, a blind prey to impulses . . . a victim to endless illusions, which make his mental existence a burden, and fill his life with barren toil and battle.[18]

Huxley however held out some comfort. The course of natural evolution, in its essentially blind unfolding, had thrown up a creature, man, who had a capacity for reflecting on that process and opposing to it a specifically human, ethical, purpose.

Social progress means a checking of the cosmic process at every step and the substitution for it of another, which may be called the ethical process; the end of which is not the survival of those who may happen to be the fittest, in respect of the whole of the conditions which obtain, but of those which are ethically the best.[19]

Thus:

That which lies before the human race is a constant struggle to maintain and improve, in opposition to the State of Nature, the State of Art of an organized polity; in which, and by which, man may develop a worthy civilization, capable of maintaining and constantly improving itself, until the evolution of our globe shall have entered so far upon its downward course that the cosmic process resumes its sway; and, once more, the State of Nature prevails over the surface of our planet.

The melancholy ending, with its reminder of the ultimate entropic impulse of the cosmos, is characteristic. Huxley concludes with a warning against facile optimism. The potentiality for constructive human effort exists, but it contends against the deeper inheritance of our animal nature:

The cosmic nature born with us, and, to a large extent, necessary for our maintenance, is the outcome of millions of years of severe training, and it would be folly to imagine that a few centuries will suffice to subdue its masterfulness to purely ethical ends. Ethical nature may count upon having to reckon with a tenacious and powerful enemy as long as the world lasts.[20]

It is not too much to say that the central tenets of Wells's philosophy, maintained to the end of his life, are all contained in this 1893 lecture by Huxley. Biology was always for Wells the master science; and he felt the force of Huxley's lectures, which he attended in his first year at the Normal School of Science, for the whole of his life.[21] Evolutionary theory, as interpreted by Huxley and modified by the law of entropy, came closest to providing the unifying framework that he always sought in all his speculations. There were indeed times when, in his more hopeful moods, he fused this grim Huxleyan view of evolution with a belief in the collective will of mankind, pressing on to mankind's fulfilment in the world state. This could make him sound very close to Bergson and Shaw, who however repudiated Darwin in their embrace of the *élan vital*.[22] Wells never abandoned Darwin and Huxley. For Bergson and Shaw the creative Life Force was within evolution, within the unfolding cosmic process. For Wells as for Huxley, the collective human will was an agency peculiar to humankind: it stood outside and against the cosmic process of evolution, challenging it with a specifically human purpose. 'If you have things that you desire,' wrote Wells, 'it is because you willed well enough to have it so. . . . Nothing comes of itself except weeds and confusion.'[23]

In recent years it has become fashionable, almost *de rigueur*, to dwell on Wells's pessimism. This view stems largely from the memoir, written some ten years after Wells's death in 1946, by his son (by Rebecca West), Anthony West. Wells had appeared to many to have renounced his life-long utopianism in the despair and bitterness of his last published work, *Mind at the End of its Tether* (1945). West challenged this conventional picture.

I cannot agree that his final phase of scolding and complaining at human folly represented any essential change in his views at all. What happened as his powers declined from 1940 onwards was that he reverted to his original profoundly-felt beliefs about the realities of the human situation. He was by nature a pessimist, and he was doing violence to his intuitions and his rational perceptions alike when he asserted in his middle period that mankind could make a better world for itself by an effort of will.[24]

One wonders whether this is simply a case of the son not having the faith or the intellectual conviction of the father, and wishing his frailty on to the dead parent. In any case it is an odd view, to put it no stronger, that takes the first and last five years of Wells's public life to express the 'essential' Wells, and regards the long 'middle period' of some forty years as an 'abberation'. Whatever one may feel about the quality of Wells's utopianism, it seems perverse to deny its real and fervently held existence, in his life and thought. Only five years after his first published work, *The Time Machine* (1895), he produced a volume of sociological speculations, *Anticipations*, which was resolutely utopian in character, and which contained in embryo practically every one of the utopian ideas that he was to develop and propagate over the next forty years. *The Time Machine* is largely anti-utopian; *Anticipations* is utopian. Are we to suppose that in five years Wells swung from the extremes of anti-utopian pessimism to utopian optimism (and in doing so betrayed his 'real' conviction as to the possibilities for the human race)? If so, the swing of the pendulum continues in a distinctly perplexing and disconcerting manner. In the same year as *Anticipations* there appeared *The First Men in the Moon* (1901), which by general agreement is, in its portrait of the ant-like civilization of the Selenites, one of Wells's key anti-utopian novels, anticipating in detail the purported anti-Wellsian critique of *Brave New World*. But in 1902 we find Wells confidently 'discovering the future', in 1903 offering another volume of utopian speculations, *Mankind in the Making*, and in 1905 publishing the first of his full-fledged utopias, *A Modern Utopia*. The to-ing and fro-ing continues. A powerful plea in the utopian mode for planetary socialism, *New Worlds for Old* (1908), appears in the same year as *The War in the Air*, in which Wells devastates the world with aerial bombardment. The dark vision of *Tono-Bungay* (1909) – 'I have called it *Tono-Bungay*, but I had far better have called it *Waste*' – which ends with a nightmare image of a world disintegrating by atomic decay, is followed by Wells's sunniest novel, *The History of Mr Polly* (1910). The disillusionment and frustration of *The New Machiavelli* (1911) and *Marriage* (1912) is succeeded by a strong reaffirmation of the utopian faith in *The World Set Free* (1914).

And so one could go on. The alternating moods of hope and despair continue throughout Wells's life, varying both with the state of the world and with the state of his personal life, physical and emotional. The First World War was a profound shock, to Wells as to all his contemporaries, but he very soon conceived of it as 'the war that will end war' – in the influential phrase that he coined – and set about preparing the way for the world government that he felt convinced must arise out of the ashes of the war. Similarly, he was disappointed in the turn that Bolshevism took in Russia, and deplored the brutality and intolerance of the Fascist movements in Italy and Germany; nevertheless, he could discern some hope in the form and style of these movements, in the evidence they offered of personal commitment and dedication to a new world order. In this sense there was indeed a life-long consistency in Wells's temperament, as Anthony West claims. But it is a consistency made up of two equal parts, the elements of confidence and despair warring throughout Wells's life. There seems no more reason than personal inclination to stress – or to deny – the pessimistic strain, or to ignore the equally powerful utopian impulse that co-existed throughout. What Wells himself said towards the end of his life seems a fair statement of his true position:

I have never thought, much less have I asserted, that progress was inevitable, though numerous people chose to fancy that about me. I have always maintained that by a strenuous effort mankind might defeat the impartial destructiveness of nature, but I have always insisted that only by incessant hard thinking and a better co-ordination of man's immense but diversified powers of self-sacrifice and heriosm was such a victory possible.'[25]

If there is any explanation for the undoubted predominance of anti-utopian themes in Wells's earliest writings, this seems to have more to do with the state of his personal and professional life at the time than with any fundamental temperamental bias. Wells wrote his brilliant early science fantasies under the direct and immediate impress of his biological studies, and of his infatuation with T. H. Huxley. The clear-eyed but cheerless view of evolution presented by Huxley haunted him and fired his burgeoning literary imagination. At the same time, these were immensely stressful and difficult years for the young Wells. He had escaped from the hated draper's apprenticeship only to fail as a science student at the Normal School of Science. He was struggling desperately to become a writer in London, doing hack work of every description. He had married his cousin Isobel and almost immediately regretted it. To cap it all, the symptoms of an early constitutional weakness, never properly understood but variously diagnosed as consumption, a crushed kidney and diabetes, repeatedly recurred with such violence as to leave Wells convinced that he would not survive beyond his thirtieth year. When taken with the general *fin de siècle* mood of pessimism prevalent among artistic intellectuals, among whom Wells was very anxious to count himself, it is not entirely surprising that his writings of these years should be coloured in sombre hues.

In 1893 Wells revised a paper of his student days and published it as 'The Man of the Year Million'. It is a fascinating piece, with its delineation of so many later Wellsian ideas and its ironic blend of the utopian and the anti-utopian. Wells projects human evolution, following present lines, to the point where man's essential organ, the brain, has usurped all other faculties and functions, and the human form is reduced to a bodiless brain. With the exception of the hand, the body will become dispensable, as 'wit and machinery and verbal agreement' will do what once required bodily toil. The men of the future have 'great hands . . . enormous brains, soft, liquid, soulful eyes. Their whole muscular system, their legs, their abdomens, are shrivelled to nothing, a dangling, degraded pendant to their minds.' The image is aesthetically unattractive, as Wells clearly means it to be. But at the same time he is teasingly posing the question, Why not? What is wrong with getting rid of our troublesome bodies and dwelling serenely in the pure realm of the mind? Why not let the fusion of mind and machinery perform effortlessly and efficiently what now costs so much pain and toil?

Projecting even further, Wells imagines all plants and animals dying away, save man and the species he protects for his own food and pleasure. Soon man dispenses even with these as he learns to process his food artificially. 'In the last days man will be alone on the earth, and his food will be won by the chemist from the dead rocks and the sunlight.' Socially, 'the irrational fellowship of man will give place to an intellectual co-operation, and emotion fall within the scheme of reason.' Peering further still, Wells sees the entropic process bringing about a great, gradual, cooling of the universe.

> And so at last comes a vision of earthly cherubim, hopping heads, great unemotional intelligences, and little hearts, fighting together and perforce and fiercely against the cold that grips them tighter . . . . The whole world will be snow-covered and piled with ice; all animals, all vegetation vanished, except this last branch of the tree of life. The last men have gone ever deeper, following the diminishing heat of the planet, and vast metallic shafts and ventilators make way for the air they need.

The vision ends with 'a glimpse of these human tadpoles, in their deep close gallery, with their boring machinery ringing away, and artificial lights glaring and casting black shadows. . . . Humanity in dismal retreat before the cold, changed beyond recognition.'[26]

A year later Wells pictured an even more ominous prospect.[27] Since evolution worked by the ceaseless extinction of species in an ever-changing environment – 'Natural Selection is selection by Death' – was there any reason to suppose that the same fate was not marked out for man? The fact that man was currently ruler of the earth was no guarantee of his continued success, still less of his permanence. Quite the contrary. The evolutionary record was littered with the fossils of species that had been extinguished at the very height of their dominance. We must not let our current ideas of perfection and progress blind us to the nature of evolution, and our own place within it. 'Evolution is no mechanical tendency making for perfection . . . . it is simply the continual adaptation of plastic life, for good or evil, to the circumstances that surround it. . . .'[28] Moreover:

> In no case does the record of the fossils show a really dominant species succeeded by its own descendants. What has usually happened in the past appears to be the emergence of some type of animal hitherto rare and unimportant, and the extinction, not simply of the previously ruling species, but of most of the forms that are at all closely related to it.

And so, in half-playful and mocking form, but with a satiric pointedness that none could miss, Wells suggested a number of possible candidates as man's successor to the lordship of the world: the Crustacea, increased to terrifying size and terrestrial capacity; the cephalopods, in the form of gigantic, man-eating, octopuses; and the ants, with their high intelligence and developed social organization. He also hypothesized the onset of new strange and terrible diseases, against which humans would be helpless, and which would wipe out not 20 or 30 per cent of the population, as had earlier plagues, but 100 per cent of humanity.

Wells ends on an apocalyptic note:

> No; man's complacent assumption of the future is too confident. We think, because things have been easy for mankind as a whole for a generation or so, we are going on to

perfect comfort and security in the future. We think that we shall always go to work at ten and leave off at four, and have dinner at seven for ever and ever. But these four suggestions, out of a host of others, must surely do a little against this complacency. Even now, for all we can tell, the coming terror may be crouching for its spring and the fall of humanity be at hand. In the case of every other predominant animal the world has ever seen, I repeat, the hour of its complete ascendancy has been the eve of its entire overthrow.

The themes of these early essays were all put to effective use in Wells's early science fantasies. This was true even of some of the details: the potential overlordship of the giant crabs turns up in *The Time Machine*, that of the cephalopods in his short story 'The Sea-Raiders', and that of the ants in 'The Empire of the Ants'. But more important were the general forecasts of the prospects and possibilities for the human race, and the universe as a whole. The early fantasies are generally characterized by an urgent, apocalyptic sense of doom and disaster, with a vengeful Providence punishing humankind for its complacency and hubris. The shadow of an impending terminal catastrophe hangs over everything, whether this takes the sudden form of invading Martians or the more drawn-out form of evolutionary processes and cosmic disasters: 'the suffocating comet, the dark body out of space, the burning out of the sun, the distorted orbit. . .'[29]

But never, even at Wells's gloomiest, does the hint of hope disappear altogether. The science fantasies are offered as so many cautionary fables, so many dreadful warnings to humanity to look to itself, to take stock of its current sick condition and remedy it before it is too late. They do not deny that, in the literal sense, the human race may be superseded and that the universe will run down. Evolution and entropy make both these things entirely possible and perhaps inevitable. But Wells wasn't concerned here – if he ever was anywhere – merely with scientific truth. He was never really interested in 'pure' science and pure sociology, pursued for their own sake. The great popular educative books that he wrote – the *Outline of History*, the *Science of Life* and the *Work, Wealth and Happiness of Mankind* – were all undergirded by his utopian philosophy. So with the science fantasies. Science acted for Wells as the mainspring of his literary imagination; and that imagination was put at the service of a social philosophy that was, in the strict sense, consistently utopian. At times he uttered dire warnings; at other times he built utopias. Increasingly, he came to do both within the confines of the same work, whether fact or fiction. And both were aspects of the same prophetic mission. In 1941, at the nadir of allied fortunes during the Second World War, Wells reprinted his 1908 cautionary 'fantasy of possibility', *The War in the Air.* The new preface of a few angry terse lines concluded: 'I told you so; you *damned* fools.' It was entirely in the spirit of his utopianism that, at the very same time, he should have been working with Lord Sankey in drawing up a world declaration of the rights of man – strikingly similar to the Universal Declaration of Human Rights later adopted by the UN General Assembly in 1948 – and making another bid, his last as it turned out, to turn the world towards Cosmopolis.

Even in the first scintillating crop of science fantasies, published between 1895 and 1901,[30] suggestions of an ultimate answer to the human predicament, a possible alternative to catastrophe, peep through. The most relentlessly bleak are the very earliest – *The Time Machine* (1895), *The Island of Dr Moreau* (1896) and *The Invisible Man* (1897). Evolution and all its works are here seen under the pitiless and uncaring gaze of the cosmic beholder. The Time Traveller, stopping in the year 802,701, finds a civilization that is a degenerate but logical descendant of the class-divided society of his own day. There are the aristocratic upper-world Eloi, who lead a leisured, decadent, Edenic existence; and there are the nether-world Morlocks, the brutalized descendants of the industrial proletariat. Machines have taken over the essential work of mankind, and the motor of social evolution has temporarily come to a stop. The result is not creativity and happiness but a wasting decay, suggests Wells in this biting comment on both the hyper-industrial civilization of Bellamy's *Looking Backward* and the post-industrial pastoral idyll of Morris's *News from Nowhere*.[31] The Golden Age has been achieved, nature has been subdued, but the human fulfilment widely expected of this state of things is conspicuously lacking. On first encountering the pretty, child-like Eloi, the Time Traveller reflects:

> The great triumph of Humanity I had dreamed of took a different shape in my mind. It had been no such triumph of moral education and general co-operation as I had imagined. Instead, I saw a real aristocracy, armed with a perfected science and working to a logical conclusion the industrial system of today. Its triumph had not been simply a triumph over nature, but a triumph over nature and the fellow-man . . . . But even on this supposition the balanced civilization that was at last attained must have long since passed its zenith, and was now far fallen into decay. The too-perfect security of the Overworlders had led them to a slow movement of degeneration, to a general dwindling in size, strength, and intelligence.

The appearance of the Morlocks, and the discovery that not only do they tend the machines that keep the Eloi in idleness, but they have revenged themselves on their exploiters by preying on them as cannibals, prompts even soberer thoughts on the age-old dream of attaining security and stability:

> I understood now what all the beauty of the over-world people covered. Very pleasant was their day, as pleasant as the day of the cattle in the field. Like the cattle, they knew of no enemies, and provided against no needs. And their end was the same.
>
> I grieved to think how brief the dream of the human intellect had been. It had committed suicide. It had set itself steadfastly towards comfort and ease, a balanced society with security and permanency as its watchword, it had attained its hopes – to come to this at last. Once, life and property must have reached almost absolute safety. The rich had been assured of his wealth and comfort, the toiler assured of his life and work. No doubt in that perfect world there had been no unemployed problem, no social question left unsolved. And a great quiet had followed.
>
> It is a law of nature we overlook, that intellectual versatility is the compensation for change, danger, and trouble. An animal perfectly in harmony with its environment is a perfect mechanism. Nature never appeals to intelligence until habit and instinct are useless. There is no intelligence where there is no change and no need of change. Only those animals partake of intelligence that have to meet a huge variety of needs and dangers.

Having observed the decline of the human race in the year 802,701, the Time Traveller proceeds 30 million years into the future and, in some of the most unforgettable passages in English literature, describes the death of the planet, as the sun dulls and darkness covers the earth. With that melancholy vision he disappears from his Edwardian home and times. In musing on his possible whereabouts in space-time, his friend the narrator contrasts his own rationalist optimism with the deep pessimism of the Time Traveller:

He may even now – if I may use the phrase – be wandering on some plesiosaurus-haunted Oolitic coral reef, or beside the lonely saline seas of the Triassic Age. Or did he go forward, into one of the nearer ages, in which men are still men, but with the riddles of our own time answered and its wearisome problems solved? Into the manhood of the race: for I, for my own part, cannot think that these latter days of weak experiment, fragmentary theory, and mutual discord are indeed man's culminating time! I say, for my own part. He, I know . . . thought but cheerlessly of the Advancement of Mankind, and saw in the growing pile of civilization only a foolish heaping that must inevitably fall back upon and destroy its makers in the end. If that is so, it remains for us to live as though it were not so.

Even that faint, mocking gesture towards a hopeful future is absent from *The Island of Dr Moreau*, Wells's second and most chilling evolutionary fable. In *The Time Machine* Wells expanded the time dimension infinitely, to show something of evolution in real time. In *Dr Moreau* he concentrated it dramatically: *Dr Moreau* is the enactment of the whole of human evolution in a few years on a small island in the Pacific.

Moreau, the renegade surgeon, uses his skill in vivisection to make men out of beasts, so imitating both the means and the ends of evolution. He symbolizes in almost equal parts God the Creator, Prometheus and Frankenstein (Wells later called his story a 'theological grotesque'). Towards his creatures the Beast-Men he is as detached, impersonal and ruthless as is God or Nature in the operations of evolution by natural selection. 'The study of Nature makes a man at last as remorseless as Nature.' The path from beast to man lies through Moreau's laboratory, the House of Torture. But there is no intention to inflict gratuitous pain or suffering in Moreau's experiments, any more than in those of Nature in her equally wayward and painful creation of man out of the original primaeval slime. Moreau's purposes are as lofty as those of the Creator: 'Each time I dip a living creature into the bath of burning pain, I say, This time I will burn out all the animal, this time I will make a rational creature of my own.'

But the Beast-Men of the island cannot be lifted up to the plane of rational creatures. At first partially, then totally and collectively, they revert to their bestial state, horribly murdering Moreau in the process, and rampaging over the whole island in a fenzied bloodthirsty horde. Prendick, the young naturalist shipwrecked on the island, almost loses his sanity in his fear, and in pondering on 'the painful disorder of this island':

A blind fate, a vast pitiless mechanism, seemed to cut and shape the fabric of existence, and I, Moreau (by his passion for research), Montgomery (by his passion for drink), the Beast-People with their instincts and mental restrictions, were torn and crushed, ruthlessly, inevitably, amid the infinite complexity of its incessant wheels.

In the face of this uncaring, unethical Nature, man has the potential to become rational and god-like, the image of his Creator. But for Wells, man, reflecting his lowly animal origins, still remains half-beast, like Moreau's Beast-Men. 'Humanity is but animal, rough-hewn to a reasonable shape and in perpetual internal conflict between instinct and injunction.'[32] The duality in man – beast and God, rationalist and sensualist, Stevenson's humane Dr Jekyll and the psychopathic Mr Hyde – remains unresolved. When Prendick manages to return to England, he suffers from a persistent haunting malady, remarkably like that of Gulliver's returned from the Houyhnhnms. He cannot help seeing his fellow-creatures as Beast-Men, just as Gulliver saw them as Yahoos, and his disgust at humankind is distinctly Swiftian:

> I could not persuade myself that the men and women I met were not also another, still passably human, Beast People, animals half-wrought into the outward image of human souls, and that they would presently begin to revert, to show first this bestial mark and then that . . . . I see faces keen and bright, others dull or dangerous, others unsteady, insincere; none that have the calm authority of a reasonable soul. I feel as though the animal was surging up through them; that presently the degradation of the Islanders will be played over again on a larger scale . . . .
>
> When I lived in London the horror was wellnigh insupportable. I could not get away from men; their voices came through the windows; locked doors were flimsy safeguards. I would go out into the streets to fight with my delusion, and prowling women would mew after me, furtive craving men glance jealously at me, weary pale workers go coughing by me, with tired eyes and eager paces like wounded deer dripping blood, old people, bent and dull, pass murmuring to themselves, and all unheeding a ragged tail of gibing children.

In *The Invisible Man*, Wells repeated the Faust–Frankenstein theme in the story of a brilliant but perverted scientist, Griffin, whose discovery of the secret of invisibility leads him gradually on to the paranoid pursuit of total power. At the climax the Invisible Man institutes a 'Reign of Terror' among the villages of southern England, and is finally clubbed to death by a terrified but enraged mob. As the literal representation of the disembodied intellect, Griffin shows both the dangers to the self of the unregulated pursuit of science and also the havoc that science can wreak. But in Wells's next two science fantasies, *The War of the Worlds* (1898) and *The First Men in the Moon* (1901), the disembodied intelligence apears in a new light. The stories are still largely in the apocalyptic, anti–utopian mode. In *The War of the Worlds*, the Martians invade the earth with terrifying violence and for unfathomable purposes; in *The First Men in The Moon*, the ant-like caste civilization of the Selenites on the moon is grotesque and inhuman in its rigid hierarchy and specialization. Cavor's description of Selenite society, indeed, shows how little Aldous Huxley had to teach H. G. Wells, and how far he was indebted to him:

> In the moon . . . every citizen knows his place. He is born to that place, and the elaborate discipline of training and education and surgery he undergoes fits him at last so completely to it that he has neither ideas nor organs for any purpose beyond it. . . . If, for example, a Selenite is destined to be a mathematician, his teachers and trainers set out at once to that end. They check any incipient disposition to other pursuits, they encourage

his mathematical bias with perfect psychological skill. His brain grows, or at least the mathematical faculties of his brain grow, and the rest of him only so much as is necessary to sustain this essential part of him. At last, save for rest and food, his one delight lies in the exercise and display of his faculty, his one interest in its application, his sole society with other specialists in his own line. His brain grows continually larger, at least so far as the portions engaging in mathematics are concerned; they bulge ever larger and seem to suck all life and vigour from the rest of his frame. His limbs shrivel, his heart and digestive organs diminish, his insect face is hidden under its bulging contours. His voice becomes a mere stridulation for the stating of formulae; he seems deaf to all but properly enunciated problems. The faculty of laughter, save for the sudden discovery of some paradox, is lost to him; his deepest emotion is the evolution of a novel computation. And so he attains his end . . . .

He loves his work, and discharges in perfect happiness the duty that justifies his being. And so it is with all sorts and conditions of Selenites – each is a perfect unit in a world machine . . . .

But Cavor has *chosen* to stay on the moon among the Selenites, unlike his companion Bedford, who escapes back to earth. Cavor is the scientist, and is attracted to the efficiency and scientific organization of society that he finds on the moon. Selenite society has carried science and technology to heights undreamt of on earth. It has abolished waste and want, along with war and political strife. In some innocent questioning of Cavor about earthly institutions, the Grand Lunar learns about war, and asks incredulously, 'you mean to say . . . that you run about over the surface of your world – this world, whose riches you have scarcely begun to scrape – killing one another for beasts to eat?' At another point Cavor comes upon 'a number of young Selenites confined in jars from which only the fore-limbs protruded, who were being compressed to become machine-minders of a special sort. The extended "hand" in this highly developed system of technical education is stimulated by irritants and nourished by injection, while the rest of the body is starved.' The sight disturbs him – 'it haunts me still' – but he wonders whether it is not 'really in the end a far more humane proceeding than our earthly method of leaving children to grow into human beings, and then making machines of them'. The tone is satiric still; but the implication is clear, in these final pages of *The First Men in the Moon*, that Wells is turning away from the apocalyptic pessimism of the earliest fantasies, towards some more constructive vision of human possibilities.[33]

The Selenites and the Martians are in fact thinly disguised versions of 'the man of the year million' that Wells had earlier sketched. Both are all brain and little body; the higher the social function the less the body. Both are the essence of intellect – the Grand Lunar is practically nothing but 'quintessential brain' – and show its crushing superiority over emotion-bound creatures. Both have developed science and technology to the point where their now otiose bodies have shrivelled away and all individual and collective activity is the product of the co-ordinated fusion of brain and machine. Just in case anyone might miss the connection between the portrait of the Martians and the future of the human species, Wells makes it explicit in *The War of the Worlds*:

It is worthy of remark that a certain speculative writer of quasi-scientific repute, writing long before the Martian invasion, did forecast for man a final structure not unlike the actual Martian condition . . . . He pointed out – writing in a foolish facetious tone – that the perfection of mechanical appliances must ultimately supersede limbs, the perfection of chemical devices, digestion – that such organs as hair, external nose, teeth, ears, chin, were no longer essential parts of the human being, and that the tendency of natural selection would lie in the direction of their steady diminution through the coming ages. The brain alone remained a cardinal necessity. Only one other part of the body had a strong case for survival, and that was the hand, 'teacher and agent of the brain'. While the rest of the body dwindled, the hand would grow larger.

There is many a true word written in jest, and here in the Martians we have beyond dispute the actual accomplishment of such suppression of the animal side of the organism by the intelligence. To me it is quite credible that the Martians may be descended from beings not unlike ourselves, by a gradual development of brain and hands . . . at the expense of the rest of the body. Without the body the brain would of course become a more selfish intelligence, without any of the emotional substratum of the human being.

The Martian invasion is a warning to mankind, as in the other cautionary fables of these years. And the cruelty and sheer destructiveness of the Martians make them very unlikely utopian exemplars. But what they and the Selenites have accomplished through the development of science and the intellect intimates certain real possibilities for mankind. Most of the earlier stories, such as *The Island of Dr Moreau*, had ended on a note of despair. But *The War of the Worlds* finds some glimmer of hope in the devastating shock that the world has suffered:

It may be that in the larger design of the universe this invasion from Mars is not without its ultimate benefit for men; it has robbed us of that serene confidence in the future which is the most fruitful source of decadence, the gifts to human science it has brought are enormous, and it has done much to promote the conception of the commonweal of mankind.

'The commonweal of mankind' always, for Wells, spelt humanity organized in the World State. With that conception, therefore, Wells had already entered Utopia.

THE MODERN UTOPIA

Between *The War of the Worlds* and *The First Men in the Moon*, Wells produced the most ambiguous of his early science fantasies, *When The Sleeper Wakes* (1899). At one level this follows the theme and pattern of the earlier romances, especially *The Time Machine*. It is Wells showing his most explicit debt to Bellamy while at the same time savagely criticizing the hyper-industrial civilization of *Looking Backward*.

Graham, the sleeper of the title, awakes in the year 2100 after a trance of two centuries to find himself in a glittering future society that he first takes to be the realization of the nineteenth-century dream of progress. As with the Time Traveller, the reality gradually dawns and he comes to see that the society is an oppressive and tyrannical slave-state. It is ruled by Ostrog, a proto-fascist believer in the Over-man theory of humanity, who has risen to power on the backs of the workers and then betrayed them. His methods of rule anticipate those of the totalitarian dictatorship of Orwell's *Nineteen Eight-Four*, not to mention the actual dictatorships of Mussolini and Hitler. The workers are debased, exploited and systematically misinformed. They are subject from an early age to 'psychic surgery', a form of thought control employing advanced techniques of hypnosis. There are 'Babble Machines', propaganda machines that manufacture 'countersuggestions in the cause of law and order'. All citizens are constantly under surveillance, and any attempted strikes or other expressions of disaffection are brutally suppressed by the Labour Police. All that the stupefied workers live for are periods of mindless leisure in the Pleasure Cities, and perhaps the chance eventually to enter the Euthanasy, 'the rich man's refuge from life'. It is, as Wells described his creation in 1921, 'a world of base servitude in hypertrophied cities'.[34]

And yet, it is not only the Sleeper who is uncertain, but the reader who remains for long puzzled as to Wells's intention in this work. For there are aspects of the future society that are glowingly described, many of which are the hallmarks of the society that Wells was later to make his distinctive Utopia. The society of the year 2100 is a triumph of science, technology and rational planning. Nature has been conquered and put to work, and then banished from the consciousness of men altogether. Machines do all the work of society, merely tended by human minders. A rational system of eugenics controls population growth and occupational needs. The world has become in effect one gigantic city, glassed-in, climate-controlled and powered by huge windmill dynamos which lie outside the city domes. There are aeroplanes for long distances, but within the city travel is by a series of ceaselessly moving platforms, suspended in mid-air and graded in speed so that passengers can move uninterruptedly from the slowest to the swiftest.[35] The scene that first greets Graham when he awakes and steps out on the balcony is a Wellsian archetype, the first of the many glimpses of the utopian city that he was to give, and following him a host of city planners and science-fiction writers:

> His first impression was of overwhelming architecture. The place into which he looked was an aisle of Titanic buildings, curving spaciously in either direction. Overhead mighty cantilevers sprang together across the huge width of the place, and a tracery of translucent material shut out the sky. Gigantic globes of cool white light shamed the pale sunbeams that filtered down through the girders and wires. Here and there a gossamer suspension bridge dotted with foot passengers flung across the chasm and the air was webbed with slender cables. A cliff edifice hung above him, he perceived as he glanced upward, and the opposite facade was grey and dim and broken by great archings, circular perforations, balconies, butresses, turret projections, myriads of vast windows, and an intricate scheme of architectural relief.[36]

When The Sleeper Wakes was in fact the first of Wells's utopian stories. The elements of utopia are there, although buried still within a largely anti-utopian fable. But Wells was now ready for a new role. He was by now a famous and successful writer. He had divorced Isobel and married his former student Catherine Robbins, who gave his home life whatever stability it was ever likely to have until her death in 1927. He had built himself a splendid new house,

Spade House, at Sandgate, where his friends and neighbours included Henry James, Joseph Conrad and Ford Madox Ford. His health had vastly improved. The movement of his mind at this time was fully revealed in the exercises in social prophecy which he published in the *Fortnightly Review* in 1901, and which appeared in the same year as a book, *Anticipations of the Reaction of Mechanical and Scientific Progress Upon Human Life and Thought.*

Wells now turned sociologist and utopist: two practices which he actually considered to be one. In a paper entitled 'The So-called Science of Sociology', he attacked the positivist views of sociology advanced by Comte and Spencer. Sociology was not a science. Society could not be studied by the experimental techniques of the physical sciences. Nor could human communities be treated as distinct types or species, and so compared and classified in the manner of the naturalist or biologist. For with humanity there was only one effective unit, the whole of evolving mankind:

> We cannot put Humanity into a museum, or dry it for examination; our one single still living specimen is all history, all anthropology, and the fluctuating world of men. There is no satisfactory means of dividing it, and nothing else in the real world with which to compare it. We have only the remotest ideas of its 'life-cycle' and a few relics of its origin and dreams of its destiny . . .[37]

Sociology had to be considered as the attempt to bring its subject, mankind, 'that vast, complex, unique Being', into 'clear, true relations with the individual intelligence'. On this view, 'sociology must be neither art simply, nor science in the narrow meaning of the word at all, but knowledge rendered imaginatively, and with an element of personality; that is to say, in the highest sense of the term, literature.' One kind of historical writing, that of the theoretical or philosophical type practised by writers such as Gibbon, Carlyle and Buckle, had come near this conception, by presenting all history, or some great period of it, 'in the light of one dramatic sequence, or as one process'.[38] But there was a more important and largely neglected aspect of the sociological task:

> There is no such thing in sociology as dispassionately considering what *is*, without considering what is *intended to be*. In sociology . . . ideas are facts. The history of civilisation is really the history of the appearance and reappearance, the tentatives and hesitations and alterations, the manifestations and reflections in this mind and that, of a very complex, imperfect, elusive idea, the Social Idea. It is that idea struggling to exist and realise itself in a world of egotisms, animalisms, and brute matter. Now, I submit it is not only a legitimate form of approach, but altogether the most promising and hopeful form of approach, to endeavour to disentangle and express one's personal version of that idea, and to measure realities from the standpoint of that idealisation. I think, in fact, that the creation of Utopias – and their exhaustive criticism – is the proper and distinctive method of sociology . . . . Sociology is the description of the Ideal Society and its relation to existing societies.[39]

So it was with the figures of Plato and More, not Marx and Comte (still less Sidney and Beatrice Webb), in front of him, and with the concept of sociology as the construction of utopias, that Wells entered the field of social enquiry proper. *Anticipations* followed this scheme of thought precisely. Wells later called this book 'the keystone to the main arch of my work'; and it is indeed aptly named, in that it prefigures practically all of his more fully developed utopian ideas. An analysis of the political, social and moral disintegration of contemporary civilization is fused with the identification and projection of certain tendencies which would reintegrate and reconstruct human society. All the later Wellsian themes are touched on here: the inevitability and necessity of war as the precipitant and catalyst of the coming changes ('war comes to simplify the issue and line out the thing with knife-like cuts'); the contempt for democracy, and for 'the people' or the proletariat as the agency of the change; the singling out of the new middle class of scientific, professional and managerial people ('the Efficients') as 'a new force in the world's history' and the natural creators and inheritors of the new society, displacing both the functionless aristocracy and the mass of unskilled workers ('the People of the Abyss'); the vision of a New Republic developing into a world state, brought into being and sustained by 'an informal and open freemasonry' or 'outspoken Secret Society' composed of the capable Efficients. Throughout, Wells insists that there is no inevitability to this desired development – not, at any rate, in any mechanical sense. The rapid breeding of the 'base and servile types' in the population gives them the enormous force of numbers, and there are power-hungry politicians everywhere willing to exploit the ignorance and credulity of the masses. The way to the world state may be, and probably will be, marked by disasters and destruction of a frightful kind.

A sombre Darwinism remains a strong undercurrent of *Anticipations*. The ethical system of the New Republic is shaped primarily by eugenic considerations, and involves the systematic elimination of 'hereditary criminals' and all 'inferior' classes and types. But Wells also purports to discern in the growing class consciousness of the new middle class the germ of what he was later to call 'the Mind of the Race', an evolving sense of the oneness of mankind and a collective commitment to the common purposes of humanity. This phenomenon allowed for at least a qualified optimism about man's future.

In the next instalment of his sociological reflections, *Mankind in the Making* (1903), Wells was more explicit and – no doubt partly owing to the huge success of *Anticipations* – more confident about the growth of the collective racial mind. He now addressed himself directly to the New Republicans, to those already feeling their way to the kind of analysis he had presented in *Anticipations*. He urged them

> to see our wills only as temporary manifestations of an ampler will, our lives as passing phases of a greater life, and to accept these facts even joyfully, to take our places in that larger scheme with a sense of relief and discovery, to go with that larger being, to serve that larger being, as a soldier marches, a mere unit in the larger being of his army, and serving his army, joyfully into battle.[40]

This echo of Bellamy was underlined in the assertion of 'the central idea of my New Republic', that 'we are passing as a race out of a state of affairs when the unconscious building of the future was attained by individualistic self-seeking . . . into a clear consciousness of our co-operative share in that process.'[41] It was in that confident spirit that, less than half a dozen years after his gloomy prognostications for the human race, Wells produced his 'modern utopia'.

A Modern Utopia (1905) is not the most finished or perfected of Wells's utopias. There are more complete accounts in *Men Like Gods* (1923) and *The Shape of Things to Come* (1933). His utopian philosophy as a whole is more clearly enunciated in the great educative enterprise summed up in his trilogy *The Outline of History* (1920), *The Science of Life* (1930) and *The Work, Wealth and Happiness of Mankind* (1932). But there are good reasons for choosing *A Modern Utopia* for special treatment in examining Wells's utopianism. It finds him at the height of his creative powers. In the previous ten years he had written the finest of his science fantasies. His best 'serious' novels had either just been written – *The Wheels of Chance* (1897), *Love and Mr Lewisham* (1900), *Kipps* (1905) – or were soon to come – *Tono-Bungay* and *Ann Veronica* (1909), *The History of Mr Polly* (1910) and *The New Machiavelli* (1911). He had only recently entered the field of social speculation and enquiry, and his ideas had not yet set so firmly in the mould as to have the rigid dogmatic qualities of his later years. As the first of his explicitly utopian works, *A Modern Utopia* reaped the benefit of Wells at his most fertile and inventive, the liveliness of his style still whetted rather than blunted by sociological themes. Later on the writing was often to be careless and mechanical, the voice strident, the manner hectoring or petulant. The didactic social purpose tended to drown everything he wrote, novel or tract. *The Shape of Things to Come*, better known because of the famous film version, *Things to Come*, is lengthily turgid and far less persuasive in its utopianism than *A Modern Utopia*. But here Wells got the balance about right. Geoffrey West, Wells's first biographer, echoes a widespread opinion when he says that *A Modern Utopia* is 'perhaps the most characteristic – the most Wellsian – of all his books, both original in form and authentic in its originality. . . . It presents a union of thinker and artist more satisfying than any of the misalliances of the later years. . . .'[42]

The attractiveness and originality of the form is undoubtedly one reason for the book's popularity and success. Unlike most utopias, *A Modern Utopia* evokes a vision as much as, and perhaps rather more than, it proclaims a programme. (Morris's *News from Nowhere* comes closest to it in this respect.) Most utopias have adopted the dialogue form of Plato's *Republic*. Some questing youths, visitors from another world or age, a stage sceptic or two, insistently and dutifully ply the sage (well-informed citizen of utopia, etc.) with questions about the social and political organization of the new society. ('But how *do* you get your citizens to do the menial tasks when all are guaranteed a tolerable income. . .?') In answering them, the sage discourses at length on the salient features of his utopia, at the same time mercilessly ridiculing the beliefs and practices of his questioners' own society. ('In your day, of course, the idea of eating your old citizens appeared horrifying. To us it seems eminently sensible and humane. . . .')

Some artfulness is obviously involved in this procedure. The authors evidently feel that the fictional form, however thin, will help to put the essentially programmatic message across, in a way less likely with a purely political tract or treatise. Wells also, as he tells us, having rejected 'from the outset the form of the argumentative essay', toyed with the idea of 'the discussion novel, after the fashion of Peacock's (and Mr Mallock's) development of the ancient dialogue'; and there are echoes of it still, as in the discussion between the earthly narrator and his Utopian *alter ego*. He also considered the model of Boswell's Johnson, 'a sort of interplay between monologue and commentator'. But what he in fact came up with was more original and more interesting. It was a distinct narrative, involving contrasting characters who chance, on a walking holiday in the Alps, to stray into another dimension of space, where they find an earth-like planet and a solar system parallel in most respects to their own.

The traveller's tale aspect of this is of course ancient and standard in the utopian genre, and the walk in the Alps itself is a favourite Wellsian device. What is novel here is that Wells does not, as is the usual custom in utopian literature, quickly drop the narrative, to pass on to the main business of the book, which is to give us a detailed picture of the good society. The narrative continues, with all that that implies by way of an emergent process of discovery: a discovery of new things about the new world the two travellers have entered, and a chastening discovery of themselves, as the creatures of a spoilt and stunted world. There is, naturally in a utopia, a good deal of discursive and speculative writing about man and society, and about the way of, and to, the good life. But Wells rarely lets it suffocate the main narrative. There is a nice air of wonderment and expectation throughout, with the climax – the appearance of the Samurai class – held back to the very end. Wells said that he aimed in this book 'at a sort of shot-silk texture between philosophical discussion on the one hand and imaginative literature on the other'.[43] It was a balance he aimed at throughout his life, in his novels as well as his sociological writings, and it is one reason why he never attempted to write a conventional utopia. He never really found that balance satisfactorily, and increasingly failed to succeed even in part. Here, however, he came as near as he ever did to bringing it off.

It is not simply in its literary and formal aspects that *A Modern Utopia* has attracted attention. Commentators on utopias have also praised it for its intellectual originality and pivotal significance within the Western utopian tradition. For Lewis Mumford it is the 'quintessential utopia', in which Wells 'sums up and clarifies the utopias of the past, and brings them into contact with the world of the present'.[44] In *A Modern Utopia*, says I. F. Clarke, 'Wells had produced the most up-to-date utopia in the history of the genre . . . . It remains the most important utopia of the twentieth century, because it made the most complete act of faith in the idea of progress, and because, by a cruel irony of fiction, it became the model from which the dominant dystopias of the last fifty years have taken their mark.'[45] Mark Hillegas also stresses its centrality for twentieth-century utopianism:

In *A Modern Utopia* Wells wrote the archetypal utopia, brought up to date, with science and technology assimilated into it as never before. It becomes the utopia transformed into an archetypal blueprint for the scientifically planned welfare state, as well as an early major statement of Wells' dream of the World State . . . . It is no wonder that utopian came to mean Wellsian for men like Forster, Huxley, and Orwell.[46]

What are the elements of Wells's utopia that proclaimed it quintessentially modern? Its evolutionary dynamism was one. In a characteristically grand opening, Wells pointed to the essential difference between past utopias and all those conceived by modern thought:

The Utopia of a modern dreamer must needs differ in one fundamental aspect from the Nowheres and Utopias men planned before Darwin quickened the thought of the world. Those were all perfect and static States, a balance of happiness won for ever against the forces of unrest and disorder that inhere in things. One beheld a healthy and simple generation enjoying the fruits of the earth in an atmosphere of virtue and happiness, to be followed by other virtuous, happy, and entirely similar generations, until the Gods grew weary. Change and development were dammed back by invincible dams for ever. But the modern Utopia must be not static, but kinetic, must shape not as a permanent state but as a hopeful stage, leading to a long ascent of stages. Nowadays we do not resist and overcome the great stream of things, but rather float upon it. We build now not citadels, but ships of state. (*AMU*, ch. 1, p. 5)

That this was not an empty flight of rhetoric was shown by the sequel that Wells wrote many years later, in which he shows his utopia at a later stage of development. In *Men Like Gods* (1923), the state of the Samurai has 'withered away', and practically the whole of the population now belong to the Samurai class. In this respect at least Wells showed himself the child of Marx as much as of Darwin.

But within *A Modern Utopia* itself, there is a continual and repeated emphasis on change and initiative as the mainspring of a modern utopia. This comes out especially in Wells's insistence that modern utopias elevate freedom above all other ends, and that this will be expressed in a necessary and creative tension between individual strivings and collective needs:

To the classical Utopists, freedom was relatively trivial. Clearly they considered virtue and happiness as entirely separable from liberty, and as being altogether more important things. But the modern view, with its deepening insistence upon individuality and upon the significance of its uniqueness, steadily intensifies the value of freedom, until at last we begin to see liberty as the very substance of life, that indeed it is life, and that only the dead things, the choiceless things, live in absolute obedience to law. (*AMU*, ch.2, p. 32)

The requirements of social life set necessary limits to individual freedom, if indeed freedom outside society has any real meaning for humankind. 'There is no freedom under Anarchy', nor necessarily servitude under communism or socialism. Both 'individualism' and 'socialism' are, 'in the absolute, absurdities; the one would make men the slaves of the violent or rich, the other the slaves of the State official.' Older utopias, such as those of Plato and More, are excessively communistic and homogeneous. Bellamy and Morris show the modern temper in their 'vivid sense of individual separation'. A modern utopia realizes that to refuse the claims of the individual is to condemn society to stagnation and a potentially lethal rigidity:

The State is to be progressive, it is no longer to be static, and this alters the general condition of the Utopian problem profoundly; we have to provide not only for food and clothing, for order and health, but for initiative. The factor that leads the World State on from one phase of development to the next is the interplay of individualities; to speak teleologically, the world exists for the sake of and through initiative, and individuality is the method of initiative. Each man and woman, to the extent that his or her individuality is marked, breaks the law of precedent, transgresses the general formula, and makes a new experiment for the direction of the life force. It is impossible, therefore, for the State, which represents all and is preoccupied by the average, to make effectual experiments and intelligent innovations, and so supply the essential substance of life. As against the individual the state represents the species, in the case of the Utopian World State it absolutely represents the species. The individual emerges from the species, makes his experiment, and either fails, dies, and comes to an end, or succeeds and impresses himself in offspring, in consequences and results, intellectual, material and moral, upon the world. (*AMU*, ch. 3, pp. 88–9)

Wells remarks that it is a failing of every Utopia – 'except, perhaps, Morris's *News from Nowhere*' – that it lacks 'individualities', that 'one sees handsome but characterless buildings, symmetrical and perfect cultivations, and a multitude of people, healthy, happy, beautifully dressed, but without any personal distinction whatever' (*AMU*, p. 9). He accepts that this is probably an inevitable limitation of the utopian literary form. But he does everything he possibly can to offset this by his constant emphasis on the life of individuals as the end of all society. 'No one wants to live in any community of intercourse really, save for the sake of the individualities he would meet there. The fertilising conflict of individualities is the ultimate meaning of the personal life, and all our Utopias no more than schemes for bettering that interplay' (*AMU*, pp. 10–11).

It is one of the happiest touches in the book, and fully in keeping with Wells's purpose, that almost the first Utopian his travellers encounter is one who has wholeheartedly *rejected* utopia. They meet a Utopian hippy, who ridicules the planning and technological complexity of utopia, and who has opted out of urban life and the opportunity to enjoy the fruits of material abundance. Wells gets a good deal of fun out of this portrait of a William Morris 'simple-lifer', who spends his spare time lecturing everywhere on 'The Need of a Return to Nature' and on 'Simple Foods and Simple Ways'. But the serious point is that the modern utopia permits such eccentricity and dissent. 'The existence of our blond bare-footed friend was evidence enough that in a modern Utopia a man will be free to be just as idle or uselessly busy as it pleases him, after he has earned the minimum wage' (*AMU*, pp. 153–4). And not only have the Utopians the right to be idle, if they choose: there is a respect for a good deal of privacy (*AMU*, pp. 41–2), and the generally public nature of property is qualified by the fact that a Utopian is allowed to own 'all those things that become, as it were, by possession, extensions and expressions of his personality': clothing, the tools of his employment, books and ornaments, and up to a point his house and furniture (*AMU*, pp. 92–3). Moreover, within the context of universal security and general economic equality, there is (as with Bellamy) ample scope for the provision of individual incentives, as the best means of stimulating individual experimentation and so social progress:

The aim . . . is not to rob life of incentives but to change their nature, to make life not less energetic, but less panic-stricken and violent and base, to shift the incidence of the struggle for existence from our lower to our higher emotions, so to anticipate and neutralise the motives of the cowardly and bestial, that the ambitious and energetic imagination which is man's finest quality may become the incentive and determining factor in survival. (*AMU*, ch. 5, p. 155)

To increase the range of individuals' experience there is well-nigh absolute world-wide mobility, by means of a system of vast trains that hurtle about the earth at 200–300 miles an hour, and are furnished like a good London club or hotel (*AMU*, pp. 43–5, 239–41). In all these ways does Wells underline his oft-repeated credo that 'the State is for individuals, the law is for freedoms, the world is for experiment, experience, and change: these are the fundamental beliefs upon which a modern Utopia must go' (*AMU*, pp. 90–1). It need scarcely be pointed out how little this squares with the usual sterotype of Wells the state-worshipper, or as the planner-architect of a soulless and bureaucratic welfare state.

To the dynamism of his utopia Wells adds, as a second necessary ingredient, its planetary dimension. In this his distinctiveness is even more marked. The classical utopias had been isolated communities. Of the more recent ones, those inspired by Marxism generally gestured towards an ultimate world system, Bellamy's has a vague world federalism, and Morris largely ignores the question. Wells makes the issue absolutely central to his modern utopia.

No less than a planet will serve the purpose of a modern Utopia. Time was when a mountain valley or an island seemed to promise sufficient isolation for a polity to maintain itself intact from outward force; the Republic of Plato stood armed ready for defensive war, and the New Atlantis and the Utopia of More in theory, like China and Japan through many centuries of effectual practice, held themselves isolated from intruders. Such late instances as Butler's satirical *Erewhon* . . . found the Tibetan method of slaughtering the inquiring visitor a simple, sufficient rule. But the whole trend of modern thought is against the permanence of any such enclosures. We are acutely aware nowadays that, however subtly contrived a State may be, outside your boundary lines the epidemic, the breeding barbarian or the economic power, will gather its strength to overcome you. The swift march of invention is all for the invader. Now, perhaps you might still guard a rocky coast or a narrow pass; but what of that near tomorrrow when the flying machine soars overhead, free to descend at this point or that? A state powerful enough to keep isolated under modern conditions would be powerful enough to rule the world, would be, indeed, if not actively ruling, yet passively acquiescent in all other human organisations, and so responsible for them altogether. World-state, therefore, it must be. (*AMU*, ch. 1, pp. 11–12)

In a spirited section on race and nationalism, Wells traces the development of the world-state idea through medieval Christendom and medieval Islam, building on the empires of antiquity. In the West, the Reformation broke up the unity of Christendom, always feeble on the secular side, but modern technology and communications have worked to redress the isolating nationalisms released at that time. Ninteenth-century positivism and imperialism, and the development of such 'synthetic ideas' as Anglo-Saxonism and pan-Germanism, have continued the universalizing movement, but these have been increasingly perverted by pseudo-scientific theories of race. Wells categorically denies the existence of pure, separable human races, with fundamental differences between them. Cultural differences there are, and education and national histories, actual and invented, can accentuate these. But so too can education, if we want it to, work in the opposite direction. A world-wide synthesis of cultures and polities need not mean either fusion or uniformity; it can mean unparalleled variety, of both physical and cultural types. Coming along a terrace in Utopia, the narrator sees

> a little figure, a little bright-eyed, bearded man, inky black, frizzy haired, and clad in a white tunic and black hose, and with a mantle of lemon yellow wrapped about his shoulders. He walks, as most Utopians walk, as though he had reason to be proud of something, as though he had no reason to be afraid of anything in the world. He carries a portfolio in his hand. It is that, I suppose, as much as his hair, that recalls the *Quartier Latin* to my mind. (*AMU*, ch. 10, p. 340)

The unitary global aspect of Wells's utopianism has always been the part that has evoked the warmest assent and support. It was what attracted to him thinkers as diverse as Lewis Mumford, Arnold Toynbee and Bertrand Russell, along with others such as Gilbert Murray and Leonard Woolf, who worked with Wells in the League of Nations Society during the First World War, and later collaborators such as Arthur Salter, Julian Huxley and Kingsley Martin during his similar efforts in the 1930s.[47] A host of recent writers too have echoed George Kateb's Wellsian view that 'the whole world must be utopian for any part of it to be. . . . This is in modern times a necessary condition for utopianism; and it is, in theory, a satisfiable condition: technology permits the dream of a world community.'[48] In an era of competing power blocs, multinational corporations, instant world-wide communications and nuclear weapons, we might truly feel that Wells's insistence on the need for an integrated world order is even more relevant now than ever before. How that can be achieved politically, however, and how prevented from becoming a world Leviathan, remain as obscure and intractable as when Wells wrote.

For Wells, as for most of his supporters and critics, the world-state idea was the essential core of his intellectual system, and the very hallmark of his thought. 'Wellsian' came to mean, primarily, the hopeful world-state concept. (Wells the late Victorian scaremonger was all but forgotten.) It had been clearly stated in *Anticipations*, and it reappeared on innumerable occasions in novels, lectures and journalistic essays, over the next half-century until Wells's death in 1946. Two world wars in less than 30 years were the plain and shocking evidence of the need for a regulated world polity. Wells saw some hope now in Bolshevism, now in fascism: the New Deal of Roosevelt and the New Plan of Stalin excited him with their revolutionary potentialities, as models for a planned world-state. For a short time he even saw the Fabian Society in Britain as supplying a similar germ of the rationally planned scientific social order.

All disappointed him. No practical attempt ever got near Wells's conception of the world-state (which was, admittedly, decidedly vague in its practical details). The League of Nations he treated with undisguised contempt as the sickly child of the great schemes of the last years of the First World War. Fascism and Bolshevism turned out corrupt and nationalistic. In the last year of his life the first atomic bomb was dropped on Hiroshima, and he glimpsed with horror and despair the dawn of the nuclear age in a world still of competing nation-states. But even in that bleak moment, old and sick as he was, he did not give up all hope.[49] And, in spite of the failure of all his urgings and ceaseless propaganda on its behalf, Wells could never abandon his faith in the world-state as the sole path to salvation. 'Cosmopolis is my city, and I shall die cut off from it.'[50] In his *Autobiography* he described the 'main story' of his brain as 'the development, the steady progressive growth of a modern vision of the world, and the way in which the planned reconstruction of human relationships in the form of the world-state became at last the frame and test of my activities'.[51] The world-state idea, Wells readily avowed, was as much his religion as Christianity and Islam were to their believers. Its *credo* was reaffirmed sufficiently often as to leave no one in any doubt about it: 'In a measurable time mankind has to constitute itself into one state and one brotherhood, or it will certainly be swept down cataracts of disaster to an ultimate destruction.'[52]

The world-state of Utopia is of course, in the broadest sense of the term, socialist. This follows logically, according to Wells, from a proper conception of the sphere of economics in human life.

> Economics in Utopia must be . . . not a theory of trading based on bad psychology, but physics applied to problems in the theory of sociology. The general problem of Utopian economics is to state the conditions of the most efficient application of the steadily increasing quantities of material energy the progress of science makes available for human service, to the general needs of mankind. (*AMU*, ch. 3, pp. 80–1)

The economic problem has to be seen in the context of a society 'whose main ends are reproduction and education in an atmosphere of personal freedom'. The state exists to nurture individual growth and experimentation; and to this end it must supply the essential bedrock of material and social security. It represents the accumulated mind and experience of the race, against and within which individuals experiment and innovate. In its economic aspect, the world-state is 'a compendium of established economic experience . . . . it is the universal rule, the common restriction, the rising level platform on which individualities stand' (*AMU*, p. 89).

To this broad social conception, the existence of privately owned property on a wide scale, with its conferment of exclusive power and privilege, is anathema. In the division of functions between the State – the collective Mind of the Race – and the Individual – the experimental germ cell – private property based on the profit motive is an anachronistic and profoundly uncreative institution. It cripples individuality instead of liberating it. Wells conceives of a world-state with very extensive economic and social powers, enough to frighten even the most modern of social-democratic liberals. But it clearly isn't power for power's sake. It is power that aims at mobilizing the collective physical and intellectual energies of the race for the sole benefit of its individual constituents:

The World State in this ideal presents itself as the sole landowner of the earth. . . . The State . . . holds all the sources of energy, and, either directly or through its tenants, farmers and agents, develops these sources, and renders the energy available for the work of life. It or its tenants will produce food, and so human energy, and the exploitation of coal and electric power, and the powers of wind and wave and water will be within its right. It will pour out this energy by assignment and lease and acquiescence and what not upon its individual citizens. It will maintain order, maintain roads, maintain a cheap and efficient administration of justice, maintain cheap and rapid locomotion and be the common carrier of the planet, convey and distribute labour, control, let, or administer all natural productions, pay for and secure healthy births and a healthy and vigorous new generation, maintain the public health, coin money and sustain standards of measurement, subsidise research, and reward such commercially unprofitable undertakings as benefit the community as a whole; subsidise when needful chairs of criticism and authors and publications and collect and distribute information. The energy developed and the employment afforded by the State will descend like water that the sun has sucked out of the sea to fall upon a mountain range, and back to the sea again it will come at last, debouching in ground rent and royalty and license fees, in the fees of travellers and profits upon carrying and coinage and the like, in death duty, transfer tax, legacy and forfeiture, returning to the sea. Between the clouds and the sea it will run, as a river system runs, down through a great region of individual enterprise and interplay, whose freedom it will sustain. In that intermediate region between the kindred heights and deeps those beginnings and promises will arise that are the essential significance, the essential substance, of life. From our human point of view the mountain and the sea are for the habitable lands that lie between. So likewise the State is for Individualities. (*AMU*, ch. 3, pp. 89–90)

It need hardly be said that, although there is nothing very Marxist about Wells's socialism, any more than there is about Bellamy's, it belongs squarely to the wider socialist tradition. Wells himself said that 'my socialism was pre-Marxian', influenced largely by Plato and More, by the modern 'primitives' such as Robert Owen, and by later non-Marxist socialists such as Henry George and Bellamy. When he at last encountered Marxism he was profoundly hostile to its doctrine of class war, which he found essentially destructive and uncreative at a time when the great task facing the race was reconstruction.[53] Socialism, he wrote in 1906, 'is no piece of political strategy, no political opposition of class to class; it is a plan for the reconstruction of human life, for the replacement of a disorder by order. . . . I hate this class war idea.'[54]

Equally repugnant to him was the 'parish pump' socialism of the Fabians, and the socialism of the anarchists and syndicalists. The former were blind to the change in scale entailed in the development of modern science and technology, which was leading to the inevitable development of the world-state; the latter, along with the Marxists, made the error of linking socialism to democracy, which had intensified the 'insurrectionary impulse' in modern societies, and inflamed the masses with unreal expectations of a massive public dole-out on the day after the revolution. Most damaging of all, these types of socialism had all been hostile to the spirit of creative organization and planning. Wells put this down partly to 'a conspicuous absence from about the cradle-side of Socialism, of men with the scientific habit of mind'. Marxism in particular had depreciated 'social inventiveness', in its virulent hostility to what it called '"utopianism" – that is, making plans'. 'Any attempt to work out the details of the world contemplated under Socialism was received by the old Marxists with contemptuous hostility.'[55] In the end, Wells came increasingly to feel that the socialist philosophy, as popularly advanced, was unsatisfactory and insufficient, a barrier to the acceptance of his ideas. Socialism had exhausted its creative possibilities. Socialism, says Clissold in *The World of William Clissold* (1926), had 'gone – gone like Chartism, like Puritanism, like the naturalism of Rousseau or the civic virtue of Robespierre. . . .' By the 1930s Wells was declaring:

Steadily now throughout the world the Socialist idea and its communist intensification sink into subordination to the ampler proposition of planning upon a planetary scale thrust upon mankind by the urgent pressure of reality. World planning takes Socialism in its stride, and is Socialism plus half a dozen other equally important constructive intentions.[56]

If Marx was firmly rejected as a guide to Utopia, the older figure of Francis Bacon is central and present throughout. For Wells, Bacon's *New Atlantis* was not simply 'the greatest of the scientific utopias' but the most important for modern utopianism:

The Utopia of Bacon's has produced more in the way of real consequences than any other Utopia that was ever written . . . . It embodies a new conception of human life, the conception of continual organized research. All the other Utopias present islands, communities and worlds of happy and exemplary completion and self-satisfaction, but the Utopia of Francis Bacon is a world of seekers after knowledge, a world growing perpetually in knowledge and wisdom and incidentally growing in power. It is a world ruled by organized Science . . . . It supplements the Utopia of Plato which would make the philosopher, king. Instead of that it tries out the idea of making not the philosopher, but scientific philosophy, king.[57]

Bacon was a truer prophet of the socialist state than Marx because the latter had obscured the fundamental, intrinsic connection between science and socialism. Marxism certainly acknowleded the importance of modern science, whose fruits were the necessary basis of the material abundance of the future socialist society. Marx's followers, too, were fond of calling themselves 'scientific socialists', to distinguish themselves by the superiority of their method of analysis from the 'primitives' of pre-Marxist socialism. But Wells always felt that the science in Marxism was spurious. Marxists were drawn to it as a symbol of modernity, and were awed by its stupendous possibilities; but they didn't really understand it, and were only too liable to stunt its potential by their insistence on the rule of the unqualified masses. Few Marxists were working scientists, and therefore they did not experience, as a matter of continuous daily routines, the practical and demonstrable connection between scientific activity and socialism. Scientists, thought Wells, by the very character of their work were naturally socialists – far more so than the proletariat. Only in the world community of scientists was the idea and ethic of socialism truly perceived and practised.

The fundamental idea upon which socialism rests is the same fundamental idea as that upon which all real scientific work is carried on. It is the denial that chance impulse and individual will and happening constitute the only possible methods by which things may be done in the world. It is an assertion that things are, in their nature, orderly; that things may be computed, may be calculated upon and foreseen. In the spirit of this belief, science aims at a systematic knowledge of material things. 'Knowledge is power', knowledge that is frankly and truly exchanged, that is the primary assumption of the *New Atlantis* which created the Royal Society and the organisation of research. The Socialist has just that same faith in the order, the knowableness of things, and the power of man in co-operation to overcome chance . . . . Just as science aims at a common organized body of knowledge, to which all its servants contribute, and in which they share, so Socialism insists upon its ideal of an organized social order which every man serves and by which every man benefits.[58]

The inspiration of and debt to Bacon is directly acknowledged in *A Modern Utopia*. Scientific research is encouraged and developed as a first priority by the Utopian rulers. There are 'great systems of laboratories' attached to every level of the administration, and every industrial establishment is obliged to conduct scientific research. Inventors are carefully searched out, supported and generously rewarded. Universities retain some limited teaching functions but are largely devoted to the pursuit of 'pure' knowledge in all the sciences, physical and social. The 'world-wide House of Saloman thus created' engages the energies of over a million men. (*AMU*, pp. 275–6)

The Baconian impulse shows itself even more strongly in the emphasis on science in the service of man and society. Here too there is a sharp contrast between the classical and modern utopia. The older utopians, says Wells, 'ran their world by hand. Continual bodily labour was a condition of social existence.' The classical utopias are fertile in political and moral inventions, but dead 'in regard to all material possibilities'. The material conditions of life are taken as given and permanent. 'Plato commenced the tradition of Utopias without machinery', and with the partial exception of *New Atlantis* this continues right up to the nineteenth century. 'It is only in the nineteenth century that Utopias appeared in which the fact is clearly recognised that the social fabric rests no longer upon human labour.' Cabet in Europe and Bellamy in America are awarded the palms for being the first to present utopias in which it is clearly shown that labour can be abolished by the use of machinery. 'There appears no limit to the invasion of life by the machine' (*AMU*, pp. 97–100).

Wells's utopianism had no patience with pastoral or arcadian visions, with 'the idea that Utopia necessarily implies something rather oaken and hand-made and primitive', such as is to be found in the utopias of W. H. Hudson, Richard Jefferies, Ruskin and Morris. He enjoys himself with these 'outright Return-to-nature Utopians', with their 'bold make-believe that all toil may be made a joy, and with that a levelling down of all society to an equal participation in labour'.

But indeed this is against all the observed behaviour of mankind. It needed the Olympian unworldliness of an irresponsible rich man of the share-holding type, a

Ruskin or Morris playing at life, to imagine as much. Road-making under Mr Ruskin's auspices was a joy at Oxford no doubt, and a distinction, and it still remains a distinction; it proved the least contagious of practices . . . . If toil is a blessing, never was blessing so effectually disguised. (*AMU*, ch. 3, pp. 100–1)

The modern utopian accepts that a certain amount of bodily and mental exercise is a good thing, as for instance in artistic production and indeed 'whenever a man is freely obeying himself'. The essence of toil, by contrast, is 'that it is imperative . . . that it excludes freedom, not that it involves fatigue'. The modern utopia sets its goal as the abolition of all such toil, which it considers degrading and unnecessary in the world offered by modern science:

So long as anything but a quasi-savage life depended upon toil, so long was it hopeless to expect mankind to do anything but struggle to confer just as much of this blessing as possible upon one another. But now that the new conditions physical science is bringing about not only dispense with man as a source of energy, but supply the hope that all routine work may be made automatic, it is becoming conceivable that presently there may be no need for anyone to toil habitually at all; that a labouring class – that is to say a class of workers without personal initiative – will become unnecessary to the world of men. (*AMU*, ch. 3, pp. 101–2)

And Wells concluded his polemic against the primitivists with what is perhaps the most famous of his panegyrics on science, and its untold potential for liberating mankind:

The plain message physical science has for the world at large is this, that were our political and social and moral devices only as well contrived to their ends as a lino-type machine, an antiseptic operating plant, or an electric tram-car, there need now at the present moment be no appreciable toil in the world, and only the smallest fraction of the pain, the fear, and the anxiety that now makes human life so doubtful in its value. There is more than enough for everyone alive. Science stands, a too competent servant, behind her wrangling underbred masters, holding out resources, devices, and remedies they are too stupid to use. And on its material side a modern Utopia must needs present these gifts as taken, and show a world that is really abolishing the need of labour, abolishing the last base reason for anyone's servitude or inferiority. (*AMU*, ch. 3, p. 102)

The society of *A Modern Utopia* has not in fact yet reached the point of abolishing labour, although that is its tendency. It is currently at a stage that we might call 'advanced Keynes–Beveridge', by reference to the kind of economic and social changes advocated by Keynes and Beveridge (and of course influentially by Wells himself) in England in the 1930s and 1940s. The right to employment is guaranteed to everyone, with a legally-fixed minimum wage. Wells relies on the hope that 'a State saturated with science and prolific in invention will stimulate new enterprises', and that this, taken with a strict policy of population control, will eliminate the problem of unemployment. But for those few not able to find employment by the normal means, which includes a world-wide system of labour exchanges, the State acts as 'the reserve employer of labour'. It employs labour either indirectly, by reducing the working day and so absorbing the excess, or directly, by embarking on public works. In any case, no citizen of Utopia need feel anxiety on this score as there is a comprehensive system of welfare, from the cradle to the grave. Everyone is properly housed; there is a guaranteed level of nutrition, a free health service, free universal education to the age of twenty, and provision for old age. All these are provided as a matter of right, as to 'shareholders in the common enterprise', not as to the recipients of public charity (*AMU*, pp. 138–41, 147–55).

But although science has not yet delivered all that it can and will, its spirit is pervasive in Utopia. It is seen, for instance, in the clean lines and functional design of the room at the inn where the two travellers spend their first night. A few details illustrate the Wellsian fascination with functionality and mechanical efficiency:

> The room has no corners to gather dirt, wall meets floor with a gentle curve, and the apartment could be swept out effectually by a few strokes of a mechanical sweeper . . . . A cake of soap drops out of a store machine on the turn of a handle, and when you have done with it, you drop that and your soiled towels and so forth, which are also given to you by machines, into a little box, through the bottom of which they drop at once, and sail down a smooth shaft . . . . You are politely requested to turn a handle at the foot of your bed before leaving the room, and forthwith the frame turns up into a vertical position, and the bedclothes hang airing . . . . You stand at the doorway and realise that there remains not a minute's work for anyone to do. Memories of the foetid disorder of many an earthly bedroom after a night's use float across your mind . . . . (*AMU*, ch. 3, pp. 104–5)

The same yearning for efficiency, simplicity and system, is seen in all the physical aspects of Utopia. Wells strongly deprecates the prejudice that machinery and technical efficiency must mean ugliness. 'Ugliness is the measure of imperfection.' It is the mismatching of product to purpose. 'Things made by mankind under modern conditions are ugly, primarily because our social organisation is ugly, because we live in an atmosphere of snatch and uncertainty . . . .' In Utopia, the designers and builders of tram roads and railways are 'artist craftsmen', who strive to 'achieve the simplicity of perfection'. They make their 'girders and rails and parts as gracious as that first engineer, Nature, has made the stems of her plants and the joints and gestures of her animals' (*AMU*, pp. 110–12). The people of Utopia too are beautiful, in a spare and rather Spartan way, with striking racial mixes. Their clothes and bearing have the grace and simplicity that call to the narrator's mind, at various times, the Knights Templars, Cromwell's Ironsides, and fifteenth-century Florentines (*AMU*, pp. 159, 226, 312–17). And the cities are a triumph of the vision of the artist-engineer, the realization of the sketches and scientific intimations of Leonardo, Michaelangelo and Dürer. The narrator does not so much describe as offer a dream-like evocation of utopian London, with its 'mighty University', 'stupendous libraries and museums' and thriving literary and artistic life. Its physical aspect is overwhelming:

> One will come into this place as one comes into a noble mansion. They will have flung great arches and domes of glass above the wider spaces of the town, the slender beauty of the perfect metal-work far overhead will be softened to a fairy-like unsubstantiality by

the mild London air. It will be the London air we know, clear of filth and all impurity, the same air that gives our October days their unspeakable clarity and makes every London twilight mysteriously beautiful. We shall go along avenues of architecture that will be emancipated from the last memories of the squat temple boxes of the Greeks, the buxom curvatures of Rome; the Goth in us will have taken to steel and countless new materials as kindly as once he took to stone. The gay and swiftly moving platforms of the public ways will go past on either hand, carrying sporadic groups of people, and very speedily we shall find ourselves in a sort of central space, rich with palms and flowering bushes and statuary. We shall look along an avenue of trees, down a wide gorge between the cliffs of crowded hotels, the hotels that are still glowing with internal lights, to where the shining morning river streams dawnlit out to the sea. (*AMU*, ch. 7, pp. 244)

The scientific spirit naturally penetrates the social organization of Utopia as much as its physical organization. Wells pays particular attention to the relations between the sexes, to the having and rearing of children, and to the problem of social 'failures' and persistent deviance. Here he is at his most briskly rational and scientific, in ways exactly calculated to upset liberals and humanists.

Breeding is strongly controlled by the State. 'In the civilized State it is now clearly possible to make the conditions of life tolerable for every living creature, providing the inferiors can be prevented from increasing and multiplying.' Wells accepts the gloomy Malthusian view that the unchecked growth of population leads to misery and pauperization. Nature's way of dealing with this is cruel and bloody. The 'ideal of a scientific civilization' is to prevent the birth of weaklings and defectives, rather than to leave them to struggle hopelessly in a society for which they are unfitted. Criminals, those who prove incapable of personally supporting themselves and the physically defective will not be permitted to bear children, although they may marry. This measure of control Wells sees as no more than an extension of the general tendency in modern society for the state to take over the responsibility for the general welfare of children: 'As it does so, its right to decide which children it will shelter becomes more and more reasonable.' But this is not 'state breeding' on the lines of Plato's *Republic*, insists Wells. There is no 'compulsory pairing'. The concern for individuality in Utopia means that the State must leave people free to seek each other out, for 'the supreme and significant expression of individuality . . . lies in the selection of a partner for procreation' (*AMU*, pp. 180–6).

Nevertheless, the State takes a close interest in marriage and parenthood. Indeed, it regards motherhood as a matter primarily of concern to society, and only incidentally as a personal matter between two people. 'When a child comes in, the future of the species comes in', and it is the State's peculiar province to be the guardian of that future. Motherhood is regarded as 'a service to the State', and is paid and supported accordingly. This gives the woman an essential degree of independence from the man. The more successful her nurturing of her children – and, *pace* Plato, Wells still considers the home as providing the best environment for this – the more she is paid and respected. 'A capable woman who has borne, bred, and begun the education of eight or nine well-built, intelligent and successful sons and daughters would be an extremely prosperous woman, quite irrespective of the economic fortunes of the man she has married.' But the State therefore has good reason to see that the marriage union, with its near inevitability of leading to motherhood, is 'neither free, nor promiscuous, nor practically universal'. Individuals wishing to marry have to satisfy certain conditions of health, education and income. Each partner receives a copy of the record of the life-history of the prospective spouse, and is given time to consider the decision. Only after this interval is the marriage allowed and registered (*AMU*, pp. 186–93).[59]

On the actual relations between the sexes, and especially the degree of equality achieved by women, Wells is tentative and somewhat evasive. He does not press for the more or less complete equality that he was to proclaim a few years later in *Ann Veronica*. Here, he hedges on whether to follow Plato in treating the sexes alike, or Aristotle in treating them as different and complementary. The evolutionary trend among mankind has been towards the differentiation of the sexes. Modern European women of the middle class have carried sexual specialization to the highest degree yet. Should Utopia follow or reverse this trend? It will clearly remove the more glaring obstacles in the way of the independence of women, especially by relieving them of their economic dependence on men by the public endowment of motherhood. Beyond that, it will leave men and women free to choose how to define their roles. Its ideal is 'an equality of spirit between men and women'. Gradual experimentation will produce the right synthesis of styles and traditions that is the aim of all Utopian organization (*AMU*, pp. 196–213). This is certainly in the spirit of Wells's very open Utopia. But it is surprising, especially in view of his warm advocacy of the feminist cause at this time – or was it perhaps because of the trouble this was getting him into? – to find him so agnostic on this topic.

No such uncertainty afflicts his attitude towards the moral and physical failures in Utopia. 'It is our business to ask what Utopia will do with its congential invalids, its idiots and madmen, its drunkards and men of vicious mind, its cruel and furtive souls, its stupid people, too stupid to be of use to the community, its lumpish, unteachable and unimaginative people.' They will not be allowed to breed, of course, and that will eventually diminish the problem. But it is in the nature of the species and society that such failures will always be thrown up to some extent. The solution is to resort 'to a kind of social surgery'. Persistent young offenders are placed in 'disciplinary schools and colleges . . . in remote and solitary regions'. More hardened adult criminals and defectives, those considered virtually incurable, are exiled to islands – the 'island of Incurable Cheats', the 'Island of Drink', etc. – where, quarantined from the rest of the Utopian population, they are allowed to be largely self-governing, conducting their own often jolly and riotous activities according to the nature of their particular criminal or deviant bent. This, says Wells, is infinitely preferable to a system of prisons, which are 'places of torture by restraint' (*AMU*, pp. 136–47).

In this echo of *When the Sleeper Wakes*,[60] with its ominous system of 'psychic surgery' here given a utopian gloss, Wells admits that 'the dreadfulness of all such proposals as this lies in the possibility of their execution falling into the hands of hard, dull, and cruel administrators.' The answer comes pat: 'In the case of a Utopia one assumes the best possible government, a government as merciful and deliberate as it is powerful and decisive. (*AMU*, p. 142). It is indeed in this quality of purposefulness that the scientific attitude shows itself most clearly in Utopia. Wells is often deliberately vague about details because he does not wish to obscure the overriding impulse and ethos of Utopia. The presence of the narrator's companion in Utopia – a vain, querulous, self-obsessed botanist – is used repeatedly to illustrate by contrast the large vision and firmness of purpose of the Utopians. The Utopians have brought order out of human chaos, the messy disorder of contemporary social existence that Wells to the last days of his life loathed and fought against. It is what forcibly strikes the narrator on his first glimpse of the Utopian landscape and people: 'The pervading quality of the whole scene was a sane order, the deliberate solution of problems, a progressive intention steadily achieving itself' (*AMU*, p. 125). The encounter with the self-opinionated 'back-to-Nature' Utopian, and the constant egotistical complaints of the botanist, provokes an angry outburst:

If we are to have any Utopia at all, we must have a clear common purpose, and a great and steadfast movement of will to override all these incurably egotistical dissentients. Something is needed wide and deep enough to float the worst of egotisms away . . . . It is manifest this Utopia could not come about by chance and anarchy, but by co-ordinated effort and a community of design . . . . (*AMU*, ch. 4, p. 128)

Later he reflects on this Utopia of 'a quite unearthly sanity, of good management and comprehensive design in every material thing' (p. 159).

Compared with our world, it is like a well-oiled engine beside a scrap-heap . . . . We of the twentieth century are not going to accept the sweetish, faintly nasty slops of Rousseauism that so gratified our great-great-grandparents in the eighteenth. We know that order and justice do not come by nature – 'if only the policeman would go away.' These things mean intention, will, carried to a scale that our poor, vacillating, hot and cold earth has never known . . . . Behind all this material order, these perfected communications, perfected public services and economic organisations, there must be men and women willing these things . . . . (*AMU*, ch. 5, pp. 171–3)

Perhaps nothing so well symbolizes this Utopian straining after order and design as the World Index of Population, 'housed in a vast series of buildings at or near Paris'. Here is a record of every citizen of the world Utopia, detailing on individual cards physical and social characteristics, family history, occupational history, criminal record, residence and all physical movements across the planet. It enables every one in the world to be promptly identified and traced.

A little army of attendants would be at work upon this index day and night. From sub-stations constantly engaged in checking back thumbmarks and numbers, an incessant stream of information would come, of births, of deaths, of arrivals at inns, of applications to post-offices for letters, of tickets taken for long journeys, of criminal convictions, marriages, applications for public doles and the like. A filter of offices would sort out the stream, and all day and all night for ever a swarm of clerks would go to and fro correcting this central register, and photographing copies of its entries for transmission to the subordinate local stations, in response to their inquiries. So the inventory of the State would watch its every man and the wide world write its history as the fabric of its destiny flowed on. (*AMU*, ch. 5, pp. 164–5)

With such innocent portraits did Wells offer his hostages to the liberals and literary intellectuals who steadily, throughout the 1920s and 1930s, mounted their assault against his vision of the scientific Utopia.

A TECHNOCRATIC UTOPIA?

The ideal society of *A Modern Utopia*, selectively interpreted and eked out with later utopian writings of Wells's, gave rise to a standard and sterotyped version of the Wellsian utopia. The Wellsian utopia was large-scale, centralized, bureaucratic and automatic. It was run by a power elite of scientists and technicians. It was planned and administered down to the last detail. It was inhuman by virtue of its scale and impersonality, and soulless in its out-and-out materialism. It was complacent, conformist, consumerist. The world-state was a servile state. 'What a narrow petty bourgeois! What a philistine!' Lenin is alleged to have exclaimed after learning of Wells's vision from the master himself.[61]

It was G. K. Chesterton, Wells's persistent critic and life-long friend, who launched one of the earliest and most damaging attacks. He was disappointed, after the exhilarating pyrotechnics of the early science fantasies, to find Wells settling conservatively in *A Modern Utopia* for the rule of 'a class of engineers'. He was particularly incensed by Wells's novel of the previous year, *The Food of the Gods* (1904). This was one of those characteristically ambiguous fables of those years in which, by the presentation of noble giants set among petty normal-sized humans, Wells seemed to be lamenting the power held by the pygmies (the traditional forces looking to the past) over the giants (the new men and women looking towards the future). While the novel did not necessarily praise bigness itself, Chesterton took it to be doing so. He referred to it as 'the tale of Jack the Giant-Killer told from the point of view of the giant', and went on to take Wells to task for this celebration of 'the Strong Man, the Caesar, the Superman'.[62]

A few years later, in a story entitled 'The Machine Stops' (1909), E. M. Forster presented a passionate critique of a dehumanized machine civilization and what was seen as its corollary, the Wellsian world-state. Forster himself described his story as 'a counterblast to one of the heavens of H. G. Wells'. But it was mostly in the period after the First World War, when Wells's reputation as a publicist and skilful popularizer was reaching its height, that his standing among the literary intelligentsia seriously began to fall. There continued to be discerning admirers from abroad, like Yevgeny Zamyatin, who saw nothing contradictory in both praising Wells's achievement and writing an anti-utopia, *We* (1920), which borrowed heavily from the Wellsian repertoire.[63] But British intellectuals largely ignored the earlier Wells, to concentrate their fire on the later propagandist of the world-state. Aldous Huxley began his series of scathing portraits of Wells and Wellsian philosophy, culminating in the onslaught on the Wellsian utopia in *Brave New World* (1932). From the height of his *haut bourgeois* Marxism, Christopher St John Sprigg ('Christopher Caudwell') echoed Lenin's contempt in denouncing Wells's utopian vision as the product of the typical *petit bourgeois*, caught between the wealthy capitalist and the proletariat, and so frustrated and frightened, like the *petit bourgeois* heroes of all Wells's social novels, 'from Kipps to Clissold'. Such a person is bound to seek escape, as Wells escaped by his writing into the bourgeoisie proper, and to construct fantasy worlds of a rationalized capitalism where humane technocrats administer a utopia free from all class conflict.[64]

But probably it was George Orwell whose attacks have had the strongest and longest-lasting influence, and who gave the widest currency to the pejorative connotation of the term 'Wellsian'. Orwell was fully alive to Wells's impact on Orwell's own generation, and in turning on the older writer he seems to have been striving partly to free himself from the mesmerizing effect of Wells's writings. As Orwell put it,

> Thinking people who were born about the beginning of this century are in some sense Wells's own creation . . . . I doubt whether anyone who was writing books between 1900 and 1920, at any rate in the English language, influenced the young so much. The minds of all of us, and therefore the physical world, would be perceptibly different if Wells had never existed.[65]

Orwell's own novels of the 1930s, such as *A Clergyman's Daughter* and *Coming Up for Air*, showed the continuing indebtedness to Wells in an almost embarrassing way. In *The Road to Wigan Pier* (1937), as if to shake this off, Orwell rounded viciously on Wells as the prophet of a grotesque and philistine 'machine-world'.

> How often have we not heard it, that glutinously uplifting stuff about 'the machines, our new race of slaves, which will set humanity free', etc., etc., etc. To these people, apparently, the only danger of the machine is its possible use for destructive purposes; as, for instance, aeroplanes are used in war. Barring war and unforeseen disasters, the future is envisaged as an ever more rapid march of mechanical progress; machines to save work, machines to save thought, machines to save pain, hygiene, efficiency, organization, more hygiene, more efficiency, more organization, more machines – until finally you land up in the by now familiar Wellsian Utopia, aptly caricatured in *Brave New World*, the paradise of little fat men.[66]

In the early years of the Second World War, Orwell went so far as to see Hitler's National Socialist state as the perverted but clearly recognizable offspring of the Wellsian Utopia:

> Much of what Wells has imagined and worked for is physically there in Nazi Germany. The order, the planning, the State encouragement of science, the steel, the concrete, the aeroplanes, are all there, but in the service of ideas appropriate to the Stone Age. Science is fighting on the side of superstition.[67]

And finally, in *Nineteen Eighty-Four* he completed the case against Wells by presenting his own brutal nightmare version of the world-state – a picture no less brilliantly frightening for owing many of its key images and ideas to Wells's earlier novels, especially *When the Sleeper Wakes* and 'A Story of the Days to Come'.[68]

The attacks on Wells were not groundless. No one could have written for half a century on such themes as Wells did without appearing to hold extreme positions on the importance of planning, technology and science. A qualified endorsement of both Leninism and fascism ('a bad good thing'), as harbingers of the scientific world-state, is clearly to be found in a number of places.[69] The belief in science, and what it could do for mankind, at times became a religion. 'Science was coming', Richard Remington learns from his father in *The New Machiavelli*, 'a spirit of light and order, to the rescue of a world groaning and travailing in muddle for the want of it. . . .' Later he and his friend Willersley project 'an ideal state, an organized state as confident and powerful as modern science, as balanced and beautiful as a body, as beneficent as sunshine, the organized state that should end muddle for ever. . .' In *Tono-Bungay* George Ponderevo is saved from a serious emotional breakdown by 'Science with her order, her inhuman distance, her steely certainties. . .'[70]

In passages such as these, Wells provided ammunition enough for his critics. And *A Modern Utopia*, as we have seen, is not lacking in them either. But of all places, *A Modern Utopia* is also the most significant refutation of conventional notions of the Wellsian utopia. It is impossible to see it as propagating an ideal of rampant consumerism and technocratic power. It is here that Wells insists most clearly that the scientifically planned and ordered world-state is an empty shell without a personal and individual life that matches it in harmony and fulfilment.

This insistence is implicit in the very form that Wells adopted for *A Modern Utopia*. Wells, 'the author', distances himself from the narrative, appearing only infrequently in italicized passages to comment on the action, and in particular to set the scene and to sum up at the end. The main narrative is given over to 'The Voice', who is ostensibly reading from his manuscript about the Utopian experiences of himself and his botanist companion. The device is not just a sly way of evading a direct commitment to the utopian philosophy expressed in the book. It allows Wells to stress the fallible, personal and individual nature of all utopian visions. But more importantly, it also allows him to explore the relationship between the objective socio-political framework of Utopia, and the subjective, personal and emotional life of ordinary, everyday mortals within it.

For the ostensible narrator, the 'Voice', is also manifestly one guise of the real life Wells, the author:

> The Owner of the Voice you must figure to yourself as a whitish plump man, a little under the middle size and age, with such blue eyes as many Irishmen have, and agile in his movements and with a slight tonsorial baldness – a penny might cover it – of the crown. His front is convex. He droops at times like most of us, but for the greater part he bears himself as valiantly as a sparrow. Occasionally his hand flies out with a fluttering gesture of illustration. And his Voice . . . is an unattractive tenor that becomes at times aggressive. (*AMU*, pp. 1–2)

This isn't a mere piece of facetiousness on Wells's part. The small plump man doesn't appear in a utopia as a trivial whimsy of the author's. It is of the very essence of Wells's conception of utopia that he should be there. His utopia would not be one of grand plans and schemes, with detailed specifications as to the organization of work and the election of rulers. 'Utopias were once in good faith, projects for a fresh creation of the world and of a most unworldy completeness; this so-called Modern Utopia is a mere story of personal adventures among Utopian philosophies' (*AMU*, p. 372). And the person who undertakes the adventure is Wells himself: not just Wells ('the author'), the successful novelist, the social prophet, but also Wells ('the Voice'), the struggling writer from Bromley, the sickly child of domestic servants-turned-shopkeepers. In reaching out for utopia, in having a dream of it, the ordinary mundane Wells saw himself, and the world which had shaped him, transfigured into the image of his deepest personal longings. No other utopia is so powerfully suffused with the sense of an intensely personal vision. Utopia for Wells is indeed 'the paradise of little fat men', but in a quite different sense from that intended by Orwell. It is not really a hedonistic after-dinner daydream of unlimited abundance and leisure produced by machines. It is more truly a vision of a world where unnecessary bodily and mental suffering have been eliminated, and where individuals are allowed to grow to their full human stature in mind and body.

The anatomy of that suffering in the unreformed world is presented largely in Wells's 'social' novels. It is this that links the social novels – *The Wheels of Chance, Love and Mr Lewisham, Kipps, Tono-Bungay, the History of Mr Polly* – with the more explicitly utopian writing. In the thinly autobiographical lower-middle-class figures of Hoopdriver, Lewisham, Kipps and George Ponderevo, Wells put all his utopian anguish and yearning. Like him, or at any rate as he often saw himself, these were 'all personalities thwarted and crippled by the defects of our contemporary civilisation', as Wells said of his characters. Describing his purpose in *Kipps*, he wrote to his publisher Macmillan: '*Kipps* is designed to present a typical member of the English lower middle class in all its pitiful limitation and feebleness, and beneath a treatment deliberately kindly and general provides a sustained and fairly exhaustive criticism of the ideals and ways of life of the great mass of middle-class English people.'[71]

In a perceptive review of *Kipps*, the Liberal politician C. F. Masterman noted the connection between the social critic and prophet of *Anticipations* and *Mankind in the Making* and the novelist of lower-middle-class life:

> All the mordant power of Mr Wells's revolt against the mess which men and women are making of their world, against the failure of life which has attained comfort but no inner serenity or passion or large and intelligible purpose of being, is woven into his picture of the struggle of Kipps to attain a footing in these regions of social advancement.[72]

Wells repeatedly refers to his own acute sense of social and physical deprivation, as the stunted product of a straitened class and a straitened world. In his *Autobiography* he says that 'until I was over forty the sense of physical inferiority was a constant acute distress to me which no philosophy could mitigate.'[73] In his seventies, now an eminent figure of world repute, he still could not suppress his anger and bitterness at the obstacles placed in his way by an unjust and corrupt social order:

I have heard other people who have had similar experiences to mine tell of the thirst for knowledge they experienced. I suppose I had that thirst in good measure, but far stronger was my anger at the paltry sham of an education that had been fobbed off upon me; angry resentment also at the dismal negligence of the social and religious organizations responsible for me, that had allowed me to be thrust into the hopeless drudgery of a shop, ignorant, misinformed, undernourished and physically under-developed, without warning and without guidance, at the age of thirteen. To sink or swim . . . . I hated them as only the young can hate, and it gave me energy to struggle, and I set about struggling for knowledge. I was bitterly determined to see my world clearer and truer, before it was too late.[74]

In Wells's social novels and utopian writing, there is a constant interplay between two types of Wellsian man. There is the Chaplinesque 'little man' of the social novels. Physically he is short and stout, and frequently dyspeptic. He is generally lower-middle-class,[75] and has the striving characteristic of that class. He is incurably romantic, a creature of infinite longings and desires. He dreams of an ideal world of reason and beauty, 'where all that is tangled and confused in human affairs has been unravelled and made straight' (*AMU*, p. 352), and where individuals find complete mental and emotional fulfilment. His attempts to break out of his bodily and social prison repeatedly meet with failure, but his hopes are never permanently extinguished.

Then there is utopian man. Utopian man is tall and noble, spare of form and rational of mind. His eyes are clear and bright, his hips lean, his stomach concave. He leads an austere and elevated life of the mind and spirit. He is a sage and an Olympian, the Utopians of *Men Like Gods* or the Samurai of *A Modern Utopia* ('who remind me of Plato's Guardians, who look like Knights Templars, who bear a name that recalls the swordsmen of Japan . . . .' (*AMU*, p. 227). The Wellsian 'little man' is constantly striving to become utopian man. Utopian man is the Ideal, the small plump man the Actual. In *A Modern Utopia* this is neatly symbolized in the encounter between the narrator and his Utopian double. (Utopia contains the suitably modified doubles of all earthly individuals.) 'My Utopian self is, of course, my better self . . .' (*AMU*, p. 247). The meeting brings home powerfully to the narrator his 'manifest inferiority', the fact that he comes 'trailing clouds of earthly confusion and weakness'. It also stirs up resentful thoughts of a spoilt unhappy life and the blighting of youthful aspirations:

I think of the confessions I have just made to him, the strange admissions both to him and myself. I have stirred up the stagnations of my own emotional life, the pride that has slumbered, the hopes and disappointments that have not troubled me for years. There are things that happened to me in my adolescence that no discipline of reason will ever bring to a just proportion for me, the first humiliations I was made to suffer, the waste of all the fine irrecoverable loyalties and passions of my youth. The dull base caste of my little personal tragi-comedy – I have ostensibly forgiven, I have for the most part forgotten – and yet when I recall them I hate each actor still. Whenever it comes to my mind . . . there it is and these detestable people blot out the stars for me. (*AMU*, ch. 8, p. 254)

It is not simply the narrator whose memories and feelings focus our attention on the individual life in Utopia. His companion, the botanist, is also put there to insist on the claims of the personal as against the public – although Wells is too much of a socialist to pit these realms mechanically against each other. Once again, as with the 'back-to-nature' Utopian dissident, Wells makes his point comically. While the narrator waxes increasingly enthusiastic at his discovery of Utopia, the botanist is largely querulous and uninterested, bored with Utopian economics and politics, and appalled at Utopian views on women, the family and race. He is obsessed with his private life on earth, and especially with a love affair going disastrously wrong. Many of the best comic effects in the book – which at times partakes very much of the spirit of *Kipps* and *Mr Polly* – come from the exasperation of the narrator, musing on noble Utopian schemes, with the petty personal preoccupations of his companion:

> It is a curiously human thing, and, upon my honour, not one I had designed, that when at last I stand in the twilight in the midst of a Utopian township, when my whole being should be taken up with speculative wonder, this man should be standing by my side, and lugging my attention persistently towards himself, towards his limited futile self. This thing perpetually happens to me, this intrusion of something small and irrelevant and alive, upon my great impressions .... And now this man, on my first night in Utopia, talks and talks and talks of his poor little love affair. (*AMU*, ch. 2, pp. 54–5)

It does not take a very close reading of this passage to detect the irony there; and indeed, it is the botanist's persistent harping on his love life that later forces the narrator to take stock of his own life, as he prepares to meet his Utopian double, and to realize the importance of the personal happiness that has passed him by. It would in fact be quite out of keeping with everything we know of Wells's life, and practically everything he wrote, to imagine that he could leave this aspect out of his utopia. For one of Wells's constant themes is that no social order is worth anything, nor in the end is workable, if it cannot provide for a fulfilling and satisfying personal life. If that is a bourgeois view, Wells had no difficulty in owning to it, as his concept of utopia was essentially of a transformed middle class. But he never departed from the position that there has to be a harmonious match between the microcosmic life of personal relations and the macrocosmic order of society; otherwise there is anarchy and unhappiness. Here too Wells strikes a note conspicuously absent from most utopias before him. It is one of the things that allow him to claim with some justice that his is the first truly modern utopia. Wells knew bitterly enough from his own life how much this 'poor little love affair' mattered in the life of the individual and society. There were times when, defying the respectable world of English society over the alleged scandalousness of *Ann Veronica* and *The New Machiavelli*, he seemed to think that it was the only thing that mattered. *The New Machiavelli* indeed comes close to asserting just this. Richard Remington, who has sacrificed a promising political career for an adulterous love affair that has driven him into exile abroad, prepares to emulate Machiavelli and to write a political treatise. But he finds that he cannot, like Machiavelli, leave sex and the passions outside the study door:

> It is this gradual discovery of sex as a thing collectively portentous that I have to mingle with my statecraft if my picture is to be true .... I began life ignoring women, they came

to me at first perplexing and dishonouring; only very slowly and very late in my life and after misadventure, did I gauge the power and beauty of the love of man and woman and learnt how it must needs frame a justifiable vision of the ordered world. Love has brought me to disaster, because my career had been planned regardless of its possibility and value. But Machiavelli, it seems to me, when he went into his study, left not only the earth of life outside but its unsuspected soul . . . .

So important did Wells regard this theme of the personal and the public realms in utopia that he chose to step out from behind the ostensible narrator and, in his own authorial voice, actually to conclude *A Modern Utopia* on it. He first stresses the extreme tentativeness and subjectivity of his utopia:

There is a common notion that the reading of a Utopia should end with a swelling heart and clear resolves, with lists of names, formation of committees, and even the commencement of subscriptions. But this Utopia began upon a philosophy of fragmentation, and ends, confusedly, amidst a gross tumult of immediate realities, in dust and doubt, with, at the best, one individual's aspiration. (*AMU*, ch. 11, pp. 371–2)

This, he says, is an inevitable feature of a dynamic, modern utopia. The movement between the private concerns of individual life and the public concerns of society is an unceasing oscillation, with no clear resolution. A modern utopia must reflect this duality in both form and content. It must show the individual life as well as the public structures that gird that life. It is real men and women who must find their way to Utopia, and a utopia therefore must show something of the imperfection of the fit between the individual and society:

For I see about me a great multitude of little souls and groups of souls as darkened, as derivative as my own . . . . Yet that is not all I see, and I am not altogether bounded by my littleness. Ever and again, constrasting with this immediate vision, come glimpses of a comprehensive scheme, in which these personalities float, the scheme of a synthetic wider being, the great State, mankind, in which we all move and go, like blood corpuscles, like nerve cells, it may be at times like brain cells, in the body of a man. But the two visions are not seen consistently together, at least by me, and I do not surely know that they exist consistently together. The motives needed for those wider issues come not into the interplay of my vanities and wishes. That greater scheme lies about the men and women I know, as I have tried to make the vistas and spaces, the mountains, cities, laws and order of Utopia lie about my talking couple, too great for their sustained comprehension. When one focuses upon these two that wide landscape becomes indistinct and distant, and when one regards that, then the real persons one knows grow vague and unreal. Nevertheless, I cannot separate these two aspects of human life, each commenting on the other. In that incongruity between great and individual inheres the incompatibility I could not resolve and which, therefore, I have had to present in this conflicting form. (*AMU*, ch. 11, pp. 372–3)

The tension between the individual and the cosmic vision always remained Wells's most characteristic stance and the source of his greatest literary strength. While the social novels typically focused on the individual and the science fantasies on the cosmic perspective, both were always present to some extent within the same work. The two were most clearly fused in *In the Days of the Comet* (1906), the story of a frustrated and resentful working class youth who is saved from committing murder by the beneficent brush of a comet's tail which miraculously brings about peace on earth and social harmony within the body of the world-state. But Wells also, in a number of places, supplied an intermediate, more concrete and historically specific, analysis of the predicament of contemporary civilization. It was meant to explain the general disorientation and lack of direction of contemporary society in terms of the absence of any creative social force which could assume the leadership of society. The account is interesting not only for its own sake, as a theory of social development, but as providing some indication of the nature of political rule in utopia.

The position is most fully stated in *Tono-Bungay*, where Wells develops his 'Bladesover theory' of English society. The hero George Ponderevo, is, like Wells, the son of a housekeeper at a typical large country house of the English gentry. 'Bladesover House' is closely modelled on Up Park, the country house of the Fetherstonhaughs on the Sussex Downs where Wells spent a highly memorable part of his boyhood. George reflects that England is still, to a large extent, Bladesover writ large. The whole social system still reverberates with the impact of the gentry culture consolidated after the Revolution of 1688.

> There have been no revolutions, no deliberate restatements or abandonments of opinion in England since the days of the fine gentry, since 1688 or thereabouts, the days when Bladesover was built; there have been changes, dissolving forces, replacing forces, if you will; but then it was that the broad lines of the English system set firmly.

That gentry class has been manifestly in decline in recent times. There have been other contenders for their leading position – merchants, industrialists, financiers. But none has had any real creative or constructive potential. Uncle Edward Ponderevo's meteoric rise to fortune on the basis of a quack medical product – 'Tono-Bungay' – illustrates the essentially empty and fraudulent nature of the claims of these new men to rule. No new class has been able to stamp its social or cultural authority on English society as did the old gentry. All have been absorbed by the old order: 'the shape is still Bladesover.' The result has been a debilitating interregnum. There is acute moral and cultural disorganization. The gentry class has lost its vitality and social power, but no new class has arisen to harness the 'great new forces, blind forces of invasion, of growth', in the system. The condition of England is dangerously unstable, with new forces struggling to break through the old gentry shell. 'England is a country of great Renascence landed gentlefolk who have been unconsciously outgrown and overgrown.' But in the absence of viable alternatives, gentry ways continue to dominate and to exercise a seductive influence over all: physically in the wealthy squares and fashionable shopping areas of London, culturally in the artistic and scientific bodies that are the outgrowths of country house activities, politically in the antiquated Houses of Parliament. 'Everybody who is not actually in the shadow of Bladesover is as it were perpetually seeking after lost orientations.'

It is not any new directing class that is needed, but one with something of the same fertilizing influence as the gentry. For gentry dominance did not simply mean the self-interested exercise of ruling power, as with other ruling classes of old. It was immensely creative, the most creative force hitherto in the modern world. In his *Autobiography* Wells elaborated this view to see gentry culture as actually preparing the way to the world-state:

Now it is one of my firmest convictions that modern civilization was begotten and nursed in the households of the prosperous, relatively independent people, the minor nobility, the gentry, and the larger bourgeoisie, which became visibly important in the landscape of the sixteenth century, introducing a new architectural element in the towns, and spreading as country houses and chateaux and villas over the continually more orderly countryside. Within these households, behind their screen of deer park and park wall and sheltered service, men could talk, think and write at their leisure. They were free from inspection and immediate imperatives. They, at least, could go on after thirteen thinking and doing as they pleased. They created the public schools, revived the waning universities, went on the Grand Tour to see and learn. They could be interested in public affairs without being consumed by them. The management of their estates kept them in touch with reality without making exhaustive demands on their time. Many, no doubt, degenerated into a life of easy dignity or gentlemanly vice, but quite a sufficient number remained curious and interested to make, foster and protect the accumulating science and literature of the seventeenth and eighteenth centuries. Their large rooms, their libraries, their collections of pictures and 'curios' retained in the nineteenth century an atmosphere of unhurried liberal enquiry, of serene and determined insubordination and personal dignity, of established aesthetic and intellectual standards. Out of such houses came the Royal Society, the *Century of Inventions*, the first museums and laboratories and picture galleries, gentle manners, good writing, and nearly all that is worthwhile in our civilization today. Their culture, like the culture of the ancient world, rested on a toiling class. Nobody bothered very much about that, but it has been far more through the curiosity and enterprise and free deliberate thinking of these independent gentlemen than through any other influences, that modern machinery and economic organization have developed so as to abolish at last the harsh necessity for any toiling class whatever. It is the country house that has opened the way to human equality, not in the form of a democracy of insurgent proletarians, but as a world of universal gentlefolk no longer in need of a servile substratum. It was the experimental cellule of the coming Modern State.'[76]

What Wells is in effect offering here is a model of the future aristocracy of the utopian world-state. Its power is derived not from military force nor even, except very indirectly, from economic position, but from its scientific and cultural enlightenment. The ideal is that of the independent, disinterested scientific worker pursuing knowledge largely for its own sake but in a position to apply its fruits to the public good. *Tono-Bungay* itself actually suggests the social evolution that Wells hoped for and prophesied. If Bladesover and the gentry represent the past, and Uncle Ponderevo and the capitalists the present, then it is George himself – aviator, scientist and socialist – who represents the future. The analysis of the disintegration of nineteenth-century English society leads Wells, by a natural progression, to the diagnosis of the predicament of contemporary civilization as a whole, and then to the prediction and prescription of a coming world order governed by the creative force of science.

The class that will fill the vacuum created by the decline of the gentry will be a new middle class of all the most progressive and modern elements in society: the scientists, technicians, engineers and managers, the 'Efficients' that he first singled out in *Anticipations*. Wells, like James Burnham later in *The Managerial Revolution*, very consciously and deliberately substituted the rule of the scientists and managers for the 'dictatorship of the proletariat' predicted by Marx. But, like Marx but unlike Burnham, he still saw the future society as essentially classless. The scientists rule, but in the course of time virtually everyone comes to belong to this class. 'My thought', wrote Wells, 'has run very close to communist lines, but my conception of a scientifically organized classless society is essentially of an expanded middle-class which has incorporated both the aristocrat and plutocrat above and the peasant, proletarian and pauper below.'[77]

It is within the terms of this understanding of the rule of science and scientists that we need to consider the Samurai, the rulers of *A Modern Utopia*. Wells's conception could not be further from the conventional notion of a power elite or ruling class. But the Samurai quickly became, for Wells's opponents, the symbol of a ruthless power-hungry technocracy. With their somewhat unfortunate echoes of the military caste of feudal Japan, it proved only too easy to present them savagely or satirically as a totalitarian elite, anticipating the Bolshevik or Fascist elites for whom Wells seemed to have at times too much enthusiasm. Wells, as so often, himself supplied fuel for the fire. Writing of the Samurai many years later in his *Autobiography*, he expressed satisfaction at the way that contemporary events seemed to be confirming the validity of his conception:

> The experience of the thirty years that have passed since I launched this scheme, and particularly the appearance of such successful organizations as the Communist Party and the Italian Fascists, has greatly strengthened my belief in the essential soundness of this conception of the governing order of the future. A Samurai Order, educated in such an ideology as I have since tried to shape out, is inevitable if the modern world-state is ever to be fully realized. We want the world ruled not by everybody, but by a politically-minded organization, open, with proper safeguards, to everybody. The problem of world revolution and world civilization becomes the problem of crystallizing, as soon as possible , as many as possible of the right sort of individuals from the social magma, and getting them into effective, conscious co-operation.[78]

Even Wells's supporters might be forgiven for missing the chink of light in this very partial and overzealous interpretation of Bolshevism and Fascism. But the account of the Samurai in *A Modern Utopia* in any case makes it plain that any identification of them with, say, the Italian Fascists as they actually were goes right against the spirit and the substance of their portrayal there. Wells called *A Modern Utopia* 'the most Platonic of my books'; and it is with reference to 'that strange class of guardians which constitutes the essential substance of Plato's *Republic*' (*AMU*, p. 259) that the narrator discusses the Samurai order with his Utopian double, himself (of course) a member of that order. The Platonic reference indeed gives the main clue to the character of the Samurai, as well as to much else in Utopian society.

Utopian society is classified according to the temperament of its citizens, rather than by 'accidental categories' such as property ownership or occupation. Plato's three classes, also based on temperament, are here further subdivided to appear as four: the Poietic, the Kinetic, the Dull and the Base. The Poietic 'or creative class' includes all the artistic and scientific types, all the moral and religious philosophers. These are *par excellence* the men of reason and the imagination. It is they who conceive and elaborate, at the highest level, the central ideas and values of the society; and it is they too who look forward, to shape 'the forms of the human future'. The Kinetic class is largely an executive class, energetic, clever and capable, but essentially uncreative. It produces the best administrators and scientific technicians, as also the best actors, politicians and preachers. The Dull are, as their name implies, those too stupid or incompetent to contribute much to the life of society. They would tend to gravitate to those categories which are forbidden to marry or breed. The Base are not so much ignorant or stupid as morally defective, lacking in the sense of social obligation and duty. Cruel and criminal types belong here, and the island prisons tend to be their ultimate destination. (*AMU*, pp. 264–70).

As with Plato's *Republic*, these classes are not hereditary castes, nor is there any attempt to develop any class by special breeding. 'They are classes to which people drift of their own accord. Education is uniform until differentiation becomes unmistakable, and each man (and woman) must establish his position with regard to the lines of this abstract classification by his own quality, choice, and development. . .' (*AMU*, ch. 9, p. 266).

But the significant difference from the *Republic* is that there is no necessary class of workers, whose labour supports the speculative and political activities of the Guardians. In Utopia all work is steadily being mechanized. The appearance of a functionally specialized division of labour, as in the *Republic*, is misleading. The Dull and the Base are not necessary to Utopia. They are superfluous and parasitic. By such policies as control over marriage and breeding, they will be reduced to the lowest possible number. (Wells never envisages the possibility of their total elimination.) Ultimately, the only classes, the only temperaments, that Utopia requires seem to be the intellectual–imaginative and the executive-administrative. The whole tendency of its development is to make the bulk of its citizens belong to these two classes. They will, in other words, largely be that 'expanded middle class' of scientists, artists, managers and technicians that Wells expected to inherit his Utopia.

Utopian history – like that of the planet Earth – has in fact been an alternation of 'poietic' and 'kinetic' phases, an oscillation between the dominance of the 'creative' and the 'efficient' type. At first the poietic statesmen develop constructive ideas about the community and the state; then they are displaced by the kinetic men of action who consolidate and expand on the basis of poietic achievements. The statesman gives way to the politician or warrior, the unstable liberal state to the efficient conservative state. But with the change to the kinetic phase, the state loses its power of initiative and change, its ability to adapt to new circumstances. Through war or revolution creative poietic energy is once more infused into the state, and the cycle begins again.[79]

Utopia has broken this cycle, still operative on Earth. It has secured progress with stability. The place of poietic activities in the state is given full recognition. Poietic types are encouraged through the educational system and, later, through the award of fellowships and scholarships. The whole apparatus of research in Utopia – 'the world-wide House of Saloman' – is an acknowledgement of the importance of poietic activities to the state. Above all, poietic activities occupy a privileged position through their cultivation by the Samurai, 'in whose hands as a class all the real power of the world resides'.

The Samurai are the founders of the utopian world-state. They came into existence as the result of what Wells was later usually to refer to as 'the Open Conspiracy'. At a time of troubles, similar to those being experienced by contemporary Earth, there arose a revolutionary organization, a 'comprehensive movement of disillusioned and illuminated men' of all classes and parties dedicated to the elaboration of a common political synthesis and the achievement of a new world order in the world-state. Eventually they prevailed. The Samurai now control the world. 'Practically the whole of the responsible rule of the world is in their hands; all our head teachers and disciplinary heads of colleges, our judges, barristers, employers of labour beyond a certain limit, practising medical men, legislators, must be Samurai, and all the executive committees . . . are drawn by lot exclusively from them (*AMU*, p. 278). Samurai are the only voters in the world-state. Utopia has got rid of the sham of 'democracy', the exploitation of an ignorant and credulous populace by skilled politicians.

But these administrative activities are not the sole function of the Samurai. They are regarded in fact by most of them as a necessary burden, undertaken for the good of the community by those most fitted. Samurai, such as the narrator's double, who is engaged in criminological research, typically prefer poietic activities, and devote as much time as possible to scientific research and philosophy. The order of the Samurai, a 'voluntary nobility', is indeed largely a device to secure the requisite balance of the poietic and the kinetic in the state. Membership of the Samurai is not hereditary; any individual can aspire to it. 'Any intelligent adult in a reasonably healthy and efficient state may, at any age after five-and-twenty, become one of the Samurai, and take a hand in universal control' (*AMU*, p. 278).

But to be admitted, the aspirant must be able to follow the Rule. The Rule is the great filtering mechanism, which permits only the most worthy and dedicated to be enrolled among the Samurai.

> The Rule aims to exclude the Dull and Base altogether, to discipline the impulses and emotions, to develop a moral habit to sustain a man in periods of stress, fatigue, and temptation, to produce the maximum co-operation of all men of good intent, and, in fact, to keep all the Samurai in a state of moral and bodily health and efficiency. (*AMU*, ch. 9, p. 280)

What this elevated end involves in practice is a severe intellectual and moral obstacle race. The minimum qualification is a certain level of educational attainment, demonstrated by the passing of an examination at roughly undergraduate finals level. This tends to weed out the majority of the Dull and the Base. The harder task is the set of moral prohibitions and injunctions that the intending Samurai must obey. They are forbidden alcohol, drugs, smoking, betting, trade, usury, games and servants. They need not be celibate, but marriage among the Samurai, as in Utopia generally, is strictly controlled. Both partners must show Samurai qualities in order to be eligible. If either subsequently falls below Samurai standards, either the marriage is dissolved or both partners quit the Samurai order.

The Puritan rigour and austerity that pervades all aspects of Samurai life, and is required at all times of its votaries, is the most daunting aspect of life at the top, and is sufficient to ensure that only the most able and committed enter the order. Few Samurai even can maintain this level for the whole of their lives, and Utopia allows that individuals may give up Samurai status and, if they wish, seek readmission at a later stage, subject to the necessary safeguards. The life of the Samurai is essentially a religious vocation. They have their 'Book of the Samurai', a Samurai bible which embodies the ideal of the order and contains 'all the guiding ideas of our modern State'. There is a strict monastic discipline of body and mind, involving a detailed regimen of eating, sleeping, reading and socializing with fellow Samurai. There is indeed a more or less formalized religion in Utopia, although one very different from most earthly religions, at least in the West. For the concept of the Fall, the Utopians have substituted the Rise of Man, in all his individuality and power. 'The leading principle of the Utopian religion is the repudiation of the doctrine of original sin; the Utopians hold that man, on the whole, is good. That is their cardinal belief' (AMU, pp. 299--300). It was this Wellsian *credo* that most shocked Chesterton. Christianity had taught that an inherently sinful mankind had abused an essentially good world. Wells was arguing that it was the world that was naturally evil, and that man had it in his power to impose his ethical will on it. This, Wells held, was no less a religious conception than the opposite view. It meant that in Utopia religion, instead of going against the grain of a presumed sinful humanity, works with human nature.

The religious impulse, like all human impulses such as hunger and sex, can be perverted by society into something gross and excessive, into superstition and idolatry. The Dull and Base in Utopia have to be guided against that temptation. But the life of the Samurai is designed to prevent that corruption. They do this partly by their disciplined and selfless activity in maintaining the common weal, in upholding and administering the world-state. But Utopian religion, which is 'saturated with the philosophy of the uniqueness of all things', places the highest value on the individual life. The most striking of the rules of the Samurai enjoins that, for seven consecutive days of each year, all Samurai 'must go right out of all the life of man into some wild and solitary place', in the remote regions of the planet. Here, entirely on their own, without books, weapons or money, with the barest of provisions, they are free from the distractions of public life and have the time and space for reflection. Here they are 'alone with Nature, necessity, and their own thoughts'. They return refreshed in mind and body.

This 'steadfast yearly pilgrimage of solitude' epitomizes the life and character of the Samurai. In its unworldly austerity and utter disregard for the normal trappings and rewards of power, it seems a most unlikely paradigm of earthly dictatorship, still less 'the paradise of little fat men'. In so far as the Samurai order can be treated in conventional political terms, it amounts to an advocacy of a meritocracy not unlike that espoused by many social democrats in the twentieth century. No doubt the Samurai can be criticized as Plato's philosopher-kings can be criticized. In both cases there is an almost cavalier disregard of the possible corruption of the rulers, and of the dangers of the lack of restraint on their power and the total absence of democracy. But no more than Plato was Wells offering a constitutional blueprint in his portrait of a world-state ruled by Samurai. Like Plato, what he was trying to show was a certain ideal of rule or government. The ideal was drawn from a conception of the self-imposed rule governing a religious order. The Samurai rule the world because they rule themselves. They have subdued their passions and their irrational, selfish impulses. By suppressing their 'lower selves' – helped by being free of any doctrine of original sin – and realizing their full intellectual and emotional potential as human beings, they have achieved that victory of man over nature which Wells, following T. H. Huxley, saw as the only hopeful possibility for mankind. The Samurai are indeed an elite, an elect, group. But it is an elite formed on a radically different basis from Communist or Fascist elites. It is an elite constituted by 'the most capable elements in humanity, dedicated with a scientist's dedication to truth, service, and racial progress'.[80]

But there is a further aspect of the Samurai that is perhaps even more relevant to the charges made against Wells. The Samurai represent the prospect of a society without any state or government in the usual sense. Wells once wrote that 'one's dreamland perfection is Anarchy'; and although he generally avoided the use of the term in anything but a pejorative sense, in *A Modern Utopia* he seems to be gesturing towards the possibility of such a condition. This is not, it should be stressed, the abolition of politics in the usual utopian style, where universal happiness has been instituted for all time, and change and conflict pose no problems of adjustment. Wells's dynamic Utopia will not allow such a Draconian solution. What the Samurai symbolize is an alternative pattern of rule, which is radically open to future development: the sovereignty not of the state, nor even of laws, but of scientific knowledge and collective enlightenment. As Utopian social policies take their effect, as education raises the general level of the population and the spirit of science increasingly penetrates Utopian society, more and more people are fitted to join the Samurai order. All citizens eventually will share in rule – or, to put the same point differently, there will no longer be a ruling class or elite. The narrator's Utopian double makes the point emphatically that this is the ultimate goal of Utopia. The Samurai, he says, are 'not an exclusive caste; subject to the most reasonable qualifications, anyone who sees fit can enter it at any time, and so, unlike all other privileged castes the world has seen, it increases relatively to the total population, and may indeed at last assimilate almost the whole population of the earth' (*AMU*, ch. 9, p. 299).

That is indeed what has happened in the utopian society of *Men Like Gods* (1932), Wells's second long look at Utopia, and an explicit projection of the society of *A Modern Utopia* at a later stage of its evolution. 'In *Men Like Gods*,'

Wells wrote, 'all the people are Samurai.' It is a happy carefree Utopia (until, that is, the Earthlings bring their conflicts and diseases to it), and its frequent references to *News from Nowhere* suggest that Wells meant it as a guarded tribute to Morris. The Utopians go about virtually naked, and cannot understand the pained reactions of the Earthlings to this, and to their abolition of marriage and the family. They have abolished the need to work, yet all Utopians work for the pleasure of it, according to their aptitudes and imagination. There is no central authority, and no government of any recognizable kind. The system of decision-making reminds Mr Barnstaple of the anarchist doctrines of the Guild Socialists on earth. 'Decisions in regard to any particular matter were made by the people who knew most about the matter.' All this has been achieved by the right system of education. Adult Utopians do not need laws or government because 'our education is our government.'[81]

Similarly, in his third and most elaborate account of Utopia, *The Shape of Things to Come* (1933), Wells tells the story of the world-state from its confused and cataclysmic origins in war, through the period of the Air Dictatorship and tutelage under the World Council, to the final inauguration of the world-state when the World Council virtually abolishes itself, and leaves only self-governing administrative organs: a more or less precise rendering of Engels's formula for the socialist society, 'from the government of men to the administration of things'. There is now, says the elder statesman Donadieu,

> no need to govern the world . . . . We have made war impossible; we have liberated ourselves from the great anti-social traditions that set man against man; we have made the servitude of man to man through property impossible. The faculties of health, education, and behaviour will sustain the good conduct of the race. The controls of food, housing, transport, clothing, supply, initiative, design, research, can do their own work. There is nothing left for a supreme government to do.[82]

It is somewhat unexpected, in view of the picture of Wells as the prophet of technocratic dictatorship, to find that his Utopia ends in an Anarchy.

'IF ONLY YOU WOULD': THE MESSIANIC VISION

Unlike his friend Joseph Conrad, Wells never, even at his most pessimistic, believed that mankind could not be reformed and saved. Humanity might need the most awful shock to shake it out of its complacency, it might have to go through generations of misery and pain, but eventually it would come to its senses and construct the world-state.

The early science fantasies had sounded the apocalyptic note most purely. They warned that the natural course of events was for the human race to perish, along with life itself. Nature would stand impassively by; it was up to man to master and control nature through the exercise of the reason and imagination that was his unique evolutionary endowment. The utopian writings of the early 1900s, from *Anticipations* onwards, were tuned in what Wells called the hopeful 'utopian key-note . . . "If only" . . .'. They showed the constructive possibilities open to mankind, based on the social developments that in their disorder and confusion were already announcing the birth of a new social order. At the same time, in the social novels, the note of 'if only' sounded at the level of the individual life, in the frustrations and aspirations of the Lewishams and Kippses.

As time went on, as class conflict increased social disharmony and divisiveness without promising any constructive resolution, as the nations embroiled themselves in a bloody world war without constructing the world order that should have been the natural consequence of such a calamity, Wells's mood became grimmer. The hopefulness of 'if only' was transposed into the bleaker 'if only you would', which Wells saw as adding the necessary warning note of 'moral edification' to a modern utopia.[83] In his novel *The Secret Places of the Heart* (1922), a Harley Street nerve specialist Dr Martineau diagnoses a new mental disease that is afflicting 'whole classes of intelligent people: the sense of a coming smash . . . a loss of confidence, so that we seem to float over abysses'. Wells now concentrated his energies on uttering dire predictions of disaster, with salvation coming, if at all, only after frightful slaughter and destruction. The sequence starts with *The War in the Air* (1908), which gives only the barest hint of a future world order arising out of the ruins of a world devastated by aerial warfare. In *The World Set Free* (1914), an atomic war annihilates the world, but the statesmen do eventually pick up the pieces and reintegrate them in the world-state. So too do the aviators and scientists of *The Shape of Things to Come* (1933), Wells's last and most elaborate statement of his utopian scheme. Here a long analysis of contemporary world civilization and its disorders is followed by an account of a long drawn-out world war which reduces societies to pre-industrial levels of technology and social organization, until finally the airmen, the only surviving scientific professionals, use their skills and mastery of the channels of communication to set up a world Air Dictatorship which gradually leads the world to the world-state ruled in, and by, the pure spirit of science.

Religious conceptions were never far below the surface of Wells's thought, the permanent legacy of his mother's fervent Evangelicalism and his early immersion in the Protestant tracts which formed the only reading matter in his early home environment.[84] Books such as *The Pilgrim's Progress* had given him the themes and imagery of millennial Puritanism: the idea of the painful pilgrimage to salvation, the Last Judgement, and the coming of the New Jerusalem of universal peace, brotherhood and wisdom. Wells very quickly dropped all formal religious beliefs, although the struggle as he describes it in his *Autobiography* was severe.[85] Only briefly, in the mood of the greatest despair towards the end of the First World War, did he revert to something like formal religion. But the Mackenzies rightly speak of 'the latent messianism in his personality', and equally plausibly postulate it as a primary influence on his utopian conceptions:

By 1896 . . . Wells had begun to secularise the Plan of Salvation which was central to the evangelical religion of his boyhood. What he had done was to equate man's animal inheritance with original sin. The Puritans had sought for a means of saving mankind from the curse of Adam: salvation now meant saving the human species from the evolutionary process which, unchecked, damned it as surely as the Fall. But only the elect could hope for salvation, their righteousness triumphing over human fallibility and establishing the Rule of the Saints on earth. Wells, who now identified himself with the elect, had defined his mission. It was to struggle against the cosmic process as energetically as his Puritan predecessors had struggled against the primal curse. In both cases the price was profound anxiety and a repressed sexual guilt which broke out into demonology and the monstrous imageries of Judgement Day.[86]

Something of this 'monstrous imagery' actually breaks out in the last pages of *A Modern Utopia*. In an ending strongly reminiscent of Julian West's 'nightmare' return to Boston at the end of *Looking Backward*, the narrator and his botanist companion have been brusquely hurled back from Utopia into their own world, the imperfect world of Earth. In the deepest despondency the narrator trudges around London, beset by tramps and whores, struck afresh by the poverty, dirt, noise and confusion around him. He sees a newspaper placard shrieking examples of human violence and idiocy:

Massacre in Odessa

Discovery of Human Remains at Chertsey

SHOCKING LYNCHING OUTRAGE IN NEW YORK STATE

German Intrigues Get a Set-back

The Birthday Honours – Full List

'Dear old familiar world!' His anguished mind conjures up a consoling fancy:

Could one but realise an apocalyptic image and suppose an angel, such as was given to each of the seven churches of Asia, given for a space to the service of the Greater Rule. I see him as a towering figure of flame and colour, standing between earth and sky, with a trumpet in his hands, over there above the Haymarket, against the October glow; and when he sounds, all the Samurai, all who are Samurai in Utopia, will know themselves and one another . . . . For a moment I have a vision of this resurrection of the living, of a vague magnificent answer, of countless myriads at attention, of all that is fine in humanity at attention, round the compass of the earth. (*AMU*, ch. 11, pp. 368–9)

In the decades of writing after *A Modern Utopia*, Wells elaborated this vision to produce something almost akin to a formula for his prophetic and utopian writings. The elements of this formula are especially evident in *The War in the Air, The World Set Free, Men Like Gods* and *The Shape of Things to Come*. Taken together, they add up to the progressive revelation and achievement of Utopia through a series of linked stages.

Stage 1 A world of discontent, disorder, waste and injustice. Civilization, avers Wells, typically goes through a phase of 'diastole' – a long period of progressive development – followed by a phase of 'systole' – a sudden sharp contraction into collapse and disorder. The modern world is in its systolic phase. There are morbid signs of restlessness and anxiety, which are also the symptoms of a new order struggling to be born. The world is in travail. There is a lowering 'sense of a coming smash'. Social thinkers, while recognizing the need for fundamental change, are confused and divided. A few far-sighted prophets can see the need for a world-state but either they themselves are too impractical or they are ignored by their fellows. Reforms are too little and too late. Disaster on a world-wide scale seems inevitable.

Stage 2 'The cleansing disillusionment' (*Shape of Things to Come*). The world is blown up, literally or metaphorically. The causes are cosmic disasters (comets, etc.), alien invasions or, usually, world wars (aerial, atomic) between competing nation-states. This total breakdown is the necessary purgatory for bringing people to their senses. There has to be a war to end war. 'I remain persuaded that there will have to be a last conflict to inaugurate the peace of mankind'.[87]

Stage 3 The period of transition. The world lies prostrated by war. Diseases and plagues are rampant. There is a reversion to more primitive forms of economic and social life. Cities decay, and are abandoned for the countryside. Local chieftains and gang-leaders set up independent domains as all central authority collapses. Trade is local. Communications are poor and unsafe. In remote corners of the globe, or in the semi-deserted cities, a 'saving remnant' of scientists and philosophers maintain a quasi-monastic existence, biding their time.

Stage 4 Salvation. After a longer or shorter period of time, the world, too exhausted now to make war, slowly recovers economically. The scientific intelligentsia takes power and, through a world organization (the Air Dictatorship, etc.), supervises the economic, social and political reconstruction of the world. The new world arises like the phoenix from the ashes of the old. The period of reconstruction culminates in the inauguration of the world-state, 'the fair and great and fruitful World State' (*A Modern Utopia*). Thus begins a new era of world history, a period of continued progress marked by peace and plenty. It is the attainment of Utopia.

This apocalyptic vision is what finally links the three main modes of Wells's writing: the science fantasies, the social novels and the utopian fiction. In this basically religious conception Wells fuses the personal, social and cosmic or evolutionary themes of his life's work. It is the vision of the Bromley-born, puritanically reared, lower-middle-class, sickly, ill-educated Wells the individual, passionate to escape from the narrow cell in which he was apparently to be confined for the rest of his life. Utopia was the land in which he could take wing, and dream of a world free from the crippling constraints of his own childhood and youth. Like the narrator of *A Modern Utopia* and Mr Barnstaple of *Men Like Gods*, Wells fell in love with Utopia. He yearned, with the yearning of one who sensed that for him, at least, it was not to be, to live in a rational, ordered world, where poverty and illness would have become no more than ancient memories of the race.

It is the vision also of Wells the sociologist, who, in his 'Bladesover theory', diagnosed the suffering and disorder in society as the consequence of the decline of a social class and a social ethic, and the failure of any new class so far to make a contribution of comparable significance. The capitalists had strikingly failed to produce a new stable order. Quite the contrary, the incessant race for profits was the source of the prodigious waste so evident, and the chief stimulus to war. The capitalists had remained the second-rate imitators and cultural prisoners of the aristocracy they had displaced. The proletariat too, despite Marx's claim, remained dependent, the prisoners, in their turn, of the capitalist system. They could be at times sullen and rebellious, but they were unable to conceive and create a new society. But around both these classes, often as their employees and 'public servants', was a growing band of scientific and technical experts and professional managers. These were the germ cells of the coming scientific world civilization which, under their guidance, would utilize their scientific knowledge not for private gain but for the benefit of all humanity.

It is the vision, lastly, of Wells the philosopher of natural and human history, the disciple of Darwin and T. H. Huxley. In his conception of Utopia, Wells showed men taking upon themselves the responsibility for their own future instead of leaving it to the blind forces of nature. Original sin was a crippling myth, perhaps the most damaging perpetrated upon the human species. It made suffering the normal and necessary part of the human condition. The real sin was the refusal to see the potential possessed by humankind to escape the fate marked out by natural selection for all other species, the fate of extinction. Men could indeed be like gods, rather than like the brutes whom they had been so assiduously imitating for most of their history. It depended upon making use of their sovereign faculty, reason. But Wells's was a *modern* Utopia. Reason was not to be conceived in the old rationalist, deductive, way. This was the mistake of all those utopias too much under the spell of Plato. There could now be only one valid conception of reason: scientific, experimental, tentative reason. The Utopia of Plato had to be fused with the Utopia of Bacon. The modern Utopia makes 'not the philosopher, but scientific philosophy, king'.

7

Science and Anti-Utopia: Aldous Huxley and *Brave New World*

'Tomorrow,' said Gumbril at last, meditatively.
'Tomorrow,' Mrs Viveash interrupted him, 'will be as awful as today.'
Aldous Huxley, *Antic Hay* (1923)

Bertie Russell, whom I've just been lunching with, says one oughtn't to mind about the superficial things like ideas, manners, politics, even wars – that the really important things, conditioned by scientific technique, go steadily on and up ... in a straight, un-undulating trajectory. It's nice to think so; but meanwhile there the superficial undulations are, and one lives superficially; and who knows if that straight trajectory isn't aiming directly for some fantastic denial of humanity?
Aldous Huxley, letter to E. M. Forster, 17 February 1935, in *Letters*, ed. Grover Smith (1969)

I remember his talking to me about Aldous Huxley, whom he regarded as the degenerate descendant of a noble grandfather. He spoke with bitterness of *Brave New World*; it was blasphemy against the religion of science. It suggested that knowledge might be the path, not to the modern Utopia, but to a new kind of servile Hell. Aldous Huxley was escaping to the United States, was he? Well – he spat it out with memorable contempt – 'that is his quality.'
Kingsley Martin, recollection of H. G. Wells, in J. R. Hammond (ed.), *H. G. Wells. Interviews and Recollections* (1980)

WELLS *CONTRA* WELLS

After the First World War, utopias were everywhere in retreat. The 1920s, 1930s and 1940s were the classic era of the 'utopia in the negative', the anti-utopia or dystopia. These were the 'devil's decades', the years of mass unemployment, mass persecution, brutal dictatorships and world war. H. G. Wells continued to practise and preach his utopianism throughout this period, but he had largely lost his audience. He had in particular little influence – except as a target – with the new generation of thinkers who had been fashioned by the disillusioning experience of the world war. For them, it was grotesque to see reason and science as the great deliverers of humanity. If reason and science provided any guide to the future, it was in the nightmare form of their perverted use. The urge to look into the future remained. That was the compliment that anti-utopia paid to utopia. But it was now a future to be feared. In a number of books of striking imagery and power–Yevgeny Zamyatin's *We*, Aldous Huxley's *Brave New world*, Arthur Koestler's *Darkness at Noon*, George Orwell's *Nineteen Eighty-Four* – the future was portrayed as a totalitarian hell in which all hope was extinguished and all exits closed.

The writers of this period certainly owed much to Wells. Anti-utopia was, as has already been suggested, at least partly a case of Wells *contra* Wells. Themes and images from the early science fantasies, especially *The First Men in the Moon* and *When the Sleeper Wakes*, were taken over and elaborated to suit the more deliberately anti-utopian purpose. The Selenite civilization of the Moon was given a terrestrial home in *Brave New World*; Ostrog's socialist dictatorship in *When the Sleeper Wakes* reappeared magnified in *Nineteen Eighty-Four*. Some of the borrowing seems to have been largely unconscious, as with Huxley and Orwell; some was indirect, mediated particularly through Zamyatin's *We*, where the debt to Wells was explicit and acknowledged. But whichever way, the importance of Wells to both utopia and anti-utopia in the twentieth century is clear and undeniable.[1]

It will not do, however – as Mark Hillegas for instance does[2] – to regard the anti-utopian literature that flourished after 1918 as merely a footnote to Wells's early writings. For one thing, Wells was by then firmly established in his role as prophet of the utopian world-state. As the ardently self-professed and most prominent apostle of the scientific utopia, any attack on the pretensions of science naturally directed itself against Wells. In popular parlance, 'Wellsian' meant, quite simply, the complex mechanized society of the future run by a scientific elite. Writers may have consciously or unconsciously used elements of the early Wells to attack this vision. But they had plenty of later Wells to attack as well; and in countering the sheer ubiquity and massive presence of the Wellsian utopia they were forced to develop a critique that went a good deal further than anything to be found in Wells's early writings.

Aldous Huxley, indeed, seems never to have been able to get Wells out of his system. In one form or another, Wells was around him for much of his earlier life. Aldous was the grandson of T. H. Huxley, Wells's revered mentor and the constant reference point in his writings. His brother Julian, the biologist, was one of the principal collaborators with Wells on *The Science of Life* , and came to embrace an almost pure form of the Wellsian philosophy of science and progress. In common with most of his contemporaries, Aldous read practically everything that Wells wrote, in a mood compounded of exasperation and indignation. His letters throughout the decades of the 1910s and 1920s are peppered with scathing references to Wells. From his undergraduate days at Oxford, in 1916: 'However, All's well that ends Wells, as the man said on reading one of H. G. W.'s articles on the future in the *Daily Chronicle* (or else, in that sublime writer's own words, let us hope that this is THE WAR that will END WELLS). . . .'[3] From Italy, in 1927: 'I don't know him at all well; but he has always struck me as a rather horrid, vulgar little man.'[4] There are frequent caricatures of Wells and Wellsian philosophy in the early novels, especially in *Crome Yellow* (1921) and *Point Counter Point* (1928). Finally came the all-out counter-blast in *Brave New World* (1932): 'a novel about the future,' wrote Huxley, 'on the horror of the Wellsian Utopia and a revolt against it'.[5]

But the relationship to Wells goes beyond this. The antagonism hid a deeper affinity to the older writer. Fundamentally, although he was at his sparkling best as an anti-utopian satirist, Huxley was a utopian. Like Wells, he was haunted throughout his life by the sense of an impending disaster for the human race. The bright and brittle Bohemian characters of his novels of the 1920s seem to be living on the edge of a precipice. Like Wells, in his earlier writings and novels he was more concerned to criticize and warn, although in an ironic and satirical mode rather than in Wells's savage and apocalyptic tones. Like Wells, there came a moment when he broke through to a constructive, utopian philosophy; and, as with Wells, it was a variety of religion that offered the solution. In the decade after *Brave New World* Huxley discovered and discoursed on 'the perennial philosophy', a form of mysticism which he saw as the basic unifying philosophy of all the world religions, and the only hope for mankind. His conversion to this view was first made explicit in his novel *Eyeless in Gaza* (1936). A Christianized version of the perennial philosophy was presented in the novel *After Many a Summer* (1939); and, in his very last novel *Island* (1962), he made full amends for the destructiveness of *Brave New World* by offering a fully realized portrait of a utopian society, in which the Buddhist form of the perennial philosophy has been successfully applied to all aspects of personal and public life.

So the movement from anti-utopia to utopia was finally completed, a year before Huxley's death. But it had absorbed the whole of the latter half of Huxley's life, and had come to dominate his writing. And, just as with Wells, critics have had cause to regret the switch from the witty, iconoclastic Huxley of the 1920s to the serious and impassioned prophet of the later years. Huxley the prophet of the perennial philosophy did not narrow his literary purpose to anything like the same extent as Wells the prophet of the world-state. But the adoption of the didactic and moralistic tone from the late 1930s onwards was accompanied, as in the case of Wells, by a distinct falling off of his literary art. As so often, the teacher came to be the enemy of the artist. Like Wells, Huxley grew impatient with purely literary form, and came to see the message as infinitely more important than the medium. There were times when he seemed concerned to remind the world that he was the descendant not simply of T. H. Huxley but also – through his mother – of that stern moralist, Matthew Arnold.

Huxley the utopian will interest us later. Here we are dealing with the anti-utopian Huxley of *Brave New World*. Unlike Wells, whose later voluminous utopian writings came to overwhelm in the public mind his anti-utopian stories, Huxley made his lasting impact upon the wider public with his brilliantly destructive satires, culminating in *Brave New World*. The Wellsian inspiration was certainly important to these works, directly and indirectly. Wells's utopian vision was the direct stimulus to Huxley's anti-utopian satire. But there was also the indirect connection, through Wells's influence on the 'science and society' movement of the 1920s; and through the importance of Yevgeny Zamyatin's

We, an anti-utopian novel that was the most powerful and complete realization of Wells *contra* Wells.[6]

Zamyatin was a Russian marine architect who had spent some time in England during the First World War, and who was a passionate admirer of English literature and all things English (to his friends he was known as 'the Englishman'). Among his favourite writers were Swift, Shaw and Wells. In a perceptive study of Wells, he praised him as the inventor of the 'mechanical, chemical fairy tale', a tale intrinsic to the modern city. The twentieth-century city, a 'place of stone, asphalt, iron, gasoline, and machines', was Wells's natural habitat. Wells had peopled his urban fairy-tales with 'mechanical goblins', such as the Martians, and had uniquely constructed his 'new urban myths' on the basis of modern science. Zamyatin was one of the first critics to suggest that Wells's basic purpose was anti-utopian rather than, as was the common opinion, utopian.

> Wells's socio-fantastic novels are not utopias. . . . There are two generic and invariable features that characterize utopias. One is the content: the authors of utopias paint what they consider to be ideal societies; translating this into the language of mathematics, we might say that utopias bear a plus sign. The other feature, organically growing out of the content, is to be found in the form: a utopia is always static; it is always descriptive, and has no, or almost no, plot dynamics. In Wells's socio-fantastic novels we shall hardly ever find these characteristics. To begin with most of his social fantasies bear the minus sign, not the plus sign. His socio-fantastic novels are almost solely instruments for exposing the defects of the existing social order, rather than building a picture of a future paradise. . . . Most of them are social tracts in the form of fantastic novels. . . . Further, in Wells's socio-fantastic novels the plot is always dynamic, built on collisions, on conflict; the story is complex and absorbing.[7]

Petrified, pre-revolutionary Russia, says Zamyatin, had lacked any real examples of Wellsian social fantasy. But 'post-revolutionary Russia, which has become the most fantastic country in modern Europe, will undoubtedly reflect this period with literary fantasy.' And he instanced his own novel of 1920, *We*, as one of the first signs of this development. The Wellsian influence could hardly be clearer in this cautionary fantasy. Wells's 'A Story of the Days to Come' and *When the Sleeper Wakes* suggest almost all its themes and a good deal of its plot and setting. The fact that Zamyatin chose to follow the anti-utopian Wells, and not the writer of 'sugary, pinkish' utopias such as *Men Like Gods*, was a melancholy comment on the mind of the one-time Bolshevik revolutionary and *Potemkin* mutineer who now observed with horror the construction of the monolithic collectivist state.

We is a story of the 'One State', the autocratic world-state ruled by the Benefactor and his Guardians. It has been in existence for a thousand years, following the 'Two Hundred Years' War' which annihilated the old civilization and decimated the world's population. There are still vast tracts of jungle and wilderness outside the cities of the One State; but the inhabitants of the cities are walled in by vast impregnable glass walls (the 'Green Walls'), outside which no one is allowed to go. Within the walls is a glittering, mechanized, fully harmonized society. It is Reason and Science concretized and completely realized in the physical, social and mental strutures of the society. All citizens have numbers, not names. Mathematics is the reigning paradigm of all thought and art; engineering is the fundamental applied mode for all social and psychological as well as physical problems. The American Frederick Winslow Taylor, the founding father of 'scientific management', is a revered ancestor, 'the greatest genius the ancients had, ... the prophet who had been able to look ten centuries ahead'.

Order and regimentation pervade every aspect of the life of the One State. All march, four abreast, at regular intervals to 'the March of the One State', composed by the Musical Factory. All activities are strictly regulated by the 'Tables of Hourly Commandments' – modelled on the old railway timetables – which 'transform each one of us into the six-wheeled hero of a great poem.'

Each morning, with six-wheeled precision, at the very same minute and the very same second we, in our millions, arise as one. At the very same hour we mono-millionedly begin work – and, when we finish it, we do so mono-millionedly. And, merging into but one body with multi-millioned hands, at the very second designated by the Tables of Hourly Commandments we bring our spoons up to our mouths; at the very same second, likewise, we set out for a walk, or go to an auditorium, or the Hall of Taylor Exercises, or retire to sleep.

Privacy is severely frowned on. Everyone lives in glass apartment blocks, open at all times to full view from the outside. Only in the twice-daily 'Personal Hours' are the blinds permitted to be drawn. Sex is the usual activity during these personal hours; but it is sex firmly divorced from love or procreation. The State controls reproduction on strict eugenic principles, and unlicensed pregnancies are punishable by death. Sex is governed by the *Lex Sexualis*, which proclaims: 'Every number has the right of availability, as a sexual product, to any other number.' Strong sexual emotions, such as jealousy, have thereby been banished. 'That which served the ancients as the source of countless and exceedingly silly tragedies we have converted to a harmonious, pleasantly useful organic function, much as we have done with sleep, physical labour, the intake of food, defecation and so forth.'

The plot of *We* focuses on the revolt against this utilitarian paradise by D–503, a prominent space engineer. He is stimulated to this by his love for E–330, a member of a dissident underground group known as the Mephi, who are in touch with the wild remnants of the old humanity outside the Green Wall. Symbolically, D–503 has 'shaggy, simian hands', an atavistic feature which suggests to E–330 that he still has 'forest blood' in him. The rebels plot to take over the space rocket, the Integral, which is to make its test flight under D–503's command. The plot is foiled, but the Mephi manage to destroy a section of the Green Wall, allowing some of the wilderness (birds, animals, hairy humans) to enter and cause orgiastic confusion for a while. Order however is quickly restored. D–503 is captured and 'fantasiectomized', an operation which rids people of 'wild fancies'. The Benefactor tells him: 'What have men, from their swaddling-clothes days, been praying for, dreaming about, tormenting themselves for? Why, to have someone tell them, once and for all, just what happiness is – and then weld them to this happiness with chains. What else are we doing now if not that?' D–503 is fully rconciled to the One State. He betrays all the plotters, including E–330, who are first publicly tortured in the Gas Bell Glass (which slowly produces a vacuum) and then executed. D–503 pours scorn on the rebels who have 'betrayed rationality. . . . For rationality must conquer.'

This bare summary – which cannot begin to do justice to Zamyatin's elegant ironic fable, with its clipped telegraphic sentences and swift ellipses – is enough to suggest *We*'s filiation both backwards – to Wells – and forwards, to *Brave New World* and *Nineteen Eighty-Four.* The attack on utilitarianism and the utopia of painless mechanized existence connects it with Huxley; the omipresent spies and surveillance, the control of thought and language and the ruthless exercise of state power point as clearly to Orwell's nightmare. '*We*,' as Zamyatin himself said in 1932, 'was written as a warning against the two-fold danger which threatens humanity: the hypertrophic power of the machines and the hypertrophic power of the State.' The three novels share too the same mood of pessimism. There is a complete failure of all attempts at revolt, and the abandonment of all hope for the future. The inception of the One State has ended the old cycle of stasis and revolution. It has brought stability for all time. As D–503 tells E–330: 'Our revolution [of the One State] was the last. There can't be any other revolutions.'

Zamyatin's attack on the scientific utopia clearly drew on the early Wells. But he went well beyond Wells in his stylistic innovations, and the depth of his critique of the scientific–rational mode of thought and existence. In *We*, unlike anywhere in Wells, the reader actually experiences through D–503's consciousness (the book's narrative is his diary) the alienation and fragmentation of personality induced by 'the mathematically perfect State'.[8] A contemporary work, which was similarly both an extension of Wells and an attack on him, was another anti-utopia from Eastern Europe that had a great success in the West, Karel Capek's play *R.U.R.* (1921). In this 'comedy of science' Capek reworked the Frankenstein theme that was one of the archetypes of the anti-utopia. Rossum's Universal Robots are a triumph of man's scientific knowledge and technological imagination: and they take over the world, displacing their creator. 'Mankind,' says Rossum's General Manager, 'will never cope with the robots, and will never have control over them. Mankind will be overwhelmed in the deluge of these dreadful living machines, will be their slave, will live at their mercy.' In a note on his play Capek explained:

> Young Rossum is the modern scientist, untroubled by metaphysical ideas; scientific experiment is to him the road to industrial production. . . . To create a Homunculus is a medieval idea; to bring it in line with the present century this creation must be undertaken on the principle of mass production. Immediately we are in the grip of industrialism; this terrible machinery must not stop, for if it does it would destroy the lives of thousands. It must, on the contrary, go on faster and faster although it destroys in the process thousands and thousands of other existences. Those who think to master the industry are themselves mastered by it: Robots must be produced. . . . The conception of the human brain has at last escaped from the control of human nature. This is the comedy of science.[9]

THE SCIENTIFIC HUBRIS: MEN LIKE GODS

These literary manifestations of the anti-utopian genre in the 1920s indicate that Huxley was to some extent swimming with the tide. His anti-utopian satire on a world formed by science and technology was fed by a current of profound revulsion against the Wellsian utopia. But there was a stimulus from within the scientific community as well, although it worked in precisely the opposite direction. The 1920s and 1930s were the principal decades of the 'science and society' movement in England. A number of prominent scientists fervently espoused the Wellsian scientific utopia in its fullest form. For them, as for Wells, the experience of world war, economic collapse and mass unemployment, far from constituting some sort of case against science, actually confirmed the need for science and scientists to take command. The rulers and politicians, trained in obsolete disciplines and shaped by class experiences that would have made them more at home in the eighteenth than the twentieth century, were the carriers of an antiquated technique and philosophy that was bringing western civilization to the brink of catastrophe. Not a turning away from science, not less but more science was the necessary antidote.

The leaders in the science and society movement in England were the biologists J. B. S. Haldane and Lancelot Hogben, the physicist J. D. Bernal, the biochemist Joseph Needham and the mathematician Hyman Levy.[10] In 1924 Haldane published *Daedalus, or Science and the Future*, in which he posed the question that was the fundamental underlying motif of the whole anti-utopian critique:

> Has mankind released from the womb of matter a Demogorgon which is already beginning to turn against him, and may at any moment hurl him into the bottomless void? Or is Samuel Butler's even more horrible vision correct, in which man becomes a mere parasite of machinery, an appendage to the reproductive system of huge and complicated engines which will successively usurp his activities, and end by ousting him from the mastery of the planet? Is the machine minder engaged on repetition work the goal and ideal to which humanity is tending?[11]

Haldane's answer was an exuberant vindication of science, its claims and possibilities. Wells – 'the very mention of the future suggests him' – he thought had been if anything too 'modest, conservative, and uimaginative' in his scientific prophecies to demonstrate sufficiently the truly emancipatory promise of modern science. Haldane was correspondingly bolder in his speculations. He foresaw the 'energy problem' posed by the exhaustion of coal and oil-fields, and proposed to solve it by the exploitation of wind and solar energy. Developments in transport and communication 'are only limited by the velocity of light', and 'we are working towards a condition when any two persons on earth will be able to be completely present to one another in not more than one-fifteen-hundredth of a second.' Novel drugs, such as acid sodium phosphate, which do not have the harmful effects of nicotine and alcohol, are proposed as beneficent stimulants to physical and mental activity. Chemistry would be applied to the production of food, so that within a century all necessary food could be artificially produced. This would eliminate agriculture and the agrarian way of life, a prospect which Haldane cheerfully looked forward to. 'Human progress in historical time has been the progress of cities dragging a reluctant countryside in their wake. Synthetic food will substitute the flower garden and the factory for the dunghill and the slaughterhouse, and make the city at last self-sufficient.'

But it was his own field, biology, that stimulated Haldane to the highest flights of fancy. Borrowing the form of 'future history' invented by Wells, *Daedalus* incorporates 'an essay on the influence of biology on history during the twentieth century, which will (it is hoped) be read by a rather stupid undergraduate member of this university [Cambridge] to his supervisor during his first term 150 years hence'. In this future world, eugenics has achieved considerable success in preventing the transmission of hereditary diseases such as syphilis and insanity. Medicine has practically abolished infectious diseases. Nitrogen-fixing in the soil has enormously increased the yield of crops, leading to a massive drop in food prices (and the ruin of purely agricultural societies). The drifting sands of the world's deserts have been bound by a new lichen, and now bloom with an abundance of produce. In 1951 the world's first 'ectogenetic child', or test-tube baby, is produced, from the egg of an ovary artificially kept alive for five years outside a woman's body. 'As we know ectogenesis is now universal, and in this country less than thirty per cent of children are now born of a woman.' The effects on human psychology and social life have been enormous. Sex and reproduction are separated. The family, no longer needed for procreation, dissolves. Some loss is admitted here, but this is greatly compensated by the advantages of a system of eugenics which regulates reproduction in the public interest.

The small proportion of men and women who are selected as the ancestors for the next generation are so undoubtedly superior to the average that the advance in each generation in any single respect, from the increased output of first-class music to the decreased conviction for theft, is very startling. Had it not been for ectogenesis there can be little doubt that civilization would have collapsed within a measurable time owing to the greater fertility of the less desirable members of the population in almost all countries.'[12]

Looking further ahead, Haldane muses:

In the future it may be possible by selective breeding to change character as quickly as institutions. I can foresee the election placards of 300 years hence, if such quaint political methods survive, which is perhaps improbable. 'Vote for Smith and more musicians'; 'Vote for O'Leary and more girls'; or perhaps finally 'Vote for Macpherson and a prehensile tail for your great-grand-children'.[13]

Haldane concludes with some further speculations: that the abolition of disease by medical advance 'will make death a physiological event like sleep: a generation that has lived together will die together'; that youth will be prolonged, especially that of women through the abolition of the menopause (by isolating and synthesizing the chemical substance which the ovary fails to produce); and that we may at last begin to tap the enormous potential of the psychological techniques of hypnotism and suggestion in learning and the modification of behaviour. These developments, together with the others predicted, would require in the end a socialistic world-state, as the best possible framework for the future growth and use of science. Haldane saw some faint hope in the League of Nations, but 'it may take another world war or two to convert the majority.'[14]

Is it not easy, perhaps too easy, to see *Brave New World* simply as the factual acceptance but the moral rejection of Haldane's projections? So many of the items here, from drugs to test-tube babies, turn up in Huxley's satire, their evaluation suitably reversed. Huxley, whose own scientific interests always leaned towards the biological and psychological, knew very well the truth of Haldane's assertion that 'not one of the practical advances which I have predicted is not already foreshadowed by recent scientific work.' He knew it to some extent from Haldane himself, who had been a close friend of his and his brother Julian's at Oxford, and at whose house he had often stayed. (Haldane is affectionately caricatured as the scientist Shearwater in Huxley's novel *Antic Hay*, and Haldane's father J. S. Haldane appears as the biologist Lord Edward Tantamount in *Point Counter Point*.) When, just after its completion, Huxley described the intention of *Brave New World* to his father, he did so in terms which strongly recall Haldane's speculations. The book was, he said,

> a comic, or at least satirical, novel about the Future, showing the appallingness (at any rate by our standards) of Utopia and adumbrating the effects on thought and feeling of such quite possible biological inventions as the production of children in bottles, (with consequent abolition of the family and all the Freudian 'complexes' for which family relationships are responsible), the prolongaton of youth, the devising of some harmless but effective substitute for alcohol, cocaine, opium etc.: – and also the effects of such sociological reforms as Pavlovian conditioning of all children from birth and before birth, universal peace, security and stability.'[15]

Haldane's little book indeed caused quite a stir. It was quickly answered in an admonitory tract by Bertrand Russell, entitled *Icarus or the Future of Science* (1924). Science, Russell argued, was more likely 'to promote the power of dominant groups than to make men happy'. Science had become the driving force of industrialism, and to that extent had been responsible for some improvement in the general welfare of the population. But industrialism had remained bound to the interests of the dominant social groups, and had served largely to increase the destructive power of the nationalist wars by which these groups conducted their ever-intensifying rivalries. While the motives and purposes of social groups remained unchanged, science was a force for evil, not for good. Eugenics would not lead to a general increase in the fitness of the population, but would be used by the state to produce a servile population. Physiology would show how the emotions could be controlled, perhaps by regulating the secretions of the ductless glands. But this would lead not to an increase in psychological health, but to the rulers' strengthening their power and stupefying the mass of the people.

We shall have the emotions desired by our rulers, and the chief business of elementary education will be to produce the desired dispositions, no longer by punishment or moral precept, but by the far surer method of injection or diet. The men who will administer this system will have a power beyond the dreams of the Jesuits . . . .

Russell concluded:

Science has not given men more self-control, more kindliness, or more power of discounting their passions in deciding upon a course of action. . . . men's collective passions are mainly evil; far the strongest of them are hatred and rivalry directed towards other groups. Therefore at present all that gives men power to indulge their collective passions is bad. That is why science threatens to cause the destruction of our civilization.[16]

Huxley undoubtedly read *Icarus*; and there are, as often pointed out, many similarities between Russell's attack on the scientific hubris and the general critique of science in *Brave New World*. Russell too had become a good friend and correspondent, through their meetings at Lady Ottoline Morrell's intellectual salon at Garsington Manor, and Huxley paid him the dubious compliment of portraying him as the cynical rationalist Scogan in his early novel *Crome Yellow*. But in any case there were many others in the 1920s who took up Haldane's challenge, accepting the promise that science held out while being more inclined to stress the dangers it posed. In 1930 the barrister and politician the Earl of Birkenhead published a popular work of synthesis, *The World in 2030 AD*, which in its mixture of complacency and criticism fairly reflected the general attitude of the educated non-scientific public. Birkenhead was particularly exercised by the problem posed by 'ectogenesis', the *in vitro* development of a child in the laboratory from an artificially fertilized cell. The danger was of a new slavery.

By regulating the choice of ectogenetic parent of the next generation, the Cabinet of the future could breed a nation of industrious dullards, or leaven the population with fifty thousand irresponsible, if gifted, mural painters. . . . If it were possible to breed a race of strong healthy creatures, swift and ductile in intricate drudgery, yet lacking ambition, what ruling class would resist the temptation? Many of the arguments brought against slavery would be powerless in such a case; for the ectogenetic slave of the future would not feel his bonds. Every impulse which makes slavery degrading and irksome to ordinary humanity would be removed from his mental equipment. His only happiness would be in his task; he would be the exact counterpart of the worker bee.'[17]

This direct anticipation of one of the leading themes of *Brave New World* cannot be considered in the nature of an 'influence'. (For one thing, Huxley had already, as we shall see, played with it as early as 1921.) It simply serves to indicate the perturbation among literary and humanist intellectuals stirred up by the strong claims of scientists in these years. Haldane's projections in their turn looked pallid when set against the extravagant vision evoked in J. D. Bernal's *The World, the Flesh, And The Devil*, published in 1929. In this, the most sparkling of the products of the 'science and society' movement, Bernal confronted 'the three enemies of the Rational Soul' and sought to rout them once and for all with science. Physics would tame 'the massive, unintelligent forces of nature'; biology would cure the problems of the human body; and psychology would control man's 'desires and fears, his imagination and stupidities'.

As far as the material world goes, Bernal quickly gets through a conventional recital of expected developments (which can be predicted with 'mathematical' exactness): the age of metals will give way to new synthetic materials, food will be synthetically and abundantly produced, and the world will banish want and achieve a high degree of leisure. Man will then reach out towards space, which will give him access to the full range of the sun's energy and so solve the energy problem virtually for ever. Space colonies, in the form of self-supporting, self-maintaining globes of 20,000 – 30,000 inhabitants each, will be established as a first step towards the colonization of other planets and stars.

> Once acclimatized to space living, it is unlikely that man will stop until he has roamed over and colonized most of the sidereal universe, or that even this will be the end. Man will not ultimately be content to be parasitic on the stars, but will invade them and organize them for his own purposes . . . . A star is essentially an immense reservoir of energy which is being dissipated as rapidly as its bulk will allow . . . . The stars cannot be allowed to continue in their old way, but will be turned into efficient heat engines.'[18]

The only limit that Bernal sees to material expansion is the second law of thermodynamics – the entropy law – and even here, he suggests, by 'intelligent organization' we can defy it for a long time, so that we may prolong the life of the universe to 'many millions of millions of times what it would be without organization'.

The flesh is not so easily subjugated, but Bernal's inventiveness is splendidly fertile. Surgery and 'physiological chemistry' will take over and speed up the process of natural bodily evolution. Undaunted by the shades of Dr Moreau, or the ridicule heaped upon Wells for a similar vision, Bernal proposes dispossessing the man of the future of his inefficient limbs and organs, and substituting for them artificial parts which could be mechanically linked to a bodiless brain that has become practically immortal. Any new powers and functions required can be met by incorporating new artificial organs, as parts of the total cerebro-motor system. 'We badly need a small sense organ for detecting wireless frequencies, eyes for infra-red, ultra-violet and X-rays, ears for supersonics, detectors of high and low temperatures, of electrical potential and current, and chemical organs of many kinds.' Through such artificial additions and modifications, 'a mechanical stage, utilizing some or all of these alterations to the bodily frame, might . . . become the regular culmination to ordinary life.'

Bernal conceives, very much in the spirit of George Bernard Shaw's *Back to Methuselah* (1921), a series of ascending stages of existence for the man of the future. 'Starting, as Mr J. B. S. Haldane so convincingly predicts, in an ectogenetic factory, man will have anything from sixty to a hundred and twenty years of larval, unspecialized existence – surely enough to satisfy the advocates of the natural life.' During this stage he can, if he so wishes, occupy his time in 'dancing, poetry, and love-making'. 'Then he will leave the body, whose potentialities he should have sufficiently explored . . . .'

The next stage is chrysalis-like, 'a complicated and rather unpleasant process of transforming the already existing organs and grafting on all the new sensory and motor mechanisms'.

There would follow a period of re-education in which he would grow to understand the functioning of his new sensory organs and practise the manipulation of his new motor mechanism. Finally he would emerge as a completely effective, mentally directed mechanism, and set about the tasks appropriate to his new capacities.'[19]

The third stage itself has several phases, consisting of a progressive complication and 'de-materialization' of 'mechanized humanity'. To start with, man is still a fairly simple machine, albeit highly artificial.

Instead of the present body struture we should have the whole framework of some very rigid material, probably not metal but one of the new fibrous substances. In shape it might well be a rather short cylinder. Inside the cylinder, and supported very carefully to prevent shock, is the brain with its nerve connections, immersed in a liquid of the nature of cerebro-spinal fluid, and kept circulating over it at a uniform temperature. The brain and nerve cells are kept supplied with fresh oxygenated blood and drained of de-oxygenated blood through their arteries and veins which connect outside the cylinder to the artificial heart-lung digestive system – an elaborate, automatic contrivance.

Bernal brushes aside the idea that there is anything 'unnatural' or 'inhuman' in this potential development of humanity.

The new man must appear to those who have not contemplated him before as a strange, monstrous and inhuman creature, but he is only the logical outcome of the type of humanity that exists at present . . . . Although it is possible that man has far to go before his inherent physiological and psychological make-up becomes the limiting factor to his development, this must happen sooner or later and it is then that the mechanized man will begin to show a definite advantage. Normal man is an evolutionary dead end; mechanical man, apparently a break in organic evolution, is actually more in the true tradition of a further evolution.[20]

In line with this manner of conceiving evolution, Bernal envisages a further phase of mechanized man in which individuals link up directly with other individuals to form 'dual or multiple organisms'. This is achieved through electrical transference of impulses from nerve endings in one brain, via wires or over the ether to the brain cells of another person. These connections between two or more units would tend to become a more and more permanent condition. The consequences of this would be nothing less than an evolutionary leap into immortality.

Once the more or less permanent compound brain came into existence, two of the ineluctable limitations of present existence would be surmounted. In the first place, death would take on a different and far less terrible aspect. Death would still exist for the mentally directed mechanism we have just described; it would merely be postponed for three hundred or perhaps a thousand years, as long as the brain cells could be persuaded to live in the most favourable environment, but not for ever. But the multiple individual would be, barring cataclysmic accidents, immortal, the older components as they died being replaced by newer ones without losing the continuity of self, the memories and feelings of the older member transferring themselves almost completely to the common stock before its death. And if this seems only a way of cheating death, we must realize that the individual brain will feel itself part of the whole in a way that completely transcends the devotion of the most fanatical adherent of a religious sect.

Such a collective being will also overcome that solipsistic individuality which has so far inevitably limited human endeavour and achievement. With the compound mind, 'feeling would truly communicate itself, memories would be held in common; and yet in all this, identity and continuity of individual development would not be lost.' Moreover, it is likely that a division of labour would soon set in, to enhance efficiency and creativity. 'To some minds might be delegated the task of ensuring the proper functioning of the others, some might specialize in sense reception, and so on. Thus would grow up a hierarchy of minds that would be more truly a complex than a compound mind.' The increase in sensitivity and power of such a complex being would be truly remarkable. Perceptions, understanding, and actions would be immeasurably extended compared with those of the individual. The collective mind could experience, directly in its senses, the movement of geological time, as much as the most rapid vibrations of the physical world. Since most of its organs would be remote from its body, the complex mind could penetrate regions where organic bodies cannot enter or hope to survive. 'The interior of the earth and the stars, the inmost cells of living things themselves, would be open to consciousness through these angels, and through these angels also the motions of stars and living things could be directed.[21]

Bernal does not stop with this Wellsian evocation of 'men like gods'. There is still the limitation imposed by the very nature of the material, the organic substance, upon which evolution has worked hitherto. Man will eventually free himself from this prison and aspire to re-order matter acording to his own will and purpose.

For men will not be content to manufacture life: they will want to improve on it. For one material out of which nature has been forced to make life, man will have a thousand; living and organized material will be as much at the call of the mechanized or compound man as metals are today, and gradually this living material will come to substitute more and more for such inferior functions of the brain as memory, reflex actions, etc., in the compound man himself; for bodies at this time would be left far behind. The brain itself would become more and more separated into different groups of cells or individual cells with complicated connections and probably occupying considerable space. This would mean loss of mobility, which would not be a disadvantage owing to the extension of the sense faculties. Every part would now be accessible for replacing or repair – and this would in itself ensure a practical eternity of existence, for even the replacement of a previously organic brain-cell by a synthetic apparatus would not destroy the continuity of consciousness.

Man is now truly god-like, as he becomes the maker of new forms of life and master of their future evolution. Bernal's final vision is almost literally blinding.

> The new life would be more plastic, more directly controllable and at the same time more variable and more permanent than that produced by the triumphant opportunism of nature. Bit by bit the heritage in the direct line of mankind – the heritage of the original life emerging on the face of the world – would dwindle, and in the end disappear effectively, being preserved perhaps as some curious relic, while the new life which conserves none of the substance and all the spirit of the old would take its place and continue its development. Such a change would be as important as that in which life first appeared on the earth's surface and might be as gradual and imperceptible. Finally, consciousness itself may end or vanish in a humanity that has become completely etherealized, losing the close-knit organism, becoming masses of atoms in space communicating by radiation and ultimately perhaps resolving itself entirely into light. That may be an end or a beginning, but from here it is out of sight.[22]

As with Haldane, it is biology that inspires Bernal with his most scintillating and ingenious fancies. When he comes to consider the problem of the devil, the difficulties appear formidable, and far less surmountable in the current state of knowledge and society. Yet, Bernal argues, dealing with the devil must have priority, if the suggestions concerning the world and the flesh are not to remain 'so doubtful, fanciful and Utopian'. 'We can abandon the world and subdue the flesh only if we first expel the devil, and the devil, for all that he has lost individuality, is still as powerful as ever.' It is no help that 'psychology is in the state of physics at the time of Aristotle.'

Bernal considers that one of the principal obstacles to progress here may well be the very disillusion and dissatisfaction with science evidenced in the work of so many intellectuals and artists. As a counter to this, he holds out the hope that, before such a malaise spreads beyond the ranks of the humanistic intelligentsia, 'science, raised to power by industrialism, may become the directing tradition' in society. Just as with religion and humanism in earlier ages, science would have it in its power to select and promote to influence in society those groups and individuals most sympathetic to its ethos and most successful in its practice. The desired psychological changes would naturally follow from the ascendancy of such social types. But he confesses that this victory, particularly in the climate of the 1920s, is very uncertain, and instances the 'hatred and fear' of mechanical civilization shown in the works of D. H. Lawrence and Aldous Huxley.

> A severe crisis in mechanical civilization brought about by its inherent technical weakness or, as is much more likely, by its failure to arrange secondary social adjustments, is likely to be seized upon by the emotional factors hostile to all mechanism, and we may be closer to such a reversion than we suppose. Two recent books representing very divergent standpoints, the latest works of Mr Aldous Huxley and Mr D. H. Lawrence, show at the same time the weakening desires and the imminent realization of futility on the part of the scientist and a turning away from the whole of mechanization on the part of the more humanely-minded. The same thought is echoed from still another angle in the writings of Mr Bertrand Russell. They may be prophets predicting truly the doom of the new Babylon, or merely lamenting over a past that is lost for ever.[23]

Time alone will judge who is right, Bernal evenhandedly suggests; but in a concluding synthesis he makes it clear that the cards will be decisively stacked in favour of science. Science, after all, alone has proved to the world that it is capable of banishing the age-old fear of hunger and want:

Permanent plenty, no longer a Utopian dream, awaits the arrival of permanent peace. Even now, through rationalized capitalism or Soviet state planning, the problem of the production and distribution of necessaries to the primary satisfaction of all human beings is being pushed forward with uniform and intelligent method. Stupidity and the perversity of separate interests may hold the consummation back for centuries, but it must come gradually and surely.

From the point of view of the mass of the population, it is this decisive victory of science over natural necessity that will matter most. Beyond this and as a more 'rational psychology' advances among them, they may be content to let the world be governed by 'the aristocracy of scientific intelligence'. Scientific bodies, formally advisory, will gradually increase in influence and power until 'real sovereignty' centres in them.

The scientists would then have a dual function: to keep the world going as an efficient food and comfort machine, and to worry out the secrets of nature for themselves. It may well be that the dream of Daedalus and the doom of Icarus may both be fulfilled. A happy prosperous humanity enjoying their bodies, exercising the arts, patronizing the religions, may be well content to leave the machine by which their desires are satisfied in other more efficient hands. Psychological and physiological discoveries will give the ruling powers the means of directing the masses in harmless occupations and of maintaining a perfect docility under the appearance of perfect freedom. But this cannot happen unless the ruling power are the scientists themselves.[24]

The ambiguity here of Bernal's concern over this foreshadowing of *Brave New World* is heightened by his evident belief that the scientists will perforce have to go their own way. They will in fact have to be the pioneers in the creation of the 'new species', the super-race of humanity evolved into a mechanized body occupying the vast reachers of interstellar space. The approximately 10 per cent of the world's population that make up the scientists and technicians may have to begin the process of transformation behind the backs of the majority, and soon it would be too late to arrest the change. There would be 'an effective bar between the altered and the non-altered humanity'. A massive programme of education, within the context of a world socialist state, might prevent 'a permanent human dimorphism' from arising. But Bernal seems to feel that even this might not prevent the virtual separation of scientists from the rest of humanity. As the scientists grew in knowledge and power, they would tend increasingly to draw away from unreconstructed mankind. They would come to constitute the nucleus of the 'new humanity' inhabiting the whole universe. And here an intriguing possibility suggests itself. It is the final image that Bernal leaves us with, and it clearly tickles him greatly:

Mankind – the old mankind – would be left in undisputed possession of the earth, to be regarded by the inhabitants of the celestial spheres with a curious reverence. The world might, in fact, be transformed into a human zoo, a zoo so intelligently managed that its inhabitants are not aware that they are there merely for the purposes of observation and experiment.[25]

Wells himself, in his move from the dystopia to the utopia of science, never dared go to these lengths of calmly and complacently standing the nightmare world of Dr Moreau on its head. But the scientists of the 1920s and 1930s were nothing if not confident, not to say cocky. Two years before Bernal's book appeared, J. B. S. Haldane proposed to rewrite the Book of Revelations from a scientific perspective. 'The Last Judgement' (1927) is an eschatological fable concerning 'the most probable end of our planet as it might appear to spectators on another'. It is presented in the 'future history' form of 'a broadcast to infants on the planet Venus some forty million years hence'. The earth's doom comes not through the usual kind of cosmic catastrophe – the sun becomes an exploding supernova, the earth collides with a gigantic meteor – but as a consequence of man's greatest technological achievement, the harnessing of the energy of the seas' tides. The thoroughgoing exploitation of this source of power brings prosperity and happiness to mankind for thousands of years, but at the unforseen cost of slowing down the earth's rotation through tidal friction. Had the energy been less greedily used, the braking action of the tides could have been slowed down for thousands of millions of years. But 'it was characteristic of the dwellers on earth that they never looked more than a million years ahead, and the amount of energy available was ridiculouly squandered.' The slowing of the earth's rotation eventually causes huge earthquakes and cataclysmic climatic changes, leading to the extinction of practically all non-human life. The only hope of salvation seems to be the colonization of other planets. Scientists by careful selection gradually produce a strain of humans capable of withstanding the great heat and lack of oxygen on Venus. There also develop among these new humans 'a tradition and an inheritable psychological disposition' to consider themselves not as individuals but as 'dedicated to membership of a super-organism'.

The psychological types which had been common among the saints and soldiers of early history were revived. Confronted once more with an ideal as high as that of religion, but more rational, a task as concrete as and infinitely greater than that of the patriot, man became once more capable of self-transcendence.[26]

Human life on earth dies out, but the new men colonize Venus, from which their descendants contemplate the re-colonization of not simply the earth but the whole galaxy and – since the life of the galaxy is 'probably only eighty million million years' – the whole universe beyond. As in Bernal's projection, the new species of humanity has evolved new senses, many of them designed to make them more efficient and committed members of the collective 'super-organism'.

After the immense efforts of the first colonizers, we have settled down as members of a super-organism with no limits to its possible progress. The evolution of the individual has been brought under complete social control, and besides enormously enhanced intellectual powers we possess two new senses. The one enables us to apprehend radiation of wave-lengths between 100 and 1200 metres, and thus places every individual at all moments of life, both asleep and awake, under the influence of the voice of the community. It is difficult to see how else we could have achieved as complex a solidarity as has been possible. We can never close our consciousness to those wave-lengths on which we are told of our nature as components of a super-organism or deity, possibly the only one in space-time, and of its past, present, and future.[27]

Not content with blasphemy – the Christian thinker C. S. Lewis was particularly incensed by Haldane's fable – the scientists frequently and repeatedly pitched in with dogmatic Wellsian claims on behalf of science. 'Until the scientific point of view is generally adopted,' said Haldane, 'our civilization will continue to suffer from a fundamental disharmony. Its material basis is scientific, its intellectual framework is pre-scientific.'

If we are to control our own and one another's actions as we are learning to control nature, the scientific point of view must come out of the laboratory and be applied to the events of daily life. It is foolish to think that the outlook which has already revolutionized industry, agriculture, war and medicine will prove useless when applied to the family, the nation, or the human race.[28]

The 1920s and 1930s were years of ceaseless scientific missionary activity, promoted by some of the best works of scientific popularization ever written. To Wells's *The Science of Life* (1930) were added two which were even more popular with the public: Lancelot Hogben's *Mathematics for the Million* (1936) and *Science for the Citizen* (1938). Julian Huxley contributed *Science and Social Needs* (1935). In 1934 a series with the title 'The Library of Science and Culture' was launched under the general editorship of Hyman Levy. The series, wrote Levy in his manifesto, will 'reveal how mankind had sought in science the means of satisfying its varied needs, and how, in turn, science is stimulating fresh aspirations, inspiring loftier deeds of progress, and awakening hopes of increasing mastery over the destiny of the race'.[29]

The scientists moreover, left no one in doubt that their claims were not merely on behalf of a superior technique or method but implied a new politics. They took from Wells, but characteristically pushed in a more radical direction, the view that capitalist civilization held out little hope for the progress of science in the service of mankind. Without being by any means all Marxists, they accepted that science and socialism were intimately connected, almost synonymous. 'Science is communism', affirmed Bernal, always the most fervent of the group. For many of these socially minded scientists, a great impression was created by the Second International Congress of the History of Science and Technology held in London in the summer of 1931. The Russians had sent a powerful delegation, and the expectations of the conference were not disappointed by the papers of Boris Hessen and Nicholai Bukharin on the social context and significance of science, issued that year along with other Soviet presentations under the title *Science at the Cross-Roads*.

The 'science and society' movement chimed in with a wider movement that was embracing most of the western world in these decades. Whatever their ostensible philosophies, and under the aegis of a variety of political parties – Conservative and Labour, Democratic and Republican – western societies in these years committed themselves irrevocably to centralized planning on a national scale. Even without the spur of the experiments in planning in the Soviet Union and Nazi Germany, the economic and social turmoil of the 1920s and 1930s made this commitment on pragmatic grounds appear inevitable to practically every thinker of the time. This is the era of John Maynard Keynes's *The General Theory of Employment, Interest, and Money* (1936), Harold Macmillan's *The Middle Way* (1938), and James Burnham's *The Managerial Revolution* (1941) – not to mention Roosevelt's New Deal. 'Planning was the keyword of the thirties,' writes A. J. P. Taylor; 'planned economy, plan for peace, planned families, plan for holidays. The standard was Utopia.'[30] Planning was to be 'scientific', of course, but also to a good extent it would necessarily be about science, its progress and application to society. This conviction was shared by all parties, but it was held with particular fervour by the progressive left-wing intelligentsia of the time. George Woodcock, who was active in these circles in the 1930s, recalls that 'the radical youth became what [Aldous] Huxley later called "nothing-but" men'.

> Whether we termed ourselves Communists, Socialists, Anarchists or Militant Pacifists, we not only believed in the ultimate power of scientific progress to lead us to Utopia; we also saw no problem that the reasonable application of social planning could not solve. Perhaps we did not hold with Rousseau that man was naturally good, but we did hold that he was naturally social; where he gave the appearance of being anti-social, we believed, the fault lay not in him but in the perverting effect of artificial and coercive institutions, puritanical rules of behaviour and unjust economic systems. Remove the institutions, clean up the economics, expel the puritans; then the naturally cooperative qualities of man could produce a society that would work without coercion and merely from its inherent tendency to mutual aid.[31]

It was thinking of this kind, and the belief in science that was virtually axiomatic within it, that stirred Huxley's deepest anxieties. Too much can be made of the purely literary influence – Forster, Zamyatin and the like – on *Brave New World.* Huxley was always inclined to be scornful of the traditional literary intelligentsia, class-bound and clinging to narrow concepts of art and 'high culture'. They provided in fact much of the material for his satires of the 1920s. In his view, they were no match for scientific intellectuals of the calibre of Haldane and Bernal. In the face of the powerful and persuasive advocacy of the men of science, these effete and antiquated aesthetes were likely to be swept away unmourned. Huxley was too knowledgeable about the world of science to be so blind to the threat posed by the scientific hubris. It is a mistake to think of Huxley as the conventional literary intellectual, with the artist's traditional ignorance of and disdain for science. His fear of the scientific ethos was strongly reinforced by his admiration for D. H. Lawrence, but he never shared in Lawrence's violent repudiation of science. He read voraciously works of science and scientific philosophy. He had many scientific friends, among them Bertrand Russell, the Haldanes, Linus Pauling and Victor Rothschild, and he paid them the compliment of reading and corresponding on their works. His family environment was saturated with science: not just through the powerful influence of his grandfather, Thomas Henry Huxley, but continuing in the work of his father Leonard Huxley, who spent many years on his biography of T. H. Huxley and his *Life* of the great botanist Joseph Hooker. Above all, there was his elder brother Julian: a famous biologist, collaborator with Wells on *The Science of Life* and an active protagonist of the 'science and society' movement. As a boy Aldous had wished to emulate his brother and to become a biologist or doctor. The onset of near-blindness at the age of 16 made both careers impossibile, but he continued to follow Julian's career with pride, sometimes mixed with affectionate irony.[32]

Huxley once said that 'I feel strongly that a man of letters should be intensely aware of the problems which surround him, of which technological and scientific problems are the most urgent.'[33] If anyone in this century can claim to have bridged the 'two cultures' of literature and science – a subject which fascinated Huxley and to which he devoted his last work[34] – it was Aldous Huxley. Echoing the words of his grandfather T. H. Huxley, he spoke of 'the great truth, that art and literature and science are one'. 'He was equally at ease with Dante and with Darwin', writes Lord David Cecil in a memoir on Huxley.[35] The physicist Denis Gabor has recalled the great impact that Huxley had on him and his fellow-scientists in the Hungary of the 1920s, for 'here at last was a writer who could touch on scientific matters without making us wince.'[36]

In *Brave New World* Huxley wrote the most powerful denunciation of the scientific world-view that has ever been written. But unlike many other such denunciations – such as those of Aldous's great-uncle Matthew Arnold or the literary critic F. R. Leavis – it came out of an absorption and immersion in science that is unmatched in the work of any other twentieth-century literary figure. Huxley knew precisely the fascination and fantastic strength of the adversary. It is of course just this that still makes *Brave New World*, more than 50 years after it appeared, so frightening.

THE WORLD OF OUR FORD: THE FUTURE AS AMERICA

Huxley was always good with epigraphs; and the remarks of Nicolas Berdiaeff which he chose as the epigraph to *Brave New World* could not have been more apposite to its central concern. The problem with utopias, says Berdiaeff, is not, as is commonly said, that they are unreal and unrealizable. Quite the contrary. It is the frightful fact that the modern world is for the first time making it possible that utopias *will* be realized. 'Les utopies sont réalisables. La vie marche vers les utopies.' The question now is how we might *avoid* their definitive realization, how we might recover and safeguard a society 'non utopique, moins "parfaite" et plus libre'.

It is Huxley's conviction in *Brave New World* that practically the whole of modern western development has been a steady descent into nightmare. Progress has been a grotesque and cruel illusion. The most characteristic and vaunted achievements of the West – the scientific revolution of the seventeenth century and the industrial revolution of the nineteenth – have been the building blocks of the sterile graveyard of twentieth-century civilization. Science and Reason, the twin components of practically all progressive and utopian conceptions since the seventeenth century, are only too clearly in the ascendant. But instead of producing the heaven on earth that the utopians confidently predicted, they have succeeded only in creating a hell. Huxley is nothing if not even-handed in meting out the blame. Progressives and Conservatives, Radicals and Reactionaries, Socialists and Capitalists – all have contributed to the mess in about equal measure. As in the old allegorical fables, Huxley gives many of his characters names which symbolize his particular *bêtes noires*. Together, they add up to a fairly comprehensive indictment of western thought and achievement since the Enlightenment.

His old enemy Wells is charitably given only a one-line, walk-on appearance ('Dr *Wells* says that a three months' Pregnancy Substitute now will make all the difference to my health for the next three or four years'). Wells's fellow-Fabian George Bernard Shaw also appears fleetingly as Dr *Shaw*, as do other free-thinkers and rationalists (Fifi *Bradlaugh, Jean-Jacques* Habibullah). The Left gets a trouncing in Polly *Trotsky,* Sarojini *Engels*, Herbert *Bakunin, Lenina* Crowne, and Bernard *Marx*. For Huxley, Socialism and Marxism, as the latest variants of scientific rationalism, differed from other varieties only in their greater arrogance and fanaticism, a judgement the Russian Revolution and the new Soviet State had done nothing to shake. He naturally had no greater faith in right-wing dictators or large capitalists, who are rebuffed in *Benito* Hoover and *Primo* Mellon, the last also doubling for capitalists along with Morgana *Rothschild*. Technology gets its due in George *Edzel*, Joanna *Diesel*, and Clara *Deterding*, and science its brick-bat in *Darwin* Bonaparte, *Bernard* Marx, and *Helmholtz* Watson. *Watson* is also Huxley's backhanded tribute to the founder of behaviourism in psychology, and therefore a key influence in the new society. (Pavlov is given star-billing as the guiding spirit behind the *Neo-Pavlovian Conditioning Rooms*.) Benito *Hoover* points up the drive towards the air-conditioned nightmare, the making of life as mindlessly effortless and physically comfortable as possible through the ceaseless quest for 'labour-saving' devices. An especially important role is marked out for *Mustapha Mond*. His name not only plays on the fact that he is one of the ten World Controllers, but also takes a side-swipe at the nationalism symbolized by Attaturk and, more importantly, refers to Alfred Mond (the later Lord Melchett), the founder and dynamic chairman of the chemical firm ICI. Mond stands for the new giant conglomerates that were coming to dominate the industrial world. He is a particularly good choice on Huxley's part, not simply as one of the new breed of scientist-industrialist, but because both the left and the right were hailing the conglomerates enthusiastically as the latest and most progressive organizational form in the modern world: the right because they were a move towards 'rationalization', the left because they were a half-way house to nationalization. H. G. Wells went so far as to use Alfred Mond as the basis of his portrait of the enlightened industrialist William Clissold, who in *The World of William Clissold* is presented as the type of the new generation of businessmen who will inaugurate the coming scientific civilization.

Pride of place is of course reserved for Our *Ford* ('or Our *Freud*, as, for some inscrutable reason, he chose to call himself whenever he spoke of psychological matters'). Henry Ford – 'this ascetic missionary and saint of the new dispensation'[37] – is elevated as the avowed deity of the future society. Here Huxley makes two points. He singles out 'Fordism' as the central ideology and practice which encapsulates all the most inhuman tendencies of scientific–industrial society; and he makes it clear that it is America, as the parent and most systematic practitioner of Fordism, that has so far travelled furthest along the road to damnation.

Fordism is a compound of the 'scientific management' of men linked to the fullest mechanization of tasks. It carries to a logical end the basic impulse of industrialism, to reduce the human being to the status of an appendage of the machine and to empty his work of all skill and significance. It employs modern science and technology to 'mass produce', cheaply and efficiently, standardized items – whether of material or non-material culture. It is equally applicable to works of art and literature as to motor cars or the production of food. For Huxley, Fordism was the latest and most destructive of the 'rationalizing' impulses in western civilization that had begun with Plato.

> Fordism, or the philosopy of industrialism, . . . demands that we should sacrifice the animal man (and along with the animal large portions of the thinking, spiritual man) . . . to the machine. There is no place in the factory, or in that larger factory which is the modern industrialized world, for animals on the one hand, or for artists, mystics, or even, finally, individuals on the other. Of all the ascetic religions, Fordism is that which demands the cruellest mutilations of the human psyche – demands the cruellest mutilations and offers the smallest spiritual returns. Rigorously practised for a few generations, this dreadful religion of the machine will end by destroying the human race.[38]

Fordism found its first and definitive expresion in the early years of the century at Henry Ford's Motor Company in Detroit. Ford's Model T, 'the people's car', had been an enormous success and created a demand that could not be met by the traditional methods of production. Between 1908 and 1914 Ford reorganized production on a revolutionary basis. He incorporated the theories and studies of Frederick Winslow Taylor, the father of 'scientific management', which has been called 'the most powerful as well as the most lasting contribution America has made to Western thought since the Federalist Papers'.[39] Scientific management (or Taylorism) sought to improve productive efficiency by a minute analysis of work tasks, breaking down the tasks into their simplest components and restricting each worker to a single component, so that worker error – as well as worker skill and initiative – was reduced to a minimum. It aimed to extract the maximum benefit from the classic industrial principle of the division of labour. Linked to the assembly-line method of production, it promised to simplify tasks to the point where they could all be automated and the human worker dispensed with altogether. The assembly line at Ford's, though not fully automated, clearly pointed in that direction.

> The key element of the new organization of labor was the endless conveyor chain upon which car assemblies were carried past fixed stations where men performed simple

operations as they passed. This system was first put into operation for various subassemblies, beginning around the same time the Model T was launched, and developed through the next half-dozen years until it culminated in January 1914 with the inauguration of the first endless chain conveyor for final assembly at Ford's Highland Park plant. Within three months, the assembly time for the Model T had been reduced to one-tenth the time formerly needed, and by 1925 an organization had been created which produced almost as many cars in a single day as had been produced, early in the history of Model T, in an entire year.[40]

The 'endless conveyor chain' was what Charlie Chaplin seized on as the distinctive image of industrial civilization in his satire *Modern Times*; and is it accidental that Huxley actually begins *Brave New World* with it? The Director of the Central London Hatchery and Conditioning Centre is showing a group of students around the plant. He explains the *in vitro* fertilization process, and especially the revolutionary 'Bokanovsky's Process' applied to the future Gammas, Deltas and Epsilons, which, by checking the normal growth of the fertilized ova, causes them to bud and to produce scores of identical embryos.

On a very slowly moving band a rackful of test-tubes was entering a large metal box, another rackful was emerging. Machinery faintly purred. It took eight minutes for the tubes to go through, he told them. Eight minutes of hard X-rays being about as much as an egg can stand. A few died; of the rest, the least susceptible divided into two; most put out four buds; some eight; all were returned to the incubators, where the buds began to develop; then, after two days, were suddenly chilled, chilled and checked. Two, four, eight, the buds in their turn budded; and having budded were dosed almost to death with alcohol; consequently burgeoned again and having budded – bud out of bud out of bud – were thereafter – further arrest being generally fatal – left to develop in peace. By which time the original egg was in a fair way to becoming anything from eight to ninety-six embryos – a prodigious improvement, you will agree, on nature. Identical twins – but not in piddling twos and threes as in the old viviparous days, when an egg would sometimes accidentally divide; actually by dozens, by scores at a time.[41]

This is Fordism with a vengeance: the conveyor-belt production not simply of goods but of human beings. It is, as the Director says, 'the principle of mass production at last applied to biology'. Human life in Brave New World is artificially manufactured in test-tubes. The embryos are bottled, labelled and passed on to the Social Predestinaton Room, where, according to the current social requirements, they are chemically treated and in other ways physiologically conditioned to result in future Alphas, Betas or members of the lower castes. After a suitable period of storage in the Embryo Store they are then decanted and sent on their way to the infant nurseries – the Neo-Pavlovian Conditioning rooms – where their biological conditioning is complemented and completed by intensive psychological and social conditioning. The whole operation is conducted with the smoothness and automatic precision of the modern factory. Human beings are made to order, and their manufacture is carried out with all the attention to grading and 'quality control' necessary in the production of the differentiated units which make up the different castes of the society. 'We decant our babies as socialized human beings, as Alphas or Epsilons, as future sewage workers or future . . . Directors of Hatcheries . . . .'

Embryos predestined to be workers in the tropics are inoculated with a love of heat and a horror of cold. 'Later on their minds would be made to endorse the judgement of their bodies. We condition them to thrive on heat . . . . Our colleagues upstairs [in the nurseries] will teach them to love it.' The students watch the predestination of some other workers.

On Rack 10, rows of next generation's chemical workers were being trained in the toleration of lead, caustic soda, tar, chlorine. The first of a batch of two hundred and fifty embryonic rocket-plane engineers was just passing the eleven hundredth metre mark on Rack 3. A special mechanism kept their containers in constant rotation. To improve their sense of balance . . . . 'Doing repairs on the outside of a rocket in mid air is a ticklish job. We slacken off the circulation when they're right way up, so that they're half starved, and double the flow of surrogate when they're upside down. They learn to associate topsy-turvydom with well-being; in fact, they're only truly happy when they're standing on their heads.' (*BNW*, ch. 1, p. 25)

Huxley did not of course have to go to America to see Fordism in operation. Fordism was, quite simply, the principle of the modern world *tout court*. But a brief visit to America in 1926 – his first – left an unforgettable impression. He got the feel of the new civilization in the making, but without any of the hope that had inspired earlier visitors. The Brave New World that had inspired such utopian strivings in the past two centuries was in the process of realizing a Brave New World of a grotesquely different kind. He visited Los Angeles, 'the great Joy City of the West', 'the City of Dreadful Joy'. Here he saw a world totally given over to hedonism, a world where the movies, jazz, cocktails, automobiles and having a Good Time had become equated with life itself. He saw too the fatigue and boredom that was the other side of the Good Time, and the deadness that lay at its centre. The girls were 'plumply ravishing, with the promise of pneumatic bliss'. But their faces were 'so curiously uniform, unindividual, and blank'.[42] In Los Angeles Huxley found his Lenina Crowne: so sexy and seductive, so shallow and synthetic.

Huxley, as Theodor Adorno notes, scorned the consolation so often seized upon by European intellectuals in relation to America: 'the notion that the frightening aspects of American civilization are ephemeral relics of its primitiveness or potent safeguards of its youth'.[43] For Huxley, America was not the rough-cut copy of Old Europe but on the contrary represented, in the fullest form then visible, the image of Europe's own future, and indeed that of the world. In an article written for *Harper's Magazine* a year after his return from the States, he wrote:

The future of America is the future of the world. Material circumstances are driving all nations along the path in which America is going. Living in the contemporary environment, which is everywhere becoming more and more American, men feel a psychological compulsion to go the American way. Fate acts within and without; there is no resisting. For good or for evil, it seems that the world must be Americanized. America is not unique; she merely leads the way along the road which the people of every nation and continent are taking. Studying the good and the evil features in American life, we are studying, in a generally more definite and highly developed form, the good and evil features of the whole world's present and immediately coming civilization. Speculating on the American future, we are speculating on the future of civilized man.[44]

The focus on America as the future of man made another point: that any future prophecy must be largely based on the study of the present. 'The future is the present projected.'[45] It is only a superficial paradox that a few years later Huxley produced a full portrait of a civilization six hundred years distant. In all his speculations Huxley very rarely departed from present conditions, and this is as true of *Brave New World* as of his many social and political essays dealing with similar themes. Huxley frequently expresssed his dislike and distrust of future speculations of the usual kind. 'Personally, I must confess, I am more interested in what the world is now than what it will be, or what it might be if improbable conditions were fulfilled.'[46] 'The utopians . . . are too much preoccupied with what ought to be to pay any attention to what is.'[47] Future thinking, moreover, always carried for him the danger of that utopianism – whether in communism, Wellsianism, or certain varieties of Christianity – which was prepared to sacrifice the present 'to a future about which the one thing that can certainly be said is that we are totally incapable of foreseeing it accurately'.[48]

In *Brave New World* Huxley put into the most effective form he ever discovered the concerns that he explored in his novels and essays of the 1920s.[49] With the help of Vilfredo Pareto and Georges Sorel, among others, and the hindrance of H. G. Wells and Sigmund Freud, among others,[50] he carried out a wide-ranging exploration of the character and prospects of the modern western world. His conclusions were almost wholly negative and pessimistic. Democracy was a sham and a fraud, based on the scientifically untenable premise that all men were equal in reason and ability. This belief, essentially a product of the eighteenth-century Enlightenment, had led to an equally unreal belief in the power of the environment and education to 'level up' the inequalities caused by differences of social origin. Human inequality was a natural fact, the result of hereditable differences in intelligence and ability. 'There is no valid reason for supposing that the two . . . infants who were to become Shakespeare and Stratford's village idiot could have been educated into exchanging their adult parts.'[51] No more could the Enlightenment presumption of a natural human tendency to moral virtue be upheld.

The doctrine of Original Sin is, scientifically, much truer than the doctrine of natural reasonableness and virtue. Original Sin in the shape of anti-social tendencies inherited from our animal ancestors, is a familiar and observable fact. Primitively, and in a state of nature, human beings were not, as the eighteenth century philosophers supposed, wise and virtuous: they were apes.[52]

Democracy in the modern world had become a shibboleth, a new religious faith subscribed to by all classes. If its theory was intellectually feeble, its practice was disastrous. It flew in the face of all the well-established facts of human nature and society. The vast majority of men and women were ignorant of and uninterested in politics, except for the rare occasions when politics directly impinged on their everyday lives. Universal suffrage consequently had led to the reign of demagogues and political swindlers. It had given the advertisers and newspaper proprietors enormous power. 'Plutocratic oligarchs, they aspire to rule, under cover of democratic institutions, impersonally and without responsibility.'[53] The gullibility and susceptibility of the mass electorate were buttressed by a system of education which ruinously treated all children alike, irrespective of their individual differences of ability, and which put all the emphasis on teaching and instruction rather than active learning. 'The over-taught child is the father of the newspaper-reading, advertisement believing, propaganda-swallowing, demogogue-led man – the man who makes modern democracy the farce it is.'[54]

Modern education had become obsessed with the need to produce socially useful skills, and to instil, as was thought, the qualities needed to be successful in the modern world. This emphasis on the good 'citizen', narrowly conceived, at the expense of the whole man resulted in one-dimensional personalities incapable of dealing either with their own individual lives or that of society at large.

> When men are brought up to be citizens and nothing else, they become, first imperfect men and then unsatisfactory citizens . . . . We have tried to make men good citizens of highly organized industrial states: we have only succeeded in producing a crop of specialists, whose dissatisfaction at not being allowed to be complete men makes them extremely bad citizens.[55]

The educational system in its turn reflected a more fundamental dissociation of personality. The decline of religion had removed the unifying mental and moral framework of the pre-industrial world. The modern substitutes, such as politics, business, art and sex, were at best too partial and unfulfilling to be fully integrative activities. The modern personality, like the modern world, was a congeries of specialized, disconnected parts, flying off in different and often contradictory directions: 'instinct' against 'intellect', 'materialism' against 'idealism', 'asceticism' against 'indulgence'. One result of the uncoordinated personality had been the explosion of promiscuity among the young, the deliberate flaunting of sex and the emotions against the claims of 'prudence' and 'reason'. Rebellious in intent, it simply confirmed their imprisonment within the disconnected compartments of the modern personality. It is a new barbarism, a new savagery, but without the taboos that provide some sort of framework for real savages.

> Our modern savages have no taboos of any sort. They copulate with the casual promiscuity of dogs; they make use of every violent emotion-producing sensation for its own sake, because it gives a momentary thrill. In the discontinuity of their emotional states they find . . . not something to be deplored and as far as possible corrected, but something curious and entertaining. They pass from state to mental state with the enjoyment of children visiting the side-shows of a fair. In one booth is lasciviousness, in the next disgust. You pay your money and you take your choice of drunken fury or drunken sentimentality.[56]

Underlying and sustaining all these perversions of modern society and the modern personality are the logic and dynamism of Fordism and the machine age, observable at their clearest in America. Huxley does not deny the real benefits brought by industrialism. He is, or at least so he claims, no Luddite. Machinery has relieved drudgery and brought leisure and prosperity to more people than ever before in history. But this increased leisure has not, as it could, led to increased culture for the masses. 'More leisure and more prosperity mean for them more dancing, more parties, more movies, more distractions in general.' Nor is this simply the fault of the masses themselves, although Huxley believes that 'a great many men and women . . . do not want to be cultured, are not interested in the higher life.'[57] It is the industrial system itself which, in its ceaseless quest for profit, breeds passivity and the consumerist mentality.

> Rationalization has led to over-production, and over-production calls insistently for a compensating over-consumption. Economic necessities easily and rapidly become moral virtues, and the first duty of the modern consumer is not to consume little, as in the pre-industrial epoch, but to consume much, to go on consuming more and more. Asceticism is bad citizenship; self-indulgence has become a social virtue.[58]

Such an attitude renders the modern consumer incapable of creatively using his new-found leisure. Leisure as a result now threatens him as boredom and 'the servitude of amusement and social duties, more pointless than work and often quite as arduous'.

Moreover, if the industrial economy is to survive, nothing can be allowed to escape the operations of Fordism. The industrial system turns on expansion. Its method is mass production, and mass production can be applied as easily to things of the mind and spirit as to material objects. Once again, a potentially culture-enhancing series of mechanical inventions is employed not to raise but to debase culture. 'The rotary press, the process block, the cinema, the radio, the phonograph are used not, as they might so easily be used, to propagate culture, but its opposite. All the resources of science are applied in order that imbecility may flourish and vulgarity cover the whole earth.'[59] In their need to appeal to the largest number of consumers, the purveyors of mass-produced culture are driven to standardize taste at the lowest common level.

What in some ways concerns Huxley even more is that this debasement and standardization is not restricted to the masses. The process also radically affects the capacity and the opportunity of the cultivated minority to pursue the finer things in life. Huxley purports to discover a Law of Diminishing Returns in the progress of industrial civilization. Industrialism promises to confer the benefits of leisure and prosperity, previously enjoyed only by the few, on the many. But in doing so it diminishes or destroys the available satisfactions for all. 'Experiences which, enjoyed by a few, were precious, cease automatically to be precious when enjoyed by many.'[60] Education, once made general, turns out not only to be disillusioning to those many incapable of appreciating its intrinsic rewards, but also socially unrewarding, since what all possess ceases to have any value or distinction.[61] Similarly, 'beauty-spots accessible to whole populations cease to be beauty-spots and become Blackpools.'[62] Travel too, once rightly considered a liberal education owing to the diversity of cultural experiences it brought, ceases to have that value when the mass media and universal education abolish the differences between cultures. The very cheapness and rapidity of mass transport hastens on that end.

There is still some point in going from Burslem to Udaipur. But when all the inhabitants of Burslem have been sufficiently often to Udaipur and all the inhabitants of Udaipur have been sufficiently often to Burslem, there will be no point whatever in making the journey. Leaving out of account a few trifling geological and climatic idiosyncracies, the two towns will have become essentially indistinguishable.[63]

The philosophy of Fordism, the principle of mechanical reproduction, so clearly reigns in industrial society that its effects can as easily be seen in art, morality and politics as in the more obvious spheres of the economy. Cubist artists rejoice in pure gometric form, Futurists worship the machine, both scorning human 'sentimentality' and personal values. Architects and planners too, such as Le Corbusier, are in love with the machine, and design their houses and cities accordingly: frequently in imitation of 'entirely fabulous Chicagos and New Yorks, where every house is a skyscraper and every skyscraper a factory full of incessantly turning wheels; where there are elevated railways in every street, aeroplanes circling round every chimney-pot, electric sky-signs on every blank wall, motor cars never doing less than sixty miles an hour, and a noise like seventy pandemoniums.'[64] In politics, interestingly, it is the new Soviet state, rather than America, which has shown the Fordian impulse in its clearest form. The Bolsheviks have elevated Economic Man as the sole political animal, and have established collectivism as the fitting political mode to match the industrial mode of production. The Bolsheviks here are only indicating the tendencies apparent in all modern mass democracies, to organize the whole of society according to the dictates and in the image of the machine.

The aim of the Communist Revolution in Russia was to deprive the individual of every right, every vestige of personal liberty . . . and to transform him into a component cell of the great 'Collective Man – that single mechanical monster who . . . is to take the place of the unregimented hordes of 'soul-encumbered' individuals who now inhabit the earth. To the Bolshevik, there is something hideous and unseemly about the spectacle of anything so 'chaotically vital', so 'mystically organic' as an individual with a soul, with personal tastes, with special talents. Individuals must be organized out of existence; the communist state requires, not men, but cogs and rachets in the huge 'collective mechanism'. To the Bolshevik idealist, Utopia is indistinguishable from one of Mr Henry Ford's factories. It is not enough, in their eyes, that men should spend only eight hours a day under the workshop discipline. Life outside the factory must be exactly like life inside. Leisure must be as highly organized as toil. Into the Christian Kingdom of Heaven men may only enter if they have become like little children. The condition of their entry into the Bolsheviks' Earthly Paradise is that they shall have become like machines.[65]

It is very evident that the critique of society contained in these essays of the 1920s springs from fairly traditional conservative sources. This is not, of course, the conservatism of the Tory Party, but that strand of cultural criticism running from Coleridge to F. R. Leavis which has used the past – usually somewhat idealized – as a reference point from which to criticize the present.[66]

Huxley in these essays speaks often with the voice and in the manner of the most influential of these critics, his great-uncle Matthew Arnold. There is the same concern with preserving 'the best', with the threat to taste and cultural standards posed by the onset of mass mechanical civilization. There is the same distrust of democracy, and the same lack of faith in the will and capacity of any of the main social classes to stem the tide of barbarism. Huxley's frequently satirical and playful tone lightens the mood – he does not often match Arnold's darker visions of disaster – but there is no missing the fundamental seriousness, or the fundamental pessimism. Essentially the same critique, in Huxley's most bitingly satirical vein, continues in *Brave New World.*

What is more surprising, in view of Huxley's later social philosophy, is the character of the alternatives he was suggesting during these years. Most of his writing, certainly his best, at this time was satirical and critical. But Huxley also felt impelled on occasion to offer something more positive and constructive, as some sort of answer to his own destructive criticism. Stimulated perhaps by his reading of Pareto and other 'elite' theorists, he came out strongly in favour of rule by an enlightened elite, a new aristocracy of intelligence. About this, too, there was nothing in itself particularly surprising or original. Elitism was the commonest and most fashionable idea of the decade. Theorists of both right and left, thinkers as different as H. G. Wells and T. S. Eliot, were proposing elitist solutions of various kinds to current predicaments. Frequently there was reference to the Bolshevik and Fascist elites of the 1920s as providing – 'in a crude form, of course' – some sort of model of this.

What makes Huxley's case interesting is that he proposes a type of elitist social organization that has almost exactly the form that he so mercilessly savages in *Brave New World.* The proposal first surfaces in Huxley's lightest and most playful manner, in his first novel, *Crome Yellow* (1921). Parading his cynical rationalism, the philosopher Scogan discourses provocatively on the founding of 'the Rational State'. 'The men of intelligence must combine,' he argues, 'must conspire, and seize power from the imbeciles and maniacs who now direct us.' What they will set up is a carefully-graded caste society.

> In the Rational State . . . human beings will be separated out into distinct species, not according to the colour of their eyes or the shape of their skulls, but according to the qualities of their mind and temperament. Examining psychologists, trained to what would now seem an almost superhuman clairvoyance, will test each child that is born and assign it to its proper species. Duly labelled and docketed, the child will be given the education suitable to members of its species, and will be set, in adult life, to perform those functions which human beings in his variety are capable of performing.

Thus graded, the citizens of the Rational State will fall into three main classes; 'the Directing Intelligences, the Men of Faith, and the Herd'. The Intelligences, those with the highest intellectual ability, will naturally rule the state. The Men of Faith will be their unwitting ideological agents. These men, of the psychological type of the religious prophets of old, will from their earliest years be trained by the Intelligences to preach the doctrines that support the Rational State. Their principal function will be to mobilize the Herd to act according to the schemes of the Directing Intelligences. As for the Herd,

In the upbringing of the Herd, humanity's almost boundless suggestibility will be scientifically exploited. Systematically, from the earliest infancy, its members will be assured that there is no happiness to be found except in work and obedience; they will be made to belive that they are happy, that they are tremendously important beings, and that everything they do is noble and significant. For the lower species the earth will be restored to the centre of the universe and man to pre-eminence on earth. Oh, I envy the lot of the commonalty in the Rational State! Working their eight hours a day, obeying their betters, convinced of their own grandeur and significance and immortality, they will be marvellously happy, happier than any race of men has ever been. They will go through life in a rosy state of intoxication, from which they will never awake. The Men of Faith will play the cup-bearers at this life-long bacchanal, filling and ever filling again with the warm liquor that the Intelligences, in sad and sober privacy behind the scenes, will brew for the intoxication of their subjects.[67]

This is all so close to Wells's Utopia – and also of course Plato's – that there can be no question of any endorsement of it here, quite apart from the fact that Huxley puts the speculation in the mouth of a grotesque rationalist. But the basic idea clearly fascinated Huxley. Only a few years later we find him proposing a system of education based on the recognition of the innate inequalities of intelligence among individuals, so that academic education is restricted to the relatively few capable of profiting from it, and more practical and vocational education given to the rest. 'The ideal educational system,' he says, 'is one which accurately measures the capacities of each individual and fits him, by means of specially adapted training, to perform those functions which he is naturally adapted to perform. A perfect education is one which trains up every human being to fit into the place he or she is to occupy in the social hierarchy . . . .'[68] This system then becomes the basis of 'a new social hierarchy, based on the facts of human nature', and a new regenerated state governed according to 'the aristocratic ideal'.

The ideal state is one in which there is a material democracy controlled by an aristocracy of intellect – a state in which men and women are guaranteed a decent human existence and are given every opportunity to develop such talents as they possess, and where those with the greatest talents rule.[69]

'That every human being should be in his place – that is the ideal of the aristocratic as opposed to the democratic state. It is not merely a question of the organization of government, but of the organization of the whole of society.' Briskly, like any good technocrat going about his business, Huxley admonishes: 'The misplacement of parts of the social machine leads to friction and consequent waste of power; in the case of the individuals concerned it leads to many varieties of suffering.'[70] This is as true of politics as of the many spheres, such as business and the professions, where the principle of competence is familiar and acknowledged. Few people are fit to govern themselves; it is in any case a serious error to suppose that the majority of people want to. This delusion of the democrats, if acted upon, could lead to social anarchy. In words that could come out of the mouth of Mustapha Mond, or the Grand Inquisitor, Huxley intones:

States function as smoothly as they do, because the greater part of the population is not very intelligent, dreads responsibility, and desires nothing better than to be told what to do. Provided the rulers do not interfere with its material comforts and its cherished beliefs, it is perfectly happy to let itself be ruled.[71]

With this Machiavellian credo Huxley has announced the principal rationale of *Brave New World*. On this showing, he could have presented *Brave New World* as a neo-Platonic utopia rather than, as he does, an anti-utopia. The comparison with Wells, once again, is fascinating. Wells began with anti-utopian themes which he transformed into utopian ones. Huxley – although admittedly not as clearly – began with utopian ideas which became the substance of his anti-utopia. The aristocracy of intellect becomes rule by the World Controllers. In a later development, and with a further twist, some of his anti-utopian themes – e.g., the use of drugs – were turned once more into utopia, although of a kind radically different from his youthful utopianism. Where the early Huxley's utopianism was elitist, that of the mature Huxley was anarchist.

What led Huxley to retreat from his elitist views? Why did he move from advocacy to admonition? One can only guess, as most of Huxley's biographers and commentators either ignore this aspect of his thought or fail to offer any explanation for the turn-about.[72] Perhaps the renewed friendship with D. H. Lawrence after 1926 had something to do with it, although, while Lawrence no doubt would scorn the faith in the intellect and reinforce Huxley's suspicion of science, he was certainly no democrat.[73] A stronger possibility concerns the progress of the Fascist movement in Italy, which Huxley, like many intellectuals, began by welcoming and ended by denouncing. Huxley lived in Italy for much of the 1920s, and so had an opportunity to witness the degeneration of Italian Fascism at first hand. Nor was the disenchantment purely objective and intellectual. An incident in which four Fascist thugs forced their way into his house seems finally to have determined him to leave Italy for good.[74] Certainly it does not appear accidental that in his novel *Point Counter Point*, published in 1928, the elitist point of view is expressed by the megalomaniac English Fascist Everard Webley – 'a Tinpot Mussolini' – whose ravings are clearly presented by Huxley for the murderous lunacy that they are.

Whatever the cause, by the time Huxley published *Music at Night* (1931) his views had undergone a perceptible shift. There are still, interestingly, signs that he is attracted to possibilities which are roundly condemned in *Brave New World*. For instance, bemoaning the fact that the modern age has produced no new pleasures, only variants of the old, he remarks (only half-seriously, it is true):

So far as I can see, the only possible new pleasure would be one derived from the invention of a new drug – of a more efficient and less harmful substitute for alcohol and cocaine . . . . If we could sniff or swallow something that would for five or six hours each day abolish our solitude as individuals, atone us with our fellows in a glowing exaltation of affection and make life in all its aspects seem not only worth living, but divinely beautiful and significant, and if this heavenly, world-transfiguring drug were of such a kind that we could wake up next morning with a clear head and an undamaged constitution – then, it seems to me, all our problems . . . would be wholly solved and earth would become paradise.[75]

There is still, too, a belief in the positive power of eugenics to improve the race. But it is now 'contemporary prophets' – not, apparently, the author, who deprecates the role – who have 'visions of future societies founded on the idea of natural inequality . . . of a ruling aristocracy and of a race slowly improved . . . by deliberate eugenic breeding'. And in speculating on the more distant future made possible by the advances of genetics and psychology, Huxley's tone modulates distinctly into the key of *Brave New World*:

We can imagine our children having visions of a new caste system based on differences in native ability and accompanied by a Machiavellian system of education, designed to give the members of the lower castes only such instruction as it is profitable for society at large and the upper castes in particular that they should have.[76]

Through the gates of the scientific Eden, Huxley glimpsed a hell contrived by the most advanced techniques and the most knowledgeable minds of the modern world. Almost as if to atone for his earlier dismissive utterances, Huxley turned prophet with a vengeance. In *Brave New World* he produced what Sir Isaiah Berlin has said is 'certainly the most influential modern expression of disillusionment with purely technological progress'.[77]

'COMMUNITY, IDENTITY, STABILITY': THE SOCIAL ORDER OF *BRAVE NEW WORLD*

It is fair to call *Brave New World* an anti-utopia of science, in fact *the* anti-utopia of science. But we should always remember that what Huxley is attacking is not science as such so much as *scientism*. It is the applications of science, in a particular social context and with a particular social purpose, that draws his fire. Huxley later wrote that 'the theme of *Brave New World* is not the advancement of science as such; it is the advancement of science as it affects human individuals.'[78] Science in the Brave New World, as Mustapha Mond points out, is actually a threatening and potentially subversive activity, along with art and religion. The pure unfettered pursuit of truth and knowledge wherever they lead might undermine the social purpose of Brave New World. 'Every discovery in pure science is potentially subversive . . . .' Science is therefore strictly controlled, in the interest of the overriding goal of social stability. Science has provided the means for the achievement of 'the stablest equilibrium in history'; it must not now be allowed to disturb that stability. The use of labour-saving inventions, for instance, is highly selective. The lower castes work a seven-and-a-half-hour day. It would be technically feasible to reduce that to three or four hours a day, but no attempt is made to do so, any more than, as would be equally possible, to synthesize all food and so dispense with the need for agricultural labour. The reason is the proven incapacity of the lower castes to make good – 'safe' – use of their increased leisure time, and the threat to the social order that this would pose. 'The experiment was tried . . . . The whole of

Ireland was put on to the four-hour day. What was the result? Unrest and a large increase in the consumption of *soma*; that was all. Those three and a half hours of extra leisure were so far from being a source of happiness that people felt constrained to take a holiday from them' (*BNW*, p. 176).

The concern with the social impact and application of science is one reason why little attention is paid in *Brave New World* to developments in physics, chemistry and engineering. Their progress is taken for granted, and is apparent in the glossy, super-technological environment in which the inhabitants of Brave New World pass their lives. Huxley was criticized for not seeing the possibilities of atomic energy as an obvious source of power in the highly mechanized and automated society he depicts. His rejoinder was that such an omission was from his point of view unimportant, as were any other particular developments, however revolutionary in their own terms, in the physical sciences. For him, 'the sciences of matter' were significant only in so far as they were used by biologists and psychologists 'to modify the natural forms and expressions of life itself'. 'It is only by means of the sciences of life that the quality of life can be radically changed . . . . The release of atomic energy marks a great revolution in human history, but not (unless we blow ourselves to bits and so put an end to history) the final and most searching revolution.'[79] It was to the sciences of biology, physiology and psychology that Huxley looked for the attainment of that final revolution, a revolution whose prophet was not Marx or Einstein but the Marquis de Sade.

> This really revolutionary revolution is to be achieved, not in the external world, but in the souls and flesh of human beings. Living as he did in a revolutionary period, the Marquis de Sade very naturally made use of this theory of revolution in order to rationalize his peculiar brand of insanity. Robespierre had achieved the most superficial kind of revolution, the political. Going a little deeper, Babeuf had attempted the economic revolution. Sade regarded himself as the apostle of the truly revolutionary revolution, beyond mere politics and economics – the revolution of individual men, women and children, whose bodies were henceforward to become the common sexual property of all and whose minds were to be purged of all natural decencies, all the laboriously acquired inhibitions of traditional civilization. Between Sadism and the really revolutionary revolution there is, of course, no necessary or inevitable connexion. Sade was a lunatic and the more or less conscious goal of his revolution was universal chaos and destruction. The people who govern the Brave New World may not be sane (in what may be called the absolute sense of that word); but they are not madmen and their aim is not anarchy but social stability. It is in order to achieve stability that they carry out, by scientific means, the ultimate, personal, really revolutionary revolution.[80]

What connects Fordism, the philosophy of industrialism, with Sadism, the philosophy of the body, is that 'mutilation of the psyche' that Huxley had seen as the central tendency of Fordism. Whatever their totalitarian intentions, the rulers of industrial society have been limited hitherto by their ideological timidity and the crudity of their technical apparatus of control. They have not been able to prevent deviance and dissent, which in the long run has always undermined their social stability. Sadism shows them how to put an end to this for ever. It offers them the essential philosophy and technique for binding the individual indissolubly to society. The rulers of Brave New World have used the advances in biology and psychology to manufacture bodies and minds according to the precise requirements of the new social order. They are the most radical of social engineers in that they have not stopped, as have most dictators, at the merely external control of bodies or the influence of the mind by propaganda. They are aware that, however skilful and intensive the forms of social control, there will always lurk hidden in the genes and the mental apparatus of the individual, potential heresy and subversion. You cannot hope to have total control of the minds and bodies of individuals unless you make these yourself, from the very beginning. However early after birth the social conditioning starts, the infant already harbours perhaps ineradicable tendencies that are potentially dangerous, the legacy of its heredity and its embryonic experience. The most elemental process of human birth and human heredity contains the seeds of heresy. The only solution is to select all the necessary parts and materials yourself and make individuals according to the specifications of the manufacturer's blueprint. Only then will individuals be safe from heresy, as they will contain nothing that you have not put in them yourself. These are, in effect, artificial or mechanical men, individuals without souls, without anything that, in a traditional understanding, can be seen as distinctly human and individual as opposed to the purely social and functional. This is the perfection of the social machine, part intermeshing smoothly with part, beyond the wildest imaginings of even the most thoroughgoing functionalist. But it has been made possible only by the 'really revolutionary revolution', the direct invasion and manipulation of the bodies and minds of men.

So in Brave New World babies are made in bottles, where they undergo direct biological conditioning to suit them to their future roles and tasks. Once decanted, they continue their socialization with a sustained period of psychological and social conditioning in the Neo-Pavlovian Conditioning Rooms. In an example of Delta conditioning, the infants are made to associate books and flowers with piercing alarm bells and unpleasant electric shocks. Books are dangerous as well as useless for Deltas; similarly, they must not acquire a liking for natural things as this might deflect them from the continuous consumption of manufactured articles: 'a love of nature keeps no factories busy.' Thus:

> Books and loud noises, flowers and electric shocks – already in the infant mind these couples were compromisingly linked; and after two hundred repetitions of the same or similar lesson would be wedded indissolubly. What man has joined, nature is powerless to put asunder . . . . 'They'll be safe from books and botany all their lives.' (*BNW*, ch. 2, p. 29)

This form of simple reflex conditioning is accompanied by the subtler form of hypnopaedia or sleep-teaching. This is used not, as in earlier experiments, to inculcate factual knowledge or abstract ideas, but to give 'moral education'. Essentially, it is a highly effective form of socialization used to fix unalterably in the minds of the infants a sense of their destined place in society and their general moral and social attitudes. Thus a Beta child hears softly and repeatedly throughout the night the following lesson in Elementary Class Consciousness:

Alpha children wear grey. They work much harder than we do, because they're so frightfully clever. I'm really awfully glad I'm a Beta, because I don't work so hard. And then we are much better than the Gammas and Deltas. Gammas are stupid. They all wear green, and Delta children wear khaki. Oh no, I *don't* want to play with Delta children. And Epsilons are still worse. They're too stupid to be able to read or write. Besides, they wear black, which is such a beastly colour. I'm *so* glad I'm a Beta. (*BNW*, ch. 2, p. 33)

Hypnopaedia, says the Director of Hatcheries and Conditioning, is 'the greatest moralizing and socializing force of all time'. Wordless conditioning, as with flowers and electric shocks, is effective but crude. For teaching 'the finer distinctions' and inculcating 'the more complex courses of behaviour', words are necessary, but 'words without reason'. Ceaselessly repeated and heard, the sleep-taught lessons bore in to the minds of the children, forming like 'drops of liquid sealing wax, drops that adhere, incrust, incorporate themselves with what they fall on. . . . .'

Till at last the child's mind *is* these suggestions, and the sum of the suggestions *is* the child's mind. And not the child's mind only. The adult's mind too – all his life long. The mind that judges and desires and decides – made up of these suggestions. But all the suggestions are *our* suggestions. . . . Suggestions from the State. (*BNW*, ch. 2, p. 34)

Huxley had for long been fascinated by mass advertising, which, though a product of the late nineteenth century, arrived with all its seductive extravagance only in the 1920s. It was for him an inescapable part of the consumerist, throw-away, 'planned obsolescence' society.[81] But its effects were not limited to goods. It was a thoroughly modern form of mass hypnosis, working upon human suggestibility with all the techniques of modern psychology to condition people unconsciously to act and think as the advertisers wanted them. Politicians during the First World War had quickly fastened on to its possibilities. Lloyd George, with his wartime slogans such as 'Homes fit for Heroes', was one of the first and most successful practitioners. Along with the other media of mass communication such as the press, radio and cinema, it clearly was capable of indefinite expansion as a tool of social conditioning and social stability – as America, again, most clearly demonstrated.[82]

Hypnopaedic slogans and sayings are the advertising jingles of Brave New World. In a way not so far removed from today, they make up the substance of much of the conversation of Brave New Worlders. They function as a kind of Orwellian Newspeak, eliminating all thought and disturbing reflection with a comforting assurance. Lenina, exposed more than most to the disconcerting and eccentric views of Bernard Marx and the Savage, has frequent resort to these slogans – or to *soma* – to counter the threats they pose to her peace of mind. There are slogans to handle all situations; and all tend to underline the social order encapsulated in the world-state's motto, 'Community, Identity, Stability', the derisive echo of the motto of the French Revolution that had inspired all 'progressive' striving during the past century. For the 'Community' that defines a collectivity in which the individual is wholly and unconditionally subordinated to the functioning of the whole (the questioning of whose end and purpose is neither permissible nor even possible), there are: 'Everyone belongs to everyone else'; 'Everyone works for everyone else'. For the 'Identity' that opposes all individual differences as threats to stability and aims at the maximum standardization of thought and behaviour, there is 'When the individual feels, the community reels.' To keep up the psychological stimulus to continuous consumption, Brave New Worlders repeat to themselves and to each other that 'ending is better than mending'. To stave off the horror of anger, pain or any other disturbing feeling, there is the invocation of the soothing wonder-drug *soma*: 'A gramme is better than a damn'; 'A gramme in time saves nine.' The dirt and disorder that the Savage brings in his wake is countered with 'Civilization is sterilization' and 'Cleanliness is next to fordliness.' The dominant philosophy of hedonism and instant gratification is bolstered by the advice, 'Never put off till tomorrow the fun you can have today.' And in any idle moment when thought might be lurking to seize the minds of Brave New Worlders, there are the vague complacent banalities to fill the vacant spaces: 'Everybody's happy now'; 'Progress is lovely'; 'Science is everything'; 'Ford's in his flivver, all's well with the world.'

All the hypnopaedic slogans, like all other mechanisms in Brave New World, go towards the maintenance of 'Stability', the prime achievement and sole end of the society. 'Stability,' says the Controller Mustapha Mond, 'stability. No civilization without social stability. No social stability without individual stability.' Brave New World has brought an end to the social dynamics that have repeatedly and regularly convulsed all previous civilizations. But it has taken catastrophic wars and economic collapse to carry the world to this timeless plateau of plenty and security. Despite the existence, as he saw it, of much of the potential for Brave New World in his own day, Huxley does not seem to have expected the new society to evolve by some sort of natural progression. Just as with the utopian writers, the 'final solution' comes only after enervating strife. Looking back from 'the year of stability', AF (After Ford) 632, the Controller, mocking the familiar Wellsian tale of the future, tells the Alpha students of the Nine Years' War that began in AF 141. It is an annihilating war, fought with all the latest biological and chemical weapons, and it leads to the great Economic Collapse. The population is decimated – a necessary condition for the stability of Brave New World. 'There was a choice between World Control and destruction . . . .' The new world order begins to emerge. The World Controllers first attempt forcible direction. There is the 'conscription of consumption', in which every one is compelled to consume so much a year, in the interests of industry. The result is 'conscientious objection on an enormous scale' and a back-to-nature movement led by the intellectuals. The Controllers react harshly. 'Eight hundred Simple Lifers were mowed down by machine gun at Golders Green.' In 'the famous British Museum Massacre . . . two thousand culture fans were gassed with dichlorethyl sulphide'. The Controllers realize that force is inefficient. They launch a massive programme of re-education involving the use of neo-Pavlovian conditioning and hypnopaedia. Ectogenesis is perfected, and viviparous reproduction discouraged and finally abolished. There is a systematic 'campaign against the Past', involving the closure of museums and the suppression of all books published before AF 150. The drug *soma* – 'euphoric, narcotic, pleasantly hallucinant' – is produced following huge government investment in pharmacology and biochemistry. By the year AF 178 the world-state was virtually stabilized. The final element was the conquest of old age by the physiologists, so that 'at sixty our powers and taste are what they were at seventeen'. (*BNW*, ch. 3, pp. 48–54)

Brave New World has achieved historical stasis. Just as individual development is abolished – individuals are frozen for the whole of their lives by their genetic and social conditioning – so too is social development. Brave New Worlders live in an eternal present, with no idea of a future or a past. 'Was and will make me ill, I take a gramme and only am', recites Lenina. History is wiped out not so much because – as in *Nineteen Eighty-Four* – it is dangerous, but because it is irrelevant.[83] 'We haven't any use for old things here', says the Controller. Our Ford's dictum, 'History is bunk', is among the most revered and frequently repeated sayings in Brave New World. It perfectly expresses the attitude of contempt towards the past that is the logical position of a civilization that has achieved complete stability. History, whose stuff is change, has traditionally inspired philosophies of social evolution, as well as acting as a storehouse of instructive examples. In an unchanging society, what need is there of any philosophy of change or development? In a society that has achived stability, 'the primal and the ultimate need' and the goal of all civilizations, what possible interest, apart from idle curiosity, can there be in the failed experiments of the past? Once success is achieved, who can care about the error-strewn path that led there? Only the Controllers have access to books and documents of the past, a recognition that the past *might* stir dangerous thoughts. And they are capable of using examples from the early days of the revolution – the Irish experiment with increased leisure, the Cyprus experiment of an all-Alpha society – as cautionary tales to counter the queries of the occasional awkward Alpha. But in general, the past can only be a horror story, a reservoir of obscene words and dim memories such as 'family', 'home', 'parents', 'democracy', 'religion'. If the more curious of the Alphas want a history lesson, they can get it pleasurably enough through a visit to the Savage Reservation. That should remind them forcibly enough of what they once were, and what they have been fortunate enough to escape from.

Just as history is redundant, so too is politics. Politics too is about to change, about making choices for the future. But the essential choices have already been made for all time. Who, apart from misanthropes, could possibly want to change the social order, to bring back instability and social anarchy? There is only one goal in Brave New World: the goal of self-perpetuation. The ten World Controllers and their subordinates constitute an administration, rather than a government in the strict sense of that term. Their task is simply to maintain the *status quo*, to keep things ticking over in an orderly and efficient way. They alone are truly aware of the momentousness of the achievement of social stability. Their entire training and lives are devoted to maintaining that stability, to eliminating any threats to it – whether from genetic accidents in the Hatcheries or the pursuit of disturbing scientific knowledge.

The rule of the Controllers is bland and benevolent to an exemplary degree. They have learned that force is crude and inefficient. It stirs up resentment and resistance. They have therefore reversed the techniques of practically all previous dictatorships. Theirs is the friendly face of totalitarianism. They do not ceaselessly watch and lecture their citizens, threatening them with the Gulag or the firing-squad if they do not give their loyalty to the state. There is no equivalent to Big Brother in Brave New World, no environment of giant tele-screens with their day and night surveillance, no frenzied Hate Weeks against putative enemies. There is in fact no atmosphere of fear or paranoia at all. The Brave New Worlders live in a milieu that is permanently sunny and seductive. They feel no threat, experience no restraint. They appear as what they actually are: happy, carefree, irresponsible children in a world of security and plenty. The Controllers and Directors, the only real adults in the society, move among them as wise and loving parents, reproving with a twinkle here, explaining with a mildly naughty joke there. Only occasionally, as with the abortive rebellion of the Savage, Helmholtz Watson and Bernard Marx, is a sterner face shown. But deviants and dissidents are not severely punished. They are too few to bother about. There is no need for the gruelling rehabilitation so necessary in the world of *Nineteen Eighty-Four*. As in Wells's *A Modern Utopia*, they are exiled to distant islands where they are permitted to carry on their deviant pursuits with others of their kind. Helmholtz chooses the Falkland Islands because it has the 'thoroughly bad climate' conducive to writing. On hearing his fate, the faint-hearted Bernard Marx at first has to be forcibly carried shouting and sobbing from the room (he later accepts it with better grace). But, as the Controller urbanely puts it to Helmholtz, 'his punishment is really a reward.'

He's being sent to an island. That's to say, he's being sent to a place where he'll meet the most interesting set of men and women to be found anywhere in the world. All the people who, for one reason or another, have got too self-consciously individual to fit into community life. All the people who aren't satisfied with orthodoxy, who've got independent ideas of their own. Everyone, in a word, who's anyone. I almost envy you, Mr Watson. (*BNW*, ch. 16, p. 178)

There are, it is true, some conventionally totalitarian features in Brave New World. The family has been abolished, and all enduring personal relationships are frowned upon and ridiculed. But these are really the offshoots of more fundamental processes, in particular the laboratory production of children and their moral conditioning against strong individual feeling. The State does not have much reason to fear the rise of unofficial intermediate associations which will threaten its sovereign and total control. It does not in fact generally have to prohibit and prevent people from doing things it disapproves of, for the simple reason that doing such things does not occur to the overwhelming majority of Brave New Worlders. Their conditioning has seen to that. And that, says the Director of Hatcheries and Conditioning, 'is the secret of happiness and virtue – liking what you've *got* to do. All conditioning aims at that: making people like their unescapable social destiny' (*BNW*, p. 24). Brave New World has solved the oldest and thorniest problem of ethics: how to get people willingly to act the way they *should* act. Huxley was very fond of quoting a line of Ovid's: *video meliora proboque; deteriora sequor* (I see the good and I approve, but I cleave to the bad). It summed up for him the principal moral dilemma of the human condition, the eternal conflict between mind and body, reason and instinct, individual desires and social needs. Brave New World has resolved the dilemma by abolishing the warring impulses. Bodies and minds are conditioned so that 'the minds endorse the judgement of the bodies.' Individual and society are reconciled, unified. 'As children of society in the literal sense, men no longer exist in dialectical opposition to society but rather are identical with it in their substance.'[84]

Othello, says the Controller Mustapha Mond to the Savage, is prohibited not because it is ideologically dangerous but because it is old and beautiful, and might lead people to hanker after old things instead of ceaselesssly pursuing the new. *Othello* is not dangerous, because the people of Brave New World literally would not be able to understand it. As if to prove the point, even Helmholtz Watson, intellectually the most clear-sighted of the rebels, is puzzled at the story of *Romeo and Juliet*, and to the Savage's chagrin bursts into uncontrollable laughter at the scene in which Juliet's parents are trying to bully her into marrying Paris:

> The mother and father (grotesque obscenity) forcing the daughter to have someone she didn't want! And the idiotic girl not saying that she was having someone else whom (for the moment, at any rate) she preferred! In its smutty absurdity the situation was irresistibly comical. (*BNW*, ch. 12, p. 147)

Helmholtz's response nicely illustrates the Controller's contention that Brave New Worlders cannot understand tragedy because their world is so totally different from that which makes for tragedy. Othello's jealousy, Juliet's passion, the conflict between desire and duty, individual values and social requirements, are all equally absurd and incomprehensible. Tragedy needs suffering and social instability, and it is precisely this that Brave New World has abolished.

> The world's stable now. People are happy; they get what they want, and they never want what they can't get. They're well off; they're safe; they're never ill; they're not afraid of death; they're blissfully ignorant of passion and old age; they're plagued with no mothers or fathers; they've got no wives, or children, or lovers to feel strongly about; they're so conditioned that they practically can't help behaving as they ought to behave. And if anything should go wrong, there's *soma*. (*BNW*, ch. 16, p. 173)

This is, indeed, some sort of earthly paradise. It contains many of the elements that, in one form or another, most of the progressive and humanitarian movements of the past have always striven for. Brave New World is the modern utopia realized, and as such it is bound to have many features that to the modern mind are highly attractive. In putting the case for Brave New World against the barely coherent protestations of the Savage, the Controller wins the contest hands down. In *Brave New World*, the devil has all the best tunes. Huxley here – especially in the central dialogues of chapters 16 and 17, where Mond confronts the defeated rebels – clearly casts the Controller in the role of Dostoyevsky's Grand Inquisitor, the apologist for human happiness at the cost of human freedom. The Savage disdains comfort. He claims freedom, he claims 'the right to be unhappy'.

'Not to mention', the Controller reminds him, 'the right to grow old and ugly and impotent; the right to have syphilis and cancer; the right to have too little to eat; the right to be lousy; the right to live in constant apprehension of what may happen tomorrow; the right to catch typhoid; the right to be tortured by unspeakable pains of every kind.' (*BNW*, ch. 17, p. 187)

In return for their liberty ('liberty to be inefficient and miserable. Freedom to be a round peg in a square hole', *BNW*, p. 47), the inhabitants of Brave New World have gained something resembling a modern Eden. They are for the whole of their lives healthy and youthful. At sixty, still looking youthful, they deteriorate swiftly and are given a painless death. The Savage's mother, Linda, is shunned not simply because she is – obscenely – a mother, but more because, although only 44, her life on the Reservation has made her look old and ugly, 'a monster of flaccid and distorted senility'.[85] Even more unseemly and disquieting is the Savage's grief at her death. As anticipated in Haldane's *Daedalus*, Brave New World has abolished the age-old terror of death. 'Death conditioning begins at eighteen months. Every tot spends two mornings a week in a Hospital for the Dying. All the best toys are kept there, and they get chocolate cream on death days. They learn to take dying as a matter of course' (*BNW*, ch. 11, p. 131).

John's outburst at Linda's bedside provokes near-panic among the nurses and their infant charges, cheerfully observing the dying patients as part of their conditioning. It is the immediate prelude to the short-lived rebellion in the hospital that he leads with Helmholtz Watson and Bernard Marx, and it indicates how important a challenge to the scientific society his traditional attitude to death and mourning poses. Linda, meanwhile, in happy conformity with the Brave New World practice of euthanasia, dies blissfully in a haze of *soma*, sweet scents and synthetic music.

In removing the fear of death the scientific society has abolished perhaps the worst terror – and one of the most important cultural strengths – of 'the bad old days'.[86] But it has been equally successful in eliminating the suffering and frustration produced by want and waiting.[87] Thirty years before the actual era of the Pill, Huxley sketched a sexual paradise based on publicy-provided contraceptives and compulsory 'Malthusian drill'. 'Everyone belongs to everyone else.' Long-term relationships are discouraged by conditioning and social ridicule. Lenina is puzzled and frightened by Bernard Marx's evident desire that they should commit themselves exclusively to each other. She is totally bewildered by the Savage's refusal to 'have' her when she offers herself. No one need go without; there is no need for self-restraint. Brave New World carries out to its logical end the Bolshevik precept that 'sex should be taken like a drink of water.' People change their sexual partners as they change their clothes, with no more tremor of feeling or fear of disturbing emotional consequences. Sexuality, for Huxley's friend Lawrence as well as Freudian radicals such as Wilhelm Reich, had long been associated with emancipation from civilized or bourgeois repressiveness. The 'pleasure principle' was to be the agent of revolt against the 'reality principle' of bourgeois society. Huxley recognized that the opposite could be equally true: that, once sexual taboos lost their force and effective contraceptive techniques were widely available, self-denial, as attempted by Bernard Marx and practised by the Savage, could become the radical gesture. In these circumstances, sexuality could become institutionalized as promiscuity, and instead of providing an avenue of escape from a repressive society could turn into a new prison.[88]

But the argument for this is subtle and by no means self-evident to the majority. The Savage pleads the virtues of self-denial and painful effort in the language of traditional religion and traditional morality. But what, protests the Controller, is the virtue of such outmoded puritanism? What is the value of patience for its own sake? Why, where there is no need, should pleasure be mixed with pain? 'There isn't any need for a civilized man to bear anything that's seriously unpleasant.' Self-restraint is vigorously discouraged in Brave New World, self-indulgence warmly promoted, both in the interests of the constantly turning wheels of industry. There can be no virtue in chastity, only the danger to society that comes from frustration and the growth of strong feelings. 'Chastity means passion, chastity means neurasthenia. And passion and neurasthenia mean instability.' The craving for excitement is in any case sufficiently satisfied by the regular administration of drugs to stimulate the adrenals, as part of the regular health regimen of all citizens.

> Violent Passion Surrogate. Regularly once a month. We flood the whole system with adrenalin. It's the complete physiological equivalent of fear and rage. All the tonic effects of murdering Desdemona and being murdered by Othello, without any of the inconveniences. (*BNW*, ch. 17, p. 187)

Something of the same function – excitement and romance without the inconvenience – is satisfied by the feelies, where the emotions of the actors in the film are directly experienced by the spectators. Other emotional indulgences and distractions include the lavish dance-halls, such as the Westminster Abbey Cabaret, with its scent- and colour-organ and its Sixteen Sexophonists, and the Community Singery where individuals join with each other in performing the Solidarity Service. The Service involves the singing of Solidarity Hymns to the accompaniment of pulsating synthetic music, the dedication of *soma* tablets, the passing around of 'the loving cup of strawberry ice-cream *soma*' and an orgiastic climax in which the congregation ecstatically sings 'Orgy-Porgy, Ford and fun' before releasing its pent-up emotions in frenzied coupling.

Bread is plentiful in Brave New World, and circuses amply provided for. But if for any reason the system should fail at any point, if unpleasant experiences and emotions do arise, there is always *soma*. *Soma*, whose name Huxley took from the plant used in ancient Indian religious rites, is the hypothetical 'world-transfiguring' drug that he had fancifully looked forward to as offering a more efficient and less harmful substitute for alcohol and cocaine. In Brave New World *soma* is omnipresent, the sovereign remedy for all discomfort and disorder, individual and social. *Soma* helps Lenina cope with Bernard and the Savage, *soma* helps Bernard make love to Lenina when he doesn't want to, *soma* helps Linda forget her ugliness and face her death, *soma* – in vapour form sprayed by gas-masked police – helps quell the riot started by the Savage in the

Hospital for the Dying. Drugs are a crucial part of the structure of social control, aiding and abetting such ritual reinforcements of the social order as the Solidarity Services. The Controller clearly points to the religious function of *soma*.

> There's always *soma* to give you a holiday from the facts, there's always *soma* to calm your anger, to reconcile you to your enemies, to make you patient and long-suffering. In the past you could only accomplish these things by making a great effort and after years of hard moral training. Now, you swallow two or three half-gramme tablets, and there you are. Anybody can be virtuous now. You can carry at least half your morality about in a bottle. Christianity without tears – that's what *soma* is. (*BNW*, ch. 17, p. 185)

In *The Scientific Outlook*, published in 1931, Bertrand Russell wrote: 'We may seek knowledge of an object because we love the object or because we wish to have power over it . . . . The scientific society of the future . . . is one in which the power impulse has completely overwhelmed the impulse of love . . . . The scientific society in its pure form . . . is incompatible with the pursuit of truth, with love, with art, with spontaneous delight, with every ideal that men have hitherto cherished.'[89] It is precisely Huxey's view. In return for 'happiness', Brave New World has abandoned art, science – in the true sense – and, what Huxley came to think most important of all, religion. Individuals need religion, says the Controller – quoting Cardinal Newman and Maine de Biran, two of Huxley's favourite authors – because they require consolation and justification for the loss of youthful power and prosperity, and the onset of old age and death. Religion consoles because it reveals the existence of a higher, more abiding, reality, independent of these worldly concerns. But Brave New World has abolished old age and the fear of death. It has removed all material worries. It has therefore removed the need for religion or God.

> There aren't any losses for us to compensate; religious sentiment is superfluous. And why should we go hunting for a substitute for youthful desires, when youthful desires never fail? A substitute for distractions, when we go on enjoying all the old fooleries to the very last? What need have we of repose when our minds and bodies continue to delight in activity? of consolation, when we have *soma*? of something immovable, when there is the social order? (*BNW*, ch. 17, p. 182)

'God,' says the Controller, 'isn't compatible with machinery and scientific medicine and universal happiness.' Modern society, says Huxley, has made its choice. Like the modern utopia, it invokes 'not the God from the machine, but the machine itself'.[90] It has opted to be secular, materialistic, hedonistic, technological, utilitarian, unhistorical – in a word, 'scientific'. In doing so, it has broken with all past societies, its own as well as all those of the non-western world. The crucial question is whether Huxley is right, whether Brave New World is the world of the future, and whether it is capable of that death-like stability that he only half-mockingly attributes to it.

A POSSIBLE FUTURE?

It is common to read a utopia as an anti-utopia, far less so the other way round. Chad Walsh reports that, to his alarm, his American college students of the late

1950s found *Brave New World* highly appealing. All that available sex and free drugs – wasn't that just paradise? For these students Huxley's anti-utopia was replete with features of the contemporary youth culture's utopia.[91] Similarly, many contemporary feminists and sexual radicals have not sympathized with Huxley but have reacted positively to Brave New World's attack on the family and its abolition of parenthood. They do not side with Huxley's implied defence of marriage and motherhood, but respond feelingly to Mustapha Mond's scathing dismissal of the home and the monogamous family of the barbarous old days.

Home, home – a few small rooms, stiflingly over-inhabited by a man, by a periodically teeming woman, by a rabble of boys and girls of all ages. No air, no space; an understerilized prison; darkness, disease, and smells . . . .

And home was as squalid psychically as physically. Psychically, it was a rabbit hole, a midden, hot with the frictions of tightly packed life, reeking with emotion. What suffocating intimacies, what dangerous, insane, obscene relationships between the members of the family group! Maniacally, the mother brooded over her children (*her* children) . . . brooded over them like a cat over its kittens; but a cat that could talk, a cat that could say, 'my baby, my baby" over and over again . . . .

Mother, monogamy, romance. High spurts the fountain; fierce and foamy the wild jet. The urge has but a single outlet. My love, my baby. No wonder those poor pre-moderns were mad and wicked and miserable . . . . What with mothers and lovers, what with the prohibitions they were not conditioned to obey, what with the temptations and the lonely remorses, what with all the diseases and the endlessly isolating pain, what with the uncertainties and the poverty – they were forced to feel strongly. And feeling strongly (and strongly, what was more, in solitude, in hopelessly individual isolation), how could they be stable?' (*BNW*, ch. 3, p. 40–3)

Reading Huxley today, says Elaine Baruch, 'it is the author rather than the inhabitants of his brave new world that seems naive. Like Mustapha Mond . . . many of us now shudder about the dangerous intimacies of family life, with its mother brooding over her children like a talking cat . . . .'[92] The radical feminist Shulamith Firestone argues that women should press for the speedy achievement of *in vitro* fertilization and foetal development, for only by rejecting their biological destiny as mothers will women have any hope of gaining true equality with men.[93] In Marge Piercy's novel of a feminist future, *Woman on the Edge of Time* (1976), monogamy and the nuclear family have been abolished, sex divorced from procreation, and the mechanization of reproduction instituted. The visitor from the past, Connie Ramos, sees through the door of an aquarium-like structure babies 'joggling slowly upside down, each in a sac of its own inside a large fluid receptacle'. She is told:

It was part of women's long revolution. When we were breaking all the old hierarchies. Finally there was that one thing we had to give up too, the only power we ever had, in return for no more power for anyone. The original production: the power to give birth. Cause as long as we were biologically enchained, we'd never be equal.

That *Brave New World* should prefigure such current concerns and anticipate such current aspirations – even if from Huxley's point of view his devil's advocacy was only too successful – points to one of its chief strengths and an important reason for its continued power to stimulate. Like almost no other modern utopia or anti-utopia, neither Wells's nor Orwell's, Huxley's has the exact feel of today. More than half a century after it was published, *Brave New World* depicts a society that is instantly recognizable to a contemporary readership. It speaks directly of our own world. Sex and *soma*, the feelies and the collective orgy-porgies, the omnipresent electric advertising signs, the colour-organs and the packed discos with their pounding synthetic music, the test-tube babies and widespread use of contraceptives, scientific riot control, mass world-wide travel: this is to an extraordinary degree of precision our 'high-tech', 'affluent', 'post-scarcity', 'Muzak'-saturated society, all the more remarkable for being portrayed during the depths of the Great Depression of the 1930s. In the 1950s and 1960s there appeared a number of influential works of social criticism, books such as David Riesman's *The Lonely Crowd*, William H. Whyte's *The Organization Man*, Vance Packard's *The Hidden Persuaders*, John Kenneth Galbraith's *The Affluent Society*, Herbert Marcuse's *One-Dimensional Man*, Theodor Roszak's *The Making of the Counter-Culture*. They dealt with such topics as social conformity, the effects of advertising and the mass media, the results of affluence, the liberating possibilities of sex and drugs. All were themes straight out of *Brave New World*, a clear testimony to the fact that Huxley had been unnervingly prophetic.

Huxley himself was gloomily confident about his prognostications. Like Keynes in the 1930s,[94] he did not believe that the Depression, serious as it was, marked an end to industrial growth or signalled the decline of industrial civilization. Even the Second World War, and the dropping of the atomic bomb, he thought would be significant not so much for teaching the nations that they should follow a new course entirely as to make them moderate their existing course, to the extent at least of avoiding all-out war. For the rest, the prewar developments would continue, but at an intensified pace. In a new 'Foreword' to *Brave New World* in 1946 – 'fifteen years further down the inclined plane of modern history' – he took stock of his earlier prophecies. He had, it appeared, been if anything too restrained, too modest in his projections. Nuclear energy would put unprecedented power in the hands of modern rulers, and the result would be economic and social changes of a rapidity and completeness he had not contemplated in his prewar writing. These changes would inevitably be directed by 'highly centralized totalitarian governments', since rapid technological changes have always produced social confusion, leading to the centralization of power and an increase in government control.

But the new totalitarianism need not, and probably would not, resemble the old. *Brave New World* had already sketched the outline of a truly modern totalitarian society, more modern than either Hitler's Germany or Stalin's Russia. It was the totalitarianism of the 'soft-sell', the totalitarianism of mass advertising and scientific techniques, whose potentialities were already there to see in American society. The new developments, Huxley believed, would continue the pattern of *Brave New World*.

Government by clubs and firing squads, by artificial famine, mass imprisonment, and mass deportation, is not merely inhumane (nobody cares much about that nowadays); it is demonstrably inefficient – and in an age of advanced technology, inefficiency is the sin against the Holy Ghost. A really efficient totalitarian state would be one in which the all-powerful executive of political bosses and their army of managers control a population of slaves who do not have to be coerced, because they love their servitude .... The most important Manhattan Projects of the future will be vast government-sponsored inquiries into what the politicians and the participating scientists will call 'the problem of happiness' – in other words, the problem of making people love their servitude.'[95]

Economic plenty and economic security for the mass of the population are assumed – again, an unusually clear-sighted vision in a world devastated by war. As early as 1946 Huxley could foresee – helped perhaps by his residence in California since 1937 – the 'economic miracle' of the 1950s and 1960s which produced in the West the first mass-consumption societies in history. But no more than in *Brave New World* is economic security held to be sufficient for enduring stability. 'Its achievement is merely a superficial, external revolution. The love of servitude cannot be established except as the result of a deep, personal revolution in human minds and bodies.' Huxley therefore looks forward to the progress of that 'really revolutionary revolution' that he had shown in *Brave New World*. There would be improved techniques of suggestion, through infant conditioning and the use of such drugs as scopolamine. There would be 'a fully developed science of human differences, enabling government managers to assign any given individual to his or her proper place in the economic and social hierarchy'. New drugs would be developed, 'a substitute for alcohol and the other narcotics, something at once less harmful and more pleasure-giving than gin or heroin'. And he foresaw the achievement of a 'foolproof system of eugenics, designed to standardize the human product and so to facilitate the task of the managers'.

This last development – the most radical accomplishment of Brave New World – Huxley admits is still a long way off. But other characteristic features of Brave New World – 'the equivalents of soma and hypnopaedia and the scientific caste system' – were 'probably not more than three or four generations away'. And one significant feature, sexual promiscuity, was already more or less established. Huxley cites the climbing divorce rate in American cities in support.

In a few years, no doubt, marriage licenses will be sold like dog licenses, good for a period of twelve months, with no law against changing dogs or keeping more than one animal at a time. As political and economic freedom diminishes, sexual freedom tends compensatingly to increase. And the dictator . . . will do well to encourage that freedom. In conjunction with the freedom to daydream under the influence of dope and movies and the radio, it will help to reconcile his subjects to the servitude which is their fate.[96]

All in all, Huxley had reason to feel that contemporary developments had borne out only too well the predictions of *Brave New World*.

All things considered, it looks as though utopia were far closer to us than anyone only fifteen years ago could have imagined. Then, I projected it six hundred years into the future. Today it seems quite possible that the horror may be upon us within a single century. That is, if we refrain from blowing ourselves to smithereens in the interval. Indeed, unless we choose to decentralize and to use applied science, not as the end to which human beings are to be made the means, but as the means to producing a race of free individuals, we have only two alternatives to choose from: either a number of national, militarized totalitarianisms, having as their root the terror of the atomic bomb and as their consequence the destruction of civilization (or, if the warfare is limited, the perpetuation of militarism); or else one supra-national totalitarianism, called into existence by the social chaos resulting from rapid technological progress in general and the atom revolution in particular, and developing, under the need for efficiency and stability, into the welfare tyranny of Utopia. You pays your money and you takes your choice.[97]

The appearance of *Nineteen Eighty-Four*, with its very different conception of an equally horrible future, did nothing to shake Huxley's conviction that he had got the future in the right perspective. He praised the book, which Orwell had sent him on publication. But he raised again, in a letter to the author, the question of the nature of 'the ultimate revolution' which *Nineteen Eighty-Four* purported to deal with, and which Huxley himself had traced back to the Marquis de Sade and 'the revolution which lies beyond politics and economics, and which aims at a total subversion of the individual's psychology and physiology'.

The philosophy of the ruling minority in *Nineteen Eighty-Four* is a sadism which has been carried to its logical conclusion by going beyond sex and denying it. Whether in actual fact the policy of the boot-on-the-face can go on indefinitely seems doubtful. My own belief is that the ruling oligarchy will find less arduous and wasteful ways of governing and of satisfying its lust for power, and that these ways will resemble those which I have described in *Brave New World*. I have had occasion recently to look into the history of animal magnetism and hypnotism, and have been greatly struck by the way in which, for a hundred and fifty years, the world has refused to take serious cognizance of the discoveries of Mesmer, Braid, Esdaile and the rest. Partly because of the prevailing materialism and partly because of prevailing respectability, ninteenth century philosophers and men of science were not willing to investigate the older facts of psychology. Consequently there was no pure science of psychology for practical men, such as politicians, soldiers and policemen, to apply in the field of government. Thanks to the voluntary ignorance of our fathers, the advent of the ultimate revolution was delayed for five or six generations. Another lucky accident was Freud's inability to hypnotize successfully and his consequent disparagement of hypnotism. This delayed the general application of hypnotism to psychiatry for at least forty years. But now psycho-analysis is being combined with hypnosis; and hypnosis has been made easy and indefinitely extensible through the use of barbiturates, which induce a hypnoid and suggestible state in even the most recalcitrant subjects. Within the next generation I believe that the world's rulers will discover that infant conditioning and narco-hypnosis are more efficient, as instruments of government, than clubs and prisons, and that the lust for power can be just as completely satisfied by suggesting people into loving their servitude as by flogging and kicking them into obedience. In other words, I feel that the nightmare of *Nineteen Eighty-Four* is destined to modulate into the nightmare of a world having more resemblance to that which I imagined in *Brave New World*. The change will be brought about as a result of a felt need for increased efficiency.[98]

Later still, looking forward from the halcyon days of the affluent fifties, Huxley felt even more strongly that a servitude based on willing compliance, rather than on brute terror, was the likeliest future of modern civilization. Once more, revisiting for the last time *Brave New World*, he was driven to conclude that 'the prophecies made in 1931 are coming true much sooner than I thought they would.' The liberalization of the Soviet Union, whose form of rule had so influenced Orwell, was itself a significant indicator of the dominant tendencies of the time.

George Orwell's *Nineteen Eighty-Four* was a magnified projection into the future of a present that contained Stalinism and an immediate past that had witnessed the flowering of Nazism. *Brave New World* was written before the rise of Hitler to supreme power in Germany and when the Russian tyrant had not yet got into his stride. In 1931 systematic terrorism was not the obsessive contemporary fact which it had become in 1948, and the future dictatorship of my imaginary world was a good deal less brutal than the future dictatorship so brilliantly portrayed by Orwell. In the context of 1948, *Nineten Eighty-Four* seemed dreadfully convincing. But tyrants, after all, are mortal and circumstances change. Recent developments in Russia and recent advances in science and technology have robbed Orwell's book of some of its gruesome verisimilitude. A nuclear war, will, of course, make nonsense of everybody's predictions. But, assuming for the moment that the Great Powers can somehow refrain from destroying us, we can say that it now looks as though the odds were more in favour of something like *Brave New World* than of something like *Nineteen Eighty-Four*.[99]

Recent studies of both animal and human behaviour, Huxley averred, had made it clear 'that control through the punishment of undesirable behaviour is less effective in the long run, than control through the reinforcement of desirable behaviour by rewards, and that government through terror works on the whole less well than government through the non-violent manipulation of the environment and of the thoughts and feelings of individual men, women and children'. This Skinnerian lesson in 'positive reinforcement' has been learned by the rulers of the Soviet state. 'The old-fashioned, *Nineteen Eighty-Four*-style dictatorship of Stalin has begun to give way to a more up-to-date form of tyranny.' For the upper levels of the social hierarchy, at any rate, for the engineers and scientists, teachers and administrators, control is increasingly exercised through incentives and the allowance of a certain degree of personal freedom, and less through fear. This has mainly been responsible for the remarkable scientific and technological achievements of the Soviet Union in recent years. The Soviet police, too, have learned – supported by Chinese success with American prisoners during the Korean War – that Pavlovian techniques of conditioning are infinitely more effective with their political prisoners than the strong-arm methods of old.[100]

The evolution of Soviet society mirrored general social and scientific developments which, Huxley argued, all tended towards Brave New World. In the face of the enormous threat posed by the over population of the globe, and as a result of the increased centralization and scale of organization produced by modern technology, a new corps of expert, scientifically trained 'social engineers' was emerging to manage the transition to a scientific dictatorship, a 'new medieval system' of hierarchical castes. 'The managerial revolution' and 'the organization man' were part of the same phenomenon: the move to a human termitary similar to that in *Brave New World*, in which de-humanized and carefully graded castes of human workers live in blissful subjection to the rule of scientific controllers. As in *Brave New World*, sex is one of the principal sweeteners of this servitude. Once more, the explosion of 'permissive' sexuality, the use of pleasure rather than pain to control, points to Brave New World rather than *Nineteen Eighty-Four*.

It is worth remarking that, in *Nineteen Eighty-Four*, the members of the party are compelled to conform to a sexual ethic of more than Puritan severity. In *Brave New World*, on the other hand, all are permitted to indulge their sexual impulses without let or hindrance. The society described in Orwell's fable is a society permanently at war, and the aim of its rulers is first, of course, to exercise power for its own delightful sake and, second, to keep their subjects in that state of constant tension which a state of constant war demands of those who wage it. By crusading against sexuality the bosses are able to maintain the required tension in their followers and at the same time satisfy their lust for power in the most gratifying way. The society described in *Brave New World* is a world-state, in which war has been eliminated and where the first aim of the rulers is at all costs to keep their subjects from making trouble. This they achieve by (among other methods) legalizing a degree of sexual freedom (made possible by the abolition of the family) that practically guarantees the Brave New Worlders against any form of destructive (or creative) emotional tension. In *Nineteen Eighty-Four* the lust for power is satisfied by inflicting pain; in *Brave New World*, by inflicting a hardly less humiliating pleasure.[101]

Pleasure, too, is the main component of the effects of the media of mass communication which have spread with such rapidity in the post war era. Newspapers and magazines, radio and television, films and records provide constant distraction to an extent surpassing all the gladiatorial shows and military reviews put on to distract the population of ancient Rome. *Brave New World* anticipated this development.

In *Brave New World* non-stop distractions of the most fascinating nature (the feelies, orgy-porgy, centrifugal bumble-puppy) are deliberately used as instruments of policy, for the purpose of preventing people from paying too much attention to the realities of the social and political situation . . . . A society, most of whose members spend a great part of their time not on the spot, not here and now and in the calculable future, but somewhere else, in the irrelevant other worlds of sport and soap opera, of mythology and metaphysical fantasy, will find it hard to resist the encroachments of those who would manipulate and control it.[102]

But the media are also powerful instruments of persuasion and propaganda, the now indispensable tools of Big Business and Big Government. Hitler was the first to demonstrate the power of modern techniques of mass propaganda. 'The Nuremberg rallies were masterpieces of ritual and theatrical art.' Madison Avenue has fully absorbed the lesson. Through 'motivational research', and with the aid of such new techniques as 'subliminal projection', they have brought into being a sinister band of 'hidden persuaders'. Politicians are marketed and sold like soap, using the same techniques of applied psychology to exploit human suggestibility. 'The art of mind-control is in the process of becoming a science.' Modern societies have not yet achieved the perfection of *Brave New World*, but they have clearly set themselves on that road. The Communists' success with methodical brainwashing shows the enormous potentialities, still largely untapped, of the new methods of conditioning.

Brainwashing, as it is now practiced, is a hybrid technique, depending for its effectiveness partly on the systematic use of violence, partly on skilful psychological manipulation. It represents the tradition of *Nineteen Eighty-Four* on its way to becoming the tradition of *Brave New World*. Under a long-established and well-regulated dictatorship our current methods of semi-violent manipulation will seem, no doubt, absurdly crude. Conditioned from earliest infancy (and perhaps also biologically predestined), the average middle- or lower-caste individual will never require conversion or even a refresher course in the true faith . . . . The upper-caste individuals will be members, still, of a wild species – the trainers and guardians, themselves only slightly conditioned, of a breed of completely domesticated animals. Their wildness will make it possible for them to become heretical and rebellious. When this happens, they will have to be either liquidated, or brainwashed back into orthodoxy, or (as in *Brave New World*) exiled to some island where they can give no further trouble, except of course to one another.[103]

The discontented Alphas can, of course, resort to *soma* – or to its real-life equivalents. In Brave New World, 'the daily *soma* ration was an insurance against personal maladjustment, social unrest and the spread of subversive ideas. Religion, Karl Marx declared, is the opium of the people. In the Brave New World . . . opium, or rather *soma*, was the people's religion.'[104] Research into 'psychopharmacology', virtually non-existent in 1931, had advanced so rapidly that 'some fairly good substitutes for the various aspects of *soma* have already been discovered.' Tranquilizers such as meprobamate and chlorpromazine, vision-producing drugs such as LSD and stimulants such as Iproniazid were all, Huxley considered, promising candidates for *soma's* triple role. 'Truth drugs' such as pentothal, which increase suggestibility and lower psychological resistance, were further potential weapons in the dictator's armoury. Huxley had by the 1950s already explored the liberating potential of mind-changing drugs, but he never forgot the uses of *soma* in Brave New World. Drugs can 'both enslave and make free, heal and at the same time destroy'.[105]

Brave New World, Huxley concluded from this survey of current trends, was imminent.

The genetic standardization of individuals is still impossible; but Big Government and Big Business already possess, or will very soon possess, all the techniques for mind-manipulation described in *Brave New World*, along with others of which I was too unimaginative to dream. Lacking the ability to impose genetic uniformity upon embryos, the rulers of tomorrow's over-populated and over-organized world will try to impose social and cultural uniformity upon adults and their children . . . . By means of ever more effective methods of mind-manipulation, the democracies will change their nature; the quaint old forms – elections, parliaments, Supreme Courts and all the rest – will remain. The underlying substance will be a new kind of non-violent totalitarianism. All the traditional names, all the hallowed slogans will remain exactly what they were in the good old days. Democracy and freedom will be the theme of every broadcast and editorial – but democracy and freedom in a strictly Pickwickian sense. Meanwhile the ruling oligarchy and its highly trained elite of soldiers, policemen, thought-manufacturers and mind-manipulators will quietly run the show as they see fit.[106]

Was there any hope of reversing 'the current drift toward totalitarian control of everything'? Huxley offered a few thoughts on educational and legislative measures to stem the tide. But his heart was clearly not in it and his head told him he was wasting his time. One of the most depressing features of the contemporary scene was that people seemed not to care about the encroaching servitude; indeed, they positively embraced it.

In the United States – and America is the prophetic image of the rest of the urban–industrial world as it will be a few years from now – recent public opinion polls have revealed that an actual majority of young people in their teens, the voters of tomorrow, have no faith in democratic institutions, see no objection to the censorship of unpopular ideas, do not believe that government of the people by the people is possible and would be perfectly content, if they can continue to live in the style to which the boom has accustomed them, to be ruled, from above, by an oligarchy of assorted experts. That so many of the well-fed young television-watchers in the world's most powerful democracy should be completely indifferent to the idea of self-government, so blankly uninterested in freedom of thought and the right to dissent, is distressing, but not too surprising .... If the bread is supplied regularly and copiously three times a day, many of them will be perfectly content to live by bread alone – or at least by bread and circuses alone. 'In the end', says the Grand Inquisitor in Dostoevsky's parable, 'in the end they will lay their freedom at our feet and say to us, "make us your slaves, but feed us."'[107]

The Grand Inquisitors of old did remarkably well, cconsidering how little they knew and how poorly they were equipped.

But their successors, the well-informed, thoroughly scientific dictators of the future, will undoubtedly be able to do a great deal better. The Grand Inquisitor reproaches Christ with having called upon men to be free and tells Him that 'we have corrected Thy work and founded it upon miracle, mystery, and authority.' But miracle, mystery and authority are not enough to guarantee the indefinite survival of a dictatorship. In my fable of *Brave New World*, the dictators had added science to the list and thus were able to enforce their authority by manipulating the bodies of embryos, the reflexes of infants and minds of children and adults. And, instead of merely talking about miracles and hinting symbolically at mysteries, they were able, by means of drugs, to give their subjects the direct experience of mysteries and miracles – to transform mere faith into ecstatic knowledge. The older dictators fell because they could never supply their subjects with enough bread, enough circuses, enough miracles and mysteries. Nor did they possess a really effective system of mind-manipulation .... Under a scientific dictator education will really work – with the result that most men and women will grow up to love their servitude and will never dream of revolution. There seems to be no good reason why a thoroughly scientific dictatorship should ever be overthrown.[108]

The question of the ultimate stability of the society of *Brave New World* will be considered shortly. But first one needs to acknowledge that, whatever one's view of the future, there can be no denying the force of Huxley's claim or the accuracy of so many of his projections. His fear concerning the use – or abuse – of drugs and behavioural conditioning has, in the eyes of many observers, been amply confirmed. Increasingly, the managers and controllers of a variety of institutions have resorted to these techniques as a more efficient and often cheaper means of achieving social control or 'cure' than costly increases in personnel or facilities. Following the practice of *Brave New World*, there has been a marked tendency towards the 'medicalization of social problems', which has sought to establish the primacy of medical methods of diagnosis and cure over 'unscientific' and 'less efficient' social diagnoses and social remedies. The approach has the great appeal of taking troublesome and intractable problems out of the messy arena of social ideology and social policy, and handing them over to the safe hands and scientific expertise of physicians and psychiatrists. Not surprisingly, the medical profession and the giant pharmaceutical industries have been active proponents of the move. Drugs have been invented to calm 'hyperactive' children in schools and unruly prisoners and mental patients in prisons and hospitals. Striking claims have been made on behalf of new 'miracle' drugs to cure or powerfully alleviate many cases of mental illness, thus obviating time-consuming and expensive psychotherapy and allowing many mental patients to be discharged from institutions and 'returned to the community'. Dissidents and deviants have been diagnosed as clinically insane and subjected to drug treatment in asylums, for their own good and the safety of society. This is not only a phenomenon of the Soviet Union. Militant blacks and other civil rights activists in the United States have similarly been regarded as psychiatrically disturbed and in need of medical treatment. And not only are the 'sick' and the 'unhealthy' the voluntary or involuntary recipients of drug therapy: we too, 'the normals', have been marked out for treatment. There are or will be drugs to soothe our fears, prevent depression, make us less aggressive, increase our energy and intelligence. 'We will see new drugs, more targeted, more specific and more potent than anything we have . . . . And many of these would be for people we would call healthy.'[109]

Behavioural conditioning too has been having a field day, especially through the influence of B. F. Skinner and his disciples. Skinnerian techniques of conditioning by 'positive reinforcement' have been widely put to use in schools, prisons, hospitals, offices and factories.[110] In a subtler form, conditioning by kindness has also come to play a prominent part in the practice of penal reformers. In an apparently liberal spirit, offenders, especially juveniles, are increasingly committed not to prisons or borstals but to 'half-way houses' or 'residential centres'. The 'de-carceration' movement has argued, on humanitarian and pragmatic grounds, the case for 'community treatment' and 'community control'. But not only has this served to deprive offenders of many of the rights and protections of formal 'due process', handing them over instead to the far more nebulous and discretionary control of social workers and psychiatrists. It has also blurred the distinction between the 'criminal' and 'non-criminal' population, establishing a comprehensive 'correctional continuum' which embraces not just actual but also *potential* offenders, such that a far larger section of the population now comes under the scrutiny of the new system than was the case in the bad old days. In *Brave New World* style, these correctional centres are non-punitive and often pleasant in appearance and situation. Offenders are not gaoled but undergo 'intensive placement'; there are no guards but 'correctional counsellors', no prisons but 'milieu therapy'. Community control, indeed, aspires to be effective by restoring the 'informal controls' of the pre-industrial community. But its methods are anything but pre-industrial. All the latest techniques of behavioural engineering and group therapy are employed to 're-direct' the energies and desires of the somewhat reluctant guests. The results so far have been inconclusive; but the intention must gladden the hearts of all would-be World Controllers.[111]

So too would the continued expansion and intensification of the mass media. Americans now watch on average seven hours of television a day, the British somewhat less; in both cases for the populations of these countries television viewing has become the dominant waking – if that is the right word – activity of their lives, outpacing the time spent in formal education or at work. Television has become, by a large margin, the principal source of information and entertainment, the preferred leisure activity, of all ages and all classes. The coming of new media technologies such as cable and satellite transmission, the spread of video-cassette recorders and the transformation of popular music by pop 'videos' clearly herald a new wave of media penetration into the lives of Western societies. The effects will be felt in work as much as in leisure. Linked to the personal or domestic computer, the television screen becomes the individual's main and perhaps only window on the world, the chief medium of his interaction with society. The home becomes in principle the chief site of all work and leisure. Public activities and encounters, which might offset media influences, dwindle; daily life is increasingly privatized, lived amidst a battery of electronic devices on a diet of media messages and media stimuli. This, admittedly, is only one possibility, amidst a diversity of possibilities theoretically opened up by the new technologies. As of old, media effects and influences are notoriously difficult to pin down, and all predictions suffer accordingly. But the sheer pervasiveness of the mass media, the clear dependence of the mass of the population on them for information and attitudes about domestic and foreign matters, their continued control by large state and private corporations, certainly suggest a powerful tendency towards a *Brave New World* pattern of more or less calculated distraction and manipulation, if not outright indoctrination.[112]

Equally in line with Huxley's prophecies have been the developments in medical science and technology, and the uses to which they have been put. The discovery of a truly effective contraceptive pill for women has since the 1960s effected a revolution in sexual *mores*, such that sex and procreation, as in *Brave New World*, have been decisively separated. Sex is now largely, as the Americans say, 'recreational'. For those women who do become involuntarily pregnant, abortion is now legal, cheap and safe in most Western countries, while in Eastern Europe it is actively promoted as the chief method of birth control. At the other end, as it were, euthanasia is now openly discussed and covertly practised in respectable circles. Eugenics, too, has once more become a serious policy issue and matter of public debate, centring largely around alleged class and racial differences in inherited intelligence, and involving such bizarre manifestations as 'sperm banks' containing the seed of famous scientists and athletes.

Advances in surgical techniques also promise the more or less imminent advent of 'modular man', whose constituent parts can be removed and renewed or replaced at will, like those of a mechanical doll or motor car. Organs can be transplanted from one human to another and from non-animals to humans. Artificial organs, such as plastic hearts, are becoming increasingly common, and it must only be a matter of time before their cheapness and superior efficiency make them the routine substitutes for defective or worn-out organs. Similarly while it is now commonplace to sew back severed limbs on to the torso, the advantages of purely artificial limbs are bound to appear compelling as they continue their remarkable progress in precision and flexibility. Nor has there been any lack of attention to the outward human appearance, spurred on by the urgent requests of ageing film stars and others who live by their looks. Sagging breasts can be lifted, multiple chins reduced in number, wrinkled flesh smoothed and polished, thinning grey hair replaced by lustrous and luxuriant locks. If we cannot yet quite, as in *Brave New World*, look 17 until the age of 60, we can at least look 30 until the age of 50, which is some sort of progress. In this Brave New World of spare-parts surgery, of rejuvenated and renewable bodies, Doctors Frankenstein and Moreau would have felt thoroughly at home; while Huxley, for his part, might have wondered at the speed and extent of present-day society's advance towards the fully artificial man.[113]

But even more, Huxley would have been startled by developments in embryology and biology. While speculations about test-tube babies had been rife throughout Huxley's lifetime, he seems always to have believed that its achievement was a very distant prospect. But in 1978 two British doctors, Patrick Steptoe and Robert Edwards, for the first time successfully re-implanted in the mother's womb an egg which had been artificially fertilised *in vitro*. Their achievement has since been repeated numerous times, by themselves and others. Now while this is not, of course, the same thing as the production and growth of an embryo entirely in the laboratory, it is a fundamental and perhaps decisive step in that direction. Many biologists, indeed, believe that it is the caution inspired by fear of unpredictable social repercussions, rather than scientific obstacles in the technical sense, that has so far prevented the advance to the laboratory production of fully grown embryos. This is a very real constraint, of course, and no one can predict at what stage society will feel able to face up to the moral and social implications of test-tube babies. But we can at least point to certain social forces which may well force the pace of advance. If it is indeed true that the scientific knowledge is there, then the urgency of the population problem (too many people in some parts of the world, too few in others), the desire of many feminists to free women of the thraldom of reproduction, and the aspirations of many governments to regulate the type as well as the number of their people may well bring test-tube babies in the relatively near future out of the realm of science fiction and into that of social fact.[114]

But probably what would have excited and alarmed Huxley most are the developments in the new field of biotechnology or 'genetic engineering', hailed by many biologists as the most far-reaching advance in biology since Francis Crick and James Watson revealed the structure of the DNA molecule in 1953. Building on that discovery, molecular biologists have been able to snip out particular genes from human DNA strands, insert them into laboratory bacteria, and get the bacteria to grow the newly-inserted genes. To date, scientists have induced bacteria to grow human insulin, human interferon and human growth hormones, all vital but scarce natural products of human cells. Companies have already been formed to manufacture these and other products for commercial purposes. And recombinant DNA technology, or 'gene splicing', holds out much more. It permits in principle the almost limitless manipulation of DNA, so that bacteria can be made to produce, in virtually unlimited quantities, anything produced naturally by animal cells. Moreover, these natural products can be broken down and recombined in a great variety of patterns, so that entirely new forms of life can be created by artificial means. These new forms can then by multiplied by cloning (cf. Huxley's 'Bokanovsky's process').

Currently, it is the commercial and industrial possibilities of genetic engineering that is creating the most excitement. The effects in agriculture, and in the chemical, pharmaceutical and food industries, could be dramatic. Genetic manipulation can be used, for instance, to speed up and improve the quality of processes now performed scarcely or clumsily by nature: photosynthesis could be made more efficient in plants, crops could be modified so that they could fix nitrogen and so produce in effect their own fertilizer. In the pharmaceutical field, genetic splicing is being used to produce artificial antibodies more finely tuned and more effective than their natural counterparts in the human body. In the chemical industry, novel enzymes are being used to grow important industrial chemicals, such as those used in plastics, and plans are afoot for the biological production of alcohol. It is admitted by all researchers that we are as yet only at the beginning of what could be a new 'scientific–industrial revolution'.

And the potential for Brave New World? 'The Brave New World that Aldous Huxley warned of is now here', declared one alarmed public interest group when the US Supreme Court ruled in June 1980 that new forms of life created in the laboratory were eligible for patents.[115] Not here yet, perhaps; but certainly Huxley would have seen in genetic engineering the closest approximation yet to the manufacture of different forms of life in the test tube that is the fundamental basis of Brave New World. Test-tube babies are one thing, but gene-splicing goes further in allowing the manipulation of the basic human genetic structures, so that the normal hereditary mechanisms can be interfered with and altered according to the scientist's purpose. The result in principle could be the production of distinct and novel human types fitted, physically and intellectually, for specific social functions: in other words, the biologically based castes of *Brave New World*. The new developments in biotechnology are indeed the most compelling evidence to date that Huxley's vision of 1932 was no mere fantasy, a simple moral fable that was thankfully unrealizable in practice. This would not have surprised a Haldane or a Bernal, who no doubt would have seized upon the hopeful and liberating potential of the new biology. Bernal in particular would surely have seen in genetic engineering the crucial first step in man's taking control of cosmic evolution, instead of leaving it to the blind forces of nature. But what would impress Huxley himself even more is that, scientifically and technically at least, Brave New World is practically on the agenda of modern societies.[116]

But *socially* too? Even if the scientific and technical competence exists for the construction of Brave New World, would it be sociologically viable? Could Brave New World survive? Stability, we may remember, is the end and ultimate justification of Brave New World; and Huxley had concluded that a dictatorship based on science was virtually impregnable. We need to ask, in concluding this discussion of *Brave New World*, whether he is right, whether the society that Huxley depicted is plausible in a sociological as well as a scientific sense. Would it indeed endure, if not for ever at least a good deal longer than most utopian communities that have been attempted?

It is interesting, and at first a little paradoxical, that Huxley should actually make the whole narrative of *Brave New World* concern itself with dissent and rebellion. Partly this is a matter of the convention of the dystopian novel (if, indeed, not a requirement of the novel form as such). As developed especially by Wells and Zamyatin, typically the strength of the dystopian society is demonstrated by pitting against it various antagonists, most of whom fail. In any case, the convention served Huxley very well. For of course the rebellion in *Brave New World* is a pathetic, half-baked affair, doomed from the start and easily crushed. Huxley seems to have wanted to underline the overwhelming strength and stability of Brave New World by showing how feeble were the threats posed to it, and how puny its opponents.

But then, the suspicion arises that Huxley has made things too easy for himself. The stability of Brave New World would surely be better demonstrated by offering it worthier opponents, in the routing of whom the impregnability of its institutions would be made manifest. (This was how, for, instance, Arthur Koestler treated Soviet Communism in *Darkness at Noon*.) Huxley seems to be unwilling to dig too deeply beneath the surface of Brave New World society, in case he exposes the contradictions buried there. This reluctance is probably related to the fact that, at the time of writing, Huxley was clear about what was wrong with industrial society but had little idea of what could be done. Hence the ironic mode of *Brave New World*. Irony has always been the natural stance of those who dislike the present, distrust attempts to resurrect the past and have no hope for the future. This had been the mood of the essays and the novels of the 1920s, and it remained the mocking, sceptical mood of the 'amused, Pyrrhonic aesthete'[117] who was the author of the fable of 1932. Given the general nature of man, Huxley seems to be saying, his preference for material happiness over moral discomfort, of comforting lies over uncomfortable truth, why not Brave New World? Why not security and stability, which is what the overwhelming majority of mankind seems to desire, even if this involves the sacrifice of the chance of art and creativity for the small minority able to cultivate and appreciate it? Is Shakespeare to be preferred to the happiness of mankind? Is Brave New World not better than the suicidal war, nationalism and class conflict that seem to be its only alternatives?[118] It is in these Grand Inquisitorial tones that the

World Controller Mustapha Mond addresses us as well as the rebels, and Huxley at the time seems to have had no real answer to him. Towards the end of the dialogue between Mustapha Mond and John the Savage, the Savage protests that all the 'pleasant vices' of Brave New World have been used to degrade man. 'Degrade him from what position?' counters the Controller.

> As a happy, hard-working, good-consuming citizen he's perfect. Of course, if you choose some other standard than ours, then perhaps you might say he was degraded. But you've got to stick to one set of postulates. You can't play electro-magnetic Golf according to the rules of Centrifugal Bumble-puppy. (*BNW*, ch. 17, p. 184)

To this, all the Savage can offer is one of his Shakespearean quotations: 'But value dwells not in particular will . . . . It holds his estimate and dignity as well wherein 'tis precious of itself as in the prizer.' The weakness and insufficiency of this, when set against Mond's powerful apology for Brave New World, seems a fair reflection of the alternatives offered by Huxley in his ambiguous dystopia. It is almost as if Huxley felt that the case that could be made for human truth and freedom as against conditioned happiness was too esoteric or elitist to carry much conviction.

But by its own standards, and Huxley's own account, Brave New World *does* fail. It does produce deviants; cracks do appear. The question is whether these cracks are merely superficial, the signs of minor failings which pose no threat to the essential stability of Brave New World, or whether on closer inspection they turn out to be symptons of more profound fissures in the social order of Brave New World, which Huxley was either unwilling or unable to see.

Take first the rebelliousness of Bernard Marx and Helmholtz Watson, the two characters whose discontent and deviance dominate the first half of the novel. Both are Alpha-Pluses; both belong, that is, to the highest social caste of Brave New World. Huxley's own account of their dissatisfaction is superficial and unconvincing. Bernard, unlike most Alphas, is physically an unattractive and clumsy specimen; 'his physique . . . hardly better than the average Gamma'. It is rumoured, apparently with truth, that 'somebody made a mistake when he was still in the bottle – thought he was a Gamma and put alcohol in his blood-surrogate.' Bernard constantly imagines himself – often with reason – to be the butt of both peers and inferiors on account of his stunted growth.

> This mockery made him feel an outsider; and feeling an outsider he behaved like one, which increased the prejudice against him and intensified the contempt and hostility aroused by his physical defects. Which in turn increased his sense of being alien and alone. (*BNW*, ch. 4, p. 60)

Helmholtz feels similarly isolated, but for quite different reasons, so that his friendship with Bernard is based less on mutual understanding than on a common resentment against their society. In Helmholtz's case, exceptional physical prowess and good looks have led to satiation and finally boredom with sport and sex. He is in search of something that will make his life more satisfying and stimulate his literary strivings. His Alpha-Plus intelligence here serves to increase his discontent.

A mental excess had produced in Helmholtz Watson effects very similar to those which, in Bernard Marx, were the result of a physical defect. Too little bone and brawn had isolated Bernard from his fellow men, and the sense of this apartness, being, by all current standards, a mental excess, became in its turn a cause of wider separation. That which had made Helmholtz so uncomfortably aware of being himself and all alone was too much ability. What the two men shared was the knowledge that they were individuals. (*BNW*, ch. 4, p. 62)

Individuals in a totally conformist society they may be; but Huxley gives them little room for development, and their ultimate failure as rebels is foreshadowed in the very causes of their deviance. Bernard becomes in effect the proud possessor of John the Savage, whom he brings back from the Reservation, and immediately his discontents evaporate. Far from responding to the Savage's criticism of Brave New World, he uses the Savage as a circus animal with which to win himself fame and popularity, as well as all the girls who have hitherto shunned him because of his physical inferiority. His alienation from his society is revealed as nothing more than resentment arising from his lack of success in Brave New World terms, and he is as easily satisfied by his social success with the Savage as he is discountenanced by the Savage's refusal to continue to play his ignoble part in Bernard's scheme. He is an unwilling and almost uncomprehending participant in the short-lived riot started by the Savage in the Hospital, and his discomfiture is completed by his cowardly and tearful collapse in the Controller's office when the sentence of exile is pronounced on him. If Bernard, in short, is the only kind of rebel that Brave New World has to deal with, it can rest assured of its stability.

Helmholtz is made of sterner stuff. He has genuinely rejected most of the values and pleasures of Brave New World. He responds enthusiastically to the Savage, finding in his reactions to Brave New World, and the scraps of Shakespeare which he brings out, a strong echo of his own feelings. As contrasted with Bernard's irresolution, he throws himself wholeheartedly and exultantly into the Savage's rebellion in the Hospital, even though he is clearly aware of its futility. And he embraces his future exile stoically, even cheerfully. Nevertheless, Huxley shows us little meaning or significance in his revolt. From the first time that we encounter Helmholtz to his final departure for the island, he remains frozen in his development. He is deeply discontented, he wants something very different from the life of Brave New World, but he is totally incapable of knowing what. His conditioning, even as an Alpha, seems to have been effective to the extent of shutting out an awareness of any real alternative to Brave New World. He can understand the Savage's protests only partly, and his incomprehension is total in the face of the tragedy of Romeo and Juliet. Helmholtz remains gloomy and oppressed throughout, but he is unable to achieve any understanding of his position. The 'voluntary blindness and deafnesss of deliberate solitude' and 'the artificial impotence of asceticism' (*BNW*, p. 63) are feeble counters to the powerful conditioning agencies of Brave New World. Helmholtz is attracted by Shakespeare's world, where there are 'so many insane, excruciating things to get excited about'. He recognizes that such emotions are necessary for creative work, but he belongs too much to

Brave New World to accept the features of the old society – lovers, fathers and mothers – that gave rise to such emotions. 'We need some other kind of madness and violence. But what? Where can one find it? . . . I don't know' (*BNW*, p. 147). In the end, his involvement in the Savage's rebellion has a strong element of suicidal despair in it, his restless and melancholy spirit at last finding an outlet in this elemental explosion of energy, however pointless. Helmholtz's rebellion, unlike Bernard's, is genuine, and represents the real threat that a powerful intelligence may pose to the conformist ethic of Brave New World. But in so far as he cannot conceive of any alternative, he remains impotent, and is unlikely to influence anyone by his verses in praise of solitude. Helmholtz remains the type of the ineffectual intellectual, a thinly sketched version of the more rounded but equally ineffectual artists and intellectuals who people Huxley's novels of the 1920s – *Crome Yellow, Antic Hay, Those Barren Leaves, Point Counter Point.* From such as these Brave New World has little to fear.

But could not Huxley have made the challenge more serious? Even the trivial-seeming cause of Bernard's queerness suggests more disorderly possibilities than Huxley appears to allow. 'Accidents will happen' (*BNW*, p. 60) in the laboratories of the Hatcheries, and indeed another such accident is recorded when Lenina, mooning over the Savage, neglects to give an embryo a sleeping-sickness injection, and 'twenty-two years eight months and four days from that moment, a promising young Alpha-Minus administrator at Mwanza-Mwanza was to die of trypanosomiasis . . . . (*BNW*, p. 148). Such episodes indicate that Brave New World may accidentally throw up a good many more Bernard Marxes and other oddities than might be comfortable to its security. A system so dependent on the precise manipulations of science and scientists is highly vulnerable to accidental malfunctioning, as the recent history of nuclear power plants and space technology makes very clear. And not only accidental. 'It is interesting,' says Jenni Calder, 'to speculate on the possibilities of a test-tube revolution. One faulty product could distort the entire human race and the future of the world simply by tampering with the test tubes.'[119]

More fundamentally, the very social structure of Brave New World contains the seeds of instability and potential dissent. Brave New World is a hierarchical caste society. Each caste is biologically and socially conditioned to perform its allotted function. The Alphas provide the principal administrators, scientists and propagandists. They too are conditioned, of course, but it is in the nature of their allotted task that they must be allowed some independence of mind. Alphas are, says the Controller, 'separate and unrelated individuals of good heredity and conditioned so as to be capable (within limits) of making a free choice and assuming responsibilities' (*BNW*, p. 174). When Bernard Marx's unorthodoxy starts to become too blatant, the Director of Hatcheries and Conditioning reproves him for abusing his Alpha endowment. 'Alphas are so conditioned that they do not *have* to be infantile in their emotional behaviour. But that is all the more reason for their making a special effort to conform. It is their duty to be infantile, even against their inclination' (*BNW*, ch. 6, p. 83).

The Controller makes a similar point about the Alpha caste when he says that 'Alphas can be completely socialized – but only on condition that you make them do Alpha work. . . . Each one of us, of course, goes through life inside a bottle . . . an invisible bottle of infantile and embryonic fixations. But if we happen to be Alphas, our bottles are, relatively speaking, enormous' (*BNW*, p. 175). This capacity is channelled and controlled by the hierarchical division of labour between the castes. The lower castes do all the routine work, thus freeing the Alphas for the more complex managerial tasks. But each caste needs the others, the Alphas no less than the lower castes. The nature of the caste system is organic, and the brain is as helpless and unconstructive without the activities of the other parts as they are without its directing intelligence. 'The optimum population,' says the Controller, 'is modelled on the iceberg – eight-ninths below the water line, one-ninth above.' A society composed wholly of Alphas would be 'unstable and miserable'. The result of 'the Cyprus experiment' showed this conclusively.

The Controllers had the island of Cyprus cleared of all its existing inhabitants and re-colonized with a specially-prepared batch of twenty-thousand Alphas. All agricultural and industrial equipment was handed over to them and they were left to manage their own affairs. The result exactly fulfilled all the theoretical predictions. The land wasn't properly worked; there were strikes in all the factories; the laws were set at naught, orders disobeyed; all the people detailed for a spell of low-grade work were perpetually intriguing for high-grade jobs, and all the people with high-grade jobs were counter-intriguing at all costs to stay where they were. Within six years they were having a first-class civil war. When nineteen of the twenty-two thousand had been killed, the survivors unanimously petitioned the World Controllers to resume the government of the island. Which they did. And that was the end of the only society of Alphas that the world has ever seen. (*BNW*, ch. 16, p. 175)[120]

But Huxley does not seem to see, or at least does not sufficiently acknowledge, the threats to Brave New World that these potentially lawless and disorderly upper-caste Alphas pose. In their very stubbornness and quarrelsome striving the Alphas show that they, alone of all Brave New Worlders, retain the vestiges of humanity. Even within the safer context of the hierarchical caste system they remain, by virtue of their necessarily lighter conditioning, a permanent source of potential dissent, as the cases of Bernard Marx and Helmholtz Watson demonstrate. Later, in *Brave New World Revisited*, Huxley admitted that the higher castes might prove a problem to the authorities. 'The members of the highest caste will have to be able to think new thoughts in response to new situations; consequently, their training will be much less rigid than the training imposed upon those whose business is not to reason why, but merely to do and die . . . .' These upper-caste individuals will be members of a still 'wild species – the trainers and guardians, themselves only slightly conditioned, of a breed of completely domesticated animals. Their wildness will make it possible for them to become heretical and rebellious.' But once again, he considered that these upper-caste rebels could be relatively easily dealt with by renewed brainwashing or the Brave New World expedient of exile.[121]

This is to ignore all the evidence of history. In the West, at any rate, the upper classes have provided both the motive and the material for some of the most explosive revolts against the established order. Plato had argued, in the

Republic, that, whatever the threats, a society was safe from revolution so long as the ruling class remained united. Dissension and division within the ruling class was the prime condition of revolution. The history of revolutions has borne out this insight admirably. There has been no major revolution that has not started without the active involvement of a significant section of the upper class. This was true of England in 1640, France in 1789 and Russia in 1917. Upper classes have, of course, a pre-eminent interest in stability, and for long periods can contain the divisions within their ranks. But precisely because so much is at stake – sovereign control of society – any failure to remain at the centre of power appears highly threatening. Upper-class individuals or groups who feel they are losing out in the competition to keep within the inner circles of power are desperate enough to stir up discontents in other sections of society, and ally themselves with these forces. The fact that they, along with the whole upper class, might be – and historically often have been – the first victims of the revolution has not prevented them from repeatedly embarking on this dangerous gamble.[122] And if not the parents, then the children. The nineteenth and twentieth centuries are rich with instances of the revolt of the *jeunesse dorée* – the latest perhaps being the 'counter-culture' of the 1960s – against the world created and ruled by their parents, and whose privileges are their due but despised inheritance.

There seems no good reason why Brave New World should be an exception to this general process. However conditioned the population as a whole, Brave New World requires a relatively free-thinking and independent upper stratum to deal with the challenges and problems that all societies, and especially one so technologically advanced as Brave New World, must face. This stratum will, like all upper classes, have by training and interest alike a strong commitment to the prevailing order. But the society of Brave New World, although founded on automation, has no automatic stabilizers. Its stability depends upon the most complex management of society, scientific knowledge and the technological environment. This is bound to be the source of constant disputes and differences of opinion, the breeding-ground of factions and struggles for power among the Alphas. This will be true, it must be stressed, even and especially while the goals of the society remain unquestioned. But it would be surprising, among such highly trained and educated people, if such divisions did not also occasionally lead to a questioning of those values and goals – if only, as with Helmholtz Watson, out of boredom with Brave New World. At any rate, it is clear that the upper-caste Alphas must always remain the Brave New Worlders most vulnerable to thoughts and temptations of an unorthodox kind.[123] They are, from the point of view of social stability, the Achilles' heel of Brave New World.

The problem can be stated in another, more familiar, way. The existence of a relatively unconditioned caste raises the question, Who conditions the conditioners? And *a fortiori*, who controls the Controllers? For, while the problem applies to all the Alphas, it is particularly pertinent in the case of the World Controllers, presumably the brightest and most independently minded of all the Alphas. Huxley's answer seems to be the same as that of Dostoyevsky's Grand Inquisitor, whose shadowy presence pervades *Brave New World*: the

Controllers, like the leaders of the Church in the legend (and not unlike Wells's Samurai), *voluntarily* dedicate themselves to the service of their society. Their rule is in the nature of a vocation, a religious duty. The vast majority of mankind are like children. They need leadership and guidance. In committing themselves to the security and happiness of these millions, the Controllers must sacrifice the happiness that they themselves, with their superior understanding, might find in the pursuit of science and art. They accept the limitation of their desires and powers that subservience to this cause entails. For it is a higher cause, above personal happiness and fulfilment. As servants of the cause they are willing to bow to its demands and subject themelves to its logic, however personally distasteful to themselves. Personal happiness is the price they must pay for their crucial part in this grand design. The leaders of the Church, says the Grand Inquisitor, 'the hundred thousand who rule, . . . who guard the mystery, shall be unhappy'. 'There will be thousands of millions of happy babes, and a hundred thousand sufferers who have taken upon themselves the curse of the knowledge of good and evil.'

This renunciation of powers, and the personal loss it entails, is fully exemplified in the case of the Controller Mustapha Mond. Mond knows his powers. 'As I make the laws here, I can also break them' (*BNW*, p. 172). He, along with the other World Controllers, alone has access to the forbidden old books such as the works of Shakespeare. He reads and censors all new scientific papers, and therefore remains abreast of all the latest scientific knowledge. It is this that qualifies him to say that 'all our science is just a cookery book, with an orthodox theory of cooking that nobody's allowed to question, and a list of recipes that mustn't be added to except by special permission from the head cook. I'm the head cook now' (*BNW*, p. 177). Mond in fact, as he tells the rebels, was once a 'real scientist', pursuing scientific knowledge in so adventurous and unorthodox a way that he was in danger of being sent into exile to an island. Permitted a choice by the authorities – science in exile or service to the state – he chose to renounce his science and to join the Controller's Council, becoming in time a Controller himself. He is clear about the personal sacrifice involved. 'Sometimes I rather regret the science. Happiness is a hard master – particularly other people's happiness. A much harder master, if one isn't conditioned to accept it unquestioningly, than truth . . . . What fun it would be if one didn't have to think about happiness!' But 'duty's duty. One can't consult one's own preferences' (*BNW*, pp. 178, 142).

It would be quite wrong to see this as cynicism or hypocrisy. In choosing to dedicate themselves to 'other people's happiness', even though a variety scorned by them, the Controllers genuinely put what they feel to be the greater good over lesser considerations of personal gratification. To this extent George Orwell was wide off the mark when he remarked of *Brave New World*:

> No society of that kind would last more than a couple of generations, because a ruling class which thought principally in terms of a 'good time' would soon lose its vitality. A ruling class has got to have a strict morality, a quasi-religious belief in itself, a mystique.[124]

Mustapha Mond does not, it is true, express himself with anything of the fervour of O'Brien in *Nineteen Eighty-Four*. But there is no doubt that he has a 'strict morality' and a 'quasi-religious belief' in his mission. And it is not the ruling class, not at any rate the Controllers, who go in for having a 'good time', but the rest of the population for whom such a life is deliberately designed by the Controllers. In so far as we get any idea what the Controllers themselves enjoy, it seems remarkably like the ascetic preference of Wells's Samurai for science and solitude – as, for instance, in the scene where Mustapha Mond admiringly studies a bold scientific paper and reluctantly rejects it for publication as subversive (*BMW*, ch. 12, pp. 141–2).

Nevertheless, Orwell has a point. The ascetic renunciation of personal happiness in the service of some higher rule or cause is fairly common in Western culture. There have been numerous attempts to inaugurate the 'Rule of the Saints' – the Calvinists in sixteenth-century Geneva, Cromwell and the Puritans in seventeenth-century England, the Jacobins under Robespierre and St Just in the French Revolution. But, apart from the fact that these attempts have been usually brief and frequently bloody, there is a fundamental difference between these episodes and what is attempted in Brave New World. The ascetic elites of history have tried, with notoriously little success it is true, to make the whole population live their own saintly lives. Cromwell and the Puritan divines offered themselves as models of proper piety and Christian character. There was to be a consistency of values across the whole society, a common thread linking the lives of rulers and ruled. In the end, with society thoroughly Christianized, there would be no need for rulers.

The aim in Brave New World is precisely the opposite. The ruled must never become like the rulers, the rulers never like the ruled. An insurmountable wall is raised between the understanding and outlook of the Controllers – and most Alphas – and that of the mass of the lower-caste population. The lower castes remain eternally children. Their whole life is given over to play and pleasure. They will never grow up to achieve adult maturity and responsibility. The Controllers, their benevolent parent-surrogates, have seen to that. By the same token, the Controllers, although they must understand their children, would lose their title and ability to rule if they became too much like them. From the Controllers' point of view, and presumably Huxley's, the divide beween the lives of rulers and ruled is the very ground and condition of the stability of Brave New World.

While superficially plausible, this balance is in fact highly unstable and precarious. In placing so much weight on the continuing purity and integrity of the rulers, Huxley is trying to solve the problem of stability by hauling himself up by his own bootstraps. He has not considered sufficiently the dynamics of the interaction between rulers and ruled. It is difficult, as Orwell's comment suggests, to imagine an ascetic ruling class persisting against this general and overwhelming background of hedonism. Unlike Cromwell's Puritans or Robespierre's Jacobins, the Controllers are not driven by the goal of remaking the whole society in their image. Their purpose is merely to maintain things as they are, to provide sufficient distractions and pleasures to keep the population contented. In Europe of old, a traditional ruling class, such as the British aristocracy, whose tastes and outlook were not so very different from those of the mass of the population, was in fact able to continue to rule on this basis for a considerable length of time. Such is not the case with Brave New World, where the elite and the mass are radically dissimilar. The expectation must surely be that the elite themselves will gradually succumb to the prevailing hedonism, or will become so out of touch with the general population as to lose control, perhaps even in the form of a coup or palace revolution. In either case, a decline or breakdown of the society is as likely as renewal; but Brave New World as Huxley conceived its order will have dissolved.

As Huxley depicts Brave New World, the Alphas and the Controllers present the only problem to arise directly and structually out of its system. The Savage, who in the second half of the book increasingly takes over from Bernard and Helmholtz the role of principal critic of the society, is an import, a force of opposition artificially thrust into the structure. Here again, Huxley seems concerned to stress that the most serious resistance to Brave New World will never come from within but, if at all, only from without. (Analogously, Huxley's later utopian society of *Island* succumbs not to internal weaknesses but to external invasion.) The Savage has been born and brought up on the New Mexico Reservation by his mother Linda, a Brave New Worlder who was lost and abandoned there when on a trip with the London Director of Hatcheries and Conditioning. In bringing them both back into Brave New World society, Bernard Marx sees the opportunity not simply of scoring off his boss, the Director, but of enhancing his own social reputation.

The opposition that the Savage offers is based on his socialization among the largely Indian population of the Reservation, eked out with ideas and impressions gathered from an understandably imperfect reading of Shakespeare. Though rejected by the Indians because of his white skin, he is attracted by the warmth of their community and the power of their religious rituals. The sterility and absence of feeling in Brave New World appals him: the coldly rational attitude towards death is what finally triggers off his abortive rebellion in the Hospital for the Dying. Against all Brave New World principle and practice, the Savage prizes heroism, cherishes self-discipline and believes in chastity. Brave New World has paid far too high a price for its comfort and 'happiness'. 'I don't want comfort. I want God, I want poetry, I want real danger, I want freedom, I want goodness. I want sin.' The Savage, as he defiantly admits to Mustapha Mond, is claiming 'the right to be unhappy' (*BNW*, p. 187).

The Savage's criticism has force, as is clearly intended by Huxley. Huxley at the time was very much under the influence of D. H. Lawrence, and the New Mexico siting of the Reservation seems a deliberate pointer to the Lawrentian 'dark gods' as the most powerful and perhaps only counter to the hedonist philosophy of Brave New World. But, as Huxley later admitted, the choices offered to the Savage are in truth neither of them very appealing. 'The Savage is offered only two alternatives, an insane life in Utopia, or the life of a primitive in an Indian village, a life more human in some respects, but in others hardly less queer and abnormal.'[125] The densely communal life of the Reservation in fact denies individuality almost as much as Brave New World; while its religion – described by Huxley as 'half fertility cult and half *Penitente* ferocity' – distinctly echoes the orgy-porgies and collective Solidarity Rites of Brave New World. As if to underline the parallel, the Savage's despairing suicide follows the collective orgy in which he finally gives way to his desire for Lenina, and which, with its self-flagellation and *soma*-induced frenzy, contains elements of both ways of life. There had, said Huxley, to be a third way, a 'sane' alternative to both the primitivism of the Reservation and the sterilized happiness of Brave New World. In such a sane community, 'economics would be decentralist and Henry-Georgian, politics Kropotkinesque and cooperative. Science and technology would be used as though, like the Sabbath, they had been made for man, not . . . as though man were to be adapted and enslaved to them.'[126] In *Island*, his last novel, such a possibility is fully pictured. But at the time of writing *Brave New World* Huxley evidently found compelling, as well as amusing, the idea that 'human beings are given free will in order to choose between insanity on the one hand and lunacy on the other.'

Is Brave New World, then, the perfected Hell that Huxley clearly conceives it to be? We have seen that there are sources of instability in it, but are there no intimations of anything more positive, something that might unfreeze its alienated strucures with the promise of a more human fulfilment? Utopias commonly contain dystopian features, unseen and unintended by their authors. Might this not also be true of dystopias, that they contain, in however distorted and diminished a form, a utopian impulse?

Brave New World offers everlasting happiness – but a happiness, Huxley makes us see, that is superficial and synthetic. It is symbolized above all in Lenina, with her Hollywood glamour and purely physical seductiveness. Against this, all that Huxley can offer is the rejection of happiness, 'the right to be unhappy'. But does not the desire and experience of happiness, however shallow and debased, itself contain the potential for change? The German Marxist Theodor Adorno once wrote: 'there is no happiness which does not promise to fulfil a socially constituted desire, but there is also none which does not promise something qualitatively different in this fulfilment.' In an incisive comment on Huxley he argued that 'were Lenina the imago of Brave New World, it would lose its horror.'[127] Lenina personifies the mechanical and reified happiness of Brave New World, but at the same time she suggests that devotion to the end of pleasure and happiness has a dialectic that cannot necessarily be anticipated or controlled by either the society or the individual. A society that promises happiness, in one set of terms, as its principal *raison d'être* cannot easily deny the right to happiness when this is sought according to a different set of terms.

This is precisely what happens to Lenina in the course of the novel. She begins by being presented as the most complete embodiment of Brave New World philosophy, the conventionalized glamour-girl to her very core. Her attitudes, expressed largely in hypnopaedic maxims, and her responses are copy-book examples of proper Brave New World behaviour, as both the Director of Hatcheries and Bernard Marx, from their very different standpoints, have occasion to observe. But her very liking for Bernard, with his queer appearance and reputation for unorthodoxy, already betrays a distinctly non-Brave New World preference, as does her excessively long (four-month) affair with Henry Foster. Thus it is not really surprising that she should fall for the Savage. But her feeling for him develops well beyond anything she has ever experienced before. His very strangeness, his explosions of anger and passion, draw her to him. She actually falls *in love* – an extraordinary and utterly reprehensible thing in Brave New World. She gazes at the moon, she becomes pale, her eyes cloud 'with an unwonted melancholy', she feels 'a sense of dreadful emptiness, a breathless apprehension, a nausea' (*BNW*, p. 139). Formally bid, she goes to bed with the Arch-Community Songster in a dispirited mood, 'wholly insensible of the honour done to her'. Quite understandably, both Henry Foster and her friend Fanny Crowne think she is seriously ill. She is, of course, in Brave New World terms; and any further progression in her attachment to the Savage could very well lead to trouble and even exile for her. Such demonstrations of feeling for one person are in the highest degree subversive. She is saved from this fate by the Savage's own violent repudiation of her and his subsequent self-seclusion and suicide.

Lenina's is hardly a 'grand passion' in the vein of a Juliet; and the Savage, with his prudish fear of sex and hypocritical disdain for Lenina's frank sexuality, is a poor Romeo. But the very suggestion of a development in Lenina, following the impulse to pursue her happiness, is an indication that the stuff of a very different sort of happiness – and the possibility of tragedy – is a potentiality of even so debased a culture as Brave New World. It would be entirely in the spirit of Huxley's ironic fable if, though unintended by him, the immaculately awful society that he created were to be undermined by happiness, its most sacred value and primary rationale. There is a sort of poetic justice in this, that the way both into and out of Brave New World might lie through Lenina's arms.

8

Politics and Anti-Utopia: George Orwell and *Nineteen Eighty-Four*

We are living in a world in which nobody is free, in which hardly anybody is secure, in which it is almost impossible to be honest and to remain alive.

George Orwell, *The Road to Wigan Pier* (1937)

Old Hitler's something different. So's Joe Stalin. They aren't like these chaps in the old days who crucified people and chopped their heads off and so forth just for the fun of it. They're after something quite new – something that's never been heard of before.

George Bowling in Orwell's *Coming Up For Air* (1939)

To say 'I accept' in an age like our own is to say that you accept concentration camps, rubber truncheons, Hitler, Stalin, bombs, aeroplanes, tinned food, machine-guns, putsches, purges, slogans, Bedaux belts, gas-masks, submarines, spies, *provocateurs*, press censorship, secret prisons, aspirins, Hollywood films and political murders.

George Orwell, *Inside the Whale* (1940)

We live in a lunatic world in which opposites are constantly changing into one another, in which pacifists find themselves worshipping Hitler, Socialists become nationalists, patriots become quislings, Buddhists pray for the success of the Japanese army, and the Stock Market takes an upward turn when the Russians stage an offensive.

George Orwell, review of Lionel Fielden's *Beggar My Neighbour, Horizon* (September 1943)

Every honest man is a Prophet. He utters his opinion both of private and public matters Thus If you go on So the Result is So. He never says such a thing Shall happen let you do what you will. A Prophet is a Seer not an Arbitrary Dictator.

William Blake

INTENTIONS AND INTERPRETATIONS

Is *Nineteen Eighty-Four*, as so many readers innocently think, a prophecy of things to come? Or is it rather more in the nature of Swiftian satire, an attack on the present and a warning of worse to come if we do nothing?[1] Are its targets more historically specific: is it largely an anatomy, in grotesque form, of the Nazi and Bolshevik regimes, and a projection of their totalitarian systems as a possible future for the world?[2] Even more specifically, is it essentially a satire on the conditions of wartime and postwar Britain, 'no more than a comic transcription of the London of the end of World War Two'?[3] Are autobiographical themes perhaps the key to the novel? Were the misery and terror that Orwell experienced at his prep school St Cyprian's, at least as he wrote of it so passionately in 'Such, Such Were the Joys', the source of a 'hidden wound', a 'masochistic guilt', that appeared repeatedly in his writings, culminating in the 'remorseless pessimism' of *Nineteen Eighty-Four*?[4] Or if not the beginning, perhaps the end of his life: is *Nineteen Eighty-Four* the last despairing product, the 'final testament', of a diseased and dying man, who turned 'sickness into art' and moved 'from his own sickness to the world's'?[5] Or is the despair something more metaphysical, a sense of isolation and loss that belongs essentially to the literature of Protestantism?[6]

Nineteen Eighty-Four is conceivably all of these things, of course. It is a novel,[7] a work of fiction, and as such can carry many strands and levels of meaning. And while this is true of all the utopian and anti-utopian works considered in this section – they are all novels of a kind – none has stirred up such controversy over its meaning and significance as has *Nineteen Eighty-Four*. The reason is not hard to find. *Nineteen Eighty-Four* was published in 1949, at the height of the first wave of Cold War hysteria. It appeared, in other words, in the midst of the development of the most important political fact of our time. Inevitably it was taken up, from the very first day of publication, as a weapon in the armoury of the Cold War. For whatever else *Nineteen Eighty-Four* might mean, it appeared clearly enough to most of its early readers and reviewers to be centrally about socialism, fascism, democracy and the prospects for all three in the contemporary world. As such, and given its undoubted literary force, it was ideally suited to serve as 'a sort of an ideological super-weapon in the cold war'.[8]

Conservatives and liberals on both sides of the Atlantic – but especially in the United States – gratefully seized on it as a stick with which to beat the Soviet Union. It was largely owing to their efforts that the concepts and images of Big Brother, 'Newspeak', 'doublethink', 'thoughtcrime' and the rest entered the political vocabulary of the West. But it was not only the enemies, but also the friends, of socialism who saw Orwell's book as fundamentally an anti-socialist tract. Fredric Warburg, Orwell's sympathetic left-wing publisher, thought that the book was 'a deliberate and sadistic attack on socialism and socialist parties generally. It seems to indicate a final breach between Orwell and Socialism . . . .'[9] (But despite thinking it 'worth a cool million votes to the Conservative Party' he rushed forward its publication: he knew when he had a best-seller on his hands.) Some left-wingers might console themselves with the reflection that the book's target was Stalinism, not socialism. But to many others it seemed only too evident – despite Orwell's disclaimers – that 'Ingsoc', the ideology of Oceania, stood for Socialism *tout court*. '*Nineteen Eighty-Four*', said Isaac Deutscher, a leading socialist theoretician and respected biographer of Trotsky and Stalin, 'is a document of dark disillusionment not only with Stalinism but with every form and shade of socialism.'[10]

There was therefore a strong inducement, on the part of some left-wing sympathizers, to turn away from a directly political interpretation, couched in terms of contemporary politics. They reached instead for a view of *Nineteen Eighty-Four* as a passionate disquisition on the nature of power in general, and the possible forms of its corruption. Seeing the work as some kind of political or moral allegory seemed a safer way of containing its potentially damaging implications for the socialist cause. Other considerations also pointed away from the more obvious political interpretations – away from political interpretation altogether. To the continuing controversy over Orwell's attitude to socialism, there was the fuel added by the imminence of the year 1984, and the status of the work as prophecy. For those who admired the book primarily as a powerful achievement of the literary imagination, it became important not to allow the falsity or otherwise of Orwell's 'predictions' to confuse the understanding and evaluation of the work. Hence, in recent years, the proliferation of interpretations of *Nineteen Eighty-Four* as allegory, satire, autobiography, religion and so forth. The old-fashioned view, that it is fundamentally a vision of a future world shaped in the image of totalitarianism, is now likely to be treated with good-natured condescension by the tribe of symbol-hunting literary critics who have largely taken over 'Orwell studies'.[11]

Some blame must, no doubt, be attached to Orwell for too blithely assuming that the mass readership soon gained by *Nineteen Eighty-Four* would know about his other writings and past attitudes and so be on their guard against too simple a reading of the novel. Moreover, the complexity and even contradictions of the book's many themes, as compared say with *Animal Farm*, made it especially easy for casual readers to fix upon the most obvious targets and symbols – Big Brother, the telescreens, the Thought Police and the other paraphernalia of the collectivist state. But at least on the issue of socialism, those who knew him, and students of his life and work, should surely have been in no doubt as to where he stood, in 1948 as much as in 1937, when *The Road to Wigan Pier* first publicly announced his commitment to socialism. 'I belong to the Left and must work inside it, much as I hate Russian totalitarianism and its poisonous influence in this country', he wrote to the Duchess of Atholl in 1945, firmly refusing her invitation to speak to the League of European Freedom because it was 'an essentially Conservative body'.[12] When some early reviews of *Nineteen Eighty-Four*, especially in America, took an exclusively anti-socialist view of the work, Orwell, though by now a very sick man, took great pains to correct this impression. In a statement to be made public through the United Automobile Workers of America he wrote:

> My recent novel is NOT intended as an attack on socialism or on the British Labour Party (of which I am a supporter) but as a show up of the perversions to which a centralized economy is liable and which have already been partly realized in Communism and Fascism. I do not believe that the kind of society I describe necessarily *will* arrive, but I believe (allowing of course for the fact that the book is satire) that something resembling it *could* arrive. I believe also that totalitarian ideas have taken root in the minds of intellectuals everywhere, and I have tried to draw these ideas out to their logical consequences. The scene of the book is laid in Britain in order to emphasize that the English-speaking races are not innately better than anyone else and that totalitarianism, *if not fought against*, could triumph anywhere.[13]

This statement already goes beyond the specific issue of socialism to lay out Orwell's intention in *Nineteen Eighty-Four* in the broadest terms. Even fuller, and clearer, was the statement of intent contained in the press release which, distressed by some reviews, he had Warburg issue in June 1949:

It has been suggested by some reviewers of NINETEEN EIGHTY-FOUR that it is the author's view that this, or something like this, is what will happen inside the next forty years in the Western world. This is not correct. I think that, allowing for the book being after all a parody, something like NINETEEN EIGHTY-FOUR *could* happen. This is the direction in which the world is going at the present time, and the trend lies deep in the political, social and economic foundations of the contemporary world situation.

Specifically, the danger lies in the structure imposed on Socialist and on Liberal capitalist communities by the necessity to prepare for total war with the USSR and the new weapons, of which of course the atomic bomb is the most powerful and the most publicized. But danger lies also in the acceptance of a totalitarian outlook by intellectuals of all colours.

The moral to be drawn from this dangerous nightmare situation is a simple one: *Don't let it happen. It depends on you.*[14]

It is of course perfectly proper to disregard this clear statement of authorial intent and to read *Nineteen Eighty-Four* in quite other ways. Authors – especially when they purport to be artists – are not always fully aware of what they have created. Even with the apparently simple fable of *Animal Farm*, Orwell had been concerned to find that some read it as 'very strong Tory propaganda'. The literary critic William Empson, who pointed this out to Orwell, warned him that 'the danger of this kind of perfection is that it means very different things to different readers . . . . The allegory is a form that has to be set down and allowed to grow like a separate creature . . . . it is a form that inherently means more than the author means, when it is handled sufficiently well.'[15] The satiric and parodic intent – even if only in part – of *Nineteen Eighty-Four* was bound to raise the same problems and same diversity of interpretation; and Orwell's distressed attempts to clarify his aims in the form of press releases and the like only showed the extent to which his novel may have gone beyond his own conscious and explicit purpose. Certainly it is not patently absurd, despite Orwell's firmly expressed socialist convictions, to read *Nineteen Eighty-Four* as a warning against socialism, especially if one conceives socialism as essentially a state-run economy and society. No more can one rule out of court autobiographical interpretations, which stress unconscious fears and desires arising out of intense childhood and later experiences. It is indeed, as Empson suggests, a testimony to Orwell's success and the power of the novel that such a range of meanings can be derived from it – however unhappy Orwell himself may have been at the implications of some of them.

Nevertheless, I propose here to treat *Nineteen Eighty-Four* largely in the terms of Orwell's own statements of intent set out above. They are reasonably clear; they cover the ostensible ground, the salient themes, of the novel more or less comprehensively; and they accord with the perceptions of most readers – even careful readers – of what the novel is truly about. In accepting them, moreover, we can eliminate at least some of the ambiguities and ambivalences joyfully heaped upon the work by the critics.

First, Orwell's account of his novel breaks down, for all practical purposes, the distinction between treating it as 'satire' and treating it as 'prophecy' which has been so insisted upon in recent years. To stress the satirical aspects of *Nineteen Eighty-Four* is to concentrate on the novel's function primarily as a warning: things are bad, don't let them get worse. That is very clearly one intended purpose, as Orwell expresses it ('*Don't let it happen. It depends on you.*') But at the same time, Orwell is equally concerned to insist that it *could* happen; and this because 'this is the direction in which the world is going at the present time.' The trend, he says, 'lies deep in the political, social and economic foundations of the contemporary world situation'. There is, in other words, something like a prophecy contained in the analysis of the contemporary world: things being (as bad) as they are, it is *very probable* that in the near future the world will resemble, will realize, the totalitarian society of *Nineteen Eighty-Four*. Orwell never believed in the doctrine of 'historical necessity' or 'historical inevitability',[16] and so he makes it abundantly clear that the direction of events is reversible – '*if . . . fought against*'. But this leaves open the calculation of how likely it is that people *will* resist the trend, given its strength; and it allows us to ask, some forty years after the appearance of *Nineteen Eighty-Four*, how far we *have* been able to resist the trend. The innocent question, the question that arises in most readers' minds today and largely accounts for the book's continuing popularity, is actually a very proper one: How much is 1984 like *Nineteen Eighty-Four*?

We shall have to return to this later. But it seems worth noting at this point that Orwell was prepared on several occasions during the 1940s to make remarkably 'prophetic' statements about the future shape of the world – and to make them, what is more, in terms that singularly anticipate the world of *Nineteen Eighty-Four*. In a letter to a Mr H. J. Willmett in 1944, for instance, he expressed his belief – 'or fear' – that 'totalitarianism, leader-worship, etc.' are 'on the increase' in the world as a whole, despite their relatively undeveloped state in countries like Britain and the United States.

Hitler, no doubt, will soon disappear, but only at the expense of strengthening (a) Stalin, (b) the Anglo-American millionaires and (c) all sorts of petty fuehrers of the type of de Gaulle. All the national movements everywhere, even those that originate in resistance to German domination, seem to take non-democratic forms, to group themselves round some superhuman fuehrer (Hitler, Stalin, Salazar, Franco, Gandhi, De Valera are all varying examples) and to adopt the theory that the end justifies the means. Everywhere the world movement seems to be in the direction of centralized economies which can be made to 'work' in an economic sense but which are not democratically organized and which tend to establish a caste system. With this go the horrors of emotional nationalism and a tendency to disbelieve in the existence of objective truth because all the facts have to fit in with the words and prophecies of some infallible fuehrer. Already history has in a sense ceased to exist, i.e. there is no such thing as a history of our own times which could be universally accepted, and the exact sciences are endangered as soon as military necessity ceases to keep people up to the mark. Hitler can say that the Jews started the war, and if he survives that will become official history. He can't say that two and two are five, because for the purposes of, say, ballistics, they have to make four. But if the sort of world that I am afraid of arrives, a world of two or three great superstates which are unable to conquer one another, two and two could become five if the fuehrer wished it.

That, so far as I can see, is the direction in which we are actually moving, though, of course, the process is reversible.[17]

The *caveat* at the end is characteristic. So is his comment that the 'comparative immunity' of Britain and the United States to totalitarianism might simply mean that they 'haven't been really tried, they haven't known defeat or severe suffering', and that there are some 'bad symptoms' as portents: for instance, the 'totalitarian outlook' of most English intellectuals, who have simply exchanged Hitler for Stalin. Orwell remained convinced for the whole of his life that the drift towards totalitarianism could be halted, that there were countries like Britain with strong traditions of freedom which could be in the forefront of resistance to the trend. But he would have considered it foolish and dishonest if he did not show the immense forces ranged on the other side, and indicate the real possibility of their triumphing. 'If one simply proclaims that all is for the best and doesn't point to the sinister symptoms, one is merely helping to bring totalitarianism nearer.'[18]

This remark clearly anticipates Orwell's later statements clarifying the purpose of *Nineteen Eighty-Four*, and serves to underline the second thing to be derived from those statements: namely, that, whatever other concerns we may find in the novel, it is centrally about totalitarianism – its nature and its prospects in the modern world. This would scarcely need saying were it not for a persistent tendency to regard *Nineteen Eighty-Four* as trafficking in the general metaphysics of power and politics, only slightly related if at all to the actual historical forms of totalitarianism that made their novel appearance in the twentieth century. In this view, *Nineteen Eighty-Four* belongs more alongside works like Kafka's *The Castle* or *The Trial* than, say, Zamyatin's *We* or Koestler's *Darkness at Noon.*

That there are Kafkaesque elements in *Nineteen Eighty-Four* no one would deny (Kafka, after all, also belongs to the era of totalitarianism). But from everything that Orwell wrote it is clear that his overriding preoccupation was with the events of his own 'tumultuous revolutionary' age, with the analysis of the chief forces shaping the twentieth-century world and the need to resist them if a decent and humane world were to be created. 'Every line of serious work that I have written since 1936 has been written, directly or indirectly, *against* totalitarianism and *for* democratic socialism, as I understand it.'[19] Orwell was a writer who stuck unusually close to the experiences of his own life and times. His works, as nearly every critic has observed, are heavily autobiographical, most clearly so in the earlier novels, from *Burmese Days* (1934) to *Coming Up for Air* (1939). But they are also, in the general sense, deeply historical, saturated wth the times and places of Orwell's life as that reflected the life of his society and civilization. If Winston Smith carries on the autobiographical tradition of Flory (*Burmese Days*), Dorothy Hare (*A Clergyman's Daughter*), Gordon Comstock (*Keep the Aspidistra Flying*) and George Bowling (*Coming Up for Air*), the proles and politics of Oceania continue the tradition of *Down and Out in Paris and London* (1933), *The Road to Wigan Pier* (1937), *Homage to Catalonia* (1938) and *Animal Farm* (1945).

This very closeness to immediate experience may be, as many have felt, the main limitation of Orwell as a novelist, in that he was never able sufficiently to transmute his experience into the universality of art. The voice of the essayist and the journalist is insistently present in all his fictional works, *Nineteen Eighty-Four* not excepted. But this should at least make us chary of treating that work too readily as allegory or metaphysics. In dozens of essays and reviews Orwell had addressed the theme of totalitarianism as the distinctive force and form of twentieth-century history. In Spain, crucially, he had encountered unforgettably its two major expressions to date, fascism and communism. Orwell really had no need – even had he had the taste and talent – to take off into general metaphysical speculation on the nature and effects of power. In his own times, in his own life, he had experienced power of so novel and frightening a kind as gave him ample scope for reflecting on the larger questions of truth, freedom and individual autonomy and integrity. In doing so, he would have thought it irresponsible and dangerous in the highest degree not to distinguish between past and present systems, past and present dangers. It was not in his character to go in for abstract political philosophy. The concreteness of his thinking, as of his observation of the world in general, is one of his hallmarks, and one of his glories. It would be strange indeed if this concreteness of time and place, this urgent sense of history, did not also inform his account of totalitarian politics in *Nineteen Eighty-Four.*

To see *Nineteen Eighty-Four* as both a warning and a prophecy, both a contemporary analysis and a vision of the future as totalitarianism triumphant, is also to place it squarely within the tradition of modern utopian and anti-utopian writing. This, too, is increasingly being denied, usually on the contention that the book is fundamentally a satire, and so belongs more with works like *Gulliver's Travels* than with what Orwell called 'the chain of Utopia books' – Wells's *When the Sleeper Wakes*, Jack London's *The Iron Heel*, Zamyatin's *We* and Huxley's *Brave New World*[20]. *Nineteen Eighty-Four*, says Bernard Crick, is 'Swiftian satire in the disguise but not in the tradition of the Utopian or dystopisn novel'. Elsewhere he refers to it as 'a mutant of social novel and satiric polemic', pointing here additionally to its place in the tradition of Orwell's own fictional and non-fictional works of 'documentary realism', which aimed to shock and stir the reader by showing how things 'really are'.[21]

Now it is true that to concentrate on *Nineteen Eighty-Four* as the product of a chain of purely literary influences is to obscure its relation to its own times, and hence its central meaning. So, for instance, referring to Orwell's undoubted debt to Wells's *When the Sleeper Wakes* and 'A Story of the Days to Come', David Lodge rightly says: 'When all the debts of Orwell to the early Wells have been totted up, the fact remains that *Nineteen Eighty-Four* derives most of its power and authenticity from Orwell's imaginative exploitation of facts, emotions, and iconography specifically associated with Stalinist Russia, Nazi Germany and World-War-II-devastated Euorpe.'[22] The same thing can no doubt also be said of the equally obvious influence of Zamyatin's *We*, which like 'A Story of the Days to Come' contains the basic narrative pattern of *Nineteen Eighty-Four*: the opposition between two lovers and a totalitarian state. But then of course precisely the same observation can be made of Zamyatin and Huxley in relation to Wells. Both of these writers clearly 'borrowed' from Wells, but in the writing of their anti-utopias they were strongly influenced by many social and political experiences – the First World War, the Russian Revolution – which had not occurred when Wells was in his anti-utopian phase. Their anti-utopian visions, as a result, were of a quite different character from his, whatever the superficial similarities of plot and detail. But in each case what they presented – with no less a satirical element than in Orwell – was the anatomy of what they considered the distinctive form and tendency of modern society, together with its projection, in magnified and grotesque proportions, into the future.

This is what Orwell also did, as he himself seemed quite happy to acknowledge. 'My new book is a Utopia in the form of a novel', he wrote to Julian Symons[23] (*not* 'a novel in the form of a Utopia', as Crick and others would rather have him say). Earlier he had written to Fredric Warburg that he was working on 'a novel about the future – that is, it is in a sense a fantasy, but in the form of a naturalistic novel.'[24] Both of these remarks suggest that Orwell was consciously working in the tradition he knew so well, the utopian tradition of Wells, London, Zamyatin and Huxley.[25] Like these, he drew as a matter of course on other than purely utopian writings – in his case, James Burnham's *The Managerial Revolution* was a particularly important influence. Like these, too, he used satire and parody to make his point: the Appendix on 'Newspeak' is a good example of this, as also his treatment of the proles. And for good measure he threw in the style and much of the content of his political essays and documentary works. Such a mixture was bound to flaw the finished work somewhat, and to leave several puzzles in the minds of his readers as to his precise intentions. But in most ways *Nineteen Eighty-Four* does function, as Orwell intended it to, as an anti-utopian novel: both a warning *and* a prophecy.[26]

There has been a marked tendency in recent years, as part of a general 'revisionist' attitude towards Orwell, to distance us from the world of *Nineteen Eighty-Four*: to see it through the perspective of 1948, to reduce it to a distillation of Nazi and Soviet experience (and so not ours), to treat it as satire or allegory. This has the effect either of placing it firmly in its own times, the 1940s, at what seems a safe remove from ours; or of taking it out of time and history altogether and giving it a metaphysical setting.[27] *Nineteen Eighty-Four* then becomes either history or myth. Orwell quite clearly intended it to be neither, and whatever historical or mythical elements it contains are put there deliberately to underline the central message: *de te fabula narratur. Nineteen Eighty-Four* is about us; it is about our own times. That, as Orwell points out, is one reason for the Englsh setting of the novel: to show that it *could* happen here. Moreover, the tendencies he describes are of so powerful and long-term a kind that it would be the shallowest optimism to think that, at this modest distance in time from him, they have simply been swallowed up by history. Nor can we comfort ourselves with the view that *Nineteen Eighty-Four* only generalizes the experience and prospects of other societies – Russia, Germany – so that, while we shudder for them, we need not feel any concern for the democracies of the West. Orwell, again, in his statements about his book, tells us this is not so: the tendencies are world-wide.

We know, in any case, well enough what a satire specifically on the Soviet Union and the theme of 'the revolution betrayed' would look like to Orwell, since he had recently written an outstanding one: *Animal Farm. Nineteen Eighty-Four* is very different from *Animal Farm*, and we should therefore surely respect the different scope and intention which the change of form and treatment imply. In 1946, the year in which he began work on *Nineteen Eighty-Four*, Orwell wrote a review of Zamyatin's *We*. He noted the obvious satire on the new Soviet regime but concluded that 'what Zamyatin seems to be aiming at is not any particular country but the implied aims of industrial civilization.'[28] It is a fair statement of his own aims in *Nineteen Eighty-Four*.

TOTALITARIANISM: THE 'DICTATORSHIP OF THEORISTS'

Orwell set his savage satire on the Soviet Union, *Animal Farm*, in an idyllic English countryside. He made the same sort of point in setting *Nineteen Eighty-Four* in 'London, chief city of Airstrip One, itself the third most populous of the provinces of Oceania'. The world of Airstrip One is, in its physical and much of its social trappings, patently the war-weary world of England in the last stages of the Second World War and the immediate postwar period. It is a drab, mean world, instantly recognizable to any of Orwell's contemporaries. One of them, Orwell's friend Julian Symons, has written:

> In one of its aspects *Nineteen Eighty-Four* was about a world familiar to anybody who lived in Britain during the war that began in 1939. The reductions in rations, the odious food, the sometimes unobtainable and always dubiously authentic drink, these were with us still when the book appeared.[29]

So we have Winston Smith's residence in the dilapidated block of flats, Victory Mansions, its hallway smelling of 'boiled cabbage and old rag mats'; the lifts that often don't work because of erratic power failures; the coarse soap, the shortages of razor blades, buttons and shoelaces, as well as of modest luxuries such as sweets and chocolates; the prole shops, where some of these things could sometimes illicitly be got (a kind of black market); the artificial or adulterated tea, coffee and sugar; the cheap Victory Gin, and Victory Cigarettes, whose tobacco usually fell out; the ill-fitting clothes and unhealthy faces of the people; the appalling institutional food in the underground canteen at Winston's place of work, the Ministry of Truth ('pinkish-grey stew . . . a filthy liquid mess that had the appearance of vomit'). Intermittently rocket bombs hit the city, but the people have become too used to this to bother to seek refuge in the tube stations. Bombsites and craters litter the city; posters bearing government slogans ('Big Brother is Watching You', 'War is Peace', etc.) cover the walls.

This is the 1940s, all right. After the glitter and glamour of *Brave New World*, the society of *Nineteen Eighty-Four* is distinctly a step backwards. But the run-down 1940s background is not so carefully and painstakingly presented simply because, as Anthony Burgess suggests, 'novels are made out of day-to-day experience',[30] and Winston's experience was Orwell's. The lack of technological sophistication is deliberate. Even where Orwell introduces innovations they are simply minor modifications of existing technology. The BBC's television service, suspended during the war, had already resumed, in

1948, and the 'telescreens' are simply two-way TV. 'Speakwrites' are simply dictaphones that type. Beyond this, 'ink-pens' are the new Biros, and the 'pneumatic tubes' that carry Winston's work in the Ministry had been used in the big department stores since the 1920s. Helicopters had already been used by the American army during the war, and rocket bombs had already fallen on London. In their never-ending wars, the three super-states of *Nineteen Eighty-Four* use conventional weapons – grenades, bombs, tanks, submarines, machine guns – although there had been a short-lived atomic war before the establishment of the new world-system.

In physical and technical terms, then, this is a world in which progress has deliberately been halted. Orwell wanted to create a sense of familiarity in his readers, to establish a point of contact with their own world, so that the discovery of a brutal political system working within it would come with shocking force. By using the familiar background of his own times, and setting the novel in the near rather than – like Wells and Huxley – the distant future, he made it impossible for the reader to escape into the realm of exoticism or science fiction. It could happen here; it *had* happened here. *De te fabula narratur.*

The squalor and ugliness of Winston's environment is used to introduce another theme: the importance of memory, and the past. The petty personal discomforts and deprivations are among the things that fuel Winston Smith's rebelliousness. As he sits resentfully in the canteen of the Ministry of Truth, he reflects that things must have been different once, and so could be again:

> Had it always been like this? Had food always tasted like this? He looked round the canteen. A low-ceilinged, crowded room, its walls grimy from the contact of innumerable bodies; battered metal tables and chairs, placed so close together that you sat with elbows touching; bent spoons, dented tray, coarse white mugs; all surfaces greasy, grime in every crack; and a sourish, composite smell of bad gin and bad coffee and metallic stew and dirty clothes. Always in your stomach and in your skin there was a sort of protest, a feeling that you had been cheated of something you had the right to. It was true that he had no memories of anything greatly different. In any time that he could accurately remember, there had never been quite enough to eat, one had never had socks or underclothes that were not full of holes, furniture had always been battered and rickety, rooms underheated, tube trains crowded, houses falling to pieces, bread dark-coloured, tea a rarity, coffee filthy-tasting, cigarettes insufficient – nothing cheap and plentiful except synthetic gin. And though, of course, it grew worse as one's body aged, was it not a sign that this was not the natural order of things if one's heart sickened at the discomfort and dirt and scarcity, the interminable winters, the stickiness of one's socks, the lifts that never worked, the cold water, the gritty soap, the cigarettes that came to pieces, the food with its strange evil tastes? Why should one feel it to be intolerable unless one had some kind of ancestral memory that things had once been different?[31]

Orwell here directly intimates that, in the unlikely event of things getting better, the past – 'ancestral memory' – rather than some new future will be the path to a more human existence. The importance of the past, as the only available storehouse of alternative values and practices, is dwelt on throughout: in the old diary and the antique glass paperweight that Winston conceals and treasures, in the old-fashioned room above the junk-shop where the lovers meet, in the dream of the 'Golden Country' which Winston thinks he may have actually seen in his youth, in memories of his mother and sister, in the word 'Shakespeare' that is on Winston's lips when he wakes from the dream (*NEF*, p. 28). So the deliberately down-at-heel 1940s setting of *Nineteen Eighty-Four* serves another purpose. It is Orwell's revenge on Wells, and his reproof to Huxley. Whether the future was glorious, as Wells hoped, or frightful, as Huxley anticipated, both expected it to be a rational, scientific super-technological world. The Wellsian utopia, the 'glittering Wells-world,' said Orwell, was one of 'science, order, progress, internationalism, aeroplanes, steel, concrete, hygiene. . . .'[32] The reality of the future, as Orwell lets Winston reflect with a certain grim relish, is however quite different:

It struck him that the truly characteristic thing about modern life was not its cruelty and insecurity, but simply its bareness, its dinginess, its listlessness. Life, if you looked about you, bore no resemblance not only to the lies that streamed out of the telescreens, but even to the ideals that the Party was trying to achieve. Great areas of it, even for a Party-member, were neutral and non-political, a matter of slogging through dreary jobs, fighting for a place on the Tube, darning a worn-out sock, cadging a saccharine tablet, saving a cigarette end. The ideal set up by the Party was something huge, terrible, and glittering – a world of steel and concrete, of monstrous machines and terrifying weapons – a nation of warriors and fanatics, marching forward in perfect unity, all thinking the same thoughts and shouting the same slogans, perpetually working, fighting, triumphing, persecuting – three hundred million people all with the same face. The reality was decaying, dingy cities where underfed people shuffled to and fro in leaky shoes, in patched-up nineteenth century houses that smelt always of cabbage and bad lavatories. He seeemed to see a vision of London, vast and ruinous, city of a million dustbins, and mixed up with it was a picture of Mrs Parsons, a woman with lined face and wispy hair, fiddling helplessly with a blocked waste-pipe. (*NEF*, pp. 62–3)

The mind-boggling future of Huxley and Wells dissolves into the banality of a drab everyday life. But Orwell goes further. Not only is the future not better than the present, it is actually worse. Technically and economically, the world of *Nineteen Eighty-Four* has suffered regression. As Emmanuel Goldstein's 'The Theory and Practice of Oligarchical Collectivism' puts it:

The world of today is a bare, hungry, dilapidated place compared with the world that existed before 1914, and still more so if compared with the imaginary future to which the people of that period looked forward. In the early twentieth century, the vision of a future society unbelievably rich, leisured, orderly, and efficient – a glittering antiseptic world of glass and steel and snow-white concrete – was part of the consciousness of nearly every literate person. Science and technology were developing at a prodigious speed, and it seemed natural to assume that they would go on developing. This failed to happen, partly because of the impoverishment caused by a long series of wars and revolutions, partly because scientific and technical progress depended on the empirical habit of thought which could not survive in a strictly regimented society. As a whole the world is more primitive today than it was fifty years ago. (*NEF*, p. 153)

The world of *Nineteen Eighty-Four* is primitive not simply in the technical sphere. There has been an all-round triumph of primitivism and barbarism, a sort of 'return of the collective repressed'. The reversion that has taken place touches the very core of the new totalitarian society. Wells had seen history as the progressive triumph of rational scientific man over irrational, romantic, primitive man. But it has not been like that. 'Creatures out of the Dark Ages have come marching into the present. . . . .' If science has been developed and put to any use, it has done so 'on the side of superstition', as in Nazi Germany.[33] Progress had turned out to be a swindle. The general liberal belief in material and moral advance had proved to be a cruel delusion. Beliefs and practices, such as slavery and genocide, which all sane, educated people had thought had vanished for ever, had reappeared with a vengeance. Even cynics like Huxley had been fooled. In some notes of 1940 Orwell wrote:

> It is as though in the space of ten years we had slid back into the Stone Age. Human types supposedly extinct for centuries, the dancing dervish, the robber chieftain, the Grand Inquisitor, have suddenly reappeared, not as inmates of lunatic asylums, but as the masters of the world . . . . Mr Aldous Huxley's *Brave New World* was a good caricature of the hedonistic Utopia, the kind of thing that seemed possible and even imminent before Hitler appeared, but it had no relation to the actual future. What we are moving towards at this moment is something more like the Spanish Inquisition, and probably far worse, thanks to the radio and the secret police.[34]

Goldstein's book, in *Nineteen Eighty-Four*, develops this point. By the 1940s all political thought had become authoritarian, despite the fact that intellectual and material progress was for the first time making democracy and equality possible. 'The earthly paradise had been discredited at exactly the moment when it became realizable.' The tension created by this paradox was resolved by the return of barbarous practices.

> In the general hardening of outlook that set in round about 1930, practices which had long been abandoned, in some cases for hundreds of years – imprisonment without trial, the use of war prisoners as slaves, and the deportation of whole populations – not only became common again, but were tolerated and even defended by people who considered themselves enlightened and progressive. (*NEF*, p. 164)

People like Wells and Huxley, said Orwell, 'are too sane to understand the modern world'. Their rationalism inhibits them from seeing the profoundly irrational, 'primitivist' roots of modern totalitarianism. They cannot understand that people can and will act on the basis of non-utilitarian motives. Hitler, on the contrary, has seen just this and capitalized on it:

> He has grasped the falsity of the hedonistic attitude to life. Nearly all western thought since the last war, certainly all 'progressive' thought, has assumed tacitly that human beings desire nothing beyond ease, security and avoidance of pain. In such a view of life there is no room, for instance, for patriotism and the military virtues . . . . Hitler, because in his own joyless mind he feels it with exceptional strength, knows that human beings don't only want comfort, safety, short working-hours, hygiene, birth-control and, in general, common sense; they also, at least intermittently, want struggle and self-sacrifice, not to mention drums, flags, and loyalty-parades. However they be as economic theories, Fascism and Nazism are psychologically far sounder than any

hedonistic conception of life. The same is probably true of Stalin's militarized version of Socialism. All three of the great dictators have enhanced their power by imposing intolerable burdens on their peoples.[35]

'The people who have shown the best understanding of Fascism,' wrote Orwell, 'are either those who have suffered under it or those who have a Fascist streak in themselves.' That is why Jack London's *The Iron Heel* (1907), for all its crudity, is 'a truer prophecy of the future than either *Brave New World* or *The Shape of Things to Come.*[36] For London 'with his love of violence and physical strength, his belief in "natural aristocracy", his animal worship and exaltation of the primitive ... had in him what one might fairly call a Fascist strain.'[37] Similarly, Zamyatin's *We* is superior to *Brave New World*, despite the similarities, because it possesses that 'intuitive grasp of the irrational side of totalitarianism – human sacrifice, cruelty as an end in itself, the worship of a Leader who is credited with divine attributes. . . . .'[38] By contrast, the liberal intelligentsia has been blinded by its rationalist prejudices:

> The energy that actually shapes the world springs from emotions – racial pride, leader-worship, religious belief, love of war – which liberal intellectuals mechanically write off as anachronisms, and which they have usually destroyed so completely in themselves as to have lost all power of action.[39]

The paradox is that the new totalitarianism is itself a creation of the intellectuals – but intellectuals of a new type. Hitler and Stalin, like Lenin and Trotsky, are men of what Orwell's friend Koestler called 'an entirely new species: militant philosophers'. The dictatorships they have created are 'dictatorships of theorists'.[40] They are the men who, largely because of their own character, have realized the precariousness of mere hedonism as the basis of rule. 'Men can only be happy when they do not assume that the object of life is happiness.'[41] They have risen to power by appealing to the non-hedonistic instincts and emotions: nationalism, leader-worship, self-abasement and self-sacrifice. It is quite wrong to see the Bolsheviks, for instance, as inhabiting the same world as rational 'sensible' men like Wells and Huxley. 'They were not introducing a Wellsian Utopia but a Rule of the Saints, which, like the English Rule of the Saints, was a military despotism enlivened by witchcraft trials.'[42] As a result, the nominal 'dictatorship of the proletariat' had to mean 'the dictatorship of a handful of intellectuals, ruling through terrorism'.[43]

The new breed of intellectuals in England, the 'Auden-Spender crowd', had for long been the target of some of Orwell's most venomous abuse. It was not simply, as he saw it, that they luxuriated in the criticism of their own class and country while living comfortably off the dividends of capitalist enterprise, and on the backs of millions of slaving natives in the colonies. More dangerous was the unconscionable power-worship of the intellectuals, the result largely of the very safeness and softness in which they pass their bookish lives.[44] At bottom, the driving force of the socialist intellectual – as seen clearly in George Bernard Shaw's admiration for fascist as well as communist dictatorship – was no different from that of the fascist.

> The underlying motive of many Socialists . . . . is simply a hypertrophied sense of order. The present state of affairs offends them not because it causes misery, still less because it makes freedom impossible, but because it is untidy; what they desire, basically, is to reduce the world to something resembling a chessboard . . . . The truth is that, to many people calling themselves Socialists, revolution does not mean a movement of the masses with which they hope to associate themselves; it means a set of reforms which 'we', the clever ones, are going to impose upon 'them', the Lower Orders.[45]

Orwell always believed that the ordinary working people had a very different conception of socialism, springing from the immediate experiences of their work and life. It was the conception that he endorsed throughout his life, and it turned on the idea of socialism as 'justice and common decency', as social equality and liberty.[46] Intellectuals, however, were not similarly protected by their way of life from a credulous and uncritical worship of force. They were the natural adherents of the movements that Orwell called 'nationalistic' – fascism, communism, Catholicism, pacifism, among others – and which he glossed as 'power-hunger tempered by self-deception'.[47] They had likewise become the most fervent converts to 'realism', that is, 'the doctrine that might is right'. Observing this in the context of a discussion of the sadistic world of certain popular novels, such as James Hadley Chase's *No Orchids for Miss Blandish*, Orwell commented that 'the interconnexion between sadism, masochism, success worship, power worship, nationalism and totalitarianism is a huge subject whose edges have barely been scratched.' He once more pointed to the affinity of fascism and communism and of both of these to the sado-masochistic world of Chase's novel:

> Fascism is often loosely equated with sadism, but nearly always by people who see nothing wrong in the most slavish worship of Stalin. The truth is, of course, that the countless English intellectuals who kiss the arse of Stalin are not different from the minority who give their allegiance to Hitler or Mussolini, nor from the efficiency experts who preached 'punch', 'drive', 'personality' and 'learn to be a Tiger man' in the nineteen-twenties, nor from the older generation of intellectuals, Carlyle, Creasy and the rest of them, who bowed down before German militarism. All of them are worshipping power and successful cruelty. It is important to notice that the cult of power tends to be mixed up with a love of cruelty and wickedness *for their own sakes* . . . . This idea colours the outlook of all sympathizers with totalitarianism . . . .
>
> [*No Orchids*] is a day-dream appropriate to a totalitarian age. In his imagined world of gangsters Chase is presenting, as it were, a distilled version of the modern political scene, in which such things as mass bombing of civilians, the use of hostages, torture to obtain confessions, secret prisons, execution without trial, floggings with rubber truncheons, drownings in cesspools, systematic falsification of records and statistics, treachery, bribery and quislingism are normal and morally neutral, even admirable when they are done in a large and bold way . . . . People worship power in the form in which they are able to understand it. A twelve-year-old boy worships Jack Dempsey. An adolescent in a Glasgow slum worships Al Capone. An aspiring pupil at a business college worships Lord Nuffield. A *New Statesman* reader worships Stalin. There is a difference in intellectual maturity but none in moral outlook.[48]

We are here of course squarely in the world of *Nineteen Eighty-Four*, and we need now to look a little more closely at what Orwell meant by totalitarianism.

In his understanding of it, he readily admitted his debt to other writers who, like himself, were 'trying to write contemporary history, but *unofficial* history, the kind that is ignored in the textbooks and lied about in the newspapers'. He remarked on the lack in England of 'what one might call concentration camp literature', and the consequent absence of 'a literature of disillusionment about the Soviet Union'. The reason was fairly simple: 'there is almost no English writer to whom it has happened to see totalitarianism from the inside.' Foreigners who had experienced totalitarianism had however done much to fill the gap. Orwell mentions particularly Ignazio Silone, André Malraux, Gaetano Salvemini, Franz Borkenau, Victor Serge and Arthur Koestler. To this list we should certainly add Trotsky and, even more, James Burnham, who provided Orwell with much of the theoretical framework for his analysis of the contemporary world. But for the subjective response, the artistic rendering, of the totalitarian experience, it was to works like Silone's *Fontamara*, Malraux's *Man's Fate* and Borkenau's *The Spanish Cockpit* that we would have to turn. Above all, perhaps, there was Koestler's *Darkness at Noon*, with its powerful and moving depiction of the arrest, interrogation and 'confession' of the Old Bolshevik, Rubashov. As *Nineteen Eighty-Four* shows at several points, Orwell never found a more fully realized account of the mentality – of both victims and executioners – displayed at the great Moscow Trials of 1936–8, when the remnants of the Old Bolsheviks were finally 'liquidated' by Stalin.[49]

But Orwell too had seen 'totalitarianism from the inside', and so was in a position to make his own contribution to the new kind of political literature. In the Spanish Civil War, as a member of the POUM militia, he had glimpsed something of the outlook of all the main totalitarian systems to date – Spanish, Italian, German, Russian. The Spanish experience crystallized decisively for him the political outlook that he was to hold with remarkable consistency for the rest of his life. Up till 1936 Orwell, like most left-wing sympathizers, had seen the main totalitarian threat as lying in fascism. The apocalyptic 'pre-figurations' of *Nineteen Eighty-Four* that are to be found in his early novels, *A Clergyman's Daughter* and *Keep The Aspidistra Flying*, are mostly drawn from the fascist repertoire: 'a thousand million slaves toiling', the stamping boot, the 'lord who rules us blood and hand and brain'. *The Road to Wigan Pier* is largely concerned with the need to prevent the middle classes from going over to fascism, as they are likely to owing to the stupidity and insensitivity of the orthodox socialists. Even as late as 1939, in the novel *Coming Up for Air*, the prophetic images have a mostly Nazi colouring: 'the rubber truncheons, the barbed wire, the coloured shirts, the slogans, the enormous faces, the machine-guns squirting out of bedroom windows'.

But in Spain Orwell had found a more insidious and more threatening enemy: Stalinist communism. 'The Spanish War and the other events of 1936–37 turned the scale and thereafter I knew where I stood.'[50] As a member of POUM he found himself denounced by the Communists in the Republican government as belonging to a Trotskyist 'Fifth Column' operating on behalf of Franco. In June 1937 the Communists launched 'a reign of terror' in Barcelona. Orwell and his wife Ellen barely escaped with their lives across the French frontier. 'When I left Spain in late June the atmosphere in Barcelona, what with the ceaseless arrests, the censored newspapers and the prowling hordes of armed police, was like a nightmare.'[51] Later he was to reflect: 'These man-hunts went on at the same time as the great purges in the USSR, and were a sort of supplement to them.'[52] What was in some ways even more traumatic for Orwell were the lies and suppressions in the left-wing press about what was really going on in Spain, and especially what the Communists were up to. He had great difficulty in telling the English public what he had seen in Spain. Gollancz refused to publish *Homage to Catalonia* – even before seeing it – and the *New Statesman* refused an article on Spain and rejected his review of Borkenau's *The Spanish Cockpit*.[53]

From this time on, there could be no separation in Orwell's mind between the threat posed by Soviet communism and that posed by German and Italian fascism. The usual distinctions between 'left' and 'right' were here meaningless. 'The sin of nearly all left-wingers from 1933 onward is that they have wanted to be anti-Fascist without being anti-totalitarian.'[54] It is in fact quite clear from nearly all of Orwell's later writings that he came to regard Soviet communism as the more menacing of the totalitarian movements. This was partly because, as he often remarked, there were plenty of socialist intellectuals in England to belabour fascism. In England at least, fascism was intellectually a weak force, especially from the late 1930s onwards when a war with Germany seemed to be more or less inevitable. On the other hand, Orwell felt that the bulk of the English intelligentsia had gone over blindly to communism, denying or suppressing the evidence of the reality of Soviet society. All the more reason then for him to turn on Soviet communism, with its spurious claims to be both truly Marxist and the rightful heir of all the democratic and progressive movements of the nineteenth century. This was not just a task of intellectual and moral honesty. It was as a committed socialist that Orwell most felt the need to expose 'the Soviet myth'. 'In my opinion, nothing has contributed so much to the corruption of the original idea of socialism as the belief that Russia is a Socialist country and that every act of its rulers must be excused, if not imitated.' Hence, he wrote, explaining his purpose in *Animal Farm*,

> It was of the utmost importance to me that people in western Europe should see the Soviet regime for what it really was. Since 1930 I had seen little evidence that the USSR was progressing towards anything that one could truly call Socialism. On the contrary, I was struck by clear signs of its transformation into a hierarchical society, in which the rulers have no more reason to give up their power than any other ruling class.[55]

By 1948, Hitler and Mussolini were both dead and fascism defeated. With Roosevelt also dead and Churchill out of office – and a Labour government in power – of the 'Big Three' who had determined the fate of the world in the past few years, only Stalin was left. Orwell must have felt that the need to expose the Soviet myth was even more urgent. Russian power dominated most of eastern and central Europe: 'Eurasia' was in the process of formation. 'Throughout eastern Europe,' wrote Orwell, 'there is a "revolution from above", imposed by the Russians, which probably benefits the poorer peasants but kills in advance any possibility of democratic Socialism.'[56] And yet it was a grave error on the part of so many critics to see *Nineteen Eighty-Four* as directed mainly at and against the Soviet Union. Well before the outbreak of the Second World War, Orwell had identified totalitarianism as a new species of politics, encompassing both the actual movements of fascism and communism as well as certain other widespread tendencies in modern industrial societies. His first impulse, before the Spanish experience, was to see the new totalitarianism in the image of a fascism grown into a world-system, 'a totalitarian world':

The advance of machine-technique must lead ultimately to some form of collectivism, but that form need not necessarily be equalitarian; that is, it need not be Socialism. *Pace* the economists, is quite easy to imagine a world-society, economically collectivist – that is, with the profit principle eliminated – but with all political, military, and educational power in the hands of a small caste of rulers and their bravos. That or something like it is the objective of Fascism. And that, of course, is the slave-state, or rather the slave-world; it would probably be a stable form of society, and the chances are, considering the enormous wealth of the world if scientifically exploited, that the slaves would be well-fed and contented.[57]

Less than two years later, shortly after his return from Spain, Orwell was noting the striking similarities between fascism and communism. In a review of a book about the Soviet Union by an American journalist Eugene Lyons, he wrote:

The system that Mr Lyons describes does not seem to be very different from Fascism. All real power is concentrated in the hands of two or three million people, the town proletariat, theoretically the heirs of the revolution, having been robbed even of the elementary right to strike; more recently, by the introduction of the internal passport system, they have been reduced to a status resembling serfdom. The GPU are everywhere, everyone lives in constant terror of denunciation, freedom of speech and of the press are obliterated to an extent we can hardly imagine. There are periodical waves of terror, sometimes the 'liquidation' of kulaks or Nepmen, sometimes some monstrous state trial at which people who have been in prison for months or years are suddenly dragged forth to make incredible confessions, while their children publish articles in the newspaper saying 'I repudiate my father as a Trotskyist serpent.' Meanwhile the invisible Stalin is worshipped in terms that would make Nero blush.[58]

In the same year – 1938 – Orwell's friend Jack Common, in a book which Orwell reviewed, saw a merging of nazism and Bolshevism into 'pyramidal states of negative socialism'.[59] Bertrand Russell's *Power* (1939) made the similar point that this was an age of dictatorships, but Orwell took him to task for his conventionally liberal view that, as in the past, these dictatorships must collapse.

Underlying this is the idea that common sense always wins in the end. And yet the peculiar horror of the present moment is that we cannot be sure that this is so. It is quite possible that we are descending into an age in which two and two will make five when the Leader says so . . . . It is quite easy to imagine a state in which the ruling caste deceive their followers without deceiving themelves. Dare anyone be sure that something of the kind is not coming into existence already?[60]

Another book about Russia, expressing the same sort of liberal faith as Russell's, gave Orwell the opportunity of stating even more strongly the conviction that '"the truth is great and will prevail" is a prayer rather than an axiom.'

The terrifying thing about the modern dictatorships is that they are something entirely unprecedented. Their end cannot be foreseen. In the past every tyranny was sooner or later overthrown, or at least resisted, because of 'human nature', which as a matter of course desired liberty. But we cannot be at all certain that 'human nature' is constant. It may be just as possible to produce a breed of men who do not wish for liberty as to produce a breed of hornless cows. The Inquisition failed, but then the Inquisition had not the resources of the modern state. The radio, press censorship, standardized education and the secret police have altered everything. Mass suggestion is a science of the last twenty-years, and we do not yet know how successful it will be.[61]

It was the Hitler–Stalin pact of 1939, thought Orwell, that finally forced people to see that nazism and communism were no more than variants of a single type. Up till then, thinkers of both right and left had argued that nazism was simply an extreme form of capitalism, 'capitalism with the lid off'. It was neither revolutionary nor, despite the party's name, had it anything to do with socialism. The Russo-German pact exploded this 'Strachey–Blimp' thesis. 'National Socialism *is* a form of Socialism, *is* emphatically revolutionary, *does* crush the property owner just as surely as it crushes the worker. The two regimes having started from opposite ends, are rapidly evolving towards the same system – a form of oligarchical collectivism.' Russia, it appeared, had the purer form of the new system, as, pushed further by its war effort, 'it is Germany that is moving towards Russia, rather than the other way about.' But it was of the essence of the Nazi system that this was a matter of supreme indifference to its leaders.

When the State has taken complete control of industry, then the so-called capitalist is reduced to the status of a manager, and when consumption goods are so scarce and so strictly rationed that you cannot spend a big income even if you earn one, then the essential structure of socialism already exists, plus the comfortless equality of war-Communism. Simply in the interest of efficiency the Nazis found themselves expropriating, nationalizing, destroying the very people they had set out to save. It did not bother them, because their aim was simply power and not any particular form of society.[62]

As the world war deepened, Orwell's view of the future became increasingly gloomy.

This is the age of the totalitarian state . . . . When one mentions totalitarianism one thinks immediately of Germany, Russia, Italy, but I think one must face the risk that this phenomenon is going to be world-wide. It is obvious that the period of free capitalism is coming to an end and that one country after another is adopting a centralized economy that one can call Socialism or state capitalism according as one prefers. With that the economic liberty of the individual, and to a great extent the liberty to do what he likes, to choose his own work, to move to and fro across the surface of the earth, comes to an end.[63]

To a *Tribune* reader who pressed the claims of Aldous Huxley's view of the future on him, he replied with a direct statement of the main theme of *Nineteen Eighty-Four*:

I think you overestimate the danger of a 'Brave New World' – i.e. a completely materialistic vulgar civilization based on hedonism. I would say that the danger of that kind of thing is past and that we are in danger of quite a different kind of world, the centralized slave state, ruled over by a small clique who are in effect a new ruling class, though they might be adoptive rather than hereditary. Such a state would not be hedonistic; on the contrary, its dynamic would come from some kind of rabid nationalism and leader worship kept going by literally continuous war . . . .[64]

It is clear that, by the end of the war, Orwell had already developed a fairly definite idea of the main political structure of *Nineteen Eighty-Four*. But he had also gone further. It was, ultimately, the capacity of totalitarian systems to control not just the external but the internal world of men that most frightened Orwell. 'The totalitarian state tries . . . . to control the thoughts and emotions of its subjects at least as completely as it controls their actions.'[65] The belief of many artists and intellectuals that, whatever the external world of censorship and repression, they could be free 'inside', to pursue their own private thoughts, he regarded as 'a very dangerous fallacy'. Whatever the practical truth of this belief under old-fashioned despotisms, with their many loopholes, the superior efficiency of modern totalitarian systems would show its essential falsity.

The greatest mistake is to imagine that the human being is an autonomous individual. The secret freedom which you can supposedly enjoy under a despotic government is nonsense, because your thoughts are never entirely your own. Philosophers, writers, artists, even scientists, not only need encouragement and an audience, they need constant stimulation from other people. It is almost impossible to think without talking. If Defoe had really lived on a desert island, he could not have written *Robinson Crusoe*, nor would he have wanted to. Take away freedom of speech, and the creative faculties dry up . . . . When the lid is taken off Europe, I believe one of the things that will surprise us will be to find how little worth-while writing of any kind – even such things as diaries, for instance – has been produced in secret under the dictators.[66]

The totalitarian ideologies – whether Fascist, Communist or Catholic – claimed possession of the absolute truth about the world. The Party or the Church was the sole repository of that truth. Its actions, however mysterious or even perverse they may at times seem to the member, were not to be questioned. All deviations from the orthodox interpretations were therefore heretical, if not actually criminal. The Party must be given complete freedom in the accomplishment of its purpose. It can lie, distort, suppress and generally treat the past and the external world as if they had no objective reality but were no more than the raw material of the Party's unchallengeable strategy. This was not merely a matter of opportunism and expediency:

It is something integral to totalitarianism . . . . From the totalitarian point of view history is something to be created rather than learned. A totalitarian state is in effect a theocracy, and its ruling caste, in order to keep its position, has to be thought of as infallible. But since, in practice, no one is infallible, it is frequently necessary to re-arrange past events in order to show that this or that mistake was not made, or that this or that imaginary triumph actually happened . . . . Totalitarianism demands, in fact, the continuous alteration of the past, and in the long run probably demands a disbelief in the very existence of objective truth.[67]

This need for tactical flexibility means that totalitarianism is not content, like the orthodoxies of the past, to fix the framework of the subject's thoughts for the whole of his life – as is the case with most of the organized religions, past and present. 'The peculiarity of the totalitarian state is that, though it controls thought, it does not fix it. It sets up unquestionable dogmas, and it alters them from day to day.'[68] What is new in totalitarianism is that its doctrines are not only unchallengeable but also unstable. The members of a totalitarian state have to accept one thing today, and a quite different thing tomorrow, to regard the Nazis with unspeakable horror at one moment and to accept them as comrades-in-arms the next. In this sense, 'totalitarianism does not so much promise an age of faith as an age of schizophrenia.'[69] In their acceptance of this attitude to reality, the intellectuals, who of all groups should be the defenders of the concepts of truth and objectivity, show their greatest capitulation to totalitarianism.

It is here, at the deepest level of the attitude to reality and the mode of its manipulation, that totalitarianism most shows its essentially modern, contemporary aspect. The past had known orthodoxy and autocracy; it had not known totalitarianism.

The despotisms of the past were not totalitarian. Their repressive apparatus was always inefficient, their ruling classes were usually either corrupt or apathetic or half-liberal in outlook, and the prevailing religious doctrines usually worked against perfectionism and the notion of human infallibility.[70]

Goldstein's book also emphasizes the novelty of the society of *Nineteen Eighty-Four*: 'By comparison with that existing today, all the tyrannies of the past were half-hearted and inefficient' (*NEF*, p. 165). At the same time he makes it clear that it was the actual historical systems of totalitarianism, 'which had appeared earlier in the century', which established the basic pattern of the new society. There is no reason to doubt that, for his picture of the totalitarian world of *Nineteen Eighty-Four*, Orwell drew largely on his understanding of German nazism and Russian communism. Practically every feature of the internal order of Oceania had been touched on by him in his essays and reviews of the previous 12 years dealing with those systems. It is also equally clear that Orwell felt free to intensify and exaggerate a good number of these features, as well as to elaborate on them with material drawn from some of his other concerns. That this sometimes obscured the relation of Oceania to the real movements and tendencies of his time was one of the penalties of the utopian genre he worked in; although critics seem to have wanted to add to this obscurity excessively. In any case, if pushed on this point Orwell could have fallen back on an admired and highly appropriate model: Jonathan Swift. Swift, he said, 'did not possess ordinary wisdom, but he did possess a terrible intensity of vision, capable of picking out a single hidden truth and then magnifying and distorting it'.[71] Just how far Orwell himself may have distorted as well as magnified the real world of people and politics is something we will need to come to presently.

THE WORLD OF OCEANIA: NEWSPEAK AND DOUBLETHINK

Following James Burnam's lead in *The Managerial Revolution* (1941), Orwell in *Nineteen Eighty-Four* presents a world divided up into three super-states: Oceania, a creation of the United States and including the Americas, the British Isles, Australasia and the southern portion of Africa; Eurasia, forged by Russia and comprising 'the whole of the northern part of the European and Asiatic land-mass, from Portugal to the Bering Strait'; and Eastasia, mainly China and Japan with a 'large but fluctuating portion of Manchuria, Mongolia, and Tibet'. Towards the end of the Second World War Orwell had become increasingly convinced that this would be the future world system. Indeed, in a letter to his publisher Roger Senhouse, correcting a misleading 'blurb', he singled out that prospect as one of the two main themes of *Nineteen Eighty-Four*:

> What it is really meant to do is to discuss the implications of dividing the world up into 'Zones of influence' (I thought of it in 1944 as a result of the Teheran Conference), and in addition to indicate by parodying them the intellectual implications of totalitarianism.[72]

The advent of the atom bomb, Orwell felt, made this prospect more rather than less probable. Given the great expense and industrial effort needed to manufacture the bomb, it was likely that only three or four countries would be capable of making it. This point was of 'cardinal importance, because it may mean that the discovery of the atomic bomb, so far from reversing history, will simply intensify the trends which have been apparent for a dozen years past'. Orwell expected that the 'two or three monstrous super-states' which possessed the bomb would use its threat to divide the world between them, while at the same time making 'a tacit agreement never to use the atomic bomb against each other'. The world situation would then bear a remarkable resemblance to that anticipated by Burnham in *The Managerial Revolution*, with the relatively minor modifications necessary due to the defeat of Germany and Japan.

> For Burnham's geographical picture of the new world has turned out to be correct. More and more obviously the surface of the earth is being parcelled off into three great empires, each self-contained and cut off from contact with the outer world, and each ruled, under one disguise or another, by a self-elected oligarchy.[73]

In the year that he was working on the first draft of *Nineteen Eighty-Four*, Orwell reverted to the possibility of the tacit agreement between the possessing powers not to use the atom bomb, and elaborated on the likely consequences of this.

> It would mean the division of the world among two or three vast super-states, unable to conquer one another and unable to be overthrown by an internal rebellion. In all

probability their structure would be hierarchic, with a semi-divine caste at the top and outright slavery at the bottom, and the crushing out of liberty would exceed anything that the world has yet seen. Within each state the necessary psychological atmosphere would be kept up by complete severance from the outer world, and by a continuously phony war against rival states. Civilizations of this type might remain static for thousands of years.[74]

It is this possibility, which Orwell seems to have considered worse than an atomic war which wiped out 'machine civilization', that has been fully realized in *Nineteen Eighty-Four.* There has indeed been a brief atomic exchange, but its consequences were so appalling that the super-powers have rapidly come to the kind of agreement contemplated by Orwell. But, as Goldstein's book explains, this does not of course mean no war. On the contrary, it means permanent and continuous war. But since the super-states cannot conquer each other, and moreover have no wish really to do so, the war is deliberately limited and controlled. It uses only conventional weapons, and it takes place almost entirely outside the heartlands of the three great northern powers that control the world. 'In the centres of civilization war means no more than a continuous shortage of consumption goods, and the occasional crash of a rocket bomb which may cause a few scores of deaths.' The violence has largely been exported to the poorer southern hemispheric regions of the world – equatorial Africa, the Middle East, southern India and the Indonesian archipelago. Here the three super-powers conduct their never-ending war, and the native populations of these areas pass from one conqueror to another. Alliances change ceaselessly. But no one power ever wins, or even seems to want to win, a permanent advantage: 'the balance of power always remains roughly even, and the territory which forms the heartland of each super-state always remains inviolate' (*NEF*, pp. 151–2).

The ostensible reason for the war is economic: to gain control of valuable raw materials and, more especially, to exploit the cheap labour abundantly available in the poverty-stricken areas where the war rages. The leaders of the three super-states quite genuinely believe this; but, in a typical act of 'doublethink', they also know that no one of them actually needs the raw materials, nor even the cheap labour power of the natives. The super-states have established self-contained economies in which production and consumption are geared to one another; among their own vast territories they can obtain practically all the raw materials they need. The labour of the natives in any case is used up almost entirely in the production of war materials which are consumed in further warfare. What, then, is the main reason for the continuous phony war? It is political and psychological. The primary aim of the war – and the leaders are conscious of this as well – is 'to use up the products of the machine without raising the general standard of living'. The disposing of the surplus of consumption goods had been the central problem of industrial society since the late nineteenth century. The early socialists had seen the great productivity of the machine as the answer to the age-old problem of human drudgery and inequality; and indeed, more or less automatically, in the last part of the nineteenth century and the beginning of the twentieth, the general standard of living of the population went up considerably. But this tendency was profoundly alarming to the elites of the existing hierarchical society. A general increase in wealth, even if not accompanied by any significant redistribution of power, threatened the long-term stability of their hierarchical society.

For if leisure and security were enjoyed by all alike, the great mass of human beings who are normally stupefied by poverty would become literate and would learn to think for themselves; and when once they had done this, they would sooner or later realize that the privileged minority had no function, and they would sweep it away. In the long run, a hierarchical society was only possible on a basis of poverty and ignorance. (*NEF*, p. 154)

The expedient, first tried, of keeping the masses in poverty by restricting the output of goods was disastrous. The economic slump of the 1920s and 1930s forced millions of people to live off state charity and stirred up opposition because the privations inflicted were so obviously unnecessary; moreover, it entailed the military weakness of the state. 'The problem was how to keep the wheels of industry turning without increasing the real wealth of the world. Goods must be produced, but they must not be distributed.' The answer was continuous warfare. In principle, 'the war effort is always so planned as to eat up any surplus that might exist after meeting the bare needs of the population.' In practice, 'the needs of the population are always underestimated, with the result that there is a chronic shortage of half the necessities of life.' But this too has advantages. The general scarcity of goods increases the importance of small luxuries and privileges, and therefore magnifies the distinction between groups – especially between Party members and the proles. 'The social atmosphere is that of a besieged city, where the possession of a lump of horseflesh makes the difference between wealth and poverty.' Generally, the war atmosphere has the healthy effect of keeping everyone keyed-up and on their toes; and the sense of danger which it generates makes the handing-over of all power to a small caste seem natural and inevitable.

The war therefore has a psychological as well as a political function. But this is aimed not so much at the population in general – the morale of the masses is not of great importance – as at the Party members. The average Party member is expected to be competent and industrious, but 'it is also necessary that he should be a credulous and ignorant fanatic whose prevailing moods are fear, hatred, adulation, and orgiastic triumph. In other words it is necessary that he should have the mentality appropriate to a state of war.' The higher up the Party one goes, the more marked this mentality. 'It is precisely in the Inner Party that war hysteria and hatred of the enemy are strongest.' Inner Party members know that in some sense the war is phony and unnecessary; but it is also important, for psychological reasons, that they should also genuinely feel that there is a life-and-death struggle going on. The technique of 'double-think' neutralizes this contradiction. 'No Inner Party member wavers for an instant in his mystical belief that the war *is* real, and that it is bound to end victoriously, with Oceania the undisputed master of the entire world' (*NEF*, 156).

What keeps the war in being, and upholds the whole structure of world power, is the fact that each super-state is a more or less exact replica of the others. The requirements are therefore in each case much the same. This fact has to be concealed from their populations, lest the fear and hatred on which their commitment depends might evaporate. Hence citizens of the three super-states are forbidden all contact with each other, and are not allowed to learn foreign languages. Consequently they do not realize that the ideology of Oceania, Ingsoc, is scarcely to be distinguished from the ideology of Eurasia, Neo-Bolshevism, or from that of Eastasia, 'Death-Worship' (the literal meaning of the Chinese term, 'better rendered as Obliteration of the Self'). Similarly, these ideologies support identical social systems. 'Everywhere there is the same pyramidal structure, the same worship of a semi-divine leader, the same economy existing by and for continuous warfare.' The three super-states therefore not only cannot conquer one another, they would gain no advantage from doing so. On the contrary, in the interests of their own internal hierarchical structure they need a state of permanent war. 'So long as they remain in conflict they prop one another up, like three sheaves of corn' (*NEF*, p. 159).

In the new age, the whole nature and meaning of war has changed. In the past, ruling groups, although recognizing their common interest, really did fight against each other for conquest. Wars had a definite beginning and end. Now war is 'a purely internal affair'. Ruling groups are not fighting against each other at all. 'The war is waged by each ruling group against its own subjects, and the object of the war is not to make or prevent conquests of territory, but to keep the structure of society intact.' Hence the war has to be continuous and, being so, it is scarcely any longer war at all, in the usual sense. Or perhaps it would be better to say that the distinction between war and peace has been obliterated for all practical purposes. So long as the internal controls remained efficient, it would make no difference if the three super-states, instead of fighting each other, agreed to live in perpetual peace, each inviolate within its own boundaries. 'For in that case each would still be a self-contained universe . . . . A peace that was truly permanent would be the same as a permanent war.' Precisely that thought occurs to Julia, with her down-to-earth scepticism of Party propaganda. She tells a surprised Winston that she does not believe there is a war. 'The rocket bombs which fell daily on London were probably fired by the government of Oceania itself, "just to keep the people frightened"' (*NEF*, p. 125). Whatever the confusion of other Party members, Julia at least understands 'the inner meaning of the Party slogan: *War is Peace*' (*NEF*, p. 161).

The first thing that must surely strike anyone about this virtuoso account – making the necessary allowances for its satiric intent – is how astonishingly good it is as prophecy. It is true that Orwell was able to see the origins of the Cold War during his own lifetime, but it was a bold stroke to work out its implications for international conflict in the way that he did. In the past 40 years, the super-powers have indeed refrained from the use of atomic weapons, but they have certainly not refrained from war. There has been what can fairly be called a 'Third World War' continuously going on since 1948. As Orwell saw, this war has not been fought in the territories of the super-powers or their main allies (organized in the NATO and Warsaw Pact alliances), but it has been exported to the countries of what it has become common to call the 'Third World'. The super-powers have conducted their wars in Cuba and Nicaragua, in Ethiopia and Mozambique, in Egypt and Lebanon, in Korea and Vietnam, and in a score of other countries in the poorer sections of the globe. In the middle of 1984 there were, according to the Secretary-General of the United Nations, at least 40 wars officially – and many more 'unofficially' – raging in various parts of the world.

Moreover, the most striking recent development on the international scene has moved us even closer to *Nineteen Eighty-Four*. Since the 1950s, two super-powers, the United States and the Soviet Union, have dominated the international system. But in the early 1970s President Nixon and his Secretary of State Henry Kissinger moved to bring China into the system as a third protagonist, and later Presidents have continued this policy of détente with China. The aim of this strategy, as Gordon Craig has explained, was not simply to put pressure on the Soviet Union but to introduce 'a triangular balance-of-power politics in which the United States, as *tertius gaudens*, maintained friendly relations with both the Soviet Union and the People's Republic of China, ideological antagonists not only of each other but of the United States as well'. Such a triangular system of mutually reinforcing but also mutually inhibiting antagonisms is of course exactly the one described in Goldstein's book. Craig interestingly remarks of this model that 'from the inherent weaknesses that vitiated all of the historical models of international order, this one is free, and there is no logical reason why it shouldn't continue forever.'[75]

Scarcely less convincing is Orwell's account of the motivation of war: the consumption of 'surplus' products and maintenance of the social order. Much of the employment, investment, research and development of the last 40 years have gone into armaments – under a variety of Orwellian names ranging from communications technology to space exploration. The 'arms race' between the super-powers has been one of the major causes of economic growth since the war. But while some of that growth has percolated through to the population at large, a good part of it is consumed, as in *Nineteen Eighty-Four*, in war. The United States during the Vietnam War dropped a greater tonnage of bombs than was expended by all combatants during the entire Second World War. And where the great powers do not use up war goods themselves, they have been assiduous in selling them to any and all comers, or giving them to favoured allies. Nothing more clearly indicates the involvement of the super-powers in the wars of the Third World than that they are fought almost exclusively with their weapons. Taking the whole period since the war, there has probably never before in history been the creation and destruction of wealth on so massive a scale. The political and psychological effects of the arms race and super-power rivalry have been equally clear for all to see: 'red scares' and McCarthyite witch-hunts on the one side, the suppression of all 'bourgeois' freedom of expression and liberal experimentation on the other. The leaders of the 'free world' and the 'workers' republics' are only too well aware of the benefits of their public displays of mutal hatred and paranoiac hysteria, whether truly felt or expediently assumed.

Thus far, considering the international system in the broadest terms, the world of 1984 is uncannily close to that of *Nineteen Eighty-Four*. What of the internal strucure of Oceania? In one of his discussions of Burnham's view of the coming world system, Orwell had remarked:

> James Burnham's theory has been much discussed, but few people have yet considered its ideological implications – that is, the kind of world-view, the kind of beliefs, and the social structure that would probably prevail in a state which was at once unconquerable and in a permanent state of 'cold war' with its neighbours.[76]

In *Nineteen Eighty-Four* Orwell set himself the task of showing just those 'ideological implications'. He again borrowed from Burnham's analysis of contemporary society in *The Managerial Revolution* and *The Machiavellians*,[77] although as we have seen he had himself reached a substantially similar view of the advent of world-wide 'oligarchical collectivism' well before his reading of Burnham. Chapter 1 of Goldstein's book sets out the main features of Oceania society. In the most ambitious and far-reaching social experiment yet attempted, Oceania is trying to freeze for ever one phase of a pattern or cycle which has recurred throughout history. In all societies hitherto, people have been divided up into three main social groups, the High, the Middle and the Low. This is 'the essential structure of society' and it has never altered. 'Even after enormous upheavals and seemingly irrevocable changes, the same pattern has always reasserted itself, just as a gyroscope will always return to equilibrium, however far it is pushed one way or the other.' What generally produces these upheavals are the attempts by the Middle to displace the High and establish a new equilibrium, with themselves in control. The High can resist these attempts for long periods, but inevitably there comes a time when their self-confidence and capacity to govern weaken, and they are overthrown. In their bid for power the Middle generally engage the Low on their side, with the promise of establishing a just and free society. For in so far as the Low have an aim – 'it is an abiding characteristic of the Low that they are too much crushed by drudgery to be more than intermittently conscious of anything outside their daily lives' – it is 'to abolish all distinctions and create a society in which all men shall be equal'. But once the Middle have securely established themselves as the new High, they invariably betray their erstwhile allies, the Low, and reduce them once more to servitude. This has been and always will be their status in history. 'No advance in wealth, no softening of manners, no reform or revolution has ever brought human equality a millimetre nearer. From the point of view of the Low, no historic change has ever meant much more than a change in the name of their masters' (*NEF*, pp. 162–3).

In the nineteenth century, it had appeared to some that for the first time this elemental pattern might be broken. Machine production promised to equalize social and economic levels without causing a loss of culture and civilization. The early Socialists had preached just this: inequality was an historical phenomenon, not an unalterable necessity of the human condition. But a later generation of Socialists, influenced perhaps by certain 'elite theorists', had begun to expound a view of Socialism which declared that equality was impossible and democracy a myth. These Socialists, speaking on behalf of new Middle groups, 'in effect proclaimed their tyranny in advance', unlike all previous Middle groups. The new movements which appeared in the middle years of the twentieth century – Ingsoc, Neo-Bolshevism, Death-Worship – had the 'conscious aim of perpetuating *un*freedom and *in*equality'. They kept the names and something of the ideologies of the older movements that they grew out of.

> But the purpose of all of them was to arrest progress and freeze history at the chosen moment. The familiar pendulum swing was to happen once more, and then stop. As usual, the High were to be turned out by the Middle, who would then become the High; but this time, by conscious strategy, the High would be able to maintain their position permanently. (*NEF*, p. 163).

The votaries of Ingsoc that have come to power in Oceania – 'after a decade of national wars, civil wars, revolutions, and counter-revolutions' – are the very same salaried middle-class professionals singled out by James Burnham as constituting the managerial oligarchy of the new post-capitalist civilization. The new High are made up 'for the most part of bureaucrats, scientists, technicians, trade-union organizers, publicity experts, sociologists, teachers, journalists, and professional politicians' (*NEF*, p. 164). They are the product of the 'barren world of monopoly industry and centralized government'. These are also the intellectuals that Orwell constantly inveighed against for their 'slavish russophilia', and whose attraction to the totalitarian outlook became something of an obsession with him in his last years. (He mentions this theme in *every* direct comment on *Nineteen Eighty-Four*.) He identified them as 'middling people who feel themselves cramped by a system that is still partly aristocratic, and are hungry for more power and more prestige'.

> These people look towards the USSR and see in it, or think they see, a system which eliminates the upper class, keeps the working class in its place, and hands unlimited power to people very similar to themselves .... Burnham, although the English russophile intelligentsia would repudiate him, is really voicing their secret wish: the wish to destroy the old, equalitarian version of Socialism and usher in a hierarchical society where the intellectual can at last get his hands on the whip.[78]

The new High employ many of the old techniques of repression – torture, public executions – to safeguard their position. But being intellectuals, they differ from past ruling groups not simply in their greater hunger for power but in their greater consciousness of what they are doing and what they must do to perpetuate their rule. They realized, for instance, that 'the only secure basis for oligarchy is collectivism. Wealth and privilege are most easily defended when they are possessed jointly.' Individually, no Party member owns anything, but collectively 'the Party owns everything in Oceania, because it controls everything, and disposes of the product as it thinks fit.'[79] The capitalists have been expropriated, but the Socialism which has followed is very different from the egalitarian kind preached by the early Socialists. 'Ingsoc, which grew out of the earlier Socialist movement and inherited its phraseology, has in fact carried out the main item in the Socialist programme; with the result, foreseen and intended beforehand, that economic inequality has been made permanent' (*NEF*, p. 166).

The general trappings and techniques of the totalitarian state established by the intelligentsia are fairly evidently taken from Nazi and Communist practice. There is the calculated and pervasive atmosphere of fear and distrust of everyone, even and especially one's friends and family. There are the 'gorilla-faced guards in black uniforms, armed with jointed truncheons', who roam outside the Ministry of Love, home of the dreaded Thought Police. There are the Party slogans plastered everywhere: 'War is Peace', 'Freedom is Slavery', 'Ignorance is Strength'. And there is the piercing, watchful gaze of Big Brother, pursuing and seeking one out everywhere. 'On coins, on stamps, on the covers of books, on banners, on posters, and on the wrappings of a cigarette packet – everwhere. Always the eyes watching you and the voice enveloping you. Asleep or awake, working or eating, indoors or out of doors, in the bath or in bed – no escape' (*NEF*, p. 25).

No more is there any escape from the regular ceremony of the Two Minutes Hate, featuring Emmanuel Goldstein, 'the Enemy of the People', author of the heretical 'book' and leader of the underground Brotherhood dedicated to the overthrow of the State. The telescreens simultaneously show threatening and fearful images of whichever super-state – Eurasia or Eastasia – Oceania happens to be at war with at the time, linking Goldstein with the hated enemy. During the Two Minutes Hate 'a hideous ecstasy of fear and vindictiveness, a desire to kill, to torture, to smash faces in with a sledge-hammer, seemed to flow through the whole group like an electric current, turning one even against one's will into a grimacing, screaming lunatic.' But always at the end of each session, as a sort of cathartic release, there appears the consoling face of Big Brother, 'black-haired, black-moustachio'd, full of power and mysterious calm, and so vast that it almost filled up the screen'. This occasions among the watching people, in a manner reminiscent of *Brave New World's* 'orgy-porgy' ceremony, a slow rhythmical chant of 'B-B! . . . B-B! . . . a heavy, murmurous sound, somehow curiously savage, in the background of which one seemed to hear the stamp of naked feet and the throbbing of tom-toms' (*NEF*, p. 17).

For the children and young people – as with the Hitler Youth and the Soviet Young Pioneers – there are the Spies, the Youth League and the Junior Anti-Sex League. Children are encouraged to spy on everybody, especially their own parents. 'It was almost normal for people over thirty to be frightened of their own children.' With good reason, as the case of Winston's neighbour, the egregious Parsons, shows. Parsons is denounced to the Thought Police by his young daughter for the 'thoughtcrime' of babbling 'Down with Big Brother' in his sleep.

Oceania has indeed carried surveillance of the population far beyond the point capable of being reached by even the most despotic tyranny of old. Spies and *agents provocateurs*, such as O'Brien and Mr Charrington, the mild-mannered owner of the junk-shop, are everywhere. The omnipresent two-way telescreens, which can never be switched off, allow for 24-hour-a-day surveillance. These, together with the rest of the police apparatus, enable the Thought Police to keep the tightest control over the people whose commitment and loyalty matter most: the Party members.

A Party member lives from birth to death under the eye of the Thought Police. Even when he is alone he can never be sure that he is alone. Wherever he may be, asleep or awake, working or resting, in his bath or in bed, he can be inspected without warning and without knowing that he is being inspected. Nothing that he does is indifferent. His friendships, his relaxations, his behaviour towards his wife and children, the expression of his face when he is alone, the words he mutters in sleep, even the characteristic movements of his body, are all jealously scrutinized. Not only any actual misdemeanour, but any eccentricity, however small, any change of habits, any nervous mannerism that could possibly be the symptom to an inner struggle, is certain to be detected. He has no freedom of choice in any direction whatever'. (*NEF*, p. 168)

The minute surveillance of Party members is crucial to the stability of the social order of Oceania. For the threat to that stability can only come from within the Party itself. Of all the factors that have caused the downfall of ruling groups in the past, this is now the only one that matters to the oligarchy. Conquest by a foreign power is no longer a threat owing to the stabilization of the world-system. A revolt of the masses is a theoretical but not a practical possibility. For, says Goldstein's book, 'the masses never revolt of their own accord, and they never revolt merely because they are oppressed.' In fact, without 'standards of comparison' they never even become aware that they are oppressed. So long as the government does not allow large-scale economic crises to develop – as it did during the 'great slump' of the 1930s – discontent will not become articulate and the masses will present no danger. The consciousness of the masses needs to be influenced only in 'a negative way', as for instance by keeping up the war scare and instilling fear of a foreign enemy. From the point of view of the present rulers, therefore, 'the only genuine dangers are the splitting-off of a new group of able, under-employed, power-hungry people, and the growth of liberalism and scepticism in their own ranks.' The problem, that is to say, is 'educational'. 'It is a problem of continuously moulding the consciousness both of the directing group and of the larger executive group that lies immediately below it' (*NEF*, p. 166).

Thus put, the problem of social control in Oceania resolves itself into a concentration on a remarkably small proportion of the population. At the apex of the pyramidal social structure is Big Brother: infallible, omniscient, all-powerful – and invisible. It is even suggested that he will never die, 'and there is already considerable uncertainty as to when he was born.' He may or may not exist in person: Winston Smith gets a characteristically equivocal reply from O'Brien to this question (*NEF*, p. 208). His function is in any case exclusively symbolic. 'Big Brother is the guise in which the Party chooses to exhibit itself to the world. His function is to act as a focusing point for love, fear and reverence, emotions which are more easily felt towards an individual than towards an organization' (*NEF*, p. 167).

Beneath Big Brother come the Party members, comprising in all no more than about 15 per cent of the population. Most of these are members of the Outer Party, with a small group, amounting to less than 2 per cent of the population of Oceania, forming the Inner Party. If the Inner Party represents the 'brain of the State', and the Outer Party its hands, the proles, who make up the remaining 85 per cent of the population, are presumably its feet – certainly the new Low. In principle, membership of these three groups is not hereditary. There are open competitive examinations for admission to either branch of the Party. In practice, however, proletarians never graduate to Party membership, and even between the Inner and the Outer Party there is only limited interchange. The appearance therefore is of a rigidly stratified, caste-like, hereditary social structure. But it would be wrong to regard the Party as a ruling class in the traditional sense of the word 'class'. It does not aim at transmitting power to its own children, and it would, if necessary to maintain its efficiency, be perfectly prepared to recruit an entire new generation from the ranks of the proletariat. The fact that the Party is an adoptive rather than an hereditary oligarchy is in fact its great strength: as witness the long-lasting quality of an adoptive organization such as the Catholic Church, compared with hereditary aristocracies.

The essence of oligarchical rule is not father-to-son inheritance, but the persistence of a certain world-view and a certain way of life, imposed by the dead upon the living. A ruling group is a ruling group so long as it can nominate its successors. The Party is not concerned with perpetuating its blood but with perpetuating itself. *Who* wields power is not important, provided that the hierarchical structure remains always the same. (*NEF*, p. 168)

It is thus on 'the beliefs, habits, tastes, emotions and mental attitudes' of its own members, the top 15 per cent of Oceania's population, that the Party has to focus. The attention has to be the closer, the orthodoxy more rigid, because there are no laws in Oceania. In his essay on Swift, Orwell had remarked on the totalitarian tendencies of societies such as that of the Houyhnhnms, which are not governed by systems of law but appeal to the self-evident dictates of 'Reason', which are supposedly voluntarily accepted by everyone. It was because this feature was especially marked in most anarchist and pacifist visions of society that Orwell, to the distress of some of his friends, found them 'implicitly' totalitatian.

In a society in which there is no law, and in theory no compulsion, the only arbiter of behaviour is public opinion. But public opinion, because of the tremendous urge to conformity in gregarious animals, is less tolerant than any system of law. When human beings are governed by 'thou shalt not', the individual can practice a certain amount of eccentricity: when they are supposedly governed by 'love' or 'reason', he is under continuous pressure to make him behave and think in exactly the same way as everyone else. The Houyhnhnms, we are told, were unanimous on almost all subjects . . . . They had apparently no word for 'opinion' in their language, and in their conversations there was no 'difference of sentiments'. They had reached, in fact, the highest stage of totalitarian organization, the stage where conformity has become so general that there is no need for a police force.[80]

Oceania does of course only too palpably have a state and a police force. But the interesting thing to notice is that its long-term aim is to dispense more or less completely with them, exactly as in anarchist or Houyhnhnm society. This has nothing to do with doctrines of 'the withering away of the state', at least as understood in traditional socialist theory. The Party in Oceania makes no pretence of that. But in another, typically distorted, sense of the old socialist slogan – in what Goldstein would call its 'inner meaning' – it does come to something like that. Irving Howe has reminded us that 'the world of *Nineteen Eighty-Four* is *not* totalitarianism as we know it, but totalitarianism after its world triumph. Strictly speaking, the society of Oceania might be called post-totalitarian.'[81] Put another way, Oceania is the society of *Animal Farm* a generation or two on from the time when the pigs betrayed the revolution and constituted themelves a new oligarchy. Clearly, there has been a good deal of consolidation of their rule since then. But we also need to remember that Oceania is itself still in a state of change. Although starting at a more advanced stage of totalitarian development than *Animal Farm*, it has been in existence for only two or three decades, since its establishment in 'the revolutionary period of the 'fifties and 'sixties' (*NEF*, p. 165). The kind of Newspeak in use in 1984, as the Appendix on Newspeak makes clear, is as yet incomplete and 'provisional', containing 'many superfluous words and archaic formations which were due to be suppressed later .... It was expected that Newspeak would have finally superseded Oldspeak ... by about the year 2050' (*NEF*, p. 241). So we have good grounds for considering what the ultimate goal and tendencies of Ingsoc might be, what 'the highest stage of totalitarian organization' might aim at.

Since there are no laws in Oceania, and since police surveillance and action must always be to some extent insufficient, the goal is to make all Party members police themselves. They must internalize the Thought Police, and thereby render it and much of the whole coercive apparatus of 'purges, arrests, tortures, imprisonments and vaporizations' redundant. It is in this sense that the Party recognizes that the problem of social stability is 'educational'. 'A Party member is required to have not only the right opinions, but the right instincts ... If he is a person naturally orthodox (in Newspeak a *goodthinker*), he will in all circumstances know, without taking thought, what is the true belief or the desirable emotion' (*NEF*, p. 169). An 'elaborate mental training' in childhood, backed by all the ideological institutions and practices of Oceania, ensures that the overwhelming majority of Party members will never need to come to the attention of the Thought Police. As Winston's colleague Syme, the specialist in Newspeak, says: 'Orthodoxy means not thinking – not needing to think. Orthodoxy is unconsciousness' (*NEF*, p. 46).

A Party member is not expected to have any private life ('ownlife') but should direct all his thoughts and emotions outwards. 'He is supposed to live in a continuous frenzy of hatred of foreign enemies and internal traitors, triumph over victories, and self-abasement before the power and wisdom of the party' (*NEF*, p. 169). The ascetic and puritanical attitude to sex in Oceania is one way of shaping the emotions of the model 'goodthinker'. Winston, reflecting on his joyless marriage to his estranged wife Katharine, believes that

> the aim of the Party was not merely to prevent men and women from forming loyalties which it might not be able to control. Its real, undeclared purpose was to remove all pleasure from the sexual act. Not love so much as eroticism was the enemy, inside marriage as well as outside it.

A Party committee has to approve all marriages between Party members, and any indication of physical attraction between the couple usually led to a refusal. 'The only recognized purpose of marriage was to beget children for the service of the Party. Sexual intercourse was to be looked on as a slightly disgusting minor operation, like having an enema.' Winston longs, even more than he longs to be loved, to 'break down the wall of virtue' sedulously built up in all Party women. 'The sexual act, successfully performed, was rebellion. Desire was thoughtcrime' (*NEF*, pp. 56–8).

The chief, almost the sole, good result of his brief affair with Julia is that together they do perform that act of rebellion. Winston exults, rather than feeling jealousy, in the fact that Julia has had hundreds of affairs with Party members. 'Anything that hinted of corruption always filled him with wild hope.' After they have made love in the forest clearing in the countryside, he is emboldened to hope that 'the animal instinct, the simple undifferentiated desire' might be the force 'that would tear the Party to pieces .... Their embrace had been a battle, the climax a victory. It was a blow struck against the Party. It was a political act' (*NEF*, p. 104).

Julia's whole strength, and the only source of her resistance to the Party, lies in her sexuality. She is 'only a rebel from the waist downwards'. She does not believe in organized revolt or in the existence of the Brotherhood. Party doctrines bore her, and Winston cannot get her interested in the principles of Newspeak or concepts like the mutability of the past. When Winston reads Goldstein's book out aloud to her she falls asleep. As Winston sees her, she is not rebelling against the Party's authority 'but simply evading it, as a rabbit dodges a dog'. But the spontaneous and instinctual nature of Julia's opposition allows her to see with clarity things that Winston's intellectualism is blind to.

> Unlike Winston, she had grasped the inner meaning of the Party's sexual puritanism. It was not merely that the sex instinct created a world of its own which was outside the Party's control and which therefore had to be destroyed if possible. What was more important was that sexual privation induced hysteria, which was desirable because it could be transformed into war-fever and leader-worship .... 'All this marching up and down and cheering and waving flags is simply sex gone sour.' (*NEF*, p. 109)[82]

Winston sees that, just as the Party had turned the dangerous sex impulse to political account, so it had done with 'the instinct of parenthood'. Parents were encouraged to be fond of their chilldren, while children were systematically turned against their parents and taught to spy on them. 'The family had become in effect an extension of the Thought Police.' O'Brien later confirms this while looking forward to an even more radical smashing of the family and the sex impulse.

> We have cut the links between child and parent, and between man and man, and between man and woman. No one dares trust a wife or a child or a friend any longer. But in the future there will be no wives and no friends. Children will be taken from their mothers at birth, as one takes eggs from a hen. The sex instinct will be eradicated. Procreation will be an annual formality like the renewal of a ration card. We shall abolish the orgasm. (*NEF*, pp. 214–15)

If the purpose of Oceania's rigid sexual puritanism is to direct the Party member's emotions into the right channels, Newspeak seeks likewise to channel his thoughts. The appendix on 'The Principles of Newspeak' states this aim concisely.

> The purpose of Newspeak was not only to provide a medium of expression for the world-view and mental habits proper to the devotees of Ingsoc, but to make all other modes of thought impossible. It was intended that when Newspeak had been adopted once and for all and Oldspeak forgotten, a heretical thought – that is, a thought diverging from the principles of Ingsoc – should be literally unthinkable, at least so far as thought is dependent on words. (*NEF*, p. 241)

The perversion and diminution of language was, in Orwell's eyes, perhaps the most heinous and unforgivable aspect of the contemporary *trahison des clercs*. Language was, *par excellence*, the intellectual's tool, and the defence of it his greatest trust. It should be his particular charge, by the careful, discriminatory and original use of language, to enlarge its range of meanings and enhance its possibilities of thought and expression. The intellectuals of Oceania are dedicated to doing just the opposite. Syme, the specialist in Newspeak, expounds to Winston, with 'a pedant's passion' and dreamy eyes, the aim of his work on the 'definitive' Eleventh Edition of the Newspeak Dictionary.

> You think, I dare say, that our chief job is inventing new words. But not a bit of it! We're destroying words – scores of them, hundreds of them, every day. We're cutting the language down to the bone . . . . It's a beautiful thing, the destruction of words . . . . Do you know that Newspeak is the only language in the world whose vocabulary gets smaller every year? . . .
>
> The whole aim of Newspeak is to narrow the range of thought. In the end we shall make thoughtcrime literally impossible, because there will be no words in which to express it. Every concept that can ever be needed, will be expressed by exactly *one* word, with its meaning rigidly defined and all its subsidiary meanings rubbed out and forgotten . . . . Every year fewer and fewer words and the range of consciousness always a little smaller. Even now, of course, there's no reason or excuse for committing thoughtcrime. It's merely a question of self-discipline, reality-control. But in the end there won't be any need even for that. The Revolution will be complete when the language is perfect. Newspeak is Ingsoc and Ingsoc is Newspeak. (*NEF*, pp. 44–5)

While Newspeak aims at simplification and reductionism in every area of life, it is not surprising to find its first and most urgent concern to be the language of politics: the *B* vocabulary, as it is known to Newspeak philologists. *B* words are all compound words, acting 'as a sort of verbal shorthand' which pack 'whole ranges of ideas into a few syllables'. The single word 'crimethink', for instance, contained all the words and ideas grouping themselves round the concepts of liberty and equality; while all words grouping themselves round the concepts of objectivity and rationalism were contained in the single world 'oldthink'. As a result, Newspeak could dispense entirely with words such as 'honour', 'justice', 'morality', 'internationalism', 'democracy', 'science'. Similarly, the sexual life of the Party member was entirely regulated by the two words 'sexcrime' (sexual immorality) and 'goodsex' (chastity). A particular category of *B* words are political euphemisms, having as their meaning almost the exact opposite of what they appear to mean: for instance 'joycamp' (forced-labour camp) and 'Minipax' (Ministry of Peace, i.e. Ministry of War). On the other hand, there are some words which display 'a frank and contemptuous understanding of the real nature of Oceanic society' – presumably so long as this understanding contained no political threat. An example of this is 'prolefeed', 'meaning the rubbishy entertainment and spurious news which the Party handed out to the masses'. All *B* words, in fact, are ideologically coloured: there are no 'neutral' or scientific words in the political vocabulary (*NEF*, pp. 244–7).

It has been impossible for all but the most literal-minded reader to take Orwell's invention of Newspeak as anything but satiric. As Bernard Crick says, 'nobody could think that he really believed that a time will come when *The Times* will praise "one of the orators of the Party as a *doubleplusgood duckspeaker*"' (*NEF*, p. 249).[83] No more is it possible to take wholly seriously the reduction of the entire preamble to the American Declaration of Independence to one word: *crimethink* (*NEF*, p. 251). The Appendix on Newspeak is in fact one of the areas where the comedy of *Nineteen Eighty-Four* most comes out. Its very extravagance and mocking tone – very different from the tone of Goldstein's book – bespeak its satiric intent: 'Ultimately it was hoped to make articulate speech issue from the larynx without involving the higher brain centres at all' (*NEF*, p. 249). A fairly obvious target, which Orwell as a journalist would have been familiar with, is journalistic 'cablese'. In his job at the Records Department of the Ministry of Truth, Winston Smith has to alter the record according to the following instructions: 'times 3.12.83 reporting bb dayorder doubleplusungood refs unpersons rewrite fullwise upsub antefiling' (*NEF*, p. 34). This has the same flavour as the well-known exchange of cables between the London *Daily Mail* and its intrepid correspondent Evelyn Waugh, covering the conflict in Abyssinia in the early 1930s:

WHY UNNEWS – UNNEWS GOODNEWS – UNNEWS UNJOB – UPSTICK JOB ASSWISE.[84]

But the fact of Newspeak's primarily satiric intent should not detract from the fundamental seriousness of Orwell's concern, nor from our seeing, again, that in so far as he is pointing to certain deep-lying tendencies, he is making a certain sort of prophecy. The relation between language, truth and politics was one that preoccupied Orwell throughout his life, as some of his best-known essays attest. He accepted that, for all practical purposes, language governed thought, and that 'to think clearly is a necessary first step towards political regeneration.'[85] The English language had an enviable simplicity and flexibility, but 'just because it is so easy to use it is easy to use it *badly*.'[86] It had been particularly susceptible to the jargon of the technical and scientific intelligentsia, and to the deadening influences of 'standard English', the flat and stilted language of the BBC and government White Papers. Above all, language like all else had suffered from the encroachments of totalitarian ideology and practice. Everywhere now 'political language . . . is designed to make lies sound truthful and murder respectable, and to give an appearance of solidity to pure wind.' It had come to consist largely of 'euphemism, question-begging and sheer cloudy vagueness'.

Defenceless villages are bombarded from the air, the inhabitants driven out into the countryside, the cattle machine-gunned, the huts set on fire with incendiary bullets; this is called *pacification*. Millions of peasants are robbed of their farms and sent trudging along the roads with no more than they can carry: this is called *transfer of population* or *rectification of frontiers*. People are imprisoned for years without trial, or shot in the back of the neck or sent to die of scurvy in Arctic lumber camps: this is called *elimination of unreliable elements*.[87]

The Appendix on Newspeak itself draws attention to certain tendencies, apparent since 'the early decades of the twentieth century', which had led to the definite formulation of the principles of Newspeak. One such was the tendency to telescope words and phrases, a feature 'most marked in totalitarian countries and organizations'. Examples were such words as 'Nazi', 'Gestapo', 'Inprecorr', 'Comintern', 'Agitprop'. In consciously adopting this practice, the theorists of Newspeak perceived that 'in thus abbreviating a name one narrowed and subtly altered its meaning by cutting out most of the associations that would otherwise cling to it.'

The words *Communist International*, for instance, call up a composite picture of universal human brotherhood, red flags, barricades, Karl Marx, and the Paris Commune. The word *Comintern*, on the other hand, sugggests merely a tightly-knit organization and a well-defined body of doctrine. It refers to something almost as easily recognized, and as limited in purpose, as a chair or table. *Comintern* is a word that can be uttered almost without taking thought, whereas *Communist International* is a phrase over which one is obliged to linger at least momentarily. (*NEF*, pp. 247–8)

Can we say that this kind of thing has declined or disappeared – or is of little importance? Is it not as ubiquitous and familiar as the party politician 'spraying forth the correct opinions as automatically as a machine gun spraying forth bullets' (*NEF*, p. 248)? We live, even more than in Orwell's time, in a world of thought-eliding acronyms and official euphemisms. Any newspaper or magazine article will be peppered with GATT, OPEC, UNCTAD, SEATO, NATO – to say nothing of the 'Nukespeak' vocabulary of SALT, ABM, ICBM and MIRV. It would be surprising if even a relatively well informed and educated person were able to give the precise derivation of all of these common acronyms; and yet they are freely used in writing and conversation with just that thing-like familiarity that Orwell mentions as eliminating the need to pause to think about their real meaning. It may not be of much help immediately to know that MIRV refers to 'multiple independently targetable re-entry vehicles'; but merely in getting out that mouthful of gibberish one might feel simply the need to find out what it means, and in doing so see something of what our leaders have in mind for us.

The military and other departments of government have of course been the great purveyors of obscure or euphemistic words and phrases, some simply ludicrous, others more sinister. Everyone will have his own favourites. I particularly like the US Environmental Protection Agency's reformulation of acid rain as 'poorly buffered precipitation', and President Reagan's terming his new taxation schemes 'revenue enhancement measures'. Less funny but far deadlier is the whole battery of Pentagon euphemisms: 'Enmity stimulation' for propaganda, 'permanent pre-hostility' for peace, 'circadian de-regulation' for death.[88] The new world of computers is also fast making its contribution to Newspeak, adding to the great strides already made by advertising and television. Many people now speak a sub-species of English called FORTRAN or sometimes COBOL, and indeed, these computer languages may well be producing a new version of official or standard English. Computers treat language as a conveyor of 'information bits', and require compound words formed very much as the *B* vocabulary of Newspeak: that is, any word should be available as noun, adverb, adjective or verb, depending on how it is used or combined with other prefixes or suffixes. A NASA official showed himself highly proficient in this vocabulary when he announced that 'the Columbia spacewalk would be upscheduled in terms of one day.'[89]

As some of these examples suggest, Newspeak is itself part and product of 'the system of thought which really embraces all the rest', and which is called in Oldspeak 'reality control' and in Newspeak 'doublethink'.

> *Doublethink* means the power of holding two contradictory beliefs in one's mind simultaneously, and accepting both of them . . . . The process has to be conscious, or it would not be carried out with sufficient precision, but it also has to be unconscious, or it would bring with it a feeling of falsity and hence of guilt. *Doublethink* lies at the very heart of Ingsoc, since the essential act of the Party is to use conscious deception while retaining the firmness of purpose that goes with complete honesty. To tell deliberate lies while genuinely believing in them, to forget any fact that has become inconvenient, and then when it become necessary again, to draw it back from oblivion for just so long as it is needed, to deny the existence of objective reality and all the time to take account of the reality which one denies – all this is indispensably necessary. Even in using the word *doublethink* it is necessary to exercise *doublethink*. For by using the word one admits that one is tampering with reality; by a fresh act of *doublethink* one erases this knowledge: and so on indefinitely, with the lie always one leap ahead of the truth. Ultimately it is by means of *doublethink* that the Party has been able – and may, for all we know, continue to be able for thousands of years – to arrest the course of history . . . . Upon no other intellectual basis could the dominion of the Party be made permanent. If one is to rule, and to continue ruling, one must be able to dislocate the sense of reality. For the secret of rulership is to combine a belief in one's own infallibility with the power to learn from past mistakes. (*NEF*, p. 171)

Doublethink, then, is the mental technique learned by all Party members which allows them to deny and remain unaware of any objective truth or reality while being able to take account of it where necessary. It involves the permanent dislocation of the sense of reality, so that no external or objective reference point exists by which the independent truth or reality of something can be judged. Of all the contortions of reality that this entails, the continuous alteration of the past is the most important to the stability of Oceania society. This is partly because no Party member, just as no prole, must be able to make comparisons with the real standards of living of past times, lest he come to feel that he is actually worse off than his forebears rather than, as the Party claims, on a constantly rising material plane. But the more important reason for the readjustment of the past is the need to safeguard the infallibility of the Party. This means not only constantly bringing up to date speeches, statistics and records of every kind, so that the predictions of the Party can be seen to have always been right: it also means never admitting that there has ever been a change of doctrine or of political alignment. For 'to change one's mind or even one's policy is a confession of weakness.' To avoid any such suspicion, history must continuously be rewritten. 'This day-to-day falsification of the past, carried out by the Ministry of Truth, is as necessary to the stability of the regime as the work of repression and espionage carried out by the Ministry of Love.' Moreover, doublethink ensures that the people who actually do the falsification can do it accurately and methodically while at the same time suppressing the memory of ever having done so. As a result, when the past has been recreated in whatever shape is needed for the time being, 'this new version *is* the past, and no different past can ever have existed.'

The mutability of the past is the central tenet of Ingsoc. Past events, it is argued, have no objective existence, but survive only in written records and in human memories. The past is whatever the records and the memories agree upon. And since the Party is in full control of all records and in equally full control of the minds of its members, it follows that the past is whatever the Party choose to make it. (*NEF*, p. 170)

The importance of the past, the *real* past, to Winston – and to Orwell – is symbolized in the toast the conspirators make in O'Brien's apartment. To what shall we drink? asks O'Brien.

'To the confusion of the Thought Police? To the death of Big Brother? To humanity? To the future?'

'To the past,' said Winston.

'The past is more important,' agreed O'Brien gravely. (*NEF*, p. 44)

Orwell further underlines the point by making the rewriting of the past Winston's job at the Ministry of Truth. Winston is in the perfect position to understand the force of the Party's slogan 'Who controls the past controls the future: who controls the present controls the past.' At one point Winston vaguely remembers that, although in 1984 ('if it was 1984'), Oceania is at war with Eurasia and in alliance with Eastasia, it had been different not so long ago. No one, of course, accepted that things had ever been other than they now were.

The party said that Oceania had never been in alliance with Eurasia. He, Winston Smith, knew that Oceania had been in alliance with Eurasia as short a time as four years ago. But where did that knowledge exist? Only in his own consciousness, which in any case must soon be annihilated. (*NEF*, p. 31)

The fragility and unreliability of human memory as any useful guide to the past is forcibly brought home to Winston in his hilarious encounter with the old prole in the pub. Winston pumps him on his past memories, hoping to get some reliable knowledge about the recent past. What he finds instead, to his intense frustration, is that the old man's memory is 'nothing but a rubbish-heap of details', lacking all clarity and coherence. He reflects that, even though there were still some survivors from the pre-revolutionary days, 'the huge and simple question, "Was life better before the Revolution than it is now?"' was already unanswerable, since the survivors from the old world were incapable of comparing one age with another.

They remembered a million useless things, a quarrel with a workmate, a hunt for a lost bicycle pump, the expression on a long-dead sister's face, the swirls of dust on a windy morning seventy years ago: but all the relevant facts were outside the range of their vision. They were like the ant, which can see small objects but not large ones. And when memory failed and written records were falsified – when that happened, the claim of the Party to have improved the conditions of human life had got to be accepted, because there did not exist, and never could exist, any standard against which it could be tested. (*NEF*, p. 78)

At another time Winston will see a different and more hopeful significance in the ant-like vision of the proles, with their limited but concrete memories and the concrete emotions that lie behind them. But as an aid to the reconstruction of the past, something much more definite than human memory is clearly necessary. More formal knowledge, such as written documents, will always be needed if there is to be any degree of certainty about the past. The power of the written record is clear to Winston in his day-to-day work, systematically altering and remaking the past by the destruction and creation of documents. It is with a certain satisfaction in the exercise of his skill that Winston invents a purely mythical figure, 'Comrade Ogilvy', and plants him firmly in the historical record as the exemplary subject of one of Big Brother's commemorative Orders for the Day (*NEF*, pp. 40–1). He even gets a certain pleasure from the completeness with which his Department, in a week of frantic work, alters the record so that Oceania can now be shown to have always been at war with Eastasia and not, as up to the previous week, with Eurasia (*NEF*, pp. 148–9). And it is with regret that he recalls his destruction of the old *Times* photograph that is the sole but indisputable proof that the 'confessions' of Jones, Aaronson and Rutherford are lies and their 'crimes' trumped-up (*NEF*, pp. 63–6). That memory is something to cling to, but it is still only memory, easily overriden by the Party's massive documentation on the case. Winston momentarily despairs at the task facing anyone who attempts to resist the Party's definition of reality. 'In the end the Party would announce that two and two made five, and you would have to believe it.' It was inherent in the logic of the Party's philosophy that they should ultimately deny not merely the validity of experience but the very existence of external reality. Reality was in the mind, and the Party controlled the mind . . . . But Winston holds on to the evidence of his eyes and ears. 'The solid world exists, its laws do not change. Stones are hard, water is wet, objects unsupported fall towards the earth's centre.' He writes in his diary: 'Freedom is the freedom to say that two plus two make four. If that is granted, all else follows' (*NEF*, p. 68).[90]

In the end, as we know, O'Brien gets Winston to accept that 2 + 2 = 5,[91] and anything else the party wants him to accept. It is the first and crucial stage of

Winston's rehabilitation. Winston's wilful obstinacy, says O'Brien, has turned him into a lunatic, 'a minority of one', and deluded him into thinking that the nature of reality is objective and self-evident. But 'reality is not external'.

> Reality exists in the human mind, and nowhere else. Not in the individual mind, which can make mistakes, and in any case soon perishes: only in the mind of the Party, which is collective and immortal. Whatever the Party holds to be the truth, is truth. It is impossible to see reality except by looking through the eyes of the Party. (*NEF*, p. 200)

O'Brien's idealist claims go beyond social and historical reality to encompass the realm of nature as well.

> We control matter because we control the mind. Reality is inside the skull . . . . There is nothing that we could not do. Invisibility, levitation – anything. I could float off this floor like a soap bubble if I wish to . . . . You must get rid of those nineteenth century ideas about the laws of Nature. We make the laws of nature. (*NEF*, pp. 212–13)

The extremism, not to say lunacy of O'Brien's assertions – 'we control life at all its levels', 'the earth is the centre of the universe', etc. – suggest that Oceania has already broken through the last 'safeguard of sanity' discussed by Goldstein. O'Brien himself concedes that 'for certain purposes' – such as navigation – it is convenient to assume that the earth goes round the sun: doublethink controls the schizophrenia. Goldstein had seen war and military necessity as the one area where, on pain of conquest or extinction, traditional dictators could not ignore the laws of physical reality. 'In philosophy, or religion, or ethics, or politics, two and two might make five, but when one was designing a gun or an aeroplane they had to make four.' But he argued that, once war was no longer a real threat, as in the new world-system, that last contact with reality could be and was being broken. Newspeak has no word for 'science', and nothing in its vocabulary that expresses the empirical mode of thought. What Oldspeak might refer to as 'science' could always be covered in Newspeak by 'Ingsoc' (*NEF*, p. 249). Since each of the three super-states is unconquerable and self-contained, 'each is in effect a separate universe within which almost any perversion of thought can be safely practised.'

> Cut off from contact with the outer world, and with the past, the citizen of Oceania is like a man in interstellar space, who has no way of knowing which direction is up and which is down. The rulers of such a state are absolute, as the Pharaohs or the Caesars could not be. (*NEF*, p. 160)

That totalitarian states were capable of an almost infinite degree of what O'Brien calls 'collective sollipsism' – limited perhaps only by the need to remain efficient for war[92] – was a conviction that Orwell had long held and frequently expressed. The free manipulation of reality appeared to him, as we have seen, 'integral' to totalitarianism. In O'Brien's ravings he may have deliberately exaggerated the point, but if so it was a matter of degree only. Once more, it was the Spanish Civil War that crystallized for Orwell the frightening possibility that 'the very concept of objective truth is fading out of the world.' 'I remember once saying to Arthur Koestler, "History stopped in 1936", at which he nodded in immediate understanding.' It was the lies and distortions of the Civil War, both those of the Fascists and their opponents within and outside Spain, that convinced Orwell that totalitarianism destroys the very possibility of any objective account of history, because it did not accept the notion of 'neutral facts' on which most people could agree.

> It is just this common basis of agreement, with its implications that human beings are all one species of animal, that totalitarianism destroys. Nazi theory indeed specificially denies that such a thing as 'the truth' exists. There is, for instance, no such thing as 'science'. There is only 'German science', 'Jewish science', etc. The implied objective of this line of thought is a nightmare world in which the Leader, or some ruling clique, controls not only the future but *the past*. If the Leader says of such and such an event, 'it never happened' – well, it never happened. If he says that two and two are five – well, two and two are five. This prospect frightens me much more than bombs . . . .[93]

It was the Spanish War, too, that gave Orwell his best insight into the 'doublethink' of intellectuals, of both right and left. He noted the abundance of atrocity stories on both sides, and the tendency for them to be believed or not believed 'solely on grounds of political predilection'. But more sinister still was the fact that 'at any moment the situation can suddenly reverse itself and yesterday's proved-to-the-hilt atrocity story can become a ridiculous lie, merely because the political landscape has changed'[94] Totalitarian doctrines were inherently unstable, and this entailed that their adherents had to learn the doublethink technique of turning hatred 'in any direction at a moment's notice, like a plumber's blow flame'.[95] Orwell saw such doublethink at its richest in the international Communist movement. 'Every Communist is in fact liable at any moment to have to alter his most fundamental convictions, or leave the Party. The unquestionable dogma of Monday may become the damnable heresy of Tuesday, and so on.'[96] Not only was there the continuous re-writing of revolutionary and post-revolutionary history, with Trotsky–Goldstein playing a multiplicity of starring roles, and heroes and villains interchanging in bewildering ways. There were also the sudden shifts of 'line' and loyalities imposed on Communists everywhere by changes in Russian foreign policy. Before 1935, in what was considered the phase of 'world revolution', Communists were expected to take the line that all bourgeois parliamentary democracies were shams, not different in kind from the Fascist regimes of Italy and Germany. With the rise of German power came the period of the 'Popular Front', during which western Communists were ordered to become good patriots and accept bourgeois parliamentarians as allies in the fight against world fascism. Then came the Nazi–Soviet pact of September 1939 and another twist. The Nazis were now the allies of the Russian people, and western Communists suddenly had to begin attacking their own governments as warmongering and imperialistic, and to call for a peace with Hitler. In June 1941 there was the German invasion of Russia, and pro-war and anti-Nazi feeling became once more the order of the day.

Turn this story around somewhat, and we can see how a similar element of doublethink was necessary in the attitudes of western populations as a whole towards the Soviet Union. Before the 1930s, Soviet communism was feared and denounced far more than Italian or German fascism. Only with the growth of Hitler's power was there a search for an alliance with Russia, and an official dampening down of criticism of Russia's internal affairs. But from 1939 to 1941 the Soviet Union had to be regarded as a hated enemy, in alliance with Hitler – only to be embraced again in June 1941 as an ally of the West. With the beginning of the Cold War in 1945, Western opinion everywhere once more had to do a quick about-turn and regard the Soviet Union as the greatest threat to freedom and world peace.

The phenomenon of doublethink is well-known as a phenomenon in both individual and collective psychopathology.[97] No doubt in totalitarian societies it reaches new heights, but its persistence in our own times and our own societies hardly requires extensive documentation. One of the simpler examples Orwell gives in *Nineteen Eighty-Four* must find a direct echo in the names and official titles of a score of ministries and public programmes today (Ministry of Defence, Medicare, Central Office of Information, etc.).

Even the names of the four Ministries by which we are governed exhibit a sort of impudence in their deliberate reversal of the facts. The Ministry of Peace concerns itself with war, the Ministry of Truth with lies, the Ministry of Love with torture, and the Ministry of Plenty with starvation. (*NEF*, p. 172)

Even more relevant is the comment on Ingsoc, the official ideology of Oceania. 'The Party rejects and vilifies every principle for which the Socialist movement originally stood, and it chooses to do this in the name of socialism.' Today, the 'free world' includes South American dictatorships and South African *apartheid*; while the 'free enterprise' system of the capitalist West, dedicated to individual initiative, is a managerial, corporatist society, governed by public and private bureaucracies with monopolistic or oligopolistic power. Most striking of all is the doublethinking that is rife in military thought in the nuclear age. 'War is horrible,' says Herman Kahn, 'but so is peace, and it is proper with the kind of calculations we are making today to compare the horror of war and the horror of peace and see how much worse it is.' It follows from this kind of thinking that we should continue to build up armaments and accept the possible destruction of 'sixty million Americans' in a nuclear war in order that there should be 'normal and happy lives for the majority of the survivors and their descendants'.[98] It is difficult to imagine that even the most skilled exponent of doublethink in Oceania would be able to produce a finer instance of the 'controlled insanity' that reigns there (*NEF*, p. 172).

PROLES AND PROLEFEED

'If there is hope . . . it lies in the proles.' Winston reflects that this must be so: 'only there, in those swarming disregarded masses, 85 per cent of the population of Oceania, could the force to destroy the party ever be generated.' He does not – contrary to Goldstein's analysis – believe that the Party can be overthrown from within. Party members were too closely watched to be able to make any collective effort at rebellion. At best, they could meet secretly in twos and threes. But the proles had been left very much to their own devices. The Party claims to have freed them from bondage to the capitalists, and in principle rules in their name. But simultaneously, 'true to the principles of doublethink', the Party taught that 'the proles were natural inferiors who must be kept in subjection, like animals, by the application of a few simple rules.'

A few agents of the Thought Police move among them, marking down and eliminating the few individuals who are judged potentially dangerous. But no attempt is made to indoctrinate them with the ideology of the Party. It was thought neither necessary nor desirable that the proles should have strong political feelings. 'All that was required of them was a primitive patriotism which could be appealed to whenever it was necessary to make them accept longer working-hours or shorter rations.' They do not have telescreens in their homes. The sexual puritanism of the Party is not imposed on them. They can marry whom they like, divorce is permitted, and promiscuity goes unpunished. As the Party slogan puts it, 'Proles and animals are free.' A good deal of crime flourishes among them, but since it affects only the proles the police largely ignore the 'world-within-a-world' of thieves, prostitutes, drug-peddlers and racketeers. Indeed, the proles as a whole exist in almost a separate world, physically and socially cut off from the remaining 15 per cent of the population, the Party members.

> Left to themselves, like cattle turned loose upon the plains of Argentina, they had reverted to a style of life that appeared to be natural to them, a sort of ancestral pattern. They were born, they grew up in the gutters, they went to work at twelve, they passed through a brief blossoming-period of beauty and sexual desire, they married at twenty, they were middle-aged at thirty, they died, for the most part, at sixty. Heavy physical work, the care of home and children, petty quarrels with neighbours, films, football, beer, and, above all, gambling, filled up the horizons of their minds. To keep them in control was not difficult. (*NEF*, p. 60)

That is certainly the official view, as expressed for instance by O'Brien when he tells Winston: 'The proletarians will never revolt, not in a thousand years or a million' (*NEF*, p. 210). It is also – not surprisingly, as the Party is its author – the view expressed in Goldstein's book, although he also makes ritual genuflexions to the ultimate overthrow of the Party by a proletarian uprising.

> From the proletarians nothing is to be feared. Left to themselves, they will continue from generation to generation, and from century to century, working, breeding, and dying, not only without any impulse to rebel, but without the power of grasping that the world could be other than it is .... What opinions the masses hold, or do not hold, is looked on as a matter of indifference. They can be granted intellectual liberty because they have no intellect. (*NEF*, p. 168)

Winston is never so certain. He thinks wistfully – but in the same animal imagery as the Party – that, if only the proles could become conscious of their strength, 'they needed only to rise up and shake themselves like a horse shaking off flies.' A memory comes back to him, of hearing in the distance a tremendous clamour of women's voices, 'a great formidable cry of anger and despair'. His heart leaps with hope: the proles are at last rebelling. What he finds when he comes on the scene is a mass of screaming, quarrelling women, squabbling over the sale of some tin saucepans. The incident typifies the problem. 'Just for a moment, what almost frightening power had sounded in that cry from only a few hundred throats! Why was it that they could never shout like that about anything that mattered?' He writes the pesssimistic reflection in his diary: 'Until they become conscious they will never rebel, and until after they have rebelled they cannot become conscious' (*NEF*, p. 60).[99]

As a directly political force, this view of the proles is reinforced by all of Winston's experiences of them. Wandering through the prole quarters, he is vividly struck by impressions of strength and endurance: the 'two monstrous women with brick-red forearms', the stoicism and good sense which the proles show in face of the rocket bombs. But then he comes across a group of working men arguing passionately over the State Lottery as if it were the most important thing in life; and he encounters the confused old prole in the pub. A sense of helplessness and despair once more settles over him. It seemed quite reasonable to say to yourself that hope lay in the proles: 'it was when you looked at the human beings passing you on the pavement that it became an act of faith' (*NEF*, p. 72).

Although unconcerned with the proles as a political threat, the Party clearly feels it desirable to confirm them in their political ignorance and apathy by keeping their minds well supplied with 'prolefeed'. The Lottery, with its weekly draw for enormous prizes, is one such device, 'the one public event to which the proles paid serious attention'. At the Ministry of Truth, there is a whole chain of separate departments producing culture for the masses.

> Here were produced rubbishy newspapers containing almost nothing except sport, crime, and astrology, sensational five-cent novelettes, films oozing with sex, and sentimental songs which were composed entirely by mechanical means on a special kind of kaleidoscope known as a versificator. (*NEF*, p. 38)

There is even a section – Pornsec, where Julia works – which exists solely to turn out cheap pornography for distribution among the proles. And, to keep up a tolerable level of nationalism and virulent xenophobia, there are such staged occasions as the Hate Week, complete with banners, processions, marching songs, propaganda films and scary rumours (*NEF*, pp. 121–2).

But it is during the showing of one of the brutally sadistic films typically churned out for the proles that Winston glimpses another possibility, another kind of hope, that may lie in the proles. The film shows, to the evident satisfaction of most of the audience, scenes of a ship full of Jewish refugees being bombed, and the efforts of the refugees to stay afloat and alive. In one scene there is a middle-aged woman in a lifeboat trying to comfort and protect her little boy. Winston's barely coherent diary entry – it is his very first – describes the image and the audience's response:

> Little boy screaming with fright and hiding his head between her breasts as if he was trying to burrow right into her and the woman putting her arms round him and

comforting him although she was blue with fright herself, all the time covering him up as much as possible as if she thought her arms could keep the bullets off him, then the helicopter planted a 10 kilo bomb in among them terrific flash and the boat went all to matchwood. Then there was a wonderful shot of a child's arm going up up up right up into the air a helicopter with a camera in its nose must have followed it up and there was a lot of applause from the party seats but a woman down in the prole part of the house suddenly kicking up a fuss and shouting they didnt oughter of showed it not in front of kids they didnt it aint right not in front of kids it aint until the police turned her out . . . . (*NEF*, p. 11)

Winston at the time does not see much significance either in the outraged response of the prole woman to the sadism – 'a typical prole reaction' – or in the passionate even through hopeless protectiveness of the mother towards her child. But later, lying in bed with Julia in the old room above the junk shop, he has a painful dream of his childhood, which he links with the image of the Jewish woman and her child in the film. The dream revives the memory of an incident just before his mother disappeared, at a time when he was living with her and his ailing three-year-old sister in their poverty-stricken home. The endless war is on, and food is scarce. His mother, although she and her daughter are virtually starving, allows Winston the greatest share of the food. Still he wants more, and when some chocolate ration unexpectedly appears Winston, dissatisfied even with his three-quarters share, grabs the last quarter from his sister and bolts for the door. His sister begins to cry, and the mother draws her arm round the child and presses its face against her breast. It is Winston's last sight of both of them: by the time he makes his shamefaced return, they have disappeared for ever.

It is that last glimpse of his mother, and that 'enveloping protective gesture of the arm', which recurs in Winston's dream, and which he now connects with the equally 'useless' and pathetic gesture of the Jewish mother, trying to protect her child against the bullets with her arm. What he now sees is that his mother, in no way unusual or intelligent, yet had possessed

a kind of nobility, a kind of purity, simply because the standards that she obeyed were private ones. Her feelings were her own, and could not be altered from the outside. It would not have occurred to her that an action which is ineffectual thereby becomes meaningless. If you loved someone, you loved him, and when you had nothing else to give you still gave him love. When the last of the chocolate was gone, his mother had clasped the child in her arms. It was no use, it changed nothing, it did not produce more chocolate, it did not avert the child's death or her own; but it seemed natural to her to do it. (*NEF*, p. 134)

And suddenly too it occurs to Winston that it is here that the real strength of the proles is to be found. The prole woman at the film had responded out of instinctive repugnance, while the Party people had applauded. The Party had made its members indifferent to 'mere feelings' and private gestures. The thing that mattered was the public significance of actions, how far they did or did not contribute to the historic destiny of the people. But perhaps the most precious legacy of the past – when it could be discerned – was that there were 'private loyalties' which one did not question. 'What mattered were individual relationships, and a completely helpless gesture, an embrace, a tear, a word spoken to a dying man, could have value in itself.' And the proles had retained these values.

> They were not loyal to a party or a country or an idea, they were loyal to one another. For the first time in his life he did not despise the proles or think of them merely as an inert force which would one day spring to life and regenerate the world. The proles had stayed human. They had not become hardened inside. They had held on to the primitive emotions which he himself had to re-learn by conscious effort. (*NEF*, p. 135)

It is a short step from this to a realization of where the essence of freedom might lie, and what the sticking-point in holding on to it. Winston has always known that sooner or later he and Julia will be caught and probably shot. 'We are the dead', he has often said to her. It is also likely that under torture and interrogation they will both confess to numerous crimes, real and pretended. But so long as they 'stayed human', so long as they did not betray one another, they would have beaten the Party. Winston affirms: 'confession is not betrayal. What you say or do doesn't matter: only feelings matter. If they could make me stop loving you – that would be the real betrayal.' Winston feels that he has at last discovered the real secret of resistance to the Party. 'With all their cleverness they had never mastered the secret of finding out what another human being was thinking.' Whatever the Party did to him, even if they killed him,

> if the object was not to stay alive but to stay human, what difference did it ultimately make? They could not alter your feelings . . . . They could lay bare in the utmost detail everything that you had done or said; but the inner heart, whose workings were mysterious even to yourself, remained impregnable. (*NEF*, p. 136)

The irony of this – for it is of course precisely this illusion that O'Brien shatters – is matched by, and probably linked to, the irony of the situation in which we and Winston last contemplate the proles. On the day that Winston rents the room above Mr Charrington's shop, he observes in the courtyard below 'a monstrous woman, solid as a Norman pillar, with brawny red forearms and a sacking apron strapped about her middle, . . . stumping to and fro between a washtub and a clothes line' (*NEF*, p. 113). This Amazonian prole sings constantly as she works, and although the song is a typically sentimental piece of rubbish turned out for the proles on the mechanical versificator, Winston finds that the woman has made it sound 'almost pleasant'. She is nearly always there, hanging out her washing and singing her song, when the lovers occupy the room. Her powerful and calming, almost timeless, figure goes with the satisfaction and peace that they enjoy there. On the day of their arrest, Winston is gazing down at the prole woman and decides that, with her 'powerful marelike buttocks' and her 'solid, contourless body, like a block of granite', she is beautiful. He feels a 'mystical reverence' for this woman, a woman with no mind but 'only strong arms, a warm heart, and a fertile belly'. And she is transformed in his mind into a symbol of all proles everywhere, 'people who had never learned to think but who were storing up in their hearts and bellies and muscles the power that would one day overturn the world'. The hope in the proles was not misplaced: the future belonged to them.

> Sooner or later it would happen, strength would change into consciousness. The proles were immortal, you could not doubt it when you looked at that valiant figure in the yard. In the end their awakening would come. And until that happened, though it might be a thousand years, they would stay alive against all the odds, like birds, passing on from body to body the vitality which the Party did not share and could not kill. (*NEF*, p. 175)

Seconds before the Thought Police burst into the room, Winston has a lyrical, prophetic, vision of a mighty impregnable proletariat that would re-shape the world:

> All round the world, in London and New York, in Africa and Brazil, and in the mysterious, forbidden lands beyond the frontiers, in the streets of Paris and Berlin, in the villages of the endless Russian plain, in the bazaars of China and Japan – everywhere stood the same solid unconquerable figure, made monstrous by work and childbearing, toiling from birth to death and still singing. Out of those mighty loins a race of conscious beings must one day come. You were the dead; theirs was the future. But you could share in that future if you kept alive the mind as they kept alive the body, and passed on the secret doctrine that two plus two make four. (*NEF*, p. 176)

Orwell here echoes Marx: 'The philosophers are the head of a revolution, the proletariat its heart.' It is not just this dubious amalgam that is disquieting – how many 'philosophers' (Winstons) in any case will there be in Oceania? – nor even the overblown language of Winston's vision. It is more the fact that the pronouncement – the revelation, almost – comes at the very moment when Winston is about to be arrested and suffer a very rude awakening at the hands of O'Brien. There is distinctly something of a last-gasp, forlorn-hope, quality about it. Does Orwell mean us to regard Winston's ultimate faith in the proles as misplaced, the product of wishful thinking? It is in any case on the moral qualities of the proles, their stubborn loyalties and instinctive humanity, that Winston rests his hopes. How are these translated into political consciousness and political action, as they must be if the proles are not to remain a segregated and powerless segment of society, however numerous? Nothing in *Nineteen Eighty-Four* suggests that they have that capacity, and a good deal – the cool analysis of Goldstein, for instance – tells in quite the opposite direction.

There is another thing that bears on this question. As many commentators have pointed out, Orwell's portrait of the proles in *Nineteen Eighty-Four* is taken with very little change from his studies and observations of the English working class in the 1930s and 1940s. The proles of Oceania are the English working class of Orwell's day planted in the totalitarian society of the near future. In *The Road to Wigan Pier* Orwell had noted many things about the working class that chime very well with his observations on the proles. He had seen at first hand their resilience and stoicism, and their loyalty to each other. He had noticed that, however untheoretical their understanding, and unlike most middle-class socialists, they had instinctively grasped that socialism means essentially 'justice and common decency'. The strength of family ties among them, and the capacity this gave them to stand up to such hardships as unemployment, struck him forcibly. And generally, Orwell felt that 'in a working-class home . . . you breathe a warm, decent, deeply human atmosphere which it is not so easy to find elswhere.'

But on the more negative side there was the passivity of the working class, the fact that a working man 'does not act, he is acted upon'. The working class had historically shown a great talent for corporate organization, in the form of trade unions and working-men's clubs; but they had displayed almost no capacity for leadership and were content to let themselves be led – usually astray – by middle-class people, 'the people who could pronounce their aitches'. Instead of protesting passionately against their appalling condition during the Slump, they had allowed themselves to be bought off with 'cheap palliatives', such as nylon stockings, tinned food, radio, the movies and the football pools (the last, as with the Lottery in Oceania, amounting almost to an obsession with working men).[100] The development of a 'mass culture', culture for the masses, seemed in fact to Orwell to prefigure very precisely the kind of culture that would be consciously promoted in a totalitarian society. In 'The Prevention of Literature' he speculated on this in terms that anticipate much of the account of 'novel-writing machines' and versificators in *Nineteen Eighty-Four*:

> Newspapers will presumably continue until television technique reaches a higher level, but apart from newspapers it is doubtful even now whether the great mass of people in the industrialized countries feel the need for any kind of literature . . . . Probably novels and stories will be completely superseded by film and radio productions. Or perhaps some kind of low-grade sensational fiction will survive, produced by a sort of conveyor belt process that reduces human initiative to the minimum. It would probaly not be beyond human ingenuity to write books by machinery. But a sort of mechanizing process can already be seen at work in the film and radio, in publicity and propaganda, and in the lower reaches of journalism. The Disney films, for instance, are produced by what is essentially a factory process, the work being done partly mechanically and partly by teams of artists who have to subordinate their individual style. Radio features are commonly written by tired hacks to whom the subject and the manner of treatment are dictated beforehand . . . . So also with the innumerable books and pamphlets commissioned by government departments. Even more machine-like is the production of short stories, serials, and poems for very cheap magazines. Papers such as the *Writer* abound with advertisements of Literary Schools, all of them offering you ready-made plots at a few shillings a time . . . . It is probably in some such way that the literature of a totalitarian society would be produced.[101]

If the proles of Oceania bear any resemblance to a working class formed by these sorts of conditions – and it is clear that they do – then the best they can do seems to be to bear silent witness to the inhumanity of the society. Political transformation does not come into it. 'Heart' is a great thing, as Orwell was the first to praise in a writer like Dickens, and which he presented as the great strength of Boxer, the noble but not overly-intelligent carthorse of *Animal Farm*; but it does not change the system.[102] Orwell once wrote that 'the manual workers in a machine civilization have certain characteristics forced upon them by the circumstances in which they live: loyalty, improvidence, generosity, hatred of privilege.' It was this that made 'the mystique of proletarian socialism' the 'idea of equality'. But the proletariat itself seemed incapable of achieving this goal. 'It would seem that what you get over and over again is a movement of the proletariat which is promptly canalized and betrayed by astute people at the top, and then the growth of a new governing class. The one thing that never arrives is equality.' The rigidity of this pattern led Orwell to entertain the 'cynical thought' that 'men are only decent when they are powerless.'[103] Cynical or not – and it certainly wasn't Orwell's last word on the subject – it seems the most fitting epitaph on the proles of Oceania.

Orwell may have made the proles of Oceania in the image of the contemporary working class for the same reason that he made so much of the physical environment of Oceania familiar to his English reader: to force a point of identification, to prevent the reader from being able to read the tale as a futuristic fantasy. But if so, he may have compensated too much in the direction of contemporaneity in this case. The timeless, naturalistic, view of a traditional working class that he presents in *Nineteen Eighty-Four* seriously mars the consistency of the picture of totalitarian society, and diffuses some of its force. For such a working class – amounting, we should remember, to fully 85 per cent of the population of Oceania – does not belong to a model of a totalitarian society. As Crick puts it,

> the proles are left passive; they are not mobilized systematically, as nearly every author who used the term 'totalitarian' had thought was of the essence of the concept . . . . The concept of totalitarianism only applies to how the Inner Party controls the Outer Party – a situation astonishingly unlike anything that Orwell himself, and his readers, would have imagined of the real regimes called totalitarian.[104]

Irving Howe states the objection most fully:

> The totalitarian state can afford no luxury, allow no exception; it cannot tolerate the existence of any group beyond the perimeter of its control; it can never become so secure as to lapse into indifference. Scouring every corner of society for rebels it knows do not exist, the totalitarian state cannot come to rest for any prolonged period of time. To do so would risk disintegration. It must always tend toward a condition of self-agitation, shaking and re-shaking its members, testing and retesting them in order to insure its power. And since . . . . the proles remain one of the few possible sources of revolt, it can hardly seem plausible that Oceania would permit them even the relative freedom Orwell describes.[105]

Orwell's own writings on totalitarianism, and all the works by Silone, Borkenau and Koestler that he admired, show a full awareness of this feature of totalitarianism. Why did he not try to imagine the impact of totalitarian rule on the common people, as he would have found for instance in Jack London's *The Iron Heel* and Zamyatin's *We*? I think Crick is probably right in arguing that here – more damagingly perhaps than at any other point in the novel – the satiric purpose overwhelms the imaginative portrayal of a totalitarian world. 'The demands of the specific satire must make the proles debased, rather than adequate human material for ideological mobilization.'[106] Orwell seems here to be registering his bitter disappointment – and that of other socialists – at the failure of popular education and a universal franchise to produce a more politically educated and ideologically conscious working class. He saw instead a working class addicted to the movies, the radio, sport and gambling: 'electronic bread and circuses'. He was as angry at the working class itself, for its submissiveness, as at the middle-class intellectuals – the Symes, Ampleforths and Tillotsons – who made their living from churning out propaganda and 'prolefeed' at the behest of the authorities: yet one more betrayal by the intellectuals. Deliberately exaggerating the debasement of the working class, he made their control in Oceania the relatively simple and routine matter of supplying sufficient prolefeed at regular intervals, just as animals in a zoo, or passengers on an aeroplane, are kept orderly by regular feeding.

We can't of course rule out the possibility that Orwell actually thought that the working class in a totalitarian society would become so degraded and alienated that this degree of attention would suffice to control them. We should remember, once more, that Oceania is a 'post-totalitarian' society. Even if the practices of Nazi Germany and Stalinist Russia were different, it is certainly not impossible to imagine a society in which a highly disciplined and well organized 15 per cent controlled the remaining fragmented and demoralized 85 per cent. This was presumably something like the position in the slave civilizations of the ancient world, and we know that Orwell often drew the comparison between these and modern totalitarian states, different as he knew them to be in many respects.[107] Moreover, there is the important point that Orwell specifically denies that the Party in Oceania rule on the basis of a legitimating ideology, and therefore ideological mobilization of the masses – as in Germany or Russia – does not arise as an issue. But we need now to consider this problematic aspect of *Nineteen Eighty-Four*, Orwell's account of power, in more detail.

POWER FOR THE SAKE OF POWER

In a harshly lit, windlowless cell deep in the heart of the Ministry of Love, Winston wonders to himself: 'If I could save Julia by doubling my pain, would I do it? Yes, I would.' But he knows that this is merely an intellectual decision; the question of what he would do in the midst of pain and suffering is unanswerable until actually put at the time. When the first blow of the truncheon shatters his elbow and almost paralyses him, he thinks he knows the answer: 'Never, for any reason on earth, could you wish for an increase of pain. Of pain you could wish only one thing: that it should stop. Nothing in the world was so bad as physical pain. In the face of pain there are no heroes . . .' (*NEF*, p. 192).

Actually, Winston is braver than he realizes. Although there is no way he can save Julia, he does not betray her – does not betray his love for her – until all the resistance has first been crushed out of him, by a lengthy process of frequent beatings, brutal torture and fierce interrogation. This may be a case of his mind refusing to do what his body pleads for, but that in itself shows O'Brien that he has a tough case on his hands. Winston's heresy has deeper roots than he may have thought, deeper even than we have been led to believe from Winston's self-doubting manner and his frequently expressed conviction that his 'rebellion' has been doomed from the start, from the very first entry in the diary.

O'Brien tells Winston that there are three stages in his 're-integration': 'There is learning, there is understanding, and there is acceptance' (*NEF*, p. 209). In effect, what this process consists of is to break down, one by one, the 'sticking-points', the axiomatic affirmations of his sanity and of the possibility of freedom, that Winston has painfully arrived at in the course of his lonely rebellion. The first thing that has to go is Winston's empiricism, his grip on reality and his belief that there is an external world independent of the consciousness of the observer: that '2 + 2 = 4' always and everywhere. This is achieved by a typical mixture of torture and the force of O'Brien's interrogation, at once patient and paternal, brutal and hysterical. Winston has quickly made all the routine confessions: to the assassination of Party members, sabotage, spying, sexual perversion and the murder of his wife. But O'Brien brushes all that impatiently aside. His pupose is to 'cure' Winston, to make him 'sane'. 'The Party is not interested in the overt act: the thought is all we care about. We do not merely destroy our enemies, we change them.' The Inquisition made the mistake of killing unrepentant heretics, thus producing martyrs who simply became the seed of fresh heresy. The Nazis and Communists went one better. Their heretics were forced to make abject confessions, publicly admitting all their crimes and the wrongness of their ways. But they too, soon after their deaths, were resurrected as martyrs, as their confessions were only too well known to have been extorted by violence and therefore untrue. There are no martyrs in Oceania. Posterity hears nothing of deviants and heretics; they are wiped clean from the record. But the Party still feels impelled to change the heretics, to cure them, even though they are 'annihilated in the past as well as in the future'. O'Brien tells Winston:

> You are a flaw in the pattern . . . . You are a stain that must be wiped out. Did I not tell you that we are different from the persecutors of the past? We are not content with negative obedience, nor even with the most abject submission. When finally you surrender to us, it must be of your own free will. We do not destroy the heretic because he resists us: so long as he resists us we never destroy him. We convert him, we capture his inner mind, we reshape him. We burn all evil and all illusion out of him; we bring him over to our side, not in appearance, but genuinely, heart and soul. We make him one of ourselves before we kill him. It is intolerable to us that an erroneous thought should exist anywhere in the world, however secret and powerless it may be. Even in the instant of death we cannot permit any deviation. In the old days the heretic walked to the stake still a heretic, proclaiming his heresy, exulting in it. Even the victim of the Russian purges could carry rebellion locked up in his skull as he walked down the passage waiting for the bullet.[108] But we make the brain perfect before we blow it out. The command of the old despotism was 'thou shalt not'. The command of the totalitarians was 'Thou shalt'. Our command is '*Thou art*'. No one whom we bring to this place ever stands out against us. Everyone is washed clean . . . .
>
> Things will happen to you from which you could not recover, if you lived a thousand years. Never again will you be capable of ordinary human feeling. Everything will be dead inside you. Never again will you be capable of love, or friendship, or joy of living, or laughter, or curiosity, or courage, or integrity. You will be hollow. We shall squeeze you empty and then we shall fill you with ourselves. (*NEF*, pp. 204–6)

Listening to O'Brien's 'dreamy' voice, his 'exaltation, the lunatic enthusiasm', Winston with one side of himself is convinced that O'Brien is mad. But O'Brien has already made Winston doubt his own sanity. The 'learning' stage of his re-education has already made reality dissolve into doubts and fitfully glimpsed illuminations – although of what Winston cannot be certain. The second stage is 'understanding'. Winston, as O'Brien reminds him, had once written in his diary, 'I understand *how*; I do not understand *why*' (*NEF*, p. 67). What he has read of Goldstein's book has helped him to understand how the Party remains in power, but not what the motive of that power is, why the Party wants power and clings to it so tenaciously. O'Brien proposes to enlighten him on that, by his usual technique of the bullying question. Why, he asks Winston, do we want power?

Winston gives the response that he thinks O'Brien wants to hear. It is the conventional rationale of most modern dictatorships, the rationale so powerfully stated by Dostoyevsky's Grand Inquisitor.

> [Winston] knew in advance what O'Brien would say. That the Party did not seek power for its own ends, but only for the good of the majority. That it sought power because men in the mass were frail cowardly creatures who could not endure liberty or face the truth, and must be ruled over and systematically deceived by others who were stronger than themselves. That the choice for mankind lay between freedom and happiness, and that, for the great bulk of mankind, happiness was better. That the Party was the eternal guardian of the weak, a dedicated sect doing evil that good might come, sacrificing its own happiness to that of others. . . . 'You are ruling over us for our own good,' he said feebly. 'You believe that human beings are not fit to govern themselves, and therefore. . . .' (*NEF*, pp. 210–11)

To Winston's consternation, and that of most of Orwell's commentators, O'Brien contemptuously rejects this account, shooting a massive electric shock through Winston's body as a measure of his angry awareness that Winston does not really believe his own reply. He answers his own question in terms that have become famous.

> The Party seeks power entirely for its own sake. We are not interested in the good of others; we are interested solely in power. Not wealth or luxury or long life or happiness: only power, pure power . . . . We are different from all the oligarchies of the past in that we know what we are doing. All the others, even those who resembled ourselves, were cowards and hypocrites. The German Nazis and the Russian Communists came very close to us in their methods, but they never had the courage to recognize their own motives. They pretended, perhaps they even believed, that they had seized power unwillingly and for a limited time, and that just round the corner there lay a paradise where human beings would be free and equal. We are not like that. We know that no one ever seizes power with the intention of relinquishing it. Power is not a means, it is an end. One does not establish a dictatorship in order to safeguard a revolution; one makes the revolution in order to establish the dictatorship. The object of persecution is persecution. The object of torture is torture. The object of power is power. (*NEF*, pp. 211–12)

In words that emphasize the parallel with Roman Catholicism[109] – the Party as the Church and the Inner Party its priesthood – O'Brien declares: 'We are the priests of power . . . . God is power.' The oblique reference to a long-enduring religious collectivity underlines Goldstein's point that modern dictatorships realize that the greatest power comes from its collective embodiment and exercise. Individuals are merely the temporary representatives and agents of the Party, which is 'all-powerful and immortal'. And, as with the Church, the power that is crucial is that over the bodies and even more the minds of men. Power over matter – 'external reality, as you would call it' – is not important, and anyway 'already our control over matter is absolute.' Power over men is best symbolized, and best recognized, in the suffering it inflicts, for otherwise 'how can you be sure that he is obeying your will and not his own?'

Power is in inflicting pain and humiliation. Power is in tearing human minds to pieces and putting them together again in new shapes of your own choosing. Do you begin to see, then, what kind of world we are creating? It is the exact opposite of the stupid hedonistic Utopias that the old reformers imagined. A world of fear and treachery and torment, a world of trampling and being trampled upon, a world which will grow not less but *more* merciless as it refines itself. Progress in our world will be progress towards more pain. The old civilizations claimed that they were founded on love or justice. Ours is founded upon hatred. In our world there will be no emotions except fear, rage, triumph, and self-abasement. Everything else we shall destroy – everything . . . . There will be no loyalty, except loyalty towards the Party. There will be no love, except the love of Big Brother. There will be no laughter, except the laugh of triumph over a defeated enemy. There will be no art, no literature, no science. When we are omnipotent we shall have no more need of science. There will be no distinction between beauty and ugliness. There will no curiosity, no enjoyment of the process of life. All competing pleasures will be destroyed. But always – do not forget this Winston – always there will be the intoxication of power, constantly increasing and constantly growing subtler. Always, at every moment there will be the thrill of victory, the sensation of trampling on an enemy who is helpless. If you want a picture of the future, imagine a boot stamping on a human face – for ever. (*NEF*, pp. 214–15)

Commentators have differed over Orwell's treatment of the proles, but they have been almost unanimous in rejecting this view of the underlying motive of totalitarian or indeed any other kind of rule. Such a system, they say, is unreal and unworkable: Orwell has outdistanced plausibility and possibility. In one of the earliest and best reviews of *Nineteen Eighty-Four*, Philip Rahv noted that O'Brien 'simultaneously recalls and refutes the ideas of Dostoevsky's Grand Inquisitor', and went on:

Undoubtedly it is O'Brien, rather than Dostoevsky's Grand Inquisitor, who reveals the real nature of total power: yet that does not settle the question of O'Brien's personal psychology, the question, that is, of his ability to live with this naked truth as his sole support; nor is it conceivable that the party elite to which he belongs could live with this truth for very long. Evil, far more than good, is in need of the pseudo-religious justifications so readily provided by the ideologies of world-salvation generated both by the Left and the Right. Power is its own end, to be sure, but even the Grand Inquisitors are compelled, now as always, to believe in the fiction that their power is a means to some other end, gratifyingly noble and supernal.[110]

Others have continued this line of criticism, but in a markedly stronger vein. Howe has remarked that, at least in the West, no modern ruling class has yet been able to dispense with ideology. All have felt an overwhelming need to rationalize their power, to proclaim some admirable objective. Nor is this mere slyness or hypocrisy; the rulers of a modern society can hardly survive without a certain degree of sincere belief in their own claims. They cling to ideology not merely to win and hold followers, but to give themselves psychological and moral assurance. Can one imagine a twentieth century ruling class capable of discarding these supports and acknowledging to itself the true nature of its motives? I doubt it.

He believes that, without some kind of ideological rationalization, a totalitarian ruling class would find it almost impossible to sustain its morale. 'It would go soft, it would become corrupted in the obvious ways, it would lose the fanaticism that is essential to its survival.'[111]

Isaac Deutscher charged that Orwell had succumbed to a 'mysticism of cruelty'. Obsessed with the irrationality of the Stalinist purges and their repercussions in Spain, he had abandoned rationalism as an approach to politics and 'increasingly viewed reality through the dark glasses of a quasi-mystical pessimism'. He came to see all politics and all political movements as dominated by only one motive – 'sadistic power-hunger'. In Oceania, 'the Party is not a social body actuated by any interest or purpose. It is a phantom-like emanation of all that is foul in human nature. It is the metaphysical, mad and triumphant, Ghost of Evil.'[112]

A more recent tactic has been to deny that we are meant to take O'Brien's position as Orwell's. O'Brien, it is said, is clearly mad. He is the quintessential modern intellectual, as seen by Orwell, and his ravings about power are the natural consequence of his being carried away by the logic of his fantastic beliefs. It is O'Brien, not Orwell, who has succumbed to the 'mysticism of cruelty'. We are to regard his wild claims, says Bernard Crick, not as 'a projection of what total power will come to' but rather as 'a savage mocking of the pretensions of the power-hungry in general . . . within the fiction the "power for the sake of power" works best as a general satire of hierarchy, that is power-hunger, holding on to office, bureaucracy. . . .'[113] George Woodcock too sees O'Brien as 'a caricature, a monstrosity . . . . He is putting in an extreme and monstrous form the pretensions of all men of power; he is stating the logical consequences of the theory of elites which writers like Burnham and his Machiavellians have posed.'[114]

These doubts and difficulties over Orwell's position are compounded by the fact that several of his own statements seem to go against the views he attributes to O'Brien. In his essays on James Burnham, he took issue with Burnham's 'Machiavellian' view that power-hunger was the only motive in politics, and that 'literally anything can become right or wrong if the dominant class of the moment so wills it.' This ignores the fact that 'certain rules of conduct have to be observed if human society is to hold together at all. Burnham, therefore, was unable to see that the crimes and follies of the Nazi regime must lead by one route or another to disaster.'[115] In a similar vein he wrote: 'It would seem that the theory that there is no such thing as a "good" motive in politics, that nothing counts except force and fraud, has a hole in it somewhere, and that the Machiavellian system fails even by its own test of material success.'[116] The problem with Burnham, Orwell said, was that he 'never stops to ask *why* people want power'. He seems to assume that power-hunger 'is a natural instinct that does not have to be explained, like the desire for food'. Power over others made sense in times when it was necessary to free some people from drudgery in order for civilization to be possible at all. Nowadays, with machine production, that reason had disappeard. 'The question that he ought to ask, and never does ask, is: Why does the lust for naked power become a major human motive exactly *now*, when the dominion of man over man is ceasing to be necessary?'[117]

Even more telling are some of Orwell's comments on Jack London's *The Iron Heel*, the book he so often praised for its understanding of totalitarian society. He selected in particular a passage which to him showed London's deep understanding of 'the nature of a ruling class – that is, the characteristics which a ruling class must have if it is to survive'. It is a passage in which London emphasizes the sense of right possessed by the ruling Oligarchs, their belief that 'they alone maintained civilization', and that without them 'anarchy would reign and humanity would drop backward into the primitive night out of which it had so painfully emerged.' The passage continues:

> I cannot lay too great stress upon this high ethical righteousness of the whole Oligarch class. This has been the strength of the Iron Heel, and too many of the comrades have been slow or loath to realize it . . . . Love of the right, desire for the right, unhappiness with anything less than the right – in short, right conduct, is the prime factor of religion. And so with the Oligarchy . . . . The great driving force of the Oligarchs is the belief that they are doing right.[118]

It seems reasonably clear that Orwell was not making any general statement about the nature of politics in the speeches he gives to O'Brien. But that surely does not mean that we therefore have to discount them, to treat them as generalized satire or caricature, rather than as Orwell's own seriously held view. For, as his comments on Burnham indicate, Orwell does seem to have believed that power hunger was the motive *now*, in the contemporary world. The bitter irony of it is that such a motive ought to be least prevalent in modern industrial societies, where its economic basis has been removed; but the fact is that here, as in so many other domains, there has been a reversion to primitivism and barbarism. Even that understates the horror of the situation. Power hunger is in fact purer now than at any other time in history, as it emerges and holds sway shorn of all possible justifications. 'A society becomes totalitarian,' Orwell once wrote, 'when its structure becomes flagrantly artificial: that is, when its ruling class has lost its function but succeeds in clinging to power by force or fraud.'[119] That is the uniqueness of modern totalitarianism. In this sense O'Brien is only stating the general rule. Oceania is not an oddity or monstrosity; it is not even a particularly exaggerated expression of the reality of twentieth-century totalitarian politics.

There is plenty of evidence to show that Orwell did think that 'power for power's sake' was an accurate conception of the basis of modern totalitarian rule. We can turn once more to *The Iron Heel*, and the famous passage which Orwell not only clearly knew but which many have thought strongly influenced the imagery in O'Brien's key speech on power. It is the Oligarchs' answer to the claims and threats of labour, and it is couched in terms of the purest power:

> We have no words to waste on you. When you reach out your vaunted strong hands for our palaces and purpled ease, we will show you what strength is. In roar of shell and shrapnel and in whine of machine guns will our answer be couched. We will grind you revolutionists down under our heel, and we shall walk upon your faces. The world is ours, we are its lords, and ours it shall remain. As for the host of labour, it has been in the dirt since history began, and I read history aright. And in the dirt it shall remain so long as I and mine and those that come after us have the power. There is the word. It is the king of words – Power. Not God, not Mammon, but Power. Pour it over your tongue till it tingles with it. Power.'[120]

Similarly, one of the things Orwell most admired in Zamyatin's *We* – and contrasted in this respect with *Brave New World* – was Zamyatin's awareness of the 'power hunger . . . sadism . . . and hardness' which must characterize the ruling elite in a totalitarian society.[121] It was just such qualities that Orwell discerned in contemporary Nazism. The Nazis, he said, had been able to carry out various kinds of 'socialistic' measures without a qualm 'because their aim was simply power and not any particular form of society. They would just as soon be Reds as Whites, provided that it left them on top.'[122] He found in the very marching style of the Nazis 'a certain philosophy of life'. 'The goose-step is one of the most horrible sights in the world, far more terrifying than a dive-bomber. It is simply an affirmation of naked power; contained in it, quite consciously and intentionally, is the vision of a boot crashing down on a face.'[123]

In 'Raffles and Miss Blandish' he linked the sadism and power-worship of *No Orchids for Miss Blandish* with contemporary fascism and Stalinism, adding that in both those cases 'it is important to notice that the cult of power tends to be mixed up with a love of cruelty and wickedness *for their own sakes*.'[124] And in his general 'Notes on Nationalism' he brought together a host of contemporary movements which had totalitarian tendencies and characterized them by their power-hunger and power-worship.

It is of course open to anyone to doubt, as do Howe and Crick, that any political regime consciously founded on the pure lust for power could survive for very long. The important thing, however, is that Orwell himself seems to have believed that such a system was not only stable but well-nigh invulnerable to internal challenge. We should remember in this context that the Nazi regime was overthrown not from within but only by defeat in war. Russian communism too has had a pretty good run, even allowing for the internal changes since Orwell wrote. Moreover, some of the most respected students of nazism and Stalinism have taken a very similar view to Orwell's of the basic driving force of these systems. Alan Bullock, for instance, has written in his biography of Hitler:

> To say that Hitler was ambitious scarcely describes the intensity of the lust for power and the craving to dominate which consumed him. It was the will to power in its crudest and purest form, not identifying itself with the triumph of a principle as with Lenin or

Robespierre – for the only principle of Nazism was power and domination for its own sake – nor finding satisfaction in the fruits of power, for, by comparison with other Nazi leaders like Göring, Hitler lived an ascetic life. For a long time Hitler succeeded in identifying his own power with the recovery of Germany's old position in the world, and there were many in the 1930s who spoke of him as a fanatical patriot. But as soon as the interests of Germany began to diverge from his own, from the beginning of 1943 onwards, his patriotism was seen at its true value – Germany, like everything else in the world, was only a means, a vehicle for his own power, which he would sacrifice with the same indifference as the lives of those he sent to the Eastern Front. By its nature this was an insatiable appetite, securing only a temporary gratification by the exercise of power, then restlessly demanding an ever further extension of it.[125]

Again, while no one has denied that the Bolsheviks based their claim to rule on ideological grounds – they were after all the 'dictatorship of the proletariat' – there have been many observers who, like Orwell, saw the Stalinist power structure as indistinguishable in everything but name from that of nazism. In particular, Stalin's own motivation has been seen as comparable in its power-seeking to Hitler's, and to O'Brien's. Alexander Weissberg, one of Stalin's victims who survived, wrote of him:

He wanted such untrammeled power that when he pressed a button the masses of the Russian people, of the oppressed peoples of Asia and of the revolutionary workers of Europe would swing into movement . . . . He wanted to be absolutely free in all his actions, and the only way open to him was to enslave the Russian people.[126]

Arthur Koestler, who also had had first-hand experience of the Stalinist tyranny, puts in Rubashov's diary in *Darkness at Noon*:

It is said that No. 1 has Machiavelli's *Prince* lying permanently by his bedside. So he should: since then, nothing really important has been said about the rules of political ethics . . . . We introduced neo-Machiavellism into this century; the others, the counter-revolutionary dictatorships, have clumsily imitated it.[127]

We should perhaps finally note, on this issue, that O'Brien's revelation of the ultimate motive of totalitarian power is not the 'official' view presented to Oceania. It is 'off the record'; it is a privileged insight vouchsafed to Winston in the course of a process of 're-integration' which ensures that it will be a worthless piece of information once O'Brien has got through with him. There is after all an ideology in Oceania – Ingsoc – and presumably that is translated to the population – or as much of it as matters – in much the same way as Marxism–Leninism to the Russian people. One such device is the cynical but enigmatic party slogans – 'War is Peace', etc. O'Brien's secret, and the madness it enshrines, is too terrifying to publicize to even so brainwashed and degraded a population as that of Oceania.

But O'Brien has not yet fully broken Winston, even though the latter's heart 'freezes' at the revelation of the Party's purpose. Winston summons up his failing energies to oppose to this his conviction that a civilization founded on fear and hatred can never survive, that 'life will defeat' the Party. O'Brien's answer is pat: 'We control life . . . . at all its levels.' There is no such thing as a 'human nature' that will be outraged and turn on the Party. 'We create human nature. Men are infinitely malleable' (*NEF*, p. 216). When Winston persists with talk of the unconquerable 'spirit of Man', O'Brien tells him he is 'the last man', and proposes to show him what sort of creature man is. Winston is ordered to strip and to walk towards a three-sided mirror. What he sees is a 'bowed, grey-coloured, skeleton-like thing' coming towards him, his own wrecked and emaciated body. This 'bag of filth,' says O'Brien, is 'the last man'; this is humanity.

Winston's body is battered, but the eyes are still 'fierce and watchful'. As he defiantly points out, he still has not betrayed Julia. Despite their telling him that Julia betrayed him 'immediately and unreservedly', they have not been able to stop him loving her. This 'sticking point' is linked in Winston's mind to his belief that the Party's power cannot penetrate to the 'inner heart', that whatever you were forced to confess, your feelings could not be altered by them. The Party might spy on you night and day, they might lock you up for ever, but 'the few cubic centimetres inside your skull' remained always your own (*NEF*, p. 25). Winston even half-hopes that the Party will shoot him soon, because then 'they would have blown his brain to pieces before they could reclaim it. The heretical thought would be unpunished, unrepented, out of their reach for ever. They would have blown a hole in their own perfection. To die hating them, that was freedom' (*NEF*, p. 226).

This last, and to him most vital, satisfaction is denied him. In the third and final stage of his re-education – what O'Brien calls 'acceptance' – his last defence is smashed and revealed for the cruel illusion that it is. In Room 101, faced with the rats that will tear out his face, Winston betrays Julia and gives over his brain and heart whole and entire to the Party. A chance encounter with Julia, who is in the same numbed and transformed state, shows how total and effective Winston's 're-integration' has been. Sitting in his corner seat at the Chestnut Tree Café, weeping 'gin-scented tears', Winston knows that he is no longer merely willing to obey Big Brother: now he loves him.

In the year that he was busy on *Nineteen Eighty-Four*, Orwell wrote: 'This business of making people *conscious* of what is happening outside their own small circle is one of the major problems of our time, and a new literary technique will have to be evolved to meet it.'[128] A new kind of world, a world of genocide and totalitarianism, required new ways to capture its unique horror and irrationality. The illusory utopias of the age, expressed above all in the myth of the Soviet Union as the ideal socialist society, were the products of people's most fervent hopes and dreams. The only effective remedy was to appeal to equally deep feelings: their fears and nightmares. The false utopia could only be countered by the anti-utopia, the need for heaven by the fear of hell. In *Nineteen Eighty-Four*, even more than in *Animal Farm*, Orwell reworked the utopian genre to produce a 'didactic fantasy' in which he found the imaginative freedom to express the concerns of his earlier writings more compellingly than ever before.[129]

One measure of his success is the sheer credibility of *Nineteen Eighty-Four*. It was a risky enterprise to fuse the England of the 1940s with the deeper trends transforming the whole of industrial civilization, and so project a picture of the entire globe in the coming decades. Such a mix of the immediate present and the near future was unusual in the utopian tradition. But the daring paid off. Orwell produced a definitive contemporary image of horror that, irrespective of political allegiances, evidently touched on widespread fears and anxieties – as witness the book's continuing popularity. Whether or not people believe that they themselves are living in it, the world of Airstrip One is a believable world, a possible world, all the more so for the sudden startling touches of homespun familiarity.

Can we be more precise about its contemporary relevance? Is *Nineteen Eighty-Four* happening *now*? Yes, much more so than people are inclined to think on hasty reflection or a superficial reading of the book. It is true that much of the overt political trappings of *Nineteen Eighty-Four* are not present or have receded – in Western Europe and North America, at least. The communist states of Eastern Europe too have moved away from the extremes of Stalinist tyranny, although, despite the rise of an articulate and sometimes active opposition, the hold of the military and political apparatus remains unshaken. But the very passage of so many 'Orwellian' terms and concepts – Big Brother, thoughtcrime, Newspeak, doublethink – into the ordinary language suggests that, however obscurely or obliquely, people recognize them as reflections of their own world and feel the need for them. Even the physical environment of many cities, with their devastated and depopulated inner areas and crumbling infrastructure of services, recall the drab, run-down appearance of the London of *Nineteen Eighty-Four*. The planned, 'high-tech' urban utopias of the 1950s and 1960s have ended in a wasteland of derelict housing estates and razed tower-blocks.

Moreover, the most obvious contrast with Oceania – the absence of directly dictatorial political control – should not blind us to more signifiant underlying similarities. The coercive apparatus of Oceania is itself, as we have seen, destined to become redundant, as the mechanisms of 'reality control' and thought-conditioning tighten their grip. Is this not also where the continuities between *Nineteen Eighty-Four* and 1984 are most evident – in the relentless advance of Newspeak and doublethink? The mass media, especially television – paradoxically, the medium least explored by Orwell – have moved right into the centre of all industrial societies. They have affected every aspect of politics, culture and ideology. Everyday speech for many people is a mixture of advertising jingles and the journalistic idioms – 'journalese' – of the popular newspapers. Snowball's 'four legs good, two legs bad' is the common idiom of political parties and orthodoxies everywhere. The language of politics and advertising have merged into a synthetic Newspeak every bit as trivializing and emasculating as in Oceania. In the 1984 campaign for the Democratic presidential nomination, the 'debate' between the two chief contenders consisted almost entirely in bandying about the popular advertising slogan of a large hamburger chain – 'where's the beef?' Television, as a kind of visual Newspeak, has itself mapped out large parts of the social and political world by the imposition of staged accounts, simplified stereotypes and crudely distorting definitions of reality. In societies where large sections of the population are 'functionally illiterate' – over 20 per cent in the United States – and the majority of the population, of all classes, get their main understanding of the world through television, the possibilities for brainwashing and manipulation are in many ways even greater than with the more primitive media technology of Oceania. The impulse now may be as much commercial as directly political, but the centralization of culture and communication that this has entailed in either case shows the difference to be of minor importance. Whether for commercial or political reasons, the effect is to produce a population reduced to an apathetic consuming 'mass', resolutely indifferent to and ignorant of the forces that control their lives. Both capitalist and commissar teach that 'Ignorance is Strength.'

If this is true of the internal life of society, it is even truer of the world picture. Nowhere has Orwell been more prescient than in his account of a world of oligarchic super-states, dominating their populations by the threat of mutual annihilation and a carefully orchestrated demonology. 'Bloated capitalists' confront 'blood-thirsty Communists' in the mutual frenzy of the Hate Weeks whipped up whenever oligarchical control is under threat, or thought to be. In *Nineteen Eighty-Four*, it is true, the threats and counter-threats of the super-states are bluffs; atomic war has already been tried, and certain grim consequences drawn. We too play our 'war games' with the declared purpose that there will be no final outcome and no winners or losers; but if the bluffs are called, war will be peace in a sense of doublethink going beyond the imagination even of the rulers of Oceania.

9

The Utopia of 'Behavioural Engineering': B. F. Skinner and *Walden Two*

This is no time to abandon notions of progress, improvement or, indeed, human perfectibility. The simple fact is that man is able, now as never before, to lift himself by his own bootstraps. In achieving control of the world of which he is a part, he may learn at last to control himself.

B. F. Skinner, 'Freedom and the Control of Men', *The American Scholar* (Winter, 1955–6)

We had read *Brave New World* and *Nineteen Eighty-Four* and were not impressed. The writing is great, the logic downright silly.

Kathleen Kinkade, *A Walden Two Experiment: The First Five Years of Twin Oaks Community* (1973)

A UTOPIA OF MEANS, NOT ENDS

In the same year – 1948 – that Orwell wrote his *Nineteen Eighty-Four*, and when hope was not a commodity to be purchased at all cheaply in world markets, the Harvard psychologist B. F. Skinner presented his optimistic utopia, *Walden Two*. It got a hot reception.[1] 'A slur upon a name, a corruption of an impulse,' wrote *Life* magazine; 'such a triumph of mortmain, or the dead hand, has not been envisaged since the days of Sparta.'[2] 'Is it not meaningful,' asked the American humanist Joseph Wood Krutch, 'to say that, whereas Plato's Republic and More's Utopia are noble absurdities, Walden Two is an ignoble one; that the first two ask men to be more than human, while the second urges them to be less?'[3] A contemporary anthology of utopian societies, *The Quest for Utopia*, denied entry to Skinner's utopia, 'out of respect for the true utopian spirit'. In a shocked comment on *Walden Two* the editors wrote: 'We have descended from the heights of confidence in man's capacities and noble aspirations for his progressive betterment to a nadir of ignominy in which he is placed on a par with pigeons.' They continued:

> While it was to be expected that sooner or later the principle of psychological conditioning would be made the basis of a serious construction of utopia . . . yet not even the effective satire of Huxley is adequate preparation for the shocking horror of the idea when positively presented. Of all the dictatorships espoused by utopists, this is the most profound, and incipient dictators might well find in this utopia a guidebook of political practice.[4]

Like many others, they at first considered *Walden Two* to be a spoof, a dystopia parading as a utopia.[5]

Why did *Walden Two* provoke such hostility? Certainly the times were not with Skinner. The historical situation could hardly have been less propitious. The Western world had just witnessed the horrors of two 'utopian' social experiments – the Nazi and the Soviet – and was in no mood for further utopian offerings, still less for one that boasted of its 'scientific' basis with a confidence reminiscent of nazism and communism. The fact that, on a quick reading, there were aspects of *Walden Two* that actually evoked the Nazi and Soviet experiments hardly helped matters. Far more to the taste of the post-war public was Orwell's gruesome anti-utopia. Skinner's book did not enjoy even the usual pecuniary rewards of a *succès de scandale*. After a brief flurry, sales languished, and the book went out of print for many years. It is clear that *Walden Two* was regarded as not only offensive but also irrelevant.

Twenty-three years later, Skinner revived the controversy over his utopia with the publication of what was virtually a manifesto, a summary of his life's work defiantly entitled *Beyond Freedom and Dignity* (1971). By this time the purely historical antipathy to utopianism had long since passed, as was evinced by the steady sales of *Walden Two*, newly re-published, along with much other utopian writing. Moreover, there was now actually in existence a number of communities explicitly founded on the principles of *Walden Two*. The best known of these was (and is) Twin Oaks in Virginia, whose founder Kathleen Kinkade published an account of the early years under the title *A Walden Two Experiment*. It was inevitable, therefore, that the arguments of *Beyond Freedom and Dignity* should be discussed at least partly within the context of *Walden Two*, especially as Skinner himself says in the former that 'the author's *Walden Two* describes a community designed essentially on the principles which appear in the present book.'[6]

It was those principles – the principles of 'behaviourism'[7] or 'behavioural conditioning' – which outraged so many humanist philosophers and critics, and which continued, and continue, to give offence long after the initial outburst of hostility to *Walden Two*. They are the principles of an experimental science of human behaviour, developed by Skinner over a forty-year period of research and writing that began with the publication in 1938 of his first major work, *The Behaviour of Organisms: An Experimental Analysis*. Skinner wrote *Walden Two*, at a fairly early stage in his career, to popularize his doctrines, and he has continued to refine them in the subsequent years. Any examination of *Walden Two*, therefore, has to come to terms with the unusually fully developed theoretical system contained both within that book and in the rest of Skinner's writing, most accessibly in *Beyond Freedom and Dignity*.

Skinner's system is one of 'behavioural' or 'cultural engineering'; and *Walden*

Two is a utopia of behavioural engineering. This gives it a distinctiveness over and above its other differences from twentieth-century utopias, and, indeed, practically all other utopias as well. Most utopias have as their main emphasis a vision of ultimate goals, a final state of society in which peace, happiness and freedom are at last realized. It is this vision which gives them their power and their enduring appeal. For if we examine the mechanisms by which these goals are achieved, and the means described for maintaining the utopia in working order, we might be very much less inclined to enter into the realm of utopia. The social machinery of most utopias is a mechanic's nightmare. It is an affair of disconnected struts, loose bolts and unattached levers, like an unfinished and abandoned contraption by Mr Heath Robinson.

It is here that *Walden Two* is unique. It is a utopia of means, not ends. In it, technique has been elevated to utopian status. Skinner has always been impatient with those who demanded to know what the social purpose or goal of his utopia is. To him, the goals of any perfected society are self-evident – better health, better education, greater knowledge, more fulfilling work and leisure, harmonious relationships. The problem of ultimate values is not a serious issue of contention. What has always flawed utopian schemes, Skinner argues, and destroyed utopian communities, is the lack of a scientific theory of human behaviour which would enable those values to be realized. Thus, while the ideals of such communities are irreproachably noble, and the striving of members perfectly genuine, the utopian enterprise founders on the rocks of everyday personal relationships. No one has sufficiently thought through how to change the dispositions and behaviour of members, such that their actions can be realistically brought into conformity with their intentions. Once the problems begin to pile up, as they inevitably do after the first exhilarating phase of boundless self-sacrifice, old habits and unreformed behaviour reassert themselves and begin to tear the community apart. So, speaking of nineteenth-century utopian communities in America, Skinner notes that, 'contrary to popular belief, most nineteenth-century communities were economically successful. If utopia continued to mean impossible, it was because there were other problems to be solved. The important ones concerned personal relations. . . .'[8]

Walden Two therefore purports to offer a method whereby human behaviour can be shaped and altered. To this extent it is like Skinner's more formal theoretical writings, and Skinner clearly sees it as such. But unlike those, *Walden Two* sets itself the further task of showing how a 'technology of behaviour' can be applied to the solution of traditional social problems, of the kind utopias have commonly attempted to resolve, both in theory and in practice. Skinner regards *Walden Two* as a 'thought experiment' in the design of cultures. It shows 'a community in which the most important problems of daily life . . . are solved'. It is 'a pilot experiment', trying out on a small scale what we may later wish to do on the large. 'If,' says Skinner, 'we want to find out how people can live together without quarrelling, can produce the goods they need without working too hard, or can raise and educate their children more efficiently, let us start with units of manageable size before moving on to larger problems.'[9] Similarly, speaking of the Twin Oaks community, Skinner says:

> It is easy to dismiss the problems faced by the founders of Twin Oaks as of local interest only, but we are all trying to solve problems like them all the time. We are all engaged in the design of cultural practices. Twin Oaks is simply the world in miniature. The problems it faces and the solutions it tries are those of a world community.[10]

We need to be careful about what we understand by 'the world in miniature', or the analogous idea that Walden Two is in some sense a microcosm of a possible society on a world scale. Skinner is not offering Walden Two – and certainly not Twin Oaks – as a small-scale model of a utopian society, a pattern which, suitably blown-up, can simply be applied to a nation-state or even the international community. His language is sometimes careless and makes it sound as if this is that he is saying. But even in *Walden Two* Frazier, the founder, explains that Walden Two is offered simply as a model for imitation by others. It does not aspire to absorb greater and greater numbers; indeed, the plan is to create new communities, new Waldens, by a process of fission as soon as numbers go much beyond one thousand. In recent years Skinner has been at pains to make this point more explicit. He has firmly identified himself with the 'small is beautiful' philosophy of E. F. Schumacher.[11] Walden Two works, it seems, to a good extent because the small scale on which it is constructed is the most effective for the employment of Skinnerian techniques of behavioural engineering. To increase the scale runs the risk of coarsening the techniques and so distorting the behavioural consequences. Consequently, if we think of Walden Two as a model for future society, we should look forward to a world of many Waldens rather than one big Walden Two.

Once again, therefore, we come back to the point that *Walden Two* is essentially a utopia of means – a 'methodological utopia', if the phrase be allowed. Its function is exemplary. Consistent with the experimental spirit of Skinner's science of behaviour, it aims to demonstrate by the design of a utopian community a particular and allegedly privileged method for solving the problems of social life. It is this which explains the otherwise puzzling use of Thoreau's *Walden* as the inspiration of Walden Two. 'We chose our name,' explains Frazier, 'in honour of Thoreau's experiment, which was in many ways like our own. It was an experiment in living. . . .'[12]

With these general remarks on the function and purpose of *Walden Two*, we can now turn to that experiment in living which has alarmed and outraged so many thoughtful and sensitive people.

THE WORLD OF WALDEN TWO: (i): A TECHNOLOGY OF BEHAVIOUR

If Skinner has any overall vision of the good life, it seems to derive primarily from his small town, middle-class Protestant background. Skinner was born and brought up in the country town of Susquehanna, which is situated in the rich, rolling farm country of Pennsylvania. He evidently had a happy childhood there,[13] and the setting and some of the activities of Walden Two echo this. Walden Two lies 'in the midst of some prosperous farm land'. Farming plays an important part in its life – as much for its moral as its economic value. Both Twin Oaks and its offspring, the community of East Wind in Southern

Missouri, have also been enthusiasts for farming, even though it causes them a lot of trouble and barely makes an economic return. In fact, they could not survive without the income from the sale of hammocks, their one great economic success.

The general ethos of Walden Two also reflects middle-class Protestant culture. It has a brisk, active attitude towards life, it sees a central value in the activity of work, and it is constantly on the alert for improvement in its practices. At the same time, it condemns toil for its own sake, and acknowledges the importance of rest and relaxation. Leisure and recreation are treated with as much seriousness and scientific experimentation as work and education.

It would be wrong therefore to bring with us too much of the imagery of Thoreau's spare and Spartan life around Walden pond.[14] Walden Two is in no sense a primitivistic utopia. It welcomes, and indeed embraces, modern science and technology. 'The secret of our economic success,' says Frazier, 'is this: we avoid the goat and the loom.' He explains: 'We avoid the temptation to return to primitive modes of farming and industry . . . . Utopias usually spring from a rejection of modern life. Our point of view here isn't atavistic, however. We look ahead, not backwards, for a better version (*WT*, pp. 75–6). Kathleen Kinkade of Twin Oaks makes a similar point in reporting the reason given by one new member for being drawn to the community: 'It made so much sense, embracing technology instead of rejecting it. Everybody else is involved in this back-to-the-land horseshit.'[15]

Indeed, Frazier's original 'prospectus' for Walden Two, published in a popular scientific magazine, sets out admirably the objectives of the new community. As reported in summary, it read:

> Political action was of no use in building a better world, and men of good will had better turn to other measures as soon as possible. Any group of people could secure economic self-sufficiency with the help of modern technology, and the psychological problems of group living could be solved with available principles of 'behavioural engineering.' (*WT*, p. 14)

Into this world come the visitors: Burris, a professor of psychology and one-time fellow graduate student of Frazier's; Burris's old student Rogers and his friend Steve Jamnik, together with their girlfriends Barbara and Mary; and Castle, a professor of philosophy and a colleague of Burris's. The book takes the form largely of a series of dialogues between Frazier and his visitors. Frazier explains, defends, urges. The messianic fervour is however tempered by a certain wariness which is used to good effect at various points in the book. Burris is the level-headed agnostic, curious, disinterested, open to conviction and at bottom sympathetic to the enterprise. His conversion is gradual but steady, and by the end of the book we are prepared for his decision to return to Walden Two as a member. (Although Skinner's first name is Burrhus, incidentally, it is clear that he speaks at least as much through Frazier as through Burris.)

Castle is Frazier's implacable antagonist. He represents the traditional literary humanist, with his axiomatic beliefs in the freedom, dignity and responsibility of every individual human being. The scientific pretensions of Frazier's philosophy are anathema to him, and the idea of 'behavioural engineering' horrifying. The exchanges with Frazier are at first friendly and bantering, but they gradually increase in heat as Castle realizes the enormity of what is being attempted at Walden Two. At the end Castle is barely coherent, and we leave him babbling into Burris's inattentive ears. In Castle, in fact, Skinner anticipates the attacks of most of his humanist critics, such as Joseph Wood Krutch, although they could scarcely have been flattered by the portrait, and were clearly unimpressed by Frazier's rebuttals.

Frazier and Castle are engaged in a battle for the hearts and minds of the young visitors, who are attentive but largely silent observers. By the end, Steve and Mary are enthusiastic converts, and are accepted into the membership of Walden Two. Rogers is clearly attracted to the Walden philosophy, but yields to the increasingly alienated Barbara. At the very least, then, we can say that Frazier wins the game 3–2: helped, of course, by Skinner's stacking of the cards.

That is all there is to the 'story' of *Walden Two*. The rest is disputation. And the heart of the dispute is the system of behavioural engineering which penetrates into every recess of the community's life, the most intimate and personal as well as the most public.

Skinner's system implies as much an attitude towards the way we do things as to any specific techniques for modifying behaviour. The visitors to Walden Two encounter an example of this at the very outset of their visit. They take tea. Tea is served by a rather effective system, involving self-service urns and drinking glasses which are large, are pleasant to drink from, don't spill and are heat-retaining. Castle reacts with amused contempt to this trivial example of the application of the scientific method. Frazier retorts:

> The actual achievement is beside the point. The main thing is, we encourage our people to view every habit and custom with an eye to possible improvement. A constantly experimental attitude towards everything – that's all we need. Solutions to problems of every sort follow almost miraculously. (*WT*, pp. 29–30)

Later the visitors are shown weightier examples of this experimental attitude. There is an elaborate system of work-scheduling ('an amazing piece of cultural engineering – the staggered schedule!'), which keeps rooms, facilities and equipment continuously in use, but whose most valuable result, according to Frazier, is psychological: 'We're utterly free of that institutional atmosphere which is inevitable when everyone is doing the same thing at the same time. Our days have a roundness, a flexibility, a diversity, a flow. It's all quite pleasing and healthful' (*WT*, p. 45).

Then there is the careful attention to the social organization and domestic technology of cooking, eating and washing up. Dining takes place on the basis of a modified cafeteria system. Small dining rooms, variously decorated in the styles of diverse historical periods and national cultures, are grouped around a central serving area. Burris notes the absence of both the appearance and the effects of production-line delivery common in most cafeteria systems: he is reminded, rather, of a buffet supper. Meals are taken from individual trays, which are recessed so that food can be served directly on to them, thus eliminating the need for plates and so saving time and labour in washing-up. More labour is saved by the fact that the trays are transparent, so that both sides can be inspected simultaneously while the trays are being cleaned. (Castle typically guffaws at this, while Frazier as typically scores a major point in putting him down[16]). All the day's washing-up is done by a few people working on a shift basis, using a simple continuous-flow system involving a mechanized moving belt and automatic soaping, rinsing and stacking. As Frazier says, Walden Two is on its way to 'industrializing housewifery'. There is the deliberate intention of freeing women (and men) from domestic labour, to enable them to play a full part in the wider life of the community.

The examples so far have however only hinted at the main principle of behavioural engineering. It is one thing to design new cultural practices; it is quite another to motivate people to accept them and to make them work. Such a concern is inescapably at the centre of the system of child-rearing and education at Walden Two. Here, above all, is where the new men and women of the behaviourist utopia are being fashioned. It is in showing his visitors the nursery and children's quarters, therefore, and explaining the practices employed there, that Frazier also expounds and defends the science of behavioural engineering.

'Each of us,' Frazier begins provocatively, 'is engaged in a pitched battle with the rest of mankind.' This alarming statement turns out to mean no more than what others have sometimes referred to as 'the vexatious fact of society'. Individuals pursue interests, some of which conflict inevitably with those of other individuals. This is experienced most commonly by each individual as the struggle between himself ('the individual') and 'society'. History is the record of attempted resolutions – or evasions – of this basic existential dilemma. The family, religion and the state are all institutions which have been pressed into service to assure at least a temporary stability. But such stability has been purchased at the cost of enormous waste and unnecessary suffering, for both the individual and society. This is largely because societies have operated through the imperfect medium of codes of ethics and religion, with their unrealistic precepts of 'good conduct' and their equally inappropriate threats of hell-fire and damnation. Where these have failed, the state has stepped in with the even more crudely punitive sanctions of the whip and the gaol-house. The problem of the relationships between ourselves, as human beings living in society, has never been subjected to properly scientific investigation, unlike the problem of our relationship to nature. And yet the questions, says Frazier guilelessly, 'are simple enough. What's the best behaviour for the individual so far as the group is concerned? And how can the individual be induced to behave in that way? Why not explore these questions in a scientific spirit?' (*WT*, p. 105).

Skinner does not, either in *Walden Two* or elsewhere, devote much time to the question of 'the best behaviour' for the individual in relation to the group. As with the question of the good life, he assumes a consensus, derived in the main from the traditional body of Western ethical systems. The individual should be co-operative, productive, truthful, free of envy and prejudice, able to sympathize with the concerns of others. The important question, as always, is how he is to be made to act in such desirable ways. Skinner's answer, in a nutshell, is that he can be scientifically conditioned to do so.

It is important to stress at the outset the differences between Skinner and the great Russian psychologist Ivan Pavlov, since both are associated in the popular mind with the theory of conditioning. Pavlov developed the theory and the technique of the 'conditioned reflex'; Skinner's contribution is towards the theory of 'operant behaviour' and the techniques of 'operant conditioning'. According to Skinner's own account, what Pavlov essentially accomplished was the conditioning of emotions and feelings, rather than behaviour in the true sense. Pavlov's dogs came to salivate at the sound of the bell alone, in the absence of the food which had previously accompanied the ringing of the bell. They salivate because they expect the food, of course, but the important point is that the getting and eating of the food is not an integral part of the conditioned response. In other words, in Pavlovian conditioning the *consequences* of the behaviour are not an essential ingredient in the production and repetition of the behaviour; quite the contrary, it is the stimulus prior to the behaviour – the sound of the bell – which produces the desired behaviour (or more correctly, perhaps, the desired sentiment). As Skinner says, 'in Pavlov's basic studies, indeed, it might be said that the organism did not receive food *for* doing anything; the salivation elicited by the conditioned stimulus did not produce the food which followed.'[17]

Pavlov's basic contribution was the concept of the 'reflex arc'. Through conditioning, a stimulus from within or without the organism sets up a state of tension that seeks for motor or secretory discharge. It is a simple stimulus–response model of action – or, better, reaction. Stimulus and response are associated in a single, indissoluble, spasm. The conjunction takes place in prior periods of learning by the organism, and in principle the effects of the behaviour in present circumstances are not relevant to modifying that behaviour. Only a process of 'unlocking' the bond between stimulus and response, by counter-conditioning, might do that.

It is – so Skinner and his disciples claim – Pavlovian, not Skinnerian, conditioning that is satirized by Huxley in *Brave New World*. Hence it is wrong to assume that *Walden Two* simply presents in a positive and rosier light the techniques so witheringly attacked by Huxley. The two utopias employ different types of conditioning. In a famous example from *Brave New World*, Delta-class babies, destined to be menials, are conditioned not to like books or natural objects, irrelevant and possibly dangerous distractions to people in their position. The technique is to put the babies on the floor near colourful books and bright flowers. When the babies touch the books or flowers, they receive electric shocks and are frightened by loud noises. After repeated experiences of this kind, the mere sight or smell of books and flowers is sufficient to stimulate an aversive response. Stimulus and response have become one single reflex arc, and the children are forever safe from the attractions of literature or nature.

By contrast, Skinner's 'operant conditioning' throws the emphasis on the conditioning effect of the consequences of behaviour. Behaviour is monitored and modified throughout by its consequences. As Harvey Wheeler has suggested, there is a real difference of scientific paradigm here between Pavlov and Skinner. 'Pavlov's *a priori* formula was in accord with classical mechanics: stimulus produces response. Skinner defines behaviour *a posteriori*: responses are shaped by consequences. This is biological rather than mechanical.'[18] Skinner has indeed come to rely increasingly on evolutionary biology as the more inclusive framework within which to situate his theory of behaviour. In Darwinian evolution, the success of a species is related to its differential ability, in competition with other species, to produce adaptive responses to challenges from the environment. These responses – which are usually chance variations of structure or behaviour – have what is called 'survival value' and are hence selected by the environment.

In Skinnerian terms, this process is expressed by saying that the environment stimulates (not necessarily automatically) behaviour which is rewarding or 'reinforcing', and which is therefore repeated over time, the more often, the more it continues to be rewarding. This is 'operant conditioning'. (Skinner uses the term 'operant' to describe 'any behaviour which operates upon the environment to produce consequences'.) In the case of the whole evolutionary history of the species, some of the behaviour thus reinforced has a genetic basis, and the individual acquires this endowment as a matter of course at birth. But with human beings, a major part of behaviour is learned in interaction with the environment after birth. This learning, however, obeys the same evolutionary laws. Behaviour which is successful or rewarding to the individual ('positively reinforcing') is strengthened (selected) over time; that which isn't successful or rewarding ('negatively reinforcing') is eliminated or abandoned. Behaviour in general, therefore, is a function of the 'contingencies of survival' in the natural and social environment.

In effect, Skinner has replaced the two-term, stimulus–response model of Pavlov's by a three-term model: stimulus–behaviour–reinforcement. The significance of this reformulation is that the environment comes to play an even more crucial part than it does in the Pavlovian model. The environment is the source not just of the stimulus but of the 'reinforcement' – the reward or punishment which is 'contingent' upon (or a consequence of) some particular piece of behaviour, and which encourages the individual to repeat the behaviour. As Skinner says,

> the environment not only prods or lashes, it *selects*. Its role is similar to that in natural selection, though on a very different time scale . . . . It is now clear that we must take into account what the environment does to an organism not only before but after it responds. Behaviour is shaped and maintained by its consequences.[19]

Skinner draws two inferences, one theoretical, one practical, from this understanding of the role of the environment. The first is that 'behaviour which operates upon the environment to produce consequences . . . can be studied by arranging environments in which specific consequences are contingent upon it.' The study of human behaviour can, in other words, become a genuinely empirical, experimental science. The second point is the practical one that 'the environment can be manipulated. It is true that man's genetic endowment can be changed only very slowly, but changes in the environment of the individual have quick and dramatic effects. A technology of operant behaviour is . . . already well advanced. . . .'[20] Linking both theoretical and practical concerns is the notion that the entire span of human behaviour is a function of what Skinner calls 'the contingencies of reinforcement', a determinate relation between environment, behaviour and reinforcement. By the judicious arrangement of the contingencies of reinforcement we are enabled to control behaviour in ways that are for all practical purposes unlimited.[21]

So – but in a more roundabout way and in less elaborate language – Frazier informs his guests. And he underlines the point that behavioural control on Skinnerian principles does not produce the automata that are the usual products of Pavlovian conditioning. This is because operant conditioning, whose focus of concern is the shaping of behaviour, is directed towards the *way* human beings satisfy their needs, rather than to the immediate gratification of needs. In Pavlovian conditioning there is no mediation between stimulus and response. The individual is 'programmed' to react in an automatic manner to discrete stimuli – thirst, hunger, sex, fear – conceived in advance. If the world were simply the laboratory, behaviour could indeed be conditioned to meet all situations. But in the real world, as Frazier says,

> you can't foresee all future circumstances, and you can't specify adequate future conduct. You don't know what will be required. Instead you have to set up certain behavioural processes which will lead the individual to design his own 'good' conduct when the time comes. We call that sort of thing 'self-control'. But don't be misled, the control always rests in the last analysis in the hands of society. (*WT*, p. 105)

This is admittedly far from clear, and Skinner has subsequently elaborated the same point elsewhere. Most utopias, he says, have been designed for the direct satisfaction of needs. They have been lands flowing with milk and honey, havens of pleasure and idleness. Huxley's *Brave New World* is directed against these 'cities of pigs', these lands of Cokaygne, and the satire is justified. Mere idleness and abundance, the total satisfaction of needs, does not make for happiness. 'The word "sad" is etymologically related to the word "sated".' What has usually gone wrong in these utopias is that the writer has allowed himself to be too influenced by the very 'reinforcers' – rewards and pleasures – which figure so prominently in his utopia.

> If we ask someone to describe the kind of world in which he would like to live, he will probably begin to list the reinforcers he would want to find in it. He will go straight to the things which make life good, and probably simply because he will be reinforced for doing so. Food, sex, security, the approval of one's fellow men, works of art, music, and literature – these are the things men want and act to get and therefore the things they mention when they are asked to describe a world in which they would like to live. The significant fact is that they seldom mention what they are to do to get them. They specify a better world simply as they wish for it, dream of it, pray for it, giving no thought to the manner of their getting it.[22]

And yet, argues Skinner, 'the manner of getting our pleasures is the key to a satisfying and fulfilled life.' 'The important thing about the good things in life is what people are doing when they get them. "Goods" are reinforcers, and a way of life is a set of contingencies of reinforcement.'[23] There is nothing wrong with pleasure *per se*, 'but the feeling of pleasure must take second place to a more important function. The things we call pleasant have an energizing or strengthening effect on our behaviour, and it is only when they have that that they make us really happy.' The traditional reinforcers – food, sex, leisure and so on – are perfectly all right so long as it is realized that that is what they are, reinforcers of appropriate behaviour, rather than ends to be pursued irrespective of the behavioural means to attaining them. 'To make men active and happy and forward-looking, we do not need to find new reinforcers, we simply need to make better use of those we have. We must arrange effective contingencies of reinforcement.'[24] In doing so, we will have designed a particular way of life; and it is that way of life that constitutes the good life. The good life, which is the aim of cultural design, is different from the good *things* in life, which are the necessary instruments of that design.

The picture of the conditioned individual that emerges from this is very different from the stereotype of anti-Skinnerian daemonology. It is not the individual as puppet or mechanical doll. What we get, rather, is a view of behaviour, and its moral significance, that brings Skinner strangely close to traditional ethical and Christian concepts of the development of *character*. For what he seems to be saying – although not as clearly as one would like – is that the 'contingencies of reinforcement' have to be arranged in such a way as to strengthen the will, effectiveness and capability of the individual in dealing with the problems of life. Given that these problems will persist in all societies, even the most perfect, and given also that (as Frazier says) many situations cannot be foreseen, the best solution is to build up a particular character structure which will *in general* be capable of dealing adequately with those problems and situations. Skinner certainly shares the utilitarian view of human nature – men are pushed and pulled by pleasure and pains – but he has a far less cynical view than the utilitarian of what can be made of this basic postualte. By the carefully contrived use of pleasures and pains as reinforcers, Skinner believes that it should be possible to produce individuals who will find their fulfilment in a confident and resourceful encounter with the world, rather than endure the frustrations of a spoilt and stunted development.

The conviction that this is Skinner's aspiration is strengthened by his distaste for the control of behaviour through punishment. Behaviour can, in principle, be reinforced both by pleasures ('positive reinforcers') and by pains or punishments ('negative reinforcers'). When reinforced by means of the latter the form of control is said to be 'aversive'. Skinner does not deny some advantages to aversive control. It is often, in the short run at least, quick and economical. For instance, it is currently much easier to prevent speeding on the roads by punitive legislation than by positive reinforcement. But aversive control also has grave disadvantages. It builds up guilt, resistance and resentment in the individual. It is wasteful, since it tends to supress in blanket fashion many desirable forms of behaviour when aiming merely at the undesirable aspects. If you lock up a creative scientist for stealing or spying you may be also holding up the progress of science.

Beyond these pragmatic considerations, however, lie deeper reasons for Skinner's rejection of punitive forms of control. For him, the belief in punishment as the principal form of control is part and parcel of the whole historical and philosophical legacy which he has unremittingly opposed: the legacy of classical liberalism, and in particular its conception of the individual and his relation to society. Liberalism postulates the free, autonomous, rational individual. To this idea of freedom, Skinner contends, the concept of punishment is a necessary correlate. Individual freedom implies the idea of individual responsibiity, and responsibility requires the threat of punishment, for otherwise no credit attaches to the individual for behaving well, nor can he be made to accept the consequences of behaving badly. What Skinner rather disparagingly calls 'the literature of freedom and dignity' has, therefore, been responsible for giving philosophic underpinning and respectability to the otherwise barbarous idea of punishment.

The support has been not simply theoretical but also practical. Liberalism as a political movement has been the main influence in establishing the conventional and commonsense view that control and punishment go hand in hand, that control in fact *means* punishment. In its temporary alliance with utilitarianism in the nineteenth century, liberalism ensured that all western legal systems were built on a largely punitive basis. The general presumption was that individuals should be left free to pursue their privately and autonomously conceived purposes. The only form of behaviour that required restraint (control) was behaviour that interfered with the like freedom of everyone else. That restraint was necessarily punitive, a nice calculation of the balance of pains over pleasure that would be just sufficient to deter the potential offender. Bentham's 'felicific calculus' governed hundreds of laws that emanated from the nineteenth-century legislatures. And because, in so many legal and political institutions, control was so widely exercised through punitive deterrents, liberalism, even when it went on the offensive, tended to confirm this view. Where restraint was thought to be excessive or illegitimate, the 'literature of freedom and dignity' supported attempts to end or evade it. But its exhortations took entirely negative forms. People were urged to escape from, break out of or rebel against laws and institutions exercising punitive control. The general impression created was that to escape punishment was to escape control, since all control was punitive. Freedom, by this light, consists essentially in the escape from punitive control. Hence liberalism was very poorly equipped to deal with those non-punitive forms of control – such as mass propaganda, advertising, television – which rely on positive reinforcement, and which have become the widespread concern of the twentieth century. In this sense liberalism promoted a concept of freedom that was dangerous and illusory.[25]

We shall return later to Skinner's general critique of liberalism. Here the thing to stress is its relation to Skinner's ultimate purpose of creating a certain kind of character-structure. To shape behaviour through punishment is to shape it through a series of denials, negations and absences. What emerges as a result is largely an unknown quantity. It is an individual of whose intentions and aspirations we are ignorant, whose behaviour is likely to be influenced in unplanned and unconscious ways, and who is in any case likely to be frequently engaged in countering the agencies of punitive control. Skinner's utopia requires individuals far more positively and purposefully shaped. Their behaviour is developed by a series of positive reinforcements, thus avoiding the conflict and resentment generated by punishment. They are taught to co-operate rather than to compete, to solve problems rather than to run away from them, to set the interests of the community over selfish interests. In a community in which all individuals have been brought up in this way, punishment is otiose. And that should be a cause for celebration, not masochistic regret.

> Our task is not to encourage moral struggle or to build or demonstrate inner virtues. It is to make life less punishing and in doing so to release for more reinforcing activities the time and energy consumed in the avoidance of punishment. . . . It should be possible to design a world in which behaviour likely to be punished seldom or never occurs.[26]

THE WORLD OF WALDEN TWO (ii): EDUCATION, FAMILY, WORK, POLITICS

We now have the main outlines of Skinner's approach to human behaviour, and can return to the world of Walden Two. Frazier also in the meantime has been expounding the principles of behavioural engineering to his guests, who are now in a position to appreciate its applications in the spheres of education, the family, work and politics.

Child-rearing and education in Walden Two resemble in many ways the practices of some of the Israeli *kibbutzim*. Infants and children live together in special children's quarters, under expert supervision, and where great care has been taken in the design of the physical and social environment. Babies spend the first year in air-conditioned cubicles, carefully controlled for temperature and humidity, in which they experience the minimum of frustration or discomfort. They then proceed in graduated stages, through similarly air-conditioned rooms, to cots in dormitories and finally to shared rooms, which they occupy to the age of 13. The general principle is to transfer control gradually from the adult authorities to the child himself, and to his peers. Supervision is slowly withdrawn as the child progressively learns the appropriate attitudes and behaviour, so that finally the young adult can be left relatively free, in the confidence that his training will ensure that he produces the appropriate responses in a wide variety of situations.

The techniques of control reflect this conception of development. In the early stages of infancy children are taught self-control through their exposure to a series of frustrating (not punitive) situations. For instance, infants are given lollipops which they are told they can eat later provided they have not licked them even once in the meantime (the lollipops are cunningly covered in powder to show up covert licks). Or tired and hungry children are made to stand for fixed periods of time in front of steaming bowls of soup. To the criticism, from

Castle, that these are forms of torture, and to Burris's milder demur that they may give rise to resentment and anxiety, Frazier makes it clear that the experiences take place within an overall environment that promises full security: 'We set up a system of gradually increasing annoyances and frustrations against a background of complete serenity. An easy environment is made more and more difficult as the children acquire the capacity to adjust' (*WT*, p. 111). In the process of adjusting to these experiences, children learn not merely self-control, but the ability to work steadily at tasks without repeated clock-watching, and the capacity to convert their frustrating experiences into constructive and pleasant social relationships with their peers. (For instance, they chat and joke with each other while waiting the stipulated period for the food.)

The more formal practices of education follow directly from this system of early training, and indeed depend very much upon it. Walden Two has few school-rooms in the traditional sense. Instead, the visitors are shown workshops, laboratories, gymnasia, individual studies and reading rooms. The visitors are favourably struck by a sense of much fluidity and diversity in the educational experience of the young, but can't help wondering about traditional pedagogic problems of discipline, motivation, grading, specialization and so forth. Frazier's response indicates the importance of a consciously planned relationship between the various environments encountered by the children.

> We can arrange things more expeditiously here because we don't need to be constantly re-educating. The ordinary teacher spends a good share of her time changing the cultural and intellectual habits which the child acquires from its family and surrounding culture. . . . . Here we can almost say that the school *is* the family, and vice versa. (*WT*, pp. 118–19)

The early training in self-discipline means that children can be allowed a far freer relationship to the community than is normally possible elsewhere. Freed from the requirement to earn grades, or to compete, children are allowed to choose their areas of interest more or less by themselves, and to seek instruction only when they feel the need for it. Although there are certain facilities set aside specifically for students, to a good extent

> education in Walden Two is part of the life of the community. We don't need to resort to trumped-up life experiences. Our children begin to work at a very early age. It's no hardship; it's accepted as readily as sport or play. And a good share of our education goes on in workshops, laboratories, and fields . . . We teach anatomy in the slaughterhouse, botany in the field, genetics in the dairy, and poultry house, chemistry in the medical building and in the kitchen and dairy laboratory. (*WT*, pp. 120–1)

Frazier is pressed on the question of what, in this relaxed and uncompetitive atmosphere, motivates the children to learn at all. His answer is that curiosity is natural in all children, and the problem is simply not to stamp it out, as usually happens in traditional schooling. Children at Walden Two are taught perseverance by controlled experiences in their early years, so that they are not put off by discouraging events. That is all that is needed in order for the natural exploratory instinct to be put to creative use. 'The motives in education,' says Frazier, 'are the motives in all human behaviour. Education should be only life itself. We don't need to create motives . . . . We appeal to the curiosity which is characteristic of the unrestrained child, as well as the alert and inquiring adult' (*WT*, p. 124).

This is of course the familiar claim of every 'progressive' school of contemporary education; and there is indeed nothing in either the philosophy or the practice of education in Walden Two to surprise anyone acquainted with radical educational theory from John Dewey through to Paul Goodman and Ivan Illich. The distinctive thing here, as so often in Walden Two, is not so much the novelty of the ideas themselves as the passion to put them to the test of experimental practice, and to ensure that this takes place in an overall context where the practices of one institution do not contradict or cancel those of another.

Something of the same comment applies to the position of the family and the attitude towards the relations of the sexes in Walden Two. It seems odd that it should have been these sections of the book which aroused the greatest feeling, both for and against. Most of the practices in Walden Two had been tried out in various nineteenth-century utopian communities, which might well have regarded Skinner's utopia as fairly conservative in this respect. Moreover, at the very time of publication of *Walden Two* it would have been possible to observe very similar practices at work in the *kibbutzim* of the new Israeli state. Perhaps the special attention received by this aspect of Walden life reflected no more than the usual voyeuristic interest in sex which has always been a strong selling-point of utopian literature. Skinner at any rate seems to have expected this to be the case, since he has Frazier say rather contemptuously that 'the all-absorbing concern of the outside world is what happens to the family in Walden Two' (*WT*, p. 137).

Walden Two decisively breaks the traditional ties between sex, marriage and the raising of a family. Sexual relations take place freely between adolescents. Girls, whether or not they marry, begin having children as early as the age of 16, and have generally finished with child-bearing by the age of 22 or 23. The children are reared communally, and the mutual dependence of parents and children is thus removed. This takes away one of the two main props of the traditional family. The other, the economic function, is also knocked away, since the family unit plays no economic role at all in the Walden Two economy. One might have thought there would be no reason for marrying at all in Walden Two, but marriages are apparently the norm and indeed most people marry very early, in their teens. Frazier gives no very convincing reason for this. 'Economically we could dispense with permanent marriage altogether,' he admits, 'but we don't. Abiding personal affection is more than a romantic rationalisation of a crude economic unit.' This very priggish remark betrays a good deal of uncertainty about the institution of marriage in Walden Two.

The sexual and familial patterns of Walden Two are all fairly standard features of modern utopian communities, most of which have directed the main force of their criticism against the modern nuclear family. Frazier echoes the burden of that criticism when he says that 'the significant history of our times is the story of the growing weakness of the family.' He lists the causes: the decline of the family as a productive unit, and as the main socializing unit; the struggle for equality for women, the entry of women into the workforce and the acceptance of birth control and divorce; the loosening of kinship ties. All these developments spell doom to the family. Walden Two 'replaces the family, not only as an economic unit, but to some extent as a social and psychological unit as well. What survives is an experimental question.' Similarly, the rearing of children communally is simply an acknowledgement of historical developments. In the right conditions of knowledge and technology, 'group care is better than parental care.' In former times children had to be brought up by parents for want of any more expert agency. 'But with the rise of a science of behaviour all is changed . . . . The requirements of good child care are well established. Where we have failed is in getting good care into the average home. We have failed to teach the average parent even the simplest scientific principles.' The failure is inevitable, given the resources of the average household. 'Home is not the place to raise children.'

Walden Two sets no great store by the supposed need of the child for a mother- and a father-figure with which to identify. It regards this as an experimental question, as yet unanswered. Walden Two children get a lot of affection from a variety of adults, and 'what the child imitates is a sort of essential happy adult. He can avoid the idiosyncrasies of a single parent.' But about the conventional pattern of identification the community has no doubts. The tie between children and a particular set of parents is systematically destroyed. 'Our goal is to have every member of Walden Two regard all our children as his own, and to have every child think of every adult as his parent.' To this end, the community looks forward to the wholesale practice of artificial insemination, thereby breaking completely the hereditary connection. Similarly, the overemphasis on the maternal role is played down. Children are cared for equally by men and women. There is no sense that child-care is 'women's work'. It is recognized that 'the work in the nursery is very close to that of a highly skilled laboratory technician.' Indeed, as Frazier emphasizes, it is quite clear that 'the community, as a revised family, has changed the place of women more radically than that of men.'[27]

Skinner's ideas about the family fall within a familiar tradition of utopian thought, and utopian practice. The Israeli *kibbutz* – in some of its forms at least – represents the most sustained effort to date to carry out some of the ideas in practice. Before that there was the short-lived Soviet *kolkhoz*, set up to replace the family at the time of the Russian Revolution. In the 1960s, many of the communes in the United States and Europe adopted similar attitudes towards the family. These experiments have probably made us almost too familiar with the ideas, and we forget how radical they are, and how little tried out on a truly widespread basis. In Skinner's case, moreover, the radicalism of the ideas is given a characteristic distinctiveness by its very hard-headed attitude towards practice. While adolescents, for instance, are permitted a good deal of freedom in their sexual relations with each other, when it comes to marriage the romantic mood is tempered by a severely scientific realism. 'When a young couple become engaged, they go to our Manager of Marriages. Their interests, school records, and health are examined. If there's any great discrepancy in intellectual ability or temperament they are advised against marrying. The marriage is at least postponed, and that usually means it's abandoned.' Once the couple have got through this rigorous screening, their lives after marriage are subjected to experimental scrutiny at every point. One experiment was designed to test whether it was better for couples to share a room or to have separate ones. 'The result was clear cut. Living in a separate room not only made the individual happier and better adjusted, it tended to strengthen the love and affection of husband and wife.' It is in this detailed, ceaselessly experimental, attention to practice, rather than in the content of the ideas themselves, that the utopianism of *Walden Two* is seen at its most individual and radical.

This point is nicely underlined by the irony that one of the most successful ideas in *Walden Two* is not Skinner's own at all but is borrowed from Bellamy's *Looking Backward* (as Frazier readily acknowledges). The organization of work in Walden Two has often been admired. It is the aspect most frequently and successfully imitated in those communities which derive their inspiration frm Skinner's book. Both Twin Oaks and East Wind report that, in so far as they still show some particular relation to Walden Two, it is in the system of work that they most display the connection.[28]

The system is simple, and depends upon two principles: equality of work, and, subject to that constraint, the freedom to do whatever work one wants. The first principle is attained by ensuring that every member works off an equal number of 'labour credits' per year, credits being reckoned as a certain quantity of time spent on a job. But since some kinds of work are seen to be more desirable than others, the system of labour credits assigns different credit values to different kinds of work on the basis of demand. Cleaning out the sewers has a high credit rating, working in the flower gardens a very low one. Since preferences are not static, credit values are adjusted from time to time according to shifts in demand. 'In the long run,' says Frazier, 'when the values have been adjusted, all kinds of work are equally desirable. If they weren't, there would be a demand for the more desirable, and the credit value would be changed' (*WT*, p. 52). A person then has the choice of making up his quota of credits either by doing a few unpleasant tasks for a short period of time, and having a lot of time off for recreation; or by working for longer hours at work which he finds rewarding in itself. In the first case, the pleasure of extended leisure is bargained against short bursts of painful work; in the second, the pain of leisure renounced is offset by the pleasure of satisfying work. In either case of this very utilitarian calculation the criteria of both equality and freedom are satisfied.

Kathleen Kinkade tells how Twin Oaks, having adopted the basic Walden Two system of work, evolved a refinement which produced an even more satisfying result. Under the original system, most people, as at Walden Two, got a reasonably acceptable 'basket of tasks' consisting of some desirable, some undesirable and some middling kinds of work. The system worked well enough to last without change for two years. As the community grew, it seemed possible that, 'in a group as large as this, we can almost always find somebody who doesn't mind a particular job as much as somebody else. It might literally be possible for us all to work just at those things we like – or at least didn't hate.' In the revised system, each individual ranks all the available jobs according to his personal preferences. The 'labour clerks' then inspect all the lists, and in working out each individual's work schedule they try to ensure that it reflects as far as possible the individual's personal preferences. High credits are now given for work that one finds *personally* disagreeable. 'Two people might be shoveling manure side by side, and the person who enjoys the work is getting less credit for it than the person who doesn't.'[29] Owing to the variety in tastes and preferences, it turns out that most people do not have to do a lot of work which they find unpleasant, although there is always a certain amount of such work.

What are the 'reinforcers' in such a system of work? In ordinary, unregenerate conditions, most people work for financial gain (positive reinforcer), or to escape the threat of indigence (negative reinforcer). Lacking both these reinforcers, why should people work in Walden Two, or Twin Oaks? We have encountered the question already with Bellamy, and have been given one kind of answer. Skinner invites the question even more urgently, given the particular character of his theory of behaviour. The curious thing is that, although Burris raises the question, Frazier side-steps it (*WT*, p. 172). He is impatient here, as so often, with the denseness of his visitors.

The answer in fact has to be a matter of inference; and, such as there is, it is remarkably similar to Bellamy's. It is supplied, we must assume, by the whole nature and purpose of Walden Two as a community. Individuals are motivated to productive and co-operative work from their earliest days, and a sense of service to the community is a 'secondary reinforcer' that begins to operate relatively early in the individual's life. Moreover, it is one of the explicit aims of Walden Two to eliminate tedious and unpleasant work, by making full use of modern technology. Hence the work that remains is to a large extent of the rewarding and fulfilling kind: it has, that is, its *own* rewards. Indeed, in a passage very reminiscent of Marx, Frazier looks forward to a 'Golden Age' in which the activities to be pursued only too evidently supply their own reinforcement. Walden Two, he says is in the process of eliminating all 'uncreative and uninteresting work', so that 'our energies can then be turned towards art, science, play, the exercise of skills, the satisfaction of curiosities, the conquest of nature, the conquest of man – the conquest of man himself, but never of other men' (*WT*, p. 76).

The question that Frazier shrugs off so impatiently is, however, a very real one for the members of Twin Oaks. People do occasionally turn up who are lazy and sponge off the labour of others. There are various mechanisms, supervised by the Labour Manager, for attempting to change this attitude, and to help the malingerer to develop new habits. If these fail, in the last resort he or she is asked to leave: this, after all, is a real community, and Twin Oaks cannot perform the fictional sleights-of-hand of Walden Two. But it is heartening to hear that the problem is not a serious one at Twin Oaks. Indeed, what is interesting is the same sense here, as in Walden Two, that special and artificial incentives are unnecessary, that it is the work itself which is reinforcing.

Skinner has often said that, in the design of cultures, the structures should be such that activities find their own natural reinforcements: in the feeling of interest, curiosity satisfied, the sense of achievement, the pleasure that comes from constructive and creative work. As Kathleen Kinkade reports it, Twin Oaks seems to show that this is not an unrealistic aim.

> We have members who have the same intense dedication to their work that characterises happy professionals in the competitive outside world. Their involvement is with the work itself and with building the Community. The credits are beside the point, as the money would be beside the point if they were working for wages. They want to get a good hammock brochure printed, or an engine rebuilt, or a new labour system perfected, or an orchard properly planted, or the kitchen remodelled. The reinforcement comes from the finished product, the purr of the new engine, the neat rows of baby trees – and from the appreciation of the other members of the community.[30]

One is strengthened in the belief that the old sceptical question, 'Why should anyone work in your utopia?', is largely due to a failure of imagination.

Mention has already been made of the 'Manager of Marriages' at Walden Two, and the 'Labour Manager' at Twin Oaks; and it is time now to consider the political and administrative arrangements at Walden Two. An initial comment must be that, in one sense, there *is* no political system, in the usual meaning of a formally delegated or elected group of people holding legislative and executive power. Throughout *Walden Two*, in fact, there is a strong hostility towards politics, and towards all governments and political doctrines. Frequent reference is made to the fact that Walden Two derives its inspiration from Thoreau not simply because of his experimental attitude towards life, but also because of his disdain for the state.

In a characteristic passage, Frazier is at one point explaining that what distinguishes Walden Two from all past utopias is that it is not removed in space or time, but 'exists in the very midst of modern civilization'. He continues:

> The one fact that I should cry from every housetop is this: the Good Life is waiting for us – here and now! . . . It doesn't depend on a change in government or on the machinations of world politics. It doesn't wait upon an improvement in human nature. At this very moment we have the necessary techniques, both material and psychological, to create a full and satisfying life for everyone.

'The trick is to put those techniques into effect,' says Castle. 'You still have to solve the practical problems of government and politics.' Frazier replies:

> Government and politics! It's not a problem of government and politics at all. That's the first plank in the Walden Two platform. You can't make progress towards the Good Life by political action. (*WT*, p. 193)

There is of course nothing surprising in finding an antipathy to politics in a utopia. Most utopias are apolitical. Politics, as an activity of an imperfect world, is, along with wearisome toil, one of the bitter fruits of original sin. It turns on the assumption of fundamental conflicts of interest. In the liberal version, its terms are compromise, concession, adjustment. Utopias, having resolved or removed fundamental conflicts of interest have no need for this sort of politics. The chapters on politics or the state in utopia are usually very thin, although few go quite to the extreme of the famous chapter in William Morris's *News from Nowhere*, which sums up the politics of that utopia in one sentence ('We are very well off as to politics – because we have none'). Political arrangements, if they exist at all, are sketchily delineated, and the general impression conveyed is that, if the reader is looking for a detailed account of politics, he has misunderstood the nature of utopia.

Skinner's attitude to politics is however more complex than this. He is at once less political than many utopian writers, and at the same time a good deal more concerned with political control than most. Skinner's utopia is conveniently apolitical in rejecting government because government means coercion, and 'you can't force a man to be happy.' It is also apolitical, to a startling degree, in its innocent contemplation of the means by which utopia will be achieved. Most modern utopias assume a considerable degree of conflict and struggle in the achievement of utopian goals. This is an important part of the account in, for instance, Bellamy and Morris. For Skinner, however, utopia in the form of Walden Two is to be had more or less for the asking. 'Any group of men of good will can work out a satisfactory life within the existing political structures of half a dozen modern governments.' Government can simply be ignored. 'All we ask is to be left alone' (*WT*, pp. 195–6).

This apolitical quietism as to means, however, by no means extends to the ends of Walden Two. It soon turns out that the hostility to government is of a very qualified kind. Walden Two, says Frazier, is not anarchist. 'I am not arguing for no government at all, but only for none of the existing forms.' What Frazier in fact objects to in current forms of government is not so much that they are coercive as that they lack proper control. That indeed is why they are coercive: 'Governments which use force are based upon bad principles of human engineering.' Their intervention is clumsy and haphazard. They cannot experiment, and so never learn. Power is passed from one group to another which repeats the errors of its predecessor. The requirement is clear: 'We want a government based upon a science of human behaviour' (*WT*, pp. 194–5).

We have, therefore, to see that there is after all government in Walden Two: quite a lot of it, by conventional standards. But it is government reduced – or elevated – to the function of planning and management, such that to members of the community politics in the old sense has little meaning and virtually no existence. Walden Two carries into effect the Saint-Simonian slogan picked up by some nineteenth-century Marxists and anarchists: 'from the government of men to the administration of things'. But as critics – often other Marxists and anarchists – were quick to point out, you do not remove politics or political power by calling it administration.

Walden Two is administered by a Saint-Simonian directorate: a group of Planners and Managers, with Scientists playing a subsidiary role. All receive labour credits for their work. There are six Planners, who make major policy decisions. They serve for ten years. They are not elected. Set up originally out of the pioneers who established the community, they select their replacements from names put up by the Managers. The Managers are specialists who are chosen by the Planners to oversee the main activities and services in the community. 'There are Managers of Food, Health, Play, Arts, Dentistry, Dairy, various industries, Supply, Labour, Nursery School, Advanced Education and dozens of others.'[31] The point is made emphatically that, as in the case of Planners, Managers are not elected by the vote of members since democratic voting is an inappropriate way of choosing expertise. 'The people are in no position to evaluate experts. And elected experts are never able to act as they think best' (*WT*, p. 267).

Twin Oaks has adopted a modified form of the Walden Two system. There is a three-person Board of Planners who appoint and replace Managers. This is in fact their main function, as most of the important decisions affecting the daily lives of the members are made by the Managers, not the Planners. (Frazier makes the same point for Walden Two.) Planners mainly adjudicate between Managers and 'decide touchy questions having to do with ideology'. Kathleen Kinkade, indeed, thinks that

> Twin Oaks would survive under a variety of governmental systems, including consensus and even democracy, as long as the managerial system was left intact. The important decisions are made at this level. It is the Construction Manager who researches sewage systems and building designs and presents them to the Community with his recommendations. The Garden and Food Managers between them determine our diet. The Clothing Manager decides whether we buy new clothes or make do with old ones, and the Health Manager makes doctor's and dentist's appointments on the basis of need. Any of these people can be overruled by the board of Planners . . . but such occasions are exceptional. Managers use their best judgement in making decisions that benefit the group as a whole. They have nothing to gain by doing otherwise.[32]

Frazier's assertion that the members of Walden Two do not resist this system of decision-making is borne out to a considerable extent by the experience of Twin Oaks. In a small face-to-face community, it is not difficult to understand how members may feel that they have sufficient influence on decisions not to wish to participate more formally. 'All decisions that are of interest to the group are discussed with the group as a whole.' No special prestige or privileges attach to the job of Planner or Manager – indeed, it is sometimes difficult to persuade people to put up for the jobs. 'Being a Planner,' says Kinkade,

> 'wasn't supposed to be a very big deal. Our idea was that decision-making, like milking a cow or sweeping a floor or teaching a class, was a job, deserving no more or less honour than other jobs . . . . A Walden Two community is not a hierarchy. Nobody is on top of anybody. The job of decision-making requires decision-making skills, just as the job of salesman requires selling skills.[33]

Since, in addition, there is complete economic equality, no one can be tempted to acquire power for the sake of enriching himself.

Finally, would-be power-seekers lack the means to enforce their wishes against the will of the majority. 'No legislation can be put across unless members are willing to go along with it. There is no police force here to carry out anybody's will. Our only technique is persuasion.'[34]

'Persuasion': it is, of course, just this that is at the heart of the controversy over Skinner's utopia. A generation nurtured on the idea of 'the hidden persuaders' is unlikely to miss a sinister significance, albeit quite unintended, in Kinkade's words. The examination of politics and government in Walden Two raises all the issues about freedom and control which have preoccupied Skinner's critics ever since the publication of the book, and which were revived with the appearance of *Beyond Freedom and Dignity*. It seems sensible, therefore, to continue our discussion within the context of the wider philosophical and political questions raised by *Walden Two* as a whole.

WALDEN TWO AND THE WORLD: A BLUEPRINT FOR HELL?

Castle, the philosopher, has been slowly building up steam, and towards the end of *Walden Two* he erupts.

> A modern, mechanized, managerial Machiavelli – that is my final estimate of you, Mr Frazier! The silent despot! . . . So far as I can see, you've blocked every path through which man was to struggle upward towards salvation. Intelligence, initiative – you have filled their places with a sort of degraded instinct, engineered compulsion. Walden Two is a marvel of efficient coordination – as efficient as an anthill! (*WT*, pp. 252–3)

Skinner clearly anticipated the terms of the attack on his utopia. It has been called fascist, communist, authoritarian, pig-like. It is the 'utopia of conditioned virtue', and hence relegates man to the level of the unreflecting brutes. The central attributes of man – freedom, autonomy, responsibility, rationality – are denied, and the moral life emptied of all meaning. At best, the inhabitants of Walden Two are like innocent but unknowing children; at worst, they are moral zombies. As the philosopher Max Black put it,

> we might justifiably regard the end product [of Skinnerian conditioning] as a dehumanization, in which men were no longer accorded the dignity of being treated as persons. A world of well-controlled bodies emitting physical movements in response to secret reinforcements, might perhaps seem hardly worth preserving. It may, after all, be better to be dead than bred – like cattle.[35]

Skinner has been only too ready to fan the flames. 'The hypothesis that man is not free is essential to the application of scientific method to the study of behaviour.'[36] 'What is being abolished,' he says of the enterprise in *Beyond Freedom and Dignity*, 'is autonomous man – the inner man, the homunculus, the possessing demon, the man defended by the literature of freedom and dignity. His abolition is long overdue. . . .'[37] In response to Castle's repeated taunts, Frazier says coolly: 'I deny that freedom exists at all. I must deny it – or my program would be absurd' (*WT*, p. 257).

It has to be said that, whatever the ultimate strength of their position, Skinner's critics often choose the weakest ground on which to attack him. The fundamental charge is that Skinner, along with other behaviourists, dehumanizes man by studying human beings as if they are not essentially different from dogs, pigeons, cats and rats. Whereas (says Krutch) the traditional

Western view of man supports Hamlet's exclamation, 'How like a god!', Pavlov emphasized, 'How like a dog!'[38] Skinner remarks curtly that 'that was a step forward', but does not deny that there are basic differences between man and other animals. What is crucial to Skinner is the attitude to the study of human behaviour. 'Man is much more than a dog, but like a dog he is within range of a scientific analysis.'[39] It is here that the general humanist critique is most uneasily and most insecurely on the defensive. It seems concerned to preserve a 'sacred' area of human life and consciousness from the scrutiny of science. Certain cherished human values – free-will, spontaneity, creativity – seem threatened by the scientific approach to human behaviour. There appears to be an anxiety that perhaps man will after all turn out not to have the god-like attributes postulated of him. If so, better perhaps not to have that knowledge, for unscrupulous people are bound to act on it. Even if the idea of human freedom is an illusion, it may be a happy one, necessary to preserve as a weapon against attempts at tyrannical control.

One of Skinner's most impressive achievements is to demonstrate how dangerous such an attitude is. To hold, as a faith, to some idea of man's 'innate' freedom and rationality, or to the essential goodness of 'human nature', or even to man's 'unconquerable spirit', is to leave him a prey to a multitude of forces, the more powerful for being unsuspected. So, for instance, Skinner argues that the liberal concept of individual freedom, far from preserving individual liberty, often sacrifices it more completely to forces of which it is ignorant, and over which therefore it has no control. In emphasizing a negative concept of liberty – freedom *from* constraint or control – liberalism has been incapable of seeing the extent to which it delivers up the individual to other aspects of the environment with more sinister controlling powers. Liberalism's historic task has been to free individuals from control by traditionally repressive agencies – the state, the church, the family. Having more or less accomplished this, it assumes that what it has done is to allow individuals their 'natural' freedom, a freedom conceived essentially in asocial terms. But this is naive. 'To refuse to control is to leave control not to the person himself, but to other parts of the social and non-social environments.'[40]

In an exchange with Frazier, Castle proposes to 'dump the science of behaviour in the ocean' and give people their freedom. 'How could you give them freedom?' asks Frazier. 'By refusing to control them.' 'But you would only be leaving the control in other hands.' 'Whose?' 'The charlatan, the demagogue, the salesman, the ward heeler, the bully, the cheat, the educator, the priest – all who are now in possession of the techniques of behavioural engineering' (*WT*, p. 256).

It is an effective response, which points to the comprehensive character of Skinner's critique of liberal philosophy. Skinner has frequently drawn attention to the fact that liberalism, owing to the mainly practical and wholly admirable concerns of its history, has remained remarkably deficient in its theory. In the changed circumstances of the twentieth century, with the rise of mass institutions outside the traditional spheres of authority, this deficiency has shown up woefully. It has expressed itself at best in an ineffectual humanism, at worst in a wilful blindness to the social forces that are shaping men's lives.

Liberalism has above all been weakened by its lack of a theory of *positive* control of behaviour: where the 'aversive control' by means of negative reinforcement (threats and punishment) gives way to 'non-aversive control' using positive reinforcers in the form of rewards and incentives. Much of the apparatus of social control that is distinctively twentieth-century relies heavily on techniques of positive reinforcement: the persuasive propaganda of states and parties, the 'soft sell' of the advertisers, the blandly 'permissive' methods of control in schools, mental hospitals and prisons. The agonized debates about censorship – of advertising, television, the press – in all Western societies attest the difficulties that liberalism faces in dealing with these agencies of positive control.

Skinner shows two consequences of this failure of liberal philosophy. The first is that liberalism has not been able to deal at all adequately with the situation of the 'happy slave' – a characteristically modern predicament. Because it has no vocabulary or concepts to deal with the shaping of behaviour by rewards and incentives, it is often short-sighted in its judgement of practices which in the long-run may have very harmful consequences for the individual or society. Thus, liberal political practice quite happily accepts a system of payments to American farmers *not* to grow food, even though in the long run this places the farmer in an utterly dependent position *vis-à-vis* the state (not to mention being irrational by other criteria). In industry it promotes an incentive system of payment by piece-work, a system apparently acceptable to both managers and workers, even though it can be shown that the 'schedule of reinforcement' can be so manipulated as to generate a great deal of work for relatively little pay, to the greater exploitation of the worker in the long run. It condones, in prisons, a practice whereby prisoners are invited to be guinea-pigs for dangerous medical experiments – for instance, with new drugs – in return for better living conditions or shortened sentences.

In all these cases, the individuals concerned are perfectly happy to pursue their various courses of behaviour – in the short run, at least. The positive reinforcers to that extent have their expected effect. Ultimately, however – as with the habitual gambler – the 'deferred aversive consequences' are brought home to the individuals, and they suffer accordingly. The problem is, as Skinner notes, that liberalism has really very little to say on how to avoid these situations, or how to alert people to them. 'The literature of freedom has been designed to make men "conscious" of aversive control, but in its choice of methods it has failed to rescue the happy slave.'[41] What is striking is the similarity of this analysis, from a quite different theoretical perspective, to that conducted by the Frankfurt School of German Marxists, such as Erich Fromm, Herbert Marcuse and Theodor Adorno. They too, especially Marcuse in *One-Dimensional Man*, have focused on the weakness of liberalism in dealing with situations – as in present-day affluent societies – where the victims of exploitation and estrangement have become willing prisoners of the system: happy in their captivity, and unable to see the bars of the prison. In any analysis of modern mass societies there is clearly a need for this kind of perception; and it says a good deal for Skinner's approach that, by what might have seemed a very unpromising and certainly very individual route, he arrives at the same critique of the theory of liberal society as the more conventionally-equipped tradition of Marxism.

Skinner's second point has to do with the variety of 'progressive' and 'permissive' techniques currently practised in many social institutions. He refers here to such techniques as the 'Socratic method' in education, the psychoanalytic method in therapy, or the 'self-help' approach in many psychiatric institutions. These are all practices encouraged by liberals. They seem to involve no control by others, but depend for their success on the striving of the individuals themselves, drawing on their own innate qualities of curiosity, resourcefulness and resilience. Individuals help themselves to learn, or to be well. They use the resources – people and things – of the environment, but they are not controlled by them.

Skinner rightly contends that, on the contrary, such techniques represent 'weak forms of social control'. The reason why this is not readily seen is that much of the environmental control has taken place in the past, and the individual now appears to be determining his own reactions. The successful practice of the techniques turns on drawing attention to certain consequences of behaviour, and this itself depends on prior learning as to how to generalize from the experience of consequences. If a child apparently 'teaches himself', it is because he has learned what it is to be taught, which will have involved – probably in a well-designed home environment – control through reinforcement. Merely a hint from the environment, when added to this past store of learned behaviour, is enough to produce the desired response.[42] Moreover, in a more obvious way, in such matters as the analyst-patient relationship, subtle forms of control are being exercised all the time, despite beliefs to the contrary on the part of the patient and perhaps even the analyst. Simply the fact that the analyst cares is reinforcing, and determining. As Skinner says 'the apparent freedom respected by weak measures is merely inconspicuous control. When we seem to turn control over to a person himself, we simply shift from one mode of control to another .... A permissive government is a government that leaves control to other sources.'[43]

That this way of putting things is not simply a matter of trivial redefinition is made clear in the following:

> The fundamental mistake made by all those who choose weak methods of control is to assume that the balance of control is left to the individual, when in fact it is left to other conditions. The other conditions are often hard to see, but to continue to neglect them and to attribute their effect to autonomous man is to court disaster. When practices are concealed or disguised, counter-control is made difficult. It is not clear from whom one is to escape or whom one is to attack.[44]

The importance of this insight can scarcely be exaggerated. Throughout the Western world, as a result partly of shifts in ideology, partly of calculations of expense, societies have been going in increasingly for 'non-punitive' forms of education, treatment and rehabilitation. The development has in many cases been entirely beneficial and humane, for instance in schools. But there has also arisen the risk that the traditional alertness and readiness to contest, that has always existed in relation to punitive forms of control, will not be forthcoming under non-punitive forms. And this is precisely for the reasons that Skinner points to: that the control is so disguised, so cocooned in benevolent intentions and 'permissive' techniques that the very awareness of control remains dormant. Unlike the position of the 'happy slave', people may not be at all contented with their lot. But their sense of what to do and how to change it may be confused to the point of helpless apathy. If they do act, their actions may come to resemble those of the resentful but impotent pupils of the ultra-progressive school, who in their frustration burn it to the ground, to the consternation and bewilderment of the liberal staff.

It is important to see that Skinner's criticism of liberal philosophy is not simply a destructive exercise. It plays a crucial part in establishing the fundamental premise of his behavioural utopia, which is that, since control is omnipresent in human life, we must consciously take hold of it and use it for desirable ends. We must not let it go by default. To think that we can avoid or escape control, as the liberals hope, is not merely a delusion but prevents us from attending to the task of making a better world.

> The literature of freedom has encouraged escape from or attack upon all controllers. It has done so by making any indication of control aversive . . . . Control is clearly the opposite of freedom, and if freedom is good, control must be bad . . . . [But] the problem is to free men, not from control, but from certain kinds of control . . . . Were it not for the unwarranted generalisation that all control is wrong, we should deal with the social environment as simply as we deal with the non-social. Although technology has freed men from certain aversive features of the environment, it has not freed them from the environment. We accept the fact that we depend upon the world around us, and we simply change the nature of the dependency. In the same way, to make the social environment as free as possible of aversive stimuli we do not need to destroy that environment or escape from it; we need to redesign it.[45]

This is Skinner at his most persuasive. It is a counter not simply to the *laissez-faire* beliefs of the liberals, but also to the 'philosophic conservatism' of Burkeans such as Michael Oakeshott, who put their trust in the 'intimations of tradition'. Both oppose intervention and interference in the social environment, and in doing so both would abandon us to the blind forces of a history we had no hand in the making.[46] Skinner opposes to these a philosophy of ceaseless activism, ceaseless intervention in the life of the community. Since we are, willy-nilly, controlling each other all the time, let us make a virtue of necessity. Let us not fear control, but make of its exercise a science for the improvement of the human condition. It is here, in this boundless confidence in the human power to reshape the world, as much as in any detailed plan of the new world, that Skinner's utopianism shines through most strongly.

The interesting thing about Skinner's utopia, *Walden Two*, is that it fails precisely at that point where Skinner deserts his own radically experimental attitude to behaviour. He does this critically in the political sphere. The ideas about the family, education and work are in many cases sound, and certainly worth trying out. They form in any case part of the thinking of many current radical social philosophies, and are indeed being put into practice in various experimental communities as well as in more partial 'pilot' schemes. Where the communities are relatively 'open', as in the Israeli *kibbutzim*, some assessment at least is possible of the success of some of these ideas. But where, as in Walden Two itself, the control of the entire experimental design remains in the hands of a self-perpetuating oligarchy, the suspicion will always remain that what we are observing is indeed the behaviour of clockwork-dolls.

There was no need for Skinner to draw back at this point. Accepting that the education of children and the organization of work should be a matter of conscious design, and not left to chance or individual caprice, still leaves open the question of the best method of controlling the environment. To go, as Skinner does, directly to the method of a controlling directorate or elite certainly simplifies matters in theory, but it is the sort of *terrible simplification* which, as the French Jacobins found out, has unpleasant and uncontrollable consequences in practice. More to the point, it goes right against the grain of Skinner's whole experimental enterprise. There are in existence scores of examples of different forms of rule – ranging from the direct democracy of the Greek city-states, through the representative democracy of modern liberal societies, to the numerous schemes of self-management and rule by committees currently being canvassed in many spheres of industry and urban planning. There is here, as in the whole tradition of Western political theory, a wealth of historical experience which Skinner could draw upon in considering the most effective ways of achieving a planned environment. His general approach certainly does not – *pace* some of his critics – commit him automatically to an authoritarian solution.[47] But such is his contempt for politics – and history[48] – that he ignores this entire store of knowledge and experience.

This wilful *naïveté* in the face of politics seriously vitiates any assessment we might make of the success of Skinnerian techniques in contemporary practice. As a utopian thinker, Skinner is exceptional in this century in the extent to which his theories have been given practical expression. There is of course nothing like Walden Two itself – not even Twin Oaks goes very far in this direction – but there has been a host of schemes of a more fragmentary kind. The techniques of operant conditioning have been widely applied in schools in the United States, especially in such elementary areas as learning to read and write. (Skinner has even patented a 'teaching machine' to this end). They have been put to work in prisons, in the psychiatric wards of hospitals, in schools for delinquent teenagers, in mental health communities and, on a smaller scale, in factories and offices. In every case, the attempt is made to change or confirm attitudes and behaviour by the use of reinforcing techniques. Reports indicate a modest degree of success, but reveal also that the 'behaviour modification' achieved is often only temporary, and that regression takes place when the individual is removed for any length of time from the controlled environment of the institution.[49]

There could scarcely be a more damning admission of the slightness of the achievement so far. The techniques of operant conditioning evidently work only so long as the individuals concerned are the involuntary subjects (or victims) of experimental practices which they are forced to submit to – however much 'positive reinforcers' are employed within those practices themselves. The total environment – usually that of a closed 'total' institution such as a boarding school or a prison – is coercive. It is no doubt possible that the techniques would work equally well in a more permissive environment. Skinner himself, as we have seen, believes that the most effective reinforcers are those that follow naturally from the desired behaviour, so that, at least for adults, the apparatus of control can gradually be dispensed with. But the proof of this, on any reasonable scale, remains to be shown. Certainly we are not likely to be reassured by Skinner's blithe remark:

> It is true that the special communities represented by hospitals for psychotics, homes for retardates, training schools for delinquents, camps, and standard classrooms are not typical communities because the population at large is not properly represented, but the problems which arise in designing communities of that sort are not far from those in communities in the utopian sense.[50]

It is perhaps not so much the representativeness of these communities, in any statistical sense, that gives cause for concern, so much as their peculiarity as formally coercive institutions. It is quite impossible, on the basis of evidence derived from such artificial and often distasteful experiments, to draw any sensible conclusions regarding the efficacy of Skinnerian conditioning in the world at large.

It is fair to say that Skinner does not ignore the issue of authoritarian control. Indeed, in a sense it might almost be said that the problem haunts him, as well it might. Frequently in his writings he raises the question, 'who controls the controllers?' The answers are however thin and evasive in the extreme. At one point he claims that there really is no problem, since 'the relation between the controller and the controlled is reciprocal.' By some rather quick movements of the hand, he purports to show that the behaviour of the controller – be he parent, teacher, employer or priest – is shaped by the response of the controllee – child, pupil or whatever – so that 'in a very real sense, the slave controls the slave driver, the child the parent, the patient the therapist, the citizen the government, the communicant the priest, the employee the employer and the student the teacher.'[51] Whatever truth there is in this position – and there is clearly some – has been better explored by others, notably Hegel on the master–slave relationship; but in no case has it led them to assert that the ultimate power of the controller is thereby abolished.

Skinner more frequently contends that the problem of control is one of the nature of the culture as a whole, so that in a properly designed culture the controllers will, so to speak, provide their own restraints.[52] This so transparently begs the question – the Planners, after all, provide their own successors – that it is hardly a candidate for serious discussion at all. Like all efforts to pull one's self up by one's boot-straps, the result is to fall flat on one's face. Such an idea refuses to consider the degree to which the founders of the society bind their successors in their own image. Subsequent controllers may indeed be controlled, but more importantly, so is the entire society by the original conception and design of the founders. The cage is gilded but it remains a cage.

Frazier in *Walden Two* adopts a number of devious strategies in response to

Castle's probing. His weakest is to deny that the problem of control arises at all, since people in Walden Two have no sense of restraint.

> We can achieve a sort of control under which the controlled, though they are following a code much more scrupulously than was ever the case under the old system, nevertheless *feel free*. They are doing what they want to do, not what they are forced to do. That's the source of the tremendous power of positive reinforcement – there's no restraint and no revolt. By a careful cultural design, we control not the final behaviour, but the *inclination* to behave – the motives, the desires, the wishes.[53] (*WT*, p. 262)

We are suspiciously close here to the cheerful marionettes, which Skinner in most places deprecates as fully as any humanist. However effortless the exercise of virtue, it loses much of its efficacy when it is not consciously thought through and understood. Most seriously, such a principle of 'good behaviour' leaves the practitioner hopelessly lost when confronted with new situations and new contingencies – a predicament which Frazier, as we have seen, has anticipated and is anxious to avoid.

After adopting the tactic of some vicious side-swipes at contemporary practices of 'democracy' – which Castle finds difficult to rebut – Frazier comes to the real defence of the politics of Walden Two. It is, quite simply, that the business of the Planners and Managers is as much a science, a skill, as the understanding of a jet engine or a motor car. There needs to be no special mechanisms by which, as in conventional democracies, people express their choices or their grievances. It is in the nature of the job to attend to such things.

> We don't need laws and a police force to compel a pilot to pay attention to a defective engine. Nor do we need laws to compel our Dairy Manager to pay attention to an epidemic among his cows. Similarly, our Behavioural and Cultural Managers need not be compelled to consider grievances. A grievance is a wheel to be oiled, or a broken pipe line to be repaired . . . . Nowadays, everyone fancies himself an expert in government and wants to have a say. Let's hope it's a temporary cultural pattern. I can remember when everyone could talk about the mechanical principles according to which his automobile ran or failed to run. Everyone was an automotive specialist and knew how to file the points of a magneto and take the shimmy out of front wheels. To suggest that these matters might be left to experts would have been called Fascism, if the term had been invented. But today no-one knows how his car operates and I can't see that he's any the less happy. In Walden Two no-one worries about the government except the few to whom that worry has been assigned. To suggest that everyone should take an interest would seem as fantastic as to suggest that everyone should become familiar with our diesel engines. Even the constitutional rights of our members are seldom thought about, I'm sure. The only thing that matters is one's day-to-day happiness and a secure future. (*WT*, pp. 269–70).

So much is governing a matter of (behavioural) science, that the inevitable corollary, familiar from so many similarly conceived utopias of the past, follows: 'As governmental technology advances, less and less is left to the decisions of governors, anyway. Eventually we shall have no use for Planners at all. The Managers will suffice' (*WT*, p. 272).[54]

This is as clear as it is familiar. It is the old principle of benevolent despotism, refurbished in the nineteenth century as the rule of the experts. Skinner in several places shows himself quite happy to accept this designation.[55] The problems of practising benevolent despotism have been thoroughly discussed, especially by Karl Popper,[56] and there is no point in repeating the arguments here. But one implication can perhaps be drawn out, especially as it relates to a defence which Skinner himself has come to rely upon increasingly.

Skinner has, as has already been indicated, latterly came to espouse an evolutionary framework for his science of behaviour. Behaviour is selected (reinforced) according to its success in meeting the challenges of the environment. Sentiments of approval and disapproval, and our very conceptions of 'good' and 'bad', are seen to be related to evolutionary success: 'Things are good (positively reinforcing) or bad (negatively reinforcing) presumably because of the contingencies of survival under which the species evolved. All reinforcers eventually derive their power from evolutionary selection.'[57]

This Darwinian framework is applied to the problem of the 'control of the controllers'. The ultimate reason why controllers will not lapse into old-fashioned corruption and despotism is that by doing so they will condemn their communities to extinction, in the competitive struggle with other communities. If, says Frazier, the Planners were to ignore the good of the community in pursuit of their own private interests, 'then the culture will eventually be replaced by competing cultures which work more effectively. Our Planners know this. They know that any usurpation of power would weaken the community as a whole and eventually destroy the whole venture' (*WT*, p. 271). Elsewhere Skinner has written that 'survival is the only value according to which a culture is eventually to be judged. . . . .'[58]

The criterion of survival may or may not be the best one by which to judge the success of a culture, although in an obvious sense it must be one of the criteria. The point here, however, is how far Skinner's utopian design furthers this end, which he himself elevates above all others. And it seems clear that a community organized on the lines of Walden Two offers, in the end, the *least* chances of survival. Skinner does not recognize this because his account of the evolutionary process is dangerously deficient – and it is so precisely on the question of the requirements for survival.

Skinner generally regards the evolutionary record as a sort of success story.

> There is a kind of natural morality in both biological and cultural evolution. Biological evolution has made the human species more sensitive to its environment and more skillful in dealing with it. Cultural evolution was made possible by biological evolution, and it has brought the human organism under a much more sweeping control of the environment.[59]

For Skinner, survival and control are inextricably intertwined. Survival is a function of more and more conscious, planned, intervention in the social environment, the bringing of more and more behaviour under rational control. This is to be carried out by experts armed with the technology of behaviour. What Skinner does not recognize is that, while intervention in general is both necessary and desirable, handing over the form and substance of intervention to any kind of elite is suicidal for a society. This is not, or need not be, because of the selfishness or corrupt intentions of elites. It follows inescapably from the logic of the situation in which elites find themselves. A benevolent elite must harness all the available resources of knowledge and human energy in a given society, to the task of making that society more efficient in its adaptation to its *current* environment, both social and physical. It has to do this, because in an environment of competing societies failure to do so would, as Frazier rightly says, invite punishment and perhaps conquest by other societies. All the pressures, therefore, are towards greater and greater efficiency in the exploitation of the current environment. Patterns of behaviour which do not subserve this end, and hence are 'inefficient', must be eliminated.

But such efficiency in the present is consequently purchased at the cost of rigidity in the face of the future. The more successfully a species or society adapts to the current environment, the less store of diversity it preserves to meet future contingencies. Evolution requires both adaptedness and adaptability, the one for success in the present, the other for future success. There is no way of foretelling the future environment. The only certainty is that the present one will change. There can be, in a strict sense, no 'planning for the future', for planning can be only in terms of current realities and current knowledge. In the face of an unknown future, the only hope lies in preserving as many varieties of thought and practice as are compatible with current survival. We do not know, but one or some of these practices may turn out to be the successful response in an altered environment. But such practices are necessarily, in the present, inefficient and 'irrational', and as such, anathema to the benevolent elite. There is therefore a persistent tendency, in a society governed by a rationalizing elite, to supress or eliminate them. With every such suppression the species or society launches itself further along the path to extinction.

Skinner recognizes the problem, as he so often does. Variety must be nurtured, in society as in nature. But his answer also shows the narrowness of his conception of the evolutionary process.

> It is true that accidents have been responsible for almost everything men have achieved to date, and they will no doubt continue to contribute to human accomplishments, but there is no virtue in an accident as such. The unplanned also goes wrong . . . . If we are looking for variety, we should not fall back upon accident . . . . The only hope is *planned* diversification, in which the importance of variety is recognized.[60]

Skinner, indeed, thinks that conscious human design can improve on nature in the production of 'accidents'. 'The behavioural scientist does not confine himself to the schedules of reinforcement which happen to occur in nature: he constructs a great variety of schedules, some of which might never arise by accident.'[61] Diversity, in other words, can be consciously manufactured, by the deliberate actions of an enlightened elite.

The weakness of Skinner's psychology, as well as his understanding of social change, is evident here. He does not allow for the waywardness and arbitrariness, the sheer randomness, inherent in human creativity and inventiveness. The 'planning of change' is an absurd contradiction. If something is planned, it reflects current thought and practice. To the extent that it comes out *as* planned, it represents the domination of the past over the future. In no sense can it be said to have brought something new – a *change* – into the world. If Skinnerian Planners had controlled society in mankind's earliest days, it is unlikely that we would have evolved out of the Stone Age. No doubt we would have perfected Stone Age techniques to the ultimate point – so long, that is, as the environment did not change so much as to consign us to the fossil record of spent species. Our only chance of progress would have come from the existence of a plurality of communities, which, despite each having a Skinnerian elite, may have exhibited a variety of different adaptations to the environment. It is important to see, though, that such evolution would be in spite of, not because of, the Skinnerian philosophy of planning. The fact that, historically, this is largely what did happen should be a matter of regret and material for sombre reflection, not a cause for celebration. It means that societies in the past have only too closely resembled Skinnerian communities, even if their intentions were less clear to themselves or to others.

It is unfair to close on too negative a note. Skinner does not solve the political problems of utopian society, but which utopian writer does? His utopianism has many attractive features: its radical environmentalism, its out-and-out experimental attitude to the problems of social life, its confidence in human reason to understand and to resolve those problems. The whole of his work breathes the spirit of the European Enlightenment; and in a period noticeable for its rejection of Enlightenment philosophy, this was both a brave and a heartening thing to see. He knew, as one can tell from *Walden Two*, that his utopia would be slandered as fascist or communist. Given that he chose to include eugenics, collective child-rearing, the destruction of the family, equality of work and rewards, common property and centralized planning, this is hardly unexpected. What needs to be emphasized is his considerable success in rescuing these practices from their disfigurement within nazism and Stalinism. He shows that, given a suitably tentative attitude towards them, they are practices with a real potential for overcoming some of the fundamental discontents of modern society. The fact that *Walden Two*, like its great namesake *Walden*, has fired the imagination of some very dedicated utopia-seekers is the best testimony to its rightful place in the grand utopian tradition.

PART III

10

Utopia and Anti-Utopia in the Twentieth Century

> Gone are the sunlit utopian meadows of William Morris and in, most unbudgably in, are the diversifying dyspeptic dystopias of our century. Those who claim to be sensitive to the collective consciousness have gone through an unparalleled regress in the mood which has accompanied riches. We are in the era of affluent pessimism.
>
> Michael Young, 'A History of the Future', Presidential Address to British Association for the Advancement of Science, 1984

> We live in the midst of a historical crisis in which our choices are between . . . utopia and the end of civilization, in which we are presented with the existential paradox of a necessary utopia.
>
> Victor Ferkiss, *The Future of Technological Civilization* (1974)

TWILIGHT OF UTOPIA?

Can there be anything more commonplace than the pronouncement that, in the twentieth century, utopia is dead – and dead beyond any hope of resurrection? The Manuels, at the end of their long journey through utopia, suggest that we are living in the 'twilight of utopia', and wonder whether we are witnessing 'a running down of the utopia-making machine of the West'. Northrop Frye notes a 'paralysis of utopian thought and imagination' in contemparary literature. And Robert Elliott points to the widely accepted reason for the fact that 'the uninhibited utopianizing imagination' has largely disappeared: 'Our history has made confident visions of the wholesale reconstitution of society, like those of the nineteenth century, impossible.'[1]

There is likewise little disagreement about the facts of that contemporary history that have rendered all utopian aspirations illusory. Already for many Western intellectuals the First World War had sounded the death-knell of the belief in progress that had for so long borne up utopian hopes.

> I am so sad [wrote D. H. Lawrence] for my country, for this great wave of civilization, 2000 years, which is now collapsing, that it is hard to live. So much beauty and pathos of

old things passing away and no new things coming . . . the winter stretches ahead, where all vision is lost and all memory dies out.[2]

The First World War, writes I. F. Clarke, destroyed 'the golden link between progress and posterity'.[3] Subsequent events did nothing to restore the link. How could utopia stand up in the face of nazism, Stalinism, genocide, mass unemployment and a second world war? Even the resilient utopianism of H. G. Wells gave way before this onslaught. In his last work, *Mind at the End of its Tether*, published in 1945, this foremost apologist of utopia, the apostle of progress and science, seemed to abandon all hope in the future and in humanity. *Homo sapiens*, he wrote, was 'at the close of his specific existence'.

This world is at the end of its tether. The end of everything we call life is close at hand and cannot be evaded. . . . Mind near exhaustion still makes its final futile movement towards that 'way out or round or through the impasse' . . . . this, its last expiring thrust, is to demonstrate that the door closes upon us for evermore. There is no way out or round or through. . . . Our universe is not merely bankrupt; there remains no dividend at all; it has not simply liquidated; it is going clean out of existence, leaving not a wrack behind. The attempt to trace a pattern of any sort is absolutely futile. . . . The human story has already come to an end and . . . . *Homo sapiens*, as he has been pleased to call himself, is in his present form played out.[4]

Wells achieved this 'cosmic pessimism' without benefit of the news of the bombing of Hiroshima, although he lived just long enough to learn of it. The Second World War ended in the defeat of the most barbarous of the combatants, but the manner of its ending, in atomic bombardment, merely added fuel to anti-utopian despair. To totalitarian tyranny and world domination was now added the spectre of nuclear annihilation. In the interwar years, according to one calculation, about three hundred 'futuristic tales' appeared in England, 'most of them marked by chronic anxieties about the future of mankind'.[5] In the years after 1945, an incalculably greater number of such tales spelled out, in even more alarming tones, the message of the mushroom-shaped cloud.

The general tenor of world events, and the apparent direction of world history, in themselves would have been enough to dampen utopian ardour. But there was a special pathos and poignancy in the fate of two particular societies, the American and the Russian. For America and the Soviet Union are the two great utopian experiments of modern times.[6] A good deal of the history of the modern utopia can be written around them, the hopes they inspired and the designs drawn up for them. America in the twentieth century continued to attract utopian hopes, but with nothing like the fervour it had previously aroused. Now it could inspire anti-utopia as readily as utopia. One of the two most influential anti-utopias of the century, Huxley's *Brave New World*, drew largely upon American practices for its picture of a benighted future world, sunk in mindless consumerism. Later, as American military power came to dominate the world, the anti-utopian image of America took on even grimmer features. The 'ugly American', brutally bent on making the world 'safe for democracy', seemed capable in this pursuit of simultaneously dissolving the world in ruins.

The disillusionment with the Soviet Union was speedier but in many ways more far-reaching. For the Soviet Union was heir to the intense utopian expectations of nineteenth-century socialism, the principal source of the contemporary utopia. For many western intellectuals in the 1920s and 1930s it represented the highest hopes of mankind, a new beginning, as Sidney and Beatrice Webb enthusiastically hailed it in their *Soviet Communism – A New Civilization* (1935). For the young Arthur Koestler, who joined the German Communist Party in 1931, 'the new star of Bethlehem had risen in the East.' André Gide, whose disillusionment began with a tour of Russia in 1936, could still later recall his 'love and admiration for the Soviet Union where an unprecedented experiment was being attempted'.

Who can ever say what the Soviet Union had been for me? Far more than the country of my choice, an example and an inspiration – it represented what I had always dreamed of but no longer dared hope; it was something towards which all my longing was directed; it was a land where I imagined Utopia was in the process of becoming reality.[7]

Koestler, following his own rude awakening from the dream during the Spanish Civil War, went on to write his *Darkness at Noon* (1940), the most brilliant and powerful unravelling of the Soviet promise and the terrible reality. His friend Orwell was never a believer in the Soviet utopia; but for all those for whom Soviet communism was 'the God that failed', Orwell's *Animal Farm* and *Nineteen Eighty-Four* were the precise and passionate expression of their own bitter feelings about the Soviet Union. Ignoring Orwell's repeated denials that socialism or even the Soviet Union were his principal targets, they could take the Orwellian anti-utopia as the sufficient response to the communist utopia. Not all who were disenchanted with the Soviet Union felt that they must also thereby renounce socialism or Marxism; but it was difficult to prevent guilt by association. The revulsion against Stalinism, and the widespread sense of a revolution not merely betrayed but fundamentally flawed, tarnished the socialist utopia to an even greater degree than in the case of the individualist American utopia. Socialists in the West hurried to rid themseves of the Soviet and even the Marxist connection, proclaiming themselves now 'social democrats', and rediscovering their non-Marxist roots. It became plausible to argue that socialism – like Christianity? – was an inspiring and creative force only so long as it remained in the imagination, as an apparently practicable but actually unrealizable goal.

Socialism shares with all other utopias the unpleasant quality of retaining its fertility only in so far as it resides in the realm of the possible. The moment it is proclaimed as accomplished, as empirical reality, it loses its creative power . . . . The two centuries of modern socialism's history extend from its majestic advent in the attire of utopia to the incapacitation arising from its alleged realization.[8]

In its evident inclination for anti-utopia, political history was at one with intellectual history. There is no direct connection between the social theory and the political events of an epoch. But it seems reasonable to suppose that the popularity of certain ideas will turn on their correspondence with the experienced and observed social reality. If the world seems to be heading for self-destruction and damnation, the views of human nature and society which purport to explain this are likely to find favour whatever their scientific deficiencies. Little in the way of scientific or systematic social theory underlay the gloomy prognostications of Oswald Spengler's *Decline of the West* (1918); nevertheless, appearing as it did in the closing years of the First World War it is easy to see why its 'evocative melancholy' should appeal so powerfully to the German people, and later to many others outside Germany equally troubled by the drift of events.[9]

In prophesying the decline of the West, Spengler employed the analogy between the individual and the social organism. Like the former, the latter too had its predictable life-cycle of birth, maturation and death. Biological metaphors and imagery, deriving a spurious legitimacy from a supposed basis in Darwinism, were rampant in the social ideologies of the early part of the century. Embodied in various schools of Social Darwinism, they offered a direct challenge to the progressivist and evolutionary pattern of the nineteenth-century utopia, especially the socialist utopia. T. H. Huxley had shown that the struggle for survival was blind and entirely lacking in any moral dimension.[10] Transferred to society, this suggested an unending process of struggle and strife, out of which the 'fittest' and 'best' would emerge in successive waves. There could be no point of utopian rest, no security in any utopian design, in an environment which was always liable to change, sometimes cataclysmically. Some utopian writers, like Bulwer-Lytton, might use Darwinism to prefigure a coming superior race or civilization. But there could be no comfort in such a vision even for those who saw themselves, in racist terms, as possible candidates for such a role in the contemporary world. For the one sure thing about achieving dominance was that it was temporary. Today's rulers were, however wise and powerful, tomorrow's victims of a changed environment. Natural selection, Darwin had said, 'works by life and death'. So it was in nature, and so in society. It was Wells, more than anyone else, who got the true measure of the Darwinian message in the brilliant anti-utopian stories of the 1890s and 1900s.

The popularity of social Darwinism meant the popularity of ideas that emphasized man not as a political or rational animal but simply as an animal. This alone would probably have been a blow to the utopian hope, premised as it generally was on the belief in man's essence as a rational being, or at least, as with Swift, in his capacity for reason. Even in Hobbes's grim view of man in the state of nature, man had been allowed the use of his faculty of reason to construct the Leviathan as a defence against the anarchy of nature. But what made twentieth-century biological views so especially hostile to utopia was not simply that human behaviour was seen primarily in biological terms; it was the *kind* of animal that man was adjudged to be. In the dominant view man was not an altruistic, peaceful, cooperative animal, as are many of his fellow primates; he was selfish, acquisitive, aggressive, even murderous and predatory, like the wolf. Worse, even his attempt to control his biological nature by the exercise of his rational faculties was liable to founder on the rocks of his unconscious urges – at best driving him into neurosis, at worst leading him to break through all civilized restraints.

Homo homini lupus – 'man is a wolf to man': that was the motto theme of Freud's *Civilization and Its Discontents* (1930). If, though not in itself an anti-utopia, Dostoyevsky's 'Legend of the Grand Inquisitor' is the key anti-utopian text of the nineteenth century, then we might say that this work of Freud's is the key anti-utopian text of the twentieth century. No one more than Freud has so powerfully and persuasively undermined the intellectual and emotional foundations of utopian hopes – what Freud contemptuously referred to as 'lullabies of heaven'. In *Civilization and Its Discontents*, as in many of his later 'metapsychological' writings, Freud portrayed a world in which pain and unhappiness are the norm and conflict and disintegration an ever-present tendency. All culture is reared on repression and instinctual renunciation. All civilized morality, all laws and institutions, are the necessary but precarious bulwarks against elemental biological drives towards aggression, destruction and domination. Civilization achieves some stability by setting up a moral 'super-ego' in the individual to guard against the destructive impulses of the unconscious, 'like a garrison in a conquered city'. But the primeval mind lodged in the unconscious is 'imperishable', breaking out regularly in individual and collective acts of violence and war. 'Judged by our unconscious wishful impulses, we . . . are . . . a gang of murderers.' 'The commandment to love one's neighbour as onself . . . is really justified by the fact that nothing else runs so strongly counter to the original nature of man.' Freud was particularly scathing about the communists' belief that the abolition of property will end aggression and possessiveness.

In abolishing private property we deprive the human love of aggression of one of its instruments, certainly a strong one, though certainly not the strongest; but we have in no way altered the differences in power and influence which are misused by aggressiveness, nor have we altered anything in its nature. Aggressiveness was not created by property. It reigned almost without limit in primitive times, when property was still very scanty, and it already shows itself in the nursery almost before property has given up its primal, anal form; it forms the basis of every relation of affection and love among people . . . . If we do away with personal rights over material wealth, there still remains prerogative in the field of sexual relations, which is bound to become the source of the strongest dislike and the most violent hostility among men who in other respects are on an equal footing. If we were to remove this factor, too, by allowing complete freedom of sexual life and thus abolishing the family, the germ-cell of civilization, we cannot, it is true, easily forsee what new paths the development of civilization could take; but one thing we can expect, and that is that this indestructible feature of human nature will follow it there.[11]

In a passage that expressed his fundamental pessimistic credo, Freud argued that 'the inclination to aggression is an original, self-subsisting instinctual disposition in man [which] constitutes the greatest impediment to civilization.' The whole of mankind's development, as of life itself, was seen as a ceaseless war between Eros, the constructive 'life instinct' and Thanatos, the destructive 'death instinct'.

Civilization is a process in the service of Eros, whose purpose is to combine single human individuals, and after that families, then races, peoples and nations into one great unity, the unity of mankind. . . . These collections of men are to be libidinally bound to each other. Necessity alone, the advantages of work in common, will not hold them together. But man's natural aggressive instinct, the hostility of each against all and of all against each, opposes this programme of civilization. This aggressive instinct is the derivative and the main representative of the death instinct which we have found alongside of Eros and which shares world-dominion with it. And now, I think, the meaning of the evolution of civilization is no longer obscure to us. It must present the struggle between Eros and Death, between the instinct of life and the instinct of destruction, as it works itself out in the human species. This struggle is what all life essentially consists of, and the evolution of civilization may therefore be simply described as the struggle for life of the human species. And it is this battle of the giants that our nurse-maids try to appease with their lullaby about Heaven.[12]

Freud refused the role of prophet and would not speculate on the likely fortunes of the two cosmic forces contending for mastery. It is clear though that, despite the presence of Eros and Freud's own stoical belief in the power of reason to impose some degree of civilized control, there is no real place for utopia in the Freudian universe. Mere survival of the species seems a full-time effort; any further blessing must appear a gift of supererogation. Moreover, as the bleak events of the 'devil's decade' of the 1930s unfolded, Freud himself came to be deeply affected by the 'current unrest . . . unhappiness, and . . . mood of anxiety' that he noted around him. He was prompted to add some concluding lines to his work, in which he warned that 'men have gained control over the forces of nature to such an extent that with their help they would have no difficulty in exterminating one another to the last man.'[13]

In the climate of the 1930s and 1940s it was indeed difficult to imagine that utopia would again play a significant part in social thought or even imaginative literature. In purely quantitative terms, utopias continued to appear in reasonable number.[14] One might even say, knowing that this says very little, that more utopias have been produced in this century than in any preceding century. Without further evidence or assessment, all that this might point to is the successful operation of the mass publishing industry of our times. Certainly this could be true of the many utopias to be found in science fiction, whose thriving career as a separate genre was launched with the founding of Hugo Gernsback's magazine *Amazing Stories* in the United States in 1926. Together with *Astounding Stories*, started in 1930, 'genre' science fiction maintained a resolutely optimistic stance up to the end of the Second World War (when the dropping of the atomic bomb gave it pause for thought). Gernsback in particular proselytized actively on behalf of modern technology, and technological utopianism was the dominant strain in science fiction for much of this period.[15]

The optimism of science fiction in the United States was matched by that of the Technocracy movement of the 1930s and 1940s. Inspired by Thorstein Veblen's idea of a 'Soviet of Technicians', the movement adopted the conventional aim of the scientific utopia, of banishing want and waste through science and technology. Harold Loeb's *Life in a Technocracy: What it Might be Like* (1933) made clear enough the derivativeness of Technocracy's ideas and its dependence on earlier forms of technological utopianism, especially that of

Bellamy's. More interesting, as an aspect of the movement, were the great world fairs of the 1930s in various Amerian cities, culminating in the World of Tomorrow fair in New York in 1939. These were based on the real achievements of industrial designers such as Raymond Loewy and Norman Bel Geddes, and reflected their technological optimism. The fairs, with their vivid futuristic urban panoramas, aspired to promote the idea that technology was on the point of realizing utopia – the World of Tomorrow fair actually set the date at 1960. They harked back also to a guiding idea of the great Crystal Palace Exhibition of 1851, that international gatherings such as world fairs could be a force for peace.[16]

America throughout the interwar period found more space for utopia than did Europe. But even there the scope was limited. Arising as they did during the depths of the Great Depression, and given a sharp check by the onset of the Second World War, Technocracy and its associated movements were bound to be fleeting and marginal. 'Caught between ribaldry and irrelevance, the technocratic dream faded as rapidly as it had arisen.'[17] The problem with all utopian strivings of the time was that they struggled against what appeared the overwhelmingly anti-utopian character of world events. Utopia survived among small pockets of utopian missionaries, but they preached to largely unhearing ears. No work of the utopian imagination appeared which caught the public fancy as had the utopias of Bellamy, Morris and Wells at the turn of the century. At another time, perhaps, so original and ambitious a utopia as Olaf Stapledon's *Last and First Men* (1930), or its successor *Star Maker* (1937), might have found a larger and more receptive audience. Many contemporary critics admired them for their style and philosophic grandeur. C. S. Lewis paid them the compliment of attacking their rationalist outlook in some of his best science fiction. Science fiction writers such as Arthur C. Clarke and James Blish acknowledged their debt to their ideas. But the books remained isolated instances, largely ignored and quickly forgotten. Stapledon was in any event an oddity. He made no attempt to connect his works with the main utopian tradition or even the new genre of science fiction. There was undoubtedly a utopian vision in them; but with their evolutionary time scale of more than two thousand million years, and their mystic philosophy of cosmic community, it was a vision that appeared supremely irrelevant to the problems at hand. Utopia, if it was to be rescued from the nadir to which it had fallen, required something less ethereal and more earthly, something that would begin to match the anti-utopia's only too obvious engagement with the contemporary world.

There remained, of course, Wells. Wells throughout these years persisted valiantly in holding aloft the utopian banner. Work after work streamed from his pen, in which he pressed with increasing urgency the case for a new world order under a world government. His last utopian novel, *All Aboard for Ararat* (1940), used the by now familiar device of a cataclysmic 'purification' – in this case a new Flood – to bring mankind to its senses and institute the new world order. In the same year he worked with a distinguished team of scientists and intellectuals in the framing of a 'Declaration of Human Rights', which set out the principles of a new international organization to be set up once the war had ended.

But the ageing Wells had largely lost his audience. The Wellsian voice sounded increasingly shrill, petulant and hectoring. Orwell wrote dismissively of 'the usual rigmarole of the World State', and provoked a bitter row with Wells. The Christian writer C. S. Lewis produced an effective anti-Wellsian science fiction trilogy, *Out of the Silent Planet* (1938), *Perelandra* (1943) and *That Hideous Strength* (1945) – the last containing a cruel portrait of Wells as a vulgar cockney journalist. Somerset Maugham, observing Wells on an American lecture tour, noted: 'His lectures were a failure. People couldn't hear what he said and didn't want to listen to what they could hear. . . . He was hurt and disappointed. He couldn't understand why they were impatient with him for saying much the same thing as he had been saying for the last thirty years. The river has flowed on and left him high and dry on the bank.'[18]

Wells, as we have seen, himself seems to have abandoned hope in the last years of his life. Would he have been surprised, then, to find the 'Declaration of Human Rights' – which all admitted to be mainly his work – repeated in all its essentials in the Universal Declaration of Human Rights adopted by the United Nations General Assembly in 1948?[19] Would the existence of the United Nations itself have seemed to him, for all its weaknesses, some grounds for hope?

The late 1940s were intensely contradictory times. Fascism had been defeated but the Cold War had been inaugurated. The United Nations had been set up but nuclear weapons remained firmly under the control of a few powerful nation-states. Colonial empires broke up and new nations were formed by the score; but the dependence of the poor ex-colonial countries of the South on the rich countries of the North became, if anything, greater than before. As communism gained a great victory in China, its appeal progressively diminished with the Soviet take-over of eastern Europe and the revelations of the brutality of Stalinism.

Anti-utopia and utopia warred, too, in a mirror reflection of this contradictory pattern. Aldous Huxley's savage post-holocaust *Ape and Essence* (1948) was followed by Orwell's *Nineteen Eighty-Four* (1949). But in those same two years also came B. F. Skinner's scientific utopia *Walden Two* (1948) and Robert Graves's pastoral utopia *Seven Days in New Crete* (1949). In 1949, too, Martin Buber published his influential *Paths in Utopia*, the immediate stimulus to which were the utopian experiments of the contemporary Israeli *kibbutzim*. The hope was qualified, but in the decentralized communal order of the *kibbutz* Buber saw the germ for the renewal of the whole communitarian tradition of utopian socialism. Given the state of Russia, Buber concluded, the choice for socialists was clear: 'Moscow' or 'Jerusalem'.[20]

The very mention of Israel, as a state created out of a bloody civil war which displaced millions of Arabs, is enough to suggest the ambivalence which must surround the idea of Jerusalem as a symbol of utopia. And that ambivalence was, more fundamentally, to accompany the whole concept of utopia into the post-war period. But what is more important to stress here is that utopia did revive. The twentieth century cannot be simply characterized, as it so commonly is, as the death of utopia. The anti-utopia certainly made most of the running in the first half of the century. But in the second half utopia has launched a vigorous challenge to its dominance. The form of utopia has fragmented somewhat, as have the constituencies to which it is directed. But overall the confident pronouncements of its death seem premature.

UTOPIA FOR A POST-INDUSTRIAL AGE

In one of the most widely-read and quoted social science books of the 1950s, a group of American social scientists made the ritual declaration: 'The age of utopias is past. An age of realism has taken its place. . . .' In the very same work, however, they went on to resurrect utopia in a new form: as the whole system of industrialism and industrial society. Industrial civilization itself, it now appeared, could become the fit object of utopian strivings. In the twentieth century, they declared, industrialism as developed by Western societies had become 'the goal of mankind and the essence of national aspiration'.[21]

The book, *Industrialism and Industrial Man*, was representative of a marked change of mood, as compared with the earlier part of the century. The recovery of the industrial nations, after the devastation of world war, surprised even the most optimistic observers by its speed. Not only the victors but even more the defeated nations – Germany and Japan – achieved rates of economic growth in the 1950s and 1960s that made Britain's historic growth as the first industrial nation appear paltry by comparison. In retrospect, and with a good deal of selectivity, the traumatic episodes of the first half of the century could now be read as the growing pains of the transition to a fully-developed and mature industrialism. Industrial society had come of age. Keynes had shown the way to avoid recurrences of the mass unemployment of the 1930s; Beveridge had set out the blueprint of 'the welfare state' which would eliminate the worst aspects of poverty and social deprivation; all societies promised to educate all their citizens to the highest level of their capacities. The planned and managed social democratic state, accepted by virtually all political parties and political ideologies in the West, seemed to promise an end to the disruptive and wasteful social conflicts of earlier times.

The 1950s proclaimed 'the end of ideology'. There seemed no basis, and no need, for rival and irreconcilable views of social and political development. Even the Soviet Union, it was asserted, in the 'thaw' following the official denunciation of Stalinism, was steadily moving closer to the Western pattern of society. Given the political will, and a continuing consensus on what constituted the good life, there was no real barrier to indefinite economic progress and long-lasting social stability (seen as two sides of the same coin). By the same token, there could be no need for any other utopia. All utopian aspirations of the past could be incorporated in the drive towards world-wide industrialization. Industrial society was the good society *tout court*.[22]

In this utopian conception, it was evident that science and technology must play a major role. For nothing more fully promised to serve the economic growth that was seen as the goal of all policy. Economic progress, all agreed, turned now as never before on fundamental research in science and technology. Hence the revival of optimism in social thought involved also a rehabilitation of these old demons of the anti-utopia. The shadow of *Brave New*

World and *Nineteen Eighty-Four* had to be lifted. The fear of science as the instrument of tyranny and mass conformity had to give way to a belief in its role as liberator and cornucopian provider.

Essentially, this meant recalling and reviving the 'science and society' movement of the 1920s and 1930s that had been one of the principal targets of the anti-utopia, and specifically of Huxley's *Brave New World.*[23] The confident, even arrogant, scientific utopianism of Haldane and Bernal had not fared well in the climate of the 1930s and 1940s, despite – or more, perhaps, because of – the proselytizing of Wells and other scientific popularizers such as Julian Huxley and Lancelot Hogben. Even more serious was the evidence of concern among the ranks of the scientists themselves. The well publicized opposition of scientists such as Einstein to the development of nuclear weapons,[24] and the later revulsion of some of the atomic scientists themselves, such as Robert Oppenheimer, intensified the feeling that science was a fearful monster that had burst loose from the control of its masters.

Fears about nuclear war were the persistent anti-utopian undercurrent to the industrial utopia of the 1950s. But they could not prevent the refurbishing of the image of the scientist. In one of the most celebrated exercises of this kind, Sir Charles Snow's Rede Lecture, *The Two Cultures and the Scientific Revolution* (1959), the scientist appeared as a kind of culture-hero, the saviour of industrial civilization against the nostalgic and reactionary influences of the literary intellectuals. 'This is the heroic age of science', Rutherford had trumpeted, and Snow heartily endorsed that Promethean view. It was the scientists who 'naturally . . . had the future in their bones', whereas the literary intellectuals responded by 'wishing the future did not exist'.[25] Far from science and scientists being amoral, as often charged, 'there is a moral component right in the grain of science itself', while morally scientists are 'the soundest group of intellectuals we have.'[26] It was the literary intellectuals, the 'natural Luddites', who were guilty of immorality in opposing the development of industrialization to the fullest extent possible. For only in this way could the world be fed and poverty eradicated. Set against the titans of MIT and the Soviet Academy of Sciences, who were transforming the world and putting men into space, the literary coteries of Chelsea and Greenwich Village were made to appear feeble and self-indulgent – certainly, in any event, irrelevant.

There was somewhat less euphoria about the role of science and scientists, and less hostility to artists, in John Kenneth Galbraith's *The New Industrial State* (1967). But he too, in an influential conception, picked out the 'technostructure', the research scientists and technical specialists, as 'the guiding intelligence – the brain – of the modern business enterprise'. In industrial society generally, committed as it now was to technology, planning and organization, it was 'the scientific and educational estate' which held strategic power, and which must set the goals. No longer could they, or should they, shield themselves behind the industrialists and politicians, as merely advisory experts. They were in effect a new ruling class, and must exercise the responsibility that this entailed. Such, too, but in a decidedly more optimistic vein, was essentially the argument of the theory of 'post-industrial' society that emerged in the 1960s, and was widely propagated by the institutes of 'futurology' that sprang up in these years. In the work especially of Herman Kahn and his associates at the Hudson Institute in America, and in such books as Daniel Bell's *The Coming of Post-Industrial Society* (1973), a new industrial age was announced, in which the scientists and technologists would be the prime movers, and their scientific knowledge the indispensable resource for economic growth and the management of society. Science and technology were the wave of the future; and futurology attempted to dispel anti-utopian fears of the future by spelling out in detail the promise of the years to come. A series of books and reports with millennial titles – Herman Kahn and Anthony Wiener's *The Year 2000* (1967), Robert Jungk and Johan Galtung's *Mankind 2000* (1969) – urged the populations of the industrial societies to turn their eyes to the future and to look to it with hope and confidence.[27]

The utopian impulse in futurology was clear, although futurology produced no formal fictional utopia. Probably the reason was the same as that which had displaced utopia in favour of social theory in the early nineteenth century: namely, that futurologists were convinced of the imminent realization of their expectations, and saw the task as one of scientific analysis and policy prescription rather than of utopian picturing.

The same conviction that what should be involved was scientific analysis and not utopian speculation characterized another development in these years, which nevertheless carried even stronger utopian overtones. Here, what seems to have inhibited the production of a utopia proper was not so much a concern with policy prescription or detailed analysis as the fact that the writing itself strayed so far into the utopian mode. What was even more important, however, was the content. For, just as science as a social force was rehabilitated in social theory, so certain aspects of scientific theory itself were reworked and reinterpreted in ways highly favourable to utopia. The significance of this was that it was the two bogeys of the contemporary utopia, Darwin and Freud, who were thus given a kinder and more hopeful aspect.

Already in the early 1950s Sir Julian Huxley, one of Wells's collaborators in the 1930s, was preaching a species of evolutionary humanism that took the sting out of Darwinism. As a distinguished biologist in his own right, and not merely a scientific popularizer, he had throughout his working life sought to counter the anti-utopian gloom spread by his brother Aldous. More to the point, he had reinterpreted and reformulated Darwinism in ways that countered the pessimistic picture presented by his even more famous grandfather, Thomas Henry Huxley. T. H. Huxley could find no evidence of purpose or progress in evolution; on the contrary, his grandson roundly declared, evolution demonstrated that 'progress is inevitable as a general fact.' It took the form not so much of specialized biological improvements as of a general increase, over the course of time, in the all-round efficiency, organizational complexity and intelligence of living matter. Where one line of advance came to a stop, another took over, in a process of 'successional replacement, where a later deployment replaces an earlier one as a dominant type'. The human species, 'as the latest successional deployment, represents the furthest step yet taken in evolutionary progress. This is not just anthropomorphic wish-fulfilment, but a direct and necessary deduction from biological fact.' This, moreover, was just the beginning of an entirely new phase of evolutionary progress. With the appearance of man, a critical divide had been crossed. 'Biological progress, in fact, has come to an end, but human progress is just beginning.' With man, mind had entered evolution, affecting decisively its future course. Further evolution would now be 'psycho-social'. Through his social and technical inventions, man had now made himself master of all further evolutionary progress.

In the light of evolutionary biology man can now see himself as the sole agent of further evolutionary advances on this planet, and one of the few possible instruments of progress in the universe at large. He finds himself in the unexpected position of business manager for the cosmic process of evolution. He no longer ought to feel separated from the rest of nature, for he is part of it – the part which has become conscious, capable of love and understanding and aspiration. He need no longer regard himself as insignificant in relation to the cosmos. He is intensely significant. In his person, he has acquired meaning, for he is constantly creating new meanings. Human society generates new mental and spiritual agencies, and sets them to work in the cosmic process: it controls matter by means of mind . . . .

Ever since he first began, man has been groping to discern the features of his destiny more clearly. In the light of the evidence now available, he could come to the realization that his destiny is to participate and lead in the creative process of evolution, whereby new possibilities can be realized for life.[28]

It was entirely fitting that it should be Huxley who introduced the work of the French Jesuit palaeontologist Pierre Teilhard de Chardin to the English-speaking public. For, as Huxley noted in his 'Introduction' to Teilhard's *The Phenomenon of Man* (1959), they had long 'been pursuing parallel roads'. But whereas Huxley formulated his belief in progress in the agnostic terms of evolutionary humanism, Teihard's was an elaborate synthesis of evolutionary biology and Christian theology, aimed at reconciling the two through a comprehensive vision of cosmic purpose.[29] *The Phenomenon of Man* is a work of extraordinary grandeur, recalling in its sweep, in addition to something of its philosophy of religious evolutionism, Winwood Reade's *The Martyrdom of Man* and Wells's *The Outline of History*. Shorn of the explicitly Christian element, it also shares much of the character of cosmic utopianism to be found in Bernal's *The World, the Flesh and the Devil* and Stapledon's *Last and First Men*. Like several of these authors, too, Teilhard inspired a considerable cult following in many Western countries, with societies and journals – several still in existence – set up to study his work and propagate his ideas.

In principle, there was nothing especially original about Teilhard's views. What most caught the public imagination, it seems, was the highly poetic language in which they were expressed, as well as some of the special terms which Teilhard invented. The world, as Teilhard conceived it, was composed of a lifeless layer of inorganic matter, the 'lithosphere', upon which was superposed the living layer of the 'biosphere' and above which, in turn, stood the 'noosphere', the 'thinking layer' or sphere of mind. But, consistent with Teilhard's argument that there is in evolution nothing wholly new, that there is always some rudiment or archetype of everything that exists or has existed, the mental activity of the noosphere is not new but has been present throughout evolution. We are 'logically forced to assume the existence in rudimentary form . . . of some sort of psyche in every corpuscle; . . . by the very fact of the individualization of our planet, a certain mass of elementary consciousness was originally imprisoned in the matter of earth.' The consciousness of the noosphere is a primal transforming force, a kind of entelechy or *élan vital*, ceaselessly at work in the course of evolution. It leads eventually to 'noogenesis', the birth of the higher consciousness among the primates, and finally to 'hominization', the advent of human consciousness and with it the beginning of the culminating stages of evolution in the pure consciousness of the noosphere.

Human social evolution itself has been a story of progressive unification and 'complexification', cultural differentiation followed by cultural convergence, so that the whole human species has now been integrated into a single 'interthinking' group based on a single self-developing framework of thought. The progressive development of human culture and creativity has 'heated up' the psychic temperature of the noosphere, increasing the energy level and tension within it, and so preparing the way for the culminating phase of 'supreme consciousness'.

It is not always very helpful to quote Teilhard in expounding his ideas, given the metaphoric and poetic quality of the prose. ('It is the style,' Medawar cruelly remarks, 'that creates the illusion of content.'[30]) But some idea of the flavour of the book can be got from the passage in which Teilhard pictures the noosphere finally 'closing in upon itself' in a more or less perfected state of self-communing consciousness. The noosphere now becomes fully autonomous and self-sufficient (like Hegel's Spirit in its final state). The life of the biosphere ceases; the planet dies as a material entity. This is 'the ultimate phase of the phenomenon of man'. It is 'the end of the world', or rather its summit, and the discovery there of the transcendental 'Omega point' to which it has throughout been tending, and to which it has been drawn by the 'supreme Someone'.

Noogenesis rises upwards in us and through us unceasingly. We have pointed to the principal characteristics of that movement: the closer association of the grains of thought; the synthesis of individuals and of nations or races; the need of an autonomous and supreme personal focus to bind elementary personalities together, without deforming them, in an atmosphere of active sympathy. And, once again: all this results from the combined action of two curvatures – the roundness of the earth and the cosmic convergence of mind – in conformity with the law of complexity and consciousness.

Now when sufficient elements have sufficiently agglomerated, this essentially convergent movement will attain such intensity and such quality that mankind, taken as a whole, will be obliged – as happened to the individual forces of instinct – to reflect upon itself at a single point; that is to say, in this case, to abandon its organo-planetary foothold so as to pivot itself on the transcendent centre of its increasing concentration. This will be the end and the fulfilment of the spirit of the earth.

The end of the world: the wholesale internal introversion upon itself of the noosphere, which has simultaneously reached the uttermost limit of its complexity and its centrality.

The end of the world: the overthrow of equilibrium, detaching the mind, fulfilled at last, from its material matrix, so that it will henceforth rest with all its weight on God-Omega.

The end of the world: critical point simultaneously of emergence and emersion, of maturation and escape.[31]

Professional biologists might be severe with all this; but that served only to enhance the work's popularity. In any case Teilhard, like Huxley, was a scientist, a working palaeontologist. His work was intended to be read, he said, 'purely and simply as a scientific treatise'. Huxley and Teilhard were important in that they conferred the prestige of practising scientists on the new benign image of Darwin. At about the same time a number of thinkers, some of them practising psychoanalysts, were doing the same for Freud. Even before Freud's death, in fact, his heretical disciple Wilhelm Reich had tried to employ Marxism to offset the pessimistic implications of Freud's theories. Freud's theory of instincts, said Reich, was bourgeois, appropriate to the bourgeois form of society in which it had arisen. The instinctual repression that Freud had seen as the necessary basis of culture was not permanent. It was valid only in an era of scarcity, when libidinal energy had to be channelled into alienated work for the sake of production. Socialism could never be built by a working class still subject to bourgeois modes of instinctual repression. Any attempt to do so on this basis would lead to authoritarianism and a new tyranny. The workers must first free themselves instinctually, regain all the power and energy of their bodies, before they could be fit material for the new society. Without sexual revolution there could be no political revolution.[32]

Few 'Freudo-Marxists'[33] went as far as Reich in the worship of the body. Later, in America, Reich went even further, discarding much of his Marxism to become a prophet of the liberating potential of the orgasm, seen as the exclusive remedy for all nervous and mental disorders. For his theory and practice of 'orgone therapy' the American authorities declared him mad and had him locked up. But the 1960s radicals enthusiastically rediscovered him, and their slogan, 'make love, not war', owed much to Reich's theories. They were equally enthusiastic about the radical sexual politics of Norman O. Brown, an American professor of classics whose *Life Against Death* (1959) was one of the bibles of the 'counter-culture' of the 1960s. Brown outdid Reich in urging the release not just of the energies of adult genital sexuality but of all the explosive forces of pre-adult, pre-genital, infantile sexuality. In the 'polymorphous perversity' of the child, Brown saw the hope for the all-round liberation and 'resurrection of the body'. What Freud had considered a threat to all that civilization and culture achieves, Brown wished to celebrate as the most vital components of the life instinct. Satisfaction of the death instinct, 'the patience and labor of the Negative', was also necessary. But in the full release of the 'erotic exuberance' of polymorphous sexuality, Brown saw the hope of an end to the cosmic struggle between Eros and Thanatos. For 'the death instinct is reconciled with the life instinct only in a life which is not repressed, which leaves no "unlived lines" in the human body, the death instinct then being affirimed in a body which is willling to die.'[34]

Brown's sexual politics were more sexual than political; and it was left to others to make a more complete fusion of Marx and Freud in the 1950s and 1960s. The early Reich had been an important influence on the Frankfurt

School of social theory.[35] With the movement of many of its members, like Reich, to America, the hopeful synthesis of Freud and Marx was continued in a culture generally more given to hope than that of Europe. But, unlike the case with Reich, the 'sociologizing' of Freud was carried to even greater lengths. In both his psychoanalytic practice and his many works of social theory, Erich Fromm in particular 'Americanized' Freud almost to the point where a certain amount of love, sympathy and humanized work seemed sufficient to overcome the aggression and destructiveness that Freud had thought primordially locked in human nature. Fromm, like many other Western intellectuals of the 1950s and 1960s, was especially affected by the rediscovery of Marx's 1844 *Economic and Philosophical Manuscripts*, and the 'utopian Marx' they contained. 'Alienation' was the concept and condition that most thinkers took from the early Marx. But they were as much inclined to see it in humanist and ethical terms as in terms of radical political economy. Fromm was not unaware of the Marxist theory of exploitation and the requirement of revolution that Marx derived from it. But, alarmed like many other radicals by the excesses of the Soviet Union, he looked less to revolutionary socialism and more to schemes of worker democracy and decentralized communities – on the Yugoslav pattern – to provide the social framework within which the life-enhancing instincts of man could flourish.[36]

But it was another transplanted representative of the Frankfurt School, Herbert Marcuse, who produced the most influential synthesis of Marx and Freud and, on this basis, signalled a renewal of utopia in the 1960s. His *Eros and Civilization* (1955) – although it possessed the singularity of not mentioning Marx's name at all – continued Reich's work of rapprochement on a broader and more philosophical plane. Freud's theory of instincts had to be put in a historical and sociological context, rather than treated as a postulate about humanity as such and for all time. The 'reality principle' that Freud had assumed must for ever, on pain of chaos, override the infantile 'pleasure principle' was in fact a bourgeois 'performance principle', adapted to the needs of bourgeois society. This, in turn, also meant that the 'instinctual dynamic' between Eros and Thanatos need not for ever take the tragic form that Freud had given it.

The particular bourgeois form of the reality principle – the 'performance principle' – was, Marcuse claimed, being undermined by historical change and the progress of society. The performance principle was premised on scarcity; industrial civilization was, on the other hand, producing abundance and surplus capacity. 'The historical factor contained in Freud's theory of instincts has come to fruition in history when the basis of Ananke (Scarcity) – which, for Freud, provided the rationale for the repressive reality principle – is undermined by the progress of civilization.'[37]

With abundance came the possibility of freedom from the alienation – especially alienated labour – that represented the dominance of the reality principle in an era of scarcity and necessity. Instinctual repression was not a necessary condition of civilization *per se*, but only of its historical phases of growth. The possibility existed now for 'non-repressive instinctual development', for the full release of the energies of Eros and the repressed 'pleasure principle'.

Under optimum conditions, the prevalence, in mature civilization, of material and intellectual wealth would be such as to allow painless gratification of needs, while domination would no longer systematically forestall such gratification. In this case, the quantum of instinctual energy still to be diverted into necessary labour (in turn completely mechanized and rationalized) would be so small that a large area of repressive constraints and modifications, no longer sustained by external forces, would collapse. Consequently the antagonistic relation between pleasure principle and reality principle would be altered in favour of the former. Eros, the life instincts, would be released to an unprecedented degree.[38]

The release of Eros in these conditions would not signify a return to 'prehistoric savagery'. For instinctual purposes and directions are not unalterably fixed for all time. Their channelling is a matter of changing historical needs. Under the regime of a 'non-repressive reality principle, with the abolition of the surplus-repression necessitated by the performance principle', the whole character of the libido would change. Its energies would no longer be dammed up, in specific personal and social ways, in the service of the performance principle.

No longer used as a full-time instrument of labour, the body would be resexualized. The regression involved in this spread of the libido would first manifest itself in a reactivation of all erotogenic zones and, consequently, in a resurgence of pre-genital polymorphous sexuality and in a decline of genital supremacy. The body in its entirety would become an object of cathexis, a thing to be enjoyed – an instrument of pleasure.[39]

But Marcuse does not stop with this foretaste of Brown, and its evident implication of the demise of the 'monogamic and patriarchal family'. For 'the process just outlined involves not simply a release but a *transformation* of the libido: from sexuality constrained under genital supremacy to erotization of the entire personality.' Under the performance principle, the process of sublimation – the displacement of libidinal energy to cultural rather than sexual purposes – necessarily has a repressive character. But under social conditions that released 'the free play of individual needs and faculties' sublimation can become non-repressive. Sexuality can be freely and fully transformed into the wider 'culture-building power' of Eros. Eros becomes spiritualized, biology becomes culture – but without the pain and neurosis that Freud has seen as the necessary concomitants. All human activities can be suffused with the full power and pleasure of the libido – all are 'eroticized'.[40]

This applies above all to the sphere of work. Referring to the writings of Schiller, Fourier and the Surrealists, Marcuse sees the prospect of the realization of what previously has only been fantasized in art and utopian speculation. 'The utopian claims of the imagination have become saturated with historical reality.' Technical progress is leading to total automation, and with it the release of individuals from the requirements of alienated labour. The 'realm of necessity' gives way to the 'realm of freedom', where alone human fulfilment is possible and human nature truly defined. Work becomes play, 'leisure' becomes no longer just relief from alienated labour but the sphere of all the 'eroticized' cultural and artistic activities of society. What art has represented in its own practice, but could celebrate for humanity as a whole in the imagination only – the overcoming of antagonistic human reality, 'the reconciliation of the individual with the whole, of desire with realization, of happiness with reason' – now becomes actuality. For Marcuse, as for Marx, the contours of utopia are ultimately aesthetic.[41]

Finally, in these new social conditions the very conflict between Eros and Thanatos changes its character. Like many a utopian before him, such as Condorcet, Marcuse refuses to allow even death to dampen utopian hopes. The basic object of the death instinct (Thanatos) is, he argues, 'not the termination of life but of pain'. In an order of abundance, life affords such gratifications and Eros is so strengthened that 'Eros would . . . absorb the objective of the death instinct.' The instinctual value of death would have changed. Death remains a fact, perhaps even a necessity, 'but a necessity against which the unrepressed energy of mankind will protest, against which it will wage its greatest struggle'. In this struggle, reason will ally with instinct. To do otherwise, to accept death passively as fate, is to introduce 'an element of surrender into life from the beginning – surrender and submission'. It is 'to betray the promise of utopia'. In contrast,

> a philosophy that does not work as the handmaiden of repression responds to the fact of death with the Great Refusal – the refusal of Orpheus the liberator. Death can become a token of freedom. The necessity of death does not refute the possibility of final liberation. Like the other necessities, it can be made rational – painless.[42]

It was this Marcuse, the Marcuse who looked forward to an end to all the pain and strife which had resulted from historic scarcity and necessity, who became the hero of the counter-culture of the 1960s. But Marcuse had, in *Eros and Civilization*, merely sketched the possibility of utopia; he had been studiedly vague about the prospects of its realization in the near future. As to that, he tended to oscillate between bouts of pessimism and optimism that seemed sometimes only obliquely related to the events of the times. Thus, in a new preface of 1962 to *Eros and Civilization*, he wrote that he had 'perhaps unduly stressed the progressive and promising aspects' of contemporary developments, and that 'the events of the last years refute all optimism.' Instead of an increase in 'non-repressive sublimation', where sexuality is put to the service of the cultural activities of Eros, he saw rather a vast increase in what he called 'repressive de-sublimation': a 'release of sexuality in modes and forms which reduce and weaken erotic energy'. In this process, as in the former, sexuality spreads into hitherto unfamiliar and tabooed areas, such as business, politics and propaganda. However, 'instead of re-creating these dimensions and relations in the images of the Pleasure Principle, the opposite tendency asserts itself: the Reality Principle extends its hold over Eros.' Totalitarianism finds fresh fields to invade and conquer, aided now by all the power and persuasiveness of sexuality. The 'liberation' claimed on behalf of these forms of repressive de-sublimation is entirely spurious. They are merely new ways by which individuals, supposing themselves to be free and even rebellious, are made the more willing agents of their own enslavement.

Repressive de-sublimation accompanies the contemporary tendencies towards the introjection of totalitarianism into the daily business and leisure of man, into his toil and into his happiness. It manifests itself in all the manifold ways of fun, relaxation, and togetherness which practice the destruction of privacy, the contempt of form, the inability to tolerate silence, the proud exhibition of crudeness and brutality . . . . All talk about the abolition of repression, about life against death, etc., has to place itself into the actual framework of enslavement and destruction. Within this framework, even the liberties and gratifications of the individual partake of the general suppression.

While commentators were already beginning to talk about the new freedom and the new 'permissiveness', Marcuse read in these the signs only of a further turn of the screw of oppression. In the form of sexual permissiveness, especially, and the accompanying glorification of hedonism, he saw a particularly 'regressive feature' of repressive de-sublimation: namely, 'the fierce and often methodical and conscious separation of the instinctual from the intellectual sphere, of pleasure from thought'. It is, he said, 'one of the most hideous forms of alienation which is imposed upon the individual by his society and "spontaneously" reproduced by the individual as his own need and satisfaction'. In general, while not denying the real satisfactions and pleasures to be gained from the break-up of old taboos and social conventions, Marcuse was inclined to stress the sinister side of the new developments.

To be sure, one can practice non-repressiveness within the framework of the established society: from the gimmicks of dress and undress to the wilder paraphernalia of the hot or cool life. But in the established society, this sort of protest turns into a vehicle of stabilization and even conformity, because it not only leaves the roots of the evil untouched, but also testifies to the personal liberties that are practicable within the framework of general oppression. That these private liberties are still practicable and practised is good – nevertheless, the general servitude gives them a regressive content. Formerly, the release from repression was, under normal conditions, the exclusive privilege of a small upper class; under exceptional conditions, it was also granted to and taken by the most underprivileged strata of the population. In contrast, the advanced industrial society democratizes release from repression – a compensation which serves to strengthen the government which allows it, and the institutions which administer the compensation.[43]

All these themes, tersely stated in the 1962 preface, were fully amplified in Marcuse's bleak *One Dimensional Man* (1964). This was published at a time when the cultural explosion of the 1960s was already leading several observers to prophesy the dawning of a new age, a new consciousness, stimulated by mass affluence and the new developments in technology. Marshall McLuhan proclaimed the advent of 'electronic man', and celebrated the 'global village' brought into being by the electronic media of communication, especially television.[44] Alan Watts and Timothy Leary followed the later Aldous Huxley in championing the hallucinogenic drugs as the road to a psychedelic 'eupsychia', a utopia of the mind and of consciousness. Watts also, along with the poet Allen Ginsberg, was prominent in the advocacy of Zen Buddhism and other types of Eastern religion and mysticism as the philosophic complement to the new age. Most of these gurus of the counter-culture agreed with the spirit of Timothy

Leary's credo, that 'the politics of the social system must give way to the politics of the nervous system.'[45] In the new consciousness of the affluent young, in their clothes and music, their attitudes to work, sex and marriage, the theorists of the counter-culture saw all the hopeful signs of a post-bourgeois, post-industrial society in the making – but painlessly, without the need for old-fashioned political revolution.

Against these, Marcuse in *One Dimensional Man* steadfastly maintained that most of these so-called 'liberations' were manifestations of an intensified unfreedom and renewed enslavement – an enslavement extending now to the inner consciousness of the mind and the very physical structure of the body. It was the message of *Brave New World* again – now used against some of the acolytes of the later Huxley, hero of the psychedelic culture. The potential for true personal and political liberation, Marcuse argued, was indeed present, on the basis of the enormous wealth created by advanced capitalism. The utopia of *Eros and Civilization* was a distinct historical possibility, intimated by the very signs of waste and disorder in contemporary industrial civilization. But it could not, painlessly, be danced or drugged, still less fucked, into being. The enormous technical bureaucratic apparatus of modern societies allowed most manifestations of the counter-culture easily to be absorbed and used in the interests of repression. Zen, existentialism, the bohemian drug culture 'are quickly digested by the status quo as part of its healthy diet'. The surplus created by modern technology was used not to abolish want but to shore up 'surplus repression'. Instead of satisfying the real human needs of all, the modern consumer industry ceaselessly stimulated new artificial needs which kept humans on the treadmill of increasing income constantly chasing ever new kinds of goods and services. The contrived condition of 'rising expectations' led to the Hobbesian war of all occupational groups, the weakest going to the wall and creating new areas of poverty amidst unprecedented riches.

Drawing on the analysis of such works of the 1950s as David Riesman's *The Lonely Crowd* (1950) and William Whyte's *The Organization Man* (1956), Marcuse painted a dismal world of passivity, mass conformity, and manipulation. Whatever protest still took place – largely of the 'counter-cultural' kind – could readily be 'incorporated' by the dominant system and rendered harmless, the material merely for the mass consumer industry and the mass media. Industrial society had become technological society, a system with its own logic and with a potential of control that tended towards the totalitarian.

> In the medium of technology, culture, politics, and the economy merge into an omnipresent system which swallows up or repulses all alternatives. The productivity and growth potential of this system stabilize the society and contain technical progress within the framework of domination. Technological rationality has become political rationality . . . . Technological rationality reveals its political character as it becomes the great vehicle of better domination, creating a truly totalitarian universe in which society and nature, mind and body are kept in a state of permanent mobilization for the defence of this universe.[46]

Most poignantly of all for a Marxist, the working class, seduced by affluence and brainwashed by the institutions of mass culture, had abandoned its historic mission as the agency of a new socialist civilization. '"The people", previously the ferment of social change, have "moved up" to become the ferment of social cohesion.' Looking around for some alternative agency of change, Marcuse professed to see some hope in 'the substratum of the outcasts and the outsiders, the exploited and persecuted of other races and other colours, the unemployed and the unemployable.' But the hope was small and severely qualified. 'The economic and technical capabilities of the established societies are sufficiently vast to allow for adjustments and concessions to the under-dog, and their armed forces sufficiently trained and equipped to take care of emergency situations.' What remained could be no more than a symbolic or poetic gesture, lacking any element of political prophecy.

> The critical theory of society possesses no concept which could bridge the gap between the present and the future; holding no promise and showing no success, it remains negative. Thus it wants to remain loyal to those who, without hope, have given and give their life to the Great Refusal . . . . 'It is only for the sake of those without hope that hope is given to us.'[47]

Towards the end of his life, in such works as *Counter-Revolution and Revolt* (1972), Marcuse returned to the sceptical analysis of *One Dimensional Man*. But in the meantime the tide of the counter-culture, borne on the wave of student revolts and the growing opposition to the war in Vietnam, seems to have swept even him up in its optimistic current. Many of Marcuse's ideas, drawn especially from *Eros and Civilization*, had entered the student culture, though not necessarily in the form or with the caveats that he had given them.[48] His message of personal liberation with political change, of authentic feeling with social justice, was intoxicating to student radicals concerned both with their personal problems on campus and with the wider political questions which were affecting their lives – such as being drafted to Vietnam. Marcuse for his part, based at one of the storm centres of student radicalism at Berkeley, California, seems to have enjoyed his new-found role as student guru. His ideas, at any rate, moved generously in the direction of their enthusiasm and optimism. At a lecture given in 1967 at another storm centre of student radicalism, the Free University of Berlin, he announced 'The End of Utopia'. But by this title he meant to express the opposite of what most thinkers had meant by this phrase. Utopia was dead not because it was impossible, or something to dread, but precisely because the possibilities of its realization were now at hand. 'Utopia' should now, Marcuse said, be used only when 'a project for social change contradicts real laws of nature', such as achieving eternal youth or restoring 'an alleged golden age'. But in the sense of ideas that had not yet met their time, as was true of much nineteenth-century socialist thought, 'utopia' was now a redundant and unnecessarily restrictive term. 'All the material and intellectual forces which could be put to work for the realization of a free society are at hand.'

Marcuse repeated much of the analysis of his previous works, but now the tone was optimistic and the mood the more hopeful one of *Eros and Civilization*. The barrier to 'the potential for liberation' no longer seemed quite so formidable or monolithic. 'The technification of domination undermines the foundation of domination.' Marcuse did not discount the dangers and regressive tendencies that still abounded – the Vietnam war was reaching its height – but he professed now to see distinct tendencies in society that 'herald a total break with the dominant needs of repressive society'. He instanced, with a due measure of caution, the 'English pop movement', intellectuals and students as 'anticapitalist forces', 'the moral–sexual rebellion' as a 'disintegrative factor', the 'beatnik and hippie movement' as an expression of 'one of the qualitative changes of need necessary for socialist transformation', and 'some of the liberation struggles in the third world', particularly those fought in the spirit of Franz Fanon and Che Guevara. 'The interstices within the established society are still open, and one of the most important tasks is to make use of them to the full.' The goal still remained a society founded on 'the aesthetic–erotic dimension.' This, the 'utopian' demand of socialists such as Fourier, must be the heart of the transformation of society. Thus, reversing Engels's famous formulation, 'we must face the possibility that the path to socialism may proceed from science to utopia and not from utopia to science.'[49]

In 1967 Marcuse arrived at the 'Dialectics of Liberation' congress at the Roundhouse in London holding a daffodil, and warmly greeted the 'flower-power' youth in the audience. In his address he paid particular attention to the hippies, as 'the appearance of new instinctual needs and values', and as a synthesis of 'sexual, moral and political rebellion' expressing 'a transvaluation of values'.[50] The congress itself, with its mix of intellectuals and activists, was part of a wave of radical movements and ideas that in the years 1967–8 seemed to be reaching some sort of climax. There were widespread student revolts on the campuses of western universities, a growing 'black power' movement, the revival of feminism and the regrouping of the New Left around the *May Day Manifesto 1968*. There were even, with the 'Czech Spring' under the Dubček regime, signs of important changes in the communist world.

All the counter-cultural and oppositional tendencies of the 1960s found their culmination in the 'May Events' of 1968 in France. Here was a 'utopian moment', if there ever was one. France, as so often in the past, seized the torch of revolution – but a revolution of a very different kind from the past. The state was not seized; it was, for a time at least, simply bypassed. The French authorities seemed paralysed; de Gaulle, for once, lost his nerve. The students reigned in Paris; elsewhere in France workers, farmers, housewives, professionals and artists of all kinds seized control of their work and workplaces and proceeded to democratize them. *Autogestion* – self-management – ruled.

The mix of ideas and influences in the May events was exotic, at times bizarre, but fully in accord with the revival of utopian thinking in the 1960s. Groucho Marx was set next to Karl Marx, Freud and Reich jostled the Surrealists Aragon and Breton, de Sade was affirmed along with Dali, and anarchists and utopian socialists such as Bakunin and Fourier were singled out for their more profound understanding of revolutionary change, as against the 'scientific socialists'. The utopian Marx and Lenin of the Paris Commune and the early *soviets* were rediscovered and rehabilitated. Liberation was seen as intrinsically and simultaneously a personal and political matter – there was to be no return to the old-style, purely political, revolution of 1789 and 1917. Either revolution was permanent and pervasive, transforming everyday life as much as political structures, or it was no revoluton. In all this, the influence of an extraordinarily fertile group of intellectuals, the 'International Situationists', could be seen everywhere. It was their journals and pamphlets which prepared the heady utopian brew that nourished the May events. It was they who fathered the many action committees with names like 'the Freud–Che Guevara Action Committee', 'the Committee of Permanent Creation', 'the Comité Revolutionnaire d'Agitation Sursexuelle'. It was their graffiti that covered the walls of Paris: 'Demand the impossible', 'All power to the imagination', 'It's the dream that is real'.[51]

Shortly before the May events Marcuse had written his most utopian work, *An Essay on Liberation* (1969). Before its publication the events in France occurred, and Marcuse was able to add a preface dedicating his book to the French rebels. In the preface he both endorsed the action of the student militants and pointed to the 'striking' correspondence between the ideas expressed in his book and those formulated by the militants in the course of action. Since those ideas were largely repetitions of earlier ones, and since Marcuse himself had been an important influence on the student radicals, this coincidence was hardly surprising. But Marcuse generously conceded that, through linking theory with practice, the French students had shown that it was possible to go beyond even his conception.

> The radical utopian character of their demands far surpasses the hypotheses of my essay; and yet, these demands were developed and formulated in the course of action itself; they are expressions of concrete political practice. The militants have invalidated the concept of 'utopia' – they have denounced a vicious ideology. No matter whether their action was a revolt or an abortive revolution, it is a turning point.[52]

The *Essay* itself looked, with even greater hope than before, to the young intelligentsia, the black ghetto population and 'the underprivileged sections of the labouring classes in backward capitalist countries' to provide the 'subjective factor' lacking in the largely inert but still necessary 'objective factor', the industrial working class. Such a combination, Marcuse averred, could be seen in the links between the various national liberation fronts and the peasants and the emerging proletariat in the Third World. The Cuban revolution and the Viet Cong had demonstrated what could be done against even the mightiest imperialist forces. But the success of Third World struggles still depended ultimately on the 'internal weakening' of the superpowers. 'The chain of exploitation must break at its strongest link.'[53]

And it was so breaking, declared Charles Reich in *The Greening of America* (1970), a book written in sections throughout the 1960s, in a state of mounting excitement and expectation which fully communicated itself to a large and enthusiastic public. Reich's book can fairly be taken as crowning the utopian decade of the 1960s. It was a book which, like most popular books, found an audience ready and waiting for its message. It offered little that was new by way of analysis – indeed, it offered very little analysis at all. But it summed up a mood. Reich merely pieced together into a mosaic elements of the 1960s – its music, its clothes, its psychedelic drugs, its personal style, its cultural politics – to announce the coming of a non-violent revolution which was lifting America – and eventually the whole industrial world – to a new plane of consciousness, 'Consciousness III'. Consciousness III reversed most of the emphases of earlier forms of consciousness in its new-found sense of personal identity and community, its opposition to large-scale technocracy, its awareness of the natural world and its desire for peace and co-operative growth. It was built on a new mood of joyful irreverence, seen at its clearest among young people but spreading to all sections of the population. And it was, despite the Vietnam war and the repressive activities of the Corporate State, irreversible and unstoppable. Reich – a middle-aged Yale professor of law – concluded on a note of pure euphoria.

> The new consciousness is sweeping the high schools, it is seen in smiles on the streets. It has begun to transform and humanize the landscape . . . . The extraordinary thing about this new consciousness is that it has emerged out of the wasteland of the Corporate State, like flowers pushing up through concrete pavement. Whatever it touches it beautifies and renews: a freeway entrance is festooned with happy hitch-hikers, the sidewalk is decorated with street people, the humorless steps of an official building are given warmth by a group of musicians. And every barrier falls before it. We have been dulled and blinded to the injustice and ugliness of slums, but it sees them as just that – injustice and ugliness – as if they had been there to see all along. We have all been persuaded that giant organizations are necessary, but it sees that they are absurd, as if the absurdity had always been obvious and apparent. We have all been induced to give up our dreams of adventure and romance in favor of the escalator of successs, but it says that the escalator is a sham and the dream is real. And these things, buried, hidden and disowned in so many of us, are shouted out loud, believed in, affirmed by a growing multitude of young people who seem too healthy, intelligent and alive to be wholly insane, who appear, in their collective strength, capable of making it happen . . . . For one who thought the world was irretrievably encased in metal and plastic and sterile stone, it seems a veritable greening of America.[54]

ECOTOPIA – A FRAGILE BALANCE

The utopian current of the 1960s flowed largely within a tide of technological optimism. The complaint was not against technology itself, but against its abuse: its restricted and perverted uses, its employment in the service of war and repression. Technology – especially the electronic technology of television and hi-fi – was an essential part of the counter-culture; and it was also the essential basis of the utopian vision of Brown and Marcuse, as of the May 1968 radicals in France. For the Freudo-Marxists, scarcity was the principal enemy of utopia. Technology could be the agent of affluence and hence of the liberation of society from its historic condition of material need. It was in this sense that the utopia of the 1960s was a 'post-industrial' utopia, whether or not every one was prepared to accept the label.

But there were always those who pushed their anxiety about the uses of technology further, and who came to see, in the very fact of large-scale industrial technology, the essential obstacle to their hopes. Technology, in whatever hands, seemed to have the same results. It had a logic that went beyond social ideology. It was largely because of his innocence in this respect that Lenin was unable to see how his embrace of large-scale American technology, and the Taylorism that necessarily went with it, would corrupt the original socialism of the revolution and deliver it up to Stalinism. Large-scale technology, wherever it appeared, produced the same effects: alienation, de-humanization and domination.

Such fears had already been often expressed in the Romantic movement of the nineteenth century. But the speed and scale of technological development in this century, spectacularly during the two world wars, suggested that a new phase had been entered, far more terrifying than anything that could have been experienced in the last century. Such were the frequently expressed views of Aldous Huxley in the post-war period, as in *Brave New World Revisited* (1958). But it was the work of a French Catholic, Jacques Ellul's *The Technological Society* (1954), that seemed most effectively to capture the fear of a nightmare world of total domination by technology. Translated into English in 1964, it rapidly found its way into the armoury of those who believed that the introduction of technique, of technological rationality, into every sphere of life was crushing individuality and driving out spirituality.

A significant sign of the renewed perception of the technological threat was its appearance in the popular genre of science fiction. A sombre mood had descended on science fiction ever since the bombing of Hiroshima. The traditional technological optimism of the genre continued with some writers. Arthur C. Clarke blended the cosmic evolutionism of Stapledon with the confidence of the working scientific community to produce a powerful paean to man's power and knowledge in his trilogy *Childhood's End* (1953), *Rendezvous with Rama* (1973) and *Imperial Earth* (1976) – the last a thinly disguised contribution to the American bicentennial celebrations. His script for Stanley Kubrick's film *2001: A Space Odyssey* (1968) took the optimistic message of a cosmic purpose and plan to an even wider audience. And there were also established genre writers such as Robert Heinlein, whose *Stranger in a Strange Land* (1961) won a cult following in the counter-culture for its genial espousal of free love and its philosophy of mystic liberation.

But for the mainstream audience outside the 'fanzines' and clubs, what chiefly came over from science fiction was a new quizzical and cynical mood, which increasingly became pessimistic and apocalyptic. A 'New Wave' of science fiction writing developed in the 1950s and 1960s, concerned as much with society as with technology, and often couched in the anti-utopian mode of 'near future' satire. A characteristic product of the 1950s was Frederik Pohl and Cyril Kornbluth's *The Space Merchants* (1953), which satirized the glossy, hi-tech world of Madison Avenue, and portrayed a servile future world run by multinational advertising corporations. Ray Bradbury's *Fahrenheit 451* (1953), a dystopia where books are burned by the state and literacy on the point of disappearing, was also a satire on the mass media but in a darker key. It foreshadowed the grimmer tone of the 1960s, as sounded by the New Wave writer J. G. Ballard: 'The only true alien planet is Earth.'

Ballard himself, in such apocalyptic works as *The Drowned World* (1962) and *The Crystal World* (1966), as well as in numerous short stories (*The Terminal Beach* (1964) and *The Disaster Area* (1967) collections), painted memorable pictures of disaster and decay in which advanced industrial civilization lies in ruins amidst abandoned spacecraft and deserted urban hells. Others turned to overpopulation and ecological catastrophe, as in Harry Harrison's *Make Room! Make Room!* (1966) and John Brunner's *Stand on Zanzibar* (1969) and *The Sheep Look Up* (1972). An ecological consciousness was also strongly urged by Frank Herbert's *Dune* (1965), with its vivid story of a desert planet whose inhabitants, the Fremen, survive only by the most ingenious and scrupulous methods of water conservation.

In works such as these, science fiction said farewell to the scientific utopia.[55] If science and technology figured at all prominently, it was as the agents of entropy, the drive to disorder and destruction in the world. But increasingly, science and technology appeared only peripherally, or as a form of alienated consciousness rather than in the shape of scientific hardware. Science fiction moved from outer space to 'inner space'. It concerned itself not with journeys to outer planets but with journeys to the interior – 'the interior of the individual in relation to surrounding scientific and technical systems'. States of consciousness became more important than intergalactic wars. One consequence of this, seen especially clearly in Ballard's work, was a displacement not just of space but of time. The speed of technical change, and the urgency of the problems it threw up, made consideration of a distant future appear idle and irrelevant. As Ballard put it:

> To some extent the future has been annexed in the present, for most of us, and the notion of the future as an alternative scheme, as an alternative world, to which we are moving, no longer exists. I think we exist in a continuum of time now, like an immense amusement arcade . . . which has no past, present, or future . . . .[56]

Developments such as these should, on past experience, have led to a strong revival of the anti-utopia. And in science fiction this was indeed a strongly marked tendency. For there was no doubt where most of the journeys into inner space ended: in hell, but in a very private hell, where the social context was often only barely hinted at. 'Institutional hells', said Ballard, were out of fashion. 'The populated infernos of the twentieth century are more private affairs. The gaps between the bars are the sutures of one's own skull.'[57] This was one sort of anti-utopia, favoured not just by science fiction but by much of the high literary culture of the time. Novelists indeed, when they ventured into utopian territory at all, seemed almost naturally to fall into the anti-utopian mode. Horror of the present and fear of the future came as it were instinctively to them. William Golding's *Lord of the Flies* (1954) and *The Inheritors* (1955) recalled the early Darwinian Wells, in their view of the thinness of the protective civilized layer keeping man from barbarism and the brutal annihilation of his kind. In all Golding's work there is the brooding sense of the darkness of the human condition born of primal sin. Anthony Burgess, in *A Clockwork Orange* (1962) and *1985* (1978), reverted to a more traditional anti-utopian form. His targets too were traditional: the Brave New World of social science and 'behavioural engineering', and the repressive potential of the collectivist state.

The failure of the radical hopes of the 1960s also seemed to point firmly to an anti-utopia of the traditional kind. By the early 1970s the student revolts were over. The Russian tanks had rolled into Prague. In the winter of 1973 the oil crisis raised in an acute form the problem of the world's supply of energy and natural resources, and placed a question mark over the whole future of the industrial system. Works such as Paul Ehrlich's *The Population Bomb* (1968), Barry Commoner's *The Closing Circle* (1971) and the Club of Rome's *Limits to Growth* (1972) supplied material in plenty for the fashioning of anti-utopias. So too, from a different direction, did Fred Hirsch's *Social Limits to Growth* (1977). Where theorists such as Marcuse had hoped to rear utopia on growth and affluence, Hirsch offered instead a grim Hobbesian picture of persistent discontent and conflict arising as the direct consequence of economic growth.[58]

But what was remarkable, and a testimony to the resilient utopian temper of recent times, was the wresting of a new utopia from this unpromising material. The revulsion against science and technology manifested in New Wave science fiction, and in certain parts of the counter-culture, did not necessarily lead to pessimism or nostalgic conservatism. Out of the elements of the anti-technology critique of Ellul and others, out of the lively and extended debate about energy and resources that took place in the wake of the 1973 oil crisis, and out of the critique of large-scale organization and technology that was a central feature of 1960s radicalism, a new utopia was constituted, an ecological utopia or 'ecotopia'. The ecotopia aspired to steer a path between the euphoric excesses of the affluent 1960s and the pessimistic propensities of the leaner 1970s and 1980s. But it abated nothing of its utopian character in this gesture towards realism. It was a utopia for new times, when the direction of social evolution seemed more uncertain and more fraught with dangers than at any time since the 1930s; but it retained the utopian vision and intensity in its conviction that a society organized according to ecological principles not only was sustainable economically and socially, but also offered the best possible life for all its members.

An important aspect of the ecotopia was the recovery of certain traditions of social thought that had tended to be subordinated to more influential accounts, seen as more in keeping with the main development of modern society. Thus the anarchist and decentralist thought of Proudhon, Bakunin and Kropotkin was revived, and works such as Kropotkin's *Fields, Factories and Workshops* (1899) and *The Conquest of Bread* (1892) came back into circulation after more than half a century of neglect. Paul Goodman, the American anarchist whose own utopian works such as *Growing Up Absurd* (1960) and *Communitas* (1960) had an important influence on the ecotopia, wrote that 'there is not one important proposition in my book [*Communitas*] that is not in *Fields, Factories and Workshops*.'[59] The importance of such anarchist thinking to the ecotopia was that it offered an analysis of how industrial and agricultural production could be carried on in modern society without the sacrifice of meaning and creativity in work, implicit in large-scale mass production. In Kropotkin's works, as in

Goodman's *Communitas*, there were suggested detailed schemes of workshop organization and decentralized production, blueprints for the design of agricultural and urban communities on a human scale, that promised a way of cutting across and reversing all the customary divides of industrial society: urban and rural, mental and manual, individual and mass.

The opposition to large-scale centralized organization was not simply on the grounds of its dehumanizing effect, in work and in life generally. It was tied to the specific ecological concern with natural resources and environmental destruction, as both a material and a moral affair. Large-scale organization presupposed as well as promoted large-scale technology, with its voracious appetite for resources and its devastating impact on the physical environment. Thus, the oppostion to large-scale technology, and the advocacy of 'intermediate', 'alternative' or 'radical' technology, became a defining feature of the ecotopia. Particularly important influences here were the writings and activities of the British economist E. F. Schumacher. Schumacher's book *Small is Beautiful* (1973) got its philosophical rationale from Buddhism and Christianity, but this was attractively linked to the hard-headed arguments of the practising economist. The book's title launched a slogan that clearly touched a chord and for a while had great currency, while Schumacher's Intermediate Technology group was active in propogating his ideas and making practical recommendations for the future development of both the wealthy industrial countries and the Third World.

Building largely on Schumacher's reputation, the 'alternative technology' movement attracted a considerable following in the 1970s. Keeping its politics mainly for internal debate, it concerned itself with advocating the use of renewable energy sources, such as wind, water and the sun, and with the invention and application of a technology that was lasting and capable of repair in modestly equipped workshops. The banner of what was explicitly called 'utopian technology' was raised, 'designed to eliminate the alienation and exploitation of the individual, and the domination of the environment by the activities of man'. Utopian technology – sometimes also called 'soft technology' – was characterized by one of its advocates as 'a technology which is satisfying to work with, can be controlled by both the producers and the community by whom the products are used, conserves natural resources, and does negligible damage to the environment'.[60]

Journals and groups sprang up on both sides of the Atlantic to spread the ecological message. In the United States there was the *Co-Evolution Quarterly*, the *Whole Earth Catalog* and the *Mother Earth News*; in Britain, Friends of the Earth, *Undercurrents* and *The Ecologist*. It was *The Ecologist* which in 1972 presented its 'Blueprint for Survival', a manifesto which in tone and content influenced much of the subsequent presentation of the ecological argument. The 'Blueprint' announced: 'The principal defect of the industrial way of life with its ethos of expansion is that it is not sustainable.' Its end was not in doubt, in one of two ways: 'either against our will in a succession of famines, epidemics, social crises and wars; or because we want it to – because we wish to create a society which will not impose hardship and cruelty upon our children – in a succession of thoughtful, humane and measured changes'. The 'Blueprint' went on to suggest a detailed series of measures necessary for this more desirable second course: a slowing down of growth to a 'steady-state' economy, a stabilizing of the population, a gradual shift to energy from renewable sources and a scaling down of political and industrial structures. The goal was 'the stable society' which, 'as well as removing the sword of Damocles which hangs over the heads of future generations, is much more likely than the present one to bring the peace and fulfilment which hitherto have been regarded, sadly, as utopian'.[61]

The Ecologist was subtitled 'Journal of the Post-Industrial Age'; and one purpose of the ecotopia was to offer an alternative 'post-industrial utopia' to that of the 1960s – one not, as with Marcuse, based on automation and large-scale technology, but one which genuinely went *beyond* industrialism and largely dispensed with the 'high-tech', high-energy structures of advanced industrialism. The ecotopia was by no means anti-technology, nor was it a nostalgic harking back to pre-industrial ways of life. It insisted that all the ingenuity of modern science and all the technical inventiveness of modern society would be required in the design of the new 'utopian technology'. But pre-industrial or non-industrial life clearly had an attraction for many of the advocates of ecotopia, and they were happy to draw on experience and knowledge of such ways in the construction of their vision of the good life. This meant that social anthropology was a major source of ecological ideas, as were the other testimonies of those who had lived and worked in tribal and peasant societies of the Third World. Underlying much of the utopian writing of Ursula Le Guin, for instance, the American science fiction writer who was a central figure in the making of the ecotopia, was the work of her father, the anthropologist Alfred Kroeber, on the Indian tribes of the American southwest.

Pre-industrial society was also a living source of ideas and institutions in the vision of Ivan Illich, the highly individual American Catholic priest who was forced by the radical nature of his work and ideas to continue his preaching and practice outside the Church. Though his talents were more critical than constructive, Illich was by any measure one of the principal architects of the ecotopia. In a series of short, vivid and wide-ranging tracts – *Deschooling Society* (1971), *Tools for Conviviality* (1973), *Medical Nemesis* (1975), *Disabling Professions* (1977) – he sketched the broad outlines of a community which restored meaning and satisfaction in work to its members, and returned to them the control over their lives that had been expropriated by monopolistic professions and massive service organizations. Against the ethic and institutions of the mass production system, which debased work and the worker, Illich erected the ideal of 'conviviality' and the project of 'convivial reconstruction'. This would involve the redesign of 'tools', broadly conceived as social instrumentalities which had the power either to enslave and oppress or to aid and extend human effort and imagination.

A convivial society should be designed to allow all its members the most autonomous action by means of tools least controlled by others. People feel joy, as opposed to mere pleasure, to the extent that their activities are creative; while the growth of tools beyond a certain point increases regimentation, dependence, exploitation, and impotence. I use the term 'tool' broadly enough to include not only simple hardware such as drills, pots, syringes, brooms, building elements, or motors, and not just large machines like cars or power stations; I also include among tools productive institutions such as factories that produce tangible commodities like corn flakes or electric current, and productive systems for intangible commodities such as those which produce 'education', 'health', 'knowledge', or 'decisions' . . . .

Tools are intrinsic to social relationships. An individual relates himself in action to his society through the use of tools that he actively masters, or by which he is passively acted upon. To the degree that he masters his tools, he can invest the world with his meaning; to the degree that he is mastered by his tools, the shape of the tool determines his own self-image. Convivial tools are those which give each person who uses them the greatest opportunity to enrich the environment with the fruit of his or her vision. Industrial tools deny this possibility to those who use them and they allow their designers to determine the meaning and expectations of others. Most tools today cannot be used in a convivial fashion.[62]

But what, in concrete detail, in lived experience, would the 'convivial society' be like? Few of the ecology-minded theorists were inclined to lay out a formal ecological utopia, a literary ecotopia, though in many of their writings the utopian impulse is very clear. Like the futurologists of the 1960s, and the socialists of the last century, most ecologists felt that the need was for systematic analysis and concrete proposals, rather than efforts of the literary imagination. But the utopian tradition was important to the ecologists, and frequently was invoked.[63] Not surprisingly, William Morris's *News from Nowhere* was the favourite among classic utopias, for it was in many ways an ecotopia 'before the name'. The strong revival of Morris's popularity in the 1960s and 1970s was clear evidence of the appeal of the decentralist, craft-based tradition of 'utopian socialism' to a new generation wary of the more orthodox Marxist utopia. So too was the new interest in Fourier and his idea of the 'phalanstery'.

But the contemporary ecotopia did produce some literary accounts of its own. From a symbolic point of view, perhaps the most striking offering was Aldous Huxley's *Island* (1962). In this his last work, the man who had probably done more than anyone else this century to give utopia a bad name now made amends by presenting a utopia that was not simply a reversal of *Brave New World*, but actually used many of its features to positive effect in its picture of the gentle, ecologically conscious people of Pala. Pala has taken the best of the West – its science – and the best of the East – its religous philosophy – and mixed them in satisfying proportions to produce an ideally balanced life. Electricity plus soviets equals communism, Lenin had said. Electricity plus Buddhism equals the good society, say the Palanese. But electricity minus heavy industry, electricity minus ever-rising consumption and ever-increasing dependence on scarce natural resources. 'We adapt our economy and technology to human beings – not our human beings to somebody else's economy and technology . . . . If it's a choice between mechanical efficiency and human satisfaction, we choose satisfaction.'[64]

Pala has – through Noyesian 'Male Continence', taught as the Tantric technique of *maithuna* – achieved zero population growth. It has also, on the basis of a balanced pattern of agriculture and industry, achieved eonomic self-sufficiency and the provision of a reasonable standard of living for its whole population. It practices a system of work rotation that combines mental and manual labour for everyone, men and women alike. All this has been done with an economic system that is neither capitalist nor socialist but 'co-operative' and decentralist, and a political system based on a federation of small self-governing units. The Palanese have made a distinct and deliberate choice not to go for continuing economic growth and increasing affluence. That way lies armies and dictators, that way lies social and individual discontent and disease. They have instead taken

> the road of applied biology, the road of fertility control and the limited production and selective industrialization which fertility control makes possible, the road that leads towards happiness from the inside out, through health, through awareness, through a change in one's attitude to the world; not towards the mirage of happiness from the outside in, through toys and pills and non-stop distractions.[65]

Education is accordingly heavily geared to the biological and ecological sciences. But 'we always teach the science of relationship in conjunction with the ethics of relationship. Balance, give and take, no excesses – it's the rule in nature and, translated out of fact into morality, it *ought* to be the rule among people.' Children are taught about the American Dust Bowl and the ecological spoliation of Africa, as exemplary warnings. They learn the lesson: 'Treat Nature well and Nature will treat you well. Hurt or destroy Nature and Nature will soon destroy you.' They are therby led 'from conservation to morality'.

> The morality to which a child goes on from the facts of ecology and the parables of erosion is a universal ethic. There are no Chosen People in nature, no Holy Lands, no Unique Historical Revelations. Conservation-morality gives nobody an excuse for feeling superior or claiming special privileges. 'Do as you would be done by' applies to our dealings with all kinds of life in every part of the world. We shall be permitted to live on this planet only for as long as we treat all nature with compassion and intelligence. Elementary ecology leads straight to elementary Buddhism.[66]

Island ends with the Palanese being overwhelmed by the forces of their rapacious neighbour Rendang, backed by the multinational oil companies. So the anti-utopian Huxley has the last word, though with clear regrets.

Island had for the time being few imitators. Though respectfully received, it had little of the wit and bite of *Brave New World* and seemed to many people inferior Huxley. It was perhaps in any case too early to contribute in a serious way to the ecological culture, which developed only towards the end of the decade. But in 1972 there appeared Theodore Roszak's *Where the Wasteland Ends*. Roszak, whose *The Making of A Counter-Culture* had influentially and sympathetically defined its subject, now went well beyond most counter-cultural theorists in espousing a radical Blakean vision that shared much of the religious mysticism of *Island*. But, though Huxley's book is affectionately referred to at various points, the attachment to Western science that Huxley always maintained is rejected out of hand. Like William Blake, Roszak prays that 'May God us keep/From Single Vision and Newton's sleep', and, again with Blake, urges us

To cast off Bacon, Locke and Newton from Albion's covering,
To take off his filthy garments and clothe him with Imagination.

The 'scientific worldview', says Roszak, 'has become the boundary condition of human consciousness within urban-industrial culture, the reigning Reality Principle, the whole meaning of sanity.' It has created an 'artificial environment' which has permitted the rise of 'the technocracy . . . as a benevolent despotism of elitist expertise'. The technocracy can be displaced only by throwing off 'the psychic style from which it draws its strength', the 'single vision' of science whose 'psychic price' is 'the death-in-life of alienation'. Politics has become deeply psychologized, and the political problem must be resolved first at the psychological level. 'But if our psychology is not itself to be debased by scientific objectification, then it must follow where liberated consciousness leads; into the province of the dream, the myth, the visionary rapture, the sacramental sense of reality, the transcendent symbol.'

If psychological reality is thus revolutionized, what political programme should follow from that?

Nothing less, I think, than that we should undertake to repeal urban-industrialism as the world's dominant style of life. We should do this, not in the spirit of grim sacrifice, but in the conviction that the reality we want most to reside in lies beyond the artificial environment. And so we should move freely and in delight toward the true postindustrialism: a world awakened from its sick infatuation with power, growth, efficiency, progress as if from a nightmare.[67]

Roszak goes on to outline a 'visionary Commonwealth', marked by substantial 'de-urbanization', an 'economics of permanence' along the lines of Schumacher's precepts for qualitative rather than quantitative growth, and a political system of federated decentralized communities, 'a confederated community of communities', that follows Kropotkin, Goodman and Gandhi. This will be liberating not just for the industrial societies, but for the Third World countries which are being forced into the global urban-industrial network, to the benefit solely of the rich developed countries. Roszak draws back from supplying a detailed utopian portrait of his visionary commonwealth, though he does supply a thumbnail utopian sketch. He looks rather to the existing points of change and growth, the 'range of fragile experimentation' being carried out in a host of communities in Europe and North America, by 'people who have integrated the great ethical issues of the time into their very eating habits'. Here is 'the brave, radical break with urban-industrialism that promises . . . a new ecology, a new democracy, a new vitality of spirit'.[68]

Roszak's extreme hostility to science *tout court* was exceptional in the ecology movement. Even he admits that 'it will take no little technical wit to dig us out of the patterns of life we are now trapped in.'[69] And generally ecologists, often themselves with scientific backgrounds, have looked forward to more inventive and more imaginative science, rather than a rejection of it, in their visions of the future. This was certainly true of Ernest Callenbach's *Ecotopia* (1975), a formal literary utopia from America's West Coast that seems to have originated the name of the ecological utopia, though in most respects it drew on standard ecological ideas. *Ecotopia* is in fact a highly pragmatic utopia, full of technical details and ideas whose adoption is urged as a matter of practical efficiency as well as social betterment along ecological lines.

Callenbach's utopia is set in the near future, when a portion of the Pacific North-West breaks away from the United States and declares itself the independent state of Ecotopia. For a time, as it sorts out its ways and institutions, Ecotopia quarantines itself off from the rest of the world. Eventually, a sceptical and hard-boiled journalist from the United States, Will Weston, is permitted a visit. Like Huxley's cynical journalist Will Farnaby in *Island*, he gradually succumbs to the charm and vitality of the new society – helped, as in Farnaby's case, by the persuasive ways of one of its enlightened young women. What Weston discovers in Ecotopia is a communal order based on collective ownership of farms and factories. All units are small ('Small is beautiful', Weston is reminded), and all employ extensive recycling of waste materials. In the society generally there is a quaint and, Weston finds, attractive mix of the old – 'medieval' street entertainments, ritual war games, bright peasant clothing, no cars – and the new – a society fully wired up by cable, factories where small teams of workers apply their creative skills to components made by advanced automated machines. The Ecotopians have stablized the growth rate and achieved a 'steady-state' economy. This has allowed them to lower the working week to 20 hours. Their work is in any case characterized by strong elements of play ('during an important discussion in a government office, suddenly everybody will decide to go to the sauna bath'), and generally they have broken down divisions of 'work' and 'leisure', just as they have of 'urban' and 'rural'. A pattern of 'minicities', linked by rail, is planned, with the old megalopolises being allowed to return to grassland, forests, orchards or gardens. Nature is throughout a strong presence – the new San Francisco has a 'bucolic atmosphere', and there are trees everywhere. There is indeed something like tree worship: trees are regarded 'as being alive in an almost human sense', and are cut and trimmed 'with religious respect'. Reforestation is a constant and prime concern.

There is also a good deal of hedonistic nature worship of the more familiar erotic kind. Ecotopians of all sexes and ages 'bathe and take steam baths together freely'. 'Naked massage is a common group amusement.' The fact that marijuana is freely 'on tap' no doubt adds to the uninhibited joy of these occasions. As is proper in a West Coast utopia, Weston's full conversion to the new ways, and his decision to remain in Ecotopia with the delightful Marissa, take place at 'Gilroy Hot Springs', in the course of a communal, open-air bath.

'Human beings are tribal animals', declare the Ecotopians. And the tribal customs and traditions of the North American Indians are a rich source of beliefs and practices for the Ecotopians, freely acknowledged, and carefully studied. Ecotopian universities do not teach political science, sociology or psychology, but they have flourishing departments of history and social anthropology. In the high schools, hunting, fishing and 'survival skills' are taught to all students. Some dwellings have 'fierce-looking totem poles' outside. Ritual ceremonies, like war games, have a strong Indian flavour. So too does the Ecotopian attitude to death: fatalistic but accepting, sustained by the belief of their 'ecological religion' that 'they too will now be re-cycled.' Weston notes in his diary:

> Many Ecotopians sentimental about Indians, and there's some sense in which they envy the Indians their lost natural place in the American wilderness. Indeed this probably a major Ecotopian myth; keep hearing references to what Indian would or wouldn't do in a given situation. Some Ecotopian articles – clothing and baskets and personal ornamentation – perhaps directly Indian in inspiration. But what matters most is the aspiration to live in balance with nature, 'walk lightly on the land,' treat the earth as mother. No surprise that to such a morality most industrial processes, work schedules, and products are suspect! Who would use an earth-mover on his own mother?[70]

North American Indian culture was also, as we have already noted, an important influence on Ursula Le Guin, in such works as *The Left Hand of Darkness* (1969). It is there too, though more subtly and with little of the 'primitivism' that often went with it, in her *The Dispossessed* (1974), the most interesting and most complex account of the ecotopia so far. Though hailed as signifying the renewal of 'the utopian impulse',[71] *The Dispossessed* is by no means a straightforward literary utopia in the traditional mode. For one thing, it is a science fiction novel, and the science fiction elements play a more important part than is customary in most utopias. The protagonist of the story, the physicist Shevek, is at work on the 'Principle of Simultaneity' which he hopes to develop into a device, the 'ansible', that will allow instantaneous communication between all parts of space. It is because of the importance of this work to the future of the League of all Worlds that Shevek is invited to the sister planet Urras to continue his research under more favourable conditions than would be possible on his poorer home planet of Anarres. His gradual discovery of the sinister purpose of his host nation on Urras, A-Io, his fight to thwart them and the restrengthening of his faith in the ways of Anarres consititute the main narrative content of the work.

The novel alternates between Anarres and Urras, allowing a more or less systematic comparison of the two societies. Here too the purely utopian character of *The Dispossessed* is qualified. Le Guin originally subtitled it 'An Ambiguous Utopia', a subtitle she later withdrew; but its significance remains clear throughout. In so far as the terms are endorsed, Anarres is utopia, Urras anti-utopia. Anarres, a former mining colony of Urras, is organized on the anarchistic and ecological principles of Odo, the female prophet who led a group of dissidents from Urras to found an independent community on Anarres. Anarres is a decentralized federation of communities, on Kropotkinesque lines. Each has its own work-syndicate where tasks are democratically decided and equally shared out. There is nothing like a sovereign state or government. The communities are bound together by the ideal of 'complex organicism'. 'The special resources and products of each region were interchanged continually with those of others, in an intricate process of balance: that balance of diversity which is the characteristic of life, of natural and social ecology.' The Anarresti accept that there has to be a coordinating centre to the system, but this is achieved through computers rather than a central bureaucracy. The computers 'coordinate the administration of things, the division of labour, and the distribution of goods . . . .' There is a network, 'Production and Distribution Coordination', which links syndicates and federatives, but it has no power to compel them or any individual member. It can persuade and publicize, no more. 'They do not govern persons; they administrate production.'[72]

The use of computers and other forms of advanced technology underlines the determination of the Anarresti from the start that they 'would not regress to pre-urban, pre-technological tribalism'. 'They knew that their anarchism was the product of a very high civilization, of a complex diversified culture, of a stable economy and a highly industrialized economy that could maintain high production and rapid transportation of goods.'[73] Science is highly developed and put to ecological purposes. There are wind-turbines and 'earth temperature-differential generators'. There is thus no shortage of power, but 'organic economy' is practised, as much on ethical as on economic grounds. 'Excess is excrement', wrote Odo.

Nevertheless, for all its success, Anarres is in many ways an inhospitable and uncomfortable place to be. The planet is bleak and arid, a barren world of 'distances, silences, desolations'. 'The air was thin . . . . the sun burned, the wind froze, the dust choked.' Life is hard for its inhabitants, involving a constant struggle with the dust and the drought. Partly as a result of this unremitting pressure, the original Odonian impulse, the libertarian ethic underlying the community, is in danger of being forgotten. The revolution has gone into a stagnant phase. It is solidifying into a rigid pattern which encourages conformity and timidity. Shevek finds his freedom to pursue his work under threat from the jealousy and conservatism of his colleagues. It is this which persuades him to accept the invitation from Urras, in defiance of the public hostility shown to anyone who wishes to visit the world of the former oppressor.

Just as the utopia of Anarres is qualified, so too Urras is not all anti-utopia. Shevek at first feels a liberating sense of ease and opulence, admidst the magnificent buildings and comfortable surroundings of this highly advanced technological society. The drabness of Anarres stands out all the more forcibly for the colour and glitter of Urras. There is room here too for private freedoms, for the exercise of individual initiative and talent, that has been missing from Anarres for some time. The strengths and attractions of Urrastian society are made plain to Shevek, again and again, as he explores this new world. As he experiences the 'superb cars and comfortable trains', sees the well-kept countryside and the prosperous villages, contemplates the wealth and resources of the university where he is staying, be begins to wonder whether his guides are not perhaps right and the Anarresti simply prejudiced.

> the Urrasti knew how to use their world. He had been taught as a child that Urras was a festering mass of inequity, iniquity, and waste. But all the people he met, and all the people he saw, in the smallest country village, were well dressed, well fed, and, contrary to his expectations, industrious . . . . The lure and compulsion of *profit* was evidently a much more effective replacement of the natural initiative than he had been led to believe.[74]

It is not long, however, before the oppression and exploitation on which this evident replica of advanced capitalism is founded become clear to Shevek. He discovers the seamy, poverty-stricken underside of the magnificent Wellsian city of Nio Esseia. Almost by accident he gets caught up in a rebellion of the lower classes made in the name of Odo, and finds that as a visitor from Anarres he is cast in something of the role of a messiah.

Shevek survives the crushing of the rebellion and is able to pass on his discovery of the 'ansible' to the Council of World Governments, so ensuring its use by all the known worlds. He returns to Anarres with a renewed sense of the vitality of its society and of its importance as a social experiment. The Odonian revolution is not over; it is a permanent revolution, with a structural capacity for change and progress. His scientific ideas now matter less to him. 'My society is also an idea. I was made by it. An idea of freedom, of change, of human solidarity.' He was wrong to think that in coming to Urras he could further the development of Anarres in any way.

> Because there is nothing, nothing on Urras that we Anarresti need! We left with empty hands, a hundred and seventy years ago, and we were right. We took nothing. Because there is nothing here but States and their weapons, the rich and their lies, and the poor and their misery. There is no way to act rightly, with a clear heart, on Urras. There is nothing you can do that profit does not enter in, and fear of loss, and the wish for power . . . . There is no freedom. It is a box – Urras is a box, a package, with all the beautiful wrapping of blue sky and meadows and forests and great cities. And you open the box and, what is inside it? A black cellar full of dust, and a dead man. A man whose hand was shot off because he held it out to others. I have been in Hell at last. . . . Hell is Urras.[75]

So, in the end, utopia and anti-utopia both find a place in *The Dispossessed*. But the line is blurred. Utopia is qualified by a wariness, a caution and a questioning, that is a fair reflection of its condition today. Anarres can be, and should be; but Urras is also, in its own terms, successful. Industrial civilization need not, Le Guin seems to be saying, end in barbarism and devastation.[76] There is, as Williams says, 'the uneasy consciousness that the superficies of Utopia, affluence and abundance, can be achieved at least for many, by non-utopian and even anti-utopian means.'[77] As the Terran ambassador says to Shevek of the rebellion in Urras: 'Why so much commotion? The government here is not despotic. The rich are very rich indeed, but the poor are not so very poor. They are neither enslaved, nor starving. Why aren't they satisfied with bread and speeches? Why are they supersensitive. . . ?'[78]

Ecotopia has, despite some pulling in that direction, so far resisted the temptation to turn into a primitivist utopia of a Rousseauist kind. It has looked to a post-industrial future, not a pre-industrial past. But its strength lies in the social and moral sphere, rather than in the economic and technological, for all its concern with 'alternative' technology. In this it is fully in tune with the classic utopian tradition as inaugurated by More. Even in the utopias of abundance of the nineteenth century, it was the tranformation of human social relationships and the quality of individual life that lay at the heart of the utopian vision. That was as true of Marx as of Morris. Ecotopia has restated that emphasis more powerfully than any other contemporary social philosophy. It is in the end this that is Shevek's answer to the Terran ambassador's question, Anarres's answer to Urras, Christ's unspoken answer to Dostoyevsky's Grand Inquisitor: man does not live by bread alone. Here, once again, we see how the terms of utopia and anti-utopia can pass into each other, the material abundance of the modern utopia being transferred, in this instance, to the anti-utopia, and the moral protest of the modern anti-utopia being embodied in an austere eclogical utopia.

It is this moral and social quality of the ecotopia that has made it appear of continuing relevance to the industrial societies in the 1970s and 1980s. The ecotopia was partly a development of, partly a response to, the utopias of the 1960s. Certain aspects of counter-cultural theory – the concern with personal and social relationships, the critique of alienation – were picked up and extended. This is clear in the case of Roszak, and some sections of the alternative technology movement. But the ecotopia rejected the almost unthinking dependence of many 1960s visions on continuing economic growth and large-scale industrial technology. It did so, it is fair to say, before the oil crisis of 1973 forced a rethinking about the nature and prospects of economic growth on the publics of Western societies. In the wake of that crisis, however, and with the continuance of low rates of growth in the later 1970s and the 1980s, ecological ideas have seemed to many to remain highly suggestive as to the future organization and direction of industrial societies. The modest but significant degree of success of the Green Parties in Europe is some testimony to this.

But ecological ideas have had a more important impact outside the formal political structures of Western societies. Utopia and political parties do not co-exist very easily; and ecological thought has always tended towards utopia, though not necessarily in the formal sense. This may be because, in reacting to some of the widespread and dominant assumptions of industrialism, ecologists have felt the need to spell out, in unusually full detail, the character of a society restructured on ecological lines. Only thus, it has been felt, will people be able to see beyond the routines of the industrial way of life that cocoon them from the moment of birth.

In doing this, but more speedily, the ecotopia has followed the pattern of nineteenth-century socialism. That too, after a period of resistance to the demand, eventually produced pictures of the socialist future in the formal socialist utopia. Hence it is particularly interesting to see, in the most recent years, a certain convergence of the socialist and the ecological utopia – or, more precisely, the modification of the socialist utopia under the influence of ecotopia. This had already been foreshadowed in some of the anarchist utopias of the nineteenth century, as in Kropotkin's and, in a somewhat different way, Morris's. But what seems to have revived that tendency, and given it a new urgency at the present time, is the growing crisis caused by developments in work, employment and technology. It is the alarming prospect of a 'world without work' – the industrial world, anyhow – which has forced upon some socialists a rethinking of the classic socialist outlook on the future.

The problem had already been stated, with force and clarity, much earlier –

but in the form of the anti-utopia. In Kurt Vonnegut Jr's *Player Piano* (1952), a Third World War has performed a Wellsian 'purging' function. The new society that emerges from the wreckage rapidly advances beyond the technological level of its predecessor into the 'Third Industrial Revolution'. Just as the first Industrial Revolution replaced human muscle by machines, and the second one mechanized routine metal work, so the third Industrial Revolution is seeing the replacement of 'the real brainwork' by advanced computers. Thus the machines have replaced 'the two greatest wonders of the world, the human mind and hand'. A giant computer, EPICAC XIV, determines all questions of industrial production, employment and skill requirements, and educational policy. There is no government, only administration: the administration of an elite of managers and technical experts. These are, indeed, the only workers required by the new society – all others are expendable. Production has largely been automated. Computer-controlled machines do most of the work, in manufacturing and services alike. The mass of workers, their skills copied by and then incorporated into the machine – as in the 'player piano' (pianola) – are made redundant. The high productivity of the machines keeps them comfortable, materially at least; and in order to give idle hands something to do, the workers are drafted into the Army or the Reconstruction and Reclamation Corps – the 'Reeks and Wrecks' – which does useless and unproductive tasks like making holes in roads and repairing them. Conscious of their irrelevance to the main business of society, disheartened by the meaninglessness of their work, the workers lose all self-respect.

In time, the demoralization of the workers generates an abortive revolt, led, in classic anti-utopian fashion, by disaffected members of the technical elite who see their own skills under threat or who can no longer tolerate the boredom of the automated society. One of them comments that the meritocratic principle of the technological society is a direct inducement to class feeling and class conflict. 'The smarter you are, the better you are. Used to be that the richer you were, the better you were. Either one is, you'll admit, pretty tough for the have-not's to take.'[79] This was the theme of Michael Young's sparkling anti-utopian satire, *The Rise of the Meritocracy* (1958). Young shows a Britain in the early years of the next century where a full and effective system of selection by merit has produced a new aristocracy based on brains. A new caste system is emerging, replacing that founded on wealth. Technology is displacing most kinds of unskilled and semi-skilled human labour, forcing workers into domestic service (the Home Help Corps) and other kinds of heavy brainless work (the Pioneer Corps). Some, in the manner of *Brave New World*, are unconscious of their degradation. Others, as in *Player Piano*, feel it bitterly. But worker opposition and ideology are both fatally disorganized and confused. The movement of the best brains out of their ranks has left only the untalented and the unenergetic behind. No longer, as in the past, are there able and intelligent working-class men and women who have not had the opportunity to rise out of their class and who could, therefore, provide vigorous leadership. Those who remain now are left with a peculiarly poignant and paralysing sense of their worthlessness.

Today all persons, however humble, know they have had every chance. They are tested again and again. If on one occasion they are off-colour, they have a second, a third, and fourth opportunity to demonstrate their ability. But if they have been labelled 'dunce' repeatedly they cannot any longer pretend; their image of themselves is more nearly a true, unflattering, reflection. Are they not bound to recognize that they have an inferior status – not as in the past because they were denied opportunity; but because they *are* inferior? For the first time in human history the inferior man has no ready buttress for his self-regard.[80]

Today what Vonnegut and Young pessimistically or satirically predicted seems to many people to be on the point of realization – and far sooner than earlier prophets had expected. The microelectronic revolution is not only completing the work of the almost total mechanization of the factory but, more seriously, is making massive inroads into the office and into other kinds of service work – shops, banking, insurance.[81] Employment in manufacturing cannot, as in the past, be compensated for by service employment. For many people, the sense of an identity through work – that is, through their job – is disappearing, caused partly by the general de-skilling of work but most evidently by the increasing lack of work at all. The question of what most people will do in the future, of how, without the structure of a job, they will occupy their time in ways fulfilling to themselves and society, becomes acute.

It is in dealing with this question, and this situation, that a group of socialists has emerged with a new 'eco-socialist' vision.[82] Again, as with many versions of the ecotopia, optimism and pessimism are held in a nice balance. The new technology may prove so productive as to make the question of future work largely one of creative play or leisure. This is something close to the original Marxist utopia, or the neo-Marxist Marcusean one. More commonly, though, such cornucopian views are left to others, and the eco-socialists see continuing problems associated with the environmental impact of economic growth – now in a world-wide context – and the dangerous dependence on finite natural resources. This is their debt to ecology. As socialists, though, they also have to make a more important theoretical modification, at least in the eyes of orthodox socialists. They have to argue that socialists must give up the idea of a proletarian revolution, and of a future socialist society made by the labour of the proletariat. For with the end of employment will come the dissolution of the proletariat. In a world without work, there cannot be workers, in the strict Marxist sense. With André Gorz, they have bid 'farewell to the working class'.

Much of this eco-socialist thinking was stimulated by Rudolf Bahro's *The Alternative in Eastern Europe* (1977). The work of a dissident East German Marxist, Bahro's work was warmly greeted by many Western Marxists for restoring the utopian dimension to Marxism.[83] Bahro had experienced bureaucratic state socialism – he was imprisoned by the East Germans for his ideas – and so was free of the illusion that a Bellamy-style socialism represented the best or the only form of the Marxist utopia. He questioned orthodox socialist assumptions about the neutrality of technology and the primacy of economic growth, and proposed instead a 'cultural revolution' in which education and aesthetic culture would shape the priorities of production and technical growth. Most significantly, Bahro urged that socialists take seriously the possibility and prospect of workers being freed in the near future from work in the formal economy. He offered a new 'economy of time', which would reformulate the theory of value in terms of units of time required for the all-round development of individuals, considered in both their economic and non-economic aspects, towards 'social universality'. The goal of communism, concluded Bahro, must be to allow individuals 'rationally to regulate their overall social process so as to both raise themselves above the realm of necessity and find in their community their freedom, an unrestricted field for self-realization in action, in thought, and in enjoyment of their personal relations.'[84]

Bahro was eventually allowed to make his way to West Germany, where he became a leading light of the Green Party.[85] The same path, from Red to Green, was trod by the French socialist André Gorz. It was Gorz who, in such works as *Farewell to the Working Class* (1980, tr. 1982) and *Paths to Paradise* (1983, tr. 1985), was the most effective in spreading the eco-socialist message to a wider public in the West. Much of the analysis consisted of an *auto-critique* of his former socialist beliefs and an attack on the orthodox Marxism of most Western socialist movements. But in the process Gorz sketched the outlines of a 'post-industrial socialism' which came to terms with the crisis in employment, and which saw real opportunities in the organization of social life 'beyond employment'. The fear of unemployment, he insisted, must be converted into a realization of the possibilities of liberation in the sphere lying outside the formal economy of production.

Gorz drew on the utopian Marx as well as thinkers of the contemporary ecotopia, such as Illich, in presenting the scheme of a 'dual society' divided into the sphere of 'heteronomy' and the sphere of 'autonomy'. Individuals would move continually between the two spheres, the heteronomous sphere of 'wage-based social labour in the general interest, requiring little time or intense personal involvement', and the autonomous sphere of 'activities which carry their end in themselves'. The traditional concern of Marxists, the organization of the workers in the heteronomous sphere of the formal economy, was now obsolete. That sphere would in any case always carry the stamp of the machine and its technical rationality – as Marx had pointed out in volume III of *Capital*. Thanks to the productivity of the new technology, a historical opportunity now existed for making a radical break with the domination of the heteronomous sphere. 'The logic of capital has brought us to the threshold of liberation.' But it is not, as in classical Marxism, the workers as producers, as a proleteriat tied to the technical routines of formal production, who will bring in the 'different rationality' of the 'realm of freedom'. Only workers freed from the demands of production, the 'non-class of non-producers', are capable of such a 'rupture'. They will relegate the necessary work of material production to a marginal and routine portion of their lives, and find their fulfilment in the autonomous sphere of cultural, educational and communal activities carried out for their own sake, for the intrinsic satisfaction they give. It was in the organisation of time between the two spheres that Gorz, like Bahro, saw the greatest challenge, to which he responded with a brief, half-playful, 'Utopia for a Possible Dual Society'.[86]

The example of continental eco-socialism seems to have been infectious. British socialists, increasingly concerned at the narrowness of much traditional Marxism, in its concentration on work and production, have also drawn on ecotopian ideas to incorporate a wider range of issues dealing with family life, the organization of culture and leisure and the protection of the natural environment. Raymond Williams, whose own work has always sought to embrace the totality of human life within his socialist outlook, has made perhaps the most radical departure from the traditional posture in his *Towards 2000* (1983). Williams's book is significant not just for – unusually within socialism – adopting a future perspective at all, but in its generosity towards movements and ideas that have grown up largely outside traditional socialism in the 1960s and 1970s: feminism, the peace movement and, especially, the ecological movement.

Thus Williams commends, as a characteristic example of ecological thinking, the Club of Rome's *The Limits to Growth*. This he sees as important both in its concern with the long-term future, and for its method of analysing the 'complex and dynamic interactions' between long-term factors such as population, food, industrial production, natural resources and pollution. He endorses many of its main propositions, including the view that 'the "equilibrium state" – a self-renewable, self-controlling but also internally variable economic order – may be a desirable option, whatever the limits to growth may be.' Williams sees the strength of ecological thought as lying in its close connection with the systematic analysis of the classic utopian tradition. Utopia has always concerned itself with a whole way of life, with 'whole social orders . . . in general structure but also in detail'. It has also served as a standing reminder, when other traditions of social thought seem to have forgotten it, that 'human beings can live in radically different ways, by radically different values, in radically different kinds of social order.'

Williams therefore welcomes what he sees as a revival of the 'utopian mode' at the present time. It is taking place partly at the level of social theory, with its renewed interest in the systematic utopia; and, in a more tentative form, in the strivings of various minorities and sub-cultures in contemporary Western society to form or reform 'desire'. In this latter form, 'it is an imaginative encouragement to feel and to relate differently, or to strengthen and confirm existing feelings and relationships which are not at home in the existing order and cannot be lived through in it.' Neither form of utopia is, on its own, sufficient. System needs desire and desire system. But, 'in the danger of the current crisis', Williams sees some hopeful signs that this realization is breaking through among the groups variously pursuing their utopian ends.

> Thus what can properly be called the utopian impulse still runs, not only against the disappointments of current politics or a more generalised despair, but also against the incorporated and marketed versions of a libertarian capitalist cornucopia (which, ironically, some of the earlier systematic utopias now strikingly resemble). Its strongest centre is still the conviction that people can live very differently, as distinct both from having different things and from becoming resigned to endless crises and wars. In a time of scarce resources, of any such kind, there can be no question of dispensing with it.[87]

THE OUTLOOK FOR UTOPIA

It has to be admitted that no utopia, ecological or other, has seized the public imagination in the latter part of this century in the way that Bellamy, Morris and

Wells were able to do at its beginning. No utopia has become the centre of public attention and debate in the manner of *Looking Backward* or *A Modern Utopia*. *Walden Two* caused something of a stir, and certainly inaugurated a more optimistic climate of thought in the 1950s and 1960s. But, as a model of an experimental community, its aim is restricted and its ambition modest. It did not aspire, in the classic utopian fashion, to visualize a whole society ordered according to some principle of rightness or goodness. Its success, therefore, in inspiring communal experiments was the implicit token of its unwillingness or inability to challenge existing society with a vision of a whole alternative social order.

Nor was Aldous Huxley's somewhat insipid *Island* able to arouse more than a respectful response in some literary circles, together with a willing assent among certain groups already attuned to 'the perennial philosophy'. It, too, opened a period of intense optimism and immensely creative experimentation, both in social theory and in practical life. But for whatever reason, this ferment of activity in the 1960s and 1970s did not generate a commanding utopia which could be the focus of discussion about the ideas and ideals of the time. Callenbach's *Ecotopia* was a good practical manual of some of the current ideas, but, in its pedestrian literary quality, hardly an inspiring vision. Le Guin's *The Dispossessed*, the best of the ecotopias, so qualified its optimism as to appear to many readers to be offering merely the material for contemplation, rather than endorsing a new order. Presented in science fiction guise, it tended in any case to find it difficult to break out of its specialized literary ghetto.

The case of *The Dispossessed* is exemplary. Utopia, in the course of this century, has fragmented, both in its form and in its audience. The classic literary utopia, invented by More, has declined: in quality if not in quantity, in relevance and appeal if not in ingenuity. Utopia can still flourish in social theory, as we have seen; and utopian social movements – cults, communes, therapeutic missions – have thrived as never before. There has even been an interesting revival of the utopian novel among certain contemporary groups, as among the feminists.[88] But this serves only to underline the weakness of the utopia as a central symbol, capable of evoking a response from society as a whole. Utopia, where it still exists, is now addressed to specific groups and constituencies, as a special mode of communication among them, and the vehicle of a largely internal debate about ultimate goals.

Why has the literary utopia declined? A satisfactory answer to this question, even supposing one were possible, would involve examining the entire history of our century – a task fortunately beyond the scope of my enquiry, not to mention my competence. It might also involve a closer investigation of the last century, for it has seemed to many people that the seeds of utopia's decay must be sought there, in the nature of nineteenth-century social thought and the accompanying social developments.[89]

Some fairly obvious and familiar general causes do however suggest themselves. There is the argument of the Manuels, that, without the presence of Christianity as a widely-shared system of beliefs, utopia loses its heart.[90] Utopia may be (as I have argued) a different thing from religion in general and Christianity in particular. But without the hope that religion ultimately offers, without specifically the paradisiac and millennial expectations that Christianity inspires, it may be that utopia becomes a lifeless shell. Utopia is not religion; but without a religious underpinning, without the structure of belief and sentiment that religion incomparably provides, it is possible that utopia is not capable of arousing a significant and heartfelt response, on anything like a mass scale. Religion is, in this sense, as I have already suggested, the 'unconscious of utopia', the subterranean source of much of its emotional force and dynamism.[91]

It seemed, for some time, as if socialism might take the place of formal religion, so supplying the emotional current to utopia. This could explain the flurry of utopias at the end of the nineteenth century, when the 'religion of socialism' was at its height. And there is no doubt that, in vast portions of the non-Western world today, socialism is still capable of providing both the substance and the sentiment of utopia. But so far as the contemporary West is concerned, socialism is 'the God that has failed'. Stalinism has largely ensured that, coupled with the increasing evidence of cynicism and disbelief in Marxism among the intelligentsia of Eastern Europe. It is possible that, in the future, the success of some other socialist society, in terms recognizably consistent with Marx's vision, will revive the utopian appeal of socialism. At the present time, however, developments in China, Cuba, Yugoslavia, Tanzania, Vietnam – all of which at various times have inspired utopian hopes – hold out little prospect for this possibility, among current candidates at least.[92]

Socialism has been, to date, the last utopia. No other comprehensive social vision has emerged as contender, no other utopia to substitute for it. It was this that made Karl Mannheim fear that Western society had approached a situation 'in which the utopian element . . . has completely . . . annihilated itself'.[93] The populations of the West may prefer to live under capitalism, and look with mistrust at socialist alternatives. But contemporary capitalism, whether in its buccaneering free-market form or its more humane welfare guise, has no more than contemporary socialism proved the stuff of utopia. The utopian fervour that accompanied its birth has, as with socialism, diminished to a pragmatic acceptance. It would probably be true to say that, for the majority of people in the West, a suitably modified and 'reformed' capitalism is considered the 'least worst' system currently available, both in its economic and its political aspect. But this is hardly fertile ground for utopian appeals.

There may be a more specific, cultural, cause of the decline of the literary utopia. Utopia is a form of fiction, a form latterly of the novel. The novel has shown no sign of dying in this century, at least if we take a quantitative measure. The output of novels has been and remains enormous. But most critics would agree that a distinct shift of outlook and interest has taken place within the novel. Not only has the genre experimented radically with its traditional form, it has abandoned much of its traditional concern with society. The great panoramic social novel of the nineteenth century, the 'realist' novel of Balzac, Dickens and Tolstoy which aimed to encompass the whole of society within its covers, is no more. The novel has retreated to private worlds. Like contemporary science fiction, it is more interested in the 'inner space' of the mind and the emotions than in the outer world of society and politics.

Psychology or even psychoanalysis, not sociology, is the master passion. If it ventures into society at all, it does so in the form of nightmare fantasy or absurdist and existentialist satire. Neither development is encouraging to the utopian novel. The retreat from the concern with the whole life of society undermines a constitutive principle of utopian social theory; while the bleakness and pessimism of the best twentieth-century fiction strike against that hopefulness that is the life-blood of utopia.

The failure of utopia has been, of course, anti-utopia's opportunity. It has seized it gleefully. Anti-utopias such as *Brave New World* and *Nineteen Eighty-Four* have not only dominated their own times, the first half of the twentieth century, but have continued to attract a considerable following in our time. As I have tried to show, Huxley's and Orwell's outlook on the modern world can readily accommodate many of the political and social developments of the postwar decades. 'Brave New World' and 'Nineteen Eighty-Four', not to mention 'Newspeak' and the rest, are still by no means irrelevant or trivial short-hand terms of the contemporary political vocabulary. The 'airconditioned nightmare' and totalitarian power are still only too evidently features of the contemporary environment. And even if there were no other reason, the shadow of nuclear war would continue to lend substance to the anti-utopian vision.

Nevertheless, the anti-utopia too has faltered, as our continuing reliance on Zamyatin, Huxley and Orwell itself suggests. Vonnegut's *Player Piano*, David Karp's *One* (1953), a totalitarian nightmare, and Burgess's *A Clockwork Orange* have continued the tradition. So, too, in a somewhat different form, have anti-utopian satires such as Young's *Rise of the Meritocracy* and the *Report from Iron Mountain* (1967), an attack on American military thinking reputedly written by the economist John Kenneth Galbraith. The science fiction literature is replete with anti-utopias, as are science fiction films. And in a more minor vein, there have been works such as Michael Frayn's *A Very Private Life* (1968) and Adrian Mitchell's *The Bodyguard* (1970): both highly derivative, like most anti-utopias of the last 30 years.

The picture here is indeed much the same as for utopia. No anti-utopia since *Nineteen Eighty-Four* has truly captured the popular imagination or become the centre of public debate. There has been no new anti-utopia to stamp its compelling image on the contemporary world, as a rival to those of Huxley's and Orwell's. Instead, as with utopia, there has been fragmentation and a narrowing focus. Recent anti-utopias have had highly specific targets – automation, educational philosophy, military policy – and have tended to address highly specific audiences – policy-makers, the humanist literati, science fiction buffs. They have kept close to immediate social and political trends, often appearing virtually indistinguishable from party tracts. Hence, unlike Huxley and Orwell, present-day anti-utopias have communicated little idea of a dominant trend or central principle in contemporary developments; nor have they been able to impose a compelling sense of a march into a nightmare future.

Here, as always in the past, the dependence of anti-utopia on utopia is made clear. Anti-utopia shares in the fate of utopia. As utopia loses it vitality, so too does anti-utopia. The power and imagery of utopia have always been the driving force and indispensable material of anti-utopia. Take away utopia's power to inspire hope with its vision of a heaven on earth, and anti-utopia loses its corresponding function as the mocker of those hopes and the adversary of that vision with its own evocation of an earthly hell.

Is there, then, today no place for utopia, the 'good place' that is nowhere or not yet? 'If you have built castles in the air,' said Thoreau, 'your work need not have been lost; that is where they should be. Now put the foundations under them.'[94] We have taken this perhaps in too narrow a spirit, certainly not in the spirit of Thoreau. We have come to concentrate on the foundations to the exclusion of the castles which are their only reason for existence. So hard-headed and 'realist' have we become, so anxious not to be thought 'utopian', that we worry away at the earthworks and ground-plans without lifting up our eyes to the structures rising up from them. We have all become converts to 'piecemeal engineering', without bothering ourselves too much with the final shape of the structure we are so busily piecing together. The result is, not surprisingly, often a monstrosity, or a wilderness without meaning or purpose. We tend then to fall into 'a feeling of despondency, a sense of doubt about the adequacy of man, amounting to . . . a failure of nerve'.

Sir Peter Medawar, who deprecates this common attitude, resolutely declares that 'to deride the hope of progress is the ultimate fatuity, the last word in poverty of spirit and meanness of mind.'[95] There can clearly be two views about this. Some social philosophers have seen in the belief in progress the most narrowing of perspectives and the most arrogant and destructive assertion of hubris. For them the anti-utopia has been the suitable vehicle of such fears. But it certainly seems true to say that the belief in progress has been a distinctive and perhaps unique feature of Western societies in modern times. It has been the source of that hope, and that striving for betterment on this earth, that have been the hallmark of modern Western civilization and arguably its greatest achievement. There can of course be alternative ways of life, not dedicated to this end. But for the West that choice, for better or worse, has long been made. It is difficult to believe that the West can now realize its own best potential and its distinctive historical mission without a belief in the reality and possibility of progress. Since the West now controls, to all intents and purposes, world development, this is no longer a matter which concerns it alone.

Utopia has, for four centuries, accompanied that hope of progress and that striving for betterment. It has been itself a principle expression of that belief and a potent agent of that impulse. It now struggles against a confused but widespread sense that this has been an illusion, or an impossible dream. A strong utopian current has persisted, as we have seen. It may be that, once invented, the utopian idea can never entirely disappear – not, that is, so long as Western society itelf continues. But utopia as a form of the social imagination has clearly weakened – whether fatally we cannot say. It has not in recent times found the power to instill its vision in the public consciousness. If it cannot do so again some time in the future, we should be aware of the seriousness of the failure. Karl Mannheim, who was as thoughtful a student of utopias as anyone, considered that the elimination of the 'reality-transcending' power of utopia would mean 'the decay of the human will'.

> The complete disappearance of the utopian element from human thought and action would mean that human nature and human development would take on a totally new character. The disappearance of utopia brings about a static state of affairs in which man himself becomes no more than a thing. We would then be faced with the greatest paradox imaginable, namely, that man, who has achieved the highest degree of rational mastery of existence, left without any ideals, becomes a mere creature of impulses. Thus, after a long tortuous, but heroic development, just at the highest stage of awareness, when history is ceasing to be blind fate, and is becoming more and more man's own creation, with the relinquishment of utopias, man would lose his will to shape history and therewith his ability to understand it.[96]

Notes

The first reference in each chapter to a work that is included in the Select Bibliography is in shortened form of author, title, year of publication and page number; complete publication information appears in the Bibliography itself.

Chapter 1 Utopianism Ancient and Modern

1 George Orwell, 'Arthur Koestler', in *The Collected Essays, Journalism and Letters of George Orwell* (4 vols), ed. Sonia Orwell and Ian Angus (Harmondsworth, Penguin Books, 1970), vol. 3, p. 274. George Kateb too speaks of utopianism as 'that system of values which places harmony at the center' of individual and social life, and asks: 'Is not this the vision of utopianism through time; is not this the substance of the longings of common humanity? Is not utopianism the moral prepossession of our race?' Kateb, *Utopia and Its Enemies* (1972), p. 9. And cf. Rosabeth Moss Kanter: 'Utopia is the imaginary society in which humankind's deepest yearnings, noblest dreams, and highest aspirations come to fulfillment. . . .' Kanter, *Commitment and Community: Communes and Utopias in Sociological Perspective* (1972), p. 1. Ernst Bloch is probably the most powerful exponent of this view of utopia: it is the 'principle of hope' basic to humanity. See Wayne Hudson, *The Marxist Philosophy of Ernst Bloch* (1982), *passim*, esp. pp. 99–109.

2 J. C. Davis, *Utopia and the Ideal Society. A Study of English Utopian Writing 1516–1700* (1983), p. 5.

3 E.g. Chad Walsh, 'Plato supplies the great archetype of utopia', *From Utopia to Nightmare* (1962), p. 40. Nell Eurich describes the *Republic* as 'the first full-scale utopia, the forefather and archetype of the literary genre as it is known. . . .' *Science in Utopia: A Mighty Design* (1967), p. 36. Similarly Karl Manheim, 'Utopia' (1934), vol. 15, p. 200: 'It was Plato who furnished, notably in his *Republic*, the general model to which all later utopian fictions have been heavily indebted.' In the latest survey, the Manuels also say: 'In the history of utopian thought Plato's influence is paramount. . . . No utopian ever laid the ghost of Plato.' Frank E. Manuel and Fritzie P. Manuel, *Utopian Thought in the Western World* (1979), p. 110.

4 The *only* true utopia, in my view. So far as I have been able to establish, nothing like the western utopia and utopian tradition exist in any non-western or non-Christian culture. Why this should be so I do not feel competent to answer, but it must almost certainly have something to do with the nature of Christianity as a religion, and its unique blending of a terrestrial and non-terrestrial, supramundane, paradise, 'a new heaven and a new earth'. See further, n. 29 below.

5 Manuel and Manuel, *Utopian Thought in the Western World*, p. 74. For the Golden Age tradition, see Arthur O. Lovejoy and George Boas, *Primitivism and Related Ideas in Antiquity* (1935), ch. 2; Eurich, *Science in Utopia*, ch. 1. For the distinction between Arcadia and utopia see Northrop Frye, 'Varieties of Literary Utopias' (1973), pp. 40–9.

6 *The Tempest*, Act II, Scene 1.

7 Manuel and Manuel, *Utopian Thought in the Western World*, p. 94. For the Pythagorean communities of southern Italy, see also John Ferguson, *Utopias of the Classical World* (1975), pp. 46–8; Bertrand Russell, *History of Western Philosophy* (London, George Allen & Unwin, 1946), pp. 48–56.

8 Lewis Mumford, 'Utopia, The City and the Machine' (1973), p. 3. Cf. also Frye: 'The utopia is primarily a vision of the orderly city and of a city-dominated society.' 'Varieties of Literary Utopias', p. 27.

9 Manuel and Manuel, *Utopian Thought in the Western World*, p. 161.

10 For an interesting account of the whole tradition, see Manfredo Tafuri, *Architecture and Utopia* (1979). See also Helen Rosenau, *The Ideal City: Its Architectural Evolution in Europe* (1983); Robert Fishman, 'Utopia in Three Dimensions: The Ideal City and the Origins of Modern Design', in Peter Alexander and Roger Gill (eds), *Utopias* (1984), pp. 95–107.

11 For the Cokaygne utopia, see especially A. L. Morton, *The English Utopia* (1969), ch. 1: 'Poor Man's Heaven'. See also Robert C. Elliott, *The Shape of Utopia: Studies in a Literary Genre* (1970), ch. 1; Manuel and Manuel, *Utopian Thought in the Western World*, pp. 78–81, 99–104.

12 Quoted in Lovejoy and Boas, *Primitivism and Related Ideas in Antiquity*, pp. 40–1.

13 I quote here from Morton's modernized version of the poem, given as an appendix to his *The English Utopia*, pp. 279–85.

14 For the widespread existence of the paradise concept, see Alfred Braunthal, *Salvation and the Perfect Society: The Eternal Quest* (1979), *passim*. See also Mircea Eliade, 'Paradise and Utopia: Mythical Geography and Eschatology', in Frank E. Manuel (ed.), *Utopias and Utopian Thought* (1973), pp. 260–80.

15 M. I. Finley, 'Utopianism Ancient and Modern' (1967), p. 6. Cf. Martin Buber's distinction: religion is 'the vision of rightness in Revelation', utopia 'the vision of rightness in the Ideal'. Buber, *Paths in Utopia* (1958), p. 8. Darko Suvin calls utopia 'a "this-worldly other world" '. Suvin, 'Defining the Literary Genre of Utopia', in his *Metamorphoses of Science Fiction* (1979), p. 42. For a similar distinction between religion and utopia, see Richard Gerber, *Utopian Fantasy. A Study of English Utopian Fiction Since the End of the Nineteenth Century* (1955), pp. 5–7. I have developed this position in K. Kumar, *Religion and Utopia* (1985).

16 It is possible to go along with the Manuels' view that 'paradise in its Judeo-Christian forms has to be accepted as the deepest archaeological layer of Western utopia, active in the unconscious of large segments of the population. . . .' But it seems overstating the case to say then that 'the history of paradise is a prolegomenon and perennial accompaniment to utopia without which the powerful religious emotion that infuses this experience can never be captured'. Manuel and Manuel, *Utopian Thought in the Western World*, p. 33. This overlooks the extent to which paradise can *divert* energy and attention away from this world to a purely contemplative and passive awaiting of redemption through divine agency, to be followed by felicity in a supramundane realm. For a recognition of the possible conflict between paradise and utopia, and generally between religion and utopia, see ibid., pp. 112, 177.

17 Miriam Eliav-Feldon, *Realistic Utopias. The Ideal Imaginary Societies of the Renaissance 1516–1630* (1982), p. 5.

18 See John Passmore, *The Perfectibility of Man* (1972), pp. 68 ff.; Russell, *History of Western Philosophy*, pp. 372–85.

19 'Following the appearance of Augustine's *City of God* there was a period of nearly a thousand years during which there was no instance of even the most meagre and

insignificant utopian literature.' Joyce Oramel Hertzler, *The History of Utopian Thought* (1965), p. 121. There is general agreement on this. See, e.g., J. C. Davis, *Utopia and the Ideal Society* (1983), p. 42; Eliav-Feldon, *Realistic Utopias*, pp. 5–6; F. Graus, 'Social Utopias in the Middle Ages' (1967), p. 6. What Graus discusses, as he himself admits, are not so much utopias as popular village Cokaygnes and myths of the Golden Age, often associated with the reigns of particular kings.

20 Fearing this, and feeling it blasphemous to proceed, Columbus withdrew to Hispaniola. For this episode, see Eliade, 'Paradise and Utopia', pp. 262–3.

21 Passmore, *The Perfectibility of Man*, p. 93.

22 See especially Gersom Scholem, 'Towards an Understanding of the Messianic Idea in Judaism', in his *The Messianic Idea in Judaism, And Other Essays on Jewish Spirituality* (1971), pp. 1–36. See also Louis Jacobs, *A Jewish Theology* (1973), pp. 292–322; Mircea Eliade, *The Myth of the Eternal Return* (1954; Princeton University Press, 1971), pp. 102–12; Fred Polak, *The Image of the Future* (1973), pp. 38–49; Hertzler, *The History of Utopian Thought*, pp. 7–50; Braunthal, *Salvation and the Perfect Society*, pp. 1–33.

23 Hertzler, *The History of Utopian Thought*, p. 53. See also Frank Manuel, *Shapes of Philosophical History* (Stanford University Press, 1965), pp. 14–19. 'If one were to ask oneself what framework . . . of universal history prior to Hegel and Marx has had the most stubborn hold upon the Western imagination, has seen the most books produced within the confines of its grand design, one would have to admit that it was probably the visions described and interpreted in the Book of Daniel.' p. 14.

24 On Joachim and his influence, see Marjorie Reeves, *The Influence of Prophecy in the Later Middle Ages: A Study in Joachimism* (Oxford, Clarendon Press, 1969); Marjorie Reeves, *Joachim of Fiore and the Prophetic Future* (London, SPCK, 1976); Karl Löwith, *Meaning in History* (1949), pp. 145–59; Manuel, *Shapes of Philosophical History*, pp. 24–45. The turbulence in the medieval monastery caused by Joachimite influence is brilliantly caught in the novel by Umberto Eco, *The Name of the Rose* (Eng. tr. 1983).

On millenarianism generally, see Norman Cohn, *The Pursuit of the Millennium* (1962); Sylvia Thrupp (ed.), *Millennial Dreams in Action* (1970); Christopher Hill, *Antichrist in Seventeenth-Century England* (Oxford University Press, 1971); Christopher Hill, *The World Turned Upside Down: Radical Ideas During the English Revolution* (New York, Viking Press, 1972); Ernest Lee Tuveson, *Millennium and Utopia: A Study in the Background of the Idea of Progress* (1964); W. H. G. Armytage, *Heavens Below: Utopian Experiments in England 1560–1960* (1961), pp. 3–73; J. F. C. Harrison, *The Second Coming: Popular Millenarianism 1780–1850* (1979); Bryan Wilson, *Magic and the Millennium* (London, Heinemann, 1973). And cf. also Passmore, *The Perfectibility of Man*, pp. 116–22.

25 Friedrich Heer, *The Medieval World* (New York, New American Library, 1962), p. 62. For the general life of the monasteries, see David Knowles, *The Monastic Order in England*, 2nd edn (Cambridge University Press, 1963) and *The Religious Orders in England* (3 vols) (Cambridge University Press, 1948–1959). See also C. H. Lawrence, *Medieval Monasticism: Forms of Religious Life in Western Europe in the Middle Ages* (London, Longman, 1984). For the methodical and 'rational' nature of monastic life, see Max Weber, *The Protestant Ethic and the Spirit of Capitalism*, tr. T. Parsons (London, Unwin University Books, 1967), pp. 118–21.

26 Manuel and Manuel, *Utopian Thought in the Western World*, p. 51.

27 On the monastic ideal in More and later utopians, see J. H. Hexter, *More's* Utopia: *The Biography of an Idea* (Princeton University Press, 1952), pp. 85–94; Davis, *Utopia and the Ideal Society*, pp. 58–9, 68–82, 371; Manuel and Manuel, *Utopian Thought in the Western World*, pp. 48–51; Marie Louise Berneri, *Journey Through Utopia* (1982), p. 55; Frye, 'Varieties of Literary Utopias', p. 35.

28 David Plath, 'Introduction' to D. Plath, *Aware of Utopia* (1971), p. xii; Manuel and Manuel, *Utopian Thought in the Western World*, p. 64; A. Koestler, in Richard Crossman, *The God That Failed* (1950), p. 25.

29 See also n. 4 above. The claim has been made that China has an authentic utopian tradition. Particular emphasis is put on the Confucian concept of *ta-t'ung*, a Golden Age of 'Great Unity' or 'Great Togetherness'; the Taoist concept of *t'ai-p'ing*, the 'Great Harmony'; and – deriving mainly from Taoism – various anarchist and communist traditions especially prevalent among the peasantry, and surfacing periodically in the great peasant rebellions such as the T'ai-p'ing Rebellion of the mid-nineteenth century. In addition, there is the strain of Buddhistic Messianism that was influential not just in China but throughout south-east Asia. See, on all this, Jean Chesneaux, 'Egalitarian and Utopian Traditions in the East', *Diogenes*, vol. 62 (1968), pp. 76–102. But, apart from the generally backward-looking, peasant character of these beliefs and movements, which Chesneaux himself stresses (pp. 99–102), the important thing surely is that none of these 'utopian' elements cohered into a true utopia as they did in the West, with its similar utopian religious and mythical 'pre-history'. Nothing like a utopian *tradition* of writing was ever established in China. There is an interesting parallel here with the story of science. China, as is well known, developed particular aspects of science and technology to a very high level, but did not break through to a *scientific revolution* (*sc.* establish a tradition of scientific theory and practice) – again, unlike the West.

Of all non-western civilizations, China does indeed come closest to developing some concept of utopia. Dr Peter Moore, Lecturer in Theology at the University of Kent, has interestingly suggested that utopia may have unique affinities with both Christianity and Buddhism because, unlike most other world religions, they are not 'legalistic': they are uniquely 'open' in their prescriptions for the right or good life on earth, leaving their adherents to settle the question in their own terms.

For the lack of a utopian tradition in Japan, see Seiji Nuita, 'Traditional Utopias in Japan and the West: A Study in Contrasts', in Plath, *Aware of Utopia*, pp. 12–32; Isao Uemichi, 'Paradise in Japanese Literature', paper presented at the Colston Research Symposium on Utopias, University of Bristol, April 1983.

30 For the suggestion that utopia is mainly secularized millenarianism, see Tuveson, *Millennium and Utopia*. A similar idea is expressed by Carl Becker, *The Heavenly City of the Eighteenth-Century Philosophers* (New Haven, Yale University Press, 1932). An interesting possibility is that, just as many (e.g. Max Weber) have held that Christianity is an inherently secularizing religion, so – and in ways probably connected – it is an inherently 'utopianizing' religion. See on this David Lodge, 'Utopia and Criticism', *Encounter*, vol. 32 (April 1969), pp. 71–2.

31 *Pansophia* was the term invented by Comenius to describe an ideal society governed by universal knowledge – especially that supplied by the new science of Galileo, Bacon and others. See Eurich, *Science in Utopia*, pp. 147 ff. See also Manuel and Manuel, *Utopian Thought in the Western World*, pp. 205 ff.

32 R. W. Chambers, *Thomas More* (London, Jonathan Cape, 1935), p. 128.

33 Thomas More, *Utopia* (London, Everyman edn, Dent and Sons, 1951), pp. 117–30.

34 Ibid., pp. 84–93.

35 Ibid., pp. 98–101, 78–9.

36 Hexter, *More's* Utopia, p. 64. See also Davis, *Utopia and the Ideal Society*, pp. 42–3.

37 Hexter, *More's* Utopia, *passim*, esp. pp. 52–6, 113–46.

38 See Chambers, *Thomas More*; W. E. Campbell, *More's* Utopia *and his Social Teaching* (London, Eyre & Spottiswoode, 1930); Edward L. Surtz, S.J., *The Praise of Pleasure* (Cambridge, Mass., Harvard University Press, 1957) and *The Praise of Wisdom* (Chicago, Loyola University Press, 1957). This is not the place to review, still less enter into, the controversy over More's meaning and intention in his *Utopia*. Hexter has reaffirmed his view of More as a Christian humanist, with equal stress on both aspects, in his 'Introduction' to *Utopia*, (ed.) Edward Surtz, S.J. and J. H. Hexter, vol. 4 of the *Yale Edition of the Complete Works of Sir Thomas More* (New Haven, Yale University Press, 1965), pp. xv–cxxiv. There is a splendid review and discussion of the whole

matter in three contributions by Quentin Skinner: 'More's *Utopia*', *Past and Present*, no. 38 (1967), pp. 153–68; *The Foundations of Modern Political Thought*, vol. 1 (1978), pp. 233, 255–62; 'Sir Thomas More's *Utopia* and the language of Renaissance humanism', in Anthony Pagden (ed.), *The Languages of Political Theory in Early–Modern Europe* (Cambridge, Cambridge University Press, 1987), pp. 123–158.

39 On the tensions between the sacred and the secular in More, see Richard Marius, *Thomas More* (London, Dent, 1984), *passim*. For the satire in *Utopia* see especially Elliott, *The Shape of Utopia*, pp. 25–49.

40 Hill, *The World Turned Upside Down*, p. 147.

41 See Thomas Molnar, *Utopia: The Perennial Heresy* (1972). For the secularism of utopia, see Eliav-Feldon, *Realistic Utopias*, pp. 5–6; and cf. her further comment: 'Another test-case which, I believe, supports the argument that utopias proper are possible only within some form of a *secular* culture is that of the Zionist utopias in the second half of the nineteenth century. Before that time there were no Jewish utopias but only expectations for the coming of the Messiah. The first genuine Jewish utopias appear simultaneously with the first generation of non-rabbinical, yet non-assimilationist, Jewish men of letters.' Ibid., p. 6, n. 7. See also Davis, *Utopia and the Ideal Society*, pp. 42, 372; Frye, 'Varieties of Literary Utopias', pp. 35–6.

42 See, e.g., Arthur E. Morgan, *Nowhere Was Somewhere* (1946).

43 Cf. Leo Marx: 'the Western habit of writing utopias is a product of the historical transition that gave rise to the modern capitalist nation state.' 'No Such Places', *New York Times Book Review* (21 October 1979). For a similar linking of utopia and modernity, see Zygmunt Bauman, *Socialism: The Active Utopia* (1976), ch. 2.

44 Letter to Peter Giles, *The Complete Works of Sir Thomas More*, vol. 4: *Utopia*, p. 251. In his *Apology for Poetry*, Sir Philip Sydney chose More's *Utopia* as an example of the superiority of fiction ('poetry') over history in teaching goodness.

45 For the Hellenistic imaginary voyages, see Ferguson, *Utopias of the Classical World*, pp. 98–129; Manuel and Manuel, *Utopian Thought in the Western World*, pp. 81–92.

46 Although it seems too much to claim that utopia *is* satire, that it is no more than 'a prose version with variations of the formal verse satire' composed by the Roman satirists. See Elliott, *The Shape of Utopia*, pp. 22–4, 29.

47 Finley, 'Utopianism Ancient and Modern', pp. 15–16.

48 *Republic*, IX, 592. That Plato's conception here of 'the city within' is so much like Augustine's City of God further underlines the mistake of treating the Republic as a utopia offered for earthly realization. For some helpful thoughts on Plato's purpose – though unwarrantedly extending this to the whole utopian tradition – see Peter Alexander, 'Grimm's Utopia: Motives and Justification', in Alexander and Gill, *Utopias*, pp. 31–42.

49 On the nature of utopian fiction, see Darko Suvin, 'Defining the Literary Genre of Utopia', in his *Metamorphoses of Science Fiction* (1979), pp. 37–62. See also Irving Howe, *Politics and the Novel* (1957), pp. 235–9; Lodge, 'Utopia and Criticism', p. 70; Frye, 'Varieties of Literary Utopias', pp. 25–32; Gerber, *Utopian Fantasy*, pp. 3–6; Elliott, *The Shape of Utopia*, pp. 102–28; Davis, *Utopia and the Ideal Society*, pp. 14–17; Glenn Negley and J. Max Patrick, *The Quest for Utopia* (1952), pp. 3–10.

50 Manuel and Manuel, *Utopian Thought in the Western World*, pp. 438, 413. The Manuels say of Rousseau that 'in virtually all of his works he had a way of falling into the discursive utopian mode.'

51 See, e.g., Crane Brinton, 'Utopia and Democracy', in Manuel, *Utopias and Utopian Thought*, pp. 50–68; Jerome Gilison, *The Soviet Image of Utopia* (1975). For the treatment of varieties of social theory as utopia, see Ralf Dahrendorf, 'Out of Utopia: Toward a Reorientation of Sociological Analysis' (1958), pp. 115–27.

52 More, *Utopia*, pp. 97–8. Utopian bondsmen are thought to deserve greater punishment than criminals from other lands 'because they being so godly brought up to virtue in so excellent a commonwealth, could not for all that be refrained from misdoing'.

53 Berneri, *Journey Through Utopia*, pp. 53–4.
54 Valentin Andreae, *Christianopolis* (1619); abridged in Berneri, *Journey Through Utopia*, p. 112.
55 See especially Joyce Oldham Appleby, *Economic Thought and Ideology in Seventeen-Century England* (Princeton University Press, 1978); Davis, *Utopia and the Ideal Society*, ch. 11: 'The Full-Employment Utopia of Seventeenth-Century England'.
56 Weber, *The Protestant Ethic and the Spirit of Capitalism*; Robert K. Merton, *Science, Technology and Society in Seventeenth-Century England*, (1938; Atlantic Highlands, NJ: Humanities Press, 1978). For the association of the new science and utopia, see Eurich, *Science in Utopia*, pp. 103 ff; René Dubos, *The Dreams of Reason: Science and Utopias* (New York, Columbia University Press, 1961); William Leiss, 'Utopia and Technology: Reflections on the Conquest of Nature', *International Social Science Journal*, vol. 22, no. 4 (1970), pp. 576–88; Robert P. Adams, 'The Social Responsibilities of Science in *Utopia, New Atlantis*, and After', *Journal of The History of Ideas*, vol. 10 (1949), pp. 374–98; Judah Bierman, 'Science and Society in the *New Atlantis* and Other Renaissance Utopias', *PMLA*, vol. 78 (1963), pp. 492–500.
57 H. G. Wells, *A Modern Utopia* (1905; Lincoln, University of Nebraska Press, 1967), p. 299. And see also below, pp. 217–18.
58 Judith Shklar, 'The Political Theory of Utopia: From Melancholy to Nostalgia', in Manuel, *Utopias and Utopian Thought*, p. 104. Shklar quotes the apt comment of the seventeenth-century utopian Gabriel de Foigny, from his *Terra Australis Incognita*: Utopia is meant 'to confound those who, calling themselves Christians, live worse than animals, although they are specially favoured with grace, while pagans, relying on the light of nature, manifest more virtue than the Reformed Church claims to uphold'. On the incompatibility of utopia and original sin, see also Kateb, *Utopia and Its Enemies*, pp. 197 ff; Lodge, 'Utopia and Criticism', pp. 71 ff; Walsh, *From Utopia to Nightmare* pp. 70 ff.
59 G. K. Chesterton, 'Mr H. G. Wells and the Giants', in his *Heretics* (London, Bodley Head, 1905), pp. 73–4.
60 Hexter, *More's* Utopia, pp. 59–60. This is perhaps the best counter to J. C. Davis's contention that utopia postulates, if not 'original sin', at least the stubbornly recalcitrant nature of man, which is a constant threat to social order: 'Utopia is a holding operation, a set of strategies to maintain social order and perfection in the face of the deficiencies, not to say hostility, of nature and the wilfulness of man.' Davis, *Utopia and the Ideal Society*, p. 37. This Hobbesian view of man and nature certainly indicates why utopian schemes are forthcoming; but by the same token it must condemn all utopias as idle fantasies or wish-fulfilments of the most unprofitable kind, since there is a contradiction between this view of human nature and the imaginative realization of a utopia which must show, in some realistic sense, humans successfully inhabiting the good society.

Another way of seeing the matter, in the terms we have already encountered, is to say that utopia is always Pelagian; anti-utopia is frequently Augustinian. See further below, pp. 100–1.
61 Davis, *Utopia and the Ideal Society*, p. 125; and ibid., pp. 124–5, for the quotations from Bacon.
62 Hill, *The World Turned Upside Down*, pp. 131–2.
63 Tommaso Campanella, *The City of the Sun* (1602–23), in Henry Morley (ed.), *Ideal Commonwealths* (1885), p. 263.
64 H. G. Wells, 'Utopias' (1939), *Science-Fiction Studies*, vol. 9, part 2 (1982), p. 120.
65 For an interesting discussion of this issue see J. C. Davis, 'Science and Utopia: The History of a Dilemma', in Everett Mendelsohn and Helga Nowotny (eds), *Nineteen Eighty-Four: Science Between Utopia and Dystopia* (1984), pp. 21–48. See also William Leiss, 'Utopia and Technology', and his *The Domination of Nature*, (1974). Leiss acknowledges Bacon's importance in linking science and utopia through the idea of the

conquest of nature, but sees this idea as posing more problems that it solves. And see also the discussion of science in *Brave New World*, pp. 254 ff below.

66 Francis Bacon, *New Atlantis* (1627), in A. Johnston (ed.), *The Advancement of Learning* and *New Atlantis* (Oxford, Clarendon Press, 1974), p. 239. For the activities of the Baconians, see Eurich, *Science in Utopia*, pp. 145 ff. As is well known, the Royal Society soon began to show some embarrassment at its utopian parentage, and its later evolution as a club for wealthy scientific amateurs meant that it was 'never able to implement the Baconian conception to which many of the Founders were attached'. A. R. Hall, *The Scientific Revolution 1500–1800*, 2nd edn (London, Longmans, 1962), p. 195.

67 *New Atlantis*, p. 214.

68 Bacon, *Novum Organum*, in J. Devey (ed.), *The Physical and Metaphysical Works of Lord Bacon* (London, Henry Bohn, 1860), pp. 446–7.

69 Quoted in Eurich, *Science in Utopia*, p. 143.

Chapter 2 Utopia in Nineteenth-Century Europe

1 Thomas More, *Utopia* (1516; London, Everyman Library, Dent and Sons, 1951), p. 71.

2 J. H. Hexter, *More's* Utopia. *The Biography of an Idea* (Princeton University Press, 1952), pp. 70–1.

3 More, *Utopia*, pp. 66, 69.

4 Tommaso Campanella, *City of the Sun*, in Henry Morley (ed.) *Ideal Commonwealths* (1885), p. 238.

5 Johann Valentin Andreae, *Christianopolis*, extracted in Marie-Louise Berneri, *Journey Through Utopia* (1982), pp. 113–14.

6 Denis Diderot, *Supplement to Bougainville's Voyage* (written 1772, first published 1796); extracted in Berneri, *Journey Through Utopia*, p. 204. See also the section in Frank E. Manuel and Fritzie P. Manuel (eds), *French Utopias: An Anthology of Ideal Societies* (1971), pp. 147–66. And cf. Robinson Crusoe's reflection on returning to England after 28 years on his island: 'indeed I had more care upon my head now, than I had in my silent state of life in the island, where I wanted nothing but what I had, and had nothing but what I wanted; whereas I had now a great charge upon me. . . .' Daniel Defoe, *Robinson Crusoe* (1719; Harmondsworth, Penguin Books, 1965), p. 281. Richard Steele, in his account of the solitary island life of the Scotsman Alexander Selkirk (on which Defoe partly based his tale), drew a like moral: 'This plain man's story is a memorable example, that he is happiest who confines his wants to natural necessities; and he that goes furthest in his desires, increases his wants in proportion to his acquisitions.' Steele's essay, published in *The Englishman* (December 1713), is reprinted as an appendix to the Penguin edition of *Robinson Crusoe*, pp. 307–10.

7 More, *Utopia*, pp. 96, 122. For the contrast between the place of science in More's and Bacon's utopias, see Robert P. Adams, 'The Social Responsibilities of Science in *Utopia*, *New Atlantis* and After', *Journal of the History of Ideas*, vol. 10 (1949), pp. 382–9.

8 For this view of the role of science in Campanella, Andreae and other early modern utopists, see J. C. Davis, *Utopia and the Ideal Society: A Study of English Utopian Writing 1516–1700* (1983), pp. 72–7; J. C. Davis, 'Science and Utopia: The History of a Dilemma', in Everett Mendelsohn and Helga Nowotny (eds), *Nineteenth Eighty-Four: Science Between Utopia and Dystopia* (1984), pp. 30–4; Judah Bierman, 'Science and Society in the *New Atlantis* and other Renaissance Utopias', *PMLA* vol. 78 (1963), pp. 492–500. Eurich is clearly wrong in treating all these contemporary utopias as sharing in a common Baconian enterprise: Nell Eurich, *Science in Utopia* (1967), *passim*, esp. pp. 200–68; although for the view that Bacon himself was more cautious and ambivalent about science and scientists than is usually thought, see Davis, 'Science and Utopia', pp. 31–2.

9 Berneri, *Journey Through Utopia*, pp. 55–6.

10 See Albert O. Hirschman, *The Passions and the Interests: Political Arguments for Capitalism before Its Triumph* (Princeton University Press, 1977). Practically the whole literature on Hobbes makes the same point.

11 Frank E. Manuel, 'Toward a Psychological History of Utopias', in Frank E. Manuel (ed.), *Utopias and Utopian Thought* (1973), pp. 72–9.

12 Judith N. Shklar, 'Rousseau's Two Models: Sparta and the Age of Gold', *Political Science Quarterly*, vol. 81, no. 1 (1966), pp. 25–51. For a fuller account, see her *Men and Citizens. A Study of Rousseau's Social Theory* (Cambridge University Press, 1969); see also Shklar, 'The Political Theory of Utopia: From Melancholy to Nostalgia', in Manuel, *Utopia and Utopian Thought*, pp. 104–5. And cf. Hansot: 'Prior to the seventeenth century, utopias were not written primarily as models for societal change. Classical utopian criticism addressed itself first and foremost to changing individual men and concerned itself only secondarily with the societal arrangements in which men live.' She dates the change to the dynamic modern utopia, which incorporates change at the societal level, to the early nineteenth century. See Elizabeth Hansot, *Perfection and Progress: Two Modes of Utopian Thought* (1974), pp. 9–20, 94–112. Soboul too sees the character of Enlightenment utopias as 'moral and speculative', lacking a sense of historical development. Albert Soboul, 'Notes Toward A History of Utopia in France in the Eighteenth Century', in Mathé Allain (ed.), *France and North America: Utopias and Utopians* (1978), p. 179. For the view that the utopias of these times *were* 'a call to action' see Robert C. Elliott, *The Shape of Utopia* (1970), pp. 56, 61.

13 Frank E. Manuel and Fritzie P. Manuel, *Utopian Thought in the Western World* (1979), p. 431.

14 'Utopian literature reached its lowest level in England during the eighteenth century.' A. L. Morton, *The English Utopia* (1969), p. 143; also pp. 126–7. For the displacement of England by France in the utopian tradition, see also Berneri, *Journey Through Utopia*, pp. 174–5; Manuel and Manuel, *French Utopias*, pp. 1–16. *Gulliver's Travels*, described as a dystopia by the Manuels (*Utopian Thought in the Western World*, p. 431), can also of course be considered to have a utopian side. For a discussion, see Elliott, *The Shape of Utopia*, pp. 50–67; Morton, *The English Utopia*, pp. 112–42; John Traugott, 'A Voyage to Nowhere with Thomas More and Jonathan Swift', *Sewanee Review*, vol. 69 (1961), pp. 534–65.

15 'There is continuity as well as an impoverishment of the utopian tradition from the sixteenth to the eighteenth century, from Thomas More and Campanella to Restif de la Bretonne and Sebastien Mercier. Enlightenment communistic utopias belong to the tradition of the two preceding centuries. But to compare the works of the sixteenth and seventeenth to those of the eighteenth is to realize the weakness in both invention and creation in the latter. Many utopias were then only reprints, translations, adaptations. Traditional themes and forms persisted, but the conceptual heritage from the preceding centuries was little enlarged. In that sense, one cannot speak of the eighteenth century as of a classical period of utopian development, despite the large number of utopias.' Soboul, 'Notes Toward a History of Utopia in France in the Eighteenth Century', p. 179. On the imitation of More, see Berneri, *Journey Through Utopia*, pp. 174–5.

16 Manuel and Manuel, *Utopian Thought in the Western World*, p. 421. On the *philosophes* as utopians, see Carl L. Becker, *The Heavenly City of the Eighteenth-Century Philosophers* (New Haven, Yale University Press, 1932); Franco Venturi, *Utopia and Reform in the Enlightenment* (1971). For the view of the Enlightenment as a misconceived and ultimately monstrous utopia, see Max Horkheimer and T. W. Adorno, *Dialectic of the Enlightenment* (1973).

17 An extract is published in Manuel and Manuel, *French Utopias*, pp. 131–48.

18 I. F. Clarke, *The Pattern of Expectation 1644–2001* (1979), p. 23.

19 Soboul, 'Notes Toward a History of Utopia . . . ', p. 179.

20 Immanuel Kant, 'An Answer to the Question: What is Enlightenment?' (1784), in

Immanuel Kant, *Perpetual Peace and Other Essays*, tr. Ted Humphrey (Indianapolis, Hackett, 1983), p. 33.

21 *Hegel's Philosophy of Right*, tr. T. M. Knox (Oxford, Clarendon Press, 1942), p. 12.

22 The view especially of George Lichtheim; see, e.g., *Marxism. An Historical and Critical Study* (London, Routledge & Kegan Paul, 1961). It is partly because of the very brief and unsatisfactory treatment of Marxism – especially nineteenth-century Marxism – that Judith Shklar can make the claim that utopia, seen as an essentially Enlightenment idea of reason, declined after the French Revolution. It is true that formal literary utopias went into abeyance (but only until the end of the nineteenth century). But what took their place were social philosophies that were utopian in all but form – Saint-Simonism, Comtism, Marxism, etc.; and what characterized most of them was precisely a hanging on to the Enlightenment faith in reason. To concentrate almost exclusively on the 'unhappy consciousness' of romantics, Christians and existentialists in the two centuries since the French Revolution is to give a remarkably distorted intellectual history of the period, however powerfully done. See Judith N. Shklar, *After Utopia: The Decline of Political Faith* (1957); and, for another view of the negative impact of the French Revolution on utopia, see David Higgs, 'Nostalgia, Utopia, and the French Revolution', in Allain, *France and North America*, pp. 25–32.

23 Soboul, 'Notes Toward a History of Utopia . . . ', p. 181. On Restif, see Mark Poster, *The Utopian Thought of Restif de la Bretonne* (New York University Press, 1971).

24 Jean Jacques Rousseau, 'A Discourse on the Origin of Inequality' (1755), in *Rousseau: The Social Contract and the Discourses*, tr. G. D. H. Cole (London, Everyman edition, Dent and Sons, 1913), pp. 198, 192.

25 Rousseau, 'Origin of Inequality', p. 228.

26 Quoted in F. Venturi, *Utopia and Reform in the Enlightenment*, p. 97.

27 Morelly, *Nature's Domain (Code de la Nature)* (1755), in Manuel and Manuel, *French Utopias*, p. 93, 102.

28 Francois Noël Babeuf, 'Manifesto of the Equals' (c. 1796), in Manuel and Manuel, *French Utopias*, pp. 247–8 (emphasis in the original).

29 Soboul, 'Notes Toward a History of Utopia . . . ', p. 182. And cf. George Lichtheim: 'The Conspiracy of the Equals marked the dividing line between Rousseauist democracy and Communism.' *The Origins of Socialism* (London, Weidenfeld & Nicolson, 1968), p. 21.

30 Venturi, *Utopia and Reform in the Enlightenment*, pp. 97–8. And cf. the similar verdict of the Manuels: 'Despite superficial resemblances to the ideas of Plato and More, the *Code de la Nature* initiated a new utopian form, a detailed secular egalitarian constitution, ready-made for promulagation in an agrarian society. . . . Morelly and other eighteenth-century utopians drafted concrete plans for future implementation that had offspring. Morelly really expected to see his code of laws adopted, and it is known to have exerted a powerful influence upon Babeuf's Conspiracy of the Equals. We are dealing here not with the egalitarian household economies of Thomas More's *Utopia*, which retain a certain individual autonomy, but with the blueprint of a full-fledged communist society and a demand for the immediate institution of equality in all things.' Manuel and Manuel, *Utopian Thought in the Western World*, p. 562. For the details of Enlightenment communist thought, see J. L. Talmon, *The Origins of Totalitarian Democracy* (1961), pp. 50–65, 167–247; Alexander Gray, *The Socialist Tradition* (London, Longmans, 1946), pp. 76–109.

31 Manuel and Manuel, *Utopian Thought in the Western World*, p. 458.

32 Immanuel Kant, 'Idea for a Universal History with a Cosmopolitan Intent' (1784), in Kant, *Perpetual Peace and Other Essays*, p. 36.

33 I have drawn largely on J. B. Bury, *The Idea of Progress* (1923); Charles Frankel, *The Faith of Reason* (New York, Columbia University Press, 1948); Ernest L. Tuveson, *Millennium and Utopia. A Study in the Background to the Idea of Progress* (1949); Becker, *The Heavenly City of the Eighteenth Century Philosophers*; Karl Löwith, *Meaning in History*

(1949), pp. 60–103; Sidney Pollard, *The Idea of Progress* (Harmondsworth, Penguin Books, 1971); Leslie Sklair, *The Sociology of Progress* (London, Routledge & Kegan Paul, 1970); John Passmore, *The Perfectibility of Man* (1972), pp. 190–238; Frank E. Manuel, *The Prophets of Paris* (Cambridge, Mass., Harvard University Press, 1962); David Bebbington, *Patterns in History* (Leicester, Intervarsity Press, 1979), pp. 68–91; Manuel and Manuel, *Utopian Thought in the Western World*, pp. 453–531. For the nineteenth-century idea of progress see also Walter E. Houghton, *The Victorian Frame of Mind 1830–1870* (New Haven, Yale University Press, 1957); J. W. Burrow, *Evolution and Society* (Cambridge University Press, 1966); J. H. Buckley, *The Triumph of Time* (1967); H. Butterfield, *The Whig Interpretation of History* (London, Bell & Sons, 1931). For a discussion with a somewhat different focus from the present one, see K. Kumar, *Prophecy and Progress: The Sociology of Industrial and Post-industrial Society* (1978), ch. 1.

34 Manuel, 'Toward a Psychological History of Utopias', p. 77. The last section of Condorcet's *Sketch* can be found in Manuel and Manuel, *French Utopias*, p. 191–215.

35 As with all aspects of utopia, older traditions persist alongside the new. Spatial utopias on earth are still to be found, for instance, in Cabet's *Voyage en Icarie*, Hertzka's *Freeland*, Howell's *Voyage to Etruria*, and Skinner's *Walden Two*. But these are still essentially modern, both in that they are squarely based on modern science and technology and, more importantly, because they recognize their own time, the utopian time, to exist within a historical development that is now making utopia possible. See, on this 'fusion of archaic form and prophetic content', Clarke, *The Pattern of Expectation 1644–2001*, pp. 119–124.

36 Henri de Saint-Simon, 'The Reorganization of the European Community' (1814), in Felix Markham (ed. and tr.), *Henri de Saint-Simon: Social Organization, The Science of Man, and Other Writings* (New York, Harper & Row, 1964), p. 68. The move from static spatial utopias to dynamic temporal utopias at the end of the eighteenth century is widely acknowledged. See especially Hansot, *Perfection and Progress*, pp. 1–20, 94–112; also Ruth Levitas, 'Sociology and Utopia', (1979), pp. 24–7; Charles J. Erasmus, *In Search of the Common Good* (1977), pp. 35–41; C. Collins, 'Zamyatin, Wells, and the Utopian Literary Tradition', *Slavonic and East European Review*, vol. 44 (1966), p. 356; Eugene Goodheart, *Culture and the Radical Conscience* (1973), p. 97; Barbara Goodwin and Keith Taylor, *The Politics of Utopia* (1982), pp. 142–9; Manuel, 'Toward a Psychological History of Utopias', pp. 79–85.

37 As shown especially by Becker, Löwith and Tuveson – see n. 33 above.

38 Manuel and Manuel, *Utopian Thought in the Western World*, p. 560.

39 Babeuf, 'Manifesto of the Equals', pp. 251–2.

40 Rousseau, 'The Origin of Inequality', pp. 220, 196.

41 Berkeley and Smith, quoted in T. S. Ashton, *An Economic History of England: The Eighteenth Century* (London, Methuen, 1955), pp. 213–14.

42 Manuel and Manuel, *Utopian Thought in the Western World*, p. 448. Cf. also Berneri, *Journey Through Utopia*, p. 210.

43 See below, pp. 233 ff.

44 Michel Foucault, *The History of Sexuality*, vol. 1 (Harmondsworth, Penguin Books, 1981), p. 145.

45 Karl Mannheim, *Ideology and Utopia* (1960), pp. 222 ff.

46 Karl Marx, 'Theses on Feuerbach', in Karl Marx and Frederick Engels, *Selected Works in Two Volumes* (Moscow, Foreign Languages Publishing House, 1962), vol. 2, p. 405.

47 Henri de Saint-Simon, 'Letters to an American' (1817), in Keith Taylor (ed. and tr.) *Henri Saint-Simon: Selected Writings on Science, Industry, and Social Organisation* (London, Croom Helm, 1975), p. 162.

48 Karl Polanyi, *The Great Transformation* (Boston, Beacon Press, 1957), p. 3 and *passim*, esp. pp. 135–50.

49 See, e.g., the writings of F. A. Hayek, such as *Law, Legislation, and Liberty*, (3 vols) (London, Routledge & Kegan Paul, 1982); and, interpreting 'free market' in the

broadest sense of the non-interventionist state, Robert Nozick, *Anarchy, State, and Utopia* (1974). In an interesting radio interview in 1985, the British Conservative Prime Minister Margaret Thatcher made it plain that capitalism and communism were to her indeed alternative and competing utopias. 'I want people to have the right to property, the right to occupational pensions, the right to shares; the right to be the same as everyone else because they have that independence. That is my dream. . . . Like Karl Marx, I want to get totally rid of class distinctions.' But the way to this, she said, was to make everyone his own capitalist, through encouraging individual initiative and achievement. This had been clearly shown by recent history. 'Marks and Spencer have triumphed over Marx and Engels', reported in *The Times* (6 May 1985).

50 So Zygmunt Bauman – see epigraph to this chapter, above. See also Adam Ulam on the 'organic connection between socialism and utopia': 'Socialism and Utopia', in Manuel, *Utopias and Utopian Thought*, p. 116. Jerome Gilison has said that 'Marx's utopia . . . is the only utopia which has ever become the guiding principle for directed, planned social change in a modern mass society.' *The Soviet Image of Utopia* (1975), p. 34.

51 There is a huge literature on those who, following Marx and Engels, have come to be called the 'utopian socialists'. Here is a selection, concerned with both their theory and their practice: Gray, *The Socialist Tradition*, pp. 136–256; Lichtheim, *The Origins of Socialism*; Martin Buber, *Paths in Utopia* (1958); Leszek Kolakowski, *Main Currents of Marxism* (1981), vol. 1: *The Founders*, pp. 182–234; Keith Taylor, *The Political Ideas of the Utopian Socialists* (London, Frank Cass, 1982); Goodwin and Taylor, *The Politics of Utopia*, pp. 119–162; Barbara Goodwin, *Social Science and Utopia* (1978); Dominique Desanti, *Les Socialistes de l'Utopie* (Paris, Payot, 1970); Frank E. Manuel, *The New World of Henri Saint-Simon* (Cambridge, Mass., Harvard University Press, 1956); Jonathan Beecher and Richard Bienvenu (eds and trs), *The Utopian Vision of Charles Fourier: Selected Texts on Work, Love and Passionate Attraction* (London, Jonathan Cape, 1972); C. H. Johnson, *Utopian Communism in France. Cabet and the Icarians 1839–1851* (Ithaca, NY, Cornell University Press, 1974); W. H. G. Armytage, *Heavens Below: Utopian Experiments in England 1560–1960* (1961), pp. 77–167; J. F. C. Harrison, *Robert Owen and the Owenites in Britain and America* (1969); Dennis Hardy, *Alternative Communities in Nineteenth Century England* (1979); Barbara Taylor, *Eve and the New Jerusalem: Socialism and Feminism in the Nineteenth Century* (1983); Morton, *The English Utopia*, pp. 165–79; Manuel and Manuel, *Utopian Thought in the Western World*, pp. 581–693.

52 It should be remembered that by the end of the nineteenth century the victory of Marxism over other kinds of socialism was by no means assured, despite the strength of Marxist influence in the Second International. The defeat of Marx by Bakunin in the First International, and the total collapse of the Second International in 1914, showed how uncertain and fragmented the whole socialist enterprise was. Since there has been no Marxist success in the West, parliamentary or revolutionary, it is only the Russian and Chinese revolutions, and their international repercussions, which have made Marxism so central a phenomenon in the twentieth century.

53 Marx's acknowledgement of his own distinctive contribution is even more modest than this suggests. On 5 March 1852 he wrote to J. Weydemeyer: ' . . . as to myself, no credit is due to me for discovering the existence of classes in modern society or the struggle between them. Long before me bourgeois historians had described the historical development of this class struggle and bourgeois economists the economic anatomy of the classes. What I did that was new was to prove: (1) that the *existence of classes* is only bound up with *particular historical phases in the development of production*, (2) that the class struggle necessarily leads to the *dictatorship of the proletariat*, (3) that this dictatorship itself only constitutes the transition to the *abolition of all classes* and to a *classless society*' (Marx's emphases). Karl Marx and Frederick Engels, *Selected Correspondence* (Moscow, Foreign Languages Publishing House, n.d.), p. 86.

54 Karl Marx, 'Author's Preface to the Second German Edition' (1873), *Capital*, vol. 1, tr. Ben Fowkes (Harmondsworth, Penguin Books, 1976), p. 99; letter to Ruge, September

1843, in Lloyd D. Easton and Kurt H. Guddat (eds and trs), *Writings of the Young Marx on Philosophy and Society* (New York, Doubleday, 1967), p. 212. Marx is also reported to have written to the English Positivist Beesley in 1869 that 'the man who draws up a programme for the future is a reactionary.' Quoted in Manuel and Manuel, *Utopian Thought in the Western World*, p. 698.

55 Liebknecht and Engels; quoted by Riederer in Sylvia E. Bowman and others, *Edward Bellamy Abroad: An American Prophet's Influence* (New York, Twayne Publishers, 1962), pp. 193–6.

56 Quoted in Buber, *Paths in Utopia*, p. 115. 'In Marx,' says Lenin, 'you will find no trace of Utopianism in the sense of inventing the "new" society and constructing it out of fantasies.' Ibid., p. 99.

57 Sidney Webb, *The Difficulties of Individualism*, Fabian Tract no. 69 (London, Fabian Society, 1894), p. 1.

58 Lichtheim, *The Origins of Socialism*, p. 230, n. 2.

59 Frederick Engels, 'Socialism: Utopian and Scientific' (1877), in Marx and Engels, *Selected Works in Two Volumes*, vol. 2, pp. 121, 128. And cf. Marx: 'So long as the proletariat is not yet sufficiently developed to constitute itself as a class, and consequently so long as the struggle itself of the proletariat with the bourgeoisie has not yet assumed a political character, and the productive forces are not yet sufficiently developed in the bosom of the bourgeoisie itself to enable us to catch a glimpse of the material conditions necessary for the emancipation of the proletariat and for the formation of a new society, these theoreticians are merely utopians who, to meet the wants of the oppressed classes, improvise systems and go in search of a regenerating science. But in the measure that history moves forward, and with it the struggle of the proletariat assumes clearer outlines, they no longer need to seek science in their minds; they have only to take note of what is happening before their eyes and to become its mouthpiece.' Marx, *The Poverty of Philosophy* (1847; New York, International Publishers, 1963), p. 125.

Martin Buber has pointed out how the use of the term 'utopian' shifted in a more polemical and pejorative direction in later Marxist vocabulary. 'Originally Marx and Engels called those people Utopians whose thinking had preceded the critical development of industry, the proletariat and the class war, and who therefore could not take this development into account; subsequently the term was levelled indiscriminately at all those who, in the estimation of Marx and Engels, did not in fact take account of it; and of these the late-comers either did not understand how to do so or were unwilling or both. The epithet "utopian" thereafter became the most potent missile in the fight of Marxism against non-Marxism socialism.' Buber, *Paths in Utopia*, p. 5.

60 Marx and Engels, 'The Communist Manifesto' (1848), in *Selected Works in Two Volumes*, vol. 1, pp. 62–3; Marx, 'The Class Struggles in France 1848–1850', ibid., pp. 222–3.

61 Marx, 'The Eighteenth Brumaire of Louis Bonaparte' (1852), *Selected Works*, vol. 1, pp. 254–5.

62 Marx, 'The Civil War in France' (1871), *Selected Works*, vol. 1, p. 523. And cf. his statement: 'It is not enough that thought should seek to realize itself; reality must also strive towards thought.' T. B. Bottomore (ed. and tr.), *Karl Marx: Early Writings* (London, Watts & Co., 1963), p. 54.

63 Engels, 'Socialism: Utopian and Scientific', pp. 123, 126–7. Elsewhere Engels wrote: 'German theoretical Socialism will never forget that it rests on the shoulders of Saint-Simon, Fourier and Owen, the three who, in spite of their fantastic notions and Utopianism, belonged to the most significant heads of all time and whose genius anticipated numerous things the correctness of which can now be proved in a scientific way . . . ' 'Preface to the Second Edition' (1874) of *The Peasant War in Germany*, in Friedrich Engels, *The German Revolutions*, ed. Leonard Krieger (University of Chicago Press, 1967), p. 17. For a judicious assessment of the similarities and differences

between Marxism and the utopian socialists, see Kolakowski, *Main Currents of Marxism*, vol. 1, pp. 218–24. Kolakowsi, like Lichtheim (*Origins of Socialism*, p. 5), is inclined to stress the differences, although he takes much of this back by seeing Marxism as utopian in other crucial respects (see below). Joseph Schumpeter, however, argues that 'utopian socialism differed from "scientific" socialism in degree rather than kind.' Schumpeter, *Capitalism, Socialism, and Democracy* (1976), p. 309. Alvin Gouldner too sees Marx as 'not the first of the scientific socialists but the last of the utopians.' *The Future of Intellectuals and the Rise of the New Class* (New York, Oxford University Press, 1979), p. 37. For an account that shows Marx's indebtedness to the utopians, see Manuel and Manuel, *Utopian Thought in the Western World*, pp. 697–716. The strongest defence of the utopian socialists, as the most creative theorists of socialism, is in Buber, *Paths in Utopia, passim.*

64 Engels, 'Karl Marx' (1878), in *Selected Works*, vol. 2, pp. 164–5.

65 Kolakowski, *Main Currents*, vol. 1, p. 375.

66 Z. Bauman, *Socialism: The Active Utopia* (1976), pp. 137–8.

67 Ibid., p. 105. Cf. Schumpeter: 'Marx fails to turn the socialist possibility into a certainty even if we grant him the breakdown theory in its entirety; if we do not, the failure follows *a fortiori*.' *Capitalism, Socialism, and Democracy*, p. 57. For similar objections to Marx's expectation, see Kolakowski, *Main Currents*, vol. 1, pp. 371–5. Kolakowsi notes (p. 371) that 'Rosa Luxemburg was the first Marxist to point out that Marx never specified the economic conditions that made the downfall of capitalism inevitable.' See also, for similar criticisms, Robert Tucker, *Philosophy and Myth in Karl Marx* (Cambridge University Press, 1961), pp. 150–6; Tom Bottomore, *Sociology and Socialism* (Brighton, Wheatsheaf Books, 1984), pp. 187–90; John Dunn, *Western Political Theory in the Face of the Future* (1979), pp. 98–9; R. N. Berki, *Insight and Vision: The Problem of Communism in Marx's Thought* (1983), pp. 48–9 and *passim.*

68 Buber, *Paths in Utopia*, pp. 10–11.

69 Kolakowski, *Main Currents*, vol. 1, p. 223; see also pp. 180–1.

70 Ernst Bloch prefers to see Marxism as a 'concrete utopianism' in contradistinction to the 'abstract utopianism' of the utopian socialists, and most other utopians. Marxism discovers 'the not yet [*noch nicht*] actual objective real possibilities in the world'. 'Genuine *designations* of the future are lacking . . . because Marx's whole work serves the future, and indeed can only be understood and carried out in the horizon of the future, not indeed as one that is depicted in an abstract utopian way, but as one that takes effect in and out of the past as well as the future.' Quoted in Wayne Hudson, *The Marxist Philosophy of Ernst Bloch* (1982), pp. 56–7. This formulation, similar to Lukacs's notion of 'the immanence of the ultimate objective', still seems to me to take Marxism too much at its own self-understanding.

71 Schumpeter, *Capitalism, Socialism, and Democracy*, p. 308, n.

72 It is this weakness that Buber points to when he says that, for all the incisiveness of its economic and political analysis, Marxism lacks a theory of *social forms*, of the social restructuring that the new society will necessarily entail. It was precisely these social forms that the utopian socialists experimented with, in theory and in practice. He quotes Max Weber's pertinent question: 'What will that "association" look like of which the Communist Manifesto speaks? What germ-cells of that kind of organization has Socialism in particular to offer if it ever gets a real chance to seize power and rule as it wills?' Buber, *Paths in Utopia*, pp. 96, 128. For a suggestive discussion of the consequences of Marxism's failure 'to specify possible futures as closely as possible', see Steven Lukes, 'Marxism and Utopia' (1984), pp. 153–67. For an attempt to fill in some of the gaps, see the essays in Leszek Kolakowski and Stuart Hampshire (eds), *The Socialist Idea* (London, Quartet Books, 1977).

73 Quoted in J. Holloway and S. Piciotto (eds), *State and Capital: A Marxist Debate* (London, Edward Arnold, 1978), p. 27.

74 Lukes, 'Marxism and Utopia', p. 160. Cf. R. N. Berki: 'It is of course true that Marx

never describes communism "in detail", but surely the point is that concepts like "real alienation" and "deprivation" are only rendered intelligible by virtue of a substantive, i.e. another concept which refers to "arrangements" and "lifestyle" where these features are *absent*.' Berki, *Insight and Vision*, p. 2.

75 Cf. Berki: 'Marx's definition of communism in its full plenitude is probably unparalleled in modern radical thought, in its metaphysical depth, in its boldness, in its absolutism. This communism is *more* than religious eschatology in that it seeks to present divine perfection without a transcendental divinity. And this communism is *more* than utopia, for unlike the utopian vision, which conjures up a perfect way of life and perfect happiness to suit human beings *as they exist*, it envisages perfection on both counts: in society as well as in individuals who must be radically, dimensionally *changed* in their nature and outlook to be able to comprehend it and live in it.' Berki, *Insight and Vision*, p. 51. Berki's is the most illuminating treatment of the future communist society as conceived by Marx. For other valuable accounts, see Bertell Ollman, 'Marx's Vision of Communism: A Reconstruction', *Critique*, no. 8 (Summer 1977), pp. 4–41; Tucker, *Philosophy and Myth in Karl Marx*, pp. 150–61, 188–202; Robert Tucker, *The Marxian Revolutionary Idea* (London, Allen & Unwin, 1969), pp. 214–25; Herbert Marcuse, *Reason and Revolution* (Boston, Beacon Press 1960), pp. 273–95; Eugene Kamenka, *The Ethical Foundations of Marxism*, rev. edn (London, Routledge & Kegan Paul, 1972); Shlomo Avineri, *The Social and Political Thought of Karl Marx* (Cambridge University Press, 1968), pp. 202–49; Shlomo Avineri, 'Marx's Vision of Future society and the Problem of Utopianism', *Dissent*, vol. 20 (Summer 1973), pp. 323–7; John Plamenatz, *Karl Marx's Philosophy of Man* (Oxford, Clarendon Press, 1975), pp. 317–472; Gilison, *The Soviet Image of Utopia*, pp. 23–57; Iring Fetscher, 'Concepts of the Communist Society of the Future', in his *Marx and Marxism* (New York, Herder & Herder, 1971), pp. 182–203; Kolakowski, *Main Currents of Marxism*, vol. 1, pp. 132–81, 297–375; J. P. Burke, L. Crocker and L. H. Legters (eds), *Marxism and the Good Society* (1981), especially articles by Richard de George and David McLellan.

76 Engels, 'Socialism: Utopian and Scientific', p. 153.

77 Marx, 'Preface to the Critique of Political Economy' (1859), *Selected Works*, vol. 1, p. 364.

78 Marx, 'Economic and Philosophical Manuscripts' (1844), in Bottomore, *Karl Marx: Early Writings*, p. 128.

79 The passage occurs at the end of vol. 3 of *Capital*. I have taken the translation from T. B. Bottomore and Maximilien Rubel (eds), *Karl Marx: Selected Writings in Sociology and Social Philosophy* (Harmondsworth, Penguin Books, 1963), pp. 259–60.

80 Karl Marx, *Grundrisse*, tr. Martin Nicolaus (Harmondsworth, Penguin Books, 1973), p. 711. Cf. also 'Free time – which is both idle time and time for higher activity – has naturally transformed its possessor into a different subject.' Ibid., p. 712.

81 Karl Marx and Frederick Engels, *The German Ideology* (1846; New York, International Publishers, 1947), p. 22. Ollman says that 'the individual's victory over the division of labour is, without a doubt, the central feature of communist society.' 'Marx's Vision of Communism', p. 22. It means not simply the end of the division between mental and manual labour, but also that between town and country, which Marx says is 'the greatest division of material and mental labour.' *The German Ideology*, pp. 20, 43 ff. The literary utopia which comes closest to a detailed realization of this aspect of Marx's vision is William Morris's *News from Nowhere*.

82 Marx, 'Excerpt-Notes of 1844', in Easton and Guddat (eds), *Writings of the Young Marx on Philosophy and Society*, p. 281.

83 Marx, *Grundrisse*, p. 705. For a discussion of Marx's intent here, and elsewhere in his work, see Herbert Marcuse, 'The Realm of Freedom and the Realm of Necessity: A Reconsideration', *Praxis*, vol. 5, no. 1 (1969), pp. 20–5. Among those who, like Marcuse, are most strongly opposed to a conceptual or empirical separation, in Marx or elsewhere, of the realms of freedom and necessity, see especially Hannah Arendt, *The*

Human Condition (New York, Doubleday Anchor, 1959), pp. 71–153; and Simone Weil, *Oppression and Liberty* (London, Routledge & Kegan Paul, 1958).

84 Marx, *Grundrisse*, p. 706.

85 Marx, *Theories of Surplus Value*; quoted in Lukes, 'Marxism and Utopia', p. 162.

86 Marx, 'Critique of the Gotha Programme' (1875), *Selected Works*, vol. 2, p. 23.

87 Ibid., p. 24.

88 Marx, 'Economic and Philosophical Manuscripts', in Bottomore, *Karl Marx*, p. 167.

89 Ibid., pp. 153–4.

90 Ibid., p. 157.

91 Ibid., pp. 163–4.

92 Ibid., pp. 159–60.

93 Ibid., pp. 161–2. Reflecting on this and similar passages, Robert Tucker argues that 'Marx's conception of ultimate communism is fundamentally aesthetic in character. His utopia is an aesthetic ideal of the future man–nature relationship, which he sees in terms of artistic creation and the appreciation of the beauty of the man-made environment by its creator. The acquisitive and therefore alienated man of history is to be succeeded by the post-historic aesthetic man who will be "rich" in a new way. . . .' *Philosophy and Myth in Karl Marx*, p. 158. For a similarly aesthetic vision of utopia, see Herbert Marcuse, *An Essay on Liberation* (1969).

94 'Economic and Philosophical Manuscripts', p. 155. David McLellan calls this passage 'almost mystical': 'Marx and Engels on the future communist society'; in Burke et al., *Marxism and the Good Society*, p. 115. Berki similarly says of this passage that it contains 'the most audaciously extravagant philosophical claims ever advanced on behalf of what at first glance appears an historical mode of being, a form of society.' *Insight and Vision*, p. 51.

95 Engels, *Anti-Dühring: Herr Eugen Dühring's Revolution in Science* (1878; Moscow, Foreign Lanuages Publishing House, 1959). It was on chapters of this book that Engels drew for his pamphlet *Socialism: Utopian and Scientific*, and so diffused even more widely the idea, expounded in the *Anti-Dühring*, that in socialist society 'the government of persons is replaced by the administration of things' and the state 'withers away' (p. 387). Engels's decision to publish Marx's 'Critique of the Gotha Programme', hitherto only circulated privately in manuscript, was also a response to the need to clarify the Marxist position on the future society. It appeared for the first time in the journal *Neue Zeit* for 1891.

96 August Bebel, *Woman Under Socialism* (1883; reprint of 1904 American edn, New York, Schoken Books, 1971). There is an abridged version under the title *Society of the Future* (Moscow, Progress Publishers, 1971).

97 Marx, 'The Civil War in France', *Selected Works*, vol. 1, p. 522.

98 For Lenin's writings on the soviets, including the *State and Revolution* and *Can the Bolsheviks Maintain State Power?* see V. I. Lenin, *Selected Works in Three Volumes* (Moscow, Foreign Languages Publishing House, n.d.), vol. 2, pp. 305 ff. For a good discussion see Marcel Liebman, *Leninism Under Lenin* (London, Merlin Press, 1980), pp. 190 ff. See also Buber, *Paths in Utopia*, pp. 106 ff.

99 Karl Marx and Friedrich Engels, *The German Ideology* (Moscow, Progress Publishers, 1964), p. 432.

100 Leon Trotsky, *Literature and Revolution* (1924; Ann Arbor, University of Michigan Press, 1960), pp. 9, 14.

101 Ibid., pp. 252–6.

102 Leszek Kolakowski, 'The Concept of the Left', in his *Toward a Marxist Humanism* (1969), pp. 70–1. Cf. Perry Anderson: 'In general, the historical capacity to project a future qualitatively beyond the confines of the present has typically involved overshooting the limits of the realizable, in transforming the horizons of the conceivable – a condition in turn of other and later liberations. This is true of themes in Marx or Lenin as well. In that sense, all creative socialist thought is likely to possess a utopian

dimension.' Anderson, *Arguments Within English Marxism* (London, New Left Books, 1980), p. 175, n. 34. Anderson here, despite being critical on the whole of William Morris's socialism, endorses E. P. Thompson's view that the case of Morris raises 'the whole problem of the subordination of the imaginative utopian faculties within the later Marxist tradition: its lack of a moral self-consciousness or even a vocabulary of desire, its inability to project any images of the future, or even its tendency to fall back in lieu of these upon the Utilitarian's earthly paradise – the maximization of economic growth.' E. P. Thompson, *William Morris: Romantic to Revolutionary* (1977), p. 792. For the importance of Morris in the revival of utopianism in the 1960s and 1970s, see below, pp. 402 ff.

103 For this sub-genre of utopia, see I. F. Clarke, *Voices Prophesying War 1763–1984* (1966).

104 Quoted in Clarke, *The Pattern of Expectation 1644–2001*, p. 139. Clarke gives a good general account of the different varieties of utopia in this period: ibid., pp. 90 ff. For other writings of the time concerned with the future, see Asa Briggs, 'The Nineteenth Century Faces the Future', in Asa Briggs (ed.), *The Nineteenth Century: The Contradictions of Progress* (London, Thames & Hudson, 1970), pp. 337–44.

105 On Wilde's Socialist utopia, see K. Kumar, *Utopia on the Map of the World* (1984 Boole Lecture; University of Cork Pamphlet Publications, 1985).

106 Quoted in Stephen Yeo, 'A New Life: The Religion of Socialism in Britain, 1883–1896', *History Workshop*, no. 4 (Autumn 1977), p. 6. Yeo's article gives a splendid account of the fervent religious climate prevailing among English socialists in the 1880s and 1890s.

107 Engels, 'Introduction' (1895) to Marx, 'The Class Struggles in France 1848–1850', *Selected Works*, vol. 1, pp. 137–8.

108 Quoted in Yeo, 'A New Life', p. 6. 'It is essential,' William Morris wrote, 'that the ideal of the new society should always be kept before the eyes of the working classes, lest the *continuity* of the demands of the people should be broken, or lest they should be misdirected.' Quoted in Thompson, *William Morris*, p. 616.

109 Winwood Reade, *The Martyrdoms of Man* (1872; London, Watts & Co., 1948), p. 407. This passage strikingly anticipates Keynes's famous 'utopian' statement of the 1930s, that 'the economic problem' can and will be solved – but not yet. 'For at least another hundred years we must pretend to ourselves and to everyone that fair is foul and foul is fair; for foul is useful and fair is not. Avarice and usury and precaution must be our gods for a little longer still. For only they can lead us out of the tunnel of economic necessity into daylight.' J. M. Keynes, 'Economic Possibilities for Our Grandchildren' (1930), in *The Collected Writings of John Maynard Keynes*, vol. 9: *Essays in Persuasion* (London, Macmillan, 1972), p. 331.

110 *The Martyrdom of Man*, pp. 413–14. It was this book, and this passage, that Beatrice Webb chose to illustrate the utopian belief in science of the late Victorian age. See *My Apprenticeship* (1926; Cambridge University Press, 1979), pp. 131–2.

111 Passmore, *The Perfectibility of Man*, p. 262.

Chapter 3 Utopia in Nineteenth-Century America

1 Quoted in J. Martin Evans, *America: The View From Europe* (New York, W. W. Norton, 1979), pp. 16–17. For a nineteenth-century expression, cf. Victor Considérant: 'We are Europeans who believe that Europe is in a state of decline, we who can no longer endure its corruption, anarchy, and despotism – and who have faith in America for the regeneration of the world, and the political and social salvation of entire humanity.' Quoted in Albert Fein, 'Fourierism in Nineteenth-Century America: A Social and Environmental Perspective', in Mathé Allain (ed.), *France and North America: Utopia and Utopians* (1978), p. 135.

2 For this tradition, see Loren Baritz, 'The Idea of the West', *American Historical Review*, vol. 66, no. 3 (1961), pp. 618–40. 'Already long before Columbus, the transfer of Eden

and the sacred mountain from Mesopotamia to America was underway; already the Renaissance utopia loomed in the imagination. . . . With the discovery of America, Edenic expectations entered the mainstream of history, assured of a prophetic fulfilment in the West. Without this westward-looking promise, the masses of Europe might never have stirred, the industrial revolution never begun, the social revolutions never launched.' Charles L. Sanford, *The Quest for Paradise: Europe and the American Moral Imagination* (1961), p. 38.

3 Quoted in Sanford, *The Quest for Paradise*, p. 57. For conceptions of the New World at the time of Columbus's voyages, see Edmundo O'Gorman, *The Invention of America* (Bloomington, Indiana University Press, 1961); Howard Mumford Jones, *O Strange New World* (1965), pp. 1–34; Hugh Honour, *The New Golden Land: European Images of America from the Discoveries to the Present Time* (London, Allen Lane, 1975); Sigmund Skard, *The American Myth and the European Mind* (Philadelphia, University of Pennsylvania Press, 1961).

4 For the relation between the Renaissance utopia – including More's – and that of the New World, see Sanford, *The Quest for Paradise*, pp. 56–73. On the view that the discovery of America influenced More and other utopian writers, see, e.g., Lewis Mumford: 'The Utopia of Sir Thomas More, and those of later men of the Renascence, arose . . . from the contrast between the possibilities that lay open beyond the seas [since the discovery of America] and the dismal conditions that attended the breakdown of the town economy of the Middle Ages.' Mumford, *The Story of Utopias* (1922), p. 114. And cf. A. L. Rowse: '*Utopia* is the first, and a most distinguished, reflection of the New World in the literature of the old.' Rowse, *The Elizabethans and America* (London, Macmillan, 1959), p. 188. See also Evans, *America*, pp. 2–12, for the view that More's *Utopia* was heavily indebted to the accounts of Columbus's and Vespucci's voyages.

5 Ronald Reagan, Presidential campaign speech, 1980; reported the *New York Times*, 13 June 1980.

6 Roderick Nash, *Wilderness and the American Mind* (1982), p. 40. In this account I have relied largely on chs 1–4 of Nash's book. See also G. H. Williams, *Wilderness and Paradise in Christian Thought* (1962), ch. 5: 'The Enclosed Garden in the Wilderness of the New World', pp. 98–131; Jones, *O Strange New World*, pp. 35–71; H. Richard Niebuhr, *The Kingdom of God in America* (New York, Harper, 1937); Leo Marx, *The Machine in the Garden: Technology and the Pastoral Ideal in America* (1967), pp. 34–72; Ellman Crasnow and Philip Haffenden, 'New Founde Land', in Malcolm Bradbury and Howard Temperley (eds), *Introduction to American Studies* (London, Longman, 1981), pp. 23–44.

7 Marx, *The Machine in the Garden*, p. 141; and, generally, pp. 73–144.

8 Henry Nash Smith, *Virgin Land: The American West as Symbol and Myth* (1970), p. 123. Smith's book is a superb study of the garden image, the 'agrarian utopia', as the dominating motif of the westward expansion. For an earlier account that is as much an expression of the frontier ideology as a study of it, see Frederick Jackson Turner, *The Frontier in American History* (1920; New York, Holt, Rinehart & Winston, 1962).

9 Mircea Eliade, 'Paradise and Utopia', in Frank E. Manuel (ed.), *Utopias and Utopian Thought* (1973), p. 264. See also Sanford, *The Quest for Paradise*, pp. 39–40, 52–5; Williams, *Wilderness and Paradise in Christian Thought*, pp. 65 ff.; Niebuhr, *The Kingdom of God in America*, pp. 88 ff.; Ernest Lee Tuveson, *Redeemer Nation: The Idea of America's Millennial Role* (1968).

10 The Civil War was less easy to encompass in these terms, but it could be, and was, interpreted as a trial and purgation, akin to the struggle with the wilderness (internal and external).

11 The literature on the American Dream is voluminous. There is a good bibliography in Robert H. Fossum and John K. Roth, *The American Dream* (British Association for American Studies, Pamphlet Series no. 6, 1981).

12 David Lodge, 'Utopia and Criticism', *Encounter*, vol. 32 (April 1969), p. 74. See also R. W. B. Lewis, *The American Adam: Innocence, Tragedy and Tradition in the Nineteenth Century* (University of Chicago Press, 1955).

13 David Martin, *A General Theory of Secularization* (New York, Harper & Row, 1978), p. 62.

14 Quoted in Peter Marshall and Ian Walker, 'The First New Nation', in Bradbury and Temperley (eds), *Introduction to American Studies*, p. 46.

15 J. Hector St John de Crèvecoeur, *Letters from an American Farmer* (1782, England; 1783, USA; New York, E. P. Dutton, 1957), pp. 38–40.

16 Henry Steele Commager, *The Empire of Reason: How Europe Imagined and America Realized the Enlightenment* (New York, Anchor Books, 1978), p. xi.

17 Marx, *The Machine in the Garden*, pp. 197 ff. See also John F. Kasson, *Civilizing the Machine: Technology and Republican Values in America, 1776–1900* (1977), pp. 41 ff; Arthur A. Ekirch, Jr, *The Idea of Progress in America, 1815–1860* (New York, Columbia University Press, 1944).

18 Alexis de Tocqueville, *Democracy in America*, ed. J. P. Mayer (New York, Anchor Books, 1969), p. 507. For a stimulating investigation of this feature of American culture, see Michael Kammen, *A Season of Youth: The American Revolution and the Historical Imagination* (New York, Oxford University Press, 1980).

19 Quoted in C. Vann Woodward, 'Playing Hookey', *New York Review of Books* (20 December 1979), p. 16. On the American 'cult of newness', see Sanford, *The Quest for Paradise*, pp. 94–113.

20 Ralph Waldo Emerson, *English Traits* (1856; Cambridge, Mass., Belknap Press, 1966), p. 203; Ralph Waldo Emerson, 'The Young American' (1844), in his *Nature, Addresses, and Lectures*, ed. Robert E. Spiller and Alfred R. Ferguson (Cambridge, Mass., Belknap Press, 1979), p. 230.

21 David M. Potter, *People of Plenty: Economic Abundance and the American Character* (University of Chicago Press, 1954).

22 This passage strongly recalls Crèvecoeur's famous paean to the land: 'What should we American farmers be without the distinct possession of the soil? It feeds us, it clothes us, from it we even draw a great exuberancy. . . . This formerly rude soil has been converted by my father into a pleasant farm, and in return it has established all our rights; on it is founded our rank, our freedom, our power as citizens, our importance as inhabitants. . . .' Crèvecoeur, *Letters from an American Farmer*, pp. 20–1.

23 All quotations are from Emerson's 'The Young American', pp. 222–44. There are interesting discussions of this text in Marx, *The Machine in the Garden*, pp. 229 ff., and Kasson, *Civilizing the Machine*, pp. 109 ff.

24 Although curiously in the twentieth century there have been several forceful portraits of America as *anti-utopia*: e.g., Sinclair Lewis, *It Can't Happen Here* (1935); Kurt Vonnegut, *Player Piano* (1952); David Karp, *One* (1953).

25 Robert Nozick, *Anarchy, State and Utopia* (1974), pp. 311–12. This distinction between utopia and meta-utopia seems to me more useful than Arthur Bestor's attempt to distinguish between communitarianism and utopianism, understood as a purely literary form: 'It is necessary . . . to distinguish between communitarianism, or the impulse which constructed these hundred model communities [in nineteenth-century America], and utopianism, or the impulse to picture in literary form the characteristics of an ideal but imaginary society. The distinction is more than verbal. A piece of utopian writing pictures a social order superior to the present, and it does so, of course, in the hope of inspiring men to alter their institutions accordingly. But a utopian work (unless it happens also to be a communitarian one) does *not* suggest that the proper way of going about such a reform is to construct a small-scale model of the desired society. Edward Bellamy's *Looking Backward*, for example, was a utopian novel, but definitely *not* a piece of communitarian propaganda, because the social transformation that Bellamy was talking about could not possibly be inaugurated by a small scale experiment; it

could come about only through a great collective effort by all citizens of the state.' Arthur E. Bestor, Jr, 'Patent-Office Models of the Good Society: Some Relationships between Social Reform and Westward Expansion', *American Historical Review*, vol. 58, no. 3 (1953), pp. 505–6 (Bestor's emphases).

26 Though it should perhaps be pointed out that the watchword of *Walden* is *simplicity* rather than *solitude*. See especially the famous declaration of intent in ch. 2: 'I went to the woods because I wished to live deliberately, to front only the essential facts of life . . .', which includes the invocation to 'simplicity, simplicity, simplicity!'

27 Friedrich Engels, 'Description of Communist Colonies Founded in Recent Times' (1845); quoted in Lewis S. Feuer, 'The Influence of the American Communist Colonies on Engels and Marx', *Western Political Quarterly*, vol. 19, no. 3 (1966), pp. 459, 461. Feuer shows how Marx and Engels later turned against the communitarian movement in both Europe and America. But, he comments: 'The dream of decentralized communist societies on the model of the American Utopias has always remained alive as a recessive theme in the socialist unconscious. Allow Marx, Engels, Lenin, or Trotsky to speculate as to their true goal, and despite their authoritarian drives, they will fall back into a vision of society as a collection of Brook Farms.' Ibid., pp. 471–2.

28 On Owen's addresses to Congress, see George B. Lockwood, *The New Harmony Movement* (New York, Appleton, 1905), pp. 69–72; Arthur Eugene Bestor, Jr, *Backwoods Utopias: The Secretarian and Owenite Phases of Communitarian Socialism in America, 1663–1829* (1950), pp. 108–12. Bestor's book gives the fullest account of the Owenite communities in America. See also J. F. C. Harrison, *Robert Owen and the Owenites in Britain and America: The Quest for the New Moral World* (1969), pp. 163–92.

29 Quoted in Feuer, 'The Influence of the American Communist Colonies on Engels and Marx', p. 471. On the Fourierist movement in America see T. Seymour Basset, 'The Secular Utopian Socialists', in D. D. Egbert and S. Persons (eds), *Socialism and American Life* (1952), vol. 1, pp. 153–204; Arthur E. Bestor, Jr, 'Albert Brisbane – Propagandist for Socialism in the 1840s', *New York History*, vol. 28 (April 1947), pp. 128–58; Albert Fein, 'Fourierism in Nineteenth-Century America' (see n. 1).

30 Quoted in Bestor, *Backwoods Utopias*, p. 6. The literature on the American communities, as with that on the utopian socialists from whom they partly derive, is vast. In addition to the works mentioned in ns 28 and 29, I have drawn largely on the following: John Humphrey Noyes, *History of American Socialisms* (Philadelphia, J. B. Lippincott, 1870); Charles Nordhoff, *The Communistic Societies of the United States* (1875; reprinted New York, Dover Publications, 1966); William Alfred Hinds, *American Communities* (1878; revised and enlarged, 1902 and 1908; reprint of first edition, New York, Corinth Books, 1961); Mark Holloway, *Heavens on Earth: Utopian Communities in America 1680–1880* (1966); Robert S. Fogarty (ed.), *American Utopianism* (1972); Robert S. Fogarty, *Dictionary of American Communal and Utopian History* (1980); Everett Webber, *Escape to Utopia: The Communal Movement in America* (1959); Rosabeth Moss Kanter, *Commitment and Community: Communes and Utopias in Sociological Perspective* (1972); Dolores Hayden, *Seven American Utopias. The Architecture of Communitarian Socialism, 1790–1975* (1976); John M. Whitworth, *God's Blueprints: A Sociological Study of Three Utopian Sects* (1975); William M. Klephart, *Extraordinary Groups*, 2nd edn (New York, St Martin's Press, 1982); Maren Lockwood, 'The Experimental Utopia in America', in Manuel, *Utopias and Utopian Thought*, pp. 183–200; Arthur Bestor, 'The Search for Utopia', in John J. Murray (ed.), *The Heritage of the Middle West* (Norman University of Oklahoma Press, 1959), pp. 97–120; John L. Thomas, 'Romantic Reform in America, 1815–1865', *American Quarterly*, vol. 18 (Winter 1965), pp. 656–81; Bestor, 'Patent-Office Models of the Good Society' (see n. 25). On individual communities, see Edward Deming Andrews, *The People Called Shakers* (New York, Dover Publications, 1963); Maren Lockwood Carden, *Oneida: Utopian Community to Modern Corporation* (New York, Harper Torchbooks, 1971).

31 Bestor, *Backwoods Utopia*, p. 7. For a detailed characterization of the sociology and theology of the American sects, see Whitworth, *God's Blueprints*, pp. 210–41.

32 E.g. Bestor: 'I shall describe as communitarian all those colonies that were established for the definite purpose of creating a richer, nobler, more equitable social life by bringing men and women together to share their lives in closely knit communities. The term is broad enough to include those societies which adopted community of goods as well as those which did not. Indeed, the communitarian ideal – the ideal of a shared community life – was actually more important than the doctrine of community of goods, even in those colonies that were both communistic and communitarian.' Bestor, 'The Search for Utopia', pp. 102–3.

33 Nordhoff, *Communistic Societies*, pp. 40–3, 109–10. And cf. his verdict on the Shakers: 'In practical life they are industrious, peaceful, honest, highly ingenious, patient of toil and extraordinarily cleanly.' Ibid., p. 118. Oneida does not fare much better: '. . . it was a common-place company', exhibiting a narrow complacency which Nordhoff attributed to the fact that the members are 'well-fed and sufficiently amused, and not overworked, and have no future to fear. The greater passions are not stirred in such a life.' Ibid., p. 288. Generally in the communities 'you look in vain for highly educated, refined, cultivated, or elegant men or women. They profess no exalted views of humanity or destiny; they are not enthusiasts; they do not speak much of the beautiful with a big B. They are utilitarians.' Ibid., p. 399. Since Nordhoff, unlike Noyes, was interested in the communities not as models of utopia but as possible solutions to the 'labor problem', these prosaic qualities were if anything likely to commend the communities in his eyes.

34 Bestor, *Backwoods Utopia*, p. 38. This is contrasted with the situation in Europe, where 'there was a definite hiatus' caused by the intervention of Enlightenment rationalism between the religious radicalism of the seventeenth century and the secular socialism of the nineteenth. But Feuer argues that the case in Europe was not so very different: see 'The Influence of the American Communist Colonies . . .', esp. p. 472, n. 51.

35 Quoted in Holloway, *Heavens on Earth*, pp. 78–9. On Shaker influence, and relations with 'the world', see Andrews, *The People Called Shakers*, pp. 204–23; Whitworth, *God's Blueprints*, pp. 44–7, 79–85; Bestor, *Backwoods Utopias*, pp. 40–53.

36 Noyes, *American Socialisms*, pp. 25–6.

37 Ibid., pp. 615–16.

38 On these practices at Oneida, see Carden, *Oneida*, pp. 49–65; Whitworth, *God's Blueprints*, pp. 121–31. Nordhoff was plainly shocked by them: see, e.g. *Communistic Societies*, pp. 271–2, 293.

39 See Carden, *Oneida*, pp. 65–77, which describes a range of techniques and practices that anticipates many of the features of *Walden Two*. Nordhoff was struck by 'the amount of ingenuity, inventive skill, and business talent' developed at Oneida. There was a general air of restless innovation. 'They seemed to me to have an almost fanatical horror of forms. Thus they change their avocations frequently; they remove from Oneida to Willow Place, or to Wallingford, on slight excuses; they change the order of their evening meetings and amusements with much care; and have changed even their meal hours.' Nordhoff, *Communistic Societies*, pp. 285–6. The importance of constant change was indeed an item of doctrine at Oneida.'It is a point of belief with us that when one keeps constantly in a rut, he is especially exposed to attacks of evil. The devil knows just where to find him! But inspiration will continually lead us into new channels by which we shall dodge the adversary,' *Oneida Circular* (25 April 1864); quoted in Klephart, *Extraordinary Groups*, p. 103.

40 Noyes quotes himself in *American Socialisms*, p. 631. See also Nordhoff, *Communistic Societies*, pp. 271, 275; Hinds, *American Communities*, pp. 125–6.

41 Whitworth, *God's Blueprints*, p. 119. Whitworth gives the best account of Noyes's theology, pp. 89–119. See also Carden, *Oneida*, pp. 11–17. Some relevant documents are gathered together in Noyes, *American Socialisms*, pp. 617–37.

42 Noyes, *American Socialisms*, pp. 142–3; see also pp. 624–33, for the quotations in this paragraph. And see Whitworth, *God's Blueprints*, pp. 95–6; Carden, *Oneida*, pp. 49–50. For Oneida's attitude to the Shakers, see also Hinds, *American Communities*, pp. 127–8.

43 Hinds, *American Communities*, p. 138. Hinds, writing in 1878, gives a picture of Oneida that markedly brings out its free-thinking character, its lack of formalism and ritual, and its appreciation of science and the arts; see esp. pp. 117–40.

44 For these developments at Oneida in the 1860s and 1870s, see Whitworth, *God's Blueprints*, pp. 135–41; Carden, *Oneida*, pp. 89–194. Carden also gives a detailed account of Oneida's later history as Oneida Ltd on pp. 113 ff.

45 Noyes, *American Socialisms*, pp. 669–70. Noyes repeats here almost exactly a passage which first appears on pp. 191–2. Bestor qualifies Noyes's claim in several respects, but also concludes: 'When Americans listened to Robert Owen or to the disciples of Charles Fourier, they reshaped the new doctrines to conform to a communitarian ideal that the religious communities had already made familiar. In effect, what these men and women thought they discovered in Owenism or Fourierism was a way of achieving the prosperity, the security, and the peace of a Shaker village without subjecting themselves to the celibacy and the narrow social conformity exacted by Shaker theology.' Bestor, *Backwoods Utopias*, p. 59. It is interesting, in this connection, to note that what most offended Owen's American critics was not his communism but what they took to be his irreligion: see *Backwoods Utopias*, pp. 122–8.

46 With the dissolution of the New Lebanon community – the original foundation and acknowledged home of the Shaker ministry – in 1947, the Shaker experiment was virtually over. By 1970 only two societies remained: Canterbury, New Hampshire, and Sabbathday Lake, Maine, with a combined population of 15 old sisters. A reporter for *Life* said of Sabbathday Lake in 1968: 'Today the television antennas sprout from their roofs and every sister has seen the movie *The Sound of Music* at least once.' See Whitworth, *God's Blueprints*, p. 242; Andrews, *The People Called Shakers*, pp. 224–9.

47 Nordhoff, who visited Corning in 1875, remarked on 'the dreary poverty of the life' there, and judged it to be 'the least prosperous of all the communities I have visited'. *Communistic Societies*, pp. 335, 339.

48 For the later phases of the communitarian movement, see William Hinds, *American Communities and Cooperative Colonies*, 2nd rev. edn (Chicago, Charles H. Kerr, 1908); R. S. Fogarty, 'American Communes, 1865–1914', *Journal of American Studies*, vol. 9, no. 2 (1975), pp. 145–62; Otohiko Okugawa, 'Annotated List of Communal and Utopian Societies, 1787–1919'; Appendix A in Fogarty, *Dictionary of American Communal and Utopian History*, pp. 173–233. For the twentieth-century movement, see Robert Hine, *California's Utopian Colonies* (New Haven, Yale University Press, 1966); Laurence Veysey, *The Communal Experience: Anarchist and Mystical Communities in Twentieth Century America* (1978); Rosabeth Moss Kanter (ed.), *Communes: Creating and Managing The Collective Life* (1973).

49 Bestor, 'The Search for Utopia', p. 114.

50 On Owenite and Fourierist influences in educational and other reform movements, see Noyes, *American Socialisms*, pp. 22–4; Holloway, *Heavens on Earth*, pp. 112–16; Bestor, *Backwoods Utopias*, pp. 133–59, 202–27; Lockwood, *The New Harmony Movement, passim*, esp. pp. 314–77; Fein, 'Fourierism in Nineteenth-Century America'. On the importance of the communities in challenging the dominant individualistic and *laissez-faire* ideology, see Bestor, 'The Search for Utopia', pp. 116–20.

51 *Report on Fabian Policy*, Fabian Tract 70 (London, 1896), p. 8. Cf. also H. J. Muller's belief in 'the futility of the utopian communities in America in the nineteenth century, the quixotic effort to realize ideals of perfection in islands within a very different society'. 'A Note on Utopia' (1970), p. 371. This verdict is echoed by George Kateb, *Utopia and Its Enemies* (New York, Schocken Books, 1972), pp. 12–13. A quite different assessment of the communal experiments is given by Martin Buber, *Paths in Utopia* (1958), pp. 58 ff.

52 Nordhoff, *Communistic Societies*, pp. 417–18; and generally, pp. 385–418. A similar conclusion is reached by Holloway, *Heavens on Earth*, pp. 222–5.

53 Quoted in Fogarty, *Dictionary of American Communal and Utopian History*, p. xiv.

54 Noyes, *American Socialisms*, pp. 138–9. Noyes's own view qualifies this somewhat: '. . . the conclusion toward which our facts and reflections point is, first, that religion, not as a mere doctrine, but as an *afflatus* having in itself a tendency to make many into one, is the first essential of successful Communism; and, secondly, that the *afflatus* must be strong enough to decompose the old family unit and make Communism the home-center.' To which he later adds: 'the *afflatus* must also be strong enough to prevail over personal leadership in its mediums, and be able, when one leader dies, to find and use another.' Ibid., pp. 148, 153. Nordhoff's view is similarly qualified: 'It is asserted by some writers who theorize about communism that a commune cannot exist long without some fanatical religious thought as its cementing force; while others assert with equal positiveness that it is possible to maintain a commune in which the members shall have diverse and diverging beliefs in religious matters. It seems to me that both these theories are wrong; but that it is true that a commune, to exist harmoniously, must be composed of persons who are of one mind upon some question which to them shall appear so important as to take the place of a religion, if it is not essentially religious; though it need not be fanatically held.' He points out that, though the Icarians reject Christianity, 'they have adopted the communistic idea as their religion.' *Communistic Societies*, p. 387. Cf. also Buber: '. . . it is precisely where a Settlement comes into being as the expression of real religious exaltation, and not merely as a precarious substitute for religion, and where it views its existence as the beginning of God's kingdom – that it usually proves its power of endurance.' *Paths in Utopia*, p. 73. Kanter argues that, while religion is the most effective bond, other forms of 'commitment mechanisms' can bring about communal success: *Commitment and Community*, pp. 136–7.

55 There can of course be successful secular utopian communities – the Israeli *kibbutzim* are good examples, as are the Walden communities such as Twin Oaks. But these all *started* as secular communes. The problem seems acute for communities, like Oneida, which have religious origins and evolve in a secular direction.

56 Carden, *Oneida*, p. 11.

57 I discuss this further in the chapter on Bellamy, below, pp. 138 ff.

58 See n. 48 above.

59 Quoted in Bestor, 'The Search for Utopia', p. 116 (Brisbane's emphasis). See also the more extended statement in the same vein by Brisbane, quoted in Bestor, 'Patent-Office Models of the Good Society', p. 506.

60 Bestor, *Backwoods Utopia*, p. 76. This points to one cause of the decline of utopian communitarianism in the second half of the nineteenth century. Elsewhere Bestor has also considered more general factors, principally the loss of the crucial condition of social 'openness' in American society. Communitarianism declined 'not because the so-called free land was exhausted nor because the frontier line had disappeared from maps of population density but simply because social patterns had become so well defined over the whole area of the United States that the possibility no longer existed of affecting the character of the social order merely by planting the seeds of new institutions in the wilderness.' 'Patent-Office Models of the Good Society', p. 525. For other accounts of the causes of decline, see Kanter, *Commitment and Community*, pp. 139–61; Holloway, *Heavens on Earth*, pp. 212–21; Lockwood, 'The Experimental Community in America', pp. 192–8.

61 Nordhoff, *Communistic Societies*, p. 418. By 1869 Horace Greeley's original Fourierist enthusiasm also seems to have modulated into a species of mild moral reformism: 'My own conviction is strong that Co-operation is the true goal of our industrial program, the application of Republican principles to Labor, and the appointed means of reducing the laboring classes from dependence, prodigality and need and establishing it on the basis of forecast, calculation, sobriety, and thrift, conducive at once to its material

culture and moral education.' Quoted in Fogarty, 'American Communes 1865–1914', p. 149.

62 David Riesman, 'Some Observations on Community Plans and Utopia' (1964), pp. 72–3.

63 Thomas C. Cochran and William Miller, *The Age of Enterprise: A Social History of Industrial America*, rev. edn (New York, Harper Torchbooks, 1961), p. 129.

64 Quoted in Alan Trachtenberg, *The Incorporation of America: Culture and Society in the Gilded Age* (New York, Hill & Wang, 1982), p. 70.

65 Quoted in Cochran and Miller, *The Age of Enterprise*, p. 143. For labour and capital in this period, see Trachtenberg, *The Incorporation of America*, pp. 70–100; Eric Foner, *Free Soil, Free Labor, Free Men: The Ideology of the Republican Party Before the Civil War* (New York, Oxford University Press, 1970); David Montgomery, *Beyond Equality: Labor and the Radical Republicans 1862–1872* (New York, Vintage Books, 1967); Herbert G. Gutman, *Work, Culture and Society in Industrializing America* (New York, Vintage Books, 1977).

66 F. Scott Fitzgerald, *The Great Gatsby* (Harmondworth, Penguin Books, 1950), p. 171.

Chapter 4 Anti-Utopia, Shadow of Utopia

1 Quoted in J. W. Mackail, *The Life of William Morris* (2 vols) (London, Longmans, Green, 1899), vol. 2, p. 134.

2 I use 'anti-utopia' as a generic term to include what is sometimes called the 'dystopia' or – more rarely – the 'cacotopia'. Jeremy Bentham seems to have invented 'cacotopia' – an evil place – and it was later joined to 'dystopia' by John Stuart Mill. As MP for Westminster, Mill in a speech in the House of Commons in 1868 mocked his opponents: 'It is, perhaps, too complimentary to call them Utopians, they ought rather to be called dys-topians, or caco-topians. What is commonly called Utopian is something too good to be practicable; but what they appear to favour is too bad to be practicable.' *Hansard Commons*, 12 March/1517/1 (1868).

3 Quoted in J. Passmore, *The Perfectibility of Man* (1972), p. 59.

4 G. W. F. Hegel, *The Philosophy of History* (1830), tr. J. Sibree (New York, Dover, 1956), p. 26. For Augustinian and Pelagian strands in the utopian tradition, see Anthony Burgess, *1985* (Boston, Little, Brown, 1978), pp. 52–8. On their general meaning and influence, see Passmore, *The Perfectibility of Man*, pp. 68–115.

5 For the quotations from Burke, see Robert A. Smith (ed.), *Edmund Burke on Revolution* (New York, Harper Torchbooks, 1968), pp. xiii, 98. On conservative social theory, see Karl Mannheim, 'Conservative Thought', in his *Essays on Sociology and Social Psychology* (London, Routledge & Kegan Paul, 1953), pp. 74–164. See also Robert A. Nisbet, *Tradition and Revolt* (New York, Vintage Books, 1970), pp. 73–91. For a powerful contemporary restatement of the conservative case against rationalism, see Michael Oakeshott, *Rationalism in Politics, and Other Essays* (London, Methuen, 1967).

6 Essay on 'Bacon', in Thomas Babington Macaulay, *Critical and Historical Essays* (2 vols) (London, Dent, Everyman edition, 1907), vol. 2, pp. 373–4. And cf. George Kateb: 'When all is said and done, the most impressive argument against utopianism, on the ground of what is needed to establish a utopian society, is the real world as it is.' *Utopia and Its Enemies* (1972), p. 67.

7 See especially the dialogue between the Controller and the Savage in chs 16–17 of *Brave New World* (and see below, pp. 261–4). The status of *The Prince* as anti-utopia is reinforced by the strong possibility that it was intended as satire. That at any rate was the interpretation given by Machiavelli himself, though admittedly only retrospectively, in a letter to a friend: 'I now come to the last branch of my charge: that I teach princes villainy, and how to enslave. If any man will read over my book . . . with impartiality and ordinary charity, he will easily perceive that it is not my intention to recommend that government or those men there described to the world, much less to teach men how to

trample upon good men, and all that is sacred and venerable upon earth, laws, religion, honesty, and what not. If I have been a little too punctual in describing these monsters in all their lineaments and colours, I hope mankind will know them, the better to avoid them, my treatise being both a *satire* against them, and a true character of them. . . .' The letter is quoted as the epigraph to James Burnham, *The Managerial Revolution: What is Happening in the World* (New York, John Day, 1941).

8 William James, 'The Dilemma of Determinism' (1884), in his *The Will to Believe, and Other Essays in Popular Philosophy* (New York, Dover, 1956), pp. 167–8. And see the discussion of this objection to utopianism in Kateb, *Utopia and Its Enemies*, pp. 126–38. For the critique of utilitarian psychology in the context of utopian strivings, see Hannah Arendt, *The Human Condition* (New York, Doubleday, 1959), and Simone Weil, *Oppression and Liberty* (London, Routledge & Kegan Paul, 1958).

9 Aldous Huxley, letter to Julian Huxley, 23 November 1942, in Grover Smith (ed.), *Letters of Aldous Huxley* (London, Chatto & Windus, 1969), p. 483.

10 D. H. Lawrence, 'Insouciance' (1928), in his *Selected Essays* (Harmondsworth, Penguin Books, 1950), p. 105.

11 Octavio Paz, 'Development and Other Mirages', in *The Other Mexico*, tr. Lysander Kemp (New York, Grove Press, 1972), p. 68.

12 Robert C. Elliott, *The Shape of Utopia* (University of Chicago Press, 1970), pp. 19, 24.

13 It is interesting to note that Plato too pits utopia against anti-utopia. In the *Timaeus* and the *Critias* he presents, as an allegedly real historical contrast, the ideal city of Athens as it used to be long ago, and the wicked city of Atlantis, later submerged. Athens is a prosperous city-state, living the life of the 'golden mean'; Atlantis a far-flung empire based on conquest, and wallowing in luxury. Plato presents these two civilizations as the two great antagonists of the ancient world.

But the myth of Atlantis, in its later development, is itself ambivalent. It also came to be identified with its happy, prosperous and virtuous state of near-perfection before its decline and fall through pride and arrogance. During the Middle Ages and beyond it became a symbol of a perfect people and a happy land (cf. Bacon's 'New Atlantis'). See Nell Eurich, *Science in Utopia* (1967), pp. 48–9.

14 A section of *Mundus Alter et Idem* is included in Henry Morley (ed.), *Ideal Commonwealths* (1885).

15 Northrop Frye, 'Varieties of Literary Utopias', in Frank E. Manuel (ed.), *Utopias and Utopian Thought* (London, Souvenir Press, 1973), p. 29.

16 See Elaine Hoffman Baruch, 'Dystopia Now', *Alternative Futures*, vol. 2, no. 3 (Summer 1979), pp. 55–67.

17 On the utopian side of Swift, and of *Gulliver's Travels*, see Eliott, *The Shape of Utopia*, pp. 50–67. On *animal rationale* and *rationis capax*, see Swift's letter to Alexander Pope, 29 September 1725, in *Gulliver's Travels, and Other Writings*, ed. Richard Quintana (New York, Random House, 1958), pp. 514–15.

18 Butler was pained to find that many reviewers did not see this, although it has to be said – and Butler himself admitted as much – that he is highly equivocal in his presentation here, whatever his later views. See the prefaces to the second and revised editions, in Samuel Butler, *Erewhon and Erewhon Revisited* (London, Dent, Everyman edition, 1962), pp. 3–8. For a discussion of this point, see Herbert L. Sussman, *Victorians and the Machine: The Literary Response to Technology* (1968) pp. 135–61.

19 For these passages, see Butler, *Erewhon and Erewhon Revisited*, pp. 146–59.

20 See Carlyle, 'Signs of the Times' (1829), in *Thomas Carlyle: Selected Writings* (Harmondsworth, Penguin Books, 1971), pp. 64–7. There is a good discussion of a representative group of Victorian thinkers in Sussman, *Victorians and the Machine*.

21 See on this H. Stuart Hughes, *Consciousness and Society: The Reorientation of European Social Thought 1890–1930* (1958); James Burnham, *The Machiavellians: Defenders of Freedom* (New York, John Day, 1943).

22 George Woodcock, 'Utopians in Negative', *Sewanee Review*, vol. 64 (1956), p. 82. Cf.

Eugen Weber: 'The utopian form traditionally eschewed the notion of reality or immediacy. Utopia was nowhere, or it was very far away. Now, this is no longer so; utopia is with us, or just around the corner, and it generates reactions based on quite concrete hopes or fears. . . . The anti-utopians recognize in the society which they criticize the fulfilment of the dreams of yesterday.' Weber, 'The Anti-Utopia of the Twentieth Century' (Summer 1959), pp. 440–1. So too Irving Howe: 'What [the anti-utopians] fear is not . . . that history will suffer a miscarriage; what they fear is that the long-awaited birth will prove to be a monster. . . . Not progress denied but progress realized, is the nightmare haunting the anti-utopian novel.' 'The Fiction of Anti-Utopia', in I. Howe (ed.), *Orwell's Nineteen Eighty-Four: Text, Sources, Criticism* (New York, Harcourt, Brace, Jovanovich, 1963), p. 176. All of these of course echo the famous passage from Nicholas Berdyaev which Huxley uses as the epigraph for *Brave New World*. See below, pp. 242 ff.

23 Judith N. Shklar, *After Utopia: The Decline of Political Faith* (1957). Another relevant study, dealing with some of the same issues but restricted to English writers, is Raymond Williams, *Culture and Society 1780–1950* (Harmondsworth, Penguin Books, 1963). For the sociological contribution, see Robert Nisbet, *The Sociological Tradition* (London, Heinemann, 1967). For all their professed Marxism, much of the work of the German Frankfurt School falls within the same tradition – see, e.g., M. Horkheimer and T. W. Adorno, *Dialectic of Enlightenment* (1973), p. 3: 'In the most general sense of progressive thought, the Enlightenment has always aimed at liberating men from fear and establishing their sovereignty. Yet the fully enlightened earth radiates disaster triumphant.'

24 Mary Shelley, *Frankenstein* (1818), in *Three Gothic Novels* (Harmondsworth, Penguin Books, 1968), pp. 314–15.

25 William Beckford, *Vathek* (1786), in *Three Gothic Novels*, p. 254. It is for its restatement of the Faust-like theme that Brian Aldiss regards the Gothic novel, and *Frankenstein* in particular, as the true origin of modern science fiction. See Brian Aldiss, *Billion Year Spree: The History of Science Fiction* (1975), pp. 7–44.

26 Shelley, *Frankenstein*, p. 298.

27 Ibid., p. 307.

28 Ibid., p. 296.

29 On these eighteenth-century experiments, see Mario Praz's 'Introductory Essay' to *Three Gothic Novels*, pp. 27–31.

30 There was a strong revival of the Frankenstein and generally anti-utopian theme in German Expressionist cinema at the beginning of this century – not just in *Metropolis* (1926), but in such films as *The Golem* (1915), *Homunculus* (1916), *The Cabinet of Dr Caligari* (1920), Fritz Lang's *Dr Mabuse* films (1922–1932), and *Nosferatu* (1922), an adaptation of Bram Stoker's *Dracula*. For a discussion of these films, see Siegfried Kracauer, *From Caligari to Hitler* (1947); see also Carlos Clarens, *An Illustrated History of the Horror Film* (1968).

31 For these developments, see the relevant entries in Peter Nicholls (ed.), *The Encyclopaedia of Science Fiction* (1981). A particularly good recent science-fiction treatment of the 'artificial man' theme is Philip K. Dick, *Do Androids Dream of Electric Sheep?* (1968).

32 Shelley, *Frankenstein*, pp. 367–8. The whole of this section presents an account of the 'humanization' of 'natural man', as the monster learns to speak, read and develop social sympathies.

33 Ibid., pp. 413, 415. Cf. P. 495, where the monster says to Walton: 'I desired love and fellowship, and I was spurned. Was there no injustice in this? Am I to be thought the only criminal, when all humankind sinned against me?'

34 Ibid., p. 364. The extent to which Mary Shelley is reworking the theme of Milton's *Paradise Lost* is especially clear in this passage – and is indeed indicated in the passage from *Paradise Lost* which she chooses as the epigraph to the novel.

35 Ibid., pp. 338–9. For a good discussion of this and other aspects of *Frankenstein*, see David Punter, *The Literature of Terror* (1980), pp. 121–8. See also Franco Moretti, *Signs Taken for Wonders* (1983), especially for the common themes in the Frankenstein and Dracula myths.
36 Charles Baudelaire, *Fusées* (1851); quoted in Karl Löwith, *Meaning in History* (1949), pp. 97–8 (Baudelaire's emphasis). And for the general critique, see Shklar, *After Utopia*, pp. 69 ff.
37 Quoted in Löwith, *Meaning in History*, p. 99. For the Arnold–Huxley anti-utopian critique, see below, pp. 247 ff.
38 F. M. Dostoyevsky, *Diary of a Writer*; quoted in Andrew A. S. Noble, 'Dostoyevsky's Anti-Utopianism', in J. Butt and I. F. Clarke (eds), *The Victorians and Social Protest* (Newton Abbot, Devon, David & Charles, 1973), p. 138.
39 For these passages see F. M. Dostoyevsky, *Letters from the Underworld* (1864), tr. C. J. Hogarth (London, Dent and Sons, Everyman edition, 1964), pp. 31–42. For a later critique of the 'science of human behaviour', see Andrew Hacker, 'The Specter of Predictable Man' (1954).
40 For all quotations see Dostoyevsky, *The Brothers Karamazov* (2 vols), tr. David Magarshack (Harmondsworth, Penguin Books, 1966), vol. 1, pp. 288–305. For an extended discussion see Vasily Rozanov, *Dostoyevsky and the Legend of the Grand Inquisitor*, tr. Spender E. Roberts (Ithaca, NY, Cornell University Press, 1972). See also Philip Rahv, 'The Legend of the Grand Inquisitor', *Partisan Review*, vol. 21. no. 3 (May–June 1954), pp. 249–71.
41 For a discussion of the 'Legend' in this context, see Andrew Hacker, 'Dostoyevsky's Disciples: Man and Sheep in Political Theory', *Journal of Politics*, vol. 17, no. 4 (1955), pp. 590–613.
42 B. F. Skinner, *Walden Two* (New York, Macmillan, 1962), p. 249.
43 Dostoyevsky, *The Brothers Karamazov*, vol. 1, p. 305.
44 For a good discussion of Dostoyevsky's politics, see Irving Howe, *Politics and the Novel* (1957), pp. 51–75. See also John Caroll, *Break-out from the Crystal Palace: The Anarcho-Psychological Critique: Stirner, Nietzsche, Dostoyevsky* (1974); Johan Goudsblom, *Nihilism and Culture* (1980), esp. pp. 36–47. Dostoyevsky was clear enough on the importance of a utopian vision. In his novel *A Raw Youth* (1875), Versilov says: 'The Golden Age is the most unlikely of all the dreams that have been, but for it men have given up their life and all their strength, for the sake of it prophets have died and been slain, without it the peoples will not live and cannot die. . . .'
45 Howe, 'The Fiction of Anti-Utopia', p. 180.
46 Frye, 'Varieties of Literary Utopias', pp. 45–6. A similar view of Morris is taken by Perry Anderson, *Arguments Within English Marxism* (London, New Left Books/Verso, 1980), pp. 157–75.
47 It may have inspired the pessimistic outburst in the letter to Mrs Burne-Jones quoted at the head of this chapter. John Fowles suggests that Morris's own *News from Nowhere* was some sort of answer to *After London*: a celebration of the medieval world against Jefferies's savage picture of it. See Fowles's 'Introduction' to Richard Jefferies, *After London, or Wild England* (1885) (Oxford University Press, 1980), p. viii.
48 For the horror novels of the 1890s, see Punter, *The Literature of Terror*, pp. 239–67. For Freud, see below, pp. 384–5.
49 *Caesar's Column* has been reprinted by the Belknap Press of Harvard University (Cambridge, Mass., 1960), with a good introduction by Walter B. Rideout. See also Alexander Saxton, '*Caesar's Column*: The Dialogue of Utopia and Catastrophe', *American Quarterly*, vol. 19, no. 2 (1967), pp. 224–38.
50 There are many reprints of *The Iron Heel* (e.g. London, Journeyman Press, 1974). For a discussion, see Paul N. Siegel, *Revolution and the 20th Century Novel* (1979), pp. 30–52. For Orwell's appreciation of London, see below, pp. 300, 341–2.
51 See below, pp. 181 ff.

52 This was almost certainly *A Modern Utopia*. See E. M. Forster's 'Introduction' to his *Collected Short Stories* (Harmondsworth, Penguin Books, 1976), p. 6. This collection includes 'The Machine Stops'.
53 See below, pp. 184–87.
54 See Jacintha Buddicom, 'The Young Eric', in M. Gross (ed.), *The World of George Orwell* (London, Weidenfeld & Nicolson, 1971), p. 4.
55 See further on this K. Kumar, *Utopia on the Map of the World* (University of Cork Pamphlet Publications, 1985).

Chapter 5 Utopia as Socialism: Edward Bellamy and *Looking Backward*

1 In the later of the two books – *Equality* (1977) – Reynolds seems to have deliberately modified his position to accommodate more of the ecological and environmental ideas that were such strong currents in the 1970s, and that are almost wholly absent – as they were in Bellamy – in Reynolds's earlier book, *Looking Backward from the Year 2000* (1973). Both books are published by Ace Books, New York.
2 'Edward Bellamy', *The American Fabian* (June 1898). The obituary is reprinted in *Edward Bellamy Speaks Again!* (Kansas City, Missouri, Peerage Press, 1937), pp. 19–22, a collection of Bellamy's articles and addresses.
3 For the publishing history, see Sylvia E. Bowman, *The Year 2000: A Critical Biography of Edward Bellamy* (New York, Bookman Associates, 1958), p. 121; Kenneth M. Roemer, *The Obsolete Necessity: America in Utopian Writings, 1888–1900* (Kent, Ohio, Kent State University Press, 1976), p. 2. According to Bowman, *Looking Backward* was still selling 6,000 copies a year in the United States in the 1950s and 1960s.
4 For Bellamy's impact abroad, see Sylvia E. Bowman and others, *Edward Bellamy Abroad: An American Prophet's Influence* (New York, Twayne Publishers, 1962).
5 Bowman, *The Year 2000*, p. 116.
6 H. Bruce Franklin, *Future Perfect: American Science Fiction in the Nineteenth Century*, rev. edn (Oxford University Press, 1978), p. 269.
7 John Dewey, 'A Great American Prophet', *Common Sense*, vol. 3, no. 4 (April 1934), p. 7.
8 See Elizabeth Sadler, 'One Book's Influence: Edward Bellamy's "Looking Backward"', *New England Quarterly*, vol. 17, no. 4 (1944), p. 553.
9 Ibid., p. 531.
10 For these influences, see Bowman and others, *Edward Bellamy Abroad*, *passim*, especially (for Britain) pp. 86–118, and (for Russia) pp. 67–85. See also Sadler, 'One Book's Influence . . .'; F. J. Osborn, 'Preface' to his edition of Ebenezer Howard, *Garden Cities of Tomorrow* (Cambridge, Mass., MIT Press, 1965), pp. 20–1; R. C. K. Ensor, *England 1870–1914* (Oxford University Press, 1936), p. 334. It is worth mentioning that the two Roosevelts, Theodore and Franklin, produced two books with titles strikingly reminiscent of Bellamy's book and the movement it produced, and which expressed a similar hostility to big business: Theodore Roosevelt's *The New Nationalism* (1910), and Franklin D. Roosevelt's *Looking Forward* (1933).
11 On the late nineteenth-century utopian novel generally, see Roemer, *The Obsolete Necessity*. Roemer comments that 'it may not be an exaggeration to say that for a decade the utopian novel was perhaps the most widely read type of literature in America.' p. 3. For Bellamy's influence, see Allyn B. Forbes, 'The Literary Quest for Utopia, 1880–1900', *Social Forces*, vol. 6, no. 2 (1927), pp. 179–89; W. Arthur Boggs, '*Looking Backward* at the Utopian Novel, 1888–1900', *New York Public Library Bulletin*, vol. 64, no. 6 (June 1960), pp. 329–36.
12 See, e.g., Bowman, *The Year 2000*, p. 133: 'the platform adopted by the People's Party was without doubt the result of the influence of *Looking Backward* and the Nationalist movement.' William Dean Howells, a close friend and follower, claimed that Bellamy 'virtually founded the Populist Party'. Bowman, *The Year 2000*, p. 134. Bellamy himself

sometimes made large claims: '... the most startling single demonstration of the rapidity and solidity of the growth of Nationalism is the fact that in the Presidential campaign of 1892 more than one million votes were polled for the People's Party, the platform of which embodied the most important features of the immediate Nationalist programme ...'. 'The Programme of the Nationalists' (March 1894), in *Edward Bellamy Speaks Again!*, p. 165; 'Nationalists may be found in all parties; but, in particular, they are active in the recently founded People's Party, which has adopted their practical programme to such an extent that it is sometimes – wrongly – called the Nationalist's Party'. 'The Programme of the Nationalists' (October 1894); reprinted as Appendix II in Bowman and others, *Edward Bellamy Abroad*, pp. 445–8, at p. 448. Erich Fromm more recently has asserted that 'the Populist Party ... was to a large extent influenced by Bellamy's ideas, and got many of its votes from his adherents.' Fromm's 'Foreword' to New American Library edition of *Looking Backward* (New York, 1960), p. vi.

The present tendency seems to be to swing strongly the other way. John Thomas, in his 'Introduction' to the John Harvard Library edition of *Looking Backward* (Cambridge, Belknap Press, 1967), says: 'At best the effect of Nationalist propaganda on the People's Party had been minimal. Nationalists had attended the conventions at Cincinnati and Omaha but with no very impressive results.' p. 81. The most recent historian of the Populist movement, Lawrence Goodwyn, sums up the position thus: 'The organ of the Nationalists, the *New Nation*, had enthusiastically hailed the formation of the People's Party, as had Bellamy himself, but, as of 1892, the Nationalists could rally little more than scattered groups of middle class liberals across the nation. Unorganised, but with intense feeling, the Nationalists disappeared into the mass of the People's Party. To a third party effort they added a few campaign contributions, a good deal of advice, and not much else.' Goodwyn, *The Populist Movement* (Oxford University Press, 1978), pp. 176–7.

This seems a clear case of the pendulum effect. The earlier opinion evidently overestimates the extent of Nationalist influence on the Populist Party. But the more general influence of *Looking Backward* on the Populists cannot be measured simply by the activities of the Nationalist Clubs. Bellamy's book was well known in Populist circles; it was frequently quoted at Populist meetings; and General Weaver himself, the People Party's presidential candidate in 1892, frequently urged his supporters to buy Bellamy's book. Thorstein Veblen later wrote that the Farmers' Alliances 'helped sell *Looking Backward* to a million people'. On all this, see Everett W. MacNair, *Edward Bellamy and the Nationalist Movement, 1889–1894* (Milwaukee, Fitzgerald Company, 1957), pp. 162–96.

13 For general accounts of the Nationalist movement, see John H. Franklin, 'Edward Bellamy and the Nationalist Movement', *New England Quarterly*, vol. 11, no. 4 (1938), pp. 739–72; Arthur E. Morgan, *Edward Bellamy* (New York, Columbia University Press, 1944), pp. 245–98; Bowman, *The Year 2000*, pp. 122–38; Thomas, 'Introduction' to John Harvard Library edition of *Looking Backward*, pp. 69–82. The most detailed account is in MacNair, *Edward Bellamy and the Nationalist Movement*, although the treatment is at times eccentric. There is now also a full and wide-ranging account in Arthur Lipow, *Authoritarian Socialism in America: Edward Bellamy and the Nationalist Movement* (Berkeley, Cal., University of California Press, 1982).

14 Edward Bellamy, 'Progress of Nationalism in the US'. *North American Review* (June 1892), in *Edward Bellamy Speaks Again!* pp. 132–3.

15 For the reorientation in social thought in this period, see R. Jackson Wilson, *In Quest of Community: Social Philosophy in the United States, 1860–1920* (New York, John Wiley, 1968).

16 Thomas, 'Introduction' to *Looking Backward*, p. 18.

17 Bellamy, *Looking Backward* (1967), p. 312.

18 Herbert G. Gutman, *Work, Culture and Society in Industrializing America* (New York, Vintage Books, 1977), p. 33.

19 Arthur M. Schlesinger, 'The City in American Civilization', in his *Paths to the Present* (New York, Macmillan, 1949), p. 225.
20 John F. Kasson, *Civilizing the Machine: Technology and Republican Values in America, 1776–1900* (1977), p. 186.
21 *The Education of Henry Adams*, ed. Ernest Samuels (1918; Boston, Riverside Editions, Houghton Mifflin, 1973), p. 382.
22 Kasson, *Civilizing the Machine*, p. 191.
23 Ardrey René, 'A Glance at the Past and a Vision of the Future', *The Nationalist* (October 1890).
24 Edward Bellamy, 'Letter to the People's Party', *The New Nation* (22 October 1892).
25 There are undoubtedly pastoral remnants in Bellamy's utopia, as there are in practically all modern utopias. But it is a far cry from noticing this to asserting that '*Looking Backward* . . . was conceived not in hope or in expectation but in nostalgia. On the most fundamental social levels, *Looking Backward* was premissed not so much on Bellamy's imaginings of the future as on his unwillingness or inability to confront the industrial city with its sytem of factories and its proletarian labor force.' R. Jackson Wilson, 'Experience and Utopia: The Making of Edward Bellamy's *Looking Backward*', *Journal of American Studies*, vol. 11, no. 1 (1977), p. 45. It is clear from this that Wilson can imagine an industrial future only in terms of factories and workers (he comments on the 'absence of smokestacks' in Boston of the year 2000). He misunderstands Bellamy's concern with the more fundamental industrial impulse of automation and 'rationalization', and therefore reads as 'pre-industrial' certain features of Bellamy's future society which should more properly be considered 'post-industrial'.
26 I. F. Clarke, *The Pattern of Expectation, 1644–2001* (1979), p. 161.
27 Albert Fried, *Socialism in America: From the Shakers to the Third International* (New York, Doubleday, 1970), p. 180.
28 For an interesting contemporary account of American socialism in this period, see Richard T. Ely, *Recent American Socialism* (Baltimore, Johns Hopkins University Studies in Historical and Political Science, 1885). See also Fried, *Socialism in America*, pp. 178–95; and Oakley C. Johnson, *Marxism in United States History Before the Russian Revolution, 1876–1917* (New York, Humanities Press, 1974). There are sometimes stimulating reflections on the early period in John H. M. Laslett and S. M. Lipset (eds), *Failure of a Dream? Essays in the History of American Socialism* (New York, Doubleday, 1974).
29 Werner Sombart, *Why is there no Socialism in the United States?* ed. C. T. Husbands (New York, M. E. Sharpe, 1976), p. 106.
30 MacNair, *Edward Bellamy and the Nationalist Movement*, p. 29. And cf. the similar assessment of Forbes: 'That a person with Bellamy's equipment should have written a book that received the serious consideration of hundreds of thousands of readers may strike one as strange. At this stage of his career, at least, he made no pretense of being in any sense of the word a student of economics. He had had, to be sure, a partial college education; he had had some experience as a journalist, and had also met with some success as a novelist. His views on the social problems of the day were not, however, the result of what would today be called trained observation or inquiry. . . . He did, however, have a keen sense of justice, a quality perhaps attributable to the fact that as a clergyman's son he grew up in an environment where non-material values were constantly stressed. Possibly it was the combination of this very quality with his layman's attitude that was the secret of his success.' Forbes, 'The Literary Quest for Utopia, 1880–1900', pp. 182–3.
31 Letter to William Dean Howells, 1888; quoted in MacNair, *Edward Bellamy and the Nationalist Movement*, p. 32.
32 Letter to William Dean Howells, 17 June 1888; quoted in Bowman, *The Year 2000*, p. 114.
33 Bowman, *The Year 2000*, p. 33. For an account of the 1886 May Day demonstration

and subsequent battle in Chicago's Haymarket Square, see Jeremy Brecher, *Strike!* (Boston, South End Press, 1972), pp. 25–50.

34 Chicago *Journal* (24 May 1898).

35 On all this see Morgan, *Edward Bellamy*, pp. 367–84; Bowman, *The Year 2000*, pp. 95–107; Bowman and others, *Bellamy Abroad*, pp. 45–58; Thomas, 'Introduction' to *Looking Backward*, pp. 20–33.

36 Bellamy, 'Why I Wrote "Looking Backward"', *The Nationalist* (May 1889), in *Edward Bellamy Speaks Again!*, p. 199.

37 Bellamy, 'How I Wrote "Looking Backward"', *Ladies Home Journal* (April 1894), in *Edward Bellamy Speaks Again!*, pp. 217–18.

38 Ibid., p. 223.

39 C. F. Boggs: '*Equality* is an economic treatise in which Bellamy developed his socialistic ideas after several years of studying major socialists, Marx, Blanc, Bebel and George. In it are many undeniable reflections and borrowings from all these authors.' Boggs, '*Looking Backward* at the Utopian Novel, 1888–1900', p. 332.

40 Like Bellamy himself, and for much the same motives, socialists were inconsistent about this. When it suited them they were quite ready to invoke *Looking Backward* as a picture of socialist society. See Bowman and others, *Edward Bellamy Abroad*, *passim*.

41 Bellamy, 'In the Interest of a Clear Use of Terms', *New Nation* (12 December 1891).

42 John Dewey, 'A Great American Prophet', *Common Sense*, vol. 3, no. 4 (1934), p. 6.

43 Fried, *Socialism in America*, pp. 2–3.

44 Edward Bellamy, 'Plutocracy or Nationalism' (Boston address, 31 May 1889), in *Edward Bellamy Speaks Again!*, p. 48.

45 Bellamy's speech, quoted by Thomas, 'Introduction' to *Looking Backward*, p. 77.

46 Bellamy, *Equality* (New York, Appleton, 1897), p. 16. The most explicit statement of this theme in *Looking Backward* occurs at the end of ch. 5.

47 For this sketch see *Equality*, ch. 2 ('Why the Revolution did not Come Earlier'), and chs 34 and 35 ('What Started the Revolution' and 'Why the Revolution Went Slow at First but Fast at Last').

48 *Equality*, p. 17. It is interesting to note that a similar theme, of the 1776 Revolution betrayed, was common in the American labour movement of the time, from the 1870s to the 1890s. The 'robber-barons' of the Gilded Age were seen as having robbed workers of their republican rights, secured to them by the Constitution. 'In America,' wrote the Pittsburg *National Labor Tribune* in 1874, 'we have realized the ideal of a republican government at least in form. America was the star of the political Bethlehem which shone radiantly out in the dark night of political misrule in Europe. The masses of the old world gazed upon her as their escape. . . . [But] these dreams have not been realized. . . . The working people of this country . . . suddenly found capital as rigid as an absolute monarchy.' Quoted in Gutman, *Work, Culture and Society in Industrializing America*, p. 52, and, generally on this theme, pp. 50–4.

49 Treves; quoted in Bowman and others, *Edward Bellamy Abroad*, p. 330.

50 Thomas, 'Introduction' to *Looking Backward*, p. 77.

51 Bellamy's difficulties, and the shifting character of the line between 'nationalism' and 'socialism', can be seen in the following articles by him: 'In the Interest of a Clear Use of Terms', *New Nation* (12 December 1891); 'Four Distinctive Principles of Nationalism', *New Nation* (9 January 1892); 'Talks on Nationalism', *New Nation* (8 August 1891). Some amends were made in the 'Introduction' to the American edition of *The Fabian Essays* of 1894. Here Bellamy came closest to identifying nationalism and socialism. He noted that 'Nationalism is the form under which socialism has thus far been chiefly brought to the notice of the American people,' and went on: 'Nationalists are socialists who, holding all that socialists agree on, go further, and hold also that the distribution of the cooperative product among the members of the community must be not merely equitable, whatever that term may mean, but must be always and absolutely equal. Of course it is not meant that many socialists are not believers in economic

equality, but only that the creed of socialism does not of necessity imply it.' See *Edward Bellamy Speaks Again!* pp. 237–8. The vast majority of socialists were – and are – of course believers in economic equality. Indeed, Bauman makes agreement on the value of social and economic equality the defining characteristics of all varieties of socialism: 'The emphatic refusal to accept the notion of equality as limited to the political sphere alone, the insistence on the importance of the numerous links with other spheres which render political equality void if other inequalities are left intact, and the determined desire to extend the ideal of equality beyond the domain of *homo politicus* were to remain the only cultural postulates shared by all shades of the socialist counter-culture.' Zygmunt Bauman, *Socialism: The Active Utopia* (1976), p. 42.

52 On this see the persuasive study by R. R. Palmer, *The Age of the Democratic Revolution* (2 vols) (Princeton University Press, 1964).

53 Émile Durkheim, *Socialism*, tr. Charlotte Sattler (New York, Collier Books, 1962), p. 177. And cf. this definition by Schumpeter: 'By socialist society we shall designate an institutional pattern in which the control over means of production and over production itself is vested with a central authority – or, as we may say, in which, as a matter of principle, the economic affairs of society belong to the public and not to the private sphere.' Joseph Schumpeter, *Capitalism, Socialism, and Democracy* (1976), p. 167.

54 Marginal comment added to the manuscript of 'The Religion of Solidarity' in 1887. The 'Religion of Solidarity' is reprinted in Joseph Schiffman (ed.), *Edward Bellamy: Selected Writings in Religion and Society* (New York, Liberal Arts Press, 1955), pp. 3–27.

55 Bellamy, 'Religion of Solidarity', p. 17. Many commentators have singled out 'The Religion of Solidarity' in searching for the emotional and intellectual origins of *Looking Backward*. Thomas remarks that '"The Religion of Solidarity" forms the focal point on which all of his fiction converges – and, more important, describes in detail the psychological structure on which the utopian society in *Looking Backward* is based.' 'Introduction' to *Looking Backward*, p. 13. George Becker refers to 'the most important ingredient of all' in Bellamy's philosophy, 'his mystical sense of human solidarity, his religion of humanity'. George J. Becker, 'Edward Bellamy: Utopia, American Plan', *Antioch Review*, vol. 14 (1954), p. 194. And see especially Schiffman, 'Introduction' to *Edward Bellamy: Selected Writings in Religion and Society*.

56 Bellamy, 'Why I wrote "Looking Backward"', in *Edward Bellamy Speaks Again!*, p. 200.

57 William James, 'The Moral Equivalent of War', in his *Memories and Studies* (London, Longmans, Green, 1911), pp. 267–96.

58 'Edward Bellamy', *American Fabian* (June 1898), in *Edward Bellamy Speaks Again!*, p. 20.

59 Edward Bellamy, *Looking Backward 2000–1887*, ed. John L. Thomas (Cambridge, Belknap Press, John Harvard Library edition, 1967), p. 253. All references in the text hereafter – as *LB* – are to this edition.

60 Bellamy, 'Why I Wrote "Looking Backward"', pp. 201–2.

61 Ibid., p. 202.

62 Emerson, quoted in Wilson, *In Quest of Community*, p. 13.

63 Bellamy, 'Plutocracy or Nationalism – Which?' (1889), in *Edward Bellamy Speaks Again!* p. 50.

64 Franklin, *Future Perfect*, p. 275.

65 Alexander Gray, *The Socialist Tradition: Moses to Lenin* (London, Longmans, Green, 1946), p. 75.

66 Lewis Mumford, *The Pentagon of Power* (New York, Harcourt Brace Jovanovich, 1970) p. 216. Bellamy's writing at times lends a good deal of weight to these views. In explaining why the victorious party of the old society chose the name 'the Nationalist Party', he says: 'it could not well have had any other name, for its purpose was to realize the idea of the nation with a grandeur and completeness never before conceived, not as an association of men for certain merely political functions affecting their happiness only remotely and superficially, but as a family, a vital union, a common life, a mighty heaven-touching tree whose leaves are its people, fed from its veins, and feeding it in

turn. The most patriotic of all possible parties, it sought to justify patriotism and raise it from an instinct to a rational devotion, by making the native land truly a father-land, a father who kept the people alive and was not merely an idol for which they were expected to die' (*LB*, pp. 260–1).

67 Bellamy himself took one such contemporary critic, General Walker, sufficiently seriously to attempt a detailed rebuttal of Walker's allegation of 'the excessively military character' of Bellamy's projected society. See '"Looking Backward" Again', in *Edward Bellamy Speaks Again!*, pp. 179–98.

68 See Robert Heilbroner, *An Inquiry Into The Human Prospect* (New York, W. W. Norton, 1974), and *Business Civilization in Decline* (Harmondsworth, Penguin Books, 1977); Fred Hirsch, *Social Limits to Growth* (1977). For a similar analysis and remedy, see also Charles Taylor, 'The Politics of the Steady State', in A. Rotstein (ed.), *Beyond Industrial Growth* (Toronto University Press, 1976) pp. 47–70.

69 For Morris's response to *Looking Backward*, and the general relationship between *Looking Backward* and *News From Nowhere*, see Paul Meier, *William Morris: The Marxist Dreamer* (1978), vol. 1, pp. 73–93. Meier points out that, so concerned was Morris to answer Bellamy, that the first part of *News from Nowhere* appeared in *Commonweal* 'a bare six months' after Morris's review of *Looking Backward*.

Since the general tendency these days is to favour Morris as against Bellamy, and to stress the fundamental differences in their respective conceptions of socialism and utopia, it is worth recording this verdict of Meier's: 'Edward Bellamy is the first Anglo-Saxon utopist, ahead of Morris, to abandon the exploration of *terrae incognitae* in order to build in his own country, and to put the time dimension in the place of geographical distance. With both of them, this new and original form comes from the urgent doctrinal concern to prove to contemporaries and compatriots that socialism is possible; but, at the same time, the need to convince gives each utopia a definite national quality which in itself has artistic validity. The Boston of the year 2000 is the result of typically American economic and cultural factors just as the England of the twenty-second century stays familiarly English. Morris wanted to write an anti-Bellamy utopia, and could not resist tinging his theoretical disagreement with anti-Americanism. But in taking his stand against Bellamy he was inevitably obliged to borrow from his opponent his very concept of utopia in all that was newest and most fundamental. Morris's debt is immense, and since he neglected to acknowledge it, we may do so on his behalf, with the deepest gratitude.' Meier, *William Morris*, vol. 1, pp. 75–6.

70 William Morris, 'Looking Backward', *The Commonweal* (22 June 1889); reprinted in May Morris, *William Morris: Artist, Writer, Socialist* (2 vols) (Oxford, Basil Blackwell, 1936), vol. 2, pp. 501–7. The passage quoted is at pp. 502–3.

71 Morris, 'Looking Backward', pp. 504–5.

72 Ibid., p. 505.

73 Ibid., p. 505.

74 Ibid., pp. 506–7.

Chapter 6 Science and Utopia: H. G. Wells and *A Modern Utopia*

1 Quoted in Lovat Dickson, *H. G. Wells: His Turbulent Life and Times* (Harmondsworth, Penguin Books, 1972) p. 289.

2 Max Nordau, *Degeneration* (London, William Heinemann, 1895) pp. 5–6. For the changing intellectual, social and political climate of the time, see Donald Reed, *England 1868–1914* (London, Longman, 1979); Samuel Hynes, *The Edwardian Turn of Mind* (Princeton University Press, 1968); Malcolm Bradbury, *The Social Context of Modern English Literature* (Oxford, Basil Blackwell, 1971); Paul Thompson, *The Edwardians* (London, Weidenfeld and Nicolson, 1975); George Dangerfield, *The Strange Death of Liberal England 1910–1914* (1935; New York, Capricorn Books, 1961).

3 Quoted in Read, *England 1868–1914*, p. 4.
4 H. G. Wells, *Experiment in Autobiography* (2 vols) (1934; London, Jonathan Cape, 1969), vol. I, p. 135. Henceforth referred to as *Autobiography*.
5 Virginia Woolf, 'Mr Bennett and Mrs Brown' (1924), in *Collected Essays* (London, Chatto & Windus, 1966), vol. I, pp. 320–1.
6 On London in this period see Asa Briggs, *Victorian Cities* (Harmondsworth, Penguin Books, 1968), ch. 8; Gareth Stedman Jones, *Outcast London* (Harmondsworth, Penguin Books, 1976); Peter Keating (ed.), *Into Unknown England 1866–1913* (London, Fontana, 1976); Donald J. Olsen, *The Growth of Victorian London* (Harmondsworth, Penguin Books, 1979).
7 Cf. *The New Machiavelli*, bk 3, ch. 3: 'London is the most interesting, beautiful, and wonderful city in the world to me, delicate in her incidental and multitudinous littleness, and stupendous in her pregnant totality.' And see also Joseph Conrad's similar but characteristically darker image of London at the opening of *The Secret Agent* (1907).
8 Briggs, *Victorian Cities*, pp. 349, 384. Wells here of course followed the conventional wisdom of his age.
9 At about the same time as Wells, American sociologists from the farmlands were discovering and dissecting the American city with great insight and sophistication. See, e.g., R. E. Park and E. W. Burgess (eds), *The City* (1925; University of Chicago Press, 1967).
10 Quoted in Hynes, *The Edwardian Turn of Mind*, p. 14.
11 H. G. Wells, *The Discovery of the Future* (London, T. Fisher Unwin, 1902), pp. 90–3, 50–1, 36–7. Wells probably knew Frederick Harrison's essay, 'A Few Words About the Nineteenth Century' (*Fortnightly Review*, April 1882), in which Harrison remarks: 'Take it all in all, the merely material, physical, mechanical change in human life in the hundred years from the days of Watt and Arkwright to our own, is greater than occurred in the thousand years that preceded, perhaps even in the two thousand years or twenty thousand years.'
12 I. F. Clarke, *The Pattern of Expectation 1644–2001* (1979), p. 167; cf. R. D. Haynes, *H. G. Wells: Discoverer of the Future* (London, Macmillan, 1980), p. 2: 'The broadest and ultimately the most far-reaching effect of his work was the introduction into literature of a new awareness of the future.'
13 See Jerome Hamilton Buckley, *The Triumph of Time: A Study of the Victorian Concepts of Time, History, Progress, and Decadence* (1967).
14 Henry George, *Progress and Poverty* (1879; New York, Robert Schalkenbach Foundation, 1954), pp. 7, 8, 10. George's book went through ten English editions by 1884. For his influence on Wells, see *Autobiography*, vol. I, pp. 177–80.
15 On entropy and its impact see Stephen Toulmin and June Goodfield, *The Discovery of Time* (Harmondsworth, Penguin Books, 1967), ch. 9.
16 Quoted in Buckley, *The Triumph of Time*, p. 66.
17 T. H. Huxley, 'Evolution and Ethics' (the Romanes Lecture, 1893); reprinted in T. H. Huxley and J. S. Huxley, *Evolution and Ethics 1893–1943* (London, Pilot Press, 1947), pp. 80, 40.
18 T. H. Huxley, 'Agnosticism', *The Nineteenth Century* (February 1889); quoted in Norman Mackenzie and Jeanne Mackenzie, *The Time Traveller: The Life of H. G. Wells* (London, Weidenfeld & Nicolson, 1973), p. 57.
19 Huxley, 'Evolution and Ethics', p. 81.
20 Ibid., pp. 60, 84.
21 For Huxley's impact on Wells, see *Autobiography*, vol. I, pp. 199–206.
22 Shaw states his opposition to Darwinism at length in the 'Preface' to *Back to Methuselah* (1921).
23 Quoted in W. Warren Wagar, *H. G. Wells and the World State* (New Haven, Conn., Yale University Press, 1961), p. 80.

24 Anthony West, 'H. G. Wells', *Encounter*, vol. 8, no. 2 (February 1957), p. 53. The extremes of the pessimistic interpretation of Wells can be seen in Jack Williamson, *H. G. Wells: Critic of Progress* (Baltimore, Mirage Press, 1973). West was by no means the first to discern the 'anti-utopian' Wells: see, for instance, Yevgeny Zamyatin, 'H. G. Wells' (1922), in Mirra Ginsburg (ed. and tr.), *A Soviet Heretic. Essays by Yevgeny Zamyatin* (University of Chicago Press, 1970), pp. 286–7.

25 H. G. Wells, *The Common Sense of War and Peace* (1940), quoted in Wagar, *H. G. Wells and the World State*, p. 85.

26 H. G. Wells, 'The Man of the Year Million', *Pall Mall Gazette*, no. 57 (November 1893); reprinted in W. Warren Wagar (ed.), *H. G. Wells. Journalism and Prophecy 1893–1946* (London, Bodley Head, 1965), pp. 3–8.

27 H. G. Wells, 'The Extinction of Man', *Pall Mall Gazette* no. 59 (September 1894); reprinted in Wells, *Certain Personal Matter* (1897; London, T. Fisher Unwin, 1901), pp. 115–19.

28 Wells, 'The Man of the Year Million', p. 4. Wells constantly reverted, in later as much as in his earlier life, to the Huxleyan theme of Nature's indifference to human values and purposes. 'Adapt or perish: that is and always has been the implacable law of life for all its children' (*The Fate of Homo Sapiens*, 1939). In his novel *The Undying Fire* (1919), Wells's mouthpiece Job Huss thus retorts to the protest that there is much loveliness in nature: 'There is no beauty one may not balance by equal ugliness. The wart-hog and the hyaena, the tapeworm and stinkhorn, are equally God's creations. Nothing you have said points to anything but a cold indifference towards us of this order in which we live. Beauty happens; it is not given. Pain, suffering, happiness; there is no heed. Only in the heart of man burns the fire of righteousness.'

29 *Tono-Bungay*, bk 3, ch. 4.

30 For an excellent study of the early science fantasies, see Bernard Bergonzi, *The Early H. G. Wells. A Study of the Scientific Romances* (Manchester University Press, 1961). See also Mark R. Hillegas, *The Future as Nightmare: H. G. Wells and the Anti-Utopians* (1967), and Frank McConnell, *The Science Fiction of H. G. Wells* (New York, Oxford University Press, 1981).

31 See Patrick Parrinder, '*News from Nowhere, The Time Machine*, and the Break-Up of Classical Realism', *Science-Fiction Studies*, vol. 3, part 3 (1976) pp. 265–74; McConnell, *The Science Fiction of H. G. Wells*, pp. 73–7.

32 cf. Darwin, in *The Descent of Man*: 'With all his noble qualities, . . . with all these exalted powers, man still bears in his bodily frame the indelible stamp of his lowly origins.' For Huxley and Wells, of course, the stamp was as much mental and emotional as physical.

33 This is by now a conventional assessment. See, e.g., Bergonzi, *The Early H. G. Wells*, pp. 140 ff., and David Lodge, 'Utopia and Criticism', *Encounter*, vol. 32 (April 1969), p. 68.

34 In the same year as *When The Sleeper Wakes*, Wells published a long short-story, 'A Story of the Days to Come' (in *Tales of Space and Time*, 1899), which is similar in many ways to *When the Sleeper Wakes*, and similarly anticipates Zamyatin, Huxley and Orwell.

35 This was one of Wells's favourite ideas, most clearly described in *Anticipations*.

36 For the impact of the Wellsian city on a later generation of architects and planners, see Rayner Banham, 'Hotel deja-quoi?', *New Society* (5 April 1979).

37 H. G. Wells, 'The So-Called Science of Sociology' (1906); reprinted in Wells, *An Englishman Looks at the World* (London, Cassel, 1914), p. 200.

38 Wells's *The Outline of History* (1920) was his own considerable contribution to this genre.

39 Wells, 'The So-Called Science of Sociology' pp. 203–4.

40 H. G. Wells, *Mankind in the Making* (1903; London, Chapman and Hall, 1906), p. 13.

41 Ibid., p. 14.

42 Geoffrey West, *H. G. Wells: A Sketch for a Portrait* (London, Gerald Howe, 1930), p. 178. The work has had a good press from the start. Henry James was enthusiastic about

it, as was his brother William, and Joseph Conrad. Wells's Fabian friends the Webbs and Sidney Olivier greeted it warmly. The critics too were full of praise. See Mackenzie and Mackenzie, *The Time Traveller*, pp. 191–2. Later commentators have been equally admiring. Van Wyck Brooks called it 'a beautiful Utopia, beautifully seen and beautifully thought'. *The World of H. G. Wells* (London, Unwin, 1915) p. 96. Chad Walsh says that 'it is one of the most plausible utopias ever written'. *From Utopia to Nightmare* (London, Geoffrey Bles, 1962), p. 56. For Hillegas it was 'the first and finest of the Utopias written by Wells'. *The Future as Nightmare*, p. 63. And I. F. Clarke, noting that 'the special charm Wells had for his readers owed much to the artful ways in which he matched style to substance in his prophecies,' comments further: 'The magic of this gift is most evident in *A Modern Utopia* where Wells combined the allurements of the high predictive manner with the ruminative philosophizing of the older ideal states.' *The Pattern of Expectation 1644–2001*, p. 213.

43 H. G. Wells, 'A Note to the Reader', *A Modern Utopia* (1905; Lincoln, Nebraska, University of Nebraska Press, 1967), p. xxxii. All references in the text hereafter – as *AMU* – are to this edition, which reprints the original 1905 text.

44 L. Mumford, *The Story of Utopia* (London, Harrap, 1923), p. 184.

45 Clarke, *The Pattern of Expectation 1644–2001*, pp. 209, 213.

46 Hillegas, *The Future as Nightmare*, p. 66.

47 For impressions of Wells by some of these figures, see J. R Hammond (ed.), *H. G. Wells: Interviews and Recollections* (London, Macmillan, 1980).

48 George Kateb, *Utopia and Its Enemies* (1972), p. 22.

49 See Mackenzie and Mackenzie, *The Time Traveller*, pp. 445–6.

50 H. G. Wells, *A Year of Prophesying* (1924); quoted in Wagar, *H. G. Wells and the World State*, p. 206.

51 *Autobiography*, vol. II, p. 505.

52 Ibid., p. 752; and for the account of the development of the world-state idea, see ibid., pp. 643–827. The best general commentary is Wagar, *H. G. Wells and the World State*, esp. pp. 206–44.

53 *Autobiography*, vol. I, pp. 177–80. For the development of Wells's ideas about socialism, including his involvement with the Fabians and his consistent hostility to Marxism, see ibid., pp. 242–66. The major statement of his socialism is *New Worlds for Old* (1908), which G. D. H. Cole said 'was certainly the most influential piece of Socialist propaganda in Great Britain since Blatchford's *Merrie England*'. One of the earliest and most perceptive discussions of Wells's socialism was Zamyatin, 'H. G. Wells' (see n. 24); for a later Russian view, see J. Kagarlitski, *The Life and Thought of H. G. Wells*, tr. Moura Budberg (London, Sidgwick & Jackson, 1966). And see also William J. Hyde, 'The Socialism of H. G. Wells in the Early Twentieth Century', *Journal of the History of Ideas*, vol. 17 (1956), pp. 217–35; Stephen J. Ingle, *Socialist Thought in Imaginative Literature* (1979), *passim*, esp. pp. 159–73.

54 Letter to S. McLure, quoted in Mackenzie and Mackenzie, *The Time Traveller*, pp. 212–13. His later verdict was equally harsh. The Marxists, he said 'sterilized Socialism for half a century. Indeed from first to last the influence of Marx has been an unqualified drag upon the progressive reorganization of human society. We should be far nearer a sanely organized world system today if Karl Marx had never been born.' *Autobiography*, vol. I, p. 264.

55 *Autobiography*, vol. I, p. 263.

56 Ibid., p. 265; cf. the earlier assessment in *New Worlds for Old* (1908), when Wells was still linking socialism with his 'mind of the race' idea: 'The Socialist movement is . . . no less than the development of the collective self-consciousness of humanity.'

57 H. G. Wells, 'Utopias' (1939), a broadcast talk given in Australia, published in *Science-Fiction Studies*, vol. 9, part 2 (1982), p. 120.

58 H. G. Wells, *New Worlds for Old* (London, Constable, 1908), pp. 22–4.

59 Wells later toughened up this view of marriage and the family. 'Socialism, if it is anything more than a petty tinkering with economic relationships, is a renucleation of society. The family can remain only as a biological fact. Its economic and educational autonomy are inevitably doomed. The modern state is bound to be the ultimate guardian of all children and it must assist, replace, or subordinate the parent as supporter, guardian and educator; and it must refuse absolutely to recognize or enforce any kind of sexual ownership.' *Autobiography*, vol. II, p. 481. For an earlier view, see *Anticipations* (1901; London, Chapman & Hall, 1904), pp. 50 ff. See also *The New Machiavelli*, bk III, ch. 4.

60 It also of course anticipates the islands for non-conformists and deviants in *Brave New World.*

61 The reporter of this remark was Trotsky, in a vituperative attack on Wells. See Mackenzie and Mackenzie, *The Time Traveller*, pp. 326–7.

62 G. K. Chesterton, 'Mr H. G. Wells and the Giants', in his *Heretics* (London, Bodley Head, 1905), pp. 62–85.

63 Zamyatin, 'H. G. Wells', pp. 259–90.

64 Christopher Caudwell, 'H. G. Wells: A Study in Utopianism', in his *Studies in a Dying Culture* (London, John Lane, Bodley Head, 1938), pp. 73–95. And cf. A. L. Morton: '. . . the Wellsian Utopia, a sterilised, hygienic, cellophane world where everything appeared to have been just polished by all the most advertised brands'. *The English Utopia* (London, Lawrence & Wishart, 1952), p. 185.

65 George Orwell, 'Wells, Hitler, and the World State' (1941), in *The Collected Essays, Journalism and Letters of George Orwell* (4 vols), ed. Sonia Orwell and Ian Angus, vol. 2: *My Country Right or Left 1940–43* (Harmondsworth, Penguin Books, 1970), pp. 170–1.

66 George Orwell, *The Road to Wigan Pier* (1937; Harmondsworth, Penguin Books, 1962), p. 169. It is ironic that, immediately after this passage, Orwell should write: 'The truth is that many of the qualities we admire in human beings can only function in opposition to some kind of disaster, pain or difficulty; but the tendency of mechanical progress is to eliminate disaster, pain, and difficulty.' Ibid., p. 170. The suppression is probably unconscious, but it is striking that this direct echo of *The Time Machine* should follow the attack on Wells.

67 Orwell, 'Wells, Hitler, and the World State', p. 170. This article deeply wounded Wells, who abused Orwell in a letter which addressed him as 'you shit'. For the quarrel and final rupture between the two men, see Bernard Crick, *George Orwell: A Life* (Harmondsworth, Penguin Books, 1982), pp. 427–31.

Many later writers have echoed Orwell's view, e.g. Lovat Dickson: 'In more than one aspect Wells's new society has an uncomfortable suggestion of strong-armed fascism about it, and with a sense of shock. . . . one is suddenly aware that the heaven Wells dreamed of in 1900 bears a distinct resemblance to the 1984 hell imagined half a century later by George Orwell.' Dickson, *H. G. Wells*, p. 112.

68 As Orwell obliquely indicated on one occasion, 'Many earlier writers have foreseen the emergence of a new kind of society, neither capitalist nor Socialist, and probably based upon slavery. . . . Jack London, in *The Iron Heel* (1909), foretold some of the essential features of Fascism, and such books as Wells's *The Sleeper Awakes* (1900), Zamyatin's *We* (1923), and Aldous Huxley's *Brave New World* (1930), all described imaginary worlds in which the special problems of capitalism had been solved without bringing liberty, equality, or true happiness any nearer.' 'James Burnham and the Managerial Revolution' (1946), in *The Collected Essays, Journalism and Letters of George Orwell*, vol. 4: *In Front of Your Nose 1945–50* (Harmondsworth, Penguin Books, 1970), p. 195. The dates, nearly all wrong, are Orwell's.

69 See especially Wells, *The Shape of Things to Come: The Ultimate Revolution* (1933), *passim*; *Autobiography*, vol. II, pp. 662–3.

70 The religious aspect of science, and its vast potentiality for human liberation, comes out very strongly in a book that Wells always admired, Winwood Reade's *The Martyrdom of*

Man (1872; London, Watts & Co., 1948). See the powerful 'Wellsian' paean to science, pp. 410–14.

71 Quoted in Dickson, *H. G. Wells*, p. 173. And, cf. Wells's 1926 preface to *Kipps*: 'I have laughed at these two people . . . but I see through the darkness the souls of my Kippses as they are . . . little, ill-nourished, ailing, ignorant children, children who feel pain . . . and suffer and do not understand why. And the claw of the beast [sc. the social system] rests upon them.' Quoted in Ingle, *Socialist Thought in Imaginative Liberature*, p. 44.

72 Masterman; quoted in Clarke, *The Pattern of Expectation 1644–2001*, p. 210.

73 *Autobiography*, vol. II, p. 582.

74 H. G. Wells, *The Outlook for Homo Sapiens* (London, Secker & Warburg, 1942), pp. 11–12.

75 From *The New Machiavelli* (1911) onwards, Wells – no doubt consonantly with his own changed status – introduced a middle-class variant of this type, frequently a disillusioned politician, scholar or businessman (Remington, Clissold), who rails against the waste and disorder of the world, and his own blighted hopes for his individual life within it. Unlike the earlier novels of the lower middle class, however, the world-state idea is usually explicitly offered as a solution in these later novels.

76 *Autobiography*, vol. I, pp. 135–6.

77 Ibid., p. 94.

78 Ibid., vol. II, pp. 659–60.

79 This philosophy of history is fully developed in *The Outline of History* (1920). Something very close to it was first sketched out by Saint-Simon, whom Wells would have known through Comte. He may also have got the idea from Walter Bagehot's *Physics and Politics* (1869), which has a similar scheme. It is certainly very similar to the concept of 'creative' and 'dominant' minorities later developed at length by Arnold Toynbee in his *Study of History* (1934 onwards).

80 Wagar, *H. G. Wells and the World State*, p. 166.

81 Wells, *Men Like Gods*, ch. 5. The faith in education was always strong: 'I believe that through a vast educational campaign the existing capitalist system can be *civilised* into a collectivist world system.' *Russia in the Shadows* (1920).

In a BBC talk of 1931, Wells reiterated the view that science in decision-making can substitute for government in the conventional sense: 'It may be asked, who will make the ultimate decision [in Utopia]. There must be a king, or an assembly, or some such body, to say 'Yes' or 'No', in the last resort. But must there be? Suppose your intellectual organization, your body of thought, your scientific men, say and prove this, that, or the other course is the *right* one. Suppose they have the common-sense of an alert and educated community to sustain them. Why should not a dictatorship – not of this or that man, nor of the proletariat, but of informed and educated common-sense – some day rule the earth? What need is there for a lot of politicians and lawyers to argue about the way things ought to be done, confusing the issues? Why make a dispute of world welfare?' *After Democracy*, quoted in Wagar, *H. G. Wells and the World State*, pp. 219–20.

82 Wells, *The Shape of Things to Come*, bk 4, ch. 7.

83 H. G. Wells, 'Utopias', *Science-Fiction Studies*, vol. 9, part 2 (1982) p. 117.

84 *Autobiography*, vol. I, pp. 66–82; Mackenzie and Mackenzie, *The Time Traveller*, pp. 23–4.

85 *Autobiography*, vol. I, pp. 159–68.

86 Mackenzie and Mackenzie, *The Time Traveller*, pp. 129–30.

87 H. G. Wells in the 1930s, on the failure of the League of Nations.

Chapter 7 Science and Anti-Utopia: Aldous Huxley and *Brave New World*

1 As is now commonly acknowledged. See, e.g., David Lodge, 'Utopia and Criticism' (1969), p. 66; W. Warren Wagar, *H. G. Wells and the World State* (New Haven, Yale University Press, 1961), p. 83.

2 Mark Hillegas, *The Future as Nightmare: H. G. Wells and the Anti-Utopians* (1967), *passim*.

3 Letter to Julian Huxley, 30 June 1916, in *Letters of Aldous Huxley*, ed. Grover Smith (New York and Evanston, Ill., Harper & Row, 1969), p. 103. Henceforth referred to as *Letters*.

4 Letter to Robert Nichols, 18 January 1927, in *Letters*, p. 281.

5 Letter to Mrs Kethven Roberts, 18 May 1931, in *Letters*, p. 348.

6 It has to be admitted that, unlike the case with Orwell, there is no clear documentary evidence of Huxley's having read *We* at the time of writing *Brave New World*, or indeed at any time thereafter. The parallels between *We* and *Brave New World* are certainly strong; but we must remember that Huxley had already briefly adumbrated the anti-utopian themes of *Brave New World* in the speeches he gives to Scogan in *Crome Yellow* (1921), as well as in several of the essays of the 1920s. The English translation of *We* – actually the first published version in *any* language, since it was not published in the original Russian until 1952 – did not appear until 1924, in the United States, and remained a rarity for so long that Orwell still had to base his review of *We* in 1946 on the French translation. Some critics however feel that Huxley must have known *We*. Orwell was one of the most definite: 'The first thing anyone would notice about *We* is the fact – never pointed out, I believe – that Aldous Huxley's *Brave New World* must be partly derived from it.' 'Review of *We*', in *The Collected Essays, Journalism and Letters of George Orwell* (4 vols), ed. Sonia Orwell and Ian Angus (Harmondsworth, Penguin Books, 1970), vol. 4, p. 96. More cautiously, George Woodcock conjectures that, 'given Huxley's omnivorous reading habits, it seems unlikely that he failed to read *We* during the seven years between its publication and that of *Brave New World*. . . .' *Dawn and the Darkest Hour: A Study of Aldous Huxley* (London, Faber & Faber, 1972), p. 174. Michael Glenny states roundly: 'Writing in 1930, Huxley undoubtedly owed to Zamyatin the basic concept of a critique of the future based on an extrapolation of certain present trends. . . .' 'Introduction' to Penguin Modern Classics edition of *We* (Harmondsworth, Penguin, 1972), p. 17. And see also D. J. Richards, *Zamyatin* (London, Methuen, 1962), p. 54, and Hillegas, *The Future as Nightmare*, p. 186, n. 2.

On the other hand, Christopher Collins quotes from a letter written to him by Huxley on 25 October 1962: 'Oddly enough I never heard of Zamyatin's book until three or four years ago. . . . *Men Like Gods* annoyed me to the point of planning a parody, but when I started writing I found the idea of a negative Utopia so interesting that I forgot about Wells and launched into *Brave New World*.' Collins, 'Zamyatin, Wells and the Utopian Literary Tradition', *Slavonic and East European Review*, vol. 44 (1966), p. 351, n. 1.

This in itself is not conclusive either, of course; but fortunately the question of a direct influence on Huxley is not critical here. What matters in the end is the affinity between the two writers, and the importance of Wells to both of them, as inspirer and antagonist. It is interesting, incidentally, that Wells himself never appears to have read Zamyatin's book, although he met him in Russia in 1920. See Collins, 'Zamyatin, Wells and the Utopian Literary Tradition', p. 352, n. 7.

7 Yevgeny Zamyatin, 'H. G. Wells' (1922), in Mirra Ginsburg (tr. and ed.), *A Soviet Heretic: Essays by Yevgeny Zamyatin* (Chicago and London, University of Chicago Press, 1970), pp. 286–8. For Zamyatin and his relationship to Wells, Huxley and Orwell, see E. J. Brown, *Brave New World, 1984, and We: An Essay on Anti-Utopia* (Ann Arbor, Michigan, Ardis, 1976); Alan Swingewood, *The Novel and Revolution* (1975), pp. 142–68; John Huntington, 'Utopian and Anti-Utopian Logic: H. G. Wells and his Successors', *Science-Fiction Studies*, vol. 9, pt 2 (July 1982), pp. 122–46; and Collins, 'Zamyatin, Wells and the Utopian Literary Tradition', who however sees Zamyatin too exclusively as a *reaction* to Wells rather than, as Zamyatin himself saw things, a continuation of him.

8 See Patrick Parrinder, 'Imagining the Future: Wells and Zamyatin', in Darko Suvin

and Robert M. Philmus (eds), *H. G. Wells and Modern Science Fiction* (London Associated Universities Press, 1977), pp. 144–58; Collins, 'Zamyatin, Wells and the Utopian Literary Tradition', p. 360. See also R. Russell, 'Literature and Revolution in Zamyatin's *My*', *Slavonic and East European Review*, vol. 51, no. 122 (1971), pp. 36–46.

9 Karel Capek, 'The Meaning of R.U.R.', *Saturday Review* (21 July 1923), p. 79.

10 See, on these and the movement generally, Gary Werskey, *The Visible College* (1978).

11 J. B. S. Haldane, *Daedalus, Or Science and the Future* (London, Kegan Paul, Trench, Trubner, 1924), p. 4. *Daedalus* was first read as a paper to the Heretics Society at Cambridge University in 1923. The book went through five impressions within the first twelve months. See Ronald W. Clark, *JBS: The Life and Work of J. B. S. Haldane* (New York, Coward-McCann, 1969), pp. 74–5.

12 Haldane, *Daedalus*, pp. 66–7.

13 Ibid., p. 69.

14 Ibid., pp. 70–4, 83–4.

15 Letter to Leonard Huxley, 24 August 1931, in *Letters*, p. 351.

16 Bertrand Russell, *Icarus or The Future of Science* (New York, E. P. Dutton, 1924), pp. 62–3.

17 Quoted in I. F. Clarke, *The Pattern of Expectation 1644–2001* (1979), pp. 240–1. In a review of Birkenhead's book, Haldane remarked: 'Certain of the phrases seemed oddly familiar. Where had I seen them before? Finally I solved the mystery. They were my own.' Clark, *JBS*, p. 94.

18 J. D. Bernal, *The World, the Flesh and the Devil: An Inquiry into the Future of the Three Enemies of the Rational Soul* (1970), pp. 29–30.

19 Ibid., p. 38.

20 Ibid., p. 42.

21 Ibid., p. 44.

22 Ibid., pp. 45–6.

23 Ibid., p. 56.

24 Ibid., pp. 68–9.

25 Ibid., p. 73.

26 J. B. S. Haldane, 'The Last Judgement', in *Possible Worlds* (London, Library Press, 1927), p. 302.

27 Ibid., p. 304.

28 J. B. S. Haldane, 'The Scientific Point of View', in *The Inequality of Man, and Other Essays* (Harmondsworth, Penguin Books, 1932), p. 13.

29 Quoted in Werskey, *The Visible College*, p. 171.

30 A. J. P. Taylor, *English History 1914–1945* (Oxford University Press, 1965), p. 299. For the planning movement in Britain in this period, see Trevor Smith, *The Politics of the Corporate Economy* (Oxford, Martin Robertson, 1979); Keith Middlemas, *Politics in Industrial Society* (London, André Deutsch, 1979).

31 Woodcock, *Dawn and the Darkest Hour*, p. 15.

32 Julian Huxley makes it clear that in the matter of science there was little that he had to teach his brother. 'Most people seem to imagine that Aldous came to me for help over the biological facts and ideas he utilized so brilliantly in *Brave New World* and elsewhere in his novels and essays. This was not so. He picked them all up from his miscellaneous reading and from occasional discussions with me and a few other biologists, from which we profited as much as he.' Julian Huxley (ed.), *Aldous Huxley 1894–1963. A Memorial Volume* (London, Chatto & Windus, 1965), p. 22. For the relationship between the Huxley brothers, see Ronald W. Clark, *The Huxleys* (New York, McGraw-Hill, 1968).

33 Huxley, *Aldous Huxley 1894–1963*, p. 100. It is worth recalling that in *Jesting Pilate* (1926), Aldous Huxley wrote: 'If I could be born again and choose what I should be in my next existence, I should desire to be a man of science. . . . Even if I could be Shakespeare, I think I should still choose to be Faraday.'

34 Aldous Huxley, *Literature and Science* (London, Chatto & Windus, 1963).

35 Huxley, *Aldous Huxley 1894–1963*, p. 14.
36 Ibid., p. 66.
37 Aldous Huxley, 'On the Charms of History and the Future of the Past', in *Music at Night, and Other Essays* (1931; London, Chatto & Windus Phoenix Library, 1932), p. 137.
38 Aldous Huxley, 'To the Puritans All Things are Impure', in *Music at Night*, pp. 180–1. And see also the fulminations against Ford uttered by the Lawrence-like character Rampion in *Point Counter Point* (1928).
39 Peter Drucker; quoted in Harry Braverman, *Labor and Monopoly Capital* (New York, Monthly Review Press, 1974), p. 88; and for scientific management generally, see ibid., pp. 85–152.
40 Braverman, *Labor and Monopoly Capital*, p. 147.
41 Aldous Huxley, *Brave New World* (1932; reprinted with additional 'Foreword' in Penguin Modern Classics, Harmondsworth, 1964), pp. 17–18. All references in the text hereafter – as *BNW* – are to this Penguin edition.
42 Aldous Huxley, 'Los Angeles. A Rhapsody', in *Jesting Pilate* (London, Chatto & Windus, 1926), p. 266. Huxley at the time thought Hollywood 'altogether too antipodean to be lived in; it gives you no chance of escape' (*Letters*, p. 269). His later decision to live in Los Angeles is just one of the many indications that Huxley was as much attracted as repelled by the Joy City – and also by the Brave New World that it foreshadowed?
43 Theodor W. Adorno, 'Aldous Huxley and Utopia', in his *Prisms*, tr. S. Weber and S. Weber (London, Neville Spearman, 1967), p. 99.
44 Aldous Huxley, 'The Outlook for American Culture: Some Reflections in a Machine Age', *Harpers Magazine*, vol. 155 (August 1927), p. 265.
45 Ibid., p. 265.
46 Aldous Huxley, *Texts and Pretexts* (1932); quoted in Peter Firchow, *Aldous Huxley: Satirist and Novelist* (Minneapolis, University of Minnesota Press, 1972), p. 119.
47 Aldous Huxley, 'Introduction' to *Proper Studies* (1927; London, Chatto & Windus, 1957), p. x.
48 Letter to Julian Huxley, 23 November 1942, in *Letters*, p. 483.
49 The most important of these are the novels *Crome Yellow* (1921), *Antic Hay* (1923), *Those Barren Leaves* (1925), *Point Counter Point* (1928), and the collections of essays *Jesting Pilate* (1926), *Proper Studies* (1927), and *Music at Night* (1931).
50 See the influences mentioned in *Proper Studies*, p. xviii.
51 'The Idea of Equality', in *Proper Studies*, p. 17.
52 Ibid., p. 19.
53 'Political Democracy', in *Proper Studies*, p. 153. And cf.: 'Only the most mystically fervent democrats, who regard voting as a kind of religious act, and who hear the voice of God in that of the People, can have any reason to desire to perpetuate a system whereby confidence tricksters, rich men, and quacks may be given power by the votes of an electorate composed in a great part of mental Peter Pans, whose childishness renders them particularly susceptible to the blandishments of demagogues and the tirelessly repeated suggestions of the rich men's newspapers.' Ibid., p. 163.
54 'Education', in *Proper Studies*, p. 114.
55 Ibid., p. 137.
56 'Personality and the Discontinuity of the Mind', in *Proper Studies*, p. 259.
57 'The Outlook for American Culture', p. 267.
58 'Obstacle Race', in *Music at Night*, pp. 163–4.
59 'The Outlook for American Culture', p. 268.
60 'Notes on Liberty and the Boundaries of the Promised Land', in *Music at Night*, p. 131. Huxley here enunciates a principle systematically elaborated – very much later – by Fred Hirsch in his influential study, *Social Limits to Growth* (1977).
61 'Foreheads Villainous Low', in *Music at Night*, p. 205.

62 'Notes on Liberty and the Boundaries of the Promised Land', p. 129.
63 Ibid., p. 128. Cf. also 'The Outlook for American Culture', p. 268. Huxley here echoes the famous remarks of Matthew Arnold: 'Your middle class man thinks it the highest pitch of development and civilization when his letters are carried twelve times a day from Islington to Camberwell, and from Camberwell to Islington, and if railway trains run between them every quarter of an hour; he thinks it nothing that the trains only carry him from an illiberal, dismal life at Islington to an illiberal, dismal life at Camberwell; and the letters only tell him that such is the life there. . . .' 'My Countrymen', *The Cornhill Magazine* (February 1866).
64 'The New Romanticism', in *Music at Night*, pp. 217–18.
65 Ibid., pp. 213–14. Lenin's admiration for the work of Frederick Winslow Taylor is well known, and underlines the basic parallelism that Huxley sees between Soviet collectivism and American Fordism.
66 For this tradition, see Raymond Williams, *Culture and Society 1780–1950* (Harmondsworth, Penguin Books, 1963).
67 *Crome Yellow* (1921; Harmondsworth, Penguin Modern Classics, 1964), pp. 128–31. And see also *Those Barren Leaves* (1925), part 1, ch. 6. Earlier Scogan has precisely prefigured another theme from *Brave New World*. Science, he says, has made it possible to 'dissociate love from propagation. . . . Where the great Erasmus Darwin and Miss Anna Seward, Swan of Lichfield, experimented – and, for all their scientific ardour, failed – our descendants will experiment and succeed. An impersonal generation will take the place of Nature's hideous system. In vast state incubators, rows upon rows of gravid bottles will supply the world with the population it requires. The family system will disappear; society, sapped at its very base, will have to find new foundations; and Eros, beautifully and irresponsibly free, will flit like a gay butterfly from flower to flower through a sunlit world.' *Crome Yellow*, p. 28.
68 'Education', in *Proper Studies*, p. 136. Cf. 'The Outlook for American Culture', p. 271.
69 'The Outlook for American Culture', p. 270. Huxley comments further: 'The active and intelligent oligarchies of the ideal state do not yet exist. But the Fascist Party in Italy, the Communist Party in Russia, the Kuomintang in China are their still inadequate precursors.' Ibid. See also 'Political Democracy', pp. 157–69; 'On the Charms of History', pp. 151–2.
70 'Political Democracy', p. 166.
71 'A Note on Eugenics', in *Proper Studies*, p. 282.
72 Woodcock, for instance, merely notes that 'Huxley soon repudiated, by implication at least, the aristocratic pretensions of *Proper Studies*.' *Dawn and the Darkest Hour*, p. 144. See also Peter Bowering, *Aldous Huxley* (London, Athlone Press, 1968), pp. 93–4; Jerome Meckier, *Aldous Huxley. Satire and Structure* (London, Chatto & Windus, 1969), p. 178.
73 For a thorough discussion of the Huxley–Lawrence relationship, see Meckier, *Aldous Huxley*, ch. 4.
74 See Sybille Bedford, *Aldous Huxley: A Biography* (New York, Alfred A. Knopf/Harper & Row, 1974), pp. 159–61; *Letters*, p. 249.
75 'Wanted, A New Pleasure', in *Music at Night*, pp. 254–5.
76 'On the Charms of History and the Future of the Past', p. 152.
77 Sir Isaiah Berlin, in Huxley, *Aldous Huxley 1894–1963*, p. 150.
78 'Foreword' (1946) to a new edition of *Brave New World*, reprinted in Penguin Modern Classics edition (see n. 41), p. 9.
79 Ibid., p. 10.
80 Ibid.
81 See 'Selected Snobberies', in *Music at Night*, pp. 221–7.
82 'The Outlook for American Culture', p. 269. Huxley had been greatly impressed by two books – Wilfred Trotter's *Instincts of the Herd in Peace and War* (1916) and Graham Wallas's *Human Nature in Politics* (1908) – which explored the potentialities of the new

mass media for social control in the conditions of the mass democracies of western industrial society. See *Proper Studies*, p. xix.

83 Jenni Calder, *Huxley and Orwell: Brave New World and Nineteen Eighty-Four* (London, Edward Arnold, 1976), p. 56. For an interesting discussion of Huxley's philosophy of history, see Robert S. Baker, *The Dark Historic Page: Social Satire and Historicism in the Novels of Aldous Huxley 1921–1939* (Madison, Wisconsin, University of Wisconsin Press, 1982). That, to the scientist, history is and has to be regarded as irrelevant is the sense of Whitehead's well-known dictum that 'a science that hesitates to forget its founder is lost.' As Thomas Kuhn puts it, from the point of view of the working scientist, 'mere historical detail, whether of science's present or its past, or more responsibility to the historical details that are presented, could only give artificial status to human idiosyncracy, error, and confusion. Why dignify what science's best and most persistent efforts have made it possible to discard? The depreciation of historical fact is deeply, and probably functionally, ingrained in the ideology of the scientific profession, the same profession that places the highest of all values upon factual details of other sorts.' Kuhn, *The Structure of Scientific Revolutions* (University of Chicago Press, 1962), p. 137. This admirably expresses Brave New World's attitude to the past.

84 Adorno, 'Aldous Huxley and Utopia', p. 100.

85 The modern cult of youth and beauty, especially in America, was a frequent theme of Huxley's essays. See, e.g., 'The Beauty Industry', in *Music at Night*, pp. 228–36.

86 In his novel *After Many a Summer* (1939), Huxley portrayed the search through science for human immortality as the ultimate degeneration of a materialist civilization, the search for a victory 'no longer of the spirit, but of the body, the well-fed body, for ever youthful, immortally athletic, indefatigably sexy' (part 1, ch. 2). In his later writing, as in the novels *Time Must Have a Stop* (1945) and *Island* (1962), holy living and holy dying become an integral part of his philosophy.

87 On the virtues of restraint and self-denial, see 'Obstacle Race', in *Music at Night*, pp. 157–72. Huxley argues there that 'no reasonable hedonist can consent to be a flat racer. Abolishing obstacles, he abolishes half his pleasures. And at the same time he abolishes most of his dignity as a human being. For the dignity of man consists precisely in his ability to restrain himself from dashing away along the flat, in his capacity to raise obstacles in his own path.' Ibid., p. 167.

88 See 'Obstacle Race', p. 163. And cf. Adorno: 'Huxley has recognized the contradiction that in a society where sexual taboos have lost their intrinsic force and have either retreated before the permissibility of the prohibited or come to be enforced by external compulsion, pleasure itself degenerates to the misery of "fun" and to an occasion for the narcissistic satisfaction of having "had" this or that person. Through the institutionalization of promiscuity, sex becomes a matter of indifference, and even escape from society is relocated within its borders. Physiological release is desirable, as part of hygiene; accompanying feelings are dispensed with as a waste of energy without social utility.' Adorno, 'Aldous Huxley and Utopia', p. 103. A similar argument, of special relevance to the 1960s, was later advanced by Herbert Marcuse in *One-Dimensional Man* (1964).

89 Bertrand Russell, *The Scientific Outlook* (New York, W. W. Norton, 1931), pp. 261–4. In this book Russell elaborated the critique of science that he had briefly sketched in *Icarus*. The portrait of the scientific society that he projects has so much in common with *Brave New World* – test-tube babies, a biologically conditioned caste system, a scientific dictatorship, among other similarities – that some have seen it as the direct inspiration of Huxley's book. Philip Thody, for instance, says that 'so much of *Brave New World* resembles *The Scientific Outlook* that one wonders at times if Huxley put any original ideas into his book.' Thody, *Aldous Huxley* (London, Studio Vista, 1973), pp. 50–1. Russell undoubtedly influenced Huxley during the 1920s; but we have only to remember that many similar ideas were around, as in the works of Haldane and Bernal, to appreciate the exaggeration in Thody's remark. In any case, as we have seen, Huxley

himself had prefigured many of the themes of *Brave New World* in his novels and essays of the 1920s, well before the appearance of *The Scientific Outlook.*

90 'Notes on Liberty and the Boundaries of the Promised Land', p. 122.
91 Chad Walsh, *From Utopia to Nightmare* (1962), p. 25.
92 Elaine Hoffman Baruch, '"A Natural and Necessary Monster": Women in Utopia', *Alternative Futures*, vol. 2, no. 1 (1979), p. 39. Mustapha Mond's diatribes against the nuclear family can be found repeated in many of the writings of the 'anti-psychiatry' movement led by R. D. Laing and David Cooper. See, e.g., David Cooper, *The Death of the Family* (New York, Pantheon Books, 1970). In a somewhat different way, Mond's strictures on the family as 'unscientific', the source of unnecessary waste and suffering, are echoed by B. F. Skinner in *Walden Two.*
93 Shulamith Firestone, *The Dialectic of Sex: The Case for Feminist Revolution* (New York, Bantam Books, 1971), pp. 206 ff. It need hardly be said that those sexual radicals who, misunderstanding Freud, think that the way to human emancipation lies through unfettered sexual activity, likewise can find little to complain of in *Brave New World.*
94 See, e.g., J. M. Keynes, 'Economic Possibilities for Our Grandchildren' (1930) in his *Essays in Persuasion* (London, Macmillian, 1972).
95 'Foreword' (1946) to *Brave New World*, Penguin edn, p. 12.
96 Ibid., p. 14.
97 Ibid.
98 Aldous Huxley to George Orwell, 21 October 1949, in *Letters*, pp. 604–5.
99 Aldous Huxley, *Brave New World Revisited* (1958; New York, Harper & Row Perennial Library, 1965), pp. 4–5.
100 Ibid., pp. 5–6, 63—4.
101 Ibid., pp. 26–7.
102 Ibid., pp. 36–7.
103 Ibid., pp. 66–7.
104 Ibid., p. 69.
105 Ibid., p. 76. On the positive use of drugs – specifically mescalin – see Huxley's *The Doors of Perception* (1954).
106 *Brave New World Revisited*, pp. 103, 110–11.
107 Ibid., p. 116.
108 Ibid., pp. 117–18.
109 J. L. Goddard, former Commissioner of the US Food and Drug Administration, quoted in I. Zola, 'Medicine as an Institution of Social Control', *Sociological Review*, vol. 20 (1972), p. 495. And see also Peter Schrag and Diane Divoky, *The Myth of the Hyperactive Child* (New York, Dell, 1975); S. Box, 'Hyperactivity: The Scandalous Silence', *New Society* (1 December 1977); any and all of the works of Thomas Szasz, e.g., *The Theology of Medicine* (Oxford University Press, 1977). An interesting science-fiction novel satirizing medical control is Ward Moore, *Caduceus Wild* (1978).
110 See chapter 9 below.
111 See Stan Cohen, 'Community Control – A New Utopia', *New Society*, (15 March 1979); Cohen, *Visions of Social Control* (1985); and, generally, A. T. Scull, *Decarceration* (Englewood Cliffs, NJ, Prentice-Hall, 1977). The new movement is effectively satirized in Anthony Burgess's anti-utopian novel, *A Clockwork Orange* (1962).
112 For a wide-ranging discussion of the new technologies and their likely impact, see the *Report of the Working Party on the New Technologies* (London, Broadcasting Research Unit, British Film Institute, 1984).
113 For a survey of these deveopments, see Vance Packard, *The People Shapers* (Boston, Little, Brown, 1977), pp. 175 ff. John Frankenheimer's film, *Seconds* (1966), chillingly explores the consequences of the totally remodelled and rejuvenated man.
114 For a full discussion, see Peter Singer and Deane Wells, *The Reproduction Revolution: New Ways of Making Babies* (1984). See also Clifford Grobstein, *From Chance to Purpose: An Appraisal of External Human Fertilization* (Reading, Mass., Addison-Wesley, 1981).

115 *The New York Times* (17 June 1980).

116 For a good introduction to genetic engineering, see Jeremy Cherfas, *Man Made Life* (Oxford, Basil Blackwell, 1982). See also Jonathan Glover, *What Sort of People Should There Be?* (1984). Huxley's scientific prescience was noted at the time by no less an authority than Joseph Needham; in a review of *Brave New World*, he wrote: 'It may well be that only biologists and philosophers will really appreciate the full force of Mr Huxley's remarkable book. For of course in the world at large, those persons, and there will be many, who do not approve of his "utopia", will say, we can't believe all this, the biology is all wrong, it couldn't happen. Unfortunately, what gives the biologist a sardonic smile as he reads it, is the fact that the *biology is perfectly right*, and Mr Huxley has included nothing in his book but what might be regarded as legitimate extrapolations from knowledge and power that we already have. Successful experiments are even now being made in the cultivation of embryos of small mammals in vitro, and one of the most horrible of Mr Huxley's predictions, the production of numerous low-grade workers of precisely identical genetic constitution from one egg, is perfectly possible. Armadillos, parasitic insects, and even sea-urchins, if treated in the right way, do it now, and it is only a matter of time before it will be done with mammalian eggs.' Needham, 'Biology and Mr Huxley', *Scrutiny* (May 1932); reprinted in Donald Watt (ed.), *Aldous Huxley. The Critical Heritage* (London, Routledge & Kegan Paul, 1975), p. 204; Needham's emphasis.

117 Huxley's description of himself in the 1946 'Foreword' to *Brave New World*.

118 Huxley's ambivalence towards the scientific society was matched by that of Bertrand Russell during the 1920s. Russell was so alarmed at the possibility of a new world war that he was prepared to accept an authoritarian, scientifically run, world-government as the lesser evil. Freedom would have to be sacrificed to security and survival (see *Icarus* and *The Scientific Outlook*). Hence, in a characteristically quizzical review of *Brave New World*, he urged Huxley's scientific society on his readers as the grim but preferable alternative to international anarchy and world-wide destruction. See his review in the *New Leader* (11 March 1932); reprinted in Watt (ed.), *Aldous Huxley*, pp. 210–12.

119 Calder, *Huxley and Orwell*, p. 35.

120 Cf. Huxley's essay, 'A Note on Eugenics', where he argues against eugenicists such as Haldane that 'a state with a population consisting of nothing but superior people could not hope to last for a year. The best is ever the enemy of the good.' *Proper Studies*, p. 282. This is yet another of the many instances where Huxley's own views of the 1920s are put into the mouth of Mustapha Mond.

121 *Brave New World Revisited*, pp. 66–7.

122 See the 'Introduction' to K. Kumar (ed.), *Revolution* (London, Weidenfield & Nicolson, 1971).

123 No one is more aware of this than the Controller Mustapha Mond. He rejects for publication a scientific paper concerned with the conception of purpose on the grounds of its subversive potential among the educated castes. 'It was the sort of idea that might easily decondition the more unsettled minds among the higher castes – make them lose their faith in happiness as the Sovereign Good and take to believing instead, that the goal was somewhere beyond, somewhere outside the present human sphere; that the purpose of life was not the maintenance of well-being, but some intensification and refining of consciousness, some enlargement of knowledge' (*BNW*, ch. 12, p. 141).

124 George Orwell, 'Prophecies of Fascism', in *The Collected Essays, Journalism and Letters of George Orwell*, vol. 2, p. 46.

125 Foreword' (1946) to *Brave New World*, p. 7.

126 Ibid., p. 8.

127 Adorno, 'Aldous Huxley and Utopia', p. 105. For the views of Adorno and other Frankfurt School theorists on 'the dialectic of happiness', see Martin Jay, *The Dialectical Imagination: A History of the Frankfurt School and the Institute of Social Research 1923–1950* (1973), pp. 180, 215 ff. It is perhaps worth noting that in *Nineteen*

Eighty-Four Julia, like Lenina, believes in 'having a good time'; and Orwell shows how, in different circumstances admittedly, 'having a good time' can become an act of political rebellion.

Chapter 8 Politics and Anti-Utopia: George Orwell and *Nineteen Eighty-Four*

1 'The novel is best read as Swiftian satire. . . .' 'It is a warning, not a prophecy, a cry of "danger" not "despair".' Bernard Crick, 'Introduction' to George Orwell, *Nineteen Eighty-Four* (Oxford, Clarendon Press, 1984), pp. 17, 112. (Crick's essay is hereafter referred to as 'Introduction'.) See also Peter Stansky, in Peter Stansky (ed.), *On Nineteen Eighty-Four* (New York and San Francisco, W. H. Freeman, 1983), p. x.

2 'If it inspires dread above all, that is precisely because its materials are taken from the real world as we know it. . . . Ingsoc, the system established in Oceania . . . is substantially little more than an extension into the near future of the present structure and policy of Stalinism.' Philip Rahv, 'The Unfuture of Utopia' (1949), in Irving Howe (ed.), *Orwell's Nineteen Eighty-Four: Text, Sources, Criticism* (New York, Harcourt Brace Jovanovich, 1963), p. 182. See also Edward Crankshaw, 'Orwell and Communism' in Miriam Gross (ed.), *The World of George Orwell* (London, Weidenfeld & Nicolson, 1971), p. 118; R. Conquest, 'Totaliterror', in Stansky (ed.), *On Nineteen Eighty-Four*, p. 179 ('the foundation of *Nineteen Eight-Four* is . . . Stalin's Russia'); Raymond Williams, *Orwell* (London, Fontana, 1971), p. 77.

3 Anthony Burgess, *1985* (Boston, Little, Brown, 1978), p. 13. Burgess's emphasis on the comic element in *Nineteen Eighty-Four* is salutary, and the discussion of Orwell in the context of the 1940s, which forms the first part of his *1985*, is lively and provocative in the best sense. The novella that forms part two is excruciatingly awful. For the 'black humour' in *Nineteen Eighty-Four* see also Crick, 'Introduction', pp. 15–16.

The importance of England in the 1940s, whether as centre or background to the novel, has been widely recognized and acknowledged, especially by Orwell's contemporaries: e.g. George Woodcock: '*Nineteen Eighty-Four* is, first of all, a satire on the world of 1948, with its build-in utopian tendencies. . . .' Woodcock, *The Crystal Spirit. A Study of George Orwell* (Boston, Little, Brown, 1966), p. 218; Tom Hopkinson: 'Orwell has imagined nothing new. . . . His world of 1984 is the wartime world of 1944, but dirtier and more cruel. . . .' Quoted in Michael Maddison, '*1984*: A Burnhamite Fantasy?' *Political Quarterly*, vol. 32, no. 1 (January–March 1961), p. 72. See also Angus Calder, *The People's War: Britain 1939–1945* (London, Panther Books, 1971), p. 578; E. J. Brown, *Brave New World, 1984, and We: An Essay on Anti-Utopia* (Ann Arbor, Mich., Ardis, 1976), p. 43.

4 Anthony West, 'Hidden Damage' (1954), in Jeffrey Meyers (ed.), *George Orwell: The Critical Heritage* (London and Boston, Routledge & Kegan Paul, 1975), pp. 71–9. Such an interpretation was first hinted at by T. R. Fyvel in his memoir of Orwell, 'A Writer's Life', *World Review* (June 1950), reprinted in Howe (ed.), *Orwell's Nineteen Eighty-Four*, pp. 239–48. It forms the basis of a wide-ranging interpretation of the whole of Orwell's life and work by Jeffrey Meyers, *A Reader's Guide to George Orwell* (London, Thames & Hudson, 1975). (For *Nineteen Eighty-Four* see esp. pp. 21–31, 43–8, 144–54.) This is not the place to discuss so complex an issue, which by itself will give the Orwell industry plenty to chew on for years to come; but a necessary corrective is Crick's less apocalyptic account of Orwell's schooldays and, especially, his re-dating of 'Such, Such Were the Joys' to around 1940. Even if the more conventional date of 1947 is accepted, it is at least as plausible to suggest, as Crick does, that St Cyprian's was 're-imagined and re-created' as Oceania as to suggest that the opposite happened – given that Orwell was hard at work on *Nineteen Eighty-Four* at the time. See Bernard Crick, *George Orwell: A Life* (Harmondsworth, Penguin Books, 1982), pp. 41–80, 526–7, 586–94, 633. Crick here broadly follows Woodcock, *The Crystal Spirit*, pp. 198–203. For a similarly critical approach to 'Such, Such Were the Joys', emphasizing its status as art rather than

straight autobiography, see Peter Stansky and William Abrahams, *The Unknown Orwell* (London, Paladin, 1974), pp. 38–83. But we should note also Crick's acknowledgement, concerning Orwell's alleged masochistic streak, that 'something odd and disturbing', something 'inexplicable', remains. Crick, *Orwell*, p. 275 n.

5 Issac Rosenfeld, 'Decency and Death' (1950), in Howe (ed.), *Orwell's Nineteen Eighty-Four*, pp. 185–8. Many commentators combine the childhood and 'final days' interpretations of *Nineteen Eighty-Four*, and see Orwell's diseased condition in the later 1940s as intensifying the despair and haunting guilt of his childhood years – see e.g., Fyvel, 'A Writer's Life', p. 240; Meyers, *A Reader's Guide*, pp. 43–7; D. S. Savage, 'The Fatalism of George Orwell', in Boris Ford (ed.), *The New Pelican Guide to English Literature*, vol. 8: *The Present* (Harmondsworth, Penguin Books, 1983), pp. 129–46. Once again it is necessary to set against this Crick's account of Orwell's last days, which shows a chirpy and decidedly unmorbid Orwell; and the evidence Crick cites, such as the 1943 outline of *Nineteen Eighty-Four*, to the effect that *Nineteen Eighty-Four* was 'long and rationally premeditated' and not 'the morbid fantasy of a fatal illness'. See Crick, *Orwell*, pp. 510 ff., 582–5; similarly Woodcock, *The Crystal Spirit*, p. 207.

6 'Orwell's instinct is that of the *Homo religiosus*: his particular source of moral and spiritual energy the Protestant dialectic.' Alan Sandison, *The Last Men in Europe. An Essay on George Orwell* (London, Macmillan, 1974), p. 6.

7 The American custom of rendering the title as a date – *1984* – rather than spelling it out – *Nineteen Eighty-Four* – disguises this somewhat. 'A date suggests a prophecy, whereas a title or name suggests a fiction.' Crick, 'Introduction', p. 20.

8 Isaac Deutscher, '*1984* – The Mysticism of Cruelty' (1954), in Howe (ed.) *Orwell's Nineteen Eighty-Four*, p. 197. Cf. also A. L. Morton: '*Nineteen Eighty-Four* is . . . the last word to date in counter-revolutionary apologetics.' Morton, *The English Utopia* (1952), p. 274. And Maddison remarks: 'No one will disagree with the assertion that the pervasive climate of the Cold War has played perhaps a major part in the process of integrating a serviceable image of Orwell within the stark philosophical citadel of Natopolis.' '*1984*: A Burnhamite Fantasy?' p. 71. For the early reception and interpretation of *Nineteen Eighty-Four*, see Crick, *Orwell*, pp. 563–71; Crick, 'Introduction', pp. 92–105.

9 Fredric Warburg's confidential report on *Nineteen Eighty-Four* is published as an appendix to Crick, 'Introduction', pp. 147–9.

10 Deutscher, '*1984* – The Mysticism of Cruelty', p. 200. Philip Rahv, in his influential 1949 review in the *Partisan Review*, also saw the novel as dealing predominantly with 'the crisis of socialism', and as an attack on the left, specifically on the idea of 'the Soviet Utopia'. Rahv, 'The Unfuture of Utopia', pp. 181–2.

11 This is plain enough not only from publishers' lists, but also from the main type of participants at the orgy of *Nineteen Eighty-Four* conferences in England and America occasioned by the year 1984.

12 Letter to the Duchess of Atholl, 15 November 1945, in Sonia Orwell and Ian Angus (eds), *The Collected Essays, Journalism and Letters of George Orwell* (4 vols) (Harmondsworth, Penguin Books, 1970) (hereafter *CEJL*), vol. IV, p. 49.

13 Letter to Francis A. Henson of the UAW, 16 June 1949, *CEJL*, vol. IV, p. 564. (Orwell's emphases). Parts of this letter were published in *Life* and the *New York Times Book Review* in July 1949.

14 Orwell's press release of 15 June 1949 is printed as an appendix to Crick, 'Introduction', pp. 152–3.

15 Letter of William Empson to George Orwell, 24 August 1945; quoted Crick, *Orwell*, pp. 491–2.

16 '"Historic necessity", or rather the belief in it, has failed to survive Hitler.' Orwell, *The Road to Wigan Pier* (Harmondsworth, Penguin Books, 1962), p. 185.

17 Letter to H. J. Willmett, 18 May 1944, *CEJL*, vol. III, p. 177.

18 Ibid., p. 178. On the strength of the English tradition, and its potentiality for resisting

totalitarianism, see especially 'The Lion and the Unicorn' (1941), *CEJL*, vol. II, pp. 74–134.

19 'Why I Write' (1946), *CEJL*, vol. I, p. 28.

20 For 'the chain of Utopia books', see the letter to F. J. Warburg, 30 March 1949, *CEJL*, vol. IV, p. 546. For *Nineteen Eighty-Four* as directly linked to the utopian and anti-utopian tradition, see also Michael Wilding, *Political Fictions* (1980), pp. 216–17.

21 Crick, 'Introduction', pp. 135, 20. The connection between *Nineteen Eighty-Four* and the works of 'documentary realism' is argued and traced by Jenni Calder, *Chronicles of Conscience* (London, Secker & Warburg, 1968).

22 David Lodge, 'Utopia and Criticism: The Radical longing for Paradise', *Encounter*, vol. 32 (April 1969), p. 68. Analogously, cf. Crick's rejoinder to the 'hidden wound' school of Orwell criticism: 'Those who are confident that they can find a psychological "hidden wound" in the young Eric and then locate *Nineteen Eighty-Four* on the map as a version of St Cyprian's, as if the vision of totalitarianism arose from prep-school terror and sufferings, may be disguising their own lack of perception of the political horrors that Orwell said were under their own noses, far more dangerous, dramatic and objective, in their shared contemporary world of the 1930s and 1940s.' Crick, *Orwell*, pp. 64–5.

23 Letter to Julian Symons, 4 February 1949, *CEJL*, vol. IV, p. 536.

24 Letter to F. J. Warburg, 31 May 1947, *CEJL*, vol. IV, p. 378.

25 The best study of Orwell's relation to earlier utopian writers is William Steinhoff, *George Orwell and the Origins of 1984* (Ann Arbor, University of Michigan Press, 1975) published in England as *The Road to 1984* (London, Weidenfeld & Nicolson, 1975), esp. pp. 5–55. It seems worth mentioning that, according to a childhood friend Jacintha Buddicom, the young Eric Blair 'greatly fancied' Wells's *A Modern Utopia* and 'said he might write that kind of book himself'. J. Buddicom, 'The Young Eric', in Gross (ed.), *The World of George Orwell*, p. 4.

26 For a similar view, see Matthew Hodgart, 'From *Animal Farm* to *Nineteen Eighty-Four*', in Gross (ed.), *The World of George Orwell*, p. 139. It is equally one-sided, of course, to emphasize the *purely* prophetic (and profoundly pessimistic) aspect of *Nineteen Eighty-Four*, as does G. C. Le Roy, 'AF632 to 1984', *College English*, vol. 12 (1950), pp. 135–8.

27 For a view of the whole of Orwell's work as Swiftian satire, as a bleak comment on the general human condition, see Stephen J. Greenblatt, 'Orwell as Satirist', in Raymond Williams (ed.), *George Orwell: A Collection of Critical Essays* (Engelwood Cliffs, NJ, Prentice-Hall, 1974), pp. 103–18.

28 'Review of *We* by E. I. Zamyatin' (1946), *CEJL*, vol. IV, p. 99.

29 Julian Symons, quoted in Crick, 'Introduction', p. 20.

30 Burgess, *1985*, p. 33. For the 1940s background to the novel, see also Meyers, *A Reader's Guide to George Orwell*, pp. 144–6; Crick, 'Introduction', pp. 19–24.

31 George Orwell, *Nineteen Eighty-Four* (1949; Harmondsworth, Penguin Books, 1954). All references in the text, as *NEF*, are to this Penguin edition, 1977 reprint.

32 'Wells, Hitler and the World State' (1941), *CEJL*, vol. II, p. 169. See also *The Road to Wigan Pier*, pp. 164 ff., for the mechanized character of the Wellsian utopia.

33 'Wells, Hitler and the World State', pp. 170, 172.

34 'Notes on the Way' (1940), *CEJL*, vol. II, pp. 30–3. Cf. the remark that, after the Great War, 'themes like revenge, patriotism, exile, persecution, race hatred, religious faith, loyalty, leader worship, suddenly seemed real again. Tamerlane and Genghis Khan seem credible figures now, and Machiavelli seems a serious thinker, as they didn't in 1910.' 'The Rediscovery of Europe' (1942), *CEJL*, vol. II, p. 239.

35 'Review of *Mein Kampf* by Adolf Hitler' (1940), *CEJL*, vol. II, p. 29.

36 'Wells, Hitler and the World State', p. 172.

37 'Prophecies of Fascism' (1940), *CEJL*, vol. II, p. 47. See also Orwell's 'Introduction to *Love of Life and Other Stories* by Jack London' (1946), *CEJL*, vol. IV, pp. 41–8.

38 'Review of *We* . . .', p. 98. And see also the appreciation of *We* in Orwell's letter to his publisher F. W. Warburg (30 March 1949), *CEJL*, vol. IV, pp. 546–7.
39 'Wells, Hitler and the World State', p. 168.
40 Arthur Koestler, *Darkness at Noon* (1940; Harmondsworth, Penguin Books, 1964), p. 53. Orwell refers to 'a dictatorship of theorists' in his letter to Humphrey House (11 April 1940), *CEJL*, vol. I, p. 583. It is also worth remembering that the pigs in *Animal Farm*, who both lead and betray the revolution, are 'brain workers', i.e. intellectuals.
41 'Arthur Koestler' (1944), *CEJL*, vol. III, p. 281. Cf.: 'The truth is that many of the qualities we admire in human beings can only function in opposition to some kind of disaster, pain, or difficulty.' *The Road to Wigan Pier*, p. 170.
42 'Wells, Hitler and the World State', p. 170.
43 'Marx and Russia', *The Observer* (15 February 1948); quoted in Steinhoff, *George Orwell and the Origins of 1984*, p. 60.
44 'Inside the Whale' (1940), *CEJL*, vol. I, pp. 565–7. 'They can swallow totalitarianism *because* they have no experience of anything except liberalism.' Orwell's attack on the intelligentsia for what he considered the most devastating and disastrous *trahison des clercs* of modern times continued with time to become even more uninhibited: 'During the past twenty-five years the activities of what are called "intellectuals" have been largely mischievous. I do not think it an exaggeration to say that, if the "intellectuals" had done their work a little more thoroughly, Britain would have surrendered in 1940.' 'Antisemitism in Britain' (1945), *CEJL*, vol. III, p. 386.
45 *The Road to Wigan Pier*, p. 157.
46 Ibid., pp. 154, 190. Cf. letter to House, *CEJL*, vol. I, p. 583.
47 'Notes on Nationalism' (1945), *CEJL*, vol. III, p. 412.
48 'Raffles and Miss Blandish' (1944), *CEJL*, vol. III, pp. 257–9.
49 All quotations in this paragraph are from 'Arthur Koestler', pp. 270–82. And see R. G. Geering, '*Darkness at Noon* and *1984*: A Comparative Study', *Australian Quarterly*, vol. 30 (September 1958), pp. 90–6. For an interesting linked discussion of Malraux, Silone and Koestler, see Irving Howe, *Politics and the Novel* (1957), pp. 203–34; and Paul N. Siegel, *Revolution and the Twentieth-Century Novel* (1979).
50 'Why I Write' (1946), *CEJL*, vol. I, p. 28. Peter Stansky and William Abrahams concur: 'Spain transformed him', politically and artistically. *Orwell: The Transformation* (London, Paladin, 1981), p. 212 and, generally, 199–238. See also Crick, *Orwell*, p. 323 and, generally, 313–52. In a letter to Cyril Connolly from his hospital bed in Barcelona in June 1937, Orwell wrote: 'I have seen wonderful things and at last really believe in Socialism, which I never did before.' *CEJL*, vol. I, p. 301. Returning to England, he wrote that the Spanish experience not only revealed to him the truth about Stalinism but also, with the 'foretaste of Socialism' that he found in the workers' militias, made his 'desire to see Socialism established much more actual than it had been before'. *Homage to Catalonia* (1938; Harmondsworth, Penguin Books, 1962), pp. 101–3.
51 'Review of *The Spanish Cockpit* by Franz Borkenau' (1937), *CEJL*, vol. I, p. 311. See also 'Spilling the Spanish Beans' (1937), *CEJL*, vol. I, pp. 301–9. In *Homage to Catalonia*, Orwell again wrote of the 'nightmare atmosphere' prevailing in Barcelona at the time. 'It was as though some huge evil intelligence were brooding over the town.' He sensed 'a peculiar evil feeling in the air – an atmosphere of suspicion, fear, uncertainty, and veiled hatred . . . a consciousness of some evil thing that was impending'. Ibid., pp. 186–9. Much of the hallucinatory quality of *Nineteen Eighty-Four* undoubtedly derived from Orwell's experience of the period of savage repression in Catalonia.
52 'Author's Preface to the Ukrainian Edition of *Animal Farm*' (1947), *CEJL*, vol. III, p. 457.
53 For Orwell's account of these episodes, see his letters to Rayner Heppenstall (31 July 1937) and to Raymond Mortimer (9 February 1938) in *CEJL*, vol. I, pp. 311–13, 333–6. The lies and distortions of the press, especially the left-wing press, are bitterly

detailed and denounced in *Homage to Catalonia*, pp. 153–72.
54 'Arthur Koestler', p. 273.
55 'Author's Preface to the Ukrainian Edition of *Animal Farm*', pp. 457–8. And cf. Orwell's comment on the view that the Soviet Union may be thought to be in a 'transitional phase' on the way to socialism. 'The trouble with transitional periods is that the harsh outlook which they generate tends to become permanent. To all appearances this is what has happened in Soviet Russia. A dictatorship supposedly established for a limited purpose has dug itself in, and Socialism comes to be thought of as meaning concentration camps and secret police forces.' 'Review of *The Soul of Man under Socialism* by Oscar Wilde' (1948), *CEJL*, vol. IV, pp. 484–5.
56 'London Letter to *Partisan Review*' (August 1945), *CEJL*, vol. III, p. 446.
57 *The Road to Wigan Pier*, p. 189.
58 'Review of *Assignment in Utopia* by Eugene Lyons' (1938), *CEJL*, vol. I, p. 370.
59 Jack Common, *The Freedom of the Streets* (1938); quoted in Crick, *Orwell*, p. 622, n. 22. Orwell's review is in *CEJL*, vol. I, pp. 371–3. A similar presentiment had occurred earlier to the Trotskyist Max Eastman: 'I feel sometimes as though the whole modern world of capitalism and Communism and all were rushing toward some enormous efficient machine-made doom of the true values of life' (1922). Quoted in Howe (ed.), *Orwell's Nineteen Eighty-Four*, p. 176.
60 'Review of *Power: A New Social Analysis* by Bertrand Russell' (1939), *CEJL*, vol. I, pp. 413–14.
61 'Review of *Russia Under Soviet Rule* by N. de Basily' (1939), *CEJL*, vol. I, p. 419. This is the closest that Orwell comes to taking a Huxleyite view of the future.
62 'Review of *The Totalitarian Enemy* by F. Borkenau' (1940), *CEJL*, vol. II, pp. 40–1.
63 'Literature and Totalitarianism' (1941), *CEJL*, vol. II, p. 162.
64 Letter to S. Moos (16 December 1943); quoted in Crick, *Orwell*, p. 468.
65 'Literature and Totalitarianism', p. 162.
66 'As I Please', *Tribune* (28 April 1944), *CEJL*, vol. III, p. 160.
67 'The Prevention of Literature' (1946), *CEJL*, vol. IV, p. 86. See also 'Notes on Nationalism' (1945), *CEJL*, vol. III, pp. 418–21.
68 'Literature and Totalitarianism', p. 163.
69 'The Prevention of Literature', p. 89.
70 Ibid., p. 88.
71 'Politics vs. Literature: An Examination of *Gulliver's Travels*' (1946), *CEJL*, vol. IV, p. 261.
72 Letter to Roger Senhouse (26 December 1948), *CEJL*, vol. IV, p. 520. At Teheran (1943) and later at Yalta (1945), the 'Big Three' – Roosevelt, Churchill and Stalin – divided the world up between them into 'spheres of influence' – and then promptly fell out, as in *Nineteen Eighty-Four*. The last pages of *Animal Farm*, as Orwell found he had to point out to less perceptive readers, also show the two ruling groups, the Men and the Pigs, falling out after scenes of harmony.
73 'You and the Atom Bomb' (1945), *CEJL*, vol. IV, pp. 4, 23–5.
74 'Toward European Unity' (1947), *CEJL*, vol. IV, p. 424.
75 Gordon Craig, 'Triangularity and International Violence', in Stansky (ed.), *On Nineteen Eighty-Four*, pp. 26, 32. In June 1984 America agreed for the first time since 1949 to sell arms and military technology to China. *New York Times* (15 June 1984).
76 'You and the Atom Bomb', p. 26.
77 'James Burnham and the Managerial Revolution' (1946), *CEJL*, vol. IV, pp. 192–215. For the debt to Burnham, see Maddison, '*1984*: A Burnhamite Fantasy?' See also R. Gerber, *Utopian Fantasy: A Study of English Utopian Fiction since the End of the Nineteenth Century* (1955), p. 67; Steinhoff, *George Orwell and the Origins of 1984*, pp. 43–54; Crick, 'Introduction', pp. 84–92. The conventional attribution of a debt to Trotsky, and specifically to *The Revolution Betrayed* – see e.g. Irving Howe, '*1984*: History as Nightmare', in Howe (ed.), *Orwell's Nineteen Eighty-Four*, p. 190 – is clearly mistaken.

78 'James Burnham and the Managerial Revolution', p. 212.

79 The new form of collective ownership was also the basis, as Burnham had seen it, of managerial rule: 'Those who control the state, those whose interests are primarily served by the state, are the ruling class under the structure of state-owned economy. . . . An economy of state ownership can . . . provide the basis for domination and exploitation by a ruling class of an extremity and absoluteness never before known.' James Burnham, *The Managerial Revolution* (1941; Harmondsworth, Penguin Books, 1962), pp. 116–17. The same argument underlies Djilas's view that a new ruling class has arisen in the communist societies of Eastern Europe: see M. Djilas, *The New Class* (London, Thames & Hudson, 1957).

80 'Politics vs. Literature', p. 252.

81 Howe, '*1984*: History as Nightmare', p. 196.

82 Cf. Wilhelm Reich: 'Every inhibition of genital gratification intensifies the sadistic impulse.' Quoted in Elaine Baruch, 'The Golden Country: Sex and Love in *1984*', in Irving Howe (ed.), *1984 Revisited* (New York, Harper & Row, 1983), p. 50. Baruch finds Julia 'the most courageous and admirable figure in the society of *1984*'. For a less sympathetic view of Orwell's treatment of women in *Nineteen Eighty-Four*, see Anne K. Mellor, '"You're Only a Rebel From the Waist Downwards": Orwell's View of Women', in Stansky (ed.), *On Nineteen Eighty-Four*, pp. 115–25. For a more complex reading of the place of sexuality in the novel, see Paul Robinson, 'For the Love of Big Brother: The Sexual Politics of *Nineteen Eighty-Four*', in Stansky (ed.), *On Nineteen Eighty-Four*, pp. 148–58.

83 Crick, 'Introduction', p. 75.

84 Quoted in Burgess, *1985*, p. 42. Steinhoff also quotes a choice specimen of 'cablese' from Eugene Lyons's *Assignment in Utopia*, which Orwell reviewed. He further suggests that Orwell got the main design of Newspeak from C. K. Ogden's *The System of Basic English* (1934), which Orwell possessed. Steinhoff, *George Orwell and the Origins of 1984*, pp. 167–9.

85 'Politics and the English Language' (1947), *CEJL*, vol. IV, p. 157.

86 'The English People' (1944), *CEJL*, vol. III, p. 42.

87 'Politics and the English Language', p. 166.

88 Quoted in E. C. Traugott, 'Newspeak: Could It Really Work?' in Stansky (ed.), *On Nineteen Eighty-Four*, p. 98. A whole euphemistic vocabulary for the nuclear age was invented by Herman Kahn in his book that aimed to make us 'think the unthinkable': *On Thermonuclear War* (Princeton University Press, 1960).

89 This and other American examples are quoted in Bernard Avishai, 'Orwell and the English Language', in Howe (ed.), *1984 Revisited*, pp. 69–71. Normal Mailer too, in his account of the American moon project, expresses his admiration for the astronauts' achievement but is saddened by their use of a peculiarly deadened, peculiarly twentieth-century form of language which insulates speaker and hearer from reality. 'Even as the Nazis and the Communists had used to speak of mass murder as liquidation, so the astronauts spoke of possible personal disasters as "contingency". The heart of astronaut talk, like the heart of all bureaucratic talk, was a jargon which could be easily converted to computer programming, a language like Fortran or Cobol or Algol. . . . Anti-dread formulations were the center of it, as if words like pills were there to suppress emotional symptoms.' Mailer, *Of a Fire On The Moon* (Boston, Little, Brown, 1971), p. 25.

90 As Crick points out, it is somewhat unfortunate that Orwell makes so much of this formula – here and elsewhere in his writings – as the touchstone of empirical truth and reality. $2 + 2 = 4$ is *not* an empirical proposition, but belongs to an 'analytical' system of thought, mathematics, the truth of whose propositions depends simply on the internal coherence and consistency of the system, not on their correspondence to the external world. Crick, 'Introduction', p. 79.

91 The $2 + 2 = 5$ equation was actually used by the Russians, according to Eugene

Lyons's account, to suggest that the Five-Year Plan could be fulfilled in four years. See Steinhoff, *George Orwell and the Origins of 1984*, p. 172.

92 'For the moment the totalitarian state tolerates the scientist because it needs him. . . . So long as physical reality cannot be altogether ignored, so long as two and two have to make four when you are, for example, drawing the blue-print of an aeroplane, the scientist has his function, and can even be allowed a measure of liberty. His awakening will come later, when the totalitarian state is firmly established.' 'The Prevention of Literature', p. 94. *Nineteen Eighty-Four* portrays that later stage.

93 'Looking Back on the Spanish War' (1943), *CEJL*, vol. II, pp. 296–7.

94 Ibid., p. 289.

95 'Review of *The Totalitarian Enemy* by Franz Borkenau', p. 41. On the instability of totalitarian doctrines, see also 'Notes on Nationalism', pp. 417–21.

96 'Inside the Whale', *CEJL*, vol. I, p. 563. See also 'The Prevention of Literature', pp. 88–9. For some priceless examples of the rewriting of history in the Soviet Union, see Conquest, 'Totaliterror', pp. 180–1.

97 Although it comes as a surprise to find it equated with that 'negative capability' that Keats so admired in Shakespeare, and defended as a valuable principle in jurisprudence. See B. A. Babcock, 'Lawspeak and Doublethink', in Stansky (ed.), *On Nineteen Eighty-Four*, pp. 86–91.

98 Herman Kahn, *On Thermonuclear War*, quoted in Erich Fromm, 'Afterword on 1984', in Howe (ed.), *Orwell's Nineteen Eighty-Four*, p. 208.

99 Orwell notes a very similar conclusion in Koestler's *Scum of the Earth*: 'Without education of the masses, no social progress; without social progress, no education of the masses.' 'Arthur Koestler', p. 279.

100 For these points, see *The Road to Wigan Pier*, pp. 43–4, 79–81, 104. For an interesting discussion of Orwell's view of the English working class, see Richard Hoggart, 'Introduction to *The Road to Wigan Pier*' in Williams (ed.), *George Orwell*, pp. 34–51. Williams is one of the many who are outraged by Orwell's treatment of the proles in *Nineteen Eighty-Four*; see his *Orwell*, ibid., p. 79.

101 'The Prevention of Literature', pp. 92–3.

102 See 'Charles Dickens' (1939), *CEJL*, vol. I, pp. 501–4; and, for the critique of 'heart' as a political force, 'Looking Back on the Spanish Civil War', p. 304. Cf. also the comment that, in the face of twentieth-century political theories, the common people of England oppose 'not another view of their own, but a moral quality which must be vaguely defined as decency'. 'The English People', p. 28. This suggests a capacity for resistance, not change.

103 'Review of *The Freedom of the Streets* by Jack Common' (1938), *CEJL*, vol. I, pp. 371–2. Cf. the remark that 'the central problem of revolution' is 'the impossibility of combining power with righteousness'. 'Arthur Koestler', p. 275.

104 Crick, 'Introduction', pp. 14–15, 47–8. For the general features of totalitarian movements and organizations, see Hannah Arendt, *The Origins of Totalitarianism*, new ed. (New York, Harcourt Brace and World, 1966), part III; Carl J. Friedrich and Z. K. Brzezinski, *Totalitarian Dictatorship and Autocracy*, (2nd edn) (New York, Praeger, 1966).

105 Howe, '*1984*: History as Nightmare', p. 194. Philip Rahv was the first to make this point about Orwell's treatment of the proles: 'All societies of our epoch, whether authoritarian or democratic in structure, are mass-societies; and an authoritarian state built on the foundations of a mass society could scarcely afford the luxury of allowing any class or group to evade its demand for complete control. A totalitarian–collectivist state is rigidly organized along hierarchical lines, but that very fact, so damaging to its socialist claims, necessitates the domination of all citizens, of whatever class, in the attempt to "abolish" the contradiction between its theory and practice by means of boundless demagogy and violence.' Rahv, 'The Unfuture of Utopia', p. 185. For similar objections see also Maddison, '*1984*: A Burnhamite Fantasy?', p. 72.

106 Crick, 'Introduction', p. 15.
107 E.g.: 'We may be heading not for general breakdown but for an epoch as horribly stable as the slave empires of antiquity.' 'You and the Atom Bomb', p. 26. See also 'The Rediscovery of Europe (1942), *CEJL*, vol. II, p. 239; 'Review of *We* by E. I. Zamyatin', p. 98.
108 This is indeed still the attitude of Rubashov, as he walks to his execution, in Koestler's *Darkness at Noon.*
109 For detailed parallels between the structure and symbolism of Oceania and those of Roman Catholicism, see Steinhoff, *George Orwell and the Origins of 1984*, pp. 184–5.
110 Rahv, 'The Unfuture of Utopia', p. 184.
111 Howe, '*1984*: History as Nightmare', p. 195. Howe has more recently seen more plausibility in Orwell's position. See his '*1984*: Enigmas of Power', in Howe (ed.), *1984 Revisited*, pp. 10–14.
112 Deutscher, '*1984*: The Mysticism of Cruelty', p. 203. Cf. George Kateb: 'There is no historical experience that would bear Orwell out. The worst Nazi lived on something besides cruelty. In so far as one can deal with the question of political motivation in the abstract, one must conclude that the heart of *1984* is unsound.' 'The Road to *1984*', in Samuel Hynes (ed.), *Twentieth Century Interpretations of 1984* (Englewood Cliffs, NJ, Prentice-Hall, 1971), p. 75.
113 Crick, 'Introduction', pp. 48–9, 65.
114 Woodcock, *The Crystal Spirit*, p. 219. And cf. Steinhoff: 'Like "A Modest Proposal", *1984* assumes the existence of certain conditions and certain tendencies of mind and attempts to work out their outrageous consequences in order to effect in the reader a revulsion against them.' Steinhoff, *George Orwell and the Origins of 1984*, p. 201.
115 'James Burnham and the Managerial Revolution', p. 214. See also 'Burnham's View of the Contemporary World Struggle' (1947), *CEJL*, vol. IV, pp. 360–74.
116 'Why Machiavellis of Today Fall Down', *Manchester Evening News* (20 January 1944); quoted in Steinhoff, *George Orwell and the Origins of 1984*, p. 203.
117 'James Burnham and the Managerial Revolution', p. 211. Cf. 'As I Please', *Tribune* (29 November 1946), *CEJL*, vol. IV, p. 289. For Orwell's critique of Burnham and its relation to the question of power in *Nineteen Eighty-Four*, see especially Kateb, 'The Road to *1984*', pp. 80–7.
118 Orwell quotes the passage in 'Introduction to *Love of Life and Other Stories* by Jack London' (1946), *CEJL*, vol. IV, p. 43. The full passage is in Jack London, *The Iron Heel* (1907; London, Journeyman Press, 1974), pp. 190–1. And see also the comments on London in 'Prophecies of Fascism', *CEJL*, vol. II, pp. 46–7.
119 'The Prevention of Literature', p. 89.
120 Jack London, *The Iron Heel*, p. 63.
121 'Review of *We* by E. I. Zamyatin', p. 97.
122 'Review of *The Totalitarian Enemy* by F. Borkenau', p. 41.
123 'The Lion and the Unicorn', p. 81.
124 'Raffles and Miss Blandish', p. 258 (Orwell's emphasis).
125 Alan Bullock, *Hitler: A Study in Tyranny*, rev. edn (Harmondsworth, Penguin Books, 1962), p. 382. This too is the only consistent thread to Hitler's personality and motives that emerges from the portrait in Albert Speer's memoirs, *Inside the Third Reich* (London, Weidenfeld & Nicolson, 1970).
126 Alexander Weisberg, *Conspiracy of Silence* (1952); quoted in Steinhoff, *George Orwell and the Origins of 1984*, p. 207. Alexander Solzhenitsyn's novel *The First Circle* (1970) contains a similar portrait of a power-mad Stalin.
127 Koestler, *Darkness at Noon*, p. 81.
128 'As I Please', *Tribune* (17 January 1947), *CEJL*, vol. IV, p. 312.
129 See the persuasive essay by Alex Zwerdling, 'Orwell and the Techniques of Didactic Fantasy', in Hynes (ed.), *Twentieth Century Interpretations of 1984*, pp. 88–101.

Chapter 9 The Utopia of 'Behavioural Engineering': B. F. Skinner and *Walden Two*

1 Skinner has often pointed out that many of the reviews of *Walden Two* were favourable, or at least dispassionate. But he admits that the hostile ones best represented the response of the general educated public of the time.
2 The *Life* review, in the form of an anonymous editorial of 28 June 1948, is reprinted by Skinner in B. F. Skinner, *The Shaping of a Behaviorist: Part Two of an Autobiography* (New York, Alfred A. Knopf, 1979), pp. 347–8. And cf. Donald C. Williams, reviewing *Walden Two* on its appearance: 'Skinner's New Atlantis must seem to most Americans both comical and repulsive. . . .' 'The Social Scientist as Philosopher and King', *Philosophical Review*, vol. 58 (1949), p. 347.
3 Joseph Wood Krutch, *The Measure of Man* (Indianapolis, Bobbs-Merrill, 1953), p. 59.
4 Glenn Negley and J. Max Patrick (eds), *The Quest for Utopia: An Anthology of Imaginary Societies* (1952), p. 590.
5 'Halfway through this contemporary utopia, the reader may feel sure, as we did, that this is a beautifully ironic satire on what has been called "behavioural engineering". The longer one stays in this better world of the psychologist, however, the plainer it becomes that the inspiration is not satiric, but messianic.' Negley and Patrick, *The Quest for Utopia*, pp. 589–90.
6 B. F. Skinner, *Beyond Freedom and Dignity* (1971; Harmondsworth, Penguin Books, 1973), pp. 215–16. All references are to this Penguin edition.
7 Something quintessential and, I suspect, importantly American in Skinner's philosophy is lost by the anglicization of the spelling of terms like 'behavior', 'behaviorism' and 'behavioral'. But in the interest of consistency and to avoid confusion, I have regretfully decided to use the anglicized versions throughout.
8 B. F. Skinner, 'Foreword' to Kathleen Kinkade, *A Walden Two Experiment: The First Five Years of Twin Oaks Community* (New York, William Morrow, 1973), p. vi.
9 B. F. Skinner, 'Walden Two Revisited', new introduction to the 1976 reprint of *Walden Two* (New York, Macmillan, 1976), pp. viii–ix.
10 Skinner, 'Foreword' to *A Walden Two Experiment*, p. x.
11 See especially Skinner, 'Walden Two Revisited'.
12 B. F. Skinner, *Walden Two* (1948; New York, Macmillan, 1962). All references in the text hereafter – as *WT* – are to this paperback edition.
13 Skinner writes with nostaligic affection of these childhood years in the first volume of his autobiography, *Particulars of My Life* (New York, Alfred A. Knopf, 1976).
14 The relation between Thoreau's *Walden* (1854) and Skinner's *Walden Two* is complex. Both are suffused with Yankee Protestantism. Both are concerned to cut down unnecessary expenditure of time and effort, and are ceaseless in their search for devices to do this. Both are contemptuous of the artificial inflation of needs, and the consequent material dependence, of the outside world. And both adopt a radically experimental attitude to the problems of living. At the same time, Walden Two embraces modern technology with a fervour which Thoreau would have scorned. For its functioning it seems to require a level of material affluence which he would have regarded as unnecessarily luxurious and probably corrupting. Above all, its whole philosophy of collective control and manipulation of the social environment would have been anathema to the uncompromisingly individualist Thoreau.

Perhaps one further difference ought to be mentioned. Thoreau lived Walden; Skinner has never lived Walden Two.
15 Skinner, *A Walden Two Experiment*, p. 12.
16 '"Mr Castle is amused," said Frazier, bearing down hard. . . . "It might be interesting to ask him to perform an experiment. Mr Castle would you mind turning one of these trays over from side to side one thousand times? Perhaps you will concede the result. Either you would work quickly and finish with painfully cramped muscles, or else slowly and be bored. Either would be objectionable. Yet some one of us would be compelled to do

just that three times a day if our trays were opaque. . .".' (*WT*, p. 48).

17 B. F. Skinner, 'Operant Behaviour', in his *Contingencies of Reinforcement: A Theoretical Analysis* (New York, Appleton-Century-Crofts, 1969), p. 107.

18 Harvey Wheeler, 'Introduction: A Nonpunitive World?' in Harvey Wheeler (ed.), *Beyond the Punitive Society* (San Francisco, W. H. Freeman, 1973), p. 9. It should be clear that the 'biology' referred to here has nothing to do with theories of the genetic determination of human behaviour, as held by many ethologists and 'socio-biologists'. Skinner is an out-and-out environmentalist.

19 Skinner, *Beyond Freedom and Dignity*, p. 23.

20 Ibid., p. 24.

21 I have not in this section tried to do more than give a very selective account of Skinner's theoretical approach. For more general accounts, see John A. Weigl, *B. F. Skinner* (Boston, Twayne Publishers, 1977); and Robert D. Nye, *What is B. F. Skinner Really Saying?* (Englewood Cliffs, NJ, Prentice-Hall, 1979). The book edited by Harvey Wheeler (n. 18 above) contains a good selection of critical essays on Skinner's approach and its general implications.

22 Skinner, 'Utopia as an Experimental Culture', in his *Contingencies of Reinforcement*, p. 37. This essay is a revision of two broadcast talks, 'Vision of Utopia' and 'Utopia through the Control of Human Behaviour', originally printed in *The Listener*, 5 and 12 January 1967.

23 Skinner, 'Utopia as an Experimental Culture', p. 37.

24 Skinner, 'Utopia through the Control of Human Behaviour', *The Listener*, 12 January 1967, p. 55.

25 For the general lines of this discussion, see Skinner, *Beyond Freedom and Dignity*, pp. 34–46, 80–3.

26 Ibid., pp. 83, 69. For a briefer discussion of the advantages of positive reinforcement over punishment, see *Walden Two*, pp. 259–61. Skinner, it should be noted, explicitly ties his theory of conditioning through positive reinforcement to Christian ethics and the Christian ideal of how to change behaviour. In defending the techniques of positive reinforcement as against punishment, Frazier says: '"We've all seen countless instances of the temporary effect of force, but clear evidence of the effect of not using force is rare. That's why I insist that Jesus, who was apparently the first to discover the power of refusing to punish, must have hit upon the principle by accident. . . ." "A touch of revelation, perhaps?" said Castle. "No, accident. Jesus discovered one principle because it had immediate consequences, and he got another thrown in for good measure". . . . "You mean the principle of 'love your enemies'," Burris said. "Exactly! To 'do good to those who despitefully use you' has two unrelated consequences. You gain the peace of mind we talked about the other day. Let the stronger man push you around – at least you avoid the torture of your own rage. *That's* the immediate consequence. What an astonishing discovery it must have been to find that in the long run you could *control the stronger man* in the same way!"' (*WT*, p. 261). Whether or not this is blasphemy, I leave others to decide.

27 The general discussion of sex, marriage and the family, from which the quotations in the text all come, is to be found on pp. 131–48 of *Walden Two*.

28 This is a convenient point at which to acknowledge my gratitude to both B. F. Skinner and Kathleen Kinkade for their discussions with me about *Walden Two*, and its relation to Twin Oaks and East Wind, both of which were founded by Kat Kinkade.

29 Kincade, *A Walden Two Experiment*, p. 44.

30 Ibid., p. 49.

31 For the general structure of government at Walden Two see *WT*, pp. 54–5.

32 Ibid., p. 55.

33 Ibid., pp. 237, 249.

34 Ibid., p. 55.

35 Max Black, 'Some Aversive Responses to a Would-be Reinforcer', in Wheeler (ed.),

Beyond the Punitive Society, p. 132. For similar attacks on Skinner along these general lines, see Krutch, *The Measure of Man, passim*; R. Puligandla, *Fact and Fiction in B. F. Skinner's Science and Utopia* (St Louis, Missouri, Warren H. Green, 1974); Carl Rogers, in Carl Rogers and B. F. Skinner, 'Some Issues Concerning the Control of Human Behaviour', *Science*, vol. 124 (1956), pp. 1057–1106. And cf. Donald C. Williams: 'except for the aggressive psychological Managers, the adults in Walden Two are the amiable zombies, the children are the colourless little larvae, which we non-psychologists would predict. . . . Mr Skinner is a spokesman for rampant scientism. . . . His railings at democracy and capitalism are in themselves hardly distinguishable from the attacks of the National Socialists and our new medievalists on the liberal way of life. . . .' Williams, 'The Social Scientist as Philosopher and King', pp. 348, 350, 357. And see Andrew Hacker: 'The conditioned man is not an autonomous man in the sense of liberal theory. Perhaps he is not even a man. . . . It must be that in any community where extensive conditioning is operative, the conditioners may be called autonomous individuals, but the conditioned may not. They may, according to taste, be regarded as robots, sheep, or buckets. For the conditioned, being merely receptacles for the 'suggestions' of their psychological–political masters, do not possess the capability of making up "their own" minds which liberal theory postulates as essential for an individual. Skinner's children and adults can hardly be called individuals after they have been subjected to "human engineering".' Hacker, 'Dostoevsky's Disciples: Man and Sheep in Political Theory', *Journal of Politics* (1955), pp. 595, 609. See also Andrew Hacker, 'The Specter of Predictable Man', *Antioch Review*, vol. 14 (1954), pp. 195–207.

There is a bad-tempered and, I think, somewhat confused attack on Skinner by Noam Chomsky: 'The Case Against B. F. Skinner', *New York Review of Books* (30 December 1971). Chomsky comments: 'As to its social implications, Skinner's science of human behaviour, being quite vacuous, is as congenial to the libertarian as to the fascist.' Of all the general discussions, the most judicious – concluding with a qualified approval of Skinner – is George Kateb, *Utopia and Its Enemies* (New York, Schocken Books, 1972), pp. 139–209.

36 B. F. Skinner, *Science and Human Behaviour* (1953; New York, Free Press of Glencoe, 1965), p. 447.

37 Skinner, *Beyond Freedom and Dignity*, p. 196.

38 Joseph Wood Krutch, 'Epitaph for an Age', *New York Times Magazine* (30 June 1967).

39 Skinner, *Beyond Freedom and Dignity*, p. 196.

40 Ibid., p. 85. I should perhaps say that I am not here trying to defend Skinner's view of man in general. I agree with many of his critics that it is an excessively narrow and reductionist view, based on a needlessly limited conception of man's capacities and potentialities. There are many things about man which are not dreamed of in Skinner's philosophy. What I do want to emphasize is that, at the level of social and political theory, the charges against Skinner have often been very feeble, and that his position contains strengths that we need to recognize and build on.

41 Ibid., p. 44. The examples in the text are discussed by Skinner on pp. 37 ff.

42 The point is developed more fully as follows: 'The illusion that freedom and dignity are respected when control seems incomplete arises in part from the probabilistic nature of operant behaviour. Seldom does any environmental condition "elicit" behaviour in the all-or-nothing fashion of a reflex; it simply makes a bit of behaviour more likely to occur. A hint will not itself suffice to evoke a response, but it adds strength to a weak response which may then appear. The hint is conspicuous, but the other events responsible for the appearance of the response are not.' Skinner, *Beyond Freedom and Dignity*, p. 97.

43 Ibid., pp. 97–8.

44 Ibid., p. 99.

45 Ibid., pp. 45–6.

46 Cf. Kateb: 'One of the most persistent themes in Skinner's writings is that there is

almost no aspect of the cultural environment that is devoid of influence on the formation of character. If this contention is correct – and is there not a *prima facie* case at least for that contention – does it not become only reasonable to see how the influence is exerted and to try to move into a position where the cultural environment, to the fullest degree possible, is made to stop working in our despite and "behind our backs"? Must not freedom begin with a consciousness of that to which the human being is subject: the prison of endowment and the prison of milieu? The more we know about both, the less we are the dupes of both.' Kateb, *Utopia and Its Enemies*, p. 151.

47 See Melvin M. Schuster, 'Skinner and the Morality of Melioration', In Peyton E. Richter (ed.), *Utopia/Dystopia?* (1975), pp. 93–108. Schuster argues that the attacks on Skinner for his authoritarianism are unfounded, since what he is essentially proposing is a politics of intervention and 'melioration', like any contemporary thinker or political party commited to a welfare state or welfare society. The only reasonable objection to Skinner must base itself on an objection to public intervention as such, to the 'meliorative hypothesis': 'What seems wrong is not the fact that people try to control the environment, improve their lives, influence one another, use conditioning, employ one method of education instead of another, and refuse to punish. The only basis for an ethical criticism is that adult people are being fashioned and their lives moulded in accordance with someone else's concept of the good. . . . The function of political society cannot be the improvement of man and the creation of the good life; for if it is, there can be no moral objection to Skinner's world.' Ibid., p. 106.

48 Skinner's antipathy to history – the fact of it, the study of it and comparisons drawn from it – comes out repeatedly. See, e.g., Frazier's comment: 'I don't care how well historical facts can be known from afar. Is it important to know them at all? I submit that history never even comes close to repeating itself. Even if we had reliable information about the past, we couldn't find a case similar enough to justify inferences about the present or immediate future. We can make no *real* use of history as a current guide. We make a false use of it – an emotive use of it – often enough' (*WT*, p. 239). 'What I am perhaps not altogether unemotional about is the assumption that the historical account has the status of a body of facts, from which we can make predictions about the success of a contemporary venture' (*WT*, pp. 156–7). Not surpringly, history does not rank high among the subjects studied at Walden Two: 'They may read all the history they like. But we don't regard it as essential in their education' (*WT*, p. 238).

49 For a full (and enthusiastic) account of the use of Skinnerian methods in various institutional contexts, see Robert L. Geiser, *Behaviour Mod and the Managed Society* (Boston, Beacon Press, 1976). See also Vance Packard, *The People Shapers* (New York, Bantam Books, 1979), pp. 29–46, 182–6. Packard reports that 'in many of the experiments subjects have undergone dramatic relapses less than six months after leaving the controlled situation.' Ibid., p. 43. Skinner's own favourite example is an experiment in behavioural conditioning involving delinquent boys at the National Training School in Washington, DC. Success here amounted to the fact that the recidivism of the boys on leaving the school, usually a matter of months for most of them, was delayed by up to three years for an appreciable proportion of them. See B. F. Skinner, 'What's Wrong With the Social Sciences', *The Listener* (30 September 1971).

50 Skinner, 'Utopia as an Experimental Culture', in his *Contingencies of Reinforcement*, p. 38.

51 Skinner, *Beyond Freedom and Dignity*, p. 166.

52 See 'Answer to my Critics', in Wheeler (ed.), *Beyond the Punitive Society*, pp. 265–6. See also Skinner, 'Utopia as an Experimental Culture', pp. 42–4. Hacker's comment on this kind of defence is apt: 'Of course the conditioner has been conditioned. But he has not been conditioned by the conscious manipulation of another *person*. No one will deny that he has been affected by his culture, the social structure, and his psychological make-up. In addition, the fact that he must always be concerned with the "happiness" of his subjects puts a limiting strait-jacket on his freedom of choice. But it is a

strait-jacket that he has willingly donned. What sets him off from those he has conditioned is that their minds are the products of his conditioning, while he has not been conditioned by anyone in particular.' Hacker, 'Dostoevsky's Disciples: Man and Sheep in Political Theory', p. 608 n.

53 In this context it is worth quoting the notorious remark of T. H. Huxley's which is one of Skinner's favourites: '. . . if some great Power would agree to make me always think what is true and do what is right, on condition of being turned into a sort of clock and wound up every morning before I got out of bed, I should instantly close with the offer.' The passage occurs in Huxley's essay, 'On Descartes' Discourse Touching the Method of Using One's Reason Rightly and of Seeking Scientific Truth' (1870). It is quoted by Skinner (slightly inaccurately) in, e.g., *Beyond Freedom and Dignity*, p. 69. The whole problem here, of course, is the idea of a set of recipes for thought and behaviour which can constitute 'eternal virtue'. In approving Huxley's sentiment, Skinner can hardly blame us if we take it at its face value, and assume that Skinnerian conditioning does indeed lead to the production of unreflecting automata. But the more general tenor of Skinner's work points against this, especially in his differences with Pavlovian conditioning.

54 Kinkade makes a similar point about Twin Oaks; see *A Walden Two Experiment*, p. 55.

55 Skinner, *Beyond Freedom and Dignity*, p. 167; 'Utopia as an Experimental Culture', p. 43.

56 Karl Popper, *The Open Society and Its Enemies* (2 vols), rev. edn (1961).

57 Skinner, *Beyond Freedom and Dignity*, p. 104.

58 Ibid., p. 134.

59 Ibid., p. 170.

60 Ibid., pp. 158–9.

61 Ibid., p. 160.

Chapter 10 Utopia and Anti-Utopia in the Twentieth Century

1 Frank E. Manuel and Fritzie P. Manuel, *Utopian Thought in the Western World* (1979), pp. 21, 801; Northrop Frye, 'Varieties of Literary Utopias', in Frank E. Manuel (ed.), *Utopias and Utopian Thought* (1973), p. 29; Robert C. Elliott, *The Shape of Utopia: Studies in a Literary Genre* (1970), p. x, also pp. 84–8.

Examples of this view can be multiplied almost indefinitely. To take just the cases of some of the literature referred to in earlier chapters, see: M. I. Finley, 'Utopianism Ancient and Modern', in K. H. Wolff and Barrington Moore, Jr (eds), *The Critical Spirit: Essays in Honor of Herbert Marcuse*, (1967), p. 19; A. L. Morton, *The English Utopia* (London, Lawrence and Wishart, 1969), p. 250; Judith Shklar, *After Utopia: The Decline of Political Faith* (1957), p. 268; Chad Walsh, *From Utopia to Nightmare* (1962), p. 14; Marie Louise Berneri, *Journey Through Utopia* (1982), p. 293; J. H. Buckley, *The Triumph of Time: A Study of the Victorian Concepts of Time, History, Progress and Decadence* (1967), p. 86; J. C. Davis, *Utopia and the Ideal Society: A Study of English Utopian Writing 1516–1700* (1983), pp. 382 ff; Dennis Gabor, *Inventing the Future* (1964), pp. 14, 19, 168, n. 2.

2 D. H. Lawrence, letter to Lady Cynthia Asquith, November 1915, in *The Collected Letters of D. H. Lawrence*, ed. Harry Moore, vol. 1, (London, Heinemann, 1962), p. 378. On the profound disillusionment caused by the First World War, see also Sigmund Freud, 'Thoughts for the Times on War and Death' (1915), in Sigmund Freud, *Civilization, Society and Religion* (1985), pp. 61 ff.

3 I. F. Clarke, *The Pattern of Expectation 1644–2001* (1979), p. 231. For the impact of the First World War on utopian thought, see George Woodcock, 'Utopias in Negative', *Sewanee Review*, vol. 64 (1956), pp. 85–6.

4 H. G. Wells, *Mind at the End of its Tether* (London, William Heinemann, 1945), pp. 1, 15, 18.

5 I. F. Clarke, 'Methods of Prediction 1918–1939', *Futures*, vol. 2, no. 4 (1970), pp. 375–9.
6 See the discussion in Walsh, *From Utopia to Nightmare*, pp. 125 ff.
7 André Gide, in Richard Crossman (ed.), *The God That Failed: Six Studies in Communism* (1950), pp. 179, 183. For Koestler, see ibid., p. 39.
8 Zygmunt Bauman, *Socialism: The Active Utopia* (1976), p. 36. And for the Soviet Union's part in this disenchantment, cf. John Passmore: 'the ruthlessness the Soviet Union displayed in agricultural collectivization, the purges of the 'thirties, the treacherous manoeuvres of the Communist Party in the Spanish Civil War, the German–Soviet Pact, the Hungarian invasions, the Czecho-Slovakian interventions – one or the other of these events has destroyed the Soviet Union as a symbol of hope in the breasts of all but a very few Western intellectuals.' Passmore, *The Perfectibility of Man* (1972), p. 264.
9 See H. Stuart Hughes, *Consciousness and Society: The Reorientation of European Social Thought 1890–1930* (1958), pp. 315 ff.
10 See above, pp. 176–7.
11 Sigmund Freud, *Civilization and its Discontents* (1963), pp. 50–1. See also 'Thoughts for the Times on War and Death', in Freud, *Civilization, Society and Religion*, pp. 73, 86; 'Why War?' (1933), ibid., pp. 345–62.
12 Freud, *Civilization and Its Discontents*, p. 59. For Eros and Thanatos, see also Freud, *Beyond the Pleasure Principle* (1922; London, The Hogarth Press, 1961).
13 Freud, *Civilization and Its Discontents*, p. 82.
14 For listings of the more important utopias of the first half of the century, see the 'Selected List' in Glen Negley and J. Max Patrick, *The Quest for Utopia: An Anthology of Imaginary Societies* (1952), pp. 19–22; see also the appendix in Richard Gerber, *Utopian Fantasy: A Study of English Utopian Fiction since the End of the Nineteenth Century* (1955), and the appropriate sections of Lyman Tower Sargent, *British and American Utopian Literature 1516–1975: An Annotated Bibliography* (1979).
15 For science fiction from the 1920s to the 1940s, see Brian Aldiss, *Billion Year Spree: The History of Science Fiction* (1975), pp. 205–77; Brian Ash, *Faces of the Future: The Lessons of Science Fiction* (1975), pp. 65–79; Robert Scholes and Eric S. Rabkin, *Science Fiction: History, Science, Vision* (1977), pp. 26–42.
16 On Technocracy, the world fairs and associated movements, see Howard P. Segal, *Technological Utopianism in American Culture* (1985), *passim*, esp. pp. 98–128, 141–5.
17 Arthur Schlesinger Jr; quoted in Segal, *Technological Utopianism in American Culture*, p. 127.
18 Quoted in Norman Mackenzie and Jeanne Mackenzie, *The Time Traveller: The Life of H. G. Wells* (London, Weidenfeld & Nicolson, 1973), p. 424.
19 The Universal Declaration of Human Rights is reprinted as an appendix to *The United Nations and Human Rights* (New York, United Nations, 1984), pp. 241–4.
20 Martin Buber, *Paths in Utopia* (1958), pp. 148–9. Buber's book was first published, in Hebrew, in 1946.
21 C. Kerr, T. Dunlop, F. Harbison and C. A. Myers, *Industrialism and Industrial Man* (1960; 2nd edn, Harmondsworth, Penguin Books, 1973), pp. 81, 264–5.
22 For these developments in social theory, see further K. Kumar, *Prophecy and Progress: The Sociology of Industrial and Post-Industrial Society* (1978), pp. 170–84.

The utopian view of Western industrial society found its most complete expression in American social science of the 1950s, especially in the functionalist approach of the sociologist Talcott Parsons. For a characterization and a critique, see Ralf Dahrendorf, 'Out of Utopia: Toward a Reorientation of Sociological Analysis', *American Journal of Sociology*, vol. 64, no. 2 (1958), pp. 115–27.

23 See above, pp. 230 ff.
24 It is well known, of course, that Einstein, though a pacifist, later supported the development of the atomic bomb by the Allies because it was feared that Germany might get there first.

25 C. P. Snow, *The Two Cultures: And a Second Look* (1963), p. 17. Snow added the footnote: 'Compare George Orwell's *1984*, which is the strongest possible wish that the future should not exist, with J. D. Bernal's *World Without War*.'

26 Snow, *The Two Cultures*, p. 19.

27 For a discussion of post-industrial theory and futurology, see Kumar, *Prophecy and Progress*, pp. 185–240. See also K. Kumar, 'Futurology', in Adam Kuper and Jessica Kuper (eds), *The Encyclopaedia of the Social Sciences* (London, Routledge, 1985) Alvin Toffler, *Future Shock* (New York, Random House, 1970). The views of the futurologists can best be studied in the journals *Futures* (UK) and *The Futurist* (USA). For the utopia of the computer scientists of this period, see Robert Boguslaw, *The New Utopians: A Study of System Design and Social Change* (1965).

28 Julian Huxley, *Evolution in Action* (London, Chatto & Windus, 1953), pp. 113–14, 132–3. For the direct challenge to T. H. Huxley, see T. H. Huxley and Julian Huxley, *Evolution and Ethics 1893–1943* (London, Pilot Press, 1947), which reprints T. H. Huxley's 1893 Romanes Lecture and Julian Huxley's own Romanes Lecture of 1943. Julian Huxley had laid out his evolutionary credo very early in his working life. See 'Progress, Biological and Other' (1923), in his *Essays of a Biologist* (1923; Harmondsworth, Penguin Books, 1939), pp. 15–61; and see also the essays in his *The Uniqueness of Man* (London, Chatto & Windus, 1941). Later, as Director-General of UNESCO, he was responsible for initiating the project of the multi-volumed *History of Mankind*, whose explicit aim was to document the human phase of evolutionary progress. As Huxley himself wrote: 'The *History of Mankind* will be the first truly scientific and comprehensive account of psycho-social evolution as a process.' *Evolution in Action*, p. 136.

29 Huxley was forced to confess that he found it 'impossible to follow [Teilhard] all the way in his gallant attempt to reconcile the supernatural elements in Christianity with the facts and implications of evolution.' Sir Julian Huxley, 'Introduction' to Pierre Teilhard de Chardin, *The Phenomenon of Man*, tr. Bernard Wall (London, Collins, 1959), p. 19. Since, as Medawar pointed out in a distinctly unfriendly review of Teilhard's book (its 'tipsy, euphoric prose-poetry', its 'tedious metaphysical conceits', etc.), this reconciliation is what the book is all about, Huxley's endorsement of its general argument is puzzling. The review is reprinted in P. B. Medawar, *The Art of the Soluble* (London, Methuen, 1967), pp. 71–81.

30 Medawar, *The Art of the Soluble*, p. 71.

31 Teilhard, *The Phenomenon of Man*, pp. 287–8, 298.

32 Reich's major works are *Character Analysis* (1933), *The Mass Psychology of Fascism* (1933), *The Function of the Orgasm* (1942) and *The Sexual Revolution* (4th edn, 1969). For a good short discussion, see Charles Rycroft, *Reich* (London, Fontana/Collins, 1971). See also Paul A. Robinson, *The Freudian Left* (New York, Harper & Row, 1969). There is an interesting attempt to apply Reichian analysis to contemporary social developments in Reimut Reiche, *Sexuality and Class Struggle* (London, New Left Books, 1970).

33 The term is used by Bruce Brown, *Marx, Freud, and the Critique of Everyday Life: Toward a Permanent Cultural Revolution* (1973). For a discussion of the Freudo-Marxist thinkers, see also Manuel and Manuel, *Utopian Thought in the Western World*, pp. 788–800.

34 Norman O. Brown, *Life Against Death: The Psychoanalytic Meaning of History* (1959), p. 308. See also, for an even more utopian conception of sexual liberation, his *Love's Body* (New York, Random House, 1966). For a discussion of Brown's role in the counter-culture of the 1960s, see Morris Dickstein, *Gates of Eden: American Culture in the Sixties* (1977), pp. 51–88. See also Theodore Roszak, *The Making of A Counter-Culture: Reflections on the Technocratic Society and Its Youthful Opposition* (1970), pp. 84–123.

35 For the work of the Frankfurt School, see Martin Jay, *The Dialectical Imagination: A*

History of the Frankfurt School and The Institute of Social Research 1923–1950 (1973).

36 See, e.g., Erich Fromm, *The Sane Society* (1963), pp. 283 ff. The earlier *Fear of Freedom* (1942; London, Routledge & Kegan Paul, 1960) maintains a stronger Marxist orientation.

37 Herbert Marcuse, *Eros and Civilization: A Philosophical Inquiry Into Freud* (1962), p. 137.

38 Ibid., p. 139.

39 Ibid., p. 184.

40 Ibid., pp. 184–94.

41 Ibid., pp. 141, 130–2.

42 Ibid., pp. 215–16.

43 Ibid., pp. ix–xi.

44 See especially Marshall McLuhan, *The Gutenberg Galaxy* (London, Routledge & Kegan Paul, 1962), and *Understanding Media: The Extensions of Man* (London, Routledge & Kegan Paul, 1964).

45 Timothy Leary, *The Politics of Ecstasy* (New York, Putnam, 1968); quoted in Roszak, *The Making of a Counter Culture*, p. 62. And generally on Watts, Ginsberg and Leary, see ibid., pp. 124–77.

46 Herbert Marcuse, *One Dimensional Man* (1964; London, Abacus/Sphere Books, 1972), pp. 14, 28.

47 Ibid., pp. 199–200. The last line is a quotation from Walter Benjamin.

48 One of these radical students later recalled what the works of Marcuse and Brown had largely meant to him and his friends: 'To me they meant not some ontological breakthrough for human nature but probably just plain fucking, lots of it – in other words, just the opposite of what they said. I was sexually starved, though I hardly knew it, and these men seemed to promise that good times were just around the corner.' Dickstein, *Gates of Eden*, p. 82.

49 The lecture and subsequent discussion is printed as 'The End of Utopia' in Herbert Marcuse, *Five Lectures: Psychoanalysis, Politics and Utopia* (1970), pp. 62–82.

50 Marcuse's address to the congress, 'Liberation from the Affluent Society', is reprinted, along with the other addresses given, in David Cooper (ed.), The *Dialectics of Liberation* (1968), pp. 175–92. Other participants included R. D. Laing, Gregory Bateson, Paul Goodman and Stokely Carmichael. For a similar view of the Hippie phenomenon as a 'utopian moment', see Stuart Hall, 'The Hippies: An American "Moment"', in Julian Nagel (ed.), *Student Power* (London, Merlin Press, 1969), pp. 170–202.

51 For a brief account of the May events, see K. Kumar, 'The May Events and the Concept of Permanent Revolution', *Universities Quarterly*, vol. 29, no. 4 (Autumn 1975), pp. 398–411. For the influence of libertarian Marxism in it, see Gabriel and Daniel Cohn-Bendit, *Obsolete Communism: The Left-Wing Alternative* (Harmondsworth, Penguin Books, 1969). For the Situationist critique see Guy Debord, *La Société du spectacle* (1967), translated as *Society of the Spectacle* (Detroit, Black & Red Books, 1970); and Raoul Vaneigem, *Traité de savoir-vivre à l'usage des jeunes générations* (1968), translated as *The Revolution of Everyday Life* (London, Practical Paradise Publications, 1972). For a selection of articles from the *International Situationist* review, see Christopher Gray (ed.), *Leaving the Twentieth Century: The Incomplete Work of the Situationist International* (London, Free Fall Publications, 1974); and see also Charles Posner (ed.), *Reflections on the Revolution in France: 1968* (Harmondsworth, Penguin Books, 1970).

52 Herbert Marcuse, *An Essay on Liberation* (1969), p. ix.

53 Ibid., p. 82.

54 Charles Reich, *The Greening of America* (1971), pp. 290–1. For an example of the kind and level of analysis, cf. the paean to 'genuine, old-fashioned, unhomogenized peanut butter, the very symbol of the world that has enjoyed technology and transcended it.' Ibid., p. 286.

55 It should be pointed out that much science fiction in the Soviet Union remained very

optimistic about science and technology. See, e.g., Ivan Yefremov's *Andromeda* (1959), a socialist utopia which enjoyed great success in Eastern Europe. But in recent years more sceptical and questioning forms of science fiction have been gaining ground, as seen in the popularity of the Polish writer Stanislaw Lem (*Solaris*, 1961; *The Futurological Congress*, 1971). For a good anthology, see Darko Suvin (ed.), *Other Worlds, Other Seas: Science Fiction Stories from Socialist Countries* (New York, Random House, 1970). See also Suvin, 'The Utopian Tradition of Russian Science Fiction', *Modern Language Review*, vol. 66 (January 1971), pp. 139–58. As far as the West is concerned, the shift to alarm and pessimism in science fiction was first and most evident in the science fiction films of the 1950s – such as *The Thing* (1951), *Invaders from Mars* (1953), *It Came From Outer Space* (1953), *Invasion of the Body Snatchers* (1955), *Forbidden Planet* (1956).

56 J. G. Ballard, interviewed for 'Ideas in Science Fiction', BBC Radio 3, 9 November 1971. With an output as enormous and varied as that of science fiction, all generalizations about its development are suspect, these here no less then elsewhere. For helpful accounts of its history in the postwar period see, in addition to the works mentioned in n. 15 above, Kingsley Amis, *New Maps of Hell* (London, Gollancz, 1961); Patrick Parrinder (ed.), *Science Fiction: A Critical Guide* (1979); Reginald Bretnor (ed.), *Science Fiction: Today and Tomorrow* (1975); Thomas D. Clareson (ed.), *SF: The Other Side of Realism* (1971). See also the individual entries in Peter Nicholls (ed.), *The Encyclopaedia of Science Fiction* (1981) – an indispensable work of reference.

57 J. G. Ballard, 'Visions of Hell', *New Worlds* (UK) (March 1966), p. 48.

58 For a discussion of Hirsch's work, see Adrian Ellis and Krishan Kumar (eds), *Dilemmas of Liberal Democracies: Studies in Fred Hirsch's Social Limits to Growth* (London, Tavistock, 1983).

59 Paul Goodman; quoted by Colin Ward in his introduction to Peter Kropotkin, *Fields, Factories and Workshops Tomorrow* (1974), p. 9. Kropotkin was also warmly praised by Lewis Mumford for being 'almost half a century in advance of contemporary economic and technical opinion'. He had, said Mumford, 'grasped the fact that the flexibility and adaptability of electric communication and electric power, along with the possibilities of intensive biodynamic farming, had laid the foundations for a more decentralized urban development in small units, responsive to direct human contact and enjoying both urban and rural advantages . . .' Mumford, *The City in History* (Harmondsworth, Penguin Books, 1966), p. 585.

60 D. Dickson, *Alternative Technology and the Politics of Technical Change* (1974), p. 101. See also Godfrey Boyle and Peter Harper (eds), *Radical Technology* (London, Wildwood House, 1976); Ernest Braun and David Collingridge, *Technology and Survival* (London, Butterworths, 1977). The reprint in 1979 by Oxford University Press of William Cobbett's *Cottage Economy* (1822) – out of print since 1916 – was no doubt also a nicely judged response to the movement.

61 'A Blueprint for Survival', *The Ecologist*, vol. 2, no. 1 (January 1972), pp. 2, 6. The 'Blueprint' was also published in revised form as Edward Goldsmith (ed.), *A Blueprint for Survival* (1972). For other discussions of 'the stable society' and 'the steady-state economy', see Herman Daly (ed.), *Economics, Ecology, Ethics: Essays Toward a Steady-State Economy* (San Francisco, W. H. Freeman, 1980); Mancur Olson and Hans H. Landsberg (eds), *The No-Growth Society* (London, Woburn Press, 1975); William Leiss, *The Limits to Satisfaction: On Needs and Commodities* (1978). For the intellectual background to ecological thought, see Donald Worster, *Nature's Economy: A History of Ecological Ideas* (1985). The environmentalist movement in Britain is examined in Stephen Cotgrove, *Catastrophe or Cornucopia: The Environment, Politics and the Future* (1982).

62 Ivan Illich, *Tools for Conviviality* (London, Calder & Boyars, 1973), pp. 20–1. In addition to the works mentioned here, see also Illich, *Celebration of Awareness* (Harmondsworth, Penguin Books, 1973), *Energy and Equity* (London, Calder & Boyars,

1974), and *Shadow Work* (London, Marion Boyars, 1981).

63 See, e.g., Murray Bookchin, *Toward an Ecological Society* (Montreal, Black Rose Books, 1980), pp. 277–86.

64 Aldous Huxley, *Island* (1962; Harmondsworth, Penguin Books, 1964), pp. 146, 154.

65 Ibid., pp. 218–19.

66 Ibid., pp. 219–20.

67 Theodore Roszak, *Where the Wasteland Ends: Politics and Transcendence in Post-Industrial Society* (London, Faber & Faber, 1973), pp. 413–14.

68 Ibid., p. 444. For 'a little Utopian brainstorming', see p. 432.

69 Ibid., p. 444. And cf. the groups Roszak looks to for performing the task: 'dissenting technicians, dropped-out professionals, young scientists who are well away into Tantric sadhanas, people's architects, advocacy city planners, hip artisans, ecological activists brimming over with better possibilities. Here are sharp minds that have seen through the mystique of expertise and the artificial environment. They have learned to solve problems *with* people and not *for* them. They have access to the right skills and tools.' Ibid., p. 445. Clearly, a good deal of scientific and technical expertise is being called on in building the visionary commonwealth.

70 Ernest Callenbach, *Ecotopia: The Notebooks and Reports of William Weston* (Berkeley, Cal., Banyan Tree Books, 1975), p. 29.

71 Raymond Williams, 'Utopia and Science Fiction', in Parrinder (ed.), *Science Fiction*, p. 65.

72 Ursula Le Guin, *The Dispossessed* (1974; London, Panther/Granada, 1975), p. 69.

73 Ibid., p. 85.

74 Ibid., p. 74.

75 Ibid., p. 286.

76 Urras is clearly our Earth, or at least the industrialized part of it. But it is our Earth projected some time ahead, with many of its problems – poverty, pollution, the threat of nuclear war – solved. Le Guin seems to wish to give contemporary capitalist civilization as fair a face as possible so that she cannot be accused of stacking the cards too obviously in favour of Anarres. But elsewhere, in what is almost an aside, she suggests a different fate for our Earth. The Terran ambassador who gives Shevek sanctuary is from our Earth, and to her Urras is 'the kindliest, most various, most beautiful of all the inhabited worlds', almost a Paradise. She explains why: 'My world, my Earth, is a ruin. A planet soiled by the human species. We multiplied and gobbled and fought until there was nothing left, and then we died. We controlled neither appetite nor violence; we did not adapt. We destroyed ourselves. But we destroyed the world first. There are no forests left on my Earth. The air is grey, the sky is grey, it is always hot. It is habitable, it is still habitable, but not as this world is. This is a living world, a harmony. Mine is a discord. You Odonians chose a desert; we Terrans made a desert. . . . We can only look at this splendid world, this vital society, this Urras, this Paradise, from the outside. . . . We forfeited our chance for Anarres centuries ago, before it ever came into being.' *The Dispossessed*, pp. 287–8.

77 Williams, 'Utopia and Science Fiction', p. 64.

78 Le Guin, *The Dispossessed*, p. 283.

79 Kurt Vonnegut Jr, *Player Piano* (1952; London, Panther/Granada, 1973), pp. 85–6.

80 Michael Young, *The Rise of the Meritocracy 1870–2033* (1967), pp. 107–8.

81 For a brief survey of developments, see Giles Merritt, *World Out of Work* (London, Collins, 1982). See also T. Forester (ed.), *The Microelectronics Revolution* (Oxford, Basil Blackwell, 1980); T. Stonier, *The Wealth of Information* (London, Methuen, 1983); Alvin Toffler, *The Third Wave* (New York, Bantam Books, 1981).

82 André Gorz, *Paths to Paradise: On The Liberation From Work* (1985), p. 3.

83 See, e.g., Perry Anderson, *Arguments Within English Marxism* (London, New Left Books/Verso, 1980), pp. 174–5.

84 Rudolf Bahro, *The Alternative in Eastern Europe* (1978), p. 453.

85 See Rudolf Bahro, *From Red to Green* (London, New Left Books/Verso, 1984).
86 André Gorz, *Farewell to the Working Class: An Essay on Post-Industrial Socialism* (1982), pp. 74, 97, 145–52. See also Gorz, *Ecology as Politics* (Boston, South End Press, 1980).
87 I quote from the American edition: Raymond Williams, *The Year 2000* (1983), p. 14; and generally, pp. 11–18, 243–69.
88 See, e.g. Marge Piercy, *Women on the Edge of Time* (1976), Joanna Russ, *The Female Man* (1975), Dorothy Bryant, *The Kin of Ata Are Waiting For You* (1976). There is a tradition here going back to Charlotte Perkins Gilman's *Herland* (1915). For a discussion, see K. Kumar, 'Primitivism in Feminist Utopias', *Alternative Futures* (USA), vol. 4 (1981), pp. 61–7.
89 Cf. the remark of the Russian poetess Nadezhda Mandelstam: 'Isn't it time we paused to wonder why the nineteenth century, with its glorification of humanism, freedom, and the rights of man, led straight to the twentieth, which has not only surpassed all previous ages in its crimes against humanity but has managed, into the bargain, to prepare the means for total destruction of life on earth?' From Radio 3 broadcast, quoted in *Radio Times* (18 January 1981).
90 The Manuels remark on 'how difficult is the search for a terrestrial paradise when man is bereft of belief both in a Garden of Eden that might serve as a restorative model and a future other-wordly heaven.' Manuel and Manuel, *Utopian Thought in the Western World*, p. 62; see also pp. 801 ff.
91 See further K. Kumar, *Religion and Utopia* (1985).
92 For some stimulating thoughts on the future of socialism, see John Dunn, *The Politics of Socialism: An Essay in Political Theory* (1984).
93 Karl Mannheim, *Ideology and Utopia* (1960), p. 225.
94 Henry David Thoreau, *Walden* (1854; New York, New American Library, 1960), p. 215.
95 Peter Medawar, 'On "The Effecting of All Things Possible"', in his *Pluto's Republic* (Oxford University Press, 1982), pp. 328, 339.
96 Mannheim, *Ideology and Utopia*, p. 236.

Select Bibliography

This bibliography is a select list of works, in English, which deal generally with utopias and anti-utopias, or which contain material of special relevance to them. For references to particular authors and works dealt with in this book, see the notes to individual chapters.

Aldiss, Brian. *Billion Year Spree: The History of Science Fiction*. London, Corgi Books, 1975.

Alexander, P. and Gill, R. (eds). *Utopias*. London, Duckworth, 1984.

Allain, M. (ed.). *France and North America: Utopias and Utopians*. Lafayette Center for Louisiana Studies, University of Louisiana, 1978.

Amis, Kingsley. *New Maps of Hell*. London, New English Library, 1969.

Anderson, Perry. 'Utopias', in *Arguments Within English Marxism*. London, New Left Books, 1980.

Arblaster, A. and Lukes, S. (eds). *The Good Society: A Book of Readings*. London, Methuen, 1971.

Armytage, W. H. G. *Heavens Below: Utopian Experiments in England 1560–1960*. London, Routledge & Kegan Paul, 1961.

Armytage, W. H. G. *Yesterday's Tomorrows: A Historical Survey of Future Societies*. London, Routledge & Kegan Paul, 1968.

Ash, Brian. *Faces of the Future: The Lessons of Science Fiction*. London, Elek/Pemberton, 1975.

Bahro, Rudolf. *The Alternative in Eastern Europe*. London, New Left Books, 1978 (first published in 1977).

Bauman, Zygmunt. *Socialism: The Active Utopia*. London, Allen & Unwin, 1976.

Bell, Daniel, *The Coming of Post-Industrial Society*. New York, Basic Books, 1973.

Berki, R. N. *Insight and Vision: The Problem of Communism in Marx's Thought*. London, Dent, 1983.

Bernal, J. D. *The World, the Flesh, and the Devil. An Inquiry into the Future of the Three Enemies of the Rational Soul*. London, Jonathan Cape, 1970 (first published 1929).

Berneri, Marie Louise. *Journey Through Utopia*. London, Freedom Press, 1982.

Bestor, Arthur, E. Jr. *Backwoods Utopias: The Sectarian and Owenite Phases of Communitarian Socialism in America 1663–1829*. Philadelphia, University of Pennsylvania Press, 1950.

Biddis, Michael D. *The Age of the Masses: Ideas and Society in Europe since 1870*. Harmondsworth, Penguin Books, 1977.

Boguslaw, Robert. *The New Utopians: A Study of System Design and Social Change*. Englewood Cliffs, NJ, Prentice-Hall, 1965.

Bookchin, Murray. *Toward an Ecological Society*. Montreal, Black Rose Books, 1980.

Bouchier, David. *Idealism and Revolution: New Ideologies of Liberation in Britain and the United States*. London, Edward Arnold, 1978.
Braunthal, Alfred. *Salvation and the Perfect Society: The Eternal Quest*. Amherst, University of Massachusetts Press, 1979.
Bretnor, R. (ed.). *Science Fiction: Today and Tomorrow*. Baltimore, Md. Penguin Books, 1975.
Brown, Bruce. *Marx, Freud, and the Critique of Everyday Life: Toward a Permanent Cultural Revolution*. New York, Monthly Review Press, 1973.
Brown, Norman O. *Life Against Death. The Psychoanalytic Meaning of History*. New York, Vintage Books, 1959.
Buber, Martin. *Paths in Utopia*. Boston, Beacon Press, 1958 (first published in Hebrew in 1946, in English in 1949).
Buckley, J. H. *The Triumph of Time: A Study of the Victorian Concepts of Time, History, Progress, and Decadence*. Cambridge, Mass., Harvard University Press, 1967.
Burke, J. P., Crocker, L. and Legters, L. H. (eds) *Marxism and the Good Society*. Cambridge, Cambridge University Press, 1981.
Bury, J. B. *The Idea of Progress*. London, Macmillan, 1923.
Caroll, John. *Break-out from the Crystal Palace: The Anarcho-Psychological Critique: Stirner, Nietzsche, Dostoyevsky*. London, Routledge & Kegan Paul, 1974.
Chesneaux, Jean. 'Egalitarian and Utopian Traditions in the East', *Diogenes*, vol. 62, 1968, pp. 76–102.
Clarens, Carlos. *An Illustrated History of the Horror Film*. New York, Capricorn Books, 1968.
Clareson, Thomas D. *SF: The Other Side of Realism*. Bowling Green, Ohio, Bowling Green University Popular Press, 1971.
Clarke, I. F. *Voices Prophesying War 1763–1984*. Oxford, Oxford University Press, 1966.
Clarke, I. F. *The Pattern of Expectation 1644–2001*. New York, Basic Books, 1979.
Cohen, Stanley. *Visions of Social Control*. Cambridge, Polity Press, 1985.
Cohn, Norman. *The Pursuit of the Millennium*. London, Mercury Books, 1962.
Cooper, David (ed.). *The Dialectics of Liberation*. Harmondsworth, Penguin Books, 1968.
Cotgrove, Stephen. *Catastrophe or Cornucopia: The Environment, Politics and the Future*. Chichester, John Wiley, 1982.
Cross, Whitney R. *The Burned-Over District: The Social and Intellectual History of Enthusiastic Religion in Western New York, 1800–1850*. New York, Harper Torchbooks, 1965.
Crossman, Richard (ed.). *The God That Failed: Six Studies in Communism*. London, Hamish Hamilton, 1950.
Dahrendorf, R. 'Out of Utopia: Toward a Reorientation of Sociological Analysis', *American Journal of Sociology*, vol. 64, no. 2, 1958, pp. 115–27.
Davis, J. C. *Utopia and the Ideal Society: A Study of English Utopian Writing 1516–1700*. Cambridge, Cambridge University Press, 1983.
Dickson, D. *Alternative Technology and the Politics of Technical Change*. London, Fontana, 1974.
Dickstein, Morris. *Gates of Eden: American Culture in the Sixties*. New York, Basic Books, 1977.
Dunn, John. *Western Political Theory in the Face of the Future*. Cambridge, Cambridge University Press, 1979.
Dunn, John. *The Politics of Socialism: An Essay in Political Theory*. Cambridge, Cambridge University Press, 1984.
Egbert, D. D. and Persons, S. (eds). *Socialism and American Life* (2 vols). Princeton, Princeton University Press, 1952.
Eliav-Feldon, Miriam. *Realistic Utopias: The Ideal Imaginary Societies of the Renaissance 1516–1630*. Oxford, Clarendon Press, 1982.
Elliott, Robert C. *The Shape of Utopia: Studies in a Literary Genre*. Chicago, University of Chicago Press, 1970.
Ellul, Jacques. *The Technological Society*. New York, Vintage Books, 1964 (first published, in French, in 1954).

Erasmus, Charles J. *In Search of the Common Good: Utopian Experiments Past and Future*. New York, Free Press, 1977.
Eurich, Nell. *Science in Utopia: A Mighty Design*. Cambridge, Mass., Harvard University Press, 1967.
Ferguson, John. *Utopias of the Classical World*. London, Thames & Hudson, 1975.
Finley, M. I. 'Utopianism Ancient and Modern', in K. H. Wolff and Barrington Moore Jr (eds), *The Critical Spirit: Essays in Honor of Herbert Marcuse*. Boston, Beacon Press, 1967.
Fishman, R. *Urban Utopias in the Twentieth Century: Ebenezer Howard, Frank Lloyd Wright and Le Corbusier*. New York, Basic Books, 1977.
Fogarty, Robert S. *American Utopianism*. Itasca, Ill., F. E. Peacock, 1972.
Fogarty, Robert S. *Dictionary of American Communal and Utopian History*. Westport, Conn., Greenwood Press, 1980.
Freud, Sigmund. *Civilization and Its Discontents*. London, Hogarth Press, 1963 (first published 1930).
Freud, Sigmund. *Civilization, Society and Religion*. Harmondsworth, Pelican Freud Library, vol. 12, 1985.
Fromm, Erich. *The Sane Society*. London, Routledge & Kegan Paul, 1963.
Frye, Northrop. 'Varieties of Literary Utopias', in Manuel (ed.), *Utopias and Utopian Thought* (q.v.), pp. 25–49.
Gabor, Dennis. *Inventing the Future*. Harmondsworth, Penguin Books, 1964.
Gendron, Bernard. *Technology and the Human Condition*. New York, St Martin's Press, 1977.
Gerber, Richard. *Utopian Fantasy: A Study of English Utopian Fiction Since the End of the Nineteenth Century*. London, Routledge & Kegan Paul, 1955.
Gilison, Jerome. *The Soviet Image of Utopia*. Baltimore, Johns Hopkins University Press, 1975.
Glover, Jonathan. *What Sort of People Should There Be? Genetic Engineering, Brain Control and Their Impact on Our Future World*. Harmondsworth, Penguin Books, 1984.
Goldsmith, Edward (ed.). *A Blueprint for Survival*. Harmondsworth, Penguin Books, 1972.
Goodheart, Eugene. *Culture and the Radical Conscience*. Cambridge, Mass., Harvard University Press, 1973.
Goodman, Paul. *Utopian Essays and Practical Proposals*. New York, Vintage Books, 1962.
Goodman, Paul and Percival. *Communitas: Means of Livelihood and Ways of Life*. New York, Vintage Books, 1960.
Goodwin, Barbara. *Social Science and Utopia*. Hassocks, Sussex, Harvester Press, 1978.
Goodwin, Barbara and Taylor, Keith. *The Politics of Utopia: A Study in Theory and Practice*. London, Hutchinson, 1982.
Gorz, André. *Farewell to the Working Class: An Essay on Post-Industrial Socialism*. London, Pluto Press, 1982 (first published in 1980).
Gorz, André. *Paths to Paradise: On The Liberation From Work*. London, Pluto Press, 1985 (first published in 1983).
Goudsblom, Johan. *Nihilism and Culture*. Oxford, Basil Blackwell, 1980.
Graus, F. 'Social Utopias in the Middle Ages', *Past and Present*, no. 38, December 1967, pp. 3–19.
Green, Martin. 'Two Surveys of the Literature of Science', in *Science and the Shabby Curate of Poetry*. London, Longmans, 1964.
Hacker, Andrew. 'The Specter of Predictable Man', *Antioch Review*, vol. 14, 1954, pp. 195–207.
Hacker, Andrew. 'Dostoevsky's Disciples: Man and Sheep in Political Theory', *Journal of Politics*, vol. 17, no. 4, 1955, pp. 590–613.
Hansot, Elizabeth. *Perfection and Progress: Two Modes of Utopian Thought*. Cambridge, Mass., MIT Press, 1974.
Hardy, Dennis. *Alternative Communities in Nineteenth Century England*. London, Longman, 1979.
Harrison, J. F. C. *Robert Owen and the Owenites in Britain and America: The Quest for the New Moral World*. London, Routledge & Kegan Paul, 1969.

Harrison, J. F. C. *The Second Coming: Popular Millenarianism 1780–1850*. London, Routledge & Kegan Paul, 1979.
Hayden, Dolores. *Seven American Utopias: The Architecture of Communitarian Socialism, 1790–1975*. Cambridge, Mass., MIT Press, 1976.
Hayek, F. A. *The Road to Serfdom*. London, George Routledge and Sons, 1944.
Hayek, F. A. *The Counter-Revolution of Science: Studies on the Abuse of Reason*. New York, Free Press of Glencoe, 1955.
Hertzler, Joyce Oramel. *The History of Utopian Thought*. New York, Cooper Square Publishers, 1965 (first published in 1923).
Hillegas, Mark R. *The Future as Nightmare: H. G. Wells and the Anti-Utopians*. New York, Oxford University Press, 1967.
Hirsch, Fred. *Social Limits to Growth*. London, Routledge & Kegan Paul, 1977.
Holloway, Mark. *Heavens on Earth: Utopian Communities in America 1680–1880*, 2nd edn, New York, Dover Publications, 1966.
Horkheimer, M. and Adorno, T. W. *Dialectic of Enlightenment*, tr. J. Cumming. London, Allen Lane, 1973 (first published in 1944).
Horsbrugh, H. J. N. 'The Relevance of the Utopian', *Ethics*, vol. 67 (1957), pp. 127–38.
Howe, Irving. *Politics and the Novel*. New York, Horizon Press, 1957.
Hudson, Wayne. *The Marxist Philosophy of Ernst Bloch*. London, Macmillan, 1982.
Hughes, H. Stuart. *Consciousness and Society: The Reorientation of European Social Thought 1890–1930*. New York, Vintage Books, 1958.
Ingle, Stephen J. *Socialist Thought in Imaginative Literature*. London, Macmillan, 1979.
Jacobs, Louis. *A Jewish Theology*. London, Darton, Longman & Todd, 1973.
Jay, Martin. *The Dialectical Imagination: A History of the Frankfurt School and the Institute of Social Research, 1923–1950*. Boston, Little, Brown, 1973.
Jones, Howard Mumford. *O Strange New World: American Culture: The Formative Years*. London, Chatto & Windus, 1965.
Kanter, Rosabeth Moss. *Commitment and Community: Communes and Utopias in Sociological Perspective*. Cambridge, Mass., Harvard University Press, 1972.
Kanter, Rosabeth Moss (ed.). *Communes: Creating and Managing the Collective Life*. New York, Harper & Row, 1973.
Kasson, John F. *Civilizing the Machine: Technology and Republican Values in America, 1776–1900*. Harmondsworth, Penguin Books, 1977.
Kateb, George. *Utopia and Its Enemies*. New York, Schocken Books, 1972 (first published 1963).
Kateb, George (ed.). *Utopia*. New York, Atherton, 1971.
Koestler, Arthur. *The Yogi and the Commissar, And Other Essays*. London, Jonathan Cape, 1945.
Kolakowski, Leszek. *Toward a Marxist Humanism: Essays on the Left Today*. New York, Grove Press, 1969.
Kolakowski, Leszek. *Main Currents of Marxism* (3 vols). Oxford, Oxford University Press, 1981.
Kolakowski, Leszek, and Hampshire, Stuart (eds). *The Socialist Idea: A Reappraisal*. London, Quartet Books, 1977.
Kracauer, Siegfried. *From Caligari to Hitler*. Princeton, Princeton University Press, 1947.
Kropotkin, Peter. *Fields, Factories, and Workshops Tomorrow*, Revised and ed. Colin Ward. London, Allen & Unwin, 1974.
Kumar, Krishan. *Prophecy and Progress: The Sociology of Industrial and Post-Industrial Society*. Harmondsworth, Penguin Books, 1978.
Kumar, Krishan. *Religion and Utopia*. Canterbury, Centre for the Study of Religion and Society, 1985.
Lasky, Melvin J. *Utopia and Revolution*. Chicago, University of Chicago Press, 1976.
Leiss, William. *The Domination of Nature*. Boston, Beacon Press, 1974.

Leiss, William. *The Limits to Satisfaction: On Needs and Commodities*. London, Marion Boyars, 1978.
Levitas, Ruth. 'Sociology and Utopia', *Sociology*, vol. 13, no. 1, 1979, pp. 19–33.
Lodge, David. 'Utopia and Criticism: The Radical Longing for Paradise', *Encounter*, vol. 32, April 1969, pp. 65–75.
Lovejoy, A. O. and Boas, G. *Primitivism and Related Ideas in Antiquity*. Baltimore, Johns Hopkins University Press, 1935.
Löwith, Karl. *Meaning in History*. Chicago, Chicago University Press, 1949.
Lukes, Steven. 'Marxism and Utopia', in Alexander and Gill (eds.), *Utopias* (q.v.), pp. 153–67.
Mannheim, Karl. 'Utopia', in E. R. A. Seligman and A. Johnson (eds), *The Encyclopaedia of the Social Sciences*, New York, Macmillan, 1934.
Mannheim, Karl. *Ideology and Utopia*. London, Routledge & Kegan Paul, 1960 (first published 1936).
Manuel, Frank E. (ed.). *Utopias and Utopian Thought*. London, Souvenir Press, 1973.
Manuel, Frank E. and Manuel, Fritzie, P. (eds). *French Utopias: An Anthology of Ideal Societies*. New York, Schocken Books, 1971.
Manuel, Frank E. and Manuel, Fritzie, P. *Utopian Thought in the Western World*. Cambridge, Mass., The Belknap Press of Harvard University Press, 1979.
Marcuse, Herbert. *Eros and Civilization: A Philosophical Inquiry Into Freud*. New York, Vintage Books, 1962 (first published 1955).
Marcuse, Herbert. *An Essay on Liberation*. London, Allen Lane, 1969.
Marcuse, Herbert. *Five Lectures: Psychoanalysis, Politics and Utopia*. Boston, Beacon Press, 1970.
Marx, Leo. *The Machine in the Garden: Technology and the Pastoral Ideal in America*. New York, Oxford University Press, 1967.
Meadows, Donella H. and others. *The Limits to Growth* (a report for the Club of Rome). London, Earth Island, 1972.
Medawar, P. B. *Pluto's Republic*. Oxford, Oxford University Press, 1982.
Meier, Paul. *William Morris: The Marxist Dreamer* (2 vols), tr. Frank Gubb. Hassocks, Sussex, Harvester Press, 1978.
Mendelsohn, Everett and Nowotny, Helga (eds). *Nineteen Eighty-Four: Science Between Utopia and Dystopia*. Dordrecht, D. Reidel, 1984.
Molnar, Thomas. *Utopia: The Perennial Heresy*. London, Tom Stacey, 1972.
Moore, Wilbert E. 'The Utility of Utopias', in *Order and Change: Essays in Comparative Sociology*. Chichester, John Wiley, 1967.
Moretti, Franco. *Signs Taken for Wonders*. London, New Left Books, 1983.
Morgan, Arthur E. *Nowhere Was Somewhere: How History Makes Utopias and How Utopias Make History*. Chapel Hill, NC, University of North Carolina Press, 1946.
Morley, Henry (ed.). *Ideal Commonwealths*. London, George Routledge and Sons, 1885.
Morton, A. L. *The English Utopia*. London, Lawrence & Wishart, 1969 (first published in 1952).
Muller, H. J. 'A Note on Utopia', in *The Children of Frankenstein*, Bloomington, Indiana University Press, 1970.
Mumford, Lewis. *The Story of Utopias*. New York, Bonni & Liverright, 1922.
Mumford, Lewis. 'Utopia, The City, and The Machine', in Manuel (ed.) *Utopias and Utopian Thought* (q.v.), pp. 3–24.
Nash, Roderick. *Wilderness and the American Mind*, 3rd edn. New Haven, Conn., Yale University Press, 1982.
Negley, Glenn. *Utopian Literature. A Bibliography with a Supplementary Listing of Works Influential in Utopian Thought*. Lawrence, Kansas, Regents Press, 1977.
Negley, Glenn and Patrick, J. Max. *The Quest for Utopia: An Anthology of Imaginary Societies*. New York, Henry Schuman, 1952.
Nicholls, Peter (ed.). *The Encyclopaedia of Science Fiction*. London, Granada, 1981.

Nozick, Robert. *Anarchy, State, And Utopia*. New York, Basic Books, 1974.
Oakeshott, Michael. *Rationalism in Politics, and Other Essays*. London, Methuen, 1967 (first published in 1962).
Parrinder, Patrick (ed.). *Science Fiction: A Critical Guide*. London, Longman, 1979.
Parrinder, Patrick. *Science Fiction*. London, Methuen, 1980.
Parrington, Vernon L., Jr. *American Dreams: A Study of American Utopias*. Providence, RI, Brown University Press, 1947.
Passmore, John. *The Perfectibility of Man*. London, Duckworth, 1972.
Patch, H. R. *The Other World, according to Descriptions in Medieval Literature*. Cambridge Mass., Harvard University Press, 1950.
Plath, David W. (ed.). *Aware of Utopia*. Urbana, Ill., University of Illinois Press, 1971.
Polak, Fred. *The Image of the Future*. Amsterdam, Elsevier, 1973.
Popper, Karl. *The Open Society and Its Enemies*, rev. edn (2 vols). London, Routledge & Kegan Paul, 1961 (first published 1945).
Punter, David. *The Literature of Terror*. London, Longman, 1980.
Reich, Charles. *The Greening of America*. London, Allen Lane, 1971.
Rhodes, Harold V. *Utopia in American Political Thought*. Tucson, University of Arizona Press, 1967.
Richter, Peyton E. (ed.). *Utopias: Social Ideals and Communal Experiments*. Boston, Holbrook Press, 1971.
Richter, Peyton E. (ed.). *Utopia/Dystopia?* Cambridge, Mass., Schenkman, 1975.
Riesman, David. 'Some Observations on Community Plans and Utopia', in *Individualism Reconsidered*, New York, Free Press, 1964.
Roemer, Kenneth M. *The Obsolete Necessity: America in Utopian Writings, 1888–1900*. Kent, Ohio, Kent State University Press, 1976.
Rosenau, Helen. *The Ideal City: Its Architectural Evolution in Europe*, 3rd edn. London, Methuen, 1983.
Roszak, Theodore. *The Making of a Counter-Culture: Reflections on the Technocratic Society and Its Youthful Opposition*. London, Faber & Faber, 1970.
Roszak, Theodore. *Where the Wasteland Ends: Politics and Transcendence in Postindustrial Society*. London, Faber & Faber, 1973.
Sanford, Charles L. *The Quest for Paradise: Europe and the American Moral Imagination*. Urbana, Ill., University of Illinois Press, 1961.
Sargent, Lyman Tower. *British and American Utopian Literature, 1516–1975: An Annotated Bibliography*. Boston, G. K. Hall, 1979.
Scholem, Gershom. *The Messianic Idea in Judaism, and Other Essays On Jewish Spirituality*. London, Allen & Unwin, 1971.
Scholes, Robert and Rabkin, Eric S. *Science Fiction: History, Science, Vision*. New York, Oxford University Press, 1977.
Schumacher, E. F. *Small is Beautiful: A Study of Economics as if People Mattered*. London, Blond & Briggs, 1973.
Schumpeter, Joseph A. *Capitalism, Socialism and Democracy*, 5th edn. London, Allen & Unwin, 1976 (first published in 1943).
Science-Fiction Studies. Special issue, 'Utopia and Anti-Utopia', vol. 9, part 2, July 1982.
Segal, Howard P. *Technological Utopianism in American Culture*. Chicago, University of Chicago Press, 1985.
Shklar, Judith N. *After Utopia: The Decline of Political Faith*. Princeton, NJ, Princeton University Press, 1957.
Siegel, Paul N. *Revolution and the Twentieth-Century Novel*. New York, Monad Press, 1979.
Singer, Peter and Wells, Deane. *The Reproduction Revolution: New Ways of Making Babies*. Oxford, Oxford University Press, 1984.
Skinner, Quentin. *The Foundations of Modern Political Thought* (2 vols). Cambridge, Cambridge University Press, 1978.
Smith, Henry Nash. *Virgin Land: The American West as Symbol and Myth*. Cambridge, Mass.,

Harvard University Press, 1970 (first published 1950).
Snow, C. P. *The Two Cultures: And A Second Look*. New York, Mentor Books, 1963.
Sorel, Georges. *The Illusions of Progress*. Berkeley, University of California Press, 1972 (first published, in French, 1908).
Spiro, M. E. *Kibbutz: Venture in Utopia*, new edn. New York, Schocken Books, 1970.
Sussman, Herbert L. *Victorians and the Machine: The Literary Response to Technology*. Cambridge, Mass., Harvard University Press, 1968.
Suvin, Darko. *Metamorphoses of Science Fiction: On the Poetics and History of a Literary Genre*. New Haven, Conn., Yale University Press, 1979.
Swingewood, Alan. *The Novel and Revolution*. London, Macmillan, 1975.
Tafuri, Manfredo. *Architecture and Utopia*. Cambridge, Mass., MIT Press, 1979.
Talmon, J. L. *The Origins of Totalitarian Democracy*. London, Mercury Books, 1961 (first published in 1952).
Talmon, J. L. *Political Messianism: The Romantic Phase*. London, Secker & Warburg, 1960.
Taylor, Barbara. *Eve and the New Jerusalem: Socialism and Feminism in the Nineteenth Century*. New York, Pantheon Books, 1983.
Teselle, Sallie (ed.). *The Family, Communes, and Utopian Socieites*. New York, Harper Torchbooks, 1972.
Thompson, E. P. *William Morris: Romantic to Revolutionary*, rev. edn. London, Merlin Press, 1977.
Thrupp, Sylvia (ed.). *Millennial Dreams in Action*. New York, Schocken Books, 1970.
Tod, I. and Wheeler, M. *Utopia: An Illustrated History*. London, Orbis Books, 1978.
Tuveson, Ernest Lee. *Millennium and Utopia: A Study in the Background of the Idea of Progress*. New York, Harper & Row, 1964 (first published in 1949).
Tuveson, Ernest Lee. *Redeemer Nation: The Idea of America's Millennial Role*. Chicago, Chicago University Press, 1968.
Tyler, Alice Felt. *Freedom's Ferment: Phases of American Social History from the Colonial Period to the Outbreak of the Civil War*. New York, Harper Torchbooks, 1962.
Venturi, Franco. *Utopia and Reform in the Enlightenment*. Cambridge, Cambridge University Press, 1971.
Veysey, Laurence. *The Communal Experience: Anarchist and Mystical Communities in Twentieth-Century America*. Chicago, University of Chicago Press, 1978.
Walsh, Chad. *From Utopia to Nightmare*. London, Geoffrey Bles, 1962.
Webber, Everett. *Escape to Utopia: The Communal Movement in America*. New York, Hastings House, 1959.
Weber, Eugen. 'The Anti-Utopia of the Twentieth Century', *South Atlantic Quarterly*, vol. 58, Summer 1959, pp. 440–7.
Werskey, Gary. *The Visible College*. London, Allen Lane, 1978.
Whitworth, John M. *God's Blueprints: A Sociological Study of Three Utopian Sects*. London, Routledge & Kegan Paul, 1975.
Wilding, Michael. *Political Fictions*. London, Routledge & Kegan Paul, 1980.
Williams, G. H. *Wilderness and Paradise in Christian Thought*. New York, Harper, 1962.
Williams, Raymond. 'Utopia and Science Fiction', in Parrinder (ed.). *Science Fiction* (q.v.), pp. 52–66.
Williams, Raymond. *The Year 2000*. New York, Pantheon Books, 1983.
Woodcock, George. 'Utopias in Negative', *Sewanee Review*, vol. 64, 1956, pp. 81–97.
Worster, Donald. *Nature's Economy: A History of Ecological Ideas*. Cambridge, Cambridge University Press, 1985.
Young Michael. *The Rise of the Meritocracy 1870—2033*. Harmondsworth, Penguin Books, 1967 (first published in 1958).

Index

Bold page numbers refer to main entries

Index by Joyce Kerr